SALLY E. STUART

CHRISTIAN WRITERS'

MARKET GUIDE

1997

Harold Shaw Publishers
Wheaton, Illinois

ISSN 1080-3955

ISBN 0-87788-158-8

Cover design by David LaPlaca

02 01 00 99 98 97

10 9 8 7 6 5 4 3 2 1

THE 1997 CHRISTIAN WRITERS' MARKET GUIDE

CONTENTS

III. PERIODICALS

VII. INDEXES AND GLOSSARY

INTRODUCTION

Last year I talked about how each edition of this guide brings us a new perspective on the Christian publishing industry. This year, with the 12th annual edition, I had no problem figuring out what that new perspective would be. Without a doubt, it is that we are leaping headlong into the electronic age. Last year I listed a few publishers with e-mail addresses, and only a couple of websites. This year, a substantial number of publishers have an e-mail address (70 book publishers and 270 periodicals), and an ever increasing number already have websites (30 book publishers and 31 periodicals), with many more planning to take the leap this year. If you are not already on the Internet, you will need to be soon in order to take advantage of the inside information these home pages provide.

It is always a challenge to find as many new publishers as I can to add to what is already the largest listing of Christian publishers in existence. This year has been no exception, with the addition of 49 new book publishers and 85 new periodicals. Another by-product of my own adventures into the electronic age is that I have been able to clean up the existing list even better than usual by faxing copies of listings for those publishers who didn't respond to the regular questionnaire. Many more than usual responded that way, and I also found those publishers who had gone out of business but hadn't notified me. The bottom line for each of you is that you will have as close as possible to an up-to-the-minute market resource.

Each year I also try to add some new features that will make your job easier. This year, many of those additions are refinements, rather that specific additions. I have added the websites for the publishers, as mentioned above. For the publicists and others who have requested it, I have noted which publishers take advertising, noted as (Ads) at the end of the main body of each listing. Since I mentioned last year that many publishers now want to know where reprints have appeared, I have added a notation that indicates not just those who take reprints, but whether you need to tell them when/where a piece has appeared previously. I've added a new section on subsidy publishing with some valuable information for those who are considering that route to publication. Listing will also indicate which publishers now want electronic rights, and which ones want a query for electronic submissions. Overall, I've tried to include more descriptive information on many of the publishers to help you better determine their slant. Under topical listings for both books and periodicals you will find a listing of all the Canadian or foreign publishers. Check the Table of Contents for a listing of other new topics.

All of that is the good news. The bad news is that the Christian publishing market is becoming even more difficult to break into. That simply underlines your need for this market guide. With it, you will know which publishers have closed their doors, and which ones still have an open-door policy toward freelancers. Fortunately, there are still a lot of them. They may, however, be different ones than you are used to submitting to. When you find a door closed at one house, I would encourage you to seek an open one in an entirely new place. As the market is narrowing in some areas, it may be broadening in others. Your job is to find those new markets just waiting for what you have to offer.

Generally, I have continued to expand the market listings for greeting cards and specialty markets, adding a new list of software developers. The agent list is growing slowly, but at this point we are losing as many as we are gaining.

Many of the new markets seem to be a part of the explosion in publishing that came with the advent of desk-top publishing a few years ago. Many of those publications are small and pay little or nothing, but they still provide a good opportunity for the beginning writer to be published. My feeling is that writing and getting published, whether you are paid or not, is good for polishing your skills and may get you in on the ground floor of a new publication that may pay later. Good writing (no matter where it is found) will eventually gain the notice of the larger, paying markets. It can be a win-win situation for both the struggling new writer and the struggling new periodical.

The groups and conferences were especially responsive to the request for updated information this year, so you will find many new opportunities in those sections. The people offering editorial services are refining their areas of expertise and honing their skills, making their services even more valuable. Even if you don't find someone offering services in your area, most of them have fax or e-mail capabilities, making it easier to work with editors anywhere in the country. The list of contests has grown, and I've added "Ethnic Fiction" as a new topic for those seeking new ethnic markets. Be sure to study the market analysis sections of this book for more insight into what's happening in the industry.

As with any new reference book, I suggest you spend some quality time becoming familiar with its contents and structure. Discover the supplementary lists available throughout the book. Read through the glossary and spend a few minutes learning terms you are not familiar with. Review the lists of writer's groups and conferences and mark those you might be interested in pursuing during the coming months. The denominational listing will help you start making the important connection between periodicals and book publishers associated with different denominations. As some of you requested, I have added a new list of publisher by publishing groups (that are not denominational). With so many publishers being bought out or merging, it will help keep you up-to-date with the new members of these "families."

Be sure to carefully study the "How to Use This Book" section. It will save you a lot of time and frustration in trying to understand the meaning of all the notations in the primary listings, and it's full of helpful hints. Remember to send for sample copies (or catalog) and guidelines for any of these publishers or periodicals you are not familiar with. Then study those carefully before submitting anything to that publisher.

Editors tell me repeatedly that they are looking for writers who understand them, their periodical or publishing house, and most of all, their unique approach to the marketplace. One of the biggest complaints I've gotten from publishers over the years is that the material they receive routinely is not appropriate for their needs. I got fewer of those complaints this year. I hope that is an indication that you are all doing a better job of marketing. With a little time and effort, you can fulfill all their expectations, distinguish yourself as a professional, and sell what you write.

Again, I wish you well as you embark on this exciting road to publication, whether for the first time or as a long-time veteran. And as I remind you every year, each of us has been given a specific mission in the field of writing. We often feel inadequate to the task, but I learned a long time ago that the writing assignments God has given me cannot be written quite as well by anyone else.

Sally E. Stuart
1647 SW Pheasant Dr.
Aloha, OR 97006
(503)642-9844
Fax (503)848-3658
E-mail: stuartcwmg@aol.com.

P.S. For information on how to receive the market guide automatically every year and freeze the price at $19.99 for future editions, or for information on getting the guide at a discounted group rate or getting books on consignment for your next seminar or conference, contact me at the address or numbers above.

HOW TO USE THIS BOOK

The purpose of this market guide is to make your marketing job easier and more targeted. However, it will serve you well only if you put some time and effort into studying its contents and using it as a springboard for discovering and becoming an expert on those publishers best suited to your writing topics and style.

Below you will find information on its general set-up and instructions for its use. In order to help you become more of an expert on marketing, I am including an explanation of each entry in the alphabetical listings for both the book section and the periodical section. Be sure to study these before trying to use this book.

1. Spend some time initially getting acquainted with the contents and set-up of this resource book. You cannot make the best use of it until you know exactly what it has to offer.

2. Study the Contents pages, where you will find listings of all the periodical and book topics. When selecting a topic, be sure to check related topics as well. Some cross-referencing will often be helpful. For example, if you have a novel that deals with doctor-assisted suicide, you might find the list for adult novels and the list for controversial issues and see which publishers are on both lists. Those would be good potential markets. In the topical sections you will find a letter "R" following publishers that accept reprints (pieces that have been printed in other publications, but for which you retain the rights).

3. The Primary/Alphabetical Listings for book and periodical publishers contain those publishers who answered the questionnaire and those who did not. The listings preceded by an asterisk (*) are those publishers who didn't respond and whose information I was unable to update from other sources. Those with a number symbol (#) were updated from their printed guidelines or other current sources. Since the information in those two groups was not verified by the publisher, you are encouraged to send for sample copies or catalogs and writer's guidelines before submitting to them.

4. In each **book-publisher listing** you will find the following information (as available), in this format:

a) Name of publisher

b) Address, phone and fax numbers, e-mail address, Website

c) Denomination or affiliation

d) Name of editor—This may include the senior editor's name, followed by the name of another editor to whom submissions should be sent. In a few cases, several editors are named with the type of books each is responsible for. Address to appropriate editor.

e) Sometimes a statement of purpose

f) Sometimes a list of imprint names

g) Number of inspirational/religious titles published per year

h) Number of submissions received annually

i) Percentage of books from first-time authors

j) Those publishers who do not accept books through agents. If it says nothing about agents, you may assume they do accept books through agents.

k) The percentage of books from freelance authors they subsidy publish (if any).

Does not refer to percentage paid by author. If percentage of subsidy is over 50%, the publisher will be listed in a separate section under Subsidy Publishers.

l) Whether they reprint out-of-print books from other publishers

m) Preferred manuscript length in words or pages

n) Average amount of royalty, if provided. If royalty is a percentage of wholesale or net, it is based on price paid by bookstores or distributors. If it is on retail price, it is based on cover price of the book.

o) Average amount paid for advances—Whether a publisher pays an advance or not is noted in the listing; if they did not answer the question, there is no mention of it.

p) Whether they make any outright purchases and amount paid. In this kind of sale, an author is paid a flat fee and receives no royalties

q) Average first printing (number of books usually printed for a first-time author).

r) Average length of time between acceptance of a manuscript and publication of the work

s) Whether they consider simultaneous submissions. This means you can send a query or complete manuscript simultaneously to more than one publisher, as long as you advise everyone involved that you are doing so.

t) Length of time it should take them to respond to a query/proposal or to a complete manuscript (when two lengths of time are given, the first generally refers to a query and the latter to a complete manuscript). Give them a one-month grace period beyond that and then send a polite follow-up letter if you haven't heard from them.

u) Whether a publisher "Accepts," "Prefers," or "Requires" the submission of an ACCEPTED manuscript on disk. Most publishers now do accept or require that books be sent on a computer disk (usually along with a hard copy), but since each publisher's needs are different, that information will be supplied to you by the individual publisher when the time comes.

(v) Availability and cost for writer's guidelines and book catalogs—If the listing says "Guidelines," it means they are available for a #10 (business-sized) SASE with a first-class stamp. The cost of the catalog (if any), the size of envelope, and amount of postage are given, if specified (affix stamps to envelope; don't send loose). Tip: If postage required is more than $1.24, I suggest you put $1.24 in postage on the envelope and clearly mark it "Special Standard Mail." (That is enough for up to 1 pound). If the listing says "free catalog," it means you need only request it; they do not ask for payment or SASE. Note: If sending for both guidelines and catalog, it is not necessary to send both envelopes; guidelines will be sent with catalog.

w) Nonfiction Section—Preference for query letter, book proposal, or complete manuscript, and if they accept phone, fax, or e-mail queries (if it does not say they accept them, assume they do not; this applies to fiction as well as nonfiction). If they want a query letter, send just a letter describing your project. If they want a query letter/proposal, you can add a chapter-by-chapter synopsis and the number of sample chapters indicated. If not specified, send one to three chapters. This is often followed by a quote from them about their needs, or what they don't want to see.

x) Fiction Section—Same information as nonfiction section

y) Special Needs—If they have specific topics they need that are not included in the subject listings, they are indicated here.

z) Ethnic Books—Usually specifies which ethnic groups they target or any particular needs aa) Also Does—Indicates which publishers also publish booklets, pamphlets or tracts.

bb) Tips—Specific tips provided by the editor/publisher

Note: At the end of some listings you will find an indication that the publisher receives mailings of book proposals from The Writer's Edge (see Editorial Services/Illinois for an explanation of that service).

5. In each **periodical listing** you will find the following information (as available), in this format:

a) Name of periodical

b) Address, phone, fax, and e-mail address, Website

c) Denomination or affiliation

d) Name of editor and editor to submit to (if different)

e) Theme of publication—This will help you understand their particular slant.

f) Format of publication, frequency of publication, number of pages and size of circulation—Tells whether magazine, newsletter, journal, tabloid, newspaper, or take-home paper. Frequency of publication indicates quantity of material needed. Number of pages usually indicates how much material they can use. Circulation indicates the amount of exposure your material will receive, and often indicates how well they might pay or probability that they will stay in business.

g) Subscription rate—Amount given is for a one-year subscription in the country of origin. I suggest you subscribe to at least one of your primary markets every year to become better acquainted with its specific focus.

h) Date established—Included only if 1993 or later

i) Openness to freelance; percentage freelance written. If they buy only a small percentage, it often means they are open but receive little that is appropriate. The percentage freelance written indicates how great your chances are of selling to them. When you have a choice, choose those with the higher percentage, but only if you have done your homework and know they are an appropriate market for your material.

j) Preference for query or complete manuscript, if they want a cover letter with complete manuscripts, and whether they will accept phone, fax, or e-mail queries. (If it does not mention cover letters or phone, fax, or e-mail queries, assume they do not accept them.)

k) Payment schedule, payment on acceptance (they pay when the piece is accepted) or publication (they pay when it is published), and rights purchased (see glossary for definitions of different rights)

l) If a publication does not pay, or pays in copies or subscription, that is indicated in bold, capital letters.

m) If a publication is not copyrighted, that is indicated. That means you should ask for your copyright notice to appear on your piece when they publish it, so your rights will be protected.

n) Preferred word lengths and average number of manuscripts purchased per year (in parentheses)

o) Response time—The time they usually take to respond to your query or manuscript submission (add at least two weeks for delays for mailing)

p) Seasonal material (also refers to holiday)—If sending holiday or seasonal material, it should reach them at least the specified length of time in advance.

q) Acceptance of simultaneous submissions and reprints—If they accept simultaneous submissions, it means they will look at submissions (usually timely topic or holiday material) sent simultaneously to several publishers. Best to send to non-overlapping markets (such as denominational), and be sure to always indicate that it is a simultaneous submission. Reprints are pieces you have sold previously, but to which you hold the rights (which means you sold only first or one-time rights to the original publisher and the rights reverted to you as soon as they were published).

r) If they accept, prefer or require submissions on disk, and whether there is extra compensation for that. Most of them seem to want a disk after the piece is accepted, but want a query or hard copy first. If it does not say they prefer or require disks, you should wait and see if they ask for them.

s) Average amount of kill fee, if they pay one. (See glossary for definition.)

t) Whether they use sidebars (see glossary for definition).

u) Their preferred Bible version is indicated. The most popular version is the NIV (New International Version). If no version is indicated, they usually have no preference. See glossary for Bible Versions list.

v) Availability and cost for writer's guidelines, theme list, and sample copies—If the listing says "Guidelines," it means they are available for a #10 SASE (business-sized) with a first-class stamp. The cost for a sample copy, the size of envelope, and number of stamps required are given, if specified (affix stamps to envelope; don't send loose). Tip: If postage required is more than $1.24, I suggest you put $1.24 in postage on the envelope and clearly mark it "Special Standard Mail." (That is enough for up to one pound). If the listing says "Free sample copy," it means you need only to request them; they do not ask for payment or SASE. Note: If sending for both guidelines and sample copy, it is not necessary to send both envelopes; guidelines will be sent with sample copy. If a listing doesn't mention guidelines or a catalog, they probably don't have them.

w) "Not in topical listings" means the publisher has not supplied a list of topics they are interested in.

x) Poetry—Name of poetry editor (if different). Average number of poems bought each year. Types of poetry; number of lines. Payment rate. Maximum number of poems you may submit at one time.

y) Fillers—Name of fillers editor (if different). Types of fillers accepted; word length. Payment rate.

z) Columns/Departments—Name of column editor. Names of columns in the periodical (information in parentheses gives focus of column); word length requirements; payment. Be sure to see sample before sending ms or query. Most columns require a query.

aa) Special Issues or Needs—Indicates topics of special issues they have planned for the year, or unique topics not included in regular subject listings

bb) Ethnic—Any involvement they have in the ethnic market

cc) Contest— Information on contests they sponsor or how to obtain that information

dd) Tips—Tips from the editor on how to break into this market or how to be successful as an author

ee) At the end of some listings you will find a notation as to where that particular periodical placed in the Top 50 Plus Christian Periodical list in 1996, and/or their place in previous years. This list is compiled annually to indicate the most writer-friendly publications. To receive a complete listing, plus a prepared analysis sheet and writer's guidelines for the top 50 of those markets, send $22 (includes postage) to: Sally Stuart, 1647 SW Pheasant Dr., Aloha OR 97006, or call (503)642-9844 for more information.

Some listings also include EPA winners. These awards are made annually by the Evangelical Press Association (a trade organization for Christian periodicals).

6. It is important that you adhere closely to the guidelines set out in these listings. If a publisher asks for a query only, do not send a complete manuscript. Following these guidelines will mark you as a professional.

7. If your manuscript is completed, select the proper topical listing and target audience, and make up a list of possible publishers. Check first to see which ones will accept a complete manuscript (if you want to send it to those that require a query, you will have to write a query letter or book proposal to send first). Please do not assume that your manuscript will be appropriate for all those on the list. Read the primary listing for each and if you are not familiar with a publisher, read their writer's guidelines and study one or more sample copies or book catalog. (The primary listings contain information on how to get these.) Be sure the slant of your manuscript fits the slant of the publisher.

8. If you have an idea for an article, short story, or book but you have not written it yet, a reading of the appropriate topical listing will help you decide on a possible slant or approach. Select some publishers to whom you might send a query about your idea. If your idea is for an article, do not overlook the possibility of writing on the same topic for a number of different periodicals listed under that topic, either with the same target audience or another from the list that indicates an interest. For example, you could write on money management for a general adult magazine, a teen magazine, a women's publication, or one for pastors. Each would require a different slant, but you would get a lot more mileage from that idea.

9. If you do not have an idea, simply start reading through the topical listings or the primary listings. They are sure to trigger any number of book or magazine ideas you could go to work on.

10. If you run into words or terms you are not familiar with, check the glossary at the back of the book for definitions.

11. If you need someone to look at your material to evaluate it or to give it a thorough editing, look up the section on Editorial Services and find someone to send it to for such help. That often will make the difference between success or failure in publishing.

12. If you are a published author with other books to your credit, you may be interested in finding an agent. Unpublished authors generally don't need or won't be able to find an agent. However, some agents will consider unpublished authors (their listing will indicate that), but you must have a completed manuscript before you approach an agent (see agent list). Christian agents are more at a premium than ever, so realize it will be extremely hard to find an agent unless you have had some success in book writing.

13. Check the group list to find a group to join in your area. Go to the conference list to find a conference you might attend this year. Attending a conference every year or two is almost essential to your success as a writer.

14. **ALWAYS SEND AN SASE WITH EVERY QUERY OR MANUSCRIPT.**

15. **DO NOT RELY SOLELY ON THE INFORMATION PROVIDED IN**

THIS MARKET GUIDE. It is just that—a guide—and is not intended to be complete in itself. It is important to your success as a freelance writer that you learn how to use writer's guidelines and study book catalogs or sample copies before submitting to any publisher. Be a professional!

ADDITIONAL RESOURCES TO HELP WITH YOUR WRITING AND MARKETING

1. **1997 Top 50+ Christian Periodical Publishers Packet**—Includes a list of the Top 50+ "writer-friendly" periodicals, pre-prepared analysis sheets, and publisher's guidelines for each of the top 50, and a master form for analyzing your own favorite markets. Saves more than $30 in postage and 25-30 hours of work. $22, postpaid. New packet every year.

2. **The 1997 Christian Writers' Market Guide on computer disk** in ASCII Text on 3½" HD disk, for quick marketing reference. This is in text form as it appears in the book, not in a database. $28 postpaid.

3. **A Market Plan for More Sales**—A step-by-step plan to help you be successful in marketing. Includes 5 reproducible forms. $4.75 postpaid.

4. **The Complete Guide to Christian Writing and Speaking**—A how-to handbook for beginning and advanced writers and speakers written by the 19 members of the editorial staff of *The Christian Communicator*. $12, postpaid.

5. **Permissions Packet**—A compilation of over 20 pages of information directly from publishers on how and when to ask permission to quote from other people's material or from Bible paraphrases. Information not available elsewhere in printed form. $5, postpaid.

6. **The Christian Writer's Book**—Here's a new book that focuses on the writing and selling of Christian books. Many valuable sections, including what an editor does, a guided tour of the book contract, an extensive bibliography of writer's resources, and a style guide for authors and editors. $18 postpaid.

7. **Copyright Law, What You Don't Know Can Cost You**—Answers all the questions about rights and copyright law that affect you as a writer. Simple Q & A format followed by the actual wording of the law. Includes reproducible copyright forms & instructions. $17 postpaid.

8. **Write on Target,** A Five-Phase Program for Nonfiction Writers, by Dennis Hensley & Holly Miller—The craft of writing, the nuts and bolts, finding your niche, selling your manuscript, and mapping your future success as a writer. $14 postpaid.

9. **100 Plus Motivational Moments for Writers and Speakers**—A devotional book specifically for writers and speakers written by successful writers and speakers. $12 postpaid.

10. **You Can Do It! A Guide to Christian Self-Publishing,** by Athena Dean. New! Dean shares insider self-publishing secrets for the Christian market. Takes you step-by-step through the project, including actual budgets and current cost estimates. $10 postpaid.

11. **1997 Internet Directory of Christian Publishers**—New! A handy listing of over 330 Christian publishers who have e-mail addresses or websites. New ones being added as they become available. $5 postpaid.

12. The following resources are all 8-page booklets on areas of specific interest, as indicated:

a. **Keeping Track of Your Periodical Manuscripts**—These pages can be duplicated to keep track of every step involved in sending out your periodical manuscripts to publishers. $4.75 postpaid.

b. **Keeping Track of Your Book Manuscripts**—A similar booklet adapted to postpaid the steps in tracking a book manuscript from idea to publication. $4.75, postpaid.

c. **How to Submit a Book Proposal to a Publisher**—Contains all you need to know to present a professional looking book proposal to a publishing house (includes a sample book proposal). $4.75 postpaid.

d. **How to Submit an Article or Story to a Publisher**—Shows how to write a query, prepare a professional-looking manuscript, and more. $4.75 postpaid.

e. **How to Write That Sure-Sell Magazine Article**—Contains a 3-step writing plan for articles, a list of article types, 12 evaluation questions, sample manuscript page, and more. $4.75 postpaid.

f. **How to Write a Picture Book**—An inside look at how to write, format, and lay out a children's picture book, with tips for those all-important finishing touches. $4.75 postpaid.

g. **How to Write Daily Devotionals That Inspire**—Includes the basic format and patterns for daily devotionals, marketing tips, 12 evaluation questions, and polishing. $4.75 postpaid.

To order any of the above resources, send a list of what you want with your check or money order to: Sally E. Stuart, 1647 SW Pheasant Dr., Aloha OR 97006, (503)642-9844. Fax: (503)848-3658.

13. **The Writer's Edge**—A service that links book writers and Christian publishers. The writer fills out a book information form and sends that along with 3 sample chapters, a synopsis, and a check for $45. The writer receives a brief critique of the manuscript and, if the manuscript is accepted by The Writer's Edge, a synopsis of the manuscript will appear in a newsletter that goes to more than 40 Christian publishers who use The Writer's Edge as a screening tool for unsolicited manuscripts. *For further information, send an SASE to The Writer's Edge, PO Box 1266, Wheaton, IL 60189.*

RESOURCES FOR WRITERS

Below you will find a variety of resources that will help you as you carry out your training or work as a freelance writer. In addition to the resources here, also check out the separate listings for groups, conferences, editorial services, contests (see periodical topics). This is only a preliminary list of resources and will be added to each year as the writer's needs grow and expand.

CORRESPONDENCE COURSES

AT HOME WRITING WORKSHOPS. Director: Marlene Bagnull, Write His Answer Ministries, 316 Blanchard Rd., Drexel Hill PA 19026. E-mail: mbagnull@aol.com. Offers 3 courses of study with 6-10 study units in each. (1) Putting Your Best Foot Forward (lays foundation for your writing ministry), 6 units, $150; (2) Nonfiction (articles, tracts, curriculum, devotionals, how-tos, etc., plus planning a nonfiction book and book proposal), 10 units, $250; (3) Fiction, 10 units, $250. Also offers an easy payment plan of $30 per unit.

CHRISTIAN WRITERS GUILD. Director: Norman B. Rohrer, 260 Fern, Hume CA 93628. (209)335-2333. Offers a 3-year home study course: Discover Your Possibilities in Writing. Includes an introduction to writing, article writing, short inspirational pieces, and fiction, plus a number of additional benefits. Send for your free Starter Kit. Cost for 3-year course is $495. Offers several payment plans and a $75 discount for full payment up front. Special offer through the Christian Writers' Market Guide: Instead of paying $150 down payment, you may pay $25 down, plus $15/month for the next 27 months as you study. Ask about the CWMG special when you request your starter kit.

CHRISTIAN WRITERS INSTITUTE CORRESPONDENCE COURSES. Call or write for information: American Christian Writers, Reg Forder, PO Box 110390, Nashville TN 37222. (800)22-WRITE.

POETRY WRITING SESSION. Mary Sayler, instructor. PO Box 730, DeLand FL 32721-0730. (904)783-3388. Fax (904)738-0169. Six units dealing specifically with poetry: purposes, content, language, meter, and much more. A unique poetry course with a Christian perspective. Cost $175.

WRITING CLASSES ON CASSETTE TAPES

CHRISTIAN WRITERS LEARNING CENTER. Hundreds of cassette tapes to choose from. Cost is $4-5 each, depending on quantity. Send SASE for list of topics to: American Christian Writers, Reg Forder, PO Box 110390, Nashville TN 37222. (800)22-WRITE.

CREATIVE CHRISTIAN MINISTRIES. Tapes on a variety of topics. $4.95 ea.; 3 or more $3.95 ea. Send SASE for list of topics: Creative Christian Ministries, PO Box 12644, Roanoke VA 24027. (703)432-7511. Also has a series called How to Turn Everyday Events into Personal Experience Articles, $19.95, plus $2.05 p/h. Request free writer's catalog.

WRITE HIS ANSWER MINISTRIES. Director: Marlene Bagnull, 316 Blanchard Rd., Drexel Hill PA 19026. E-mail: mbagnull@aol.com. Tapes on 20+ topics, $5 ea. Topics include: Taking the Pain Out of Marketing; Self-publishing; and Turning Personal Experience Into Print. Marlene's day-long seminars (four 90-minute sessions) are $18.95. All tapes include handouts. Also offers a Ministry/Marketing Packet with over 60 resources for $10; and an ABC's of Marketing Packet for $5.

GROUPS/ORGANIZATIONS OF INTEREST

AMERICAN CHRISTIAN WRITERS, PO Box 110390, Nashville TN 37222. (800)21-WRITE. Reg Forder, director.

THE AMY FOUNDATION. Sponsors two annual contests for prizes up to $10,000. One for publication in the secular media and the other for publication in the religious media. For details on both contests, and a copy of last year's winning entries, contact: The Amy Foundation, PO Box 16091, Lansing MI 48901-6091. (517)323-6233. Website: http://www.amyfound.org.

ASSOCIATED CHURCH PRESS, PO Box 30215, Phoenix AZ 85046-0215. (602)569-6371. John Stapert, executive director.

CHRISTIAN BOOKSELLERS ASSN., PO Box 200, Colorado Springs CO 80901-0200. (800)252-1950. Bill Anderson, president.

EVANGELICAL CHRISTIAN PUBLISHERS ASSN., 3225 S. Hardy Dr., Ste. 101, Tempe AZ 85282. (602)966-3998. Doug Ross, pres./CEO.

EVANGELICAL PRESS ASSN., 485 Panorama Rd., Earlysville VA 22936. (804)973-5941. Ronald E. Wilson, director.

INTERNATIONAL CHRISTIAN WRITERS GROUP. Stanley C. Baldwin, director, 12900 SE Nixon, Milwaukie OR 97222. E-mail: SCBaldwin@juno.com. A point of contact for writers around the world.

INTERNATIONAL SMALL PRESS PUBLISHING INSTITUTE. Sponsors 6-8 educational forums a year for publishers and authors. Contact: David Rattigan, director, at e-mail: d.rattigan@smallpress.com, or Theresa Nelson, Jenkins Group, Inc., 121 E. Front St., 4th Fl., Traverse City MI 49684. (616)933-0445. Fax (616)933-0448. E-mail: theresa.nelson@smallpress.com. Website: http://www.smallpress.com.

NATIONAL RELIGIOUS BROADCASTERS., 7839 Ashton Ave., Manassas VA 22110. (703)330-7000. Request information on the Directory of Religious Media.

RELIGION NEWS SERVICE, 1101 Connecticut Ave. NW, Ste 350, Washington DC 20036. (202)463-8777. Fax (202)463-0033. Dale Hanson Bourke, publisher.

RELIGIOUS NEWSWRITERS ASSN. An organization formed to advance the professional standards of religion reporting in the secular media. Joan Connell, Newhouse News Service, 200 Pennsylvania Ave., NW, Washington DC 20006. (202)785-0101.

ON THE INTERNET

CHRISTIAN WRITER'S WORKSHOP. This is an interactive Christian writer's group that meets once a week on the Internet for discussion and has a weekly newsletter that comes by e-mail. To find the club at 9:00 ET on Thursday nights, go to Key Word: Writers—Writer's Club—Chat rooms. Select the Writer's Workshop chat room. They will tell you how to sign up for the newsletter. Contact person is Bill Yates, e-mail: WTYates@aol.com.

CROSSSEARCH is an online directory that offers Internet users a search engine for Christian and religion-related resources. Includes links to nearly 40 ministries on Gospel Communications Network. Website: http://www.cross-search.com.

INTERNET FOR CHRISTIANS, a book by Quentin J. Schultze, Gospel Films, Inc., $12.95. Available at your local Christian bookstore. Author also offers a free newsletter, Internet for Christians. To subscribe send the message "SUBSCRIBE and your e-mail address" to: ifc-request@gospelcom.net. Website: http://www.gospelcom.net/ifc (includes hyperlinks to all listed sites).

JUNO OFFERS FREE E-MAIL SERVICE. This service is free and an easy solution for those who want an e-mail address and the ability to correspond with others by e-mail, but don't need or want additional access to the Internet. There is no obligation for requesting the software or trying it out. E-mail your request to: signup@juno.com, or call (800)654-5866. This service is advertiser supported, and membership is limited to the US for now (although you can communicate with e-mail users in other countries). Since they release a limited number of memberships a day, it may take 6-8 weeks to have your request fulfilled.

RESOURCES FOR WRITERS ON THE WEB. Website: http://www.inter-log.com/ohi/www/writesource.html. To subscribe to Inklings, an electronic newsletter that covers online resources for writers, send e-mail to: majordomo@samuri.com, with the message "subscribe inklings" in the message box.

WEBSITES FOR WRITERS

GENERAL:

Christian Book Distributors (CBD): http://www.christianbook.com. Check out what's selling in the marketplace. Books can be found by publisher, author or subject.

Web Page of Links for Christian Writers: http://users.aol.com/kayhall/ cwise.html. Maintained by Kay Hall.

Internet for Christians: http://www.gospelcom.net/ifc/.

SPECIALTY TOPICS:

Bible Prophecy: http://www.sel-mor.com/armageddon. Links to every Bible Prophecy site on the Web.

Christian Comics International: http://members.aol.com/ChriCom/ or, http://members.aol.com/ChriCat/. Nate Butler can be reached by e-mail at: ChrisCom@aol.com. Also a bimonthly newsletter for writers of Christian Comics is available: New Creation, Kevin Yong, PO Box 254, Dept. C, Temple City CA 91780, or e-mail: Densign888%aol.com. The first issue is free on request. Another contact person for writers interested in scripting a comic or other aspects of comic ministry is: Len Cowan, 519 - 164th Pl. SE, Bothell WA 98012, e-mail: clcowan@xc.org.

    1. **Homeschooling:** http://www.learnathome.com/. For writers in home schooling market.

    2. **Parent Soup:** http://www.parentsoup.com. For writers of parenting articles.

3. **Poetry:** An online version of Poetry Update from London, England. Also sponsors contests with e-mail for information: info@poetry.co.uk. Website: http://www.poetry.co.uk. E-mail for Eric Goldsworthy, the editor/director, is: eric@poetry.co.uk.

SERVICES

CHRISTIAN INFORMATION MINISTRY/RESEARCH SERVICE. Provides fee-based custom research for authors, publishers, ministries, churches and individuals; primarily Bible, theology and Christian living. Basic research fee is $25/hr, plus expenses, such as photocopying. Cecil R. Price, TH.M., PO Box 141055, Dallas TX 75214. (214)827-0057.

CREATIVE RESOURCES: CONSULTING & MEDIA SERVICES. Don S. Otis, PO Box 1665, Sandpoint ID 83864. (208)263-8055. Fax (208)263-9055. E-mail: CMResources@aol.com. A publicist for Christian authors and para-church agencies.

INTERACTIVE DATA MANAGEMENT. David Gibby, 1786 NW Jay St., Roseburg OR 97470, (541)957-1786. Can help you develop a web page; design business logos or brochures; develop interactive CD magazines and books; put all your articles, artwork, or other data on a CD; plus much more. Call or write for information.

CORRESPONDENCE COURSE FOR MANUSCRIPT EDITING. The University of Wisconsin offers a correspondence course in manuscript editing for those wanting to do editing on a professional level or for writers wanting to improve their personal editing skills. Reasonable cost. Contact: U of Wisconsin Extension, 432 N. Lake St., Madison WI 53706. Ask about Manuscript Editing A52.

SOFTWARE

AMERICAN CHRISTIAN WRITERS SOFTWARE FOR WRITERS, PO Box 110390, Nashville TN 37222. (800)21-WRITE. Reg Forder, director. Send a #10 SASE/1 stamp for an 8-page catalog of software (mostly shareware) of special interest to writers.

BESTSELLER: A SUBMISSION TRACKING SOFTWARE FOR WRITERS. For a demo copy send $12 US or $17.50 CAN; for complete program, send $73.95 US or $99.45 CAN (prices include postage) to: Salt Spring Island Software, 137 McPhillips Ave., Salt Spring Island BC, V8K 2T6 Canada. For more information call (604)537-4339.

WRITER'S PUBLICATIONS/SPECIALIZED

THE CHRISTIAN MUSIC DIRECTORY. Easy-to-use guide to the Christian music, film, and video business. James Lloyd Group, PO Box 448, Jacksonville OR 97530. (541)899-8888. Fax (541)488-0418. (Call for current price). Also has The Christian Artist Survival Guide, How to Produce, Manufacture, Distribute & Promote an Independent Christian Record., $33.45, incl. postage.

HEREIN IS LOVE. A bimonthly, 4-page newsletter for inspirational romance writers (those who write romance novels for the Christian market). $15/yr. Jane LaMunyon, 1943 Inyo St., Mojave CA 93501.

TAX TIPS FOR WRITERS. A book that deals with tax law and tax return preparation from a writer's standpoint. Cost is $8.95, plus $1.55 postage. Tower Enterprises, 2130 Sunset Dr., #47, Vista CA 92083. (619)941-9293.

TOPICAL/SUBJECT LISTINGS OF BOOK PUBLISHERS

One of the most difficult aspects of marketing is trying to determine which publishers might be interested in the book you want to write. This topical listing was designed to help you do just that.

First, look up your topic of interest in the following lists. If you don't find the specific topic, check the list of topics in the table of contents and find any related topics. Once you have discovered which publishers are interested in a particular topic, the next step is to secure writer's guidelines and book catalogs from those publishers. Don't assume, just because a particular publisher is listed under your topic, that it would automatically be interested in your book. It is your job to determine whether your approach to the subject will fit within the unique scope of that publisher's catalog. It is also helpful to visit a Christian bookstore to actually see some of the books produced by each publisher you are interested in pursuing.

Note, too, that the primary listings for each publisher indicate what the publisher prefers to see in the way of a query, book proposal, or complete manuscript.

R—Indicates which publishers reprint out-of-print books from other publishers.

APOLOGETICS

ACU Press
Baker Books—R
Baldwin & Knowlton
Bethany House
Black Forest—R
Brentwood—R
Bridge/Logos—R
Broadman & Holman
Christendom Press—R
Christian Univ. Press—R
College Press—R
Concordia
Cornerstone Press
Cornerstone Pub.
Crossway Books
Destiny Image—R
Dry Bones Press—R
Eerdmans Publishing—R
Evangel Publishing—R
Faith Publishing
FOG Publishing
Franciscan Univ. Press—R
Gospel Folio Press
GROUP Publishing
HarperSanFrancisco—R
Harvard House
Harvest House—R
Hendrickson—R
Hensley, Virgil—R
InterVarsity Press

Kregel—R
Loyola Press—R
Magnus Press
Master Books—R
Morehouse—R
Our Sunday Visitor—R
Oxford University
Presbyterian & Reformed
PROBE Ministries
Read 'N Run—R
Regnery Publishing—R
Review & Herald—R
Riehle Foundation
Rose Publishing
Selah House—R
Servant—R
Son-Rise
Still Waters Revival—R
Sword of the Lord—R
Trinity Foundation—R
Tyler Press—R
United Methodist—R
Vital Issues Press—R
Zondervan/Trade—R
Zondervan/Academic

ARCHAEOLOGY

Aanvil Press
Appaloosa—R
Baker Books—R
Baldwin & Knowlton

Bob Jones—R
Brentwood—R
Broadman & Holman
Christian Univ. Press—R
Christopher Publishing
College Press—R
Concordia
Destiny Image—R
Discus Press
Eerdmans Publishing—R
HarperSanFrancisco—R
Hendrickson—R
Fortress Press—R
Monument Press
Morning Star Press—R
New Leaf Press—R
North Point Press—R
Oxford University
Ragged Edge—R
Rainbow Books—R
Read 'N Run—R
Review & Herald—R
TEACH Services—R
Trinity Press Intl.—R
Tyler Press—R
U of Ottawa Press
University Press/America—R
Westminster/John Knox
Winston-Derek—R
Yale Univ. Press—R
Zondervan/Trade—R
Zondervan/Academic

AUTOBIOGRAPHY

Aanvil Press
Appaloosa—R
Baldwin & Knowlton
Bantam Books
Bethany House
Blue Dolphin
Brentwood—R
Bridge/Logos—R
Christian Lit. Crusade
Christopher Publishing
Cornerstone Pub.
Cross Cultural—R
Dabar Publishing—R
Design Commun.—R
Destiny Image—R
Discus Press
Dry Bones Press—R
Eerdmans Publishing—R
Fairway Press—R
FOG Publishing
Guernica Editions—R
HarperSanFrancisco—R
Intl. Awakening Press
Lydia Press—R
MasterMedia
North Point Press—R
Paraclete Press—R
Read 'N Run—R
Regnery Publishing—R
Shaw Publishers, Harold—R
Son-Rise
Southern Baptist Press—R
Still Waters Revival—R
TEACH Services—R
Tyler Press—R
University Press/America—R
VESTA
Vital Issues Press—R
Westminster/John Knox
Windflower—R
Zondervan/Trade—R

BIBLE/BIBLICAL STUDIES

Accent Publications
ACU Press
Alba House—R
Baker Books—R
Baldwin & Knowlton
Bantam Books
Bethany House
Bible Discovery
Brentwood—R
Bridge/Logos—R
Broadman & Holman

Brown-ROA
Chalice Press
Christian Ed Pub.
Christian Lit. Crusade
Christopher Publishing
College Press—R
Concordia
Contemporary Drama Service
Continuum Publishing—R
Cornell Univ Press—R
Cornerstone Pub.
Creation House
Cross Cultural—R
Crossroad Publishing—R
CSS Publishing
Dabar Publishing—R
Destiny Image—R
Discipleship Resources
Eden Publishing
Eerdmans Publishing—R
Evangel Publishing—R
Fairway Press—R
Faith & Life Press
FOG Publishing
Fortress Press—R
Franciscan Univ. Press—R
Goetz Publishing, B.J.
Gospel Folio Press
GROUP Publishing
HarperSanFrancisco—R
Harrison House—R
Harvest House—R
Hendrickson—R
Hensley, Virgil—R
Herald Press
HI-TIME
Holy Cross—R
InterVarsity Press
Judson Press—R
Kindred Productions
Kregel—R
Libros Liguori
Loizeaux (commentary)
Lydia Press—R
Magnus Press
Mercer University Press
Miracle Publishing
Morehouse—R
Morning Star Press—R
New City Press—R
New Hope—R
Our Sunday Visitor—R
Oxford University
Pastoral Press
Pauline Books
Paulist Press
Pentecostal Publishing
Presbyterian & Reformed

Promise Publishing
Ragged Edge—R
Rainbow/Daybreak
Rainbow Publishers
Read 'N Run—R
Regal Books
Resource Publications
Review & Herald—R
Roper Press—R
Royal Productions—R
St. Anthony Messenger—R
Schoettle Publishing—R
Seaside Press—R
Selah House—R
Shaw Publishers, Harold—R
Sheed & Ward—R
Shining Star
Shoestring Press
Son-Rise
Southern Baptist Press—R
Sword of the Lord—R
Treasure Publishing
Trinity Press Intl.—R
Tyler Press—R
United Church Press
United Church Pub.
United Methodist—R
U of Ottawa Press
University Press/America—R
Upper Room Books—R
VESTA
Vital Issues Press—R
Wadsworth—R
Warner Press
Westminster/John Knox
Woman's Miss. Union—R
Wood Lake Books
World Bible Pub.—R
Yale Univ. Press—R
Zondervan/Trade—R
Zondervan/Academic

BIOGRAPHY

Aanvil Press
Alba House—R
Appaloosa—R
Baldwin & Knowlton
Bantam Books
Barbour & Co.—R
Bethany House
Blue Dolphin
Bob Jones—R
Brentwood—R
Cameron Press—R
Catholic Univ/America—R
Christian Lit. Crusade
Christian Univ. Press—R

Christopher Publishing
College Press—R
Cornell Univ. Press—R
Cross Cultural—R
Crossroad Publishing—R
CSS Publishing
Design Commun.—R
Destiny Image—R
Dimension Books—R
Discus Press
Dry Bones Press—R
Eerdmans Publishing—R
Fairway Press—R
Faith Publishing
Friends United Press—R
Good Book
HarperSanFrancisco—R
ICS Publications—R
Impact Christian Books
Intl. Awakening Press
Kaleidoscope Press—R
Kregel—R
Lifetime Book—R
Light and Life—R
Loyola Press—R
Lydia Press—R
MasterMedia
Middle Atlantic—R
Morehouse—R
Morrow and Co., Wm
Mt. Olive College Press
New Hope—R
North Point Press—R
Northstone—R
Our Sunday Visitor—R
Oxford University
Paraclete Press—R
PREP Publishing
Read 'N Run—R
Regnery Publishing—R
Revell, Fleming H.
Review & Herald—R
Riehle Foundation
Royal Productions—R
St. Bede's—R
Servant—R
Shaw Publishers, Harold—R
Son-Rise
Southern Baptist Press—R
Still Waters Revival—R
Sword of the Lord—R
TEACH Services—R
Tyler Press—R
United Church Press
University Press/America—R
Upper Room Books—R
VESTA
Vital Issues Press—R

Warner Press
Westminster/John Knox
Windflower—R
Woman's Miss. Union—R
Yale Univ. Press—R
Zondervan/Trade—R

BOOKLETS

Albury Publishing—R
Barbour & Co.—R
Black Forest Press—R
Cameron Press—R
Christendom Press—R
Christian Lit. Crusade
Christian Publications
Church Growth Inst.
Comments Publishing—R
Cornerstone Pub.
Design Commun.—R
Discipleship Resources
Dry Bones Press—R
Faith & Life Press
Faith Publishing
Forward Movement—R
Franciscan Univ. Press—R
Good Book
Gospel Folio Press
GROUP Publishing
Harvest House—R
Hearth Publishing—R
HI-TIME
Holy Cross—R
InterVarsity Press
Kindred Productions
Libros Liguori
Liguori Publications
Loizeaux
Master Books—R
Middle Atlantic—R
Miracle Publishing
Moody Press (series only)
Our Sunday Visitor—R
Pacific Press—R
Paradise Research
Pauline Books
Pilgrim Press—R
Purple Pomegranate—R
Read 'N Run—R
Riehle Foundation
Rose Publishing
Royal Productions—R
Shaw Publishers, Harold
Sword of the Lord—R
United Methodist—R
Wine Press Publishing
TEACH Services—R
Trinity Foundation—R

Tyler Press—R
United Methodist—R
Vital Issues Press—R
Woman's Miss. Union—R
Wood Lake Books

*CANADIAN/FOREIGN

Cerdic Publications
Essence Publishing
Guernica Editions
Herald Press Canada
Hunt and Thorpe
Inheritance Publications
Kindred Productions
Northstone Publishing
Shoestring Press
Still Waters
Summit Publishing
United Church Pub. Hs
Univ. of Ottawa Press
Vesta Publications
Windflower Communications
Wood Lake Books

CELEBRITY PROFILES

Appaloosa—R
Blue Dolphin
Bridge/Logos—R
Cameron Press—R
Chariot Family Pub.
Christopher Publishing
Destiny Image—R
Discus Press
Cornerstone Pub.
Crossroad Publishing—R
Destiny Image—R
Lifetime Books—R
MasterMedia
Morning Star Press—R
Multnomah Books
New Leaf Press—R
Read 'N Run—R
Revell, Fleming H.
Royal Productions—R
Selah House—R
Shaw Publishers, Harold—R
Wood Lake Books
Zondervan/Trade—R

CHILDREN'S PICTURE BOOKS

Alba House—R
Appaloosa—R
Bay Public., Mel—R
Bethel Publishing—R

Black Forest—R
CEF Press
Chariot Books
Concordia
Cornerstone Pub.
Design Commun.—R
Destiny Image—R
Eerdmans Publishing—R
Fairway Press—R
Gold 'n' Honey Books
GROUP Publishing
Hunt & Thorpe
Illumination Arts
Kaleidoscope Press—R
Lion Publishing
Living the Good News
Lydia Press—R
Morehouse—R
Morris, Joshua
National Baptist—R
Pansophic Publishing
Pauline Books
Paulist Press
Pelican Publishing—R
Read 'N Run—R
Regina Press
Revell, Fleming H.
Roper Press—R
Royal Productions—R
Son-Rise
Standard
Sword of the Lord—R
Treasure Publishing
United Methodist—R
Victor Books
Vital Issues Press—R
Woman's Miss. Union—R
Zondervan/Trade—R

CHRISTIAN EDUCATION

Accent Publications
ACU Press
Alba House—R
Appaloosa—R
Baker Books—R
Bantam Books
Black Forest—R
Brentwood—R
Bristol House—R
Broadman & Holman
Brown-ROA
Chalice Press
Christendom Press—R
Christian Ed Pub.
Christopher Publishing
Concordia
Contemporary Drama Service

Cornerstone Pub.
Cross Cultural—R
CSS Publishing
Destiny Image—R
Discipleship Resources
Eden Publishing
Educational Ministries
Eerdmans Publishing—R
Fairway Press—R
Faith & Life Press
Faith Publishing
Goetz Publishing, B.J.
GROUP Publishing
Harrison House—R
Harvest House—R
Hearth Publishing—R
Hensley, Virgil—R
Hunt & Thorpe
Judson Press—R
Kindred Productions
Libros Liguori
Liguori Publications
Liturgical Press
Loyola Press—R
Master Books—R
Moody Press
Morehouse—R
Morning Star Press—R
National Baptist—R
New Hope—R
New Leaf Press—R
Our Sunday Visitor—R
Paraclete Press—R
Presbyterian & Reformed
PROBE Ministries
Ragged Edge—R
Rainbow/Daybreak
Rainbow Publishers
Read 'N Run—R
Regal Books
Religious Education
Resource Publications
Revell, Fleming H.
Review & Herald—R
Riehle Foundation
Rose Publishing
Royal Productions—R
Scripture Press
Smyth & Helwys
Southern Baptist Press—R
Standard
Still Waters Revival—R
Sword of the Lord—R
Tabor Publishing
TEACH Services—R
Trinity Foundation—R
Tyler Press—R
United Church Press

United Church Pub.
United Methodist—R
VESTA
Vital Issues Press—R
Warner Press
Westminster/John Knox
Windflower—R
Winston-Derek—R
Woman's Miss. Union—R
Wood Lake Books
Zondervan/Trade—R

CHRISTIAN HOME SCHOOLING

Appaloosa—R
Baker Books—R
Bantam Books
Bay Public., Mel—R
Brentwood—R
Brown-ROA
College Press—R
Cornerstone Pub.
Crossway Books
CSS Publishing
Design Commun.—R
Destiny Image—R
Eden Publishing
Eerdmans Publishing—R
Fairway Press—R
Faith & Life Press
Faith Publishing
Shaw Publishers, Harold—R
Hensley, Virgil—R
Hunt & Thorpe
Kaleidoscope Press—R
Morehouse—R
Rainbow/Daybreak
Rainbow Publishers
Rainbow's End
Read 'N Run—R
Revell, Fleming H.
Review & Herald—R
Riehle Foundation
Royal Productions—R
Servant—R
Son-Rise
Standard
Still Waters Revival—R
Sword of the Lord—R
TEACH Services—R
Trinity Foundation--R
Tyler Press—R
Vision House—R
Vital Issues Press—R

CHRISTIAN LIVING

Aanvil Press
ACTA Publications
Alba House—R
Albury Publishing—R
Appaloosa—R
Augsburg—R
Baker Books—R
Bantam Books
Barbour & Co.—R
Barclay Press—R
Bethany House
Bethel Publishing—R
Black Forest—R
Brentwood—R
Bridge/Logos—R
Bristol House—R
Broadman & Holman
Chalice Press
Chariot Family Pub.
Chosen Books
Christian Lit. Crusade
Christian Publications
Christopher Publishing
College Press—R
Concordia
Cornerstone Pub.
Creation House
Cross Cultural—R
Crossroad Publishing—R
Crossway Books
Dabar Publishing—R
Destiny Image—R
Discus Press
Eden Publishing
Eerdmans Publishing—R
Element Books—R
Fairway Press—R
Faith Publishing
FOG Publishing
Forward Movement—R
Franciscan Univ. Press—R
Garborg's—R
GROUP Publishing
HarperSanFrancisco—R
Harrison House—R
Harvest House—R
Haworth Press—R
Hearth Publishing—R
Hendrickson—R
Hensley, Virgil—R
HI-TIME
Holy Cross—R
Honor Books—R
Horizon House—R
Howard Publishing
Innisfree Press

InterVarsity Press
Judson Press—R
Kregel—R
Life Cycle Books—R
Light and Life—R
Liguori Publications
Lion Publishing
Liturgical Press
Loyola Press—R
Lydia Press—R
Magnus Press
MasterMedia
Moody Press
Morehouse—R
Morning Star Press—R
Multnomah Books
Nelson, Thomas
New City Press—R
New Leaf Press—R
Pacific Press—R
Paraclete Press—R
Presbyterian & Reformed
Ragged Edge—R
Rainbow/Daybreak
Rainbow Publishers
Read 'N Run—R
Regal Books
Resurrection Press—R
Revell, Fleming H.
Review & Herald—R
Riehle Foundation
Roper Press—R
Royal Productions—R
St. Bede's—R
Selah House—R
Servant—R
Shaw Publishers, Harold—R
Sheed & Ward—R
Shining Star
Small Helm Press—R
Son-Rise
Standard
Still Waters Revival—R
Sword of the Lord—R
TEACH Services—R
Tyler Press—R
United Church Press
United Methodist—R
Upper Room Books—R
VESTA
Victor Books
Vision House
Vital Issues Press—R
Warner Press
Wellness
Westminster/John Knox
Woman's Miss. Union—R
Wood Lake Books

Zondervan/Trade—R

CHRISTIAN SCHOOL BOOKS

Appaloosa—R
Baker Books—R
Concordia
Cornerstone Pub.
Cross Cultural—R
Fairway Press—R
Faith Publishing
Hensley, Virgil—R
Hunt & Thorpe
Kaleidoscope Press—R
Morehouse—R
Rainbow Publishers
Read 'N Run—R
Riehle Foundation
Royal Productions—R
Son-Rise
Southern Baptist Press—R
Sword of the Lord—R
Tyler Press—R

CHURCH LIFE

ACTA Publications
ACU Press
Alban Institute
Albury Publishing—R
Appaloosa—R
Baker Books—R
Bethany House
Bethel Publishing—R
Black Forest—R
Brentwood—R
Bristol House—R
Broadman & Holman
Cerdic Publications
Chalice Press
Christendom Press—R
Christian Publications
Christian Univ. Press—R
Christopher Publishing
Church Growth Inst.
College Press—R
Concordia
Cornerstone Pub.
Cross Cultural—R
Crossroad Publishing—R
CSS Publishing
Destiny Image—R
Discipleship Resources
Eden Publishing
Eerdmans Publishing—R
Fairway Press—R
Faith Publishing

Forward Movement—R
Friends United Press—R
HarperSanFrancisco—R
Harrison House—R
Hearth Publishing—R
Hendrickson—R
Hensley, Virgil—R
Holy Cross—R
InterVarsity Press
Judson Press—R
Kregel—R
Light and Life—R
Liguori Publications
Loyola Press—R
Moody Press
Morehouse—R
New Leaf Press—R
Our Sunday Visitor—R
Pacific Press—R
Presbyterian & Reformed
Ragged Edge—R
Rainbow/Daybreak
Read 'N Run—R
Regal Books
Revell, Fleming H.
Review & Herald—R
Riehle Foundation
Selah House—R
Shaw Publishers, Harold—R
Sheed & Ward—R
Sword of the Lord—R
Tyler Press—R
United Church Press
United Methodist—R
Upper Room Books—R
VESTA
Vision House—R
Vital Issues Press—R
Warner Press
Wood Lake Books
Zondervan/Trade—R

CHURCH RENEWAL

ACTA Publications
Alban Institute
Baker Books—R
Barclay Press—R
Bethany House
Bethel Publishing—R
Black Forest—R
Brentwood—R
Bridge/Logos—R
Bristol House—R
Broadman & Holman
Cerdic Publications
Chosen Books
Christian Publications

Church Growth Inst.
College Press—R
Concordia
Crossroad Publishing—R
Crossway Books
Dabar Publishing—R
Destiny Image—R
Dimension Books—R
Discipleship Resources
Eden Publishing
Eerdmans Publishing—R
Evangel Publishing—R
Fairway Press—R
Faith Publishing
Fortress Press—R
Franciscan Univ. Press—R
HarperSanFrancisco—R
Harrison House—R
Harvest House—R
Hendrickson—R
Hensley, Virgil—R
InterVarsity Press
Judson Press—R
Kregel—R
Light and Life—R
Loyola Press—R
Middle Atlantic—R
Moody Press
Morehouse—R
Morning Star Press—R
Pacific Press—R
Paraclete Press—R
Pastoral Press
Pastor's Choice
Presbyterian & Reformed
Ragged Edge—R
Read 'N Run—R
Royal Productions—R
Regal Books
Renewal Press
Resurrection Press—R
Revell, Fleming H.
Review & Herald—R
Royal Productions—R
Riehle Foundation
Selah House—R
Servant—R
Sheed & Ward—R
Southern Baptist Press—R
Tyler Press—R
United Church Press
United Church Pub.
United Methodist—R
Upper Room Books—R
VESTA
Vision House—R
Vital Issues Press—R
Westminster/John Knox

Wood Lake Books
Zondervan/Trade—R
Zondervan/Academic

CONTROVERSIAL ISSUES

Baker Books—R
Bantam Books
Black Forest—R
Blue Dolphin
Brentwood—R
Bridge/Logos—R
Chalice Press
Chosen Books
Christendom Press—R
Christian Publications
Continuum Publishing—R
Cornerstone Pub.
Crossroad Publishing—R
Crossway Books
Destiny Image—R
Discus Press
Dry Bones Press—R
Element Books—R
Faith & Life Press
Faith Publishing
FOG Publishing
Fortress Press—R
GROUP Publishing
HarperSanFrancisco—R
Harvest House—R
Haworth Press—R
Hendrickson—R
InterVarsity Press
Judson Press—R
Kregel—R
Lifetime Books—R
Light and Life—R
Lydia Press—R
Magnus Press
MasterMedia
Monument Press
Morehouse—R
Northstone—R
Pilgrim Press—R
Presbyterian & Reformed
PROBE Ministries
Read 'N Run—R
Regnery Publishing—R
Revell, Fleming H.
Review & Herald—R
Riehle Foundation
Selah House—R
Still Waters Revival—R
Sword of the Lord—R
Trinity Foundation—R
Tyler Press—R

United Methodist—R
University Press/America—R
Vision House—R
Vital Issues Press—R
Winston-Derek—R

COOKBOOKS

Appaloosa—R
Bantam Books
Barbour & Co.—R
Brentwood—R
Christopher Publishing
Design Commun.—R
Fairway Press—R
Hearth Publishing—R
Morrow & Company, Wm.
Mt. Olive College Press
North Point Press—R
Read 'N Run—R
Revell, Fleming H.
Royal Productions—R
Son-Rise
Southern Baptist Press—R
Starburst Publishers
TEACH Services—R
Tyler Press—R

COUNSELING AIDS

Accent Publications
Baker Books—R
Bethany House
Black Forest—R
Brentwood—R
Broadman & Holman
Brown-ROA
Chosen Books
Christopher Publishing
College Press—R
Concordia
Continuum Publishing—R
Crossroad Publishing—R
Destiny Image—R
Dimension Books—R
Dry Bones Press—R
Eden Publishing
Eerdmans Publishing—R
Fairway Press—R
Fortress Press—R
GROUP Publishing
HarperSanFrancisco—R
Haworth Press—R
Hensley, Virgil—R
Herald Press
InterVarsity Press
Judson Press—R
Kaleidoscope Press—R

Life Cycle Books—R
Liguori Publications
Loyola Press—R
Morehouse—R
Neibauer Press—R
New Leaf Press—R
Northstone—R
Pastor's Choice
Presbyterian & Reformed
Rainbow's End
Read 'N Run—R
Regal Books
Resource Publications
Resurrection Press—R
Revell, Fleming H.
Review & Herald—R
Royal Productions—R
Servant—R
Shaw Publishers, Harold—R
Son-Rise
Southern Baptist Press—R
Starburst Publishers
Tyler Press—R
United Methodist—R
VESTA
Warner Press
Westminster/John Knox
Zondervan/Trade—R
Zondervan/Academic

CREATION SCIENCE

Aanvil Press
Albury Publishing—R
Black Forest—R
Christopher Publishing
Destiny Image—R
Discus Press
Hensley, Virgil—R
Kaleidoscope Press—R
Multnomah Books
Northstone—R
Pacific Press—R
Presbyterian & Reformed
Rainbow's End
Read 'N Run—R
Revell, Fleming H.
Rose Publishing
Shoestring Press
Sword of the Lord—R
TEACH Services—R

CULTS/OCCULT

Albury Publishing—R
Baker Books—R
Bantam Books
Bethany House

Bridge/Logos—R
Broadman & Holman
Christian Lit. Crusade
Comments Publishing—R
Concordia
Destiny Image—R
Faith Publishing
GROUP Publishing
HarperSanFrancisco—R
Harvard House
Harvest House—R
Hendrickson—R
InterVarsity Press
Kregel—R
Lydia Press—R
Monument Press
Moody Press
Morning Star Press—R
New Leaf Press—R
Open Court—R
Our Sunday Visitor—R
Presbyterian & Reformed
PROBE Ministries—R
Read 'N Run—R
Revell, Fleming H.
Review & Herald—R
Riehle Foundation
Rose Publishing
Selah House—R
Servant—R
Son-Rise
Sword of the Lord—R
TEACH Services—R
Tyler Press—R
U of Ottawa Press
VESTA
Vital Issues Press—R
Zondervan/Trade—R
Zondervan/Academic

CURRENT/SOCIAL ISSUES

Aanvil Press
Alba House—R
Appaloosa—R
Baker Books—R
Baldwin & Knowlton
Bantam Books
Barclay Press—R
Baylor University Press
Beacon Hill Press
Bethany House
Black Forest—R
Blue Dolphin
Brentwood—R
Bridge/Logos—R
Bristol House—R

Broadman & Holman
Chalice Press
Chosen Books
Christendom Press—R
Christian Media—R
Christian Publications
Christian Univ. Press—R
Christopher Publishing
College Press—R
Concordia
Continuum Publishing—R
Cornell Univ. Press—R
Cross Cultural—R
Crossroad Publishing—R
Dabar Publishing—R
Destiny Image—R
Discus Press
Dry Bones Press—R
Eerdmans Publishing—R
Element Books—R
Fairway Press—R
Faith & Life Press
Faith Publishing
FOG Publishing
Fortress Press—R
Forward Movement—R
Friendship Press
GROUP Publishing
HarperSanFrancisco—R
Harvest House—R
Haworth Press—R
Hearth Publishing—R
Hendrickson—R
Herald Press
Horizon House—R
Howard Publishing
InterVarsity Press
Judson Press—R
Kregel—R
Libros Liguori
Life Cycle Books—R
Lifetime Books—R
Liguori Publications
Living the Good News
Loyola Press—R
Lydia Press—R
MasterMedia
Moody Press
Morehouse—R
Multnomah Books
New Hope—R
North Point Press—R
Northstone—R
Oxford University
Paulist Press
Presbyterian & Reformed
Ragged Edge—R
Rainbow Books—R

Read 'N Run—R
Regal Books
Regnery Publishing—R
Resurrection Press—R
Revell, Fleming H.
Review & Herald—R
Riehle Foundation
Selah House—R
Shaw Publishers, Harold—R
Small Helm Press—R
Son-Rise
Still Waters Revival—R
Success Publishers—R
Sword of the Lord—R
Trinity Foundation—R
Tyler Press—R
United Methodist—R
U of Ottawa Press
University Press/America—R
VESTA
Vision House
Vital Issues Press—R
Westminster/John Knox
Woman's Miss. Union—R
Zondervan/Trade—R

CURRICULUM

Accent Bible Curric.
Augsburg—R
Christian Ed Pub.
Christian Univ. Press—R
Church Growth Inst.
Destiny Image—R
Concordia
CSS Publishing
Educational Ministries
GROUP Publishing
Group's Hands-On
Hensley, Virgil—R
Lydia Press—R
Master Books—R
Morehouse—R
Rainbow Publishers
Read 'N Run—R
Regal Books
Rose Publishing
Royal Productions—R
Scripture Press
Smyth & Helwys
Standard
Tyler Press—R
United Church Press
United Methodist—R
University Press/America—R
Wellness
Winston-Derek—R
Wonder Time (mag.)

*DEATH/DYING

ACTA Publications
Albury Publishing—R
Appaloosa—R
Augsburg Books—R
Bridge/Logos—R
Black Forest—R
Blue Dolphin
Broadman & Holman
Christopher Publishing
Conari Press—R
Continuum Publishing—R
CSS Publishing
Fairway Press—R
Fortress Press—R
Forward Movement—R
Harvest House—R
Haworth Press—R
Judson Press—R
Life Cycle Books—R
Liguori Publications
Liturgy Training
Morehouse—R
North Point Press—R
Northstone—R
Paraclete Press—R
PREP Publishing
Read 'N Run—R
Resurrection Press—R
Revell, Fleming H.
Selah House—R
Servant—R
Shaw Publishers, Harold—R
Sheed & Ward—R
So. Methodist Univ.
Sword of the Lord—R
United Methodist—R
Wood Lake Books

DEVOTIONAL BOOKS

Aanvil Press
ACU Press
Alba House—R
Albury Publishing—R
Appaloosa—R
Augsburg—R
Barbour & Co.—R
Barclay Press—R
Beacon Hill Press
Bethel Publishing—R
Bible Discovery
Black Forest—R
Brentwood—R
Bridge/Logos—R
Broadman & Holman
Chariot Books

Chariot Family Publishing
Chosen Books
Christian Lit. Crusade
Christian Publications
Christopher Publishing
Church Street Press
Concordia
Contemporary Drama Service
Continuum Publishing—R
Cornerstone Pub.
Cross Cultural—R
Crossroad Publishing—R
CSS Publishing
Dabar Publishing—R
Design Commun.—R
Destiny Image—R
Discus Press
Dry Bones Press—R
Eden Publishing
Eerdmans Publishing—R
Fairway Press—R
Faith Publishing
FOG Publishing
Franciscan Univ. Press—R
Friends United Press—R
Garborg's—R
Gilgal
Gospel Folio Press
GROUP Publishing
HarperSanFrancisco—R
Harrison House—R
Harvest House—R
Hearth Publishing—R
Hendrickson—R
Hensley, Virgil—R
Herald Press
Honor Books—R
Howard Publishing
Kindred Productions
Kregel—R
Libros Liguori
Light and Life—R
Liguori Publications
Lion Publishing
Loyola Press—R
Lydia Press—R
Morehouse—R
Morning Star Press—R
Multnomah Books
Nelson, Thomas
New Leaf Press—R
Northstone—R
Our Sunday Visitor—R
Pacific Press—R
Paraclete Press—R
Pauline Books
Promise Publishing
Rainbow/Daybreak

Rainbow Publishers
Rainbow's End
Read 'N Run—R
Regal Books
Resurrection Press—R
Revell, Fleming H.
Review & Herald—R
Riehle Foundation
St. Anthony Messenger—R
Selah House—R
Servant—R
Shaw Publishers, Harold—R
Sheed & Ward—R
Sheer Joy! Press
Son-Rise
Standard (for kids)
Sword of the Lord—R
TEACH Services—R
Tyler Press—R
United Church Pub.
United Methodist—R
Upper Room Books—R
VESTA
Victor Books
Vision House—R
Warner Press
Westminster/John Knox
Wood Lake Books
World Bible Pub.—R
Zondervan/Trade—R

DISCIPLESHIP

Accent Publications
ACU Press
Albury Publishing—R
Baker Books—R
Barclay Press—R
Beacon Hill Press
Bethany House
Bethel Publishing—R
Black Forest—R
Brentwood—R
Bridge/Logos—R
Bristol House—R
Broadman & Holman
Chalice Press
Chariot Family Pub.
Chosen Books
Christian Lit. Crusade
Christian Publications
Church Growth Inst.
College Press—R
Concordia
Creation House
Crossway Books
Dabar Publishing—R
Destiny Image—R

Discipleship Resources
Eerdmans Publishing—R
Fairway Press—R
Faith & Life Press
Faith Publishing
Friends United Press—R
GROUP Publishing
HarperSanFrancisco—R
Harvest House—R
Hendrickson—R
Hensley, Virgil—R
Herald Press
Horizon House—R
Howard Publishing
Intl. Awakening Press
InterVarsity Press
Judson Press—R
Kregel—R
Libros Liguori
Light and Life—R
Lydia Press
Middle Atlantic—R
Moody Press
Morehouse—R
Neibauer Press—R
New Hope—R
New Leaf Press—R
Pacific Press—R
Paraclete Press—R
Presbyterian & Reformed
Rainbow/Daybreak
Read 'N Run—R
Regal Books
Revell, Fleming H.
Review & Herald—R
Riehle Foundation
Roper Press—R
Selah House—R
Shaw Publishers, Harold—R
Sheed & Ward—R
Southern Baptist Press—R
Standard
Sword of the Lord—R
Tyler Press—R
United Church Press
United Methodist—R
Upper Room Books—R
VESTA
Vision House
Vital Issues Press—R
Westminster/John Knox
Zondervan/Trade—R

DIVORCE

Aanvil Press
ACTA Publications
Albury Publishing—R

Baker Books—R
Baldwin & Knowlton
Bantam Books
Beacon Hill Press
Bethany House
Brentwood—R
Cerdic Publications
Concordia
Destiny Image—R
Discipleship Resources
Forward Movement—R
Gilgal
HarperSanFrancisco—R
Harvest House—R
Haworth Press—R
Judson Press—R
Libros Liguori
Lydia Press
MasterMedia
Monument Press
Morehouse—R
Northstone—R
PREP Publishing
Presbyterian & Reformed
Read 'N Run—R
Regnery Publishing—R
Resurrection Press—R
Revell, Fleming H.
Review & Herald—R
Shaw Publishers, Harold—R
Sheer Joy! Press
Southern Baptist Press—R
Sword of the Lord—R
TEACH Services—R
Tyler Press—R
United Methodist—R
University Press/America—R
VESTA
Vital Issues Press—R
Zondervan/Trade—R

DOCTRINAL

ACU Press
Albury Publishing—R
Baker Books—R
Bethany House
Brentwood—R
Broadman & Holman
Cerdic Publications
Christendom Press—R
Christian Lit. Crusade
Christian Publications
Christian Univ. Press—R
Concordia
Cross Cultural—R
Crossway Books
Destiny Image—R

Discipleship Resources
Dry Bones Press—R
Eerdmans Publishing—R
Evangel Publishing—R
Fairway Press—R
Faith Publishing
Fortress Press—R
Friends United Press—R
Gospel Folio Press
HarperSanFrancisco—R
Harrison House—R
Hendrickson—R
Intl. Awakening Press
InterVarsity Press
Kregel—R
Libros Liguori
Light and Life—R
Liturgical Press
Loizeaux
Loyola Press—R
Magnus Press
Moody Press
Paulist Press
Pilgrim Press—R
Presbyterian & Reformed
Read 'N Run—R
Revell, Fleming H.
Review & Herald—R
Royal Productions—R
Riehle Foundation
Shaw Publishers, Harold—R
Sheed & Ward—R
Shoestring Press
Southern Baptist Press—R
Still Waters Revival—R
Sword of the Lord—R
Trinity Foundation—R
Tyler Press—R
United Methodist—R
University Press/America—R
VESTA
Vision House—R
Westminster/John Knox
Zondervan/Trade—R

DRAMA

Appaloosa—R
Baker Books—R
Baker's Plays
Baldwin & Knowlton
Black Forest—R
Brentwood—R
Christian Media—R
Church Street Press
Concordia
Contemporary Drama Service
CSS Publishing

Discus Press
Eldridge Pub.
Fairway Press—R
Faith Publishing
GROUP Publishing
Lillenas
Loyola Press—R
Meriwether—R
Miracle Publishing
New Hope—R (missions)
Read 'N Run—R
Resource Publications
Riehle Foundation
Sheer Joy! Press
Southern Baptist Press—R
So. Methodist Univ.
Standard
Tyler Press—R
United Methodist—R (juv)
Windflower—R
Woman's Miss. Union—R
Wood Lake Books

ECONOMICS

Aanvil Press
Brentwood—R
Broadman & Holman
Cerdic Publications
Christopher Publishing
Concordia
Destiny Image—R
Dimension Books—R
Discus Press
Dry Bones Press—R
Eerdmans Publishing—R
FOG Publishing
HarperSanFrancisco—R
Haworth Press—R
MasterMedia
Moody Press
Northstone—R
Oxford University
Paulist Press
Pilgrim Press—R
Read 'N Run—R
Regnery Publishing—R
Review & Herald—R
Starburst Publishers
Trinity Foundation—R
Tyler Press—R
U of Ottawa Press
University Press/America—R
Vital Issues Press—R
Zondervan/Trade—R

ENVIRONMENTAL ISSUES

Aanvil Press
Appaloosa—R
Baker Books—R
Baldwin & Knowlton
Bantam Books
Blue Dolphin
Broadman & Holman
Chalice Press
Christopher Publishing
Concordia
Continuum Publishing
Cornerstone Pub.
Cross Cultural—R
Destiny Image—R
Discus Press
Eerdmans Publishing—R
Element Books—R
Faith & Life Press
Forward Movement—R
Friendship Press
HarperSanFrancisco—R
Haworth Press—R
HI-TIME
Holy Cross—R
Judson Press—R
Liturgy Training
Monument Press
Morehouse—R
North Point Press—R
Northstone—R
Oxford University
Paulist Press
Read 'N Run—R
Resurrection Press—R
Royal Productions—R
Southern Baptist Press—R
So. Methodist Univ.
Starburst Publishers
Trinity Foundation—R
Tyler Press—R
United Methodist—R
U of Ottawa Press
University Press/America—R
Vital Issues Press—R
Zondervan/Trade—R

ETHICS

Aanvil Press
ACU Press
Alba House—R
Baker Books—R
Baldwin & Knowlton
Bantam Books
Baylor University Press

Beacon Hill Press
Bethany House
Black Forest—R
Brentwood—R
Bridge/Logos—R
Broadman & Holman
Chalice Press
Christian Publications
Christian Univ. Press—R
Christopher Publishing
College Press—R
Concordia
Cornell Univ. Press—R
Creation House
Crossroad Publishing—R
Crossway Books
Destiny Image—R
Discus Press
Dry Bones Press—R
Eerdmans Publishing—R
Evangel Publishing—R
Faith Publishing
Fortress Press—R
Forward Movement—R
Friendship Press
HarperSanFrancisco—R
Haworth Press—R
Holy Cross—R
Howard Publishing
InterVarsity Press
Judson Press—R
Kregel—R
Life Cycle Books—R
Lifetime Books—R
Loyola Press—R
MasterMedia
Mercer University Press
Morehouse—R
New Leaf Press—R
North Point Press—R
Northstone—R
Open Court—R
Our Sunday Visitor—R
Oxford University
Paulist Press
Pilgrim Press—R
Presbyterian & Reformed
PROBE Ministries
Read 'N Run—R
Regnery Publishing—R
Resource Publications
Review & Herald—R
Riehle Foundation
Royal Productions—R
Selah House—R
Servant—R
Sheed & Ward—R
So. Methodist Univ.

Still Waters Revival—R
Sword of the Lord—R
Trinity Foundation—R
Trinity Press Intl.—R
Tyler Press—R
United Church Pub.
United Methodist—R
U of Ottawa Press
University Press/America—R
Upper Room Books—R
VESTA
Vision House—R
Vital Issues Press—R
Wadsworth—R
Westminster/John Knox
Yale Univ. Press—R
Zondervan/Trade—R
Zondervan/Academic

ETHNIC/CULTURAL

ACU Press
Augsburg—R
Baker Books—R
Bantam Books
Barclay Press—R
Beacon Hill Press
Black Forest—R
Broadman & Holman
Chalice Press
Christian Univ. Press—R
Christopher Publishing
College Press—R
Concordia
Cornerstone Pub.
Cross Cultural—R
Dabar Publishing—R
Discipleship Resources
Eerdmans Publishing—R
Evangel Publishing—R
Faith & Life Press
Fortress Press—R
Forward Movement—R
Franciscan Univ. Press—R
Friendship Press
Guernica Editions—R
Haworth Press—R
Hensley, Virgil
Herald Press
Holy Cross —R
InterVarsity Press
Judson Press—R
Kaleidoscope Press—R
Kregel—R
Libros Liguori
Liguori Publications
Lydia Press—R
Middle Atlantic—R

Monument Press
Morehouse—R
National Baptist—R
Nelson, Thomas
North Point Press—R
Northstone—R
Pacific Press—R
Palisades
Pelican Publishing—R
Pilgrim Press—R
Read 'N Run—R
Revell, Fleming H.
St. Anthony Messenger—R
Shaw Publishers, Harold—R
So. Methodist Univ.
Standard (few)
United Church Press
United Methodist—R
University Press/America—R
VESTA Publications
Winston-Derek—R
Woman's Miss. Union—R
World Bible Publishers
Zondervan/Trade

EVANGELISM/ WITNESSING

Accent Publications
ACU Press
Albury Publishing—R
Appaloosa—R
Baker Books—R
Beacon Hill Press
Bethany House
Bethel Publishing—R
Black Forest—R
Brentwood—R
Bridge/Logos—R
Bristol House—R
Broadman & Holman
Chosen Books
Christian Publications
Christopher Publishing
Church Growth Inst.
College Press—R
Concordia
Cornerstone Pub.
Crossway Books
Destiny Image—R
Discipleship Resources
Discus Press
Eden Publishing
Eerdmans Publishing—R
Evangel Publishing—R
Fairway Press—R
Faith & Life Press
Faith Publishing

Friends United Press—R
Gospel Folio Press
GROUP Publishing
HarperSanFrancisco—R
Harrison House—R
Harvest House—R
Hensley, Virgil—R
Herald Press
Horizon House—R
Intl. Awakening Press
InterVarsity Press
Judson Press—R
Kregel—R
Langmarc
Light and Life—R
Middle Atlantic—R
Miracle Publishing
Moody Press
Morehouse—R
Morning Star Press—R
Multnomah Books
Neibauer Press—R
Nelson, Thomas
New Hope—R
New Leaf Press—R
Pacific Press—R
Presbyterian & Reformed
Ragged Edge—R
Read 'N Run—R
Regal Books
Resurrection Press—R
Revell, Fleming H.
Review & Herald—R
Riehle Foundation
Roper Press—R
Rose Publishing
Royal Productions—R
Selah House—R
Shaw Publishers, Harold—R
Sheer Joy! Press
Son-Rise
Southern Baptist Press—R
Still Waters Revival—R
Sword of the Lord—R
TEACH Services—R
Tyler Press—R
United Church Press
United Methodist—R
VESTA
Vision House—R
Vital Issues Press—R
Warner Press
Westminster/John Knox
Woman's Miss. Union—R
Wood Lake Books
Zondervan/Trade—R
Zondervan/Academic

EXPOSÉS

Appaloosa—R
Brentwood—R
Christian Publications
Destiny Image—R
Discus Press
Faith Publishing
Harvest House—R
Lifetime Books—R
MasterMedia
Multnomah Books
Open Court—R
Read 'N Run—R
Riehle Foundation
Revell, Fleming H.
Southern Baptist Press—R
Tyler Press—R
Vital Issues Press—R
Zondervan/Trade—R

FAMILY LIFE

Aanvil Press
ACTA Publications
ACU Press
Alba House—R
Albury Publishing—R
Appaloosa—R
Augsburg—R
Baker Books—R
Bantam Books
Barclay Press—R
Beacon Hill Press
Bethany House
Bethel Publishing—R
Black Forest—R
Blue Dolphin
Brentwood—R
Bridge/Logos—R
Broadman & Holman
Chalice Press
Chariot Family Pub.
Christian Publications
Christopher Publishing
Church Growth Inst.
College Press—R
Concordia
Continuum Publishing—R
Cornerstone Pub.
Crossroad Publishing—R
Crossway Books
Destiny Image—R
Discipleship Resources
Discus Press
Eden Publishing
Eerdmans Publishing—R
Fairway Press—R

Faith & Life Press
Faith Publishing
Friends United Press—R
Garborg's—R
GROUP Publishing
HarperSanFrancisco—R
Harrison House—R
Harvest House—R
Haworth Press—R
Hensley, Virgil—R
Herald Press
Holiday House
Honor Books —R
Howard Publishing
Innisfree Press
InterVarsity Press
Judson Press—R
Kindred Productions
Kregel—R
Langmarc
Libros Liguori
Life Cycle Books—R
Light and Life—R
Liguori Publications
Lion Publishing
MasterMedia
Moody Press
Morehouse—R
Multnomah Books
New City Press—R
New Hope—R
New Leaf Press—R
Northstone—R
Our Sunday Visitor—R
Pacific Press—R
Pauline Books
Pelican Publishing—R
PREP Publishing
Presbyterian & Reformed
PROBE Ministries (values)
Ragged Edge—R
Rainbow/Daybreak
Rainbow Publishers
Rainbow's End
Read 'N Run—R
Recovery Communications
Regal Books
Resurrection Press—R
Revell, Fleming H.
Review & Herald—R
Riehle Foundation
Seaside Press—R
Selah House—R
Shaw Publishers, Harold—R
Son-Rise
Southern Baptist Press—R
So. Methodist Univ.
Sower's Press

Still Waters Revival—R
Sword of the Lord—R
Tyler Press—R
United Methodist—R
University Press/America—R
Upper Room Books—R
VESTA
Victor Books
Vision House—R
Vital Issues Press—R
Warner Press
Wellness
Westminster/John Knox
Windflower—R
Wood Lake Books
Zondervan/Trade—R

FICTION: ADULT/ RELIGIOUS

Aanvil Press
Appaloosa—R
Baker Books—R
Baldwin & Knowlton
Bantam Books
Barbour & Co.—R
Beacon Hill Press
Bethany House
Bethel Publishing—R
Black Forest—R
Blue Dolphin
Bridge/Logos—R
Broadman & Holman
Cameron Press—R
Christian Publications
Christopher Publishing
Cornerstone Press
Cornerstone Pub.
Creation House
Cross Cultural—R
Crossway Books
Destiny Image—R
Discus Press
Dry Bones Press—R
Eerdmans Publishing—R
Faith Publishing
Friends United Press—R
Guernica Editions—R
Harvest House—R
Heartsong Presents
Hearth Publishing—R
Herald Press
Horizon House—R
Kregel—R
Lion Publishing
Morrow & Company, Wm.
Mt. Olive College Press
Multnomah Books

Nelson, Thomas
Pacific Press—R
Palisades
Pansophic Publishing
Pelican Publishing—R
PREP Publishing
Rainbow's End
Read 'N Run—R
Revell, Fleming H.
Riehle Foundation
Roper Press—R
Selah House—R
Servant—R
Shaw Publishers, Harold—R
Sheer Joy! Press
Shoestring Press
So. Methodist Univ.
Starburst Publishers
Upper Room Books—R
VESTA
Victor Books
Vision House—R
Windflower—R
Zondervan/Trade—R

FICTION: ADVENTURE

Aanvil Press
Appaloosa—R
Baldwin & Knowlton
Bantam Books
Barbour & Co.—R
Bethany House
Bethel Publishing—R
Black Forest—R
Bob Jones—R
Brentwood—R
Bridge/Logos—R
Broadman & Holman
Christian Ed Pub.
Christian Publications
Christopher Publishing
Concordia
Cornerstone Pub.
Crossway Books
Destiny Image—R
Discus Press
Dry Bones Press—R
Eerdmans Publishing—R
Fairway Press—R
GROUP Publishing (juv/teen)
Hearth Publishing—R
Illumination Arts (juv)
Kaleidoscope Press—R (juv)
Morehouse—R
Morris, Joshua
Morrow & Co., Wm. (juv)
Multnomah Books

Nelson, Thomas
Palisades
PREP Publishing
Read 'N Run—R
Revell, Fleming H.
Selah House—R
Servant—R
Shoestring Press
Southern Baptist Press—R
Starburst Publishers
Sword of the Lord—R
Vision House—R
Windflower—R
Zondervan/Trade—R

FICTION: ALLEGORY

Aanvil Press
Appaloosa—R
Baldwin & Knowlton
Black Forest—R
Bridge/Logos—R
Creation House
Destiny Image—R
Discus Press
Dry Bones Press—R
Eerdmans Publishing—R
Fairway Press—R
Friends United Press—R
GROUP Publishing
Morris, Joshua
Morehouse—R
Multnomah Books
Palisades
Read 'N Run—R
Selah House—R
Sword of the Lord—R
Vision House—R

FICTION: BIBLICAL

Aanvil Press
Appaloosa—R
Baldwin & Knowlton
Beacon Hill Press
Bethel Publishing—R
Black Forest—R
Brentwood—R
Bridge/Logos—R
Christopher Publishing
College Press—R
Concordia
Cornerstone Pub.
Creation House
CSS Publishing
Design Commun.—R
Destiny Image—R
Discus Press

Eerdmans Publishing—R
Fairway Press—R
Faith Publishing
Friends United Press—R
GROUP Publishing
Harvest House—R
Herald Press
Kregel—R
Middle Atlantic—R (juv)
Morehouse—R
Morris, Joshua
Multnomah Books
New Hope—R (juv)
Palisades
Pacific Press—R
Ragged Edge—R (juv)
Read 'N Run—R
Revell, Fleming H.
Riehle Foundation
Selah House—R
Sheer Joy! Press
Southern Baptist Press—R
Sword of the Lord—R
Vision House—R
Windflower—R
Zondervan/Trade—R

FICTION: CONTEMPORARY

Aanvil Press
Appaloosa—R
Baker Books—R
Baldwin & Knowlton
Bantam Books
Barbour & Co.—R
Beacon Hill Press
Bethany House
Bethel Publishing
Black Forest—R
Bob Jones—R
Brentwood—R
Bridge/Logos—R
Broadman & Holman
Christian Ed Pub.
Christian Publications
Christopher Publishing
Concordia
Cornerstone Press
Creation House
Cross Cultural—R
Crossway Books
Destiny Image—R
Discus Press
Eerdmans Publishing—R
Fairway Press—R
Friends United Press—R
Guernica Editions—R

HarperSanFrancisco—R
Harvest House—R
Heartsong Presents
Kindred Productions
Lion Publishing
Middle Atlantic—R (juv)
Morehouse—R
Morris, Joshua
Mt. Olive College Press
Multnomah Books
National Baptist—R
Nelson, Thomas
Palisades
Read 'N Run—R
Revell, Fleming H.
Selah House—R
Shaw Publishers, Harold—R
Southern Baptist Press—R
So. Methodist Univ.
Starburst Publishers
Victor Books
Vision House—R
Windflower—R
Zondervan/Trade—R

*FICTION: ETHNIC

Baker Books—R
Black Forest—R
Blue Dolphin
Cornerstone Pub.
Eerdmans Publishing—R
Guernica Editions—R
Hearth Publishing—R
Kaleidoscope Press—R (juv)
Multnomah Books
Palisades
Pelican Publishing—R
Shaw Publishers, Harold—R
VESTA

FICTION: FANTASY

Aanvil Press
Appaloosa—R
Baldwin & Knowlton
Bantam Books
Destiny Image—R
Discus Press
Dry Bones Press—R
Eerdmans Publishing—R
Fairway Press—R
Illumination Arts (juv)
Multnomah Books
Palisades
Read 'N Run—R
Shaw Publishers, Harold—R
Starburst Publishers

Zondervan/Trade—R

FICTION: FRONTIER

Aanvil Press
Appaloosa—R
Baldwin & Knowlton
Bantam Books
Beacon Hill Press
Bethany House
Bethel Publishing—R
Brentwood—R
Broadman & Holman
Christian Publications
Christopher Publishing
Destiny Image—R
Discus Press
Fairway Press—R
Harvest House—R
Kaleidoscope Press—R (juv)
Multnomah Books
Nelson, Thomas
Palisades
Read 'N Run—R
Revell, Fleming H.
Roper Press—R
Servant—R
Southern Baptist Press—R
Starburst Publishers
Windflower—R
Zondervan/Trade—R

FICTION: FRONTIER/ROMANCE

Aanvil Press
Appaloosa—R
Baldwin & Knowlton
Bantam Books
Barbour & Co.—R
Beacon Hill Press
Bethany House
Bethel Publishing—R
Brentwood—R
Christian Publications
Christopher Publishing
Destiny Image—R
Discus Press
Fairway Press—R
Harvest House—R
Heartsong Presents
Hearth Publishing—R
Multnomah Books
Nelson, Thomas
Palisades
Proclaim Publishing
Read 'N Run—R
Revell, Fleming H.

Roper Press—R
Servant—R
Shoestring Press
Southern Baptist Press—R
Zondervan/Trade—R

FICTION: HISTORICAL

Aanvil Press
Appaloosa—R
Baldwin & Knowlton
Bantam Books
Beacon Hill Press
Bethany House
Bethel Publishing—R
Black Forest—R
Bob Jones—R
Brentwood—R
Broadman & Holman
Cameron Press—R
Christian Publications
Christopher Publishing
Cornerstone Press
Cross Cultural—R
Crossway Books
Destiny Image—R
Discus Press
Eerdmans Publishing—R
Fairway Press—R
HarperSanFrancisco—R
Harvest House—R
Hearth Publishing—R
Herald Press
Holiday House
Horizon House—R
Kregel—R
Lion Publishing
Misty Hill Press
Morehouse—R
Morris, Joshua
Morrow & Company, Wm.
Multnomah Books
Nelson, Thomas
North Point Press—R
Pacific Press—R
Palisades
Pansophic Publishing
PREP Publishing
Ragged Edge—R (juv)
Read 'N Run—R
Revell, Fleming H.
Servant—R
Shoestring Press
Son-Rise
Southern Baptist Press—R
So. Methodist Univ.
Starburst Publishers
Sword of the Lord—R

Victor Books
Vision House
Windflower—R
Zondervan/Trade—R

FICTION: HISTORICAL/ROMANCE

Aanvil Press
Appaloosa—R
Baldwin & Knowlton
Bantam Books
Barbour & Co.—R
Beacon Hill Press
Bethany House
Bethel Publishing—R
Black Forest—R
Brentwood—R
Christian Publications
Christopher Publishing
Creation House
Crossway Books
Destiny Image—R
Discus Press
Fairway Press—R
Harvest House—R
Heartsong Presents
Hearth Publishing—R
Horizon House—R
Kregel—R
Multnomah Books
Nelson, Thomas
Pacific Press—R
Palisades
PREP Publishing
Read 'N Run—R
Revell, Fleming H.
Servant—R
Southern Baptist Press—R
Sword of the Lord—R
Zondervan/Trade—R

FICTION: HUMOR

Aanvil Press
Appaloosa—R
Baldwin & Knowlton
Bantam Books
Bethel Publishing—R
Black Forest—R
Bob Jones—R
Broadman & Holman
Christian Publications
Christopher Publishing
Cornerstone Pub.
Destiny Image—R
Discus Press
Dry Bones Press—R

Fairway Press—R
Friends United Press—R
Hearth Publishing—R
Holiday House
Kaleidoscope Press—R (juv)
Morehouse—R
Morris, Joshua
Multnomah Books
Nelson, Thomas
Palisades
PREP Publishing
Read 'N Run—R
Servant—R
Shaw Publishers, Harold—R
Sheer Joy! Press
Sword of the Lord—R

FICTION: JUVENILE (Ages 8-12)

Appaloosa—R
Barbour & Co.—R
Bay Public., Mel—R
Bethany House
Bethel Publishing—R
Black Forest—R
Bob Jones—R
Broadman & Holman
CEF Press
Christian Publications
Concordia
Cornerstone Press
Cornerstone Pub.
Crossway Books
Design Commun.—R
Destiny Image—R
Eerdmans Publishing—R
Fairway Press—R
Forward Movement—R
Friends United Press—R
Gold 'n' Honey
GROUP Publishing
Hearth Publishing—R
Herald Press
Holiday House
Horizon House—R
Illumination Arts
Kaleidoscope Press—R
Kindred Productions
Living the Good News
Lydia Press—R
Misty Hill Press
Morehouse—R
Morris, Joshua
Pacific Press—R
Pansophic Publishing
Pauline Books
PREP Publishing

Read 'N Run—R
Revell, Fleming H.
Roper Press—R
Sheer Joy! Press
Sword of the Lord—R
Tyler Press—R
Woman's Miss. Union—R
Zondervan/Trade—R

FICTION: LITERARY

Aanvil Press
Appaloosa—R
Baker Books—R
Baldwin & Knowlton
Black Forest—R
Christian Publications
Destiny Image—R
Discus Press
Eerdmans Publishing—R
FOG Publishing
Guernica Editions—R
Morrow & Company, Wm.
Mt. Olive College Press
Multnomah Books
Palisades
PREP Publishing
Read 'N Run—R
Shaw Publishers, Harold—R
So. Methodist Univ.
Sword of the Lord—R
VESTA

FICTION: MYSTERY

Aanvil Press
Appaloosa—R
Baker Books—R
Baldwin & Knowlton
Bantam Books
Bethany House
Bethel Publishing—R
Black Forest—R
Bob Jones—R
Broadman & Holman
Christian Ed Pub.
Christian Publications
Concordia
Cornerstone Pub.
Destiny Image—R
Discus Press
Dry Bones Press—R
Eerdmans Publishing—R
Lion Publishing
Morehouse—R
Morrow & Company, Wm.
Multnomah Books
Nelson, Thomas

Palisades
PREP Publishing
Prescott Press—R
Read 'N Run—R
Revell, Fleming H.
Roper Press—R
Shaw Publishers, Harold—R
Sword of the Lord—R
Victor Books
Vision House—R
Zondervan/Trade—R

FICTION: MYSTERY/ROMANCE

Aanvil Press
Appaloosa—R
Baldwin & Knowlton
Bantam Books
Barbour & Co.—R
Bethany House
Black Forest—R
Brentwood—R
Christian Publications
Destiny Image—R
Discus Press
Fairway Press—R
Harlequin
Harvest House—R
Heartsong Presents
Multnomah Books
Nelson, Thomas
Palisades
PREP Publishing
Rainbow's End
Read 'N Run—R
Revell, Fleming H.
Roper Press—R
Shaw Publishers, Harold—R
Southern Baptist Press—R

FICTION: PLAYS

Aanvil Press
Baker's Plays
Baldwin & Knowlton
Bantam Books
Bay Public., Mel—R
Brentwood—R
Creatively Yours
CSS Publishing
Discus Press
Eldridge Pub. (& musicals)
Fairway Press—R
Lillenas
Meriwether—R
Mt. Olive College Press
National Baptist—R

Pansophic Publishing
Read 'N Run—R
Resource Publications
Sheer Joy! Press
Southern Baptist Press—R
So. Methodist Univ.

FICTION: ROMANCE

Aanvil Press
Appaloosa—R
Baldwin & Knowlton
Bantam Books
Barbour & Co.—R
Bethany House
Black Forest—R
Christian Publications
Destiny Image—R
Discus Press
Fairway Press—R
Harlequin
Harvest House—R
Heartsong Presents
Hearth Publishing—R
Morrow & Company, Wm.
Multnomah Books
Nelson, Thomas
Palisades
Read 'N Run—R
Revell, Fleming H.
Sheer Joy! Press
Starburst Publishers
Zondervan/Trade—R

FICTION: SCIENCE FICTION

Aanvil Press
Appaloosa—R
Baldwin & Knowlton
Bantam Books
Black Forest—R
Cornerstone Pub.
Destiny Image—R
Discus Press
Dry Bones Press—R
Eerdmans Publishing—R
GROUP Publishing
Morrow & Company, Wm.
Multnomah Books
Nelson, Thomas
Read 'N Run—R
Shaw Publishers, Harold—R
Shoestring Press
Vision House—R

FICTION: SHORT STORY COLLECTION

Aanvil Press
Appaloosa—R
Baldwin & Knowlton
Black Forest—R
Christopher Publishing
Concordia
Cornerstone Pub.
CSS Publishing
Design Commun.—R
Destiny Image—R
Discus Press
Dry Bones Press—R
Fairway Press—R
GROUP Publishing
Kaleidoscope Press—R (juv)
Morehouse—R
Mt. Olive College Press
Multnomah Books
National Baptist—R
Northstone—R (juv)
Pelican Publishing—R
Read 'N Run—R
Revell, Fleming H.

FICTION: TEEN/YOUNG ADULT

Aanvil Press
Appaloosa—R
Baldwin & Knowlton
Bay Public., Mel—R
Bethany House
Bethel Publishing—R
Black Forest—R
Bob Jones—R
Bridge/Logos—R
Christian Publications
Cornerstone Pub.
Destiny Image—R
Discus Press
Dry Bones Press—R
Eerdmans Publishing—R
Fairway Press—R
Friends United Press—R
GROUP Publishing
Hearth Publishing—R
Horizon House—R
Living the Good News
Lydia Press—R
Morris, Joshua
Multnomah Books
Palisades
Ragged Edge—R
Read 'N Run—R
St. Mary's Press

Selah House—R
Sheer Joy! Press
Sword of the Lord—R
Windflower—R
Zondervan/Trade—R

GAMES/CRAFTS

Appaloosa—R
Bay Public., Mel—R
Brown-ROA
CEF Press
Concordia
Contemporary Drama Service
CSS Publishing
Educational Ministries
Garborg's—R
GROUP Publishing
Hunt & Thorpe
Judson Press—R
Kaleidoscope Press—R
Meriwether—R
Morehouse—R
Pacific Press—R
Rainbow/Daybreak
Rainbow Publishers
Read 'N Run—R
Shaw Publishers, Harold—R
Shining Star
Standard
Tyler Press—R
United Methodist—R
Wood Lake Books
Zondervan/Trade—R

GIFT BOOKS

Albury Publishing—R
Appaloosa—R
Augsburg—R
Baker Books—R
Barbour & Co.—R
Berrie, Russ
Black Forest—R
Bridge/Logos—R
Calligraphy Collection
Chariot Family Publishers
Christian Publications
Church Street Press
Conari Press—R
Contemporary Drama Service
Cornerstone Pub.
Creation House
Destiny Image—R
Eerdmans Publishing—R (art)
Element Books—R
Garborg's—R
HarperSanFrancisco—R

Honor Books—R
Howard Publishing
Hunt & Thorpe
Image Craft
Kaleidoscope Press—R
Lion Publishing
Living the Good News
Manhattan Greeting Card
Miracle Publishing
Morehouse—R.
Morning Star Press—R
Mt. Olive College Press
Multnomah Books
New Leaf Press—R
Our Sunday Visitor—R
Painted Hearts & Friends
Palisades (romantic)
Read 'N Run—R
Resurrection Press—R
Revell, Fleming H.
Selah House—R
Servant—R
Shaw Publishers, Harold—R
Sunrise Publications
United Methodist—R
Upper Room Books—R
Victor Books
Vision House—R
Warner Press
Westminster/John Knox
Zondervan/Trade—R

GROUP STUDY BOOKS

Alban Institute
Baker Books—R
Brentwood—R
Bridge/Logos—R
Church Growth Inst.
College Press—R
Concordia
Dabar Publishing—R
Destiny Image—R
Discipleship Resources
Fairway Press—R
Faith & Life Press
Faith Publishing
FOG Publishing
GROUP Publishing
HarperSanFrancisco—R
Hendrickson—R
Hensley, Virgil—R
Herald Press
InterVarsity Press
Judson Press—R
Kregel—R
Langmarc
Miracle Publishing

Morehouse—R
Morning Star Press—R
New Hope—R
New Leaf Press—R
Our Sunday Visitor—R
Presbyterian & Reformed
Ragged Edge—R
Rainbow/Daybreak
Rainbow Publishers
Rainbow's End
Read 'N Run—R
Resource Publications
Review & Herald—R
Riehle Foundation
Roper Press—R
Selah House—R
Shaw Publishers, Harold—R
Sheed & Ward—R
Southern Baptist Press—R
Standard
Sword of the Lord—R
Tyler Press—R
United Methodist—R
Upper Room Books—R
VESTA
Vision House—R
Woman's Miss. Union—R
Wood Lake Books
Zondervan/Trade—R

HEALING

Albury Publishing—R
Baker Books—R
Bantam Books
Bethany House
Black Forest—R
Blue Dolphin
Brentwood—R
Bridge/Logos—R
Chosen Books
Christian Lit. Crusade
Christian Publications
Christopher Publishing
Conari Press—R
Concordia
Continuum Publishing—R
Cornerstone Pub.
Crossroad Publishing—R
Dabar Publishing—R
Destiny Image—R
Eerdmans Publishing—R
Elder Books—R
Element Books—R
Fairway Press—R
Faith Publishing
Gilgal
HarperSanFrancisco—R

Harrison House—R
Haworth Press—R
Hensley, Virgil—R
Judson Press—R
Libros Liguori
Lifetime Books—R
Loyola Press—R
MasterMedia
Middle Atlantic—R
Miracle Publishing
Morehouse—R
Morning Star Press—R
Northstone—R
Our Sunday Visitor—R
Paraclete Press—R
Paradise Research
Read 'N Run—R
Recovery Communications
Resource Publications
Resurrection Press—R
Revell, Fleming H.
Review & Herald—R
Riehle Foundation
Selah House—R
Son-Rise
Southern Baptist Press—R
So. Methodist Univ.
Stillpoint Publishing
Success Publishers—R
TEACH Services—R
Tyler Press—R
United Methodist—R
Upper Room Books—R
VESTA
Wood Lake Books

HEALTH

Alba House—R
Albury Publishing—R
Appaloosa—R
Baker Books—R
Bantam Books
Bethany House
Black Forest—R
Blue Dolphin
Bob Jones—R
Brentwood—R
Bridge/Logos—R
Broadman & Holman
Christopher Publishing
Concordia
Continuum Publishing—R
Cornerstone Pub.
Destiny Image—R
Discus Press
Dry Bones Press—R
Eerdmans Publishing—R

Elder Books—R
Element Books—R
Fairway Press—R
Good Book
HarperSanFrancisco—R
Haworth Press—R
Hensley, Virgil—R
Kaleidoscope Press—R
Libros Liguori
Life Cycle Books—R
Lifetime Books—R
Loyola Press—R
MasterMedia
Morehouse—R
Northstone—R
Pacific Press—R
Paraclete Press—R
Paradise Research
Read 'N Run—R
Recovery Communications
Regnery Publishing—R
Revell, Fleming H.
Review & Herald—R
Selah House—R
Servant—R
Shaw Publishers, Harold—R
Shoestring Press
Son-Rise
Southern Baptist Press—R
So. Methodist Univ.
Starburst Publishers
Stillpoint Publishing
TEACH Services—R
Tyler Press—R
United Methodist—R
University Press/America—R
Upper Room Books—R
VESTA
Vital Issues Press—R
Wellness
Zondervan/Trade—R

HISTORICAL

Albury Publishing—R
Appaloosa—R
Baldwin & Knowlton
Bantam Books
Baylor University Press
Bethany House
Black Forest—R
Bob Jones—R
Brentwood—R
Broadman & Holman
Catholic Univ./America—R
Cerdic Publications
Christian Publications
Christian Univ. Press—R

Christopher Publishing
Cistercian Publications
College Press—R
Concordia
Continuum Publishing—R
Cornell Univ. Press—R
Crossroad Publishing—R
Custom Communications
Destiny Image—R
Dimension Books—R
Discus Press
Dry Bones Press—R
Eerdmans Publishing—R
Element Books—R
Evangel Publishing—R
Faith Publishing
Fortress Press—R
Good Book
HarperSanFrancisco—R
Harrison House—R
Hearth Publishing—R
Holiday House
Holy Cross—R
Intl. Awakening Press
InterVarsity Press
Kregel—R
Libros Liguori
Light and Life—R
Loyola Press—R
Mercer University Press
Middle Atlantic—R
Morehouse—R
Morning Star Press—R
Morrow & Company, Wm.
Our Sunday Visitor—R
Oxford University
Pansophic Publishing
Paradise Research
Ragged Edge—R
Read 'N Run—R
Regnery Publishing—R
Review & Herald—R
Riehle Foundation
St. Anthony Messenger—R
St. Bede's—R
Shoestring Press
Son-Rise
Southern Baptist Press—R
So. Methodist Univ.
Still Waters Revival—R
TEACH Services—R
Trinity Foundation—R
Tyler Press—R
United Church Press
United Methodist—R
University Press/America—R
VESTA
Vital Issues Press—R

Windflower—R
Winston-Derek—R
Zondervan/Trade—R
Zondervan/Academic

HOW-TO

Note: See Self-Help, now listed
separately.

Accent Publications
ACTA Publications
Alba House—R
Albury Publishing—R
Appaloosa—R
Augsburg—R
Baker Books—R
Bantam Books
Bethany House
Bethel Publishing—R
Black Forest—R
Blue Dolphin
Brentwood—R
Bridge/Logos—R
Broadman & Holman
Brown-ROA
Chosen Books
Christian Publications
Christopher Publishing
Church Street Press
Concordia
Continuum Publishing—R
Cornerstone Pub.
Crossroad Publishing—R
CSS Publishing
Dabar Publishing—R
Design Commun.—R
Destiny Image—R
Discus Press
Dry Bones Press—R
Elder Books—R
Element Books—R
Fairway Press—R
Faith Publishing
Gilgal
GROUP Publishing
HarperSanFrancisco—R
Harrison House—R
Hensley, Virgil—R
Howard Publishing
InterVarsity Press
Judson Press—R
Kaleidoscope Press—R
Libros Liguori
Lifetime Books—R
Living the Good News
Loyola Press—R
Lydia Press—R

MasterMedia
Miracle Publishing
Morehouse—R
Morning Star Press—R
Morrow & Company, Wm.
Mt. Olive College Press
New City Press—R
New Leaf Press—R
Northstone—R
Our Sunday Visitor—R
Pansophic Publishing
Paradise Research
Pauline Books
Pentecostal Publishing
Rainbow Books—R
Rainbow's End
Read 'N Run—R
Recovery Communications
Resource Publications
Revell, Fleming H.
Review & Herald—R
Riehle Foundation
Royal Productions—R
Selah House—R
Servant—R
Shaw Publishers, Harold—R
Sheed & Ward—R
Son-Rise
Southern Baptist Press—R
Standard
Starburst Publishers
Still Waters Revival—R
Success Publishers—R
Sword of the Lord—R
TEACH Services—R
Tyler Press—R
Vital Issues Press—R
Westminster/John Knox
Zondervan/Trade—R

HUMOR

Aanvil Press
Albury Publishing—R
Appaloosa—R
Baldwin & Knowlton
Bantam Books
Barbour & Co.—R
Bethel Publishing—R
Black Forest—R
Blue Dolphin
Bob Jones—R
Brentwood—R
Bridge/Logos—R
Broadman & Holman
Christian Publications
Christopher Publishing
Concordia

Cornerstone Pub.
CSS Publishing
Destiny Image—R
Dimension Books—R
Discus Press
Dry Bones Press—R
Fairway Press—R
Faith Publishing
Friends United Press—R
Garborg's—R
GROUP Publishing
HarperSanFrancisco—R
Harvest House—R
Hearth Publishing—R
Holiday House
Honor Books—R
Howard Publishing
InterVarsity Press
Kaleidoscope Press—R
Light and Life—R
MasterMedia
Meriwether—R
Moody Press
Morehouse—R
Multnomah Books
New Leaf Press—R
Pacific Press—R
PREP Publishing
Read 'N Run—R
Regnery Publishing—R
Revell, Fleming H.
Review & Herald—R
Riehle Foundation
Selah House—R
Servant—R
Son-Rise
Southern Baptist Press—R
Tyler Press—R
United Methodist—R
Upper Room Books—R
Vital Issues Press—R
Zondervan/Trade—R

INSPIRATIONAL

Aanvil Press
ACU Press
Albury Publishing—R
Appaloosa—R
Augsburg—R
Baker Books—R
Bantam Books
Barbour & Co.—R
Beacon Hill Press
Bethany House
Bethel Publishing—R
Black Forest—R
Blue Dolphin

Brentwood—R
Bridge/Logos—R
Broadman & Holman
Cameron Press—R
Catholic Book Publishing
Chariot Family Pub.
Christian Lit. Crusade
Christian Publications
Christopher Publishing
Conari Press—R
Concordia
Cornerstone Pub.
Crossroad Publishing—R
Dabar Publishing—R
Design Commun.—R
Destiny Image—R
Discus Press
Elder Books—R
Element Books—R
Fairway Press—R
Faith Publishing
FOG Publishing
Franciscan Univ. Press—R
Friends United Press—R
Garborg's—R
Gilgal
HarperSanFrancisco—R
Harvest House—R
Hendrickson—R
Hensley, Virgil—R
Honor Books—R
Howard Publishing
ICS Publications—R
InterVarsity Press
Kaleidoscope Press—R
Kindred Productions
Langmarc
Libros Liguori
Lifetime Books—R
Light and Life—R
Loyola Press—R
Lydia Press—R
MasterMedia
Middle Atlantic—R
Miracle Publishing
Moody Press
Morehouse—R
Morning Star Press—R
Multnomah Books
Nelson, Thomas
New Leaf Press—R
Northstone—R
Our Sunday Visitor—R
Pacific Press—R
Paradise Research
Pelican Publishing—R
PREP Publishing
Ragged Edge—R

Rainbow/Daybreak
Read 'N Run—R
Resurrection Press—R
Revell, Fleming H.
Review & Herald—R
Riehle Foundation
St. Anthony Messenger—R
Selah House—R
Servant—R
Shaw Publishers, Harold—R
Sheed & Ward—R
Sheer Joy! Press
Son-Rise
Southern Baptist Press—R
Success Publishers—R
Sword of the Lord—R
TEACH Services—R
Tyler Press—R
United Church Press
United Methodist—R
Upper Room Books—R
VESTA
Victor Books
Vision House—R
Vital Issues Press—R
Wellness
Westminster/John Knox
Winston-Derek—R
World Bible Pub.—R
Zondervan/Trade—R

LEADERSHIP

ACU Press
Albury Publishing—R
Appaloosa—R
Baker Books—R
Bantam Books
Beacon Hill Press
Bethel Publishing—R
Black Forest—R
Bridge/Logos—R
Broadman & Holman
Chalice Press
Christian Publications
Christopher Publishing
Church Growth Inst.
College Press—R
Continuum Publishing—R
Cornerstone Pub.
Creation House
Destiny Image—R
Discipleship Resources
Discus Press
Faith Publishing
Fortress Press—R
GROUP Publishing
Harvest House—R

Hensley, Virgil—R
Honor Books—R
InterVarsity Press
Judson Press—R
Kregel—R
Lifetime Books—R
Light and Life—R
MasterMedia
Middle Atlantic—R
Moody Press
Morehouse—R
Multnomah Books
New Leaf Press—R
Paulist Press
Rainbow/Daybreak
Read 'N Run—R
Regal Books
Revell, Fleming H.
Riehle Foundation
Selah House—R
Shaw Publishers, Harold—R
Standard
Success Publishers—R
Tyler Press—R
United Methodist—R
Upper Room Books—R
Victor Books
Vision House—R
Vital Issues Press—R

LITURGICAL STUDIES

Alba House—R
American Cath. Press—R
Blue Dolphin
Brentwood—R
Catholic Book Publishing
Chalice Press
Christendom Press—R
Christian Univ. Press—R
Christopher Publishing
Concordia
Cornell Univ. Press—R
Crossroad Publishing—R
CSS Publishing
Discipleship Resources
Dry Bones Press—R
Eerdmans Publishing—R
Fairway Press—R
Faith Publishing
GROUP Publishing
HarperSanFrancisco—R
Hendrickson—R
Holy Cross—R
Judson Press—R
Liturgy Training
Morehouse—R
Morning Star Press—R

Oxford University
Pastoral Press
Paulist Press
Presbyterian & Reformed
Ragged Edge—R
Read 'N Run—R
Resource Publications
Riehle Foundation
St. Bede's—R
Sheed & Ward—R
Southern Baptist Press—R
Trinity Press Intl.—R
Tyler Press—R
United Methodist—R
U of Ottawa Press
University Press/America—R
Upper Room Books—R
VESTA
Westminster/John Knox
Wood Lake Books

MARRIAGE

ACTA Publications
Alba House—R
Albury Publishing—R
Appaloosa—R
Baker Books—R
Baldwin & Knowlton
Bantam Books
Beacon Hill Press
Bethany House
Bethel Publishing—R
Bantam Books
Black Forest—R
Brentwood—R
Bridge/Logos—R
Broadman & Holman
Cerdic Publications
Chalice Press
Chariot Family Pub.
College Press—R
Concordia
Continuum Publishing—R
Cornerstone Pub.
Crossroad Publishing—R
Crossway Books
CSS Publishing
Dabar Publishing—R
Destiny Image—R
Discipleship Resources
Discus Press
Eerdmans Publishing—R
Fairway Press—R
Faith Publishing
Focus on the Family
Fortress Press—R
Forward Movement—R

Garborg's—R
HarperSanFrancisco—R
Harrison House—R
Harvest House—R
Haworth Press—R
Hensley, Virgil—R
Herald Press
Holy Cross—R
Honor Books—R
Howard Publishing
InterVarsity Press
Judson Press—R
Kregel—R
Libros Liguori
Lifetime Books—R
Liguori Publications
Lion Publishing
Loyola Press—R
MasterMedia
Morehouse—R
Multnomah Books
New Leaf Press—R
Northstone—R
Pacific Press—R
Pauline Books
Presbyterian & Reformed
Ragged Edge—R
Rainbow/Daybreak
Read 'N Run—R
Regal Books
Resource Publications
Resurrection Press—R
Revell, Fleming H.
Review & Herald—R
Riehle Foundation
St. Anthony Messenger—R
Selah House—R
Servant—R
Shaw Publishers, Harold—R
Sheed & Ward—R
Sheer Joy! Press
Southern Baptist Press—R
Sower's Press
So. Methodist Univ.
Standard
Still Waters Revival—R
Sword of the Lord—R
Tyler Press—R
United Methodist—R
University Press/America—R
Upper Room Books—R
VESTA
Victor Books
Vision House—R
Vital Issues Press—R
Westminster/John Knox
Wood Lake Books
Zondervan/Trade—R

MEN'S BOOKS

Aanvil Press
ACTA Publications
Albury Publishing—R
Augsburg—R
Baker Books—R
Bantam Books
Beacon Hill Press
Bethany House
Bethel Publishing—R
Black Forest—R
Blue Dolphin
Bridge/Logos—R
Broadman & Holman
Chalice Press
Chariot Family Pub.
Christian Publications
Concordia
Continuum Publishing
Cornerstone Pub.
Crossroad Publishing—R
Crossway Books
Destiny Image—R
Discipleship Resources
Discus Press
Faith Publishing
Focus on the Family
Forward Movement—R
Harvest House—R
Hensley, Virgil—R
Honor Books—R
Kregel—R
Liguori Publications
MasterMedia
Moody Press
Morehouse—R
Multnomah Books
New Leaf Press—R
Northstone—R
Our Sunday Visitor—R
Pacific Press—R
Pilgrim Press—R
Presbyterian & Reformed
Rainbow/Daybreak
Read 'N Run—R
Regal Books
Resource Publications
Resurrection Press—R
Revell, Fleming H.
Riehle Foundation
Selah House—R
Servant—R
Shaw Publishers, Harold—R
SonRise
Sword of the Lord—R
Tyler Press—R
United Church Press

United Methodist—R
University Press/America—R
Vision House—R
Vital Issues Press—R
Winston-Derek—R

MIRACLES

Albury Publishing—R
Appaloosa—R
Baker Books—R
Baldwin & Knowlton
Black Forest—R
Brentwood—R
Bridge/Logos—R
Broadman & Holman
Chosen Books
Christian Publications
Cornerstone Pub.
Destiny Image—R
Fairway Press—R
Faith Publishing
FOG Publishing
Friends United Press—R
HarperSanFrancisco—R
Harrison House—R
Honor Books—R
MasterMedia
Miracle Publishing
Morning Star Press—R
Our Sunday Visitor—R
Paraclete Press—R
Read 'N Run—R
Revell, Fleming H.
Review & Herald—R
Riehle Foundation
Royal Productions—R
Selah House—R
Servant—R
Shaw Publishers, Harold—R
Shoestring Press
Southern Baptist Press—R
Sword of the Lord—R
Tyler Press—R
United Methodist—R
Upper Room Books—R
VESTA
Vision House

MISSIONARY

ACU Press
Albury Publishing—R
Barbour & Co.—R
Bethany House
Black Forest—R
Bob Jones—R
Brentwood—R

Chosen Books
Christian Lit. Crusade
Christian Publications
Christian Univ. Press—R
Christopher Publishing
Concordia
Cross Cultural—R
Destiny Image—R
Discus Press
Eerdmans Publishing—R
Fairway Press—R
Faith Publishing
Friendship Press
Friends United Press—R
HarperSanFrancisco—R
Horizon House—R
Middle Atlantic—R
Miracle Publishing
New Hope—R
Promise Publishing
Read 'N Run—R
Review & Herald—R
Riehle Foundation
Southern Baptist Press—R
Sword of the Lord—R
TEACH Services—R
Tyler Press—R
United Methodist—R
VESTA
Vital Issues Press—R
Westminster/John Knox
Woman's Miss. Union—R
Zondervan/Academic

MONEY MANAGEMENT

Alban Institute
Appaloosa—R
Baker Books—R
Bantam Books
Bethany House
Blue Dolphin
Brentwood—R
Broadman & Holman
Chariot Family Pub.
Christopher Publishing
Church Growth Inst.
Concordia
Cornerstone Pub.
Destiny Image—R
Discus Press
Fairway Press—R
HarperSanFrancisco—R
Hensley, Virgil—R
Howard Publishing
Lifetime Books—R
MasterMedia
Miracle Publishing

New Leaf Press—R
Read 'N Run—R
Regnery Publishing—R
Revell, Fleming H.
Review & Herald—R
Servant—R
Shaw Publishers, Harold—R
Southern Baptist Press—R
Starburst Publishers
TEACH Services—R
Tyler Press—R
United Methodist—R
Vision House—R
Winston-Derek—R
Zondervan/Trade—R

MUSIC-RELATED BOOKS

ACU Press
Albury Publishing—R
American Cath. Press—R
Appaloosa—R
Bay Public., Mel—R
Christian Media—R
Christopher Publishing
Church Street Press
Concordia
Contemporary Drama Service
Cornell Univ. Press—R
Cornerstone Press
Destiny Image—R
Dimension Books—R
Discipleship Resources
GROUP Publishing
HarperSanFrancisco—R
Judson Press—R
Lifetime Books—R
Lillenas
Liturgy Training
Middle Atlantic—R
Morehouse—R
North Point Press—R
Paraclete Press—R
Pastoral Press
Ragged Edge—R
Read 'N Run—R
Standard
Sword of the Lord—R
Tyler Press—R
United Methodist—R
Upper Room Books—R
Windflower—R
Wood Lake Books

PAMPHLETS

American Cath. Press—R
Black Forest—R

Cameron Press—R
Christian Univ. Press—R
Comments Publishing—R
Cornerstone Pub.
Design Commun.—R
Dry Bones Press—R
Faith Publishing (maybe)
Forward Movement—R
Franciscan Univ. Press—R
Good Book
Gospel Folio Press
Hearth Publishing—R
HI-TIME
Kindred Productions
Libros Liguori
Life Cycle Books
Liguori Publications
Master Books—R
Middle Atlantic—R
Miracle Publishing
Neibauer Press—R
Our Sunday Visitor—R
Pacific Press—R
Paradise Research
Pauline Books
Purple Pomegranate—R
Read 'N Run—R
Riehle Foundation (maybe)
Rose Publishing
Royal Productions—R
Shaw Publishing, Harold—R
Sword of the Lord—R
TEACH Services—R
Wine Press Publishing

PARENTING

Aanvil Press
ACTA Publications
ACU Press
Albury Publishing—R
Appaloosa—R
Augsburg—R
Baker Books—R
Bantam Books
Beacon Hill Press
Bethany House
Black Forest—R
Brentwood—R
Bridge/Logos—R
Broadman & Holman
Chalice Press
Chariot Family Pub.
Christian Publications
Christopher Publishing
Church Growth Inst.
College Press—R
Conari Press—R

Concordia
Cornerstone Pub.
Crossroad Publishing—R
Crossway Books
CSS Publishing
Dabar Publishing—R
Destiny Image—R
Discus Press
Eden Publishing
Eerdmans Publishing—R
Fairway Press—R
Faith & Life Press
Faith Publishing
Focus on the Family
Forward Movement—R
Garborg's—R
GROUP Publishing
HarperSanFrancisco—R
Harrison House—R
Harvest House—R
Hensley, Virgil—R
Horizon House—R
Howard Publishing
InterVarsity Press
Judson Press—R
Kaleidoscope Press—R
Libros Liguori
Liguori Publications
Lion Publishing
Living the Good News
Loyola Press—R
MasterMedia
Morehouse—R
Multnomah Books
New Leaf Press—R
Northstone—R
Our Sunday Visitor—R
Pacific Press—R
Pauline Books
Presbyterian & Reformed
Ragged Edge—R
Rainbow Books—R
Rainbow/Daybreak
Read 'N Run—R
Regal Books
Resurrection Press—R
Revell, Fleming H.
Review & Herald—R
Riehle Foundation
Selah House—R
Servant—R
Shaw Publishers, Harold—R
Sheed & Ward—R
Standard
Starburst Publishers
Still Waters Revival—R
Success Publishers—R
Sword of the Lord—R

Tabor Publishing
TEACH Services—R
Tyler Press—R
United Church Press
United Methodist—R
Upper Room Books—R
VESTA
Victor Books
Vital Issues Press—R
Westminster/John Knox
Wood Lake Books
Zondervan/Trade—R

PASTORS' HELPS

Accent Publications
ACTA Publications
Alba House—R
Alban Institute
Albury Publishing—R
Baker Books—R
Beacon Hill Press
Bethany House
Bridge/Logos—R
Black Forest—R
Brentwood—R
Bristol House—R
Broadman & Holman
Brown-ROA
Christian Lit. Crusade
Christian Publications
Christopher Publishing
Church Growth Inst.
College Press—R
Concordia
CSS Publishing
Destiny Image—R
Discipleship Resources
Discus Press
Eerdmans Publishing—R
Evangel Publishing—R
Fairway Press—R
Fortress Press—R
GROUP Publishing
HarperSanFrancisco—R
Harrison House—R
Haworth Press—R
Hendrickson—R
Hensley, Virgil—R
Judson Press—R
Kregel—R
Langmarc
Libros Liguori
Liguori Publications
Loizeaux
Miracle Publishing
Morehouse—R
Multnomah Books

Neibauer Press—R
New Leaf Press—R
Our Sunday Visitor—R
Pacific Press—R
Pastor's Choice
Paulist Press
Presbyterian & Reformed
Read 'N Run—R
Regal Books
Religious Education
Resurrection Press—R
Revell, Fleming H.
Review & Herald—R
Selah House—R
Southern Baptist Press—R
Standard
Sword of the Lord—R
Tyler Press—R
United Church Press
United Methodist—R
Vital Issues Press—R
Wellness
Westminster/John Knox
Wood Lake Books
Zondervan/Trade—R

PERSONAL EXPERIENCE

Bantam Books
Beacon Hill Press
Black Forest—R
Brentwood—R
Christian Lit. Crusade
Concordia
Dabar Publishing—R
Design Commun.—R
Destiny Image—R
Discus Press
Dry Bones Press—R
Eerdmans Publishing—R
Fairway Press—R
Friends United Press—R
Gilgal
HarperSanFrancisco—R
Innisfree Press
Loyola Press—R
Lydia Press—R
Miracle Publishing
Pacific Press—R
Rainbow's End
Read 'N Run—R
Review & Herald—R
Shaw Publishers, Harold—R
Son-Rise
Southern Baptist Press—R
Sword of the Lord—R
TEACH Services—R

Tyler Press—R
United Methodist—R
VESTA
Vital Issues Press—R
Windflower—R
Zondervan/Trade—R
Hensley, Virgil—R

PERSONAL RENEWAL

Baker Books—R
Barclay Press—R
Beacon Hill Press
Bethany House
Black Forest—R
Blue Dolphin
Broadman & Holman
Chosen Books
Christian Publications
Christopher Publishing
College Press—R
Creation House
Crossroad Publishing—R
Destiny Image—R
Discus Press
Eerdmans Publishing—R
Faith Publishing
Forward Movement—R
Friends United Press—R
Garborg's—R
GROUP Publishing
Haworth Press—R
Hendrickson—R
Intl. Awakening Press
Libros Liguori
Lydia Press
Middle Atlantic—R
Rainbow/Daybreak
Read 'N Run—R
Regal Books
Revell, Fleming H.
Riehle Foundation
Shaw Publishers, Harold—R
Tyler Press—R
United Methodist—R
Vision House—R

PHILOSOPHY

Aanvil Press
ACU Press
Alba House—R
Appaloosa—R
Baldwin & Knowlton
Bantam Books
Black Forest—R
Brentwood—R
Catholic Univ./America—R

Christendom Press—R
Christian Univ. Press—R
Christopher Publishing
Concordia
Continuum Publishing—R
Cornell Univ. Press—R
Cornerstone Press
Cross Cultural—R
Crossroad Publishing—R
Destiny Image—R
Discus Press
Eerdmans Publishing—R
Element Books—R
Fairway Press—R
Faith Publishing
Friends United Press—R
HarperSanFrancisco—R
Hendrickson—R
InterVarsity Press
Loyola Press—R
Mercer University Press
North Point Press—R
Northstone—R
Open Court—R
Oxford University
Pansophic Publishing
Paulist Press
Read 'N Run—R
Regnery Publishing—R
Riehle Foundation
Still Waters Revival—R
Tabor Publishing
Trinity Foundation—R
United Methodist—R
U of Ottawa Press
University Press/America—R
VESTA
Vital Issues Press—R
Wadsworth—R
Winston-Derek—R
Yale Univ. Press—R
Zondervan/Trade—R
Zondervan/Academic

POETRY

Appaloosa—R
Black Forest—R
Brentwood—R
Christian Lit. Crusade
Christopher Publishing
Destiny Image—R
Cornerstone Press
Creatively Yours
Design Commun.—R
Destiny Image—R
Dry Bones Press—R
Fairway Press—R

Garborg's—R
Guernica Editions—R
HarperSanFrancisco—R
Illumination Arts (juv.)
Image Books—R
Middle Atlantic—R
Miracle Publishing
Morrow & Company, Wm.
Mt. Olive College Press
Poets Cove Press
Rainbow's End
Read 'N Run—R
Shaw Publishing, Harold—R
Southern Baptist Press—R
Sword of the Lord—R
TEACH Services—R
Tyler Press—R
VESTA
Vital Issues Press—R
Westminster/John Knox
Windflower—R

POLITICAL THEORY

Appaloosa—R
Bantam Books
Baylor University Press
Brentwood—R
Catholic Univ./America—R
Christian Univ. Press—R
Christopher Publishing
Concordia
Crossroad Publishing—R
Faith Publishing
Friendship Press
HarperSanFrancisco—R
Judson Press—R
Loyola Press—R
MasterMedia
North Point Press—R
Northstone—R
Open Court—R
Pilgrim Press—R
PROBE Ministries
Read 'N Run—R
Regnery Publishing—R
Riehle Foundation
Still Waters Revival—R
Trinity Foundation—R
Tyler Press—R
United Methodist—R
U of Ottawa Press
University Press/America—R
VESTA
Vital Issues Press—R

PRAYER

ACTA Publications
ACU Press
Alba House—R
Albury Publishing—R
Appaloosa—R
Augsburg—R
Baker Books—R
Bantam Books
Barbour & Co.—R
Barclay Press—R
Beacon Hill Press
Bethany House
Bethel Publishing—R
Black Forest—R
Brentwood—R
Bridge/Logos—R
Bristol House—R
Broadman & Holman
Brown-ROA
Catholic Book Publishing
Chosen Books
Christian Lit. Crusade
Christian Publications
Concordia
Continuum Publishing
Creation House
Cross Cultural—R
Crossroad Publishing—R
CSS Publishing
Dabar Publishing—R
Design Commun.—R
Destiny Image—R
Eerdmans Publishing—R
Fairway Press—R
Faith & Life Press
Faith Publishing
FOG Publishing
Forward Movement—R
Friends United Press—R
Garborg's—R
GROUP Publishing
HarperSanFrancisco—R
Harrison House—R
Harvest House—R
Hendrickson—R
Hensley, Virgil—R
Holy Cross—R
Howard Publishing
ICS Publications—R
Intl. Awakening Press
InterVarsity Press
Judson Press—R
Kregel—R
Libros Liguori
Light and Life—R
Liguori Publications

Lion Publishing
Liturgy Training
Living the Good News
Loyola Press—R
Lydia Press—R
Middle Atlantic—R
Miracle Publishing
Moody Press
Morehouse—R
Morning Star Press—R
Multnomah Books
Nelson, Thomas
New Hope—R
New Leaf Press—R
Our Sunday Visitor—R
Pacific Press—R
Paraclete Press—R
Pastoral Press
Pauline Books
Presbyterian & Reformed
Read 'N Run—R
Regal Books
Regina Press
Resource Publications
Resurrection Press—R
Revell, Fleming H.
Review & Herald—R
Riehle Foundation
Rose Publishing
Royal Productions—R
St. Anthony Messenger—R
St. Bede's—R
Selah House—R
Servant—R
Shaw Publishers, Harold—R
Sheed & Ward—R
Southern Baptist Press—R
Standard
Still Waters Revival—R
Sword of the Lord—R
TEACH Services—R
Tyler Press—R
United Church Press
United Methodist—R
Upper Room Books—R
VESTA
Victor Books
Vision House—R
Vital Issues Press—R
Warner Press
Westminster/John Knox
Winston-Derek—R
Woman's Miss. Union—R
Wood Lake Books
World Bible Pub.—R
Zondervan/Trade—R

PROPHECY

Aanvil Press
Albury Publishing—R
Appaloosa—R
Baldwin & Knowlton
Black Forest—R
Blue Dolphin
Brentwood—R
Bridge/Logos—R
Chosen Books
Cornerstone Pub.
Creation House
Destiny Image—R
Discus Press
Element Books—R
Fairway Press—R
Faith Publishing
FOG Publishing
Friends United Press—R
HarperSanFrancisco—R
Harvard House
Harvest House—R
Hendrickson—R
Hensley, Virgil—R
Miracle Publishing
Morning Star Press—R
Multnomah Books
New Leaf Press—R
Read 'N Run—R
Regal Books
Revell, Fleming H.
Riehle Foundation
Rose Publishing
Schoettle Publishing—R
Selah House—R
Small Helm Press
Southern Baptist Press—R
Still Waters Revival—R
Sword of the Lord—R
TEACH Services—R
Tyler Press—R
VESTA
Vision House—R
Vital Issues Press—R
Zondervan/Trade—R

PSYCHOLOGY

Aanvil Press
Alba House—R
Appaloosa—R
Baker Books—R
Baldwin & Knowlton
Bantam Books
Barclay Press—R
Bethany House
Black Forest—R

Blue Dolphin
Brentwood—R
Broadman & Holman
Christopher Publishing
Conari Press—R
Concordia
Continuum Publishing
Cornerstone Pub.
Crossroad Publishing—R
Destiny Image—R
Dimension Books—R
Discus Press
Dry Bones Press—R
Eden Publishing
Eerdmans Publishing—R
Elder Books—R
Element Books—R
Fairway Press—R
Faith Publishing
Good Book
HarperSanFrancisco—R
Haworth Press—R
InterVarsity Press
Liguori Publications
Loyola Press—R
Lydia Press—R
MasterMedia
Morehouse—R
Morning Star Press—R
Mt. Olive College Press
North Point Press—R
Northstone—R
Open Court—R
Oxford University
Pansophic Publishing
PREP Publishing
Read 'N Run—R
Recovery Communications
Religious Education
Resurrection Press—R
Revell, Fleming H.
Review & Herald—R
Riehle Foundation
Shaw Publishers, Harold—R
Southern Baptist Press—R
Starburst Publishers
Tabor Publishing
Tyler Press—R
U of Ottawa Press
University Press/America—R
VESTA
Vital Issues Press—R
Yale Univ. Press—R
Zondervan/Trade—R
Zondervan/Academic

RECOVERY BOOKS

Baker Books—R
Beacon Hill Press
Black Forest—R
Bridge/Logos—R
Christopher Publishing
Church Growth Inst.
Continuum Publishing—R
Cornerstone Pub.
Destiny Image—R
Eden Publishing
Elder Books—R
Forward Movement—R
Good Book
HarperSanFrancisco—R
Haworth Press—R
Hensley, Virgil—R
Libros Liguori
Liguori Publications
Lydia Press—R
Morehouse—R
Mt. Olive College Press
Our Sunday Visitor—R
Paradise Research
PREP Publishing
Rainbow's End
Read 'N Run—R
Recovery Communications
Resource Publications
Revell, Fleming H.
Rose Publishing
Selah House—R
Tyler Press—R
United Methodist—R

REFERENCE BOOKS

Aanvil Press
Baker Books—R
Bantam Books
Baylor University Press
Bethany House
Black Forest—R
Brentwood—R
Broadman & Holman
Christian Univ. Press—R
Concordia
Continuum Publishing—R
Crossroad Publishing—R
CSS Publishing
Destiny Image—R
Discus Press
Dry Bones Press—R
Eerdmans Publishing—R
Element Books—R
Evangel Publishing—R
Fairway Press—R

Fortress Press—R
GROUP Publishing
HarperSanFrancisco—R
Hendrickson—R
Intl. Awakening Press
InterVarsity Press
Kaleidoscope Press—R
Kregel—R
Lifetime Books—R
Middle Atlantic—R
Morehouse—R
Northstone—R
Our Sunday Visitor—R
Oxford University
Presbyterian & Reformed
Ragged Edge—R
Read 'N Run—R
Review & Herald—R
Southern Baptist Press—R
Still Waters Revival—R
Sword of the Lord—R
Tyler Press—R
United Methodist—R
U of Ottawa Press
University Press/America—R
VESTA
Victor Books
Westminster/John Knox
Zondervan/Trade—R
Zondervan/Academic

RELIGION

Aanvil Press
ACU Press
Alba House—R
Appaloosa—R
Baker Books—R
Baldwin & Knowlton
Bantam Books
Bethany House
Bethel Publishing—R
Black Forest—R
Blue Dolphin
Brentwood—R
Broadman & Holman
Catholic Univ./America—R
Cerdic Publications
Christendom Press—R
Christian Univ. Press—R
Christopher Publishing
Concordia
Continuum Publishing
Cornell Univ. Press—R
Cross Cultural—R
Crossroad Publishing—R
Crossway Books
CSS Publishing

Destiny Image—R
Dimension Books—R
Discus Press
Dry Bones Press—R
Eerdmans Publishing—R
Element Books—R
Fairway Press—R
Faith Publishing
FOG Publishing
Fortress Press—R
Forward Movement—R
Franciscan Univ. Press—R
Friendship Press
Friends United Press—R
Garborg's—R
GROUP Publishing
HarperSanFrancisco—R
Harvest House—R
Hendrickson—R
Herald Press
Holy Cross—R
InterVarsity Press
Kregel—R
Libros Liguori
Light and Life—R
Liguori Publications
Liturgy Training
Living the Good News
Loyola Press—R
MasterMedia
Mercer University Press
Middle Atlantic—R
More Press, Thomas
Morehouse—R
Morning Star Press—R
Morrow & Co, Wm.
Mt. Olive College Press
New Hope—R
North Point Press—R
Northstone—R
Open Court—R
Our Sunday Visitor—R
Oxford University
Pansophic Publishing
Paraclete Press—R
Paulist Press
Pilgrim Press—R
Presbyterian & Reformed
Ragged Edge—R
Read 'N Run—R
Regnery Publishing—R
Religious Education
Resurrection Press—R
Review & Herald—R
Riehle Foundation
Rose Publishing
St. Bede's—R
Shaw Publishers, Harold—R

Sheed & Ward—R
Sheer Joy! Press
Southern Baptist Press—R
Starburst Publishers
Still Waters Revival—R
Sword of the Lord—R
Tabor Publishing
TEACH Services—R
Trinity Press Intl.—R
Tyler Press—R
United Church Press
United Church Pub.
United Methodist—R
U of Ottawa Press
University Press/America—R
VESTA
Vital Issues Press—R
Wadsworth Publishing
Westminster/John Knox
Wood Lake Books
Yale Univ. Press—R
Zondervan/Trade—R
Zondervan/Academic

RETIREMENT

Aanvil Press
ACTA Publications
Baker Books—R
Bethany House
Black Forest—R
Broadman & Holman
Chalice Press
College Press—R
Concordia
Destiny Image—R
Elder Books—R
Fairway Press—R
HarperSanFrancisco—R
Judson Press—R
Liguori Publications
MasterMedia
Northstone—R
Read 'N Run—R
Regnery Publishing—R
Revell, Fleming H.
Review & Herald—R
Shaw Publishers, Harold—R
Southern Baptist Press—R
Tyler Press—R
United Methodist—R
Upper Room Books—R
VESTA
Westminster/John Knox
Zondervan/Trade—R

SCHOLARLY

Aanvil Press
Appaloosa—R
Baker Books—R
Baldwin & Knowlton
Baylor University Press
Black Forest—R
Broadman & Holman
Christian Univ. Press—R
Continuum Publishing—R
Crossroad Publishing—R
Cross Cultural—R
Crossway Books
Discus Press
Dry Bones Press—R
Eerdmans Publishing—R
Evangel Publishing—R
Faith Publishing
Fortress Press—R
Haworth Press—R
Hendrickson—R
Holy Cross—R
Intl. Awakening Press
Monument Press
Morehouse—R
North Point Press—R
Our Sunday Visitor—R
Oxford University
Paulist Press
Pilgrim Press—R
Presbyterian & Reformed
Ragged Edge—R
Read 'N Run—R
Religious Education
Riehle Foundation
Royal Productions—R
St. Bede's—R
Shaw Publishers, Harold—R
Shoestring Press
So. Methodist Univ.
Trinity Foundation—R
Trinity Press Intl.—R
Tyler Press—R
United Methodist—R
U of Ottawa Press
University Press/America—R
Vital Issues Press—R

SCIENCE

Appaloosa—R
Baldwin & Knowlton
Bantam Books
Bob Jones—R
Christopher Publishing
Cornell Univ. Press—R
Discus Press

Dry Bones Press—R
Eerdmans Publishing—R
HarperSanFrancisco—R
Harvard House
InterVarsity Press
Kaleidoscope Press—R
Master Books—R
North Point Press—R
Northstone—R
Open Court—R
Oxford University
Rainbow Books—R
Read 'N Run—R
Royal Productions—R
Shoestring Press
Regnery Publishing—R
Review & Herald—R
Shaw Publishers, Harold—R
Trinity Foundation—R
Tyler Press—R
U of Ottawa Press
Vital Issues Press—R

*SELF-HELP

Note: This year, How-To and Self-Help are listed separately. All markets listed when they were combined are still under How-to, so check that topic.

Albury Publishing—R
Appaloosa—R
Beacon Hill Press
Black Forest—R
Blue Dolphin
Bridge/Logos—R
Broadman & Holman
Christian Publications
Christopher Publishing
Cornerstone Pub.
CSS Publishing
Design Commun.—R
Fairway Press—R
Good Book
Harvest House—R
Howard Publishing
InterVarsity Press
Libros Liguori
Liguori Publications
Living the Good News
Morehouse—R
Mt. Olive College Press
Nelson, Thomas
Northstone—R
Pansophic Publishing
Paradise Research
Ragged Edge—R

Rainbow Books—R
Read 'N Run—R
Resurrection Press—R
Review & Herald—R
Revell, Fleming H.
Selah House—R
Shaw Publishers, Harold—R
Sheed & Ward—R
Starburst Publishers
United Methodist—R

SENIOR ADULT CONCERNS

Aanvil Press
ACTA Publications
Appaloosa—R
Augsburg—R
Baker Books—R
Baldwin & Knowlton
Bethany House
Bethel Publishing—R
Black Forest—R
Bridge/Logos—R
Broadman & Holman
Chalice Press
Chariot Family Pub.
Christopher Publishing
Church Growth Inst.
Concordia
Destiny Image—R
Discus Press
Fairway Press—R
Faith Publishing
HarperSanFrancisco—R
Haworth Press—R
Hensley, Virgil—R
Horizon House—R
Howard Publishing
Judson Press—R
Langmarc
Liguori Publications
Loyola Press—R
MasterMedia
Morehouse—R
Multnomah Books
New Leaf Press—R
Northstone—R
Read 'N Run—R
Revell, Fleming H.
Review & Herald—R
Riehle Foundation
Selah House—R
Shaw Publishers, Harold—R
Southern Baptist Press—R
Tyler Press—R
United Methodist—R
Westminster/John Knox

Woman's Miss. Union—R
Zondervan/Trade—R

SERMONS

Albury Publishing—R
Black Forest—R
Brentwood—R
Christian Univ. Press—R
Concordia
CSS Publishing
Destiny Image—R
Eerdmans Publishing—R
Fairway Press—R
HarperSanFrancisco—R
Intl. Awakening Press
Kregel—R
Liguori Publications
Liturgical Press
Morning Star Press—R
Our Sunday Visitor—R
Pastor's Choice
Proclaim Publishing
Read 'N Run—R
Review & Herald—R
Southern Baptist Press—R
Still Waters Revival—R
Sword of the Lord—R
Tyler Press—R
United Church Press
United Methodist—R
VESTA
Vital Issues Press—R
Wood Lake Books

SINGLES ISSUES

Albury Publishing—R
Baker Books—R
Bethany House
Black Forest—R
Brentwood—R
Bridge/Logos—R
Broadman & Holman
Church Growth Inst.
Concordia
Dabar Publishing—R
Destiny Image—R
Discipleship Resources
Faith Publishing
GROUP Publishing
HarperSanFrancisco—R
Harvest House—R
Hensley, Virgil—R
Horizon House—R
InterVarsity Press
Judson Press—R
Langmarc

Liguori Publications
MasterMedia
Miracle Publishing
Morehouse—R
New Leaf Press—R
Northstone—R
Read 'N Run—R
Revell, Fleming H.
Review & Herald—R
Riehle Foundation
Selah House—R
Sword of the Lord—R
Tyler Press—R
United Methodist—R
VESTA
Vital Issues Press—R
Zondervan/Trade—R

SOCIAL JUSTICE ISSUES

Aanvil Press
Alban Institute
Appaloosa—R
Baker Books—R
Baldwin & Knowlton
Bantam Books
Barclay Press—R
Bethany House
Black Forest—R
Brentwood—R
Bridge/Logos—R
Chalice Press
Chosen Books
Concordia
Continuum Publishing—R
Cornerstone Pub.
Cross Cultural—R
Crossway Books
Destiny Image—R
Discus Press
Dry Bones Press—R
Eerdmans Publishing—R
Faith & Life Press
Faith Publishing
Fortress Press—R
Forward Movement—R
Friendship Press
GROUP Publishing
HarperSanFrancisco—R
Haworth Press—R
Herald Press
Judson Press—R
Libros Liguori
Life Cycle Books—R
Lifetime Books—R
Liguori Publications
Liturgy Training
Loyola Press—R

MasterMedia
Monument Press
Morehouse—R
Northstone—R
Oxford University
Paulist Press
Pilgrim Press—R
Ragged Edge—R
Read 'N Run—R
Regnery Publishing—R
Resurrection Press—R
Review & Herald—R
Riehle Foundation
Selah House—R
Shaw Publishers, Harold—R
Sheed & Ward—R
Still Waters Revival—R
Tyler Press—R
United Church Pub.
United Methodist—R
University Press/America—R
VESTA
Vital Issues Press—R
Westminster/John Knox
Winston-Derek—R
Woman's Miss. Union—R
Wood Lake Books
Zondervan/Trade—R
Zondervan/Academic

SOCIOLOGY

Aanvil Press
Alba House—R
Appaloosa—R
Baker Books—R
Baldwin & Knowlton
Bethany House
Black Forest—R
Brentwood—R
Christopher Publishing
Continuum Publishing—R
Cornerstone Pub.
Crossroad Publishing—R
Destiny Image—R
Discus Press
Faith Publishing
HarperSanFrancisco—R
Haworth Press—R
InterVarsity Press
Loyola Press—R
North Point Press—R
Northstone—R
Oxford University
Pansophic Publishing
Paulist Press
Read 'N Run—R
Review & Herald—R

Riehle Foundation
Stillpoint Publishing
Still Waters Revival—R
U of Ottawa Press
University Press/America—R
Vital Issues Press—R
Zondervan/Trade—R
Zondervan/Academic

SPIRITUALITY

ACTA Publications
ACU Press
Alba House—R
Alban Institute
Appaloosa—R
Augsburg—R
Baker Books—R
Bantam Books
Barclay Press—R
Beacon Hill Press
Bethany House
Black Forest—R
Blue Dolphin
Brentwood—R
Bridge/Logos—R
Broadman & Holman
Chalice Press
Chariot Family Publishing
Chosen Books
Christian Lit. Crusade
Christian Publications
Christopher Publishing
Cistercian Publications
Conari Press—R
Continuum Publishing—R
Cornerstone Pub.
Cross Cultural—R
Crossroad Publishing—R
Crossway Books
Dabar Publishing—R
Destiny Image—R
Dimension Books—R
Dry Bones Press—R
Eerdmans Publishing—R
Elder Books—R
Element Books—R
Fairway Press—R
Faith Publishing
Forward Movement—R
Franciscan Univ. Press—R
Friends United Press—R
Garborg's—R
GROUP Publishing
HarperSanFrancisco—R
Hendrickson—R
Hensley, Virgil—R
HI-TIME

Holy Cross—R
Honor Books—R
Innisfree Press
Intl. Awakening Press
InterVarsity Press
Judson Press—R
Kregel—R
Libros Liguori
Light and Life—R
Liguori Publications
Living the Good News
Loyola Press—R
MasterMedia
More Press, Thomas
Morehouse—R
Morning Star Press—R
Mt. Olive College Press
Northstone—R
Our Sunday Visitor—R
Oxford University
Pacific Press—R
Paraclete Press—R
Paradise Research
Pastoral Press
Pauline Books
Pilgrim Press—R
PREP Publishing
Ragged Edge—R
Read 'N Run—R
Regal Books
Regnery Publishing—R
Resurrection Press—R
Revell, Fleming H.
Review & Herald—R
Riehle Foundation
St. Anthony Messenger—R
St. Bede's—R
Selah House—R
Servant—R
Shaw Publishers, Harold—R
Sheed & Ward—R
Southern Baptist Press—R
Stillpoint Publishing
Sword of the Lord—R
TEACH Services—R
Tyler Press—R
United Church Press
United Methodist—R
U of Ottawa Press
Upper Room Books—R
VESTA
Vision House—R
Vital Issues Press—R
Westminster/John Knox
Winston-Derek—R
Wood Lake Books
Zondervan/Trade—R
Zondervan/Academic

SPIRITUAL WARFARE

Aanvil Press
Albury Publishing—R
Appaloosa—R
Baldwin & Knowlton
Black Forest—R
Bridge/Logos—R
Chosen Books
Christian Publications
Cornerstone Pub.
Creation House
Destiny Image—R
Discus Press
Eden Publishing
Faith Publishing
GROUP Publishing
Harvest House—R
Hendrickson—R
Hensley, Virgil—R
InterVarsity Press
Lydia Press—R
Miracle Publishing
Multnomah Books
Read 'N Run—R
Revell, Fleming H.
Riehle Foundation
Selah House—R
Servant—R
Shaw Publishers, Harold—R
Shoestring Press
Sword of the Lord—R
Vision House—R

SPORTS/RECREATION

ACTA Publications
Appaloosa—R
Bantam Books
Christopher Publishing
Destiny Image—R
Lifetime Books—R
MasterMedia
Multnomah Books
New Leaf Press—R
North Point Press—R
Rainbow Books—R
Read 'N Run—R
Revell, Fleming H.
Royal Productions—R
Starburst Publishers
Tyler Press—R
Zondervan/Trade—R

STEWARDSHIP

Albury Publishing—R
Baker Books—R

Black Forest—R
Bridge/Logos—R
Chalice Press
Church Growth Inst.
Creation House
Destiny Image—R
Discipleship Resources
Eerdmans Publishing—R
Faith Publishing
Forward Movement—R
Hensley, Virgil—R
InterVarsity Press
Judson Press—R
Kregel—R
Libros Liguori
Miracle Publishing
Morehouse—R
Neibauer Press
North Point Press—R
Pacific Press—R
Presbyterian & Reformed
Read 'N Run—R
Riehle Foundation
Selah House—R
Shaw Publishers, Harold—R
Sword of the Lord—R
TEACH Services—R
Tyler Press—R
United Methodist—R
Upper Room Books—R
Vision House—R
Vital Issues Press—R

THEOLOGICAL

Aanvil Press
ACU Press
Alba House—R
Appaloosa—R
Baker Books—R
Bethany House
Black Forest—R
Blue Dolphin
Brentwood—R
Bridge/Logos—R
Broadman & Holman
Catholic Univ./America—R
Cerdic Publications
Chalice Press
Christendom Press—R
Christian Publications
Christian Univ. Press—R
Christopher Publishing
Cistercian Publications
Concordia
Continuum Publishing—R
Cross Cultural—R
Crossroad Publishing—R

Crossway Books
Destiny Image—R
Dimension Books—R
Dry Bones Press—R
Eerdmans Publishing—R
Evangel Publishing—R
Fairway Press—R
Faith Publishing
FOG Publishing
Fortress Press—R
Friends United Press—R
HarperSanFrancisco—R
Harvest House—R
Hendrickson—R
Herald Press
Holy Cross—R
Intl. Awakening Press
InterVarsity Press
Kregel—R
Light and Life—R
Liguori Publications
Liturgical Press
Liturgy Training
Loyola Press—R
Magnus Press
Mercer University Press
Morehouse—R
Morning Star Press—R
Multnomah Books
New City Press—R
New Leaf Press—R
North Point Press—R
Open Court—R
Our Sunday Visitor—R
Oxford University
Pastoral Press
Paulist Press
Pilgrim Press—R
Presbyterian & Reformed
Ragged Edge—R
Read 'N Run—R
Religious Education
Resurrection Press—R
Review & Herald—R
Riehle Foundation
St. Anthony Messenger—R
St. Bede's—R
Schoettle Publishing—R
Selah House—R
Shaw Publishers, Harold—R
   (lay)
Sheed & Ward—R
Southern Baptist Press—R
So. Methodist Univ.
Still Waters Revival—R
Sword of the Lord—R
Trinity Foundation—R
Trinity Press Intl.—R

Tyler Press—R
United Church Press
United Church Pub.
United Methodist—R
U of Ottawa Press
University Press/America—R
VESTA
Vision House—R
Vital Issues Press—R
Westminster/John Knox
Wood Lake Books
Zondervan/Trade—R
Zondervan/Academic

TRACTS

American Tract Society
Black Forest—R
Comments Publishing—R
Cornerstone Pub.
Design Commun.—R
Dry Bones Press—R
Faith, Prayer & Tract
Faith Publishing (maybe)
Forward Movement—R
Franciscan Univ. Press—R
Good News Publishers
Gospel Folio Press
 Impact Christian Books
Liguori Publications
Middle Atlantic—R
Neibauer Press—R
Purple Pomegranate—R
Read 'N Run—R
Riehle Foundation (maybe)
Rose Publishing
Royal Productions—R
St. Hilda's Press
Sword of the Lord—R
TEACH Services—R
Trinity Foundation—R
Woman's Miss. Union—R

TRAVEL

Appaloosa—R
Bob Jones—R
Brentwood—R
Christopher Publishing
Design Commun.—R
Destiny Image—R
Discus Press
Eerdmans Publishing—R
Image Books—R
Morehouse—R
Mt. Olive College Press
North Point Press—R
Pansophic Publishing

Pelican Publishing—R
Read 'N Run—R
Revell, Fleming H.

WOMEN'S ISSUES

Aanvil Press
Alban Institute
Albury Publishing—R
Appaloosa—R
Augsburg—R
Baker Books—R
Baldwin & Knowlton
Bantam Books
Barbour & Co.—R
Baylor University Press
Beacon Hill Press
Bethany House
Black Forest—R
Blue Dolphin
Bridge/Logos—R
Broadman & Holman
Cerdic Publications
Chalice Press
Chariot Family Pub.
Christian Publications
Christian Univ. Press—R
Christopher Publishing
Conari Press—R
Concordia
Continuum Publishing
Cornell Univ. Press—R
Cornerstone Pub.
Creation House
Cross Cultural—R
Crossroad Publishing—R
Crossway Books
Dabar Publishing—R
Destiny Image—R
Discus Press
Eerdmans Publishing—R
Elder Books—R
Element Books—R
Fairway Press—R
Faith Publishing
Fortress Press—R
Forward Movement—R
Garborg's—R
Guernica Editions—R
HarperSanFrancisco—R
Harvest House—R
Haworth Press—R
Hensley, Virgil—R
Honor Books—R
Horizon House—R
Howard Publishing
Innisfree Press
InterVarsity Press

Judson Press—R
Kregel—R
Life Cycle Books—R
Liguori Publications
MasterMedia
Monument Press
Moody Press
Morehouse—R
Morning Star Press—R
Mt. Olive College Press
Multnomah Books
New Hope—R
New Leaf Press—R
North Point Press—R
Northstone—R
Pacific Press—R
Pastoral Press
Pelican Publishing—R
Pilgrim Press—R
PREP Publishing
Rainbow Books—R
Rainbow/Daybreak
Read 'N Run—R
Regal Books
Resurrection Press—R
Revell, Fleming H.
Review & Herald—R
Riehle Foundation
St. Anthony Messenger—R
Selah House—R
Servant—R
Shaw Publishers, Harold—R
Sheed & Ward—R
Son-Rise
Southern Baptist Press—R
Still Waters Revival—R
Tyler Press—R
United Church Press
United Church Pub.
United Methodist—R
U of Ottawa Press
University Press/America—R
VESTA
Vision House—R
Vital Issues Press—R
Westminster/John Knox
Winston-Derek—R
Woman's Miss. Union—R
Wood Lake Books
Zondervan/Trade—R
Zondervan/Academic

WORLD ISSUES

Aanvil Press
Appaloosa—R
Baker Books—R
Baldwin & Knowlton

Bantam Books
Barclay Press—R
Bethany House
Black Forest—R
Blue Dolphin
Bridge/Logos—R
Broadman & Holman
William Carey Library
Chalice Press
Christopher Publishing
Cross Cultural—R
Crossway Books
Destiny Image—R
Discus Press
Dry Bones Press—R
Faith Publishing
Guernica Editions—R
HarperSanFrancisco—R
InterVarsity Press
Judson Press—R
Liguori Publications
Loyola Press—R
Morehouse—R
New Leaf Press—R
North Point Press—R
Northstone—R
Orbis Books
Pilgrim Press—R
PROBE Ministries
Read 'N Run—R
Regal Books
Regnery Publishing—R
Revell, Fleming H.
Riehle Foundation
Selah House—R
Shaw Publishers, Harold—R
Still Waters Revival—R
Trinity Foundation—R
Tyler Press—R
United Methodist—R
University Press/America—R
VESTA
Vision House—R
Vital Issues Press—R
Zondervan/Trade—R

WORSHIP RESOURCES

Baker Books—R
Barclay Press—R
Bethany House
Black Forest—R
Bridge/Logos—R
Broadman & Holman
Catholic Book Publishing
Chalice Press
Church Growth Inst.
Church Street Press

Concordia
Crossroad Publishing—R
CSS Publishing
Design Commun.—R
Destiny Image—R
Discipleship Resources
Discus Press
Educational Ministries
Eerdmans Publishing—R
Fairway Press—R
Forward Movement—R
GROUP Publishing
HarperSanFrancisco—R
Hendrickson—R
Herald Press
Judson Press—R
Liturgical Press
Liturgy Training
Loyola Press—R
Morehouse—R
Pastoral Press
Read 'N Run—R
Royal Productions—R
St. Anthony Messenger—R
Selah House—R
Sheed & Ward—R
Standard
Tyler Press—R
United Church Press
United Church Pub.
United Methodist—R
VESTA
Vital Issues Press—R
Westminster/John Knox
Wood Lake Books
Zondervan/Trade—R

*WRITING HOW-TO

Black Forest—R
Bridge/Logos—R
Cornerstone Pub.
Design Commun.—R
Fairway Press—R
Judson Press—R
Promise Publishing
Selah House—R
Sheed & Ward—R

YOUTH BOOKS (Nonfiction)

Note: Listing denotes books for 8- to 12-year-olds, junior highs or senior highs. If all three, it will say "all."

Albury Publishing—R (all)

Appaloosa—R (all)
Augsburg—R (8-12)
Baker Books—R (all)
Barbour & Co.—R (8-12)
Bethany House (all)
Bible Discovery (all)
Black Forest—R (all)
Bob Jones—R (all)
Bridge/Logos—R (Jr/Sr High)
Broadman & Holman (all)
CEF Press (8-12)
Chariot Books (8-12)
Christian Ed Pub. (8-12)
Christian Lit. Crusade (Jr/Sr
   High)
Concordia (all)
Contemporary Drama Service
Cornerstone Pub. (all)
Creation House (Sr High)
Crossway Books (8-12)
Design Commun.—R (8-12)
Dry Bones Press—R (all)
Eden Publishing (8-12)
Eerdmans Publishing—R (8-
   12/Jr High)
Fairway Press—R (all)
Faith & Life Press (Sr high)
Faith Publishing (Sr high)
GROUP Publishing (all)
Harvest House—R (Jr/Sr
   High)
Horizon House—R (Jr/Sr
   High)
Kaleidoscope Press—R (8-12)
Langmarc (Jr/Sr High)

Libros Liguori (all)
Liguori Publications (all)
Lion Publishing (8-12)
Living the Good News
Lydia Press—R (Sr High)
MasterMedia
Meriwether—R (8-12)
Miracle Publishing (all)
Morehouse—R (all)
Morris, Joshua (all)
Multnomah Books (all)
New Hope—R (8-12)
Pacific Press—R (8-12)
Pauline Books—R (all)
Ragged Edge—R (8-12)
Rainbow/Daybreak (all)
Rainbow Publishers (8-12)
Read 'N Run (all)
Regal Books (Jr/Sr High)
Royal Productions—R (8-12)
Resurrection Press—R
Revell, Fleming H. (8-12)
Review & Herald—R (all)
Riehle Foundation (Sr High)
St. Anthony Messenger—R
   (Jr/Sr High)
Selah House—R (Jr/Sr High)
Shining Star (8-12)
Son-Rise (all)
So. Baptist Press—R (all)
Still Waters Revival—R (all)
Sword of the Lord—R (all)
TEACH Services—R (8-12/Jr
   High)
Tyler Press—R (all)

United Church Press (all)
United Methodist—R (all)
Upper Room Books—R
Vital Issues Press—R
Windflower—R (all)
Woman's Miss. Union—R
Wood Lake Books (8-12)
World Bible Pub.—R (all)
Zondervan/Trade—R (all)

YOUTH PROGRAMS

Baker Books—R
Church Growth Inst.
Concordia
Contemporary Drama Service
Discipleship Resources
Educational Ministries
Fairway Press—R
GROUP Publishing
Hensley, Virgil—R
Judson Press—R
Langmarc
Liguori Publications
Miracle Publishing
Morehouse—R
Morris, Joshua
Read 'N Run—R
Regal Books
Resurrection Press—R
St. Anthony Messenger—R
Sheer Joy! Press
Standard
Vital Issues Press—R
Wood Lake Books

ALPHABETICAL LISTINGS OF BOOK PUBLISHERS

(*) An asterisk before a listing indicates no or unconfirmed information update.

(#) A number symbol before a listing indicates it was updated from their guidelines or other current sources.

(+) A plus sign before a listing indicates it is a new listing this year and was not included last year.

+AANVIL PRESS, PO Box 881, Boothbay Harbor ME 04538. (207)633-5748. Diane Dorbin, ed/pub. To create a forum where new writers can get the Word out. Publishes 1 title/yr. Receives 15-20 submissions annually. 90% of books from first-time authors. No mss through agents. Prefers 75,000-100,000 words or 300-400 pgs. Royalty 10-12% on retail; negotiable advance. Average first printing 4,500. Publication within 7 mos. Considers simultaneous submissions. Responds in 3 wks. Free guidelines; no catalog.

  Nonfiction: Complete ms. Looking for social justice issues, inspirational and world issues.

  Fiction: Complete ms. Also does horror and gothic fiction.

  Tips: "We're most open to fiction. Be patient. "

ABINGDON PRESS—See **The United Methodist Publishing House**.

ACCENT BIBLE CURRICULUM, PO Box 36640, Colorado Springs CO 80936-3664. (719)536-0100. Cook Communications Ministries. Mary B. Nelson, mng. ed. Buys all rts as work for hire of assigned projects. Writers must be Baptist or baptistic. Submit query letter explaining qualifications to write curriculum; experience; published works. No freelance submissions.

  Special Needs: Writers for kindergarten, junior and adult.

ACCENT PUBLICATIONS, PO Box 36640, Colorado Springs CO 80936-3664. (719)536-0100x3337. Imprint of Cook Communications Ministries. Mary B. Nelson, mng. ed. Publishes 8 titles/yr. Receives 500 submissions annually. 90% of books from first-time authors. No mss through agents. Royalty on retail or outright purchase; no advance. Publication within 1 yr. Considers simultaneous submissions. Responds in 4-8 wks. Guidelines; catalog for 9x12 SAE/3 stamps.

  Nonfiction: Query letter only; no phone query. "Looking for church resource products that promote the work of the local church in any ministry aspect; also series ideas for Bible studies/group study books."

  Tips: "Be fresh, creative, and in tune with the needs and ministries of the local church's Christian education programs."

ACTA PUBLICATIONS, 4848 N. Clark St., Chicago IL 60640-4711. (312)271-7399. E-mail: acta@one.org. Catholic. Gregory F. Augustine Pierce, co-pub. Resources for the "end-user" of the Christian faith. Imprints: Buckley Publications; National Center for the Laity. Publishes 10 titles/yr. Receives 200 submissions annually. 20% of books from first-time authors. Prefers 150-200 pgs. Royalty

10% of net; no advance. Average first printing 3,000. Publication within 1 yr. Disk accepted. Responds in 4 wks. Guidelines; catalog for 9x12 SAE/2 stamps.

Nonfiction: Query or proposal/1 chapter; no phone/e-mail query.

Tips: "Most open to books that are useful to a large number of average Christians. Read our catalog and one of our books first."

*ACU PRESS, 1648 Campus Ct., Abilene TX 79601. (915)674-2720. Church of Christ/Abilene Christian University. Thom Lemmons, ed. Guidance in the religious life for members and leaders of the denomination. Publishes 10 titles/yr. Receives 100 submissions annually. 10% of books from first-time authors. Royalty 10%. Average first printing 5,000. Publication within 3 mos. Considers simultaneous submissions. Responds in 1 mo. Catalog.

Nonfiction: Proposal/3 chapters.

#ALBA HOUSE, 2187 Victory Blvd., Staten Island NY 10314. (718)761-0047. Fax (718)761-0057. Catholic/Society of St. Paul. Aloysius Milella, ed. Publishes 30 titles/yr. Receives 750 submissions annually. 50% of books from first-time authors. Reprints books. Royalty 10% on retail; no advance. Publication within 9 mos. Responds in 1 month. Guidelines; catalog for SASE.

Nonfiction: Query.

#THE ALBAN INSTITUTE, INC., 4550 Montgomery Ave., Ste. 433N, Bethesda MD 20814-3341. (301)718-4407. Fax (301)718-1958. Episcopal Church. Celia A. Hahn, ed-in-chief. Publishes 10 titles/yr. Receives 100 submissions annually. No mss through agents. Prefers 100 pgs. Royalty 7-10% of net; outright purchases for $50-100 for 450-2,000 wd articles on congregational life; advance $100. Publication within 1 yr. Responds in 4 mos. Guidelines; catalog for 9x12 SAE/3 stamps.

Nonfiction: Proposal only first. Books for clergy and laity.

Tips: "Books on congregational issues: problems and opportunities in congregational life; the clergy role and career; the ministry of the laity in church and world." Intelligent/liberal audience.

+ALBURY PUBLISHING, PO Box 470406, Tulsa OK 74147-0406. (918)496-2200. Fax (918)496-7702. Mark Norris, ed. mng. Charismatic Christian lifestyle and doctrinal issues. Publishes 12 titles/yr. Receives 96 submissions annually. 2% of books from first-time authors. Reprints books. Prefers 160 pgs. Royalty; advance. Average first printing 10,000. Publication within 8 mos. No simultaneous submissions. Responds in 2 mos. Guidelines; catalog for 9x12 SAE/2 stamps.

Nonfiction: Query only. "Want well-written and compelling content, whether the topic has to do with personal or corporate Christian experience."

Also Does: Booklets.

*AMERICAN CATHOLIC PRESS, 16565 State St., South Holland IL 60473-2025. (708)331-5485. Catholic worship resources. Father Michael Gilligan, ed. dir. Publishes 8 titles/yr. Reprints books. Pays $25-100 for outright purchases only. Average first printing 3,000. Publication within 1 yr. Considers simultaneous submissions. Responds in 2 mos. Catalog for SASE.

Nonfiction: Query first.

Tips: "We publish only materials on the Roman Catholic liturgy. Especially interested in new music for church services."

+APPALOOSA PUBLICATIONS, 106 N. Main St., Ste. B, Nicholasville KY

40356-1234. (606)887-5935. Fax (606)887-4331. E-mail: Deerinalit@aol.com. Sovereign Publications. Stephanie Baker, sr. ed.; submit to Amy Franklin, acq. ed. New publisher; 8 titles/yr. Receives 300 submissions annually. 75% of books from first-time authors. **SUBSIDY PUBLISHES 19%** (some 1st time authors). Reprints books. Prefers 70-125,000 wds. Royalty 10-15% on retail; no advance. Publication within 18 mos. Considers simultaneous submissions. Responds in 4-6 wks. Requires disk. Guidelines; no catalog.

> **Nonfiction:** Query/synopsis & complete ms. Short fax/e-mail query OK. For all ages. "Looking for historical, biography, autobiography, humor and especially cookbooks. "

> **Fiction:** Query/synopsis & complete ms. All genres. For all ages. "Looking for historical novels. "

+ASLAN PUBLISHING, 3595 Webb Bridge Rd., Alpharetta GA 30202. (770)442-1500 The Aslan Group. New publisher. Not included in topical listings.

> **Nonfiction:** Only.

AUGSBURG FORTRESS—See **AUGSBURG BOOKS** and **FORTRESS PRESS**.

AUGSBURG BOOKS, 426 S. 5th St., Box 1209, Minneapolis MN 55440. (612)330-3300. Fax (612)330-3215. Evangelical Lutheran Church in America. Ron Klug, dir. of publishing; Alice Peppler, children's acq. ed; Robert Klausmeier, acq. ed. Publishes 35 titles/yr. Receives 1,500 submissions annually. 10% of books from first-time authors. Reprints books. Prefers 32-160 pgs. Royalty; advance. Average first printing 4,000. Publication within 12-18 mos. Considers simultaneous submissions. Responds in 3 mos. Requires disk. Guidelines; catalog for 9x12 SAE/5 stamps.

> **Nonfiction:** Query only; fax query OK.

> **Special Needs:** Books on spirituality, family, and for over 50s.

> **Ethnic Books:** African-American, Hispanic, Asian-American, native American; contextual theology.

> **Tips:** "Query us first. Describe the project, the readership, how you think the book meets a need, your credentials for writing, and how your book differs from similar books already published."

> ****Note:** This publisher serviced by The Writer's Edge.

BAKER BOOKS, Box 6287, Grand Rapids MI 49516-6287. (616)676-9185. Fax (616)676-9573. E-mail: JSchrier@bakerbooks.com. Website: http://www.baker books.com. Evangelical. Allan Fisher, dir. of publications; submit to Jane Schrier, asst. Imprint: Raven's Ridge. Publishes 120 titles/yr. Receives 2,000 submissions annually. 10% of books from first-time authors. Reprints books. Prefers 150-300 pgs. Royalty 14% of net; some advances. Average first printing 5,000. Publication within 1 yr. Considers simultaneous submissions. Responds in 3 mos. No disk. Guidelines; catalog for 9x12 SAE/6 stamps.

> **Nonfiction:** Proposal/3 chapters. "Request our brochure on how to prepare a proposal."

> **Fiction:** Query. "We are interested in mysteries and contemporary women's fiction from a Christian world view without being preachy. Our fiction is more literary than popular. Request summary of contemporary women's fiction."

> **Ethnic Books:** Would be interested in publishing specifically for the Afri-

can-American market; also multicultural fiction.

Tips: "Please prepare a complete, well-organized proposal. Request our guidelines for guidance." Note: At press time they had just bought Bridge-Point, the academic and professional imprint of Victor Books (from Cook Communications Ministries).

**Note: This publisher serviced by The Writer's Edge.

+BAKER'S PLAYS, 100 Chauncy St., Boston MA 02111-1783. (617)482-1280. Fax (617)482-7613. Raymond Pape, assoc. ed. Publishes 1-5 plays/yr. Receives 200 submissions annually. 50% of plays from first-time authors. Production royalty 50%, book royalty 10%; no advance. Average first printing 1,000. Publication within 6-8 mos. Considers simultaneous submissions. Accepts disk. Responds in 3-4 mos. Guidelines; free catalog.

> **Plays:** Query or complete ms; fax query OK.
>
> **Tips:** "We currently publish full-length or one-act plays, theater texts and musicals, with a separate division which publishes plays for religious institutions. The ideal time to submit work is from September to April."

+BALDWIN & KNOWLTON BOOKS, 3023 N. Clark St. #859, Chicago IL 60657-5205. (312)854-5844. Fax (312)281-4844. R.B. Harris, ed. To provide a forum for new voices with traditional family values. Publishes 2 titles/yr. Receives 150 submissions annually. 95% of books from first-time authors. Prefers 70,000 wds or 300 pgs. Royalty 10-12% on retail; negotiable advance. Average first printing 4,500. Publication within 6-8 mos. Considers simultaneous submissions. Responds in 2-3 wks. Free guidelines; no catalog.

> **Nonfiction:** Complete ms. Looking for prophecy, marriage and social issues.
>
> **Fiction:** Complete ms. Teens and adults. All types, but looking for fantasy, mystery and romance with family values at the core.
>
> **Tips:** "Open equally to fiction and nonfiction. Be creative, research your markets, ask questions, and follow guidelines. "

+BALLANTINE BOOKS, 201 E. 50th St., New York NY 10022. (212)751-2600. Fax (212)572-4912. A Division of Random House. Linda Grey, pub. General publisher that does a few religious books. No guidelines or catalog. Not included in topical listings.

> **Nonfiction & Fiction:** Proposal/2 chapters.

#BANTAM BOOKS, 1540 Broadway, New York NY 10036. (212)354-6500. General trade publisher with a religious/inspirational list. Thomas Cahill, dir. Accepts mss only through agents. Prefers at least 80,000-100,000 wds. Royalty 4-15%; advance. Publication within 8 mos. Considers simultaneous submissions from agents. Responds in 1 mo. Catalog for SASE.

> **Nonfiction:** Proposal/2-3 chapters. "Want all types of religious/inspirational books." No humor, no triumph over tragedy unless subject is well known or a celebrity.
>
> **Fiction:** Proposal/2-3 chapters. "Books must cross over into the trade market."
>
> **Tips:** "We want books that appeal to a large, general audience and fresh ideas. Be sure to investigate the competition and include an author bio. The author's relevant experience and authority is very important to us."

BARBOUR & CO., INC., 1810 Barbour Dr., PO Box 719, Uhrichsville OH 44683.

(614)922-6045. Fax (614)922-5948. E-mail: booksbarbour@tusco.net. Susan Johnson, mng ed. Imprints: Barbour Books (nonfiction) and Heartsong Presents (fiction—see separate listing); Inspirational Library. Publishes 75-80 titles/yr. Receives 500 submissions annually. 10% of books from first-time authors. No mss through agents. Reprints books. Prefers 50,000-60,000 wds or 300 pgs. Outright purchases $750-2,500; advance is half of outright purchase. Average first printing 15,000-20,000. Publication within 9-12 mos. Considers simultaneous submissions. Responds in 9-12 wks. No disk. Guidelines; catalog for 9x12 SAE/4 stamps.

> **Nonfiction:** Proposal/2 chapters; no phone/fax/e-mail query.
>
> **Fiction:** Proposal/2 chapters to Rebecca Germany, fiction ed. "We are interested in a mystery/romance series." See separate listing for Heartsong Presents.
>
> **Also Does:** Booklets.
>
> **Tips:** "A great idea is more important than a great agent here."

BARCLAY PRESS, 110 S. Elliott Rd., Newberg OR 97132-2120. (503)538-7345. Fax (503)538-7033. E-mail: info@barclaypress.com. Website: http://www.barclaypress.com. Friends/Quaker. Dan McCracken, general manager. Publishes 2 titles/yr. Receives 180 submissions annually. 50% of books from first-time authors. Reprints books. Prefers 100-200 pgs. Royalty 10%; no advance. Average first printing 2,000. Publication within 1 yr. Considers simultaneous submissions. Responds in 6 wks. Free catalog.

> **Nonfiction:** Proposal/2 chapters. "Looking for books on spirituality and current social issues."
>
> ****Note:** This publisher serviced by The Writer's Edge.

*MEL BAY PUBLICATIONS, INC., #4 Industrial Dr., Pacific MO 63069. (314)257-3970. William Bay, VP; submit to L. Dean Bye, gen mgr. Imprints: Cathedral Music Press; Creative Keyboard Publications. Publishes 25 inspirational/religious titles/yr. Reprints books. Royalty 10% on retail; no advance. Publication within 6-9 mos. Responds in 1-6 wks. Free guidelines/catalog.

> **Nonfiction:** Proposal/chapters (photocopy only).
>
> **Fiction:** Complete ms or proposal. Children's picture books, juvenile, plays.
>
> **Tips:** Specializes in music books. "In case of musical submissions, we appreciate a cassette recording."

BAYLOR UNIVERSITY PRESS, PO Box 97363, Waco TX 76798-7363. Baptist. Janet Burton, ed. Academic press producing scholarly books on religion and social sciences; separation of church and state. Publishes 1 title/yr. Receives 120 submissions annually. Royalty 10% of net; no advance. Average first printing 1,000. Publication within 6 mos. Responds in 3-6 mos. Free catalog.

> **Nonfiction:** Proposal/1-2 chapters; no phone query.

BEACON HILL PRESS OF KANSAS CITY, PO Box 419527, Kansas City MO 64141. (816)931-1900. Fax (816)753-4071. E-mail: bhp@nazarene.org. Church of the Nazarene. Bonnie Perry, mng. ed. Imprint: Beacon Hill Books. Publishes 30 titles/yr. Receives 1,000 submissions annually. 20% of books from first-time authors. No mss through agents. Prefers 200-300 pgs. Royalty 12% of net; advance. Average first printing 3,000. Publication within 1 yr. Considers simultaneous submissions. Responds in 8-12 wks. Free guidelines/catalog.

Nonfiction: Proposal/2 chapters; no phone/fax query. "Looking for practical, lay-oriented books on personal growth, applied Christianity."

Fiction: Proposal/2 chapters. For adults. "Must be wholesome, Christian fiction."

Ethnic Books: Spanish division—Casa Nazarena De Publicaciones. Publishes in several languages.

BETHANY HOUSE PUBLISHERS, 11300 Hampshire Ave. S, Minneapolis MN 55438. (612)829-2500. Fax (612)829-2768. A ministry of Bethany Fellowship, Inc. Sharon Madison, ms review ed. To publish information that communicates biblical truth and assists people in both spiritual and practical areas of life. Publishes 125 titles/yr. Receives 3,000 submissions annually. 2% of books from first-time authors. Standard royalty & advance. Publication within 18 mos. Considers simultaneous submissions. Responds in 8-12 wks. Guidelines for fiction/nonfiction/juvenile; catalog for 9x12 SAE/5 stamps.

Nonfiction: Cover letter, synopsis, 3 chapters; no phone/fax query. "Seeking well-planned and developed books in the following categories: personal growth, devotional, contemporary issues, marriage & family, reference, applied theology and inspirational."

Fiction: Cover letter/synopsis/3 chapters. "PORTRAITS is our new contemporary fiction line. We also publish adult historical fiction, teen/young adult fiction, and children's fiction series (7-12 yrs; no picture books). Send SASE for guidelines."

Tips: "Seeking high quality fiction and nonfiction that will inspire and challenge our audience—the man and woman in the pew. "

**Note: This publisher serviced by The Writer's Edge.

BETHEL PUBLISHING, 1819 S. Main, Elkhart IN 46516. (800)348-7657. Fax (800)230-8271. Missionary Church. Rev. Richard Oltz, pres.; submit to Senior Editor. Books to build up and encourage the body of Christ. Publishes 3-5 titles/yr. Receives 1,200 submissions annually. 90% of books from first-time authors. Reprints books. Prefers 30,000 wds. Royalty 5-10% of net; no advance. Average first printing 10,000. Publication within 10 mos. Considers simultaneous submissions. Responds in 30 days. Guidelines; catalog for 9x12 SAE/3 stamps.

Nonfiction: Query; fax query OK.

Fiction: Query. Adult/teen/juvenile.

Also Does: Board games.

*BIBLE DISCOVERY, Chariot Family Publishing, 4050 Lee Vance View, Colorado Springs CO 80918. (719)536-0100. Cook Communications Ministries. To acquaint children of all ages (1-14 yrs) with the truths of God's Word. See Chariot Family Publishing for details.

Nonfiction: Summary of idea and sample; complete ms for books for very young children. "Most open to accurate, quality Bible stories and devotional material that effectively bridges Scripture to a child's life. We look for unique ideas that are clear, concise, and age-appropriate."

Special Needs: Bible portions/devotional material; new ways to utilize Scripture for 8-14 year olds. Bible storybooks; product ideas for using Scripture text; devotional; Bible portions for 0-3s and 3-8 year olds.

BLUE DOLPHIN PUBLISHING, INC., PO Box 8, Nevada City CA 95959.

(916)265-6925. Fax (916)265-0787. E-mail: Bdolphin@netshel.net. Paul M. Clemens, pub. Imprint: Pelican Pond. Books that help people grow in their social awareness. Publishes 5-7 titles/yr. Receives 2,000 submissions annually. 90% of books from first-time authors. Prefers about 60,000 wds or 200 pgs. Royalty 10-15% of net; no advance. Average first printing 3,000-5,000. Publication within 6-8 mos. Considers simultaneous submissions. No disk. Responds in 1-3 mos. Guidelines; catalog for 6x9 SAE/2 stamps.

Nonfiction: Proposal/1 chapter; e-mail query OK: "Looking for books on interspecies and relationships."

Fiction: Query/2-pg synopsis.

Tips: "We look for topics that would appeal to the general market, are interesting, different and that will aid in the growth and development of humanity."

BOB JONES UNIVERSITY PRESS, Light Line and Pennant Books Imprints (for children & youth only), Greenville SC 29614. (864)242-5100x4316. Fax (864)298-0268. E-mail: grepp@wpo.bju.edu. Gloria Repp, acq. ed. Imprints: Light Line and Pennant Books. Goal is to publish books for children that excel in both literary and moral content. Publishes 6-10 titles/yr. Receives 400 submissions annually. 30% of books from first-time authors. Reprints books. Prefers 3,000-60,000 wds (depends on age group). Royalty on net; outright purchases of $1,000 (for first-time authors; advance $1,000. Average first printing 5,000. Publication within 12-18 months. Considers simultaneous submissions. Accepts disks. Responds in 2 mos. Guidelines; catalog for 9x12 SAE/2 stamps.

Nonfiction: Query or proposal/5 chapters; e-mail query OK. "Looking for juvenile biography with a good moral tone."

Fiction: Proposal/5 chapters or complete ms. "Looking for humor; problem realism; historical fiction."

Also Does: Story cassettes and book sets.

Tips: "Most open to realistic or historical fiction for upper elementary through teens."

+BOOKS-BUY-EMAIL, PO Box 271982, Fort Collins CO 80527. (719)633-6599. E-mail: books@books-buy-email.com. Website: http://www.books-buy-email.com. Frank Meyer, ed. E-mail: fmeyer@his-designs.com. Publishes book on the Internet. Costs $595 to put your book in the electronic bookstore. Details available on the Internet, or send $5 for a printed copy of their information packet.

BRIDGE/LOGOS, 1300 Airport Rd. #E, North Brunswick NJ 08902-1700. (908)435-8700. Fax (908)435-8701. E-mail: BLOGOS@aol.com. Catherine J. Barrier, ed.; submit to Hollee Chadwick-Loney. Imprints: Logos, Bridge, Haven, Open Scroll. Publishes 25-35 titles/yr. Receives 350-400 submissions annually. 50% of books from first-time authors. **SUBSIDY PUBLISHES 20%.** Reprints books. Prefers 200-280 pgs. Royalty 10-15% of net; advance. Average first printing 5,000-10,000. Publication within 3-6 mos. Considers simultaneous submissions. Responds in 6-8 wks. Requires disk. Free guidelines/catalog.

Nonfiction: Proposal/3 chapters; phone query OK. "Most open to evangelism, spiritual growth, self-help and education."

Fiction: Proposal/3 chapters. For teens and adults. "In general we don't consider fiction."

Tips: "Have a great message, a well-written manuscript, and a willingness, as well as ways, to market your book. "

BRISTOL HOUSE, LTD., PO Box 4020, Anderson IN 46013-0020. (317)644-0856. Fax (317)622-1045. Sara Anderson, sr. ed. Imprint: Bristol Books. Publishes 4 titles/yr. Receives 35-55 submissions annually. Few books from first-time authors. Reprints books. **SOME SUBSIDY.** Prefers 160-240 pgs. Royalty 14% of net; no advance. Average first printing 1,000. Publication within 6-9 mos. Responds in 4 mos. Requires disk. Catalog for 9x12 SAE/2 stamps.

> **Nonfiction:** Proposal/2 chapters; fax/e-mail query OK. "Looking for books on renewal. Most of our books are Methodist/Wesleyan in emphasis."

BROADMAN & HOLMAN PUBLISHERS, 127 9th Ave. N, Nashville TN 37234. (615)251-3638. Fax (615)251-2000. Southern Baptist. Richard Rosenbaum, ed. dir. Publishes 45-50 titles/yr. Receives 1,500-2,000 submissions annually. 10-20% of books from first-time authors. Variable royalty on net & advance. Average first printing 5,000. Publication within 8-12 mos. Considers simultaneous submissions. Responds in 2 mos. Guidelines (2 stamps); catalog for 9x12 SAE/3 stamps.

> **Nonfiction:** Proposal/2 chapters (see guidelines for format); no phone query.
>
> **Fiction:** No unsolicited fiction.
>
> **Ethnic:** Spanish translations.
>
> **Tips:** "Follow guidelines when submitting. Be informed about the market in general and specifically related to the book you want to write."
>
> ****Note:** This publisher serviced by The Writer's Edge.

*BROWN PUBLISHING-ROA MEDIA, 1665 Embassy West Dr., Dubuque IA 5200-2259. (319)588-1451. Fax (319)589-4705. Catholic. Mary Jo Graham, sr. ed. Publishes 50-100 titles/yr. Receives 100-300 submissions annually. Variable royalty or outright purchase; rarely pays advance. Average first printing 1,000-3,000. Publication within 1 yr. Considers simultaneous submissions. Responds in 2 mos. Free catalog.

> **Nonfiction:** Complete ms. "Looking primarily for school and parish text books and easy-to-use help books."

CAMERON PRESS, INC., 155 Thornwood Dr., Marlton NJ 08053. (609)983-5937. Fax (609)983-5331. Website: http://www.communityweb.com/cameronpress. Evangelical. Lynn Guise, sr. ed. Publishes 8 titles/yr. Receives 150 submissions annually. 33% of books from first-time authors. **SUBSIDY PUBLISHES 25%.** Reprints books. Prefers 261 pgs or less. Royalties 10% of net (subsidy is 50% of net); no advance. Average first printing 3,000. Publication within 1 yr. Considers simultaneous submissions. Requires disk. Guidelines.

> **Nonfiction:** Query letter only; fax query OK. "Nonfiction accepted on subsidy basis only."
>
> **Fiction:** Proposal/3 chapters. Adult historical fiction. No science fiction or books on the occult.
>
> **Contest:** Sponsors an annual essay contest. Winners are published. Send SASE for details.
>
> **Tips:** "Most open to historical fiction of a classical nature that can be marketed to Christian high schools. Also inspirational nonfiction."
>
> ****Note:** This publisher serviced by The Writer's Edge.

+WILLIAM CAREY LIBRARY, 1705 N. Sierra Bonita Ave., Pasadena CA 91104. (818)798-4067. Fax (818)794-0477. David Shaver, gen. mgr. Publishes 10-15 titles/yr. Not included in topical listings.

Nonfiction: Query only. "As a specialized publisher, we do only books and studies of church growth and world missions. "

+CATHOLIC BOOK PUBLISHING CORP., 77 West End Rd., Totowa NJ 07512. (201)890-2400. Fax (201)890-2410. Catholic. Anthony Buono, mng. ed. Inspirational books for Catholic-Christians. Publishes 15-20 titles/yr. Receives 75 submissions annually. 30% of books from first-time authors. No mss through agents. Variable royalty or outright purchases; no advance. Average first printing 3,000. Publication within 12-15 mos. No simultaneous submissions. Responds in 2-3 mos. Guidelines; catalog for 9x12 SAE/5 stamps.

Nonfiction: Query letter only; no phone/fax query.

Tips: "We accept mss with sound, mainline Catholic theology; children's books with various themes related to Catholic faith. We highly consider Marian publications, Bibles and Missals. Most open to prayer books."

THE CATHOLIC UNIVERSITY OF AMERICA PRESS, 620 Michigan Ave. NE, Washington DC 20064. (202)319-5052. Fax (202)319-4985. E-mail: cua-press @cua.edu. Website: http://www.cua.edu/www/cupr. Catholic. Dr. David L. McGonagle, dir. Publishes 15-20 titles/yr. Receives 100 submissions annually. 50% of books from first-time authors. No mss through agents. Reprints books. Prefers 80,000-200,000 wds. Variable royalty on net; no advance. Average first printing 750. Publication within 1 yr. Considers simultaneous submissions. Responds in 3 mos. Guidelines; catalog for SASE.

Nonfiction: Proposal/1 chapter, bio & credits; phone/fax/e-mail query OK. "Looking for history, literature, philosophy, political theory and theology."

Tips: "We publish only works of original scholarship of interest to practicing scholars and academic libraries; works that are aimed at college and university classrooms. We do not publish for the popular religious audience."

+CEF PRESS, PO Box 348, Warrenton MO 63383-0348. (314)456-4321. Fax (314)456-2078. Betty Johnson, ed. Produces evangelizing resources for teachers, leaders and evangelists of children. Publishes 40+ titles/yr. 5% of books from first-time authors. Prefers 200 pgs. Royalty; no advance. Average first printing 5,000. Publication within 4 mos. Accepts disks. No guidelines or catalog.

Nonfiction: Query only; fax query OK.

Fiction: Query only. For children.

Also Does: Pamphlets, booklets and tracts.

*CERDIC PUBLICATIONS, PJR-RIC, 11, rue Jean Sturm, 67520 Nordheim, France. Phone (88)87. Marie Zimmerman, ed. Publishes 3-5 titles/yr. Most books from first-time authors. Prefers 230 pgs. The first print run in the field of law in religion does not make money. Average first printing 200. Publication within 6 mos. Considers simultaneous submissions. Responds in 4 wks. Free catalog.

Nonfiction: Complete ms; fax query OK. "Looking for books on law and religion."

Tips: "We publish original studies in law of religion (any) with preference for young, beginning authors."

CHALICE PRESS, Box 179, St. Louis MO 63166-0179. (314)231-8500. Fax

(314)231-8524. E-mail: CHALICEBKS@aol.com. Christian Church (Disciples of Christ). Dr. David P. Polk, ed. Books for a thinking, caring church. Publishes 15-20 titles/yr. Receives 200+ submissions annually. 15% of books from first-time authors. No mss through agents. Prefers 144 pgs. Royalty 12-18% of net; no advance. Average first printing 2,500-3,000. Publication within 1 yr. Disk required on acceptance. Responds in 1-3 mos. Guidelines; catalog for 9x12 SAE/2 stamps.

Nonfiction: Proposal/2 chapters; fax/e-mail query OK. "Looking for books that treat current issues perceptively, especially from a moderate-to-liberal perspective."

Ethnic Books: African American & Hispanic.

*CHARIOT BOOKS, 4050 Lee Vance View, Colorado Springs CO 80918. (719)536-0100. Cook Communications Ministries. Liz Duckworth, mng ed. Books to bring the Bible to life for children. Publishes 30-35 titles/yr. 5% of books from first-time authors. Royalty on net; advance; some outright purchases. Average first printing 10,000. Publication within 18 mos. Considers simultaneous submissions. Responds in 3 mos. Guidelines.

Nonfiction & Fiction: Proposal/2 chapters; complete ms for picture books. Children's picture books and devotional books for children 8-12 years.

Tips: "We try to help parents train their children in the Christian faith, putting Deut. 6:5-9 into action."

**Note: This publisher serviced by The Writer's Edge.

*CHARIOT FAMILY PUBLISHING, 4050 Lee Vance View, Colorado Springs CO 80918. (719)536-0100. Cook Communications Ministries. Imprints: Chariot Books (children); and Bible Discovery (children's Bibles & biblical reference). Karl Schaller, dir. of product development; Julie Smith, mng ed. Publishes 50-60 titles/yr. Receives 1,500 submissions annually. 0% of adult books from first-time authors. Royalty on net; advance. Average first printing 10,000. Publication within 12 mos. Considers simultaneous submissions. Responds in 3 mos. Guidelines. Note: See Chariot Books & Bible Discovery for details on children's books.

Nonfiction: Proposal/2 chapters. Adult books on parenting and family life.

Fiction: Proposal/2 chapters. Adult fiction.

**Note: This publisher serviced by The Writer's Edge.

CHOSEN BOOKS, Division of Baker Book House, 3985 Bradwater St., Fairfax VA 22031-3702. (703)764-8250. Fax (703)764-3995. E-mail: JECampbell@aol.com. Charismatic. Jane Campbell, ed. Publishes 8 titles/yr. Receives 300 submissions annually. 15% of books from first-time authors. Prefers minimum 60,000 wds or 160 pgs. Royalty; possible advance. Average first printing 5,000-7,500. Publication within 18 mos. Considers simultaneous submissions. Responds in 2-3 mos. Prefers disk. Guidelines for #10 SASE/1 stamp.

Nonfiction: Proposal/1-2 chapters (summary, outline, author resume); e-mail query OK. "Looking for books that help the reader live a more empowered and effective life for Jesus Christ."

Tips: "State your theme clearly in your cover letter, along with your qualifications for writing on that subject, and be sure to enclose an SASE."

**Note: This publisher serviced by The Writer's Edge.

CHRISTENDOM PRESS, 134 Christendom Dr., Front Royal VA 22630. (540)636-2900. Fax (540)636-1655. Christendom College/Catholic. John Janaro, dir. Publishes important works of Catholic scholarship and commentary. Publishes 6 titles/yr. Receives 100 submissions annually. **LESS THAN 10% SUBSIDY.** Reprints books. Prefers 62,500 wds or 250 pgs. Royalty 20% on net (after production costs); no advance. Average first printing 1,000. Publication within 24 mos. Responds in 6-8 mos. Free catalog.

> **Nonfiction:** Complete ms.
>
> **Special Needs:** Catholic theology faithful to Catholic church's magisterium; philosophy (especially Thomism); history, political science, literary criticism, and educational theory from a Catholic point of view.
>
> **Tips:** "Most open to a book that provides intelligent, firm and well-balanced reflection in liberal arts, from an unashamedly Catholic point of view. We want books by responsible Catholic scholars and thinkers."

CHRISTIAN ED. PUBLISHERS, Box 26639, San Diego CA 92196. (619)578-4700. Carol Rogers, mng. ed. An evangelical publisher of Bible Club materials for ages two through high school. Publishes 80 titles/yr. Receives 120 submissions annually. 10% of books from first-time authors. No mss through agents. Outright purchases for .03/wd; no advance. Publication within 1 yr. Considers simultaneous submissions. Responds in 1-2 mos. Guidelines; catalog for 9x12 SAE/4 stamps.

> **Nonfiction:** Query first. Bible studies, curriculum and take-home papers.
>
> **Fiction:** Query first. Juvenile fiction for take-home papers. "Each story is about 1,000 wds. Write for an application."
>
> **Tips:** "All writing done on assignment. Need Bible-teaching ideas for preschool through sixth grade. Also publishes Bible stories for primary take-home papers, 300 wds."

*CHRISTIAN LITERATURE CRUSADE, 701 Pennsylvania Ave., Fort Washington PA 19034. (215)542-1242. Fax (215)542-2580. E-mail: 76043.3053@compuserve.com. Willard Stone, publications coordinator. Publishes 6-8 titles/yr. Receives 100+ submissions annually. Few books from first-time authors. No mss through agents. Prefers 120 pgs & up. Royalty 10-15% on retail; some $300-500 advances. Average first printing 3,000-5,000. Publication within 4-5 mos. Considers simultaneous submissions. Responds in 1-3 wks. Free guidelines/catalog.

> **Nonfiction:** Query letter; phone/fax query OK. Missions oriented or deeper life.
>
> **Also Does:** Booklets.

CHRISTIAN MEDIA, Box 448, Jacksonville OR 97530. (541)899-8888. Fax on request. James Lloyd, ed/pub. Publishes 5 titles/yr. Receives 12 submissions annually. Most books from first-time authors. Would consider reprints. Prefers 200 pgs. Royalty on net; no advance. Considers simultaneous submissions. Responds in 3 wks. Catalog for 9x12 SAE/2 stamps.

> **Nonfiction:** Query; phone query OK. Works dealing with the internal workings of the media industry; publishing, broadcasting, records, etc.
>
> **Tips:** "Produces manuals, instructional or otherwise. Exposés; also books of prophetic interpretation, end times, eschatology, interpolations of political events, etc."

CHRISTIAN PUBLICATIONS, 3825 Hartzdale Dr., Camp Hill PA 17011. (717)761-7044. Fax (717)761-7273. E-mail: editor@cpi-horizon.com. Christian and Missionary Alliance. David E. Fessenden, mng. ed. To serve the evangelical community worldwide through the publishing of materials that emphasize the deeper Christian life. Imprint: Horizon Books. Publishes 25 titles/yr. Receives 1,000+ submissions annually. 25% of books from first-time authors. **SUBSIDY PUBLISHES 5%.** Prefers 160-304 pgs. Royalty 5-10% of retail or net; outright purchases $100-400 (booklets); advance. Average first printing under 3,000. Publication within 12-15 mos. Considers simultaneous submissions. Disk preferred. Responds in 1-3 mos. Catalog for 9x12 SAE/7 stamps.

> **Nonfiction:** Proposal/2 chapters (include 1st); on-page fax/e-mail query OK. "Looking for books that lead the reader to a deeper walk with God; living as a servant."
>
> **Tips:** "Looking for a topic of importance for a lay audience, one that emphasizes commitment, servanthood, and self-sacrifice for the gospel. The Lordship of Christ in all areas is what gives a green light for us."
>
> ****Note:** This publisher serviced by The Writer's Edge.

CHRISTIAN UNIVERSITIES PRESS, 7831 Woodmont #345, Bethesda MD 20814. (301)654-7414. Fax (301)654-7336. E-mail: AUSTINISP@aol.com. An imprint of International Scholar's Publications. Dr. Robert West, ed-in-chief. Mainstream scholarship with a Christian theme. Publishes 15-20 titles/yr. Receives 350 submissions annually. 50% of books from first-time authors. No mss through agents. Reprints books. Prefers 250+ pgs. Royalty 8-12% of net; no advance. Average first printing 500. Publication within 6-8 mos. Considers simultaneous submissions. Responds in 2 mos. Accepts disk. Guidelines; catalog for 9x12 SAE/2 stamps.

> **Nonfiction:** Proposal/2 chapters; fax/e-mail query OK. "Looking for ethics, parish history, or African religion."
>
> **Ethnic Books:** Hispanic or African.
>
> **Also Does:** Pamphlets.
>
> **Tips:** "Most open to scholarly monograph/dissertation."

THE CHRISTOPHER PUBLISHING HOUSE, 24 Rockland St., Hanover MA 02339. (617)826-7474. Fax (617)826-5556. Nancy A. Lucas, mng. ed. Publishes 6-8 titles/yr. Receives 200+ submissions annually. 90% of books from first-time authors. **SUBSIDY PUBLISHES 8-10%.** Prefers 100+ pgs. Prefers 120 pgs. Royalty 5-30% of net; no advance. Average first printing 2,000. Publication within 12-14 mos. Considers simultaneous submissions. Responds in 4-6 wks. Accepts disk. Guidelines; catalog for #10 SAE/2 stamps.

> **Nonfiction:** Complete ms. Most topics; no juvenile material.
>
> **Fiction:** Complete ms. Adult only. About 100 pgs.

+CHURCH & SYNAGOGUE LIBRARY ASSN., PO Box 19357, Portland OR 97280-0357. (503)244-6919. Fax (503)977-3734. E-mail: CSLA@worldaccess.com. Sarah Moore, ed. An interfaith group set up to help librarians set up and organize/reorganize their religious libraries. Publishes 6 titles/yr. No mss through agents. Advance. Average first printing 750. Catalog.

CHURCH GROWTH INSTITUTE, PO Box 7000, Forest VA 24551. (804)525-0022. Fax (804)525-0608. Ephesians Four Ministries. Cindy G. Spear, ed. Publishes 10 titles/yr. Receives 52 submissions annually. 7% of books from first-time authors. No mss through agents. Prefers 64-160 pgs. Royalty 5% on retail or outright purchase; no advance. Average first printing 500. Publication within 1 yr. Considers simultaneous submissions. Responds in 2 mos. Requires disk. Guidelines; catalog for 9x12 SAE/4 stamps.

> **Nonfiction:** Proposal/1 chapter; fax query OK. "We prefer our writers to be experienced in what they write about, to be experts in the field."
>
> **Special Needs:** Topics that help churches grow spiritually and numerically; leadership training; attendance & stewardship programs; new or unique ministries (how-to).
>
> **Tips:** "Most open to a practical manual or complete resource packet for the pastor or other church leaders. Write with a conservative Christian slant; be very practical. "

*CHURCH STREET PRESS, 127 Ninth Ave. N., Nashville TN 37234. (800)436-3689. Genevox Music Group. New publisher. Does music, academic, how-to, drama and coffee table books.

CISTERCIAN PUBLICATIONS INC., Wallwood Hall, WMU Station, Kalamazoo MI 49008. (616)387-8920. Fax (616)387-8921. St. Joseph's Abbey/Catholic/Order of Cistercians of the Strict Observance. Dr. E. Rozanne Elder. ed. dir. Publishes 8-14 titles/yr. Receives 30 submissions annually. 50% of books from first-time authors. No mss through agents. Prefers 204-286 pgs. Variable payment. Average first printing 1,500. Publication within 2-10 yrs. Free guidelines/catalog.

> **Nonfiction:** Proposal/1 chapters. History, spirituality and theology.
>
> **Tips:** "We publish only on the Christian Monastic Tradition."

COLLEGE PRESS PUBLISHING CO., INC., 223 W. Third St.(94801), Box 1132, Joplin MO 64802. (417)623-6280. Fax (417)623-8250. E-mail: college press@ collegepress.com. Christian Church/Church of Christ. John M. Hunter, ed. Imprint: Forerunner Books. Christian materials that will help fulfill the Great Commission and promote unity on the basis of biblical truth and intent. Publishes 30 titles/yr. Receives 400+ submissions annually. 1-5% of books from first-time authors. Reprints books. Prefers 250-300 pgs (paperback) or 300-600 pgs (hardback). Royalty 10% of net; no advance. Average first printing 2,000. Publication within 6 mos. Considers simultaneous submissions. Responds in 2-3 mos. Guidelines; catalog for 9x12 SAE/5 stamps.

> **Nonfiction:** Query only, then proposal/2-3 chapters; no phone/fax/e-mail query. "Looking for apologetics and preparation for life in the 21st century."
>
> **Ethnic Books:** Reprints their own books in Spanish.
>
> **Tips:** "Most open to conservative, biblical exposition with an 'Armenian' view and/or 'amillennial' slant."

CONARI PRESS, 2550 - 9th St., Ste. 101, Berkeley CA 94710-2551. (510)596-8199. Fax (510)654-7259. Website: http://www.conan.com. Claudia Schaab, ed. assoc. Focus is on the human experience. Publishes 5 titles/yr. Receives 500 submissions annually. 50% of books from first-time authors. Reprints bks. Royalty 8-12%; $1,500 advance. Average first printing 10,000. Publication within 2 yrs. Considers simultaneous submissions. Responds in 1-3 mos. Guidelines; catalog for 7x10 SAE/3 stamps.

> **Nonfiction:** Proposal/3 chapters; no phone/fax query.

CONCORDIA PUBLISHING HOUSE, 3558 S. Jefferson Ave., St. Louis MO 63118-3968. (314)268-1000. Fax (314)268-1329. Lutheran Church/Missouri Synod. Ruth Geisler, Creative Director-Family & Children's Resources. Publishes 60 titles/yr. Receives 2,000 submissions annually. 10% of books from first-time authors. Royalty 6-10% on retail; some outright purchases. Publication within 1 yr. Considers simultaneous submissions. Responds in 2 mos. Prefers disk. Guidelines.

    Nonfiction: Proposal/2 chapters.

    Fiction: Proposal/2 chapters; fax query OK. For children (5-8, 6-9, or 8-12; series only) or teens only; also picture books. Fiction guidelines available on request. Christian fiction only.

    Ethnic Books: Publishes books for Hispanic, Chinese, African-American, Hmong, and Vietnamese.

    Tips: "Most open to family, inspirational/devotional, children's, and teachers' resource books."

    **Note: This publisher serviced by The Writer's Edge.

CONTEMPORARY DRAMA SERVICE—See **Meriwether Publishing, Ltd.**

THE CONTINUUM PUBLISHING COMPANY, 370 Lexington Ave., Ste. 1700, New York NY 10017-6503. (212)953-5858. Fax (212)953-5944. Website: http://www.continuum-books.com. Frank Oveis, ed. dir. Publishes 30 titles/yr. Receives 150 submissions annually. 40-50% of books from first-time authors. Reprints books. Prefers 160-200 pgs. Royalty 6-15% on retail or net; advance. Average first printing 2,500-3,500. Publication within 1 yr. Some simultaneous submissions. Responds in 4-6 wks. Disk required. Free guidelines/catalog.

    Nonfiction: Proposal/1 chapter; phone/fax/e-mail query OK.

COOK COMMUNICATIONS MINISTRIES—See Chariot Family Publishing, Chariot Books, and Bible Discovery.

DAVID C. COOK PUBLISHING CO.—See Chariot Family Publishing.

*CORNELL UNIVERSITY PRESS, Box 250, 124 Roberts Pl., Ithaca NY 14851. (607)257-7000. Fax (607)257-3552. Nondenominational. Bernard Kendler & Roger Hayden, eds. Publishes 6-8 titles/yr. Receives 20 submissions annually. 50% of books from first-time authors. Reprints books. Prefers 100,000 wds. Royalty 5-10%; rarely pays advance. Average first printing 1,250. Publication within 1 yr. May consider simultaneous submission. Responds in 3 mos. Free guidelines/catalog.

    Nonfiction: Query first. "Looking for historical (esp. medieval and early modern) and philosophical books."

*CORNERSTONE PRESS, 939 W. Wilson Ave., Ste. 202C, Chicago IL 60640. (312)561-2450. Fax (312)989-2076. Jane Hertenstein, ed. Imprint: Mere Bones. Publishes 4 titles/yr. Receives 60 submissions annually. Prefers 200-250 pgs. Royalty 12%. Average first printing 2,000-3,000. Publication within 1 yr. Considers simultaneous submissions. Catalog for SASE.

    Nonfiction: Proposal/1 chapter.

    Fiction: Proposal/1 chapter. Children, teen, adults.

CORNERSTONE PUBLISHING, INC., PO Box 2896, Virginia Beach VA 23450. (757)431-9244. Fax (757)431-6938. E-mail: healthy1@erols.com. Wendy O'Rourke, ed.; submit to A.M. Gates. A major provider of resources for writers;

multicultural books; and resources that motivate, educate and inspire. Publishes 12-15 titles/yr. Receives 250-300 submissions annually. 75% of books from first-time authors. **SUBSIDY PUBLISHES 25%.** Prefers 25,000 wds or 125 pgs. Royalty10-50% on net; no advance. Average first printing 2,000. Publication within 7 mos. Considers simultaneous submissions. Disk OK. Responds in 4-6 wks. Free guidelines/catalog.

Nonfiction: Proposal/3 chapters; phone/fax/e-mail query OK. "Looking for books on angels, miracles and testimonies; how to live the Christian life in the 21st century; humor."

Fiction: Proposal/3 chapters. All ages. "Looking for novels on spiritual warfare."

Ethnic Books: Books for all ethnic markets.

Also Does: Booklets, pamphlets, tracts; greeting cards and bookmarks.

CREATION HOUSE, 600 Rinehart Rd., Lake Mary FL 32746-4872. (407)333-3132. Fax (407)333-7100. Strang Communications. Submissions Editor. To provide the charismatic market with books on Spirit-led living. Publishes 20+ titles/yr. Receives 600 submissions annually. 5% of books from first-time authors. Prefers 40,000 wds or 200 pgs. Royalty 7-18% on net; variable advance. Average first printing 5,000. Publication within 6-9 mos. Considers simultaneous submissions. Responds in 2+ mos. No disk. Free guidelines; no catalog.

Nonfiction: Proposal/3 chapters; fax query OK. "Looking for books of Spirit-filled interest, devotional life, practical Christian living, and Bible study/foundational."

**Note: This publisher serviced by The Writer's Edge.

*CREATIVELY YOURS, 2906 W. 64th Pl., Tulsa OK 74132. Phone/fax (918)446-2424. Creatively Yours Puppetry. Jill Morris, pub. Publishes individual scripts and books of plays, poems, and related material; general religious. Send complete ms. Responds in 2 mos or less. Pays $25 for plays; $5 for poems (4-20 lines/action), and $10 for choral readings. Buys all rts. Guidelines; free brochure.

Tips: "Try the material on children—if they don't like it, don't send it to us. Use humor whenever possible. The plays we publish can be used with puppets or children, so don't overload on characters, props, or setting—keep it simple."

Note: Since this publisher wants individual plays or poems, it is listed in the topical section for periodicals.

CROSS CULTURAL PUBLICATIONS, INC., PO Box 506, Notre Dame IN 46556. (219)272-0889. Fax (219)273-5973. Cyriac K. Pullapilly, gen. ed. Promotes intercultural and interfaith understanding. Imprint: Crossroads Books. Publishes 10-15 titles/yr. Receives 2,000-3,000 submissions annually. 60% of books from first-time authors. Prefers 200-250 pgs. Royalty 5-10% of net; no advance. Average first printing 1,000. Publication within 3-5 mos. Considers simultaneous submissions. Requires disk. Responds in 30-60 days. Free catalog.

Nonfiction: Query or complete ms; fax query OK.

Fiction: Complete ms. Adult.

Special Needs: Seeks to serve the cross cultural, intercultural, and multicultural aspects of religious traditions.

Tips: "Most open to solidly researched, well-written books on serious issues.

Do a thorough job of writing/editing, etc."

THE CROSSROAD PUBLISHING CO., 370 Lexington Ave., New York NY 10017. (212)532-3650. Fax (212)532-4922. Michael Leach, pub. Imprints: Crossroad and Crossroad Herder. Publishes 70 titles/yr. Receives 1,000+ submissions annually. 10% of books from first-time authors. Rarely subsidy publishes (2%). Reprints books. Prefers 50,000-60,000 wds or 200 pgs. Royalty 6-10% on retail; advance $1,000 (more for established authors). Average first printing 4,000. Publication within 8-10 mos. Considers simultaneous submissions. Responds in 4-12 wks. No disk. Free catalog.

> **Nonfiction:** Complete ms/author bio and letter selling your idea; fax query OK.

CROSSWAY BOOKS, 1300 Crescent St., Wheaton IL 60187. (630)682-4300. Fax (630)682-4785. A division of Good News Publishers. Leonard G. Goss, VP editorial. To make a difference in people's lives for Christ. Publishes 45-50 titles/yr. Receives 3,000 submissions annually. 3% of books from first-time authors. Prefers 25,000 wds & up. Royalty 15-21% on net; advance. Average first printing 5,000-10,000. Publication within 18 mos. Considers simultaneous submissions. Requires disk (compatible with Macintosh and Microsoft Word). Responds in 6-8 wks. Guidelines; catalog for 9x12 SAE/6 stamps.

> **Nonfiction:** Query only; no phone/fax query.
>
> **Fiction:** Proposal/2 chapters. Adult; children's books for 8-14 year olds, series only.
>
> **Also Does:** Tracts. See Good News Publishers.
>
> **Tips:** "Most open to books that are consistent with what the Bible teaches and stand within the stream of historic Christian truth; books that give a clear sense that the author is a genuine Christian seeking to live a consistent Christian life." Not seeking new projects until winter of 1997.
>
> ****Note:** This publisher serviced by The Writer's Edge.

C.S.S. PUBLISHING CO., PO Box 4503, 517 S. Main St., Lima OH 45802-4503. (419)227-1818. Fax (419)228-9184. Tom Lentz, acq. ed. Publishes 60 titles/yr. Receives 450 submissions annually. 50% of books from first-time authors. No mss through agents. **SUBSIDY PUBLISHES 20%** through Fairway Press. Prefers 100-125 pgs. Royalty or outright purchases for $25-400. Average first printing 2,000. Publication within 1-2 yrs. Considers simultaneous submissions. Responds in 1-6 mos. Prefers disk. Guidelines; free catalog.

> **Nonfiction:** Complete ms; phone/fax query OK. "Need worship resources, sermon illustrations."
>
> **Fiction:** Complete ms. Inspirational; plays (Advent/Christmas); short story collections. Children's books, 6-12 years, series or single books.

*CUSTOM COMMUNICATIONS SERVICES, INC./SHEPHERD PRESS/CUSTOMBOOK, 77 Main St., Tappan NJ 10983. (914)365-0414. Norman Shaifer, pres. Publishes 50-75 titles/yr. 50% of books from first-time authors. No mss through agents. Royalty on net; some outright purchases for specific assignments. Publication within 6 mos. Responds in 1 month. Guidelines.

> **Nonfiction:** Query/proposal/chapters. "Histories of individual congregations, denominations, or districts."
>
> **Tips:** "Find stories of larger congregations (750 or more households) who

have played a role in the historic growth and development of the community or region."

DABAR PUBLISHING CO., PO Box 35377, Detroit MI 48235. (313)531-7534. Fax (313)531-7660. U. Francis Osaigbovo, acq. ed. Books for African-American Christian women. Publishes 2-5 titles/yr. Receives 30-40 submissions annually. 75% of books from first-time authors. Reprints books. Prefers 200-250 pgs. Outright purchase of $3,000-5,000 (plus additional royalties based on sales); $500 advance. Average first printing 4,000. Publication within 6-9 mos. Considers simultaneous submissions. Responds in 1 mo, if interested; rejected mss not returned. Guidelines.

Nonfiction: Proposal/3 chapters; phone/fax query OK (leave your phone #).

Ethnic Books: "Books that will help African-American Christian women face day-to-day personal/family relationships, community, economic, health, spiritual growth and maturity."

Tips: "We're small, so author will have to be willing to be involved in many phases, including promotion. Author does not have to be an African-American woman, but the message should be one that will be of interest to this group. Established speakers among African-American female audiences are especially desired."

+DESIGN COMMUNICATIONS, INC., PO Box 206, Rosenhayn NJ 08352. (609)451-4499. Fax (609)451-7686. E-mail: designpubl@aol.com. Pat Swart, ed. To inform, educate and serve the reader, church or ministry. Publishes 3 titles/yr. Receives 300+ submissions annually. 90% of books from first-time authors. **SUBSIDY PUBLISHES 15%.** Reprints books. Open length. Royalty on net; no advance. Average first printing 300-500 (100 for groups). Publication within 3 mos. Considers simultaneous submissions. Accepts disk. Responds in 2 wks. Guidelines/catalog for #10 SAE/1 stamp.

Nonfiction: Proposal/1chapter; fax/e-mail query OK.

Fiction: Proposal/1chapter. All ages.

Also Does: Pamphlets, booklets and tracts.

*DIMENSION BOOKS, INC., Box 811, Denville NJ 07835. (201)627-4334. Catholic. Thomas P. Coffey, ed. Publishes 12 titles/yr. Receives 800 submissions annually. 2% of books from first-time authors. Reprints books. Prefers 200 pgs. Royalty 10-15% on retail; advance. Average first printing 6,000-20,000. Publication within 6 mos. Considers simultaneous submissions. Responds in 2-5 wks. Catalog for #10 SAE/1 stamp.

Nonfiction: Query. Christian spirituality, music, biography and psychology.

DIMENSIONS FOR LIVING—See THE UNITED METHODIST PUBLISHING HOUSE.

*DISCIPLESHIP RESOURCES, Box 840, Nashville TN 37202-0840. (615)340-7068. (800)814-7833. Fax (615)340-7006. United Methodist. Craig Gallaway, ed. dir. Publishes 30 titles/yr. Receives 450 submissions annually. 20% of books from first-time authors. Prefers 96-144 pgs. Royalty 5-10% on retail or outright purchase, $250-1,500; $250 advance. Average first printing 4,000. Publication within 6 mos. Responds in 2 mos. Guidelines; catalog for 9x12 SAE/3 stamps.

Nonfiction: Proposal/2 chapters; phone/fax query OK. "Looking for leadership in ministry in the 21st century; ministry of laity—spiritual gifts."

Ethnic Books: Produces titles related to ministries for African-American, Hispanic, and Asian-American. Also sponsors writing workshops for ethnic groups. Call for information.

Also Does: Some booklets.

Tips: "Most open to a book that examines a specific area of ministry in the church and understands that leading this area is part of the total system of ministry in the church. Stay in touch with the real needs in the church."

*DISCOVERY PUBLISHING HOUSE, Box 3566, Grand Rapids MI 49501. Radio Bible Class. Robert DeVries, pub.; submit to Carol Holquist, assoc. pub. Guidelines. Not included in topical listings.

**Note: This publisher serviced by The Writer's Edge.

+DISCUS PRESS, 3389 Sheridan St. #308, Hollywood FL 33021. (954)894-9703. Karen Weiss, ed/pub. A vehicle for family values. Publishes 1 title/yr. Receives 54 submissions annually. 89% of books from first-time authors. Prefers 89,000 wds or 396 pgs (max.). Royalty 10-12% on net; negotiable advance. Average first printing 5,200. Publication within 9 mos. Considers simultaneous submissions. Responds in 2-3 wks. Free guidelines; no catalog.

Nonfiction: Complete ms. Looking for creation science, spiritual warfare, or prophecy.

Fiction: Complete ms. Teen & adult. All types.

Tips: "Don't bind ms. Electronic submissions for Macintosh OK. Most open to fiction. Include a cover letter, synopsis, and a brief note of information on the author."

DOUBLEDAY PUBLISHERS, 1540 Broadway, New York NY 10036. (212)782-8745. Fax (212)782-8911. Bantam Doubleday Dell/Bertlesmann. Eric Manor. VP of Religion. Imprints: Image, Galilee, Doubleday Hardcover, Anchor Bible. Publishes 45 titles/yr. Receives 2,500 submissions annually. 3% of books from first-time authors. Reprints books. Any length. Royalty/advance. Average first printing 10,000. Publication within 10 mos. Rarely considers simultaneous submissions. Responds in 1-2 wks. Free catalog.

Nonfiction: Accepts mss ONLY through agents.

Also Does: CD-ROM reference.

Tips: "Most open to a book that has a big and well-defined audience. Have a clear proposal, lucid thesis and specified audience."

EDEN PUBLISHING, 815 N Center St., Newberg OR 97132. (503)538-9032. Fax (503)537-0146. Nondenominational. Barbara Griffin, ed/pub. Strongly biblical, inspirational books for all ages. Publishes 3-4 titles/yr. Receives 300 submissions annually. 66% of books from first-time authors. No mss through agents. Prefers 60-90,000 wds or up to 150. Royalty 6-12% on retail; no advance. Average first printing 3-5,000. Publication within 3 mos. Considers simultaneous submissions. Disk on request. Responds in 2-3 wks. Catalog for #10 SAE/1 stamp.

Nonfiction: Query first; brief phone query OK. "We've been moving toward home schooling, but will consider children's books (devotional), books related to ministry (non-didactic); must motivate and inspire people to change."

Tips: "We look for quality writing on subjects that address special needs of

Christian, individuals and families. These can range from ministry to children, to ministries to grieving individuals, mentally challenged, special needs kids, etc."

*EDITORIAL CARIBE, 9300 S. Dadeland Blvd. Ste. 203, Miami FL 33156. (800)322-7423. Subsidiary of Thomas Nelson. Targets the needs and wants of the Hispanic community.

*EDITORIAL PORTAVOZ, PO Box 2607, Grand Rapids MI 49333. (616)451-4775. (800)733-2607. Fax (616)451-9330. Spanish Division of Kregel Publishing.

WM B. EERDMANS PUBLISHING CO., 255 Jefferson Ave. SE, Grand Rapids MI 49503. (616)459-4591. Fax (616)459-6540. Protestant/Academic/Theological. Jon Pott, ed-in-chief; Amy Eerdmans, children's book ed.; Nueva Creacion, Spanish imprint. Publishes 140 titles/yr. Receives 1,200-1,500 submissions annually. 5% of books from first-time authors. Reprints books. Royalty 7-10% on retail; occasional negotiable advance. Average first printing 4,000. Publication within 1 yr. Considers simultaneous submissions. Disk on request. Responds in 3-4 wks Guidelines; free catalog.

Nonfiction: Proposal/2 chapters; fax query OK. "Looking for religious approaches to contemporary issues; spiritual growth; scholarly works; biography for middle readers through young adults; children's picture books expressing positive family values."

Fiction: Query letter only. Children/teen/adult. "Our readers are educated and fairly sophisticated, so we are looking for novels with literary merit. For children. We look for manuscripts that help a child explore life in God's world, and to foster a child's exploration of his/her faith. "

Ethnic Books: Spanish imprint.

Tips: "Most open to material with general appeal, but well researched, cutting-edge material that bridges the gap between evangelical and mainline world."

**Note: This publisher serviced by The Writer's Edge.

#ELDER BOOKS, PO Box 490, Forest Knolls CA 94933. (415)488-9002. Fax (415)488-4720. Carmel Sheridan, dir. Publishes 6-10 titles/yr. Receives 250 submissions annually. 50% of books from first-time authors. Reprints books. Prefers 130 pgs. Royalty 7% of retail; no advance. Average first printing 3,000. Publication within 9 months. Responds in 3 mos. Free catalog.

Nonfiction: Proposal/2 chapters; fax query OK. "Most open to parenting, health, women's or seniors' issues."

ELDRIDGE PUBLISHING CO., INC., PO Box 1595, Venice FL 34284. (800)95-CHURCH. (941)496-4679. Fax (941)493-9680. E-mail: info@95church.com. Website: http://www.95church.com. Independent Christian drama publisher. Nancy Vorhis, sr. ed. To provide superior religious drama to enhance preaching and teaching, whatever your Christian faith. Publishes 25 plays/yr. Receives 250-300 plays annually. 50% of plays from first-time authors. One-act to full-length plays. Outright purchases of $200-500; royalty for full-length plays. Publication within 1 yr. Considers simultaneous submissions. Responds in 9 wks. Requires disk. Guidelines; free play catalog.

Plays: Complete ms; e-mail query OK. For children, teens and adults.

Special Needs: Always looking for high quality Christmas and Easter plays but open to other holiday and "anytime" Christian plays too. Can be biblical or current day, for performance by all ages, children through adult.

Tips: "Have play produced at your church and others prior to submission, to get out the bugs. At least try a stage reading. T-shirts, posters and sound effects tapes accompany our dramas."

*ELEMENT BOOKS, 42 Broadway, Rockport MA 01966. (508)546-1044. Fax (508)546-9882. Paul Cash, acq. ed. Books for broad religious market. Publishes 25 titles/yr. Receives hundreds of submissions annually. 15% of books from first-time authors. Reprints books. Prefers 125-250 pgs. Variable royalty & advance. Average first printing 3,000-5,000. Publication within 18 mos. Considers simultaneous submissions. Responds in 6-8 wks. Free guidelines & catalog.

Nonfiction: Query only.

Tips: "Try to reach a broad-based market—no books on very scholarly or limited-interest subjects."

*EVANGEL PUBLISHING HOUSE, 2000 Evangel Way, PO Box 189, Nappanee IN 46550. (219)773-3164. Fax (219)773-5934. Brethren in Christ Church. Gary Freymiller, ed. Provides resources helpful in biblical and theological foundations for Christian ministry. Publishes 15 titles/yr. Receives 25 submissions annually. 0% from first-time authors. **SUBSIDY PUBLISHES 25%.** Reprints books. Royalty 8-12% on retail; no advance. Average first printing 2,500. Publication within 4 mos. considers simultaneous submissions. Guidelines; catalog for 2 stamps.

Nonfiction: Proposal/2-3 chapters. "Looking for resources for ministry; biblical studies, theology and biblical theology."

Ethnic: Hispanic.

Tips: "Authors should have excellent credentials/experience to give credibility to work. Ph.D. preferred, but not required."

FAITH & LIFE PRESS, PO Box 347, Newton KS 67114. (316)283-5100. Fax (316)283-0454. E-mail: flp@gcmc.org. Mennonite. Susan Janzen, ed. dir. Publishes 10-12 titles/yr., plus curriculum series for all ages. Receives 35-50 submissions annually. 50% of books from first-time authors. No mss through agents. Royalty 7-12% on net or outright purchases for $500-2,000; advance $750. Average first printing 2,500. Publication in 8-10 mos. Considers simultaneous submissions. Responds in 2-3 mos. Guidelines; free catalog.

Nonfiction: Query; phone/fax/e-mail query OK.

Tips: "We have shifted from publishing a lot of unsolicited mss on a wide range of topics to a focused approach in narrower subject areas: Christian education resources, curriculum (SS & VBS), and worship/spirituality. Most are assigned."

*FAITH, PRAYER & TRACT LEAGUE, Grand Rapids MI 49504-1390. Tracts only. No information on openness to freelance submissions.

FAITH PUBLISHING CO., PO Box 237, Milford OH 45150-0237. (513)576-6400. Fax (513)576-0022. Catholic. Bill Reck, pres. Publishes 6-12 titles/yr. 50% of books from first-time authors. No mss through agents. Prefers 100-300 pgs. Negotiable terms; no advance. Average first printing 5,000-7,000. Publication within 1-3 mos. Considers simultaneous submissions. Responds in 3-6 mos.

Prefers disk. Free guidelines/catalog.

Nonfiction: Complete ms; fax query OK.

Fiction: Complete ms. Biblical/religious only. "Fiction must draw the reader to a deeper knowledge of and devotion to God."

Also Does: Booklets; would consider pamphlets or tracts.

FOCUS ON THE FAMILY PUBLISHERS, 8605 Explorer Dr., Colorado Springs CO 80920-1051. (719)531-3496. Fax (719)531-3484. Al Janssen, acq. ed. Dedicated to the preservation of marriage and the family. Publishes 18-20 titles/yr. Receives 2,000 submissions annually. 10% of books from first-time authors. Prefers 200 pgs. Royalty on retail; advance. Average first printing 25,000. Publication within 18 mos. Considers simultaneous submissions. Responds in 4-6 wks. Free guidelines/catalog.

Nonfiction: Submit ONLY a 1-pg query letter.

Tips: "Need highly practical books—tell how to do something and don't make it too complicated. Also looking for writers who are verbal and can do a good, lively interview."

**Note: This publisher serviced by The Writer's Edge.

+FOG (FRIENDS OF GOD) PUBLISHING HOUSE, PO Box 2703, Houston TX 77252-2703. (713)759-0207. Submit to The Editor. To be a servant of God, so that all will boast in the Lord and know His grace. Publishes 5+ titles/yr. Receives 200 submissions annually. 20% of books from first-time authors. Negotiated royalty; no advance. Average first printing 5,000. Publication within 8 mos. Considers simultaneous submissions. Requires disk on request. Responds in 2 mos. Guidelines; no catalog.

Nonfiction: Complete ms only; no phone query.

Fiction: Complete ms only. "Must be classic/timeless stories stressing values gained through learned experience "

Special Needs: Will consider computer games, especially if created for MACINTOSH.

Tips: "Must be extremely well researched and well written. We toss anything remotely unprofessional." Does not return manuscripts.

FORTRESS PRESS, Box 1209, 426 S. 5th St., Minneapolis MN 55440. (612)330-3433. Fax (612)330-3215. Dr. Marshall D. Johnson, dir. of pub. Academic imprint of Augsburg Fortress/Evangelical Lutheran. Publishes 37 titles/yr. Receives 300 submissions annually. 15% of books from first-time authors. Rarely reprints books. Prefers 80-120,000 wds or 250 pgs. Royalty 8-10% on net; advance $500. Average first printing 3,500. Publication within 15 mos. Considers simultaneous submissions. Responds in 3 mos. Disk required. Free guidelines/catalog.

Nonfiction: Proposal/1 chapter; phone/fax query OK. "Looking for cutting-edge scholarship from recognized authorities in the areas of biblical studies, early Christianity, Reformation, historical and systematic theology, Christian social ethics, African American religion, etc."

Ethnic Books: Publishes books for African American and Hispanic Christians.

Tips: "Most open to creative advances in scholarship in the areas of biblical studies, theology, ethics. Also creative works in African American religious life and thought."

FORWARD MOVEMENT PUBLICATIONS, 412 Sycamore St., Cincinnati OH 45202. (513)721-6659. Fax (513)421-0315. E-mail: forward.movement@ ecunet.org. Episcopal. Edward S. Gleason, ed/dir. Publishes 8 titles/yr. Receives 50 submissions annually. 25% of books from first-time authors. No mss through agents. Rarely reprints books. Prefers 150 pgs. One-time honorarium; no advance. Average first printing 5,000. Publication within 9 mos. Reluctantly considers simultaneous submissions. Responds in 1-3 mos. Guidelines; catalog for 3 stamps.

Nonfiction: Query for book, complete ms if short; fax/e-mail query OK.

Fiction: "We publish almost no fiction, but will look at fiction for children."

Ethnic Books: Pamphlets in Spanish.

Also Does: Booklets, 4-32 pgs; and pamphlets 4-8 pgs.

Tips: "We sell primarily to a mainline Protestant audience."

FRANCISCAN UNIVERSITY PRESS, University Blvd., Steubenville OH 43952. (614)283-6357. Fax (614)283-6427. E-mail: FUSPRESS@aol.com. Website: http://www.esoptron.umd.edu/fusfolder/press.html. Catholic/Franciscan University of Steubenville. Submit to The Editor. To provide literature to inform and inspire readers on their pilgrimage of faith. Publishes 4-5 titles/yr. Receives 50 submissions annually. Rarely books from first-time authors. Reprints books. Prefers 300 pgs. Royalty 10% on net; no advance. Average first printing 3,000. Publication within 6-12 mos. Considers simultaneous submissions. Prefers disk. Responds 1-3 mos. Free guidelines/catalog.

Nonfiction: Query only. "Looking for Catholic apologetic/catechetical books in a popular vein."

Ethnic Books: "Spanish translations of our best-selling devotional works."

Also Does: Pamphlets, booklets, tracts.

Tips: "Most of our books are solicited from university professors and associates."

*FRIENDSHIP PRESS, 475 Riverside Dr., Room 860, New York NY 10115. (212)870-2496. Fax (212)870-2550. National Council of Churches of Christ. Margaret Larom, ed.; submit to Audrey A. Miller, dir. Publishes 12 titles/yr. Receives 180 submissions annually. 50% of books from first-time authors. Prefers 40-130 pgs. Royalty; some outright purchases; advance. Average first printing 10,000. Publication within 1-2 yrs. Considers simultaneous submissions. Responds in 2-3 mos. Guidelines; catalog for 9x12 SAE.

Nonfiction: Complete ms. "Looking for books on life in a multicultural society, the churches, and the United Nations."

Special Needs: Global perspective, mission education and political and religious issues, peace and justice education, cultural understanding and appreciation, spiritual reflection and development related to mission and social action.

Ethnic Books: All books have a multicultural theme.

Tips: "Most open to a book that fits a theme stated in our guidelines (one global/one topical), or one with a secured market. Church people primary audience."

FRIENDS UNITED PRESS, 101 Quaker Hill Dr., Richmond IN 47374. (317)962-7573. Fax (317)966-1293. Friends United Meeting (Quaker). Ardith Talbot, ed.

To gather persons into a fellowship where Jesus Christ is known as Lord and Teacher. Publishes 4-6 titles/yr. Receives 80-100 submissions annually. 85% of books from first-time authors. No mss through agents. Reprints books. Prefers 200-300 pgs. Royalty 7.5% of net; no advance. Average first printing 1,000. Publication within 1 yr. Considers simultaneous submissions. Disk required. Guidelines; free catalog.

Nonfiction: Query or complete ms; phone/fax query OK.

Fiction: Query or complete ms. For teens and adults. Must have Quaker tie-in.

Special Needs: Spirituality.

Tips: "We are restricted to Quaker authors, history, doctrine, etc."

GARBORG'S, 2060 W. 98th St., Bloomington MN 55431. (612)888-5727. Fax (612)888-4775. Wendy Greenberg, ed. To develop irresistibly creative ways to present God's Word to the world. Publishes 30-35 titles/yr. Receives 50-70 submissions annually. Reprints books. Prefers gift book length. Royalty 5% of net or outright purchase; advance. Average first printing 20,000. Publication within 6-12 mos. Considers simultaneous submissions. Responds in 4-6 wks. No disk. Guidelines; catalog for 9x12 SAE/2 stamps.

Nonfiction: Proposal/2 chapters or complete ms; no phone/fax query.

Also Does: Gift products. Main product is the DayBrightner, a perpetual, page-a-day calendar.

Tips: "Most open to a book that's original writing, not a collection of quotes or scripture verses. We are looking for uplifting and insightful writing that can be packaged in beautifully designed gift books."

GILGAL PUBLICATIONS, Box 3386, Sunriver OR 97707. (541)593-8418. Fax (541)593-5604. Judy Osgood, exec. ed. Focuses on collections of meditations on specific themes. Publishes 1 title/yr. Receives 400 submissions annually. 30% of books from first-time authors. No mss through agents. Pays $25/meditation on acceptance. Average first printing 3,000. Publication within 18 mos. Responds in 1-2 mos. No disk. Guidelines (required); catalog for SASE.

Nonfiction: Complete ms (after reading guidelines); fax query OK. "Our books are all anthologies on coping with stress and resolving grief. Not interested in other book mss. Currently interested in meditations on bereavement of various kinds."

B.J. GOETZ PUBLISHING CO., 3055 W. John Beers Rd., Stevensville MI 49127. (616)429-6442. Fax (616)429-5353. B.J. Goetz, pub. Specializes in materials to enhance Christian education programs; experiential/environmental concepts. Publishes 1 title/yr. Receives 12 submissions annually. 100% of books from first-time authors. Variable payment for outright purchase. Average first printing 1,000. Responds in 1-3 mos. Catalog.

Nonfiction: Proposal or complete ms. "We need an interdenominational approach in Christian education programs or Bible studies for children 5-12."

GOLD 'N' HONEY BOOKS/QUESTAR, Box 1720, Sisters OR 97759. (541)549-1144. Children's book imprint of Questar Publishers. Thomas Womack, ed.; submit to Brenda Saltzer. Publishes 20 titles/yr. Receives 500 submissions annually. 5% of books from first-time authors. Prefers not to work with agents. Royalty 5-18% of net. Publication with 10 mos. Responds in 2 mos. Catalog $2.

Nonfiction: Query. Illustrated books.

Fiction: Query. Religious picture books.

GOOD BOOK PUBLISHING COMPANY, 2747 S. Kihei Rd. #G102, Kihei HI 96753. Phone/fax (808)874-4876. Christian/Protestant Bible Fellowship. Ken Burns, pres. Researches and publishes books on the biblical/Christian roots of Alcoholics Anonymous. Publishes 2 titles/yr. Receives 5 submissions annually. 10% of books from first-time authors. No mss through agents. Prefers 300 pgs. Royalty 10%; no advance. Average first printing 1,000. Publication within 2 mos. Considers simultaneous submission. Responds in 1 wk. Accepts disk. Catalog for 9x12 SAE/2 stamps.

Nonfiction: Query; no phone/fax query. Books on the spiritual history and success of A.A.

Also Does: Pamphlets & booklets.

GOOD NEWS PUBLISHERS, 1300 Crescent St., Wheaton IL 60187. (630)682-4300. Fax (630)682-4785. Tracts only. Want $2\frac{1}{2}$ manuscript pages, 40 characters/line. Send to Tract Editor. Responds in 4 wks. Guidelines.

+GOSPEL FOLIO PRESS, PO Box 2041, Grand Rapids MI 49501. (616)456-9166. Fax (616)456-5522. E-mail: gospelfoli@aol.com. Uplook Ministries. J.B. Nicholson, Jr., ed; submit to Caroline Cairns. To build up the saints with clear, scriptural teaching. Publishes 6-10 titles/yr. Receives 20 submissions annually. Up to 1% of books from first-time authors. No mss through agents. Reprints books. Prefers 160 pgs. Often our authors donate our work. Average first printing 3,000. Publication within 3-6 mos. Considers simultaneous submissions. Responds in 1 mo. No guidelines; free catalog.

Nonfiction: Proposal/3 chapters; fax/e-mail query OK. "Virtually all our books are solicited mss or pre-arranged with the author."

Also Does: Pamphlets, booklets, tracts.

Tips: "Almost all our writers are Plymouth Brethren. We are a conservative, fundamental, evangelical organization. Books must be clearly presented and doctrinally sound according to our beliefs."

GOSPEL LIGHT PUBLICATIONS—See **REGAL BOOKS**.

GROUP PUBLISHING, INC., Box 481, Loveland CO 80539. (970)669-3836. Fax (970)669-3269. E-mail: GREditor@aol.com. Website: http://www.group.publishing. com. Imprint: Group Books. Attn.: Children's, Youth or Adult Acq. Ed. Encourages Christian growth in children, youth and adults. Publishes 20-30 titles/yr. Receives 900 submissions annually. 30% of books from first-time authors. No mss through agents. Prefers 150-250 ms pgs. Royalty to 10% of net; some outright purchases; $1,000 advance. Average first printing 5,000-7,000. Publication within 18 mos. Considers simultaneous submissions. Responds in 1 mo. Accepts disk. Writer test; catalog for 9x12 SAE/4 stamps.

Nonfiction: Query; fax/e-mail query OK. "Looking for pastor/church leader how-to books; youth ministry (something new in theory or practice); or children's programming ideas."

Fiction: Query. For children or teens. "Most need children's picture books that can be produced in a CD-ROM format."

Also Does: Booklets.

Tips: "Study our line of books before you approach us. Most open to programming books for children, youth or adults. Submissions received are only kept on file for 30 days."

GROUP'S HANDS-ON BIBLE CURRICULUM, Box 481, Loveland CO 80539. (970)669-3836. Fax (970)669-3269. E-mail: GREditor@aol.com. Kerri Nance, ed. asst. Publishes 24 titles/yr. Receives 200 submissions annually. 40% of books from first-time authors. No mss through agents. Outright purchase. Publication within 12-18 mos. Considers simultaneous submissions. Responds in 3-6 mos. Accepts disk. Trial assignment guidelines/catalog for 9x12 SAE/2 stamps.

> **Nonfiction:** Query requesting a trial assignment; phone/fax query OK. Produces curriculum for preschoolers, 1st-2nd, 3rd-4th, and 5th-6th graders. Submissions received are only kept on file for 30 days

GUERNICA EDITIONS, PO Box 117, Stn. P, Toronto ON M5S 2S6 Canada. Phone/fax (416)658-9880. Toward creating an essential library. Antonio D'Alfonso, ed. Publishes 1 religious title/yr. Receives 50 submissions annually. 10% of books from first-time authors. No mss through agents. Reprints books. Prefers 128 pgs. Royalty 7-10% of net; advance $1,000. Average first printing 1,000. Publication within 18-24 mos. Responds in 1 mo. Requires disk. For catalog send money order for stamps (if from US).

> **Nonfiction:** Query first; no phone query. "Looking for books on world issues."
>
> **Fiction:** Query first. Interested in ethnic and translations.
>
> **Ethnic Books:** Concentration on Italian culture. "We are involved in translations and ethnic issues."

*HANNIBAL BOOKS, 921 Center, Hannibal MO 63401. Phone/fax (314)221-2464. Hefley Communications. Marti Hefley, ed. To impact readers for Christ. Publishes 4-6 titles/yr. Receives 40 submissions annually. Almost no books from first-time authors. Prefers 200 pgs. Variable royalty on net; no advance. Average first printing 4,000.

> **Nonfiction:** Query letter only. Phone query only if you know editor.
>
> **Fiction:** Query letter only. Rarely does fiction.
>
> **Tips:** "Most open to a crossover book. Send an intelligent query."

+HARLEQUIN/LOVE INSPIRED, 300 E. 42nd St., New York NY 10017. (212)682-6080. Fax (212)682-4539. Steeple Hill. Christian romance imprint. Anne Canedeo, sr. ed. Pubishes 36 titles/yr. 10% of books from first-time authors. Rarely reprints books. Prefers 75,000-80,000 wds or 300-320 pgs. Royalty on net; advance. Publication within 12-24 mos. Responds in 4-6 wks. No disk. Guidelines.

> **Fiction:** Query letter or 3 chapters and up to 5-page synopsis. Contemporary romance and mystery romance. "Portray Christian characters learning an important lesson about the powers of truth and faith. Include humor, drama, and the many challenges of life and faith. "

HARPERSANFRANCISCO, 1160 Battery St., San Francisco CA 94111-1213. (415)477-4455. Fax (415)477-4444. Imprint of HarperCollins. Submit to the Editor. Publishes 100 titles/yr. Receives 10,000 submissions annually. 5% of books from first-time authors. Reprints books. Prefers 160-256 ms pgs. Royalty 10-15% on cloth, 7.5% on paperback, on retail; advance. Average first printing

7,500-10,000. Publication within 18 mos. Considers simultaneous submissions. Responds in 2 mos. Requires disk. Free guidelines/catalog.

Nonfiction: Query or proposal/chapters; fax query OK.

**Note: This publisher serviced by The Writer's Edge.

*HARRISON HOUSE PUBLISHERS, Box 35035, Tulsa OK 74153. (918)494-5944. Evangelical/Charismatic. Submit to Editorial Asst. Publishes 36 titles/yr. Receives 1,500 submissions annually. 1% of books from first-time authors. No books through agents. Reprints books. Prefers 128-160 pgs. Royalty on net; no advance. Average first printing 10,000. Publication within 18 mos. Considers simultaneous submissions. Responds in 6 wks. Guidelines.

Nonfiction: Query only. "Looking for charismatic teaching books from active ministers. Historical books should be on revivalists."

Tips: "Books should teach the power of the name of Jesus, the authority of the believer and a revelation of God's grace for mankind."

HARVEST HOUSE PUBLISHERS, 1075 Arrowsmith, Eugene OR 97402. (541)343-0123. Fax (541)342-6410. Evangelical. Carolyn McCready, ed. dir.; submit to Manuscript Coordinator. Books that help the hurts of people. Imprint: Marcon Publishers. Publishes 80 titles/yr. Receives 4,000 submissions annually. 3-5% of books from first-time authors. Reprints books. Prefers 200 pgs. Royalty 14-18% of net; no advance. Average first printing 10,000. Publication within 9-12 mos. Considers simultaneous submissions. Disk required, on acceptance. Responds in 2-8 wks. Guidelines; catalog for 9x12 SAE/8 stamps.

Nonfiction: Proposal/3 chapters; no phone/fax query.

Fiction: Proposal/3 chapters. Adult.

Tips: "Request guidelines and follow through for types of submissions we accept and procedure for submitting them."

**Note: This publisher serviced by The Writer's Edge.

THE HAWORTH PASTORAL PRESS, An imprint of The Haworth Press, 10 Alice St., Binghamton NY 13904-1580. (607)722-5857. Fax (607)722-6362. Bill Palmer, mng ed. Publishes 10 titles/yr. Receives 100 submissions annually. 50% of books from first-time authors. Reprints books. Prefers up to 250 pgs. Royalty 7-15% of net; no advance. Average first printing 1,500. Publication within 1 yr. Requires disk. Responds in 1 mo. Guidelines; free catalog.

Nonfiction: Proposal/3 chapters; no phone/fax query. "Looking for books on psychology/social work, etc., with a pastoral perspective."

HEARTSONG PRESENTS, Imprint of Barbour and Company, Inc., PO Box 719, 1810 Barbour Dr., Uhrichsville, OH 44683. (614)922-6045. Fax (614)922-5948. E-mail: barbour@tusco.net. Website: http://www.barbourbooks.com. Rebecca Germany, ed. Publishes contemporary and historical fiction. Publishes 52 titles/yr. Receives 200-300 submissions annually. 20% of books from first-time authors. Prefers 50,000-55,000 wds. Royalty on net; outright purchases; $500 advance. Average first printing 20,000. Publication within 6-8 months. Considers simultaneous submissions. Responds in 9-12 wks. Requires disk. Guidelines.

Fiction: Proposal/3-4 chapters; fax/e-mail query OK. All types of inspirational romances.

+HEARTH PUBLISHING, PO Box L, Hillsboro KS 67063. (316)947-3966. Fax (316)947-3392.Stan Thiessen, ed/dir. Wholesome literature of a classic nature, not necessarily religious. Publishes 4-8 titles/yr. Receives 300-500 submissions annually. 83% of books from first-time authors. No mss through agents. **SUBSIDY PUBLISHES 25%.** Reprints books. Prefers 75,000-80,000 wds or 224 pgs (poetry 96 pgs). Negotiable royalty and advance. Average first printing 1,500-30,000. Publication within 8-12 mos. Considers simultaneous submissions. Responds in 2 wks. Prefers disk. Guidelines; catalog for 9x12 SAE/5 stamps.

Nonfiction: Proposal/4-6 chapters or complete ms; phone/fax query OK." Any topic including genealogy and cookbooks."

Fiction: Proposal/4-6 chapters or complete ms. "Looking for juvenile and young adult (7-12) series or single books, classic adventure, fun to read; should fit secular markets as well as religious. Call about on-going anthologies."

Also Does: Booklets and chapbooks.

Tips: "All works must have integrity as characterized by traditional values and biblical Christian principles."

HENDRICKSON PUBLISHERS, 140 Summit St., PO Box 3473, Peabody MA 01961. (508)532-6546. Fax (508)531-8146. E-mail: DPenwell@hendrickson.com. Dan Penwell, mngr. of trade products. To provide biblically oriented books for reference, learning and personal growth. Publishes 15-20 titles/yr. Receives 100-150 submissions annually. 25% of books from first-time authors. No mss through agents. Reprints books. Prefers 200-500 pgs. Royalty 10-14% of net; some advances. Average first printing 2,500. Publication within 9-12 mos. Considers simultaneous submissions. Responds in 1-2 mos. Requires disk. No guidelines; catalog for 9x12 SAE/6 stamps.

Nonfiction: Query/summary or sample chapters; phone/fax/e-mail query OK.

Special Needs: Books that help the reader's confrontation and interaction with Scripture, leading to a positive change in thought and action; books that give a hunger to studying, understanding and applying Scripture; books that encourage and facilitate personal growth in such areas as personal devotions and a skillful use of the Bible.

Tips: "A well-organized, thought provoking, clear and accurate proposal has the best chance of being read and accepted."

**Note: This publisher serviced by The Writer's Edge.

VIRGIL HENSLEY PUBLISHING, 6116 E. 32nd St., Tulsa OK 74135. (918)664-8520. Terri Kalfas, ed. To edify and challenge the readers to a higher level of spiritual maturity in their Christian walk. Publishes 4-10 titles/yr. Receives 800 submissions annually. 50% of books from first-time authors. Reprints books. Prefers up to 250 pgs. Royalty 5% on net; some outright purchases; no advance. Average first printing 5,000. Publication within 6-18 mos. Considers simultaneous submissions. Disk required in MAC format. Responds in 8 wks. Guidelines; catalog for 9x12 SAE/3 stamps.

Nonfiction: Query, proposal/3 consecutive chapters, or complete ms; no phone query. "If it's good we'll consider it even if it doesn't fit the categories we've indicated."

Ethnic Books: Will have a limited number of titles available this year.

Tips: "Most open to a Bible study that can be used by anyone; no denominational influences."

HERALD PRESS, 616 Walnut Ave., Scottdale PA 15683-1999. (412)887-8500. Fax (412)887-3111. E-mail: garber%mph@mcimail.com. Canadian Address: Herald Press Canada, 490 Dutton Dr., Waterloo ON N2L 6H7 Canada. Mennonite Church. S. David Garber, book ed. To publish books consistent with scriptures interpreted in the Anabaptist/Mennonite tradition. Publishes 24 titles/yr. Receives 1,000+ submissions annually. 15% of books from first-time authors. Rarely reprints books. Prefers 160-192 pgs. Royalty 10-12% on retail; no advance. Average first printing 3,500-5,000. Publication within 10 mos. Dislikes simultaneous submissions. Accepts disks. Responds in 2 mos. Free guidelines; catalog for 2 stamps.

> **Nonfiction:** Query only; phone/fax /e-mail query OK.
>
> **Fiction:** Query first. Juvenile (for 9-14 year olds; series or single books); adult. "Wants Amish-Mennonite themes if writer has direct experience and knowledge."
>
> **Ethnic Books:** Native American (California focus); Amish and Mennonite.
>
> **Also Does:** Rarely publishes pamphlets and booklets.
>
> **Tips:** "All work must be oriented to Anabaptist-Mennonite faith. Get guidelines and ask for brochure on Mennonites if not familiar with denomination."
>
> ****Note:** This publisher serviced by The Writer's Edge.

*HI-TIME PUBLISHING CORP., 12040L W. Feerick St., PO Box 13337, Milwaukee WI 53213-0337. (414)466-2420. Catholic. Lorraine Kukulski, sr. ed. Sound, contemporary resources to help Catholic teens and adults live out and develop their faith. Publishes 2-3 titles/yr. Receives 15-20 submissions annually. 50% of books from first-time authors. Negotiates royalty or outright purchase; negotiable advance. Publication within 6 mos. Responds in 2-5 wks. Free guidelines/catalog.

> **Nonfiction:** Proposal/1 chapter; phone query OK.
>
> **Also Does:** Pamphlets & booklets.

*HIGLEY PUBLISHING CORP., Box 5398, Jacksonville FL 32247. (904)396-1918. Wesley C. Reagan, ed. Publishes 1 title/yr. No mss through agents. Outright purchase of $900-3,600. Average first printing 70,000. Not in topical listings. Guidelines.

> **Tips:** "Our purpose is to publish an annual undenominational resource for adult teachers, based on International Sunday school outlines."

HOLY CROSS ORTHODOX PRESS, 50 Goddard Ave., Brookline MA 02146. (617)731-3500. Fax (617)566-9075. Greek Orthodox. Anton C. Vrame, mng ed. Academic and general works of interest to Orthodox Christians in church history, worship, spirituality and life. Publishes 8-10 titles/yr. Receives 15-20 submissions annually. 50% of books from first-time authors. No mss through agents. Reprints bks. Prefers 200-300 pgs. Royalty 8-12% on retail; no advance. Average first printing 750-1,000. Publication within 12 mos. Considers simultaneous submissions. Requires disk (MAC). Responds in 3-4 mos. Free catalog.

> **Nonfiction:** Proposal/2 chapters & introduction; fax query OK. Also open to saints and iconography. "Most open to a book on historic Orthodox Christianity with a sound theological basis."
>
> **Ethnic Books:** Greek (orthodox).

HONOR BOOKS, 2448 E. 81st St., Ste. 4800, Tulsa OK 74155. (918)496-9007. Fax (918)496-3588. Evangelical. Cristine Bolley, ed-in-chief. Publishes 72 titles/yr.

2% of books from first-time authors. Reprints books. Prefers 160+ pgs. Royalty 5-15% on net or outright purchase; advance. Publication within 10 mos. Considers simultaneous submissions. Responds in 8-10 wks. Guidelines.

Nonfiction: Proposal/2 chapters.

Special Needs: Seasonal gift books; third-person stories reflecting God's wisdom applied to everyday life.

Tips: "We do 85% of our titles on assignment to work-for-hire writers. Show us writing samples if you are interested in writing or compiling our own creative ideas."

HORIZON BOOKS, Imprint of Christian Publications, 3825 Hartzdale Dr., Camp Hill PA 17011. (717)761-7044. David Fessenden, ed. See listing for Christian Publications for details.

+HOWARD PUBLISHING CO., INC., 3117 N. 7th St., West Monroe LA 71291. 318)396-3122 Fax (318)397-1882. E-mail.Howardpublishing@howardco.com. John Howard, pres.; submit to Gary Myers, VP To inspire holiness in the lives of believers. Publishes 10-12 titles/yr. Receives 100 submissions annually. 20% of books from first-time authors. Prefers 200-250 pgs. Negotiable royalty & advance. Average first printing 5,000. Publication within 1 yr. Considers simultaneous submissions. Responds in 4-6 wks. No disk. Free guidelines/catalog.

Nonfiction: Proposal/3 chapters; phone query OK.

Tips: "Our authors must first be Christ-centered in their lives and writing, then qualified to write on the subject of choice. Public name recognition is a plus. Authors who are also public speakers usually have a ready-made audience. "

HUNT AND THORPE, Laurel House, Station Approach, New Alresford Hants, UK S024 95H. (01962) 735320. John Hunt, ed. Children's books for the international Christian market. Publishes 25 titles/yr. Receives 100 submissions annually. 1% of books from first-time authors. Prefers 1,000 wds or 10 pgs for color books. Royalty 5-10% on net; advance $500. Average first printing 20,000. Publication within 2 yrs. No simultaneous submissions. Responds in 1 mo. No disk. Free catalog.

Nonfiction: Proposal/1 chapter; no phone query.

HUNTINGTON HOUSE PUBLISHERS—See **VITAL ISSUES PRESS.**

*ICHTHUS PUBLICATIONS, 2348 Third Pl. NW, Birmingham AL 35215. (205)853-5183. David Hudson, ed. Royalties 50%. Send ms on 3.5" disk in text format.

Fiction: For young teens to age 20. No children's.

ICS PUBLICATIONS, 2131 Lincoln Rd NE, Washington DC 20002. (202)832-8489. Fax (202)832-8967. Website: http://www.ocd.or.at/ics. Catholic/Institute of Carmelite Studies. Steven Payne, OCD, ed. dir. For those interested in the Carmelite tradition with focus on prayer and spirituality. Publishes 8 titles/yr. Receives 30 submissions annually. 10% of books from first-time authors. Reprints books. Prefers 200 pgs. Royalty 2-6% on retail; some outright purchases; advance $500. Average first printing 3,000-7,000. Publication within 2 yrs. Considers simultaneous submissions. Responds in 2 mos. Guidelines; catalog for 7x10 SAE/2 stamps.

Nonfiction: Query or outline/1 chapter; phone query OK. "Most open to translation of Carmelite classics; popular introductions to Carmelite themes which show a solid grasp of the tradition."

+IGNATIUS PRESS, 2515 McAllister St., San Francisco CA 94118. (415)387-2324. Fax (415)387-0896. Catholic. Joseph Fessio, ed. Publishes 40 titles/yr. Query.

ILLUMINATION ARTS PUBLISHING CO., INC., PO Box 1865, Bellevue WA 98009. (206)646-3670. Fax (206)646-4144. E-mail: Barb@Scanet.com. Ruth Thompson, ed dir. Books for children with enduring moral and spiritual value. Publishes 1 title/yr. Receives 50 submissions annually. 75% of books from first-time authors. Prefers 1,500-3,500 wds. Royalty on retail; advance to illustrator only. Average first printing 10,000. Publication within 18 mos. Considers simultaneous submissions. Responds in 1 mo. Guidelines/flyer for #10 SAE/1 stamp.

> **Fiction:** Query or complete ms. Phone/fax/e-mail query OK. "Universal spiritual values without any reference to a specific religion."

> **Tips:** "Most open to adventure stories with plot and character development, and with an underlying spiritual theme, or poetry."

+IMPACT CHRISTIAN BOOKS, 332 Leffingwell Ave. Ste. 101, Kirkwood MO 63122. (314)822-3309. William D. Banks, pres.

> **Nonfiction:** Tracts, outstanding personal testimonies, and Christ-centered books.

+INHERITANCE PUBLICATIONS, Box 154, Neerlandia AB T0G 1R0 Canada. (403)674-3949.

+INNISFREE PRESS (formerly **LURAMEDIA**), 136 Roumfort Rd., Philadelphia PA 19119-1632. (215)247-4085. Fax (215)247-2343. E-mail: InnisfreeP@aol.com. Marcia Broucek, ed-in-chief. Specializes in books that go beyond traditional boundaries to investigate all aspects of spirituality. Publishes 6-8 titles/yr. Receives 500 submissions annually. 60% of books from first-time authors. Prefers 125-225 pgs. Royalty 10% of net; seldom offers advance, $500. Average first printing 5,000. Publication within 18 mos. Considers simultaneous submissions. Responds in 3 mos. Guidelines: catalog for 9x12 SAE/2 stamps.

> **Nonfiction:** Proposal/outline/synopsis/sample writing/assessment of book's uniqueness. "Especially interested in books that explore the spiritual dimensions of everyday living, in the home, family, workplace, and global community."

> **Tips:** "Looking for books that match our company's byline, 'A Call to the Deep Heart's Core.'" Books with personal experience and women's perspective are of special interest.

INTERNATIONAL AWAKENING PRESS, 139 N. Washington, PO Box 232, Wheaton IL 60189. Phone/fax (630)653-8616. Intl. Awakening Ministries, Inc. Richard Owen Roberts, pres. Scholarly books on religious awakenings or revivals. Publishes 4 titles/yr. Receives 12 submissions annually. Variable payment. Average first printing 3,000. Publication within 6 mos. Responds in 4 wks. Requires disk. Catalog.

> **Nonfiction:** Complete ms; phone/fax query OK.

INTERVARSITY PRESS, Box 1400, Downers Grove IL 60515. (630)887-2500. Fax (630)887-2520. E-mail: staff@ivpress.com. InterVarsity Christian Fellowship. Andrew T. LePeau, ed. dir. To communicate the Lordship of Christ in all of life through a serious-minded approach to Scripture, the church and the world. Imprints: Ediciones Certeza; LifeGuide Bible Studies; Saltshaker Books. Publishes 75 titles/yr. Receives 1,900 submissions annually. 15% of books from first-time authors. Prefers 140-240 pgs; 35,000-70,000 wds. Negotiable royalty on retail; outright purchases of $1,000 & up; negotiable advance. Average first printing 6,000. Publication within 1 yr. Considers simultaneous submissions. Requires disk. Responds in 1-3 mos. Guidelines; catalog for 9x12 SAE/5 stamps.

Nonfiction: All unsolicited mss (from people they have had no previous contact with) are referred to The Writer's Edge (see their listing under Editorial Services—IL); phone/fax/e-mail query OK. "Looking for academic and ethnic books."

Ethnic Books: Black, Hispanic, Asian.

Also Does: Booklets.

Tips: "We look for a thoughtful approach. We shy away from black and white treatments. Writers who are nuanced, subtle, discerning and perceptive will get farther at IVP."

**Note: This publisher serviced by The Writer's Edge.

+JOSSEY-BASS INC., PUBLISHERS/RELIGION IN PRACTICE, 350 Sansome St., San Francisco CA 94104. (415)433-1740. Fax (415)433-0499. Simon & Shuster, Inc. Sara Polster, ed.

Nonfiction: Query."We are starting a new line of books for religious professionals (called Religion in Practice) that will address the issues of leadership and empowerment, similar to those we deal with in our secular lines."

JUDSON PRESS, Box 851, Valley Forge PA 19482-0851. (610)768-2130. Fax (610)768-2441. American Baptist Churches USA Mary Nicol, ed. mngr; Kristy Arneson Pullen, acq. ed. Publishes 15-20 titles/yr. Receives 1,000+ submissions annually. 50% of books from first-time authors. Reprints books. Prefers 120-150 pgs. Royalty 7.5% on retail; advance $300. Average first printing 2,000-3,000. Publication within 5 mos. Considers simultaneous submissions. Responds in 2-3 mos. Requires disk. Free guidelines; catalog for 9x12 SAE/4 stamps.

Nonfiction: Proposal/1-2 chapters; phone/fax query OK. "Looking for practical how-to for local church leaders and pastors."

Ethnic Books: African-American; occasionally Hispanic and Asian.

Tips: "Develop a proposal before you write the whole ms."

KALEIDOSCOPE PRESS, 2507—94th Ave. E., Edgewood WA 98371. Phone/fax (206)848-1116. Penny Lent, ed/pub. Providing tools for growth and enrichment that are unavailable. Publishes 7 titles/yr. Receives 175 submissions annually. 90% of books from first-time authors. No mss through agents. Reprints books. Variable length. Royalty 10% on retail; no advance. Average first printing 2,000. Publication within 1 yr. Considers simultaneous submissions. Responds in 2 mos. Requires disk Guidelines; catalog for #10 SAE/1 stamp.

Nonfiction: Query letter only; no phone/fax query. "Actively seeking submissions of inspiration, short poetry, anecdotes, humor, short poetry, quips & quotes, and bizarre rejections from/about writers, for a book in progress."

Fiction: For children only; also picture books. Query only. "Show us in your query how the piece is unique or needed in the marketplace."

Tips: "Most open to nonfiction that fills a need. Do and show your market research. Grab our interest."

KINDRED PRODUCTIONS, 169 Riverton Ave., Winnipeg MB R2L 2E5 Canada. (204)669-6575. Fax (204)654-1865. E-mail: kindred@cdnmbconf.ca. Mennonite Brethren. Marilyn Hudson, mngr. To resource the churches within the denomination. Publishes 2-3 titles/yr. Receives 70 submissions annually. 90% of books from first-time authors. No mss through agents. **SUBSIDY PUBLISHES 10%.** Prefers 200 pgs. Royalty 10-15% on retail; no advance. Average first printing 1,000-2,000. Publication within 1 yr. Considers simultaneous submissions. Responds within 4-5 mos. Free guidelines/catalog.

> **Nonfiction:** Proposal/2-3 chapters; fax/e-mail query OK. Also does pamphlets & booklets. "Looking for Christian education and inspirational."

KREGEL PUBLICATIONS, PO Box 2607, Grand Rapids MI 49501. (616)459-4775. Fax (616)451-9330. E-mail: kregelpub@aol.com. Evangelical/Conservative. Dennis R. Hillman, sr. ed. To provide tools for ministry and Christian growth from a conservative, evangelical perspective. Publishes 60 titles/yr. Receives 200+ submissions annually. 20% of books from first-time authors. Reprints books. Length open. Royalty 10-18% of net; $1,000-2,000 advance. Average first printing 3,000. Publication within 1 yr. Considers simultaneous submissions. Requires disk. Responds in 3 mos. Guidelines; catalog for 9x12 SAE/3 stamps.

> **Nonfiction:** Query only.
> **Fiction:** Query only. Open to historical fiction or historical romance from a biblical perspective.
> **Ethnic Books:** Spanish division: Editorial Portaroz.
> **Tips:** "Most open to biblically-based books of practical Christian teaching or books of interest to the vocational Christian worker."
> ****Note:** This publisher serviced by The Writer's Edge.

LANGMARC PUBLISHING, PO Box 33817, San Antonio TX 78265. (210)822-2521. Fax (210)822-5014. Lutheran. Lois Qualben, pub. Focuses on spiritual growth of readers. Publishes 4 titles/yr. Receives 200 submissions annually. 50% of books from first-time authors. No mss through agents. Prefers 150-300 pgs. Royalty 8-10% on retail; no advance. Average first printing 1,500. Publication usually within 1 yr. Considers simultaneous submissions. Responds in 2-4 mos. Requires disk. Catalog for SASE.

> **Nonfiction:** Proposal/3 chapters; phone query OK. "Most open to inspirational, congregational leadership, or materials for teens."
> **Fiction:** Does some.

+LIBROS LIGUORI, 1 Liguori Dr., Liguori MO 63057-9999. (314)464-2500. Fax (314)464-8449. Spanish division of Liguori Publications. Vincent A. Hamon, ed. To spread the gospel in the Hispanic community by means of low-cost publications. Publishes 12 titles/yr. Receives 3-4 submissions annually. **SOME SUBSIDY PUBLISHING.** Prefers 48-96 pgs. Royalty or outright purchases of $400 (book and booklet authors get royalties; pamphlet authors get $400 on acceptance and royalties thereafter); no advance. Average first printing 2,500. Publication within 8 mos. No simultaneous submissions. Requires disk. Responds in 2 mos. No guidelines; free catalog.

> **Nonfiction:** Query first. "Looking for issues families face today—substance abuse, unwanted pregnancies, etc.; family relations; religion's role in immigrant's experiences."

Ethnic Books: Focuses on Spanish-language products.

Also Does: Pamphlets and booklets.

Tips: "Keep it concise; avoid academic/theological jargon; and stick to the tenets of the Catholic faith—avoid abstract arguments."

LIFE CYCLE BOOKS, Box 420, Lewiston NY 14092. (416) 690-8532. Fax (416)690-5860. E-mail: pbroughton@lcbooks.com. Website: http://www. lcbooks.com. Paul Broughton, gen. mgr. Publishes 1-3 pro-life titles/yr. Receives 50 submissions annually. 50% of books from first-time authors. Reprints books. Royalty 8% of net; outright purchase of brochure material, $250+; advance $100-300. **SUBSIDY PUBLISHES 10%.** Publication within 10 mos. Responds in 6 wks. Free catalog.

Nonfiction: Query or complete ms. "Our emphasis is on pro-life and pro-family titles."

Tips: "We are most involved in publishing leaflets of about 1,500 wds, and welcome submissions of mss of this length."

#LIFETIME BOOKS, 2131 Hollywood Blvd., Hollywood FL 33020. (954)925-5242. Fax (954)925-5244. E-mail: lifetime@shadow.net. Website: http://www. lifetimebooks.com. Brian Feinblum, sr. ed. General publisher that publishes 2-4 religious titles/yr. Receives 100 submissions annually. 60% of books from first-time authors. Reprints books. Prefers 60,000 wds or 250-300 pgs. Royalty 6-10% on retail; rare advance of $500-5,000. Average first printing 10,000. Publication within 9 mos. Considers simultaneous submissions. Responds in 1 mo. Guidelines; catalog for 9x12 SAE/5 stamps.

Nonfiction: Proposal/2 chapters; fax query OK.

Tips: "Spirituality is fine, but books predicting world doom, God's powers, or interpretations of the Bible won't sell. Include a clear marketing and promotional strategy."

LIGHT AND LIFE COMMUNICATIONS (formerly Light and Life Press), PO Box 535002, Indianapolis IN 46253-5002. Submissions go to editor at 1233 Holiday Ln. E., Brownsburg IN 46112. (317)852-8767. Free Methodist. Robert Haslam, ed. Denominational publisher; publishes books that minister. Publishes 30 titles/yr. Receives 60 submissions annually. 33% of books from first-time authors. Reprints books. Royalty & advance negotiable. Publication within 6-12 mos. Reluctantly accepts simultaneous submissions. Responds in 6 wks. (or after next acquisitions committee meeting). Requires disk. Guidelines.

Nonfiction: Proposal/3 chapters.

Tips: "Most open to books that have obvious marketability; and books that speak more to the heart than to the head."

LIGUORI PUBLICATIONS, 1 Liguori Dr., Liguori MO 63057-9999. (314)464-2500. Fax (314)464-8449. Catholic/Redemptorists. Robert Pagliari, CSSR, dir. Publishes 50 titles/yr. Receives 650 submissions annually. 25% of books from first-time authors. Prefers 35,000-40,000 wds. Royalty 9-11% on retail; outright purchase of 24-page pamphlets for $400 (variable depending on size); no advance. Average first printing 3,500-5,000 on books & booklets, 10,000 on pamphlets. Publication within 1 yr. Accepts disks. Responds in 10-15 wks. Free guidelines.

Nonfiction: Proposal/2 chapters (complete ms for pamphlets). "Looking for books on teen issues."

Fiction: Complete ms. "Generally we don't do fiction, but will consider children's picture books, allegory or biblical books for children. Must be accompanied by art."

Ethnic Books: Publishes books in Spanish. See separate listing for Libros Liguori.

Also Does: Booklets, pamphlets & tracts; computer games and screen savers.

Tips: "Manuscripts accepted by us must have a strong, practical application."

LILLENAS PUBLISHING CO., Program Builder Series and Other Drama Resources, Box 419527, Kansas City MO 64141-6527. (816)931-1900. Fax (816)753-4071. E-mail: drama@lillenas.com. Paul M. Miller, ed. Publishes 15 drama resource books and 5 program builders/yr. Royalty 10% for drama resources; outright purchase of program builder material; no advance. No simultaneous submissions. Responds in 3 mos. Guidelines; catalog.

Nonfiction: Query (preferred) or complete ms.; phone/fax/e-mail queries OK. Accepts readings, one-act and full-length plays, puppet scripts, program and service features, monologues, and sketch collections.

Tips: "We have added a new line of full-length plays for use in schools and dinner theater that are wholesome but not specifically religious."

LION PUBLISHING, 4050 Lee Vance View, Colorado Springs CO 80918. (719)536-0100. Cook Communications. Julie Smith, mng ed; submit to David Horton. Children's books suitable for a general (crossover) market, not specifically a Christian market. Publishes 4-5 titles/yr. 5% of books from first-time authors. Royalty on net or outright purchase; advance. Average first printing 7,500. Publication within 9-12 mos. Considers simultaneous submissions. Responds in 3 mos. Guidelines.

Nonfiction & Fiction: Query letter only; no phone query.

Tips: "When writing for Lion, assume the reader has no knowledge of or background in Christianity."

*THE LITURGICAL PRESS, PO Box 7500, St. John's Abbey, Collegeville MN 56321. (612)363-2213. Fax (800)445-5899. St. John's Abbey (a Benedictine group). Imprints: Michael Glazier Books and Pueblo Books. Mark Twomey, mng. ed. Publishes 100 titles/yr. Prefers 100-600 pgs. Royalty 10% of net; some outright purchases; no advance. Responds in 2 mos. Guidelines; free catalog.

Nonfiction: Query/proposal. Adult only.

Tips: "We publish liturgical, scriptural, and pastoral resources."

LITURGY TRAINING PUBLICATIONS, Office of Divine Worship, 1800 N. Hermitage Ave., Chicago IL 60622-1101. (773)486-8970. Fax (773)486-7094. E-mail: editors@LTP.org. Catholic/Archdiocese of Chicago. Victoria Tufano, sr. acq. ed. Resources for liturgy in Christian life. Publishes 25 titles/yr. Receives 150 submissions annually. 50% of books from first-time authors. Variable royalty. Average first printing 2,000-5,000. Publication within 1 yr. Considers simultaneous submissions. Responds in 2-10 wks. Requires disk. Catalog.

Nonfiction: Proposal/1 chapter; phone/fax/e-mail query OK.

+LIVING THE GOOD NEWS, 600 Grant St., Ste. 400, Denver CO 80203. Fax (303)832-4971.Division of the Morehouse Group. Liz Riggleman, ed. admin. Publishes 15 titles/yr. Royalty. Publication within 1 yr. Considers simultaneous submissions. Responds in 2 mos. Guidelines; catalog for 9x12 SAE/4 stamps.

Nonfiction: Query or proposal/1 chapter. "Seeking books on practical, personal, spiritual growth for all ages."

Fiction: Query with synopsis. For children and teens; also picture books.

Special Needs: Grandparenting and storytelling.

Tips: "Readers are mainly from liturgical and mainline church backgrounds. Seeking creative ways to connect with self, others, God and the earth."

+LOIZEAUX, PO Box 277, Neptune NJ 07754-0277. (908)922-6665. Fax (908)922-9487. Evangelical. Marjorie Carlson, mng. ed. Publishes 10 titles/yr. Receives 180+ submissions annually. 25% of books from first-time authors. No mss through agents. Any length. Negotiable royalty; no advance. Average first printing 4,000-5,000. Publication time varies. No simultaneous submissions. Responds in 2-9 wks. Free guidelines/catalog.

Nonfiction: Query only; no phone/fax query. Bible commentaries and pastor's helps.

Also Does: Booklets.

LOYOLA PRESS, 3441 N. Ashland Ave., Chicago IL 60657-1397. (773)281-1818. Fax (773)281-0885. Catholic. Loyola Press Trade Books (Jeremy Langford, mng. ed.); Imprints: Jesuit Way (Joseph F. Downey S.J., ed. consultant); and Wild Onion Books (June Skinner Sawyers, ed); Seeker Series. Publishes 15 titles/yr. Receives 200 submissions annually. 20% of books from first-time authors. Usually no mss through agents. Reprints books. Prefers 60,000-80,000 wds or 200-250 pgs. Royalty 10% of net; seldom pays advance. Average first printing 3,000-5,000. Publication within 1 yr. Considers simultaneous submissions. Responds in 9 wks. Requires disk. Free guidelines/catalog.

Nonfiction: Query; phone/fax query OK. "Most open to professionally written mss, more or less in the Catholic tradition (but not conservative), written out of solid field training and experience."

*LYDIA PRESS, PO Box 417, Galloway OH 43119-0417. Phone/fax (614)851-9448. Nondenominational. Alaine Pakkala, pres.; submit to Carolyn Reynolds. Specializes in discipleship and encouragement materials to rebuild shattered lives. Publishes 10-15 titles/yr. 60% of books from first-time authors. **SUBSIDY PUBLISHES 2%.** Reprints books. Prefers 200 pgs. Royalty 25-50% on net; no advance. Average first printing 2,000. Publication within 10 mos. Considers simultaneous submissions. Responds in 4 wks. Guidelines.

Nonfiction: Query; phone/fax query OK.

Fiction: Query. For children & teens; also picture books.

Ethnic Books: Encouragement and discipleship for black youth.

Also Does: CD-ROM discipleship materials for teens.

+MAGNUS PRESS, PO Box 41157, San Jose CA 95160. Fax (408)226-2334. Warren Angel, ed. dir. To publish biblical studies which are written for the average person and which minister life to Christ's Church. New company. Prefers 125-375 pgs. Graduated royalty on retail; no advance. Average first printing 10,000. Publication schedule unknown. Considers simultaneous submissions. No disks. Responds in 1 mo. Guidelines; no catalog yet.

Nonfiction: Query or proposal/2-3 chapters; fax query OK. "Looking for biblical studies, any subject, including apologetics and controversial issues."

*MASTER BOOKS, PO Box 726, Green Forest AR 72638-0726. (501)438-5288. Fax (501)438-5120. New Leaf Press. Ron Hillestad, gen. mngr. Publishes 8-10 titles/yr. Receives 100 submissions annually. 10% of books from first-time authors. No mss through agents. **SUBSIDY PUBLISHES 5-15%.** Reprints books. Royalty 10-15% of net; no advance. Average first printing 5,000. Publication within 6 mos. Considers simultaneous submissions. Responds in 7-10 days. Free catalog.

> **Nonfiction:** Query. "Looking for biblical creationism; biblical science; creation/evolution debate material."

> **Also Does:** Pamphlets and booklets; computer games.

*MASTERMEDIA LTD., 9 W. 57th St., Fl. 20, New York NY 10019. (212)546-7650. Fax (212)546-7638. Merry Clark, mng. ed.; submit to Melinda Lombard. The Heritage Imprint. Religious/inspirational line est. 1995. Publishes 7 titles/yr. Receives 20-30+ submissions annually. 10% of books from first-time authors. Accepts mss through agents. Prefers 224 pgs. Negotiable royalty; usually no advance. Average first printing 30,000. Publication within 8 mos. Responds in 1 mo. Free catalog.

> **Nonfiction:** Proposal/5 chapters.

> **Note:** Has a full-service speakers' bureau.

+MERCER UNIVERSITY PRESS, 1400 Coleman Ave., Macon GA 31207. (912)752-2880. Fax (912)752-2264. Edd Rowell, dir.

> **Nonfiction:** Proposal/chapters."We are looking for books on history, philosophy, theology and religion, including history of religion, philosophy of religion, Bible studies and ethics."

MERIWETHER PUBLISHING LTD., 885 Elkton Dr., Colorado Springs CO 80907-3557. (719)594-4422. Fax (719)594-9916. Primarily a publisher of plays for Christian and secular; must be acceptable for use in a wide variety of Christian denominations. Arthur L. Zapel, ed. Publishes 3 titles/yr.; 35 plays/yr. Receives 1,200 submissions annually (mostly plays). 50% of books from first-time authors. Reprints books. Prefers 150-200 pgs. Royalty 10% on retail; some outright purchases of $250-2,500; no advance. Average first printing of books 1,500-3,500, plays 500. Publication within 6 mos. Considers simultaneous submissions. Accepts disk. Responds in 2-5 wks. Guidelines; catalog $1/9x12 SAE.

> **Nonfiction:** Query letter only; no phone/fax query. "Looking for creative worship books, i.e., drama, using the arts in worship, how-to books with ideas for Christian education."

> **Fiction:** Plays only. Always looking for Christmas and Easter plays. Send complete ms.

> **Tips:** "We prefer mainstream religious titles. Most open to drama-related books. Always looking for Easter plays for children."

+MIDDLE ATLANTIC REGIONAL PRESS, 100 Bryant St. NW, Washington DC 20001. (202)265-7609. Middle Atlantic Regional Gospel Ministries. Myron Noble, pres. Helps publish works of unpublished African American authors. Publishes 1-3 titles/yr. Receives 8-12 submissions annually. 75% of books from first-time authors. **SUBSIDY PUBLISHES 20%.** Reprints books. Prefers 80-125 pgs. Royalty 10-15% of net; no advance. Average first printing 5,000. Publication within 6-18 mos. Considers simultaneous submissions. Responds in 3-6 mos. No disk. Guidelines; free catalog.

Nonfiction: Proposal/3 chapters or complete ms; phone query OK.
Fiction: Query.
Ethnic Books: African American.
Also Does: Pamphlets, booklets, tracts.

+A MIRACLE PUBLISHING CO., INC. PO Box 310210, Atlanta GA 31131. (404)505-8321. Fax (404)766-2966. Jennipher Thomas, pres. To encourage and comfort the church, win the lost to Christ and finance the end-time harvest of souls. Publishes 10-50 titles/yr. Receives 100 submissions annually. 50% of books from first-time authors. No mss through agents. Prefers 50-250 pgs. Outright purchases. Average first printing 10,000. Publication time varies. Considers simultaneous submissions. Response time varies. Accepts disk. Guidelines.

> **Nonfiction:** Query only; fax query OK. "Looking for financial testimonies and miracles, provisional testimonies and miracles. Also books on single parenting and dreams & visions."
> **Also Does:** Pamphlets and booklets.

*MISTY HILL PRESS, 5024 Turner Rd., Sebastopol CA 95472. (707)823-7437. Small press that does some religious titles. Sally C. Karste, ed. Publishes 1 title/yr. Negotiable royalty. Responds in 1 week. Guidelines; catalog for 9x12 SAE/2 stamps.

> **Fiction:** Query first. Historical fiction for children.

MONUMENT PRESS, PO Box 140361, Irving TX 75014-0361. Phone/fax (972)686-5332. Member of the consortium Publishers Associates (8 publishers). Belinda Buxjom, sr. ed.; submit to Mary Markal. Publishes only scholarly books. Other imprints: Ide House and Tangelwuld. Publishes 10 titles/yr. Receives 240 submissions annually. 70% of books from first-time authors. No mss through agents. Any length. Royalty 2-8% on retail; no advance. Average first printing 3,000. Publication within 24 mos. No simultaneous submissions. Prefers disk. Responds in 4 mos (goes to all houses in the consortium). Guidelines.

> **Nonfiction:** Query only; no phone/fax query.
> **Ethnic:** Publishes for all ethnic groups.

MOODY PRESS, 820 N. LaSalle Blvd., Chicago IL 60610. (312)329-2120. Fax (312)329-4157. Imprint: Northfield Publishing. Julie-Allyson Ieron, mng ed. To provide books that evangelize, edify the believer, and educate concerning the Christian life. Publishes 50 titles/yr. Receives 2,000 submissions annually. 5% of books from first-time authors. Occasionally reprints books. Royalty on net; variable advance. Average first printing 10,000. Publication within 1 yr. Considers simultaneous submissions. Responds in 8-12 wks. Guidelines; catalog for 9x12 SAE.

> **Nonfiction:** Proposal/2-3 chapters; no phone/fax query.
> **Also Does:** Booklets in series only.
> **Tips:** "Most open to books where the writer is a recognized expert and already has a platform to promote the book."
> ****Note:** This publisher serviced by The Writer's Edge.

*THOMAS MORE PRESS, 200 E. Bethany Dr., Allen TX 75002. (214)390-6300. Catholic/Tabor Publishing. Blake Bergen, ed. dir. Publishes 6-10 titles/yr. Receives 150 submissions annually. 100% of books from first-time authors. Prefers 40,000 wds. Royalty 7.5% on retail; advance. Average first printing 2,500-25,000.

Publication within 1 yr. Considers simultaneous submissions. Responds in 6-9 wks. Guidelines; free catalog.

Nonfiction: Proposal/1 chapter. Religion and spirituality.

Tips: "Looking for books on theology, commentary, reflection, spirituality and reference—for the serious, but non-scholarly reader."

MOREHOUSE PUBLISHING CO., 871 Ethan Allen Hwy., Ste. 204, Ridgefield CT 06877. (203)431-3927. Fax (203)431-3964. E-mail: eakelley@aol.com. Episcopal/ecumenical. Deborah Grahame-Smith, sr. ed. Academic, devotional, reference, and Bible study materials for Christians of all denominations. Publishes 30 titles/yr. Receives 5,000-7,000 submissions annually. 10% of books from first-time authors. Reprints books. Prefers 80-150 pgs. Royalty 6-12% on net; advance $350-750. Average first printing 2,500-3,500. Publication within 9 mos. Considers simultaneous submissions. Responds in 2-6 wks. Guidelines; catalog for 9x12 SAE/4 stamps (#10 SAE if children's catalog only). Outside US, include one IRC for each ounce.

Nonfiction: Proposal/2 chapters; no phone/fax query. "Looking for books on marriage, parenting skills, single parenting, relations, marriage counseling helps for clergy, stewardship, Bible studies, dealing with grief/loss, and current social issues."

Fiction: Proposal/2 chapters. For children/teens.

Tips: "Most open to a book aimed at a specific market/readership, which has perhaps evolved from a workshop or study program (field-tested and fine-tuned by interested Christians); a book that answers a specific need or fills a specific gap in the bookstores."

*MORNING STAR PRESS, Box 1095, Grand Central Station, New York NY 10163. (212)661-4304. Morning Star Chapel. Rev. Kathleen Shedaker, pub. Publishes 2 titles/yr. Receives 3 submissions annually. 50% of books from first-time authors. No books through agents. Reprints books. Prefers 120 pgs. Royalty 10% on retail; no advance. Publication within 6 mos. Considers simultaneous submissions. Responds in 3-6 wks.

Nonfiction: Query first. "Only religious/inspirational books."

Tips: "We encourage members of all denominations to live a more Christian life."

+MORNING STAR PUBLICATIONS, 16000 Lancaster Hwy., Charlotte NC 28277-2061. Rick Joyner, ed.

*JOSHUA MORRIS PUBLISHING, 355 Riverside Ave., Westport CT 06880-4810. Anglican/Evangelical. Sally Lloyd Jones, editorial dir.; submit to Wendy Mass, sr. ed. A Christian children's book packager. Publishes 75-100 titles/yr. Receives 200 submissions annually. 5% of books from first-time authors. Makes outright purchases. Average first printing 25,000-50,000. Publication within 1 yr. Considers simultaneous submissions. Responds in 3-4 mos.

Nonfiction: Proposal/1 chapter. "Looking for educational books on biblical or general theme with a Christian approach."

Fiction: Proposal/1 chapter. Children/teens.

Special Needs: Produces board games and all kinds of novelty books for children.

Tips: "Most open to novelty books for children ages 3-5 based on biblical themes." Prefers series of 2 or more.

#WILLIAM MORROW AND CO., 1350 Avenue of the Americas, New York NY 10019. (212)261-6500. Fax (212)261-6595. General trade publisher that does a few religious titles. Debbie Mercer-Sullivan, mng. ed. Publishes 5 religious titles/yr. Receives 10,000 submissions annually. 30% of books from first-time authors. Accepts most mss through agents. Prefers 50,000-100,000 wds. Standard royalty on retail; advance varies. Publication within 2 yrs. Considers simultaneous submissions. Responds in 3 mos.

Nonfiction & Fiction: Query only; mss and proposals accepted only though an agent.

Note: Morrow Junior Books accepts no unsolicited manuscripts.

MULTNOMAH BOOKS/QUESTAR, Box 1720, Sisters OR 97759. (541)549-1144. Fax (541)549-2044. Linda Bennett, ed. asst. Imprint for youth and adult books. Publishes 75 titles/yr. Receives 1,800 submissions annually. 5-10% of books from first-time authors. Length depends on project. Negotiable royalty on net and advance. Average first printing 12,500. Publication within 6-12 mos. Considers simultaneous submissions. Responds in 30-60 days. Requires disk. Guidelines; catalog for 9x12 SAE/3 stamps.

Nonfiction: Proposal/3 chapters; no phone/fax query.

Fiction: Proposal/3 chapters. Teen/adult, all genres. "Looking for clean, moral, uplifting fiction—not necessarily religious."

Tips: "We do not consider poetry, 'end-times' fiction, recovery, issues books, devotionals, academic texts or curriculum."

**Note: This publisher serviced by The Writer's Edge.

*NATIONAL BAPTIST PUBLISHING BOARD, 6717 Centennial Blvd., Nashville TN 37209. (615)350-8000. Fax (615)350-9018. National Missionary Baptist Convention of America. Rev. Kenneth H. Dupree, dir. of publications. To provide quality Christian education resources to be used by African-American churches. Receives 200 submissions annually. 30% of books from first-time authors. Reprints books. Prefers 130 pgs. Outright purchases; advance. Average first printing 20,000. Publication within 1 yr.

Nonfiction: Complete ms; phone query OK.

Fiction: Complete ms. "We need biblically based fiction for children."

Ethnic Books: African-American publisher.

Tips: "Most open to religious books that can be used for Christian education."

NAVPRESS/PIÑON PRESS, Box 35001, Colorado Springs CO 80935. (719)548-9222. "We are no longer accepting *any* unsolicited submissions, proposals, queries, etc."

**Note: This publisher serviced by The Writer's Edge.

NAZARENE PUBLISHING HOUSE —See **BEACON HILL PRESS OF KANSAS CITY**

NEIBAUER PRESS, 20 Industrial Dr., Warminster PA 18974. (215)322-6200. Fax (215)322-2495. E-mail: Nathan@Neibauer.com. Evangelical/Protestant clergy and church leaders. Nathan Neibauer, ed. Publishes 8 titles/yr. Receives 100 submissions annually. 5% of books from first-time authors. No mss through agents. Reprints books. Prefers 200 pgs. Royalty on net; some outright purchases.

SOME SUBSIDY. Publication within 6 mos. Considers simultaneous submissions. Responds in 2 wks. Requires disk. Catalog for 9x12 SAE.

Nonfiction: E-mail query OK

Tips: "Need religious books on stewardship and church enrollment, stewardship and tithing, and church enrollment tracts. Also pamphlets."

THOMAS NELSON PUBLISHERS, Nashville TN. No phone query. Additional imprints: Mystery Ink, Tommy NELSON (juvenile), Royal Media. No longer accepting queries or proposals at the publishing office listed above (except as noted below). Send brief prosaic resume, 1-pg synopsis, and 1 sample chapter to acquisitions editors at the following locations: Janet Thoma, Janet Thoma Books. 1157 Molotai, Tega Cay SC 29715, fax (803)548-2684. Victor Oliver, Oliver-Nelson Books, 1360 Center Dr., Ste. 102-B, Atlanta GA 30338, fax (770)391-9784. Rick Nash, Thomas Nelson Trade Book Div., PO Box 141000, Nashville TN 37214-1000, fax (615)391-5225. For Biblical Reference Books contact: Phil Stoner, Nelson Biblical Reference Publishing (Nashville address), fax (615)391-5225. Publishes 150-200 titles/yr. Prefers 250 pgs. Variable royalty or outright purchase; advance. Average first printing 7,500. Publication within 12-24 mos. Considers simultaneous submissions (if indicated). Responds in 8-12 wks. Catalog for 9x12 SAE.

Nonfiction: See information above. "Looking for inspirational, motivational, devotional, self-help, Christian living, prayer and evangelism."

Fiction: See information above. "Seeking successfully published commercial fiction authors who write for adults from a Christian perspective."

**Note: This publisher serviced by The Writer's Edge.

NEW CITY PRESS, 202 Cardinal Rd., Hyde Park NY 12538. (914)229-0335. Fax (914)229-0351. E-mail: PATNCP@aol.com. Catholic. Pat Markey, ed. Focus is on Christian living and unity. Publishes 12 titles/yr. Receives 60 submissions annually. 5% of books from first-time authors. Reprints books. Prefers 56,000 wds. Royalty 10% on net; no advance. Average first printing 5,000. Publication with 16 mos. Considers simultaneous submissions. Responds in 3 mos. Requires disk. Free catalog.

Nonfiction: Query only; fax/e-mail query OK. "Looking for how-to and family topics."

NEW HOPE, Box 12065, Birmingham AL 35202-2065. (205)991-8100. Fax (205)991-4990. Website: http://www.wmu.com/wmu. Woman's Missionary Union; Auxiliary to Southern Baptist Convention. Cindy McClain, ed. dir. To promote a missions lifestyle and greater missions awareness among its membership. Publishes 10-12 titles/yr. Receives 80-100 submissions annually. 50% of books from first-time authors. Rarely reprints books. Prefers 150-250 pgs. Royalty on retail or outright purchases; no advance. Average first printing 5,000-10,000. Publication within 18 mos. Considers simultaneous submissions. Responds in 6 mos. Guidelines; catalog for 9x12 SAE/4 stamps.

Nonfiction: Complete ms or proposal/3-4 chapters; no phone/fax query."All that we publish must have a missions/ministry emphasis."

Fiction: Complete ms or proposal/3-4 chapters. Children's storybooks, especially with a multicultural aspect.

Tips: "Most open to books which lead to spiritual growth toward a missions lifestyle; books that address ministry issues or social/moral issues; books that lead to involvement in missions or support of missions."

#NEW LEAF PRESS, PO Box 726, Green Forest AR 72638-0726. (501)438-5288. Fax (501)438-5120. Pentecostal/Charismatic. Submit to Editorial Board. Imprint: Master Books. Publishes 15-20 titles/yr. Receives 400 submissions annually. 15% of books from first-time authors. Reprints books. Prefers 100-400 pgs. Royalty 10% on net; no advance. Average first printing 10,000. Publication within 10 mos. Considers simultaneous submissions. Responds in 3 mos. Guidelines; catalog for 9x12 SAE/5 stamps.

> **Nonfiction:** Complete ms; phone/fax query OK. "Looking for devotional, gift books and Christian living."
>
> **Tips:** "Tell us why this book is marketable and why it will be a blessing and fulfill the needs of others."

NORTH POINT PRESS, 19 Union Square W., New York NY 10003. (212)741-6900. Fax (212)633-9385. Division of Farrar, Straus and Giroux. Ethan Nosowsky, ed. Publishes a variety of titles, including religion, philosophy and literature. Publishes 4 titles/yr. Receives 250 submissions annually. 30% of books from first-time authors. Reprints books. Any length. Variable royalty on retail; advance. Average first printing 7,500. Publication within 18 mos. Considers simultaneous submissions. Responds in 2 mos. Guidelines; no catalog.

> **Nonfiction:** Query only, then proposal/1 chapter; no phone/fax query.
>
> **Tips:** "We publish serious literary works and no inspirational/self-help books."

+NORTHSTONE PUBLISHING, INC., 330 - 1980 Cooper Rd., Kelowna BC V1Y 9G8 Canada. (604)766-2926. Fax (604)766-1201. E-mail: info@northstone.com. Website: http://www.northstone.com. Michael Schwartzentruber, ed. To provide high quality products promoting positive social and spiritual values. Publishes 14-20 titles/yr. Receives 150-200 submissions annually. 30% of books from first-time authors. Will consider reprints. Prefers 55,000-80,000 wds or 192-256 pgs. Royalty 8-12% on retail; some advances $1,500. Average first printing 4,000. Publication within 1 yr. Considers simultaneous submissions. Responds in 6 mos. Requires disk. Guidelines/flyer; catalog $2.50.

> **Nonfiction:** Proposal/no chapters; fax/e-mail query OK.
>
> **Fiction:** Complete ms. "We produce a one-volume collection of children's stories each year (ages 5-12)."
>
> **Tips:** "Although we publish from a Christian perspective, we seek to attract a general audience. Our target audience is interested in spirituality and values, but may not even attend church (nor do we assume that they should)."

*OPEN COURT PUBLISHING CO., 332 S. Michigan Ave., Ste. 2000, Chicago IL 60604-9968. David Ramsey Steele, ed. dir. Publishes 4 religious titles/yr. Receives 600 submissions annually. 20% of books from first-time authors. Reprints books. Prefers 350-400 pgs. Royalty 5-12% of net; advance $1,000-2,000. Average first printing 500 (cloth), 1,500 (paperback). Publication within 1-3 yrs. Considers simultaneous submissions. Responds in 6 mos. Free catalog.

> **Nonfiction:** Proposal/2 chapters. "We're looking for works of high intellectual quality for a scholarly or general readership on comparative religion, philosophy of religion, and religious issues."

*ORBIS BOOKS, PO Box 308, Maryknoll NY 10545-0308. (914)941-7590. Fax (914)945-0670. Catholic Foreign Mission Society. Robert Ellsberg, ed. Publishes 50-55 titles/yr. Receives 2,200 submissions annually. 2% of books from first-time authors. Accepts few mss through agents. Prefers 250-350 pgs. Royalty 10-15% of net; advance $500-3,000. Publication within 15 mos. Responds in 2 mos. Free guidelines/catalog.

Nonfiction: Proposal/1 chapter. "Global justice and peace; religious development in Asia, Africa, and Latin America; Christianity and world religions."

OUR SUNDAY VISITOR, INC., 200 Noll Plaza, Huntington IN 46750-4303. (219)356-8400. Fax (219)359-9117. E-mail: Jmanney@aol.com. Catholic. James Manney, acq. ed. To assist Catholics to be more aware and secure in their faith and capable of relating their faith to others. Publishes 20-30 titles/yr. Receives 100+ submissions annually. 10% of books from first-time authors. Rarely reprints books. Prefers 175 pgs. Royalty 8-12% on net; advance $1,000. Average first printing 3,000-5,000. Publication within 1 yr. Considers simultaneous submissions. Responds within 3 mos. Requires disk. Guidelines/catalog for 9x12 SASE.

Nonfiction: Proposal/3 chapters; fax/e-mail query OK. "Most open to devotional books (not 1st person), church histories, heritage & saints, the parish, prayer and family."

Also Does: Pamphlets & booklets.

Tips: "All books published must relate to the Catholic Church. Give as much background information as possible on why the topic was chosen. Follow our guidelines. "

#OXFORD UNIVERSITY PRESS, 198 Madison Ave., New York NY 10016-4314. (212)679-7300. Website: http://www.oup-usa.org/. Academic press. Laura Brown, trade ed. Service to academic community. Imprint: Clarendon Press. Publishes 60+ titles/yr. Receives hundreds of submissions annually. 40% of books from first-time authors. Prefers 300 pgs. Royalty 0-15% on net or retail; advances $0-40,000. Average first printing 1,500. Publication within 10 mos. Considers simultaneous submissions. Responds in 3 mos. Free catalog.

Nonfiction: Proposal/2 chapters. "Most open to academic books."

PACIFIC PRESS PUBLISHING ASSN., Box 5353, Nampa ID 83653.5353. (208)465-2570. Fax (208)465-2531. E-mail: kenwad@pacificpress.com. Website: http://www.pacificpress.com. Seventh-day Adventist. Kenneth Wade, acq. ed. Publishes 35 titles/yr. Receives 600 submissions annually. 35% of books from first-time authors. Prefers 40,000-70,000 wds or 128-256 pgs. Royalty 8-16% of net; advance $300-1,500. Average first printing 6,000. Publication within 10 mos. Considers simultaneous submissions. Responds in 3 mos. Prefers disk. Guidelines.

Nonfiction: Query or proposal; fax/e-mail query OK.

Fiction: Adults and children (7-12 years old, series or single books). Query or proposal. "Must be true-to-life. No talking animals."

Ethnic Books: Occasionally publishes for ethnic market.

Tips: "Our Website has the most up-to-date information, including samples of recent publications. Do not send full manuscript unless we request it after reviewing your proposal."

PALISADES/QUESTAR, PO Box 1720, Sisters OR 97759. (541)549-1144. Fax

(541)549-2044. Questar Publishers. Karen Ball, ed. Publishes 14 titles/yr. (12 fiction, 2 nonfiction). Receives 120 submissions annually. 20% of books from first-time authors. Accepts ms through agents. Prefers 70,000 wds. Royalty rates based on experience; $2,500 advance. Average first printing 15,000. Publication within 6 mos. Considers simultaneous submissions. Responds in 3 mos. Guidelines; catalog for 9x12 SAE/3 stamps.

Nonfiction: Proposal/3 chapters.

Fiction: Proposal/3 chapters. 80% contemporary romances and 20% historical romances.

Ethnic Books: Ethnic contemporary romances needed.

Tips: "Most open to fiction that features credible characters and entertaining plot lines, while continuing to uphold strong Christian values."

Note: This publisher serviced by The Writer's Edge.

+PANSOPHIC PUBLISHING, 2308 S. 18th, St. Joseph MO 64503. (816)364-1623. Christina Shelhorn, pub. Publishes 4 titles/yr. Receives 20 submissions annually. 90% of books from first-time authors. Royalty 8-15%; no advance. Publication within 2 yrs. Considers simultaneous submissions. Responds in 4 mos. Guidelines.

Nonfiction: Query/outline.

Fiction: Query/outline. Juvenile and adult; picture books.

PARACLETE PRESS, PO Box 1568, Orleans MA 02653. (508)255-4685. Fax (508)255-5705. DavidManuel@paraclete-press.com. Website: http://www.paralete-press.com. Ecumenical. David Manuel, sr. ed. Publishes 15 titles/yr. Receives 50 submissions annually. Few books from first-time authors. Reprints few books. Prefers 150-250 pgs. Royalty 8-12% on retail or net; no advance. Average first printing 5,000. Publication within 18 mos. Responds in 3-4 wks. Requires disk. Guidelines; catalog for 9x12 SAE/4 stamps.

Nonfiction: Proposal/1 chapter; phone/fax/e-mail query OK. "Looking for books on deeper spirituality that appeal to all denominations."

Tips: Vision statement -"In all times, in different branches of the Christian family, there are people who have written, sung, or spoken things that encouraged us to give our lives to God and to listen for His voice. We gather and share these treasures."

PARADISE RESEARCH PUBLICATIONS, 2747 S. Kihei Rd. #G102, Kihei HI 96753. Phone/fax (808)874-4876. Imprint of Good Book Publishing Co. Ken Burns, ed. Publishes 4 titles/yr. Receives 5 submissions annually. 100% of books from first-time authors. No mss through agents. Royalty 10% on retail; no advance. Average first printing 1,000. Publication within 2 mos. Considers simultaneous submission. Responds in 1 wk. Accepts disk. Catalog for 9x12 SAE/2 stamps.

Nonfiction: Query; no phone/fax query. Books on the spiritual history and success of Alcoholics Anonymous.

Also Does: Pamphlets & booklets.

THE PASTORAL PRESS, PO Box 1470, Laurel MD 20725. (800)976-9669. Fax (800)979-9669. Catholic/National Assn. of Pastoral Musicians. Lawrence Johnson, dir. Publishes 16 titles/yr. Receives 12 submissions annually. 60% of books from first-time authors. Prefers 250 pgs. Royalty 10% of net; no advance.

Publication within 10 mos. Considers simultaneous submissions. Responds in 2 mos. Free catalog.

Nonfiction: Complete ms.

Tips: "Most open to theology and planning of Roman Catholic liturgies."

PAULINE BOOKS & MEDIA, 50 St. Paul's Ave., Boston MA 02130. (617)522-8911. Fax (617)541-9805. E-mail: pbm_edit@interramp.com. Website: http://www. pauline.org. Catholic. Sr. Mary Mark, F.S.P., acq. ed. To help clarify Catholic belief and practice for the average reader. Publishes 35 titles/yr. Receives 1,300 submissions annually. 75% of books from first-time authors. No ms through agents. Royalty 8-12% of net; advance $200. Average first printing 3,000. Publication within 2 yrs. Responds in 3 mos. No disk. Guidelines; catalog for 9x12 SAE/4 stamps.

Nonfiction: Query only, fax query OK. "Looking for books on faith and moral values, spiritual growth and development, and Christian formation for families."

Fiction: Query only. Children's picture books, 150-500 wds; easy-to-read, 750-1,500 wds; and middle reader, 15,000-25,000 wds. No adult fiction.

Tips: "Open to religion teacher's resources and adult catechetics. No biographical or autobiographical material."

PAULIST PRESS, 997 Macarthur Blvd., Mahwah NJ 07430. (201)825-7300. Fax (201)825-8345. Catholic. Donald Brophy, mng. ed; Karen Scialabba, children's book ed. Imprints: Integration Books; Newman Press; Stimulus Books. Publishes 90-100 titles/yr. Receives 500 submissions annually. 5-8% of books from first-time authors. Prefers 100-400 pgs. Royalty 10% on retail; advance $500. Average first printing 3,500. Publication within 10 mos. Responds in 2 mos. Guidelines.

Nonfiction: Proposal/2 chapters. "Looking for theology (Catholic and ecumenical Christian), popular spirituality, liturgy, and religious education texts." Children's books for 5-7 years or 8-10 years; complete ms.

Tips: "Most open to progressive, world-affirming, theologically sophisticated, growth-oriented, well-written books. Have strong convictions but don't be pious. Stay well-read. Pay attention to contemporary social needs."

PELICAN PUBLISHING CO., INC., PO Box 3110, Gretna LA 70054-3110. (504)368-1175. Nina Kooij, ed. Imprints: Creager Publishing; Hope Publishing; Marmac. Publishes 5 titles/yr. Receives 500 submissions annually. 35% of books from first-time authors. Reprints books. Prefers 180+ pgs. Royalty 10%; some advances. Average first printing 6,000. Publication within 9-18 mos. Responds in 1 mo. Guidelines; catalog for 9x12 SAE/10 stamps.

Nonfiction: Proposal/2 chapters; no phone query.

Fiction: Proposal/2 chapters. Children/adults. "Currently publish multicultural stories (Jewish, Kwanzaa, etc.)."

Ethnic Books: Fiction for blacks, Hispanics, Native Americans, Asian-Americans, etc. Ethnic history for above groups.

Tips: "On inspirational titles we need a high-profile author who already has an established speaking circuit so books can be sold at these appearances. Travel guides and picture books must have a specific target audience."

+PENTECOSTAL PUBLISHING HOUSE, 8855 Dunn Rd., Hazelwood MO 63042. (314)837-7300. Fax (314)837-4503. United Pentecostal Church Intl.

Marvin Curry, gen mgr. Imprint: World Aflame Press. Publishes 10-15 titles/yr.
Nonfiction: Query. "We look for books on Protestant Pentecostalism, Bible studies, and self-help."

+PETER LANG PUBLISHING, 275 7th Ave., Fl 28, New York NY 10001-6708. (212)647-7700. Fax (212)647-7707. E-mail: MaryM@plang.com. Website: http://www.peterlang.com. General publisher that does some religious books. Mary McLaughlin, ed. 75% of books from first-time authors. Royalty 10-20% on net; no advance. Publication within 1 yr. Responds in 2 mos. Free catalog.
Nonfiction: Complete ms.

PILGRIM PRESS, 700 Prospect Ave. E., Cleveland OH 44115-1100. (216)736-3700. Fax (216)736-3703. E-mail: stavet@ucc.org. United Church of Christ. Timothy G. Staveteig, ed. Scholarly and trade books on social issues and the moral life. Publishes 25 titles/yr. Receives 500 submissions annually. 50% of books from first-time authors. Reprints books. Prefers 50,000 wds. Royalty 8% of net; negotiable advance. Publication within 1 yr. Might consider simultaneous submissions. Disk required. Responds in 12 wks. Free guidelines/catalog.
Nonfiction: Query only; phone/fax/e-mail query OK. "Looking for books on vocation (as in the workplace)."
Ethnic Books: Black, Hispanic and Asian. Always interested in books on pluralism and multiculturalism.
Also Does: Booklets; journal/calendar for women.
Tips: "Looking for a timely topic with a fresh thesis."

PREP PUBLISHING, 1110 1/2 Hay St., Fayetteville NC 28305. (910)483-6611. Fax (910)483-2439. PREP, Inc. Anne McKinney, mng ed. Books to help the reader grow spiritually. Publishes 3-7 titles/yr. Receives 2,000 submissions annually. 50% of books from first-time authors. Reprints books. Royalty 10%; no advance. Average first printing 3,000. Publication within 18 mos. Considers simultaneous submissions. Responds in 2-3 mos. Guidelines/catalog for #10 SAE/1 stamp.
Nonfiction: Query only; no phone/fax query.
Fiction: Query only. All ages.

PRESBYTERIAN AND REFORMED PUBLISHING CO., Box 817, Phillipsburg NJ 08865. (908)454-0505. Fax (908)859-2390. Not a denominational house. Thom E. Notaro, ed. All books must be consistent with the Westminster Confession of Faith. Imprints: Craig Press; Evangelical Press. Publishes 8-10 titles/yr. Receives 185 submissions annually. 20% of books from first-time authors. Prefers 140-260 pgs. Royalty 5-14% of net; no advance. Average first printing 3,000. Publication within 8-10 mos. Considers simultaneous submissions. Disk required. Responds in 4-8 wks. Free guidelines/catalog.
Nonfiction: Proposal/3 chapters; fax query OK.
Tips: "Clear, engaging, and insightful applications of reformed theology to life. Offer us fully developed proposals and polished sample chapters."

+PRESERVATION PRESS, PO Box 612, 25 Russell Mill Rd., Swedesboro NJ 08085. (609)467-8902. Fax (609)467-3183. Seeks to release titles that speak to the restoration of the orthodox faith. Est. 1994.

*PROBE MINISTRIES INTL., 1900 Firman Dr., Ste. 100, Richardson TX 75081-6796. (214)480-0240. Fax (214)644-9664. Evangelical Council for Financial Accountability. Louis D. Whitworth, sr. ed. To support goals of the ministry and to equip Christians to respond to challenges of our culture. Publishes 2-3 titles/yr. No mss through agents. Prefers 120-250 pgs. Pays variable royalty; no advance. Average first printing 2,000. Publication within 6-9 mos. Considers simultaneous submissions. Responds in 2 mos. Free copy.

Nonfiction: Query only; phone query OK. "Christian approaches to all the academic disciplines; national issues: political, social, medical; education; family values."

Tips: "Most open to a popular level book on apologetics with sound theology and a Christian world view written by a well-educated person of credible reputation and scholarship."

PURPLE POMEGRANATE PRODUCTIONS, 60 Haight St., San Francisco CA 94102. (415)864-2600. E-mail: jfj@jews-for-jesus.org. Jews for Jesus. Steven Lawson, Director of Publications. Jewish evangelism. Publishes 3-5 titles/yr. Receives few submissions annually. No mss through agents. Reprints books. Royalty on net; no advance. Average first printing 5,000-10,000. Publication within 6-12 mos. No guidelines.

Nonfiction: Query; no phone/e-mail query. "We only do Jewish evangelism or messianic topics."

Also Does: Pamphlets, booklets, tracts.

Note: They are not generally open to submissions, but they did say: "We would like to hear from Jewish believers who are writers. We do have a need from time to time for editing and freelance ghost writing, and on a rare occasion have published a book by someone who is not on our staff. But we would like to establish a relationship with such a person, rather than seeing a manuscript without any previous contact."

QUESTAR PUBLISHERS—See **MULTNOMAH BOOKS** (youth and adult), **PALISADES** (romance fiction), or **GOLD 'N' HONEY BOOKS** (children).

RAGGED EDGE, 353 Ragged Edge Rd., Chambersburg PA 17201. (717)263-5132. Fax (717)532-7704. White Mane Publishing Co., Inc. Harold E. Collier, acq. ed. Christian, social science and self-help books; to make a difference in people's lives. Publishes 10-15 titles/yr. Receives 50-75 submissions annually. 50% of books from first-time authors. **SUBSIDY PUBLISHES 20%.** Reprints books. Prefers 200 pgs. Variable royalty on net; advance. Average first printing 3,000. Publication within 1 yr. Considers simultaneous submissions. Responds in 60 days. Free guidelines/ catalog.

Nonfiction: Query only; fax query OK.

Fiction: Query only. For children (8-12) or teens (12-17).

Tips: "Most open to a Protestant book in the middle of the spectrum."

RAINBOW BOOKS, PO Box 430, Highland City FL 33846-0430. Phone/fax (941)648-4420. E-mail: NAIP@aol.com. Betsy A. Lampe, sr. ed. To provide solutions to real problems on an ethical level. Publishes 5 titles/yr. Receives 60 submissions annually. 90% of books from first-time authors. Reprints books. Any length. Royalty 6-10% on retail; outright purchases $50 & up; variable advance. Average first printing 5,000. Publication within 8 mos. Considers simultaneous submissions. Disk OK. Responds in 6 wks. Guidelines; copy for 6x9 SAE/4 stamps.

Nonfiction: Query only first, then proposal/2 chapters; fax/e-mail query OK.

Looking for something refreshing from the religious left; nothing from the religious right.

Tips: "We want to see books that deal with real world problems and provide solutions on a very ethical level."

+RAINBOW PUBLISHERS/DAYBREAK, PO Box 261129, San Diego CA 92196. (619)271-7600. Fax (619)578-4795. Christy Allen, ed. Growth and development books for the evangelical Christian. Publishes 12 titles/yr. Receives 250 submissions annually. 75% of books from first-time authors. Prefers 200 pgs. Royalty; no advance; outright purchases $500. Average first printing 2,500. Publication within 1 yr. Considers simultaneous submissions. Responds in 6 wks. Requires disk. Guidelines; catalog for 9x12 SAE/2 stamps.

Nonfiction: Query letter only. "Looking for growth and development, Bible-teaching books.

Tips: "Check the market for your book and tell us why yours fills a void or enhances the reader's spiritual life."

RAINBOW PUBLISHERS/RAINBOW BOOKS, Box 261129, San Diego CA 92196. (619)271-7600. Fax (612)578-4795. Christy Allen, ed. Publishes 12 titles/yr. Receives 400 submissions annually. 50% of books from first-time authors. No mss through agents. Prefers 64 pgs. Outright purchases $500. Average first printing 2,500. Publication within 6-9 mos. Considers simultaneous submissions. Responds in 6 wks. Requires disk. Guidelines; catalog for 9x12 SAE/2 stamps.

Nonfiction: Query only. "Looking for 64-pg. activity books (reproducible) for teachers to use in teaching the Bible to children."

Tips: "Most open to book of creative activities that encourage Bible learning for Christian educators to use with children age 2 through grade 6."

READ 'N RUN BOOKS, PO Box 294, Rhododendron OR 97049. (503)622-4798. Crumb Elbow Publishing. Michael P. Jones, pub. Books of lasting interest. Publishes 6 titles/yr. Receives 25 submissions annually. 100% of books from first-time authors. Reprints books. Royalty on net or copies; no advance; **SOME COOPERATIVE PUBLISHING.** Average first printing 1,000. Publication with 6 mos. Considers simultaneous submissions. Responds in 2 mos. Guidelines; catalog $3.

Nonfiction: Complete ms; no phone query. "Looking for historical (particularly Old West); the Pacific Northwest; missionary work among American Indians; fur trade and environmental."

Fiction: Complete ms. Any type; any age. "Historical fiction would be great, especially if it involves the Old West or the Pacific NW."

Ethnic Books: Open to.

Tips: "We're really interested in NW books, but are open to reading about anything."

*REGAL BOOKS, 2300 Knoll Dr., Ventura CA 93003. (805)644-9721. Gospel Light Publications. Kyle Duncan, assoc. pub.; Jean Daly, curriculum ed. Publishes 15-20 titles/yr. Receives 800 submissions annually. 5% of books from first-time authors. No mss through agents. Prefers 200-300 pgs. Royalty 10-15% of net (10% on curriculum books); advance $1,500-5,000. Average first printing 10,000-15,000. Publication within 12-18 mos. Responds in 4-8 wks.

Nonfiction: NOT ACCEPTING MSS OR QUERIES AT THIS TIME. All unsolicited mss will be returned unopened.

*THE REGINA PRESS, 10 Hub Dr., Melville NY 11747-3503. (516)694-8600. Fax (516)694-2205. Catholic/Christian. George Malhame, juvenile ed. Publishes 5-10 titles/yr. Royalty on net; some outright purchases; some advances. Sometimes sends free catalog.

Fiction: Query/proposal. Children's picture books for ages 3-8; coloring books.

#REGNERY PUBLISHING, 422 1st St. SE, #300, Washington DC 20003-1803. (202)546-5005. Fax (202)546-8759. Trade publisher that does scholarly Catholic books and evangelical Protestant books. Richard Vigilante, exec. ed; submit to Submissions Editor. Imprint: Gateway Editions. Publishes 2-4 religious titles/yr. Receives 30-50 submissions annually. Few books from first-time authors. Reprints books. Prefers 250-500 pgs. Royalty 8-15% on retail; advances to $50,000. Average first printing 5,000. Publication within 1 yr. Considers simultaneous submissions. Responds in 6 mos. Free catalog.

Nonfiction: Proposal/1-3 chapters. Looking for history, popular biography and popular history.

Tips: "Religious books should relate to politics, history, current affairs, biography, and public policy. Most open to a book that deals with a topical issue from a conservative point of view—something that points out a need for spiritual renewal; or a how-to book on finding spiritual renewal."

RELIGIOUS EDUCATION PRESS, 5316 Meadow Brook Rd., Birmingham AL 35242-3315. (205)991-1000. Fax (205)991-9669. E-mail: releduc@ix.netcom. com. Nancy J. Vickers, mng. ed. Imprint: Doxa Books. Mission is specifically directed toward helping fulfill, in an interfaith and ecumenical way, the Great Commission. Publishes 4-5 titles/yr. Receives 300+ submissions annually. 30% of books from first-time authors. No book through agents (generally). Prefers 350 pgs. Royalty 10% on net; no advance. Average first printing 1,500-2,000. Publication within 9 mos (varies). Disk required. Responds in 2 mos. Guidelines; free catalog for 9x12.

Nonfiction: Proposal/1 chapter & resume; fax query OK. Also publishes books on religious psychology and pastoral care.

Tips: "Personally examine 2-4 of our books first to see if your book fits representative specifications. Our books are intentionally multifaith, written for an ecumenical audience."

*RENEWAL PRESS, INC., 1117 Hellmers Ln., Ocean Springs MS 39564. (601)875-4128. Southern Baptist. Grant Shipp, pres. Publishes 1 title/yr. Receives 1 submission annually. 100% of books from first-time authors. No mss through agents. Prefers 175 pgs. Average first printing 2,000. Publication within 3 mos. Responds in 2 wks. Free guidelines/brochure.

Nonfiction: Query first. "Information and procedures concerning church renewal, and small groups."

+RENLOW PUBLISHING, PO Box 951, Middletown OH 45042. A general publisher that does a few inspirational or religious titles. D.E. Margerum, ed/pub. Send proposal/sample chapters. Not in topical listings.

RESOURCE PUBLICATIONS, INC., Ste. 290, 160 E. Virginia St., San Jose CA 95112. (408)286-8505. Fax (408)287-8748. E-mail: MdrnLitrgy@aol.com.

Website: http://www.rpinet.com. Nick Wagner, ed. dir. Publishes 20 titles/yr. Receives 450 submissions annually. 20% of books from first-time authors. Prefers 50,000 wds. Royalty 8% of net: no advance. Average first printing 3,000. Publication within 1 yr. Considers simultaneous submissions. Responds in 1-3 mos. Prefers disk. Guidelines; catalog for 9x12 SAE/2 stamps.

Nonfiction: Proposal/1 chapter; phone/fax/e-mail query OK.

Fiction: Query. Adult/teen/children. Only short skits or read-aloud stories for storytellers. "Must be useful in ministerial, counseling, or educational settings."

Also Does: Computer programs; aids to ministry or education.

Tips: "Know our market. We cater to ministers in Catholic and mainstream Protestant settings. We are not an evangelical house or general interest publisher."

RESURRECTION PRESS LTD, PO Box 248, Williston Park NY 11596. (516)742-5686. Fax (516)746-6872. Catholic. Imprint: Spirit Life Series. Emilie Cerar, sr. ed. Publishes 8 titles/yr. Receives 200 submissions annually. 30% of books from first-time authors. No mss through agents. Reprints books. Prefers 150 pgs (no more than 200). Royalty 5-10% on retail; advance $250-2,000. Average first printing 3,000. Publication within 1 yr. Considers simultaneous submissions. Responds in 1-2 mos. Free guidelines & catalog.

Nonfiction: Proposal/2 chapters; fax query OK. "Most open to pastoral resources, self-help, and spirituality for the active Christian."

FLEMING H. REVELL CO., 6030 E. Fulton, Ada MI 49301. (616)676-9185. Fax (616)676-9573. E-mail: lholland@bakerbooks.com. Subsidiary of Baker Book House. Imprints: Revell, Chosen, Spire, Paver Books. Linda Holland, ed. dir. Publishes 75 titles/yr. Receives 1,750 submissions annually. 1% of books from first-time authors. Occasionally reprints bks. Prefers 200-450 pgs. Royalty on net; advance. Average first printing 5,000. Publication within 8-12 mos. Considers simultaneous submissions. Disk required. Responds in 60-90 days. Guidelines; free catalog.

Nonfiction: Proposal/2-3 chapters; fax/e-mail query OK.

Fiction: Proposal/3-4 chapters or complete ms. Children and adult.

Tips: "Research the market for what's needed; maintain excellence; address a felt need; use good clarity and focus on topic."

**Note: This publisher serviced by The Writer's Edge.

REVIEW AND HERALD PUBLISHING ASSN., 55 W. Oak Ridge Dr., Hagerstown MD 21740-7390. (301)791-7000. Fax (301)790-9734. Seventh-day Adventist. Jeannette Johnson, acq. ed. Publishes 40-50 titles/yr. Receives 500 submissions annually. 2-3% of books from first-time authors. Reprints books. Prefers 128-160 pgs or 45,000 wds. Royalty 12-16% of net; advance $500+. Average first printing 3,500. Publication within 12-18 mos. Considers simultaneous submissions. Responds in 3 mos. Requires disk. Guidelines; catalog $3.

Nonfiction: Proposal/2-3 chapters or complete ms; fax/e-mail query OK.

THE RIEHLE FOUNDATION, PO Box 7, Milford OH 45150-0007. (513)576-0032. Fax (513)576-0022. Catholic. Bill Reck, pres. Publishes 6-12 titles/yr. 50% of books from first-time authors. No mss through agents. Prefers 100-200 pgs. Terms negotiated; no advance. Average first printing 5,000-7,000. Publication in

3-6 mos. Considers simultaneous submissions. Responds in 1-3 mos. Free guidelines/catalog.

Nonfiction: Complete ms; fax query OK. "Looking for apologetics, evangelism/witnessing, inspirational, miracles, personal renewal, prophecy, spirituality, spiritual warfare, Marian devotion, eschatology; objectivity vs. subjectivity themes, and divine mercy."

Fiction: Complete ms. Adult biblical/religious. "Must draw the reader to a deeper knowledge of and devotion to God."

Tips: "Most open to non-'gloom-and doom'-based themes which receive Roman Catholic approval, or which regard local Church-approved phenomena with worldwide scope of interest."

*ROPER PRESS, 829 S. Shields St., Fort Collins CO 80521-3541. Evangelical. Donna J. Hoskins, pres. Publishes 4-6 titles/yr. Receives 150 submissions annually. Less than 10% of books from first-time authors. Reprints books. Royalty on net; no advance; or outright purchase. Publication within 9 mos. Considers simultaneous submissions. Responds in 2-3 mos. Guidelines; catalog for 9x12 SAE/2 stamps.

Nonfiction: Proposal/3 chapters or complete ms; phone/fax query OK. "Most interested in Bible study and Bible stories."

Fiction: Proposal/3 chapters. Adult. "Christian principles must be integral to the story, not a tacked-on afterthought."

Tips: "Finish the title before submission; have an independent reader evaluate it; provide complete background on author."

*ROSE PUBLISHING, 4455 Torrance Blvd. #259, Torrance CA 90503. (310)316-4780. Fax (310)316-4401. Nondenominational. Carol Witte, mng. ed. Publishes only large Sunday school charts and teaching materials. Publishes 5 titles/yr. Receives 1-2 submissions annually. 5% of books from first-time authors. Outright purchases. Publication within 6-12 mos. Free catalog.

Special Needs: Query with sketch of proposed chart (non-returnable); fax query OK. Large teaching charts for Sunday schools; church history time lines; charts for children & youth. Also books on church history and scholarship.

ROYAL PRODUCTIONS, 7127 Little River Turnpike, 2nd Floor, Ste. 206, Annandale VA 22003. (703)642-9416. Fax (703)642-0832. Nondenominational Christian & educational publisher. Fidelis Iyebote, mng ed. Publishes 8 titles/yr. 50% of books from first-time authors. Reprints books. Prefers 200 pgs. Royalty on net; no advance. Average first printing 5,000. Publication within 6 mos. Responds in 3 mos. Guidelines/catalog.

Nonfiction: Query only. Looking for Christian school books, celebrity profiles, environmental issues, ethics and sports, biographies/autobiographies of Christian music, entertainment or sports stars.

Fiction: Children's picture books.

Special Needs: Considering ideas for production of educational audio and video films, instructional and study aid material for math, biology, chemistry, physics, French & Spanish, and Christian education.

ST. ANTHONY MESSENGER PRESS, 1615 Republic St., Cincinnati OH 45210. (513)241-5615. (800)488-0488. Fax (513)241-0399. E-mail: StAnthony@

AmericanCatholic.org, or, saintanth@aol.com. Catholic. Lisa Biedenbach, mng. ed. Seeks to publish affordable resources for living a Catholic Christian life. Imprint: Franciscan Communications. Publishes 16-20 titles/yr. Receives 250 submissions annually. 5% of books from first-time authors. No mss through agent. Reprints books. Prefers 25,000-50,000 wds or 100-250 pgs. Royalty 10-12% of net; advance $1,000. Average first printing 5,000-7,500. Publication within 12-18 mos. Responds in 4-6 wks. Guidelines; catalog for 9x12 SAE/4 stamps.

Nonfiction: Query only; fax/e-mail query OK. "Looking for resources for prayer & spirituality; sacraments; and Catholic identity, "

Ethnic Books: Hispanic, occasionally.

Tips: "Books should be written in popular (not academic style), use anecdotes or stories liberally, and reflect the best of modern Catholic teaching."

ST. BEDE'S PUBLICATIONS, Box 545, Petersham MA 01366-0545. (508)724-3407. Fax (508)724-3574. E-mail: scrilly@stbedes.org. Website: http://www.stbedes. org. Catholic. Sr. Scholastica Crilly, OSB, ed. Publishes 10 titles/yr. Receives 200 submissions annually. 30% of books from first-time authors. Reprints books. Prefers 150-200 pgs. Royalty 5-7% on retail; advance. Average first printing 500-1,500. Publication within 36 mos. Accepts simultaneous submissions. Responds in 1 mo. Accepts disk. Guidelines; catalog for 9x12 SAE/2 stamps.

Nonfiction: Query first. E-mail query OK.

Tips: "Just state what you've got simply without gimmicks or attention-getting ploys that usually turn off editors before they've even read your proposal. If your work is worthy of publication, it will stand on its own."

*ST. HILDA'S PRESS, c/o Longstreet Press, 2150 Newmarket Parkway, Ste. 102, Marietta GA 30067. (404)980-1488. Episcopal Press of the western NC diocese. Gail Godwin, ed. Publishes artistic and spiritual books, tracts, and music. Not included in topical listings.

+ST. MARY'S PRESS, 702 Terrace Heights, Winona MN 55987-1320. (507)457-7900. (800)533-8095. Fax (507)457-7990. E-mail: yanovel@smp.org. Catholic. Stephan Nagel, ed-in-chief. Fiction for teens, ages 14-17. Prefers up to 40,000 wds. Royalty. Accepts simultaneous submissions. Guidelines.

Fiction: Query/outline & chapters; e-mail query OK.

Tips: "Books that give insight into the struggle of teens to become healthy, hopeful adults and also shed light on Catholic experience, history or cultures."

+SCHOCKEN BOOKS, INC., 201 E. 50th St., New York NY 10022. (212)572-2402. Fax (212)572-6030. Arthur Samuelson, ed. dir.; submit to Bonny Fetterman, ed. Religious imprint of Pantheon Books/Random House. Publishes 75 titles/yr. Query. Not in topical listings.

*SCHOETTLE PUBLISHING, PO Box 1246, Hayesville NC 28904. (706)896-3333. Deeper Life—Deeper Truth Books. Dr. Lewis Schoettle, ed/pub. Publishes 0-28 titles/yr. Receives 8 submissions annually. Most books from first-time authors. Reprints books. Prefers 150-1,000 pgs. Royalty 7-10% on net; no advance. Average first printing 10,000. Publication within 3 mos. Considers simultaneous submissions. Free catalog.

Nonfiction: Query. Publishes only Bible studies, prophecy, theology and books on Christian accountability—Judgment Seat of Christ/Millennial Kingdom.

SCRIPTURE PRESS—See **VICTOR BOOKS**.

SEASIDE PRESS, 1506 Capitol Ave. #101, Plano TX 75074. (972)423-0092. Fax (972)881-9147. Imprint of Wordware Publishing, Inc. Russell A. Stultz, pub. Publishes 2 titles/yr. Receives 50 submissions annually. 5% of books from first-time authors. **SUBSIDY PUBLISHES 5%** Reprints books. Prefers 150 pgs. Royalty 8-10% of net; no advance. Average first printing 5,000. Publication within 6 mos. No simultaneous submissions. Requires disk. Responds in 3 wks. Free guidelines/catalog.

> **Nonfiction:** Query only; fax/e-mail query OK. Bible studies or family life.
>
> **Tips:** Not presently publishing many religious books.

SERVANT PUBLICATIONS/, 1143 Highland Dr., Ste. E, PO Box 8617, Ann Arbor MI 48107. (313)677-6490. Fax (313)677-6685. Imprints: Vine Books for Evangelical Christians; Charis Books for Catholics. Heidi S. Hess, mng ed; submit to Peg VandeVoorde. Materials which spread the gospel of Jesus Christ, help Christians live in accordance with the gospel, promote renewal in the church and bear witness to Christian unity. Publishes 50 titles/yr. Receives 600+ submissions annually. 10% of books from first-time authors. Reprints books. Prefers 120-300 pgs. Royalty & advance. Average first printing 5,000. Publication within 1 yr. Considers simultaneous submissions. Responds in 6 mos. Guidelines; catalog for 9x12 SAE/5 stamps.

> **Nonfiction:** Query letter only; no phone/fax query.
>
> **Fiction:** Query letter only. Adult. Only from previously published fiction authors.
>
> ****Note:** This publisher serviced by The Writer's Edge.

HAROLD SHAW PUBLISHERS, Box 567, Wheaton IL 60189. (630)665-6700. Fax (630)665-6793. Joan Guest, ed. dir; Mary Horner Collins, Bible study ed; Lil Copan, literary series. Publishes a "full circle," broad range of books on topics relevant to Christians of all types. Imprint: Wheaton Literary Series, Northcote Books, North Wind. Publishes 40-45 titles/yr. Receives 1,000 submissions annually. 10-20% of books from first-time authors. Reprints books. Royalty on retail; outright purchases $375-2,000 (for Bible Studyguides and compilations); advance. Average first printing 5,000. Publication within 9-18 mos. Prefers no simultaneous submissions. Responds in 12-18 wks. Guidelines; catalog for 9x12 SAE/5 stamps.

> **Nonfiction:** Proposal/3 chapters. Brief fax query OK. "Looking for stellar books on felt need just developing in the marketplace."
>
> **Fiction:** Proposal/3 chapters. Prefers high-quality, literary fiction.
>
> **Tips:** "Most open to well-written, practical books from evangelical worldview. Avoid sensational or highly sectarian topics. Interested in mental health issues and books that fill a void in the marketplace."
>
> ****Note:** This publisher serviced by The Writer's Edge.

SHEED & WARD, Box 419492, Kansas City MO 64141. (816)531-0538. Fax (816)968-2280. E-mail: NCR@aol.com. National Catholic Reporter Publishing Co. Robert Heyer, ed-in-chief. Publishes 30 titles/yr. Receives 200 submissions annually. 10% of books from first-time authors. No mss through agents. **SUB-**

SIDY PUBLISHES 2%. Reprints books. Prefers 100-200 pgs. Royalty 6/8/10% on retail; some work-for-hire; flexible advance. Average first printing 2,000. Publication within 6 mos. Responds in 3 mos. Requires disk. Guidelines; catalog for 7x11 SAE/2 stamps.

Nonfiction: Complete ms; phone/fax/e-mail query OK. "Looking for parish ministry (euthanasia, health care, spirituality, leadership, sacraments, small group or priestless parish facilitating books)."

Tips: "Be in touch with needs of progressive/changing parishes."

SHINING STAR PUBLICATIONS, 1209 Buchanan St., Carthage IL 62321. (217)357-6093. Fax (217)357-6095. Division of Burdett Ginn. Mary Tucker, ed. Publishes 20 titles/yr. Receives 30-40 submissions annually. 25% of books from first-time authors. No mss through agents. Prefers 48-96 pgs. Outright purchases $20/pg.; no advance. Average first printing 3,000. Publication within 12 mos. No simultaneous submissions. No disks. Responds in 2 mos. Guidelines; free catalog.

Nonfiction: Query first; phone/fax query OK. "We need reproducible workbooks to teach Scriptures and Christian values; Bible activities; Bible story crafts; skits and songs with a Christian emphasis."

Tips: "We publish only Bible activity books with reproducible pages for teachers and parents to use in home or church teaching situations; no picture books or children's novels."

*SHOESTRING PRESS, Box 1223, MPO, Edmonton AB T5J 2M4 Canada. (403)439-3681. Fax (403)426-0853. A. Mardon, ed; submit to Stephanie Liu. Publishes 1-2 titles/yr. Receives 10 submissions annually. 60% of books from first-time authors. SUBSIDY PUBLISHES 10%. Prefers 200 pgs. Royalty 5-10% on net; no advance. Average first printing 500. Publication within 13 mos. Considers simultaneous submissions. Responds in 1-2 mos.

Nonfiction: Complete ms/synopsis & resume; fax query OK.

Fiction: Complete ms/synopsis & resume. Adult.

Tips: "We look at everything. Send Canadian SASE or IRCs."

*SMALL HELM PRESS, 622 Baker St., Petaluma CA 94952-2525. (707)763-5757. Alice Pearl Evans, pub. Interprets direction in contemporary life. Publishes 1 title/yr. Receives few submissions. Reprints books. Prefers 96-224 printed pgs. Outright purchase, negotiable. Average first printing 1,000-2,000. Considers simultaneous submissions. Responds in 2-4 wks. Catalog for 9x12 SAE/3 stamps.

Nonfiction: Query, proposal or complete ms; prefers phone query.

Tips: "Most open to nonfiction of interest to general public and based on cultural or philosophical issues with a Christian worldview. Write with conviction and credibility."

+SMYTH & HELWYS PUBLISHING INC., 6316 Peake Rd., Macon GA 31210-3960. (912)752-2217. Christian education publisher.

Nonfiction: Publishes Sunday school curriculum, educational books; online services.

SOUTHERN METHODIST UNIVERSITY PRESS, PO Box 415, Dallas TX 75275. (214)768-1433. Fax (214)768-1428. Southern Methodist. Kathryn Lang, sr. ed. Publishes nonfiction and literary fiction. Publishes 10-15 titles/yr. Receives

1,000 submissions annually. 75% of books from first-time authors. Royalty 8-10% of net; $500 advance. Average first printing 2,000. Publication within 1 yr. Responds in 2 wks. to a query, 6-12 mos to complete ms. No disk. Catalog.

Nonfiction: Proposal/3 chapters. "We publish nonfiction in the following areas: human values, medical ethics, death & dying; film/theater; Southwest studies; and theological studies."

Fiction: Query/synopsis, chapters and author bio. No genre fiction, poetry, sci-fi, romance; stay away from experimental fiction. Adult only.

Tips: "Pay attention to our stated areas of interest."

+SOWER'S PRESS, PO Box 666306, Marietta GA 30066. (770)565-8202. Fax (770)977-3784. Jamey Wood, ed. Books to further establish the ministries of speakers and teachers. Publishes 2-3 titles/yr. Responds in 1 mo.

Nonfiction: Proposal/chapters. Marriage & family books.

STANDARD PUBLISHING, 8121 Hamilton Ave., Cincinnati OH 45231. (513)931-4050. Fax (513)931-0950. Diane Stortz, dir. of new product development; Theresa Hayes, acq. coord. An evangelical Christian publisher of curriculum, classroom resources, teen resources, children's books, and drama. Publishes 150 titles/yr. Receives 1,500 submissions annually. 25% of books from first-time authors. Royalty 4-10% of net; outright purchases $500-2,000; advance. Average first printing 20,000. Publication within 18 mos. Considers simultaneous submissions. Responds in 2 mos. Prefers disk. Guidelines; catalog $3.

Nonfiction: No unsolicited mss. Send complete proposal, including sample chapters, to Christian Education Team, Children's Editor, Teen Editor, Drama Team, or Adult Editor.

Tips: "Many titles developed by in-house staff or on assignment. Most open now to teachers helps and ideas for ages 8-12."

**Note: This publisher serviced by The Writer's Edge.

STARBURST PUBLISHERS, PO Box 4123, Lancaster PA 17604. (717)293-0939. Evangelical. Ellen Hake, ed. dir. A Christian publisher having success with crossover books. Publishes 5-10 titles/yr. Receives 1,000+ submissions annually. 40% of books from first-time authors. Prefers 200+ pgs. Royalty 6-16% of net; advances only to top prospects. Average first printing 5,000+. Publication within 1 yr. Considers simultaneous submissions. No disks. Responds in 6-8 wks. Guidelines; catalog for 9x12 SAE/4 stamps.

Nonfiction: Proposal/3 chapters; no phone query. "Looking for health, self-help/how-to, and inspirational books."

Fiction: Proposal/3 chapters. Adult. "We are looking for good, wholesome fiction."

Tips: "Most open to nonfiction that can be sold in both Christian and general markets."

+STILLPOINT PUBLISHING INTERNATIONAL., INC., PO Box 640, Meetinghouse Rd., Walpole NH 03608. (603)756-9281. Fax (603)756-92812. Stillpoint Publishing & Institute for Life Healing. Dorothy Seymour, sr. ed. Publishes 5-10 titles/yr.

Nonfiction: Query/bio/contents/samples. "Our focus is human consciousness and spiritual ecology; spirituality in business, community, and society."

*STILL WATERS REVIVAL BOOKS, 4710—37A Ave., Edmonton AB T6L 3T5

Canada. (403)450-3730. Reformed Church. Reg Barrow, pres. Publishes 15 titles/yr. Receives few submissions. Very few books from first-time authors. Reprints books. Prefers 128-160 pgs. Negotiated royalty or outright purchase. Considers simultaneous submissions. Catalog for 9x12 SAE/2 stamps.

Nonfiction: Proposal/2 chapters. "Reformed and Reconstructionistic books of scholarly value, for the use of educated laymen." No non-Reformed or premillennial.

Tips: "Most open to books based on the system of doctrine found in the Westminster confession of faith, as it applies to our contemporary setting."

*SUCCESS PUBLISHERS, One Oakglade Cir., Hummelstown PA 17036. (717)566-0468. Fax (717)566-6423. Markowski Intl. Publishers Group. Marjorie L. Markowski, ed-in-chief. Publishes 6-10 titles/yr. Receives 500 submissions annually. 80% of books from first-time authors. No mss through agents. Reprints books. Prefers 35,000-125,000 wds or 128-336 pgs. Royalty 6-15% on retail; some advances. Average first printing 5,000-50,000. Publication in 6-12 mos. Considers simultaneous submissions. Responds in 2-3 wks. Guidelines (2 stamps); catalog for 6x9 SAE/2 stamps.

Nonfiction: Proposal or complete ms; phone/fax query OK. "Looking for books that meet recognized and emerging needs of our society."

Tips: "Make a professional presentation on paper, and send an audio or video tape of you in action, if possible. Persistence is important in getting our attention."

+SUMMIT PUBLISHING, LTD., Denvigh House, Denvigh Rd., Milton Keynes MK1 1YP, England. Charismatic. Noel Halsey, pres. Send query with a summary, table of contents, and excerpts from the manuscript.

+SWORD OF THE LORD PUBLISHERS, 224 Bridge Ave., Murfreesboro TN 37129-3574. Fax (615)895-7446. Independent Baptist. Dr. Shelton L. Smith, pres./ed; submit to Guy King, dir. Publishes 12-18 titles/yr. Receives 50-60 submissions annually. 10% of books from first-time authors. No mss through agents. Reprints books. Royalty; no advance. Average first printing 7,500. Publication within 1 yr. Considers simultaneous submissions. Disk OK. Responds in 12 mos. Guidelines; catalog $2.25.

Nonfiction & Fiction: Complete ms.; phone query OK. Prefers King James version.

Also Does: Booklets, pamphlets, and tracts.

Tips: "Check spelling and grammar. "

TEACH SERVICES, INC., RR 1 Box 182, Brushton NY 12916. (518)358-2125. Fax (518)358-3028. Timothy Hullquist, pres.; submit to Wayne Reid. To publish uplifting books for the lowest price. Publishes 68 titles/yr. Receives 130 submissions annually. 35% of books from first-time authors. No mss through agents. **SUBSIDY PUBLISHES 10%** (author has to pay for first printing, then publisher keeps it in print). Reprints books. Prefers 35,000 wds or 100 pgs. Royalty 5-10% on retail; no advance. Average first printing 2,000. Publication within 5-6 mos. Disk accepted. Responds in 1-2 wks. Catalog for 3 stamps.

Nonfiction: Query only; phone/fax query OK. "Looking for books on health and fitness; vegetarian cookbooks."

Also Does: Pamphlets, booklets and tracts. IBM (music typesetting).

+TOCCOA FALLS PRESS, Toccoa Falls College, PO Box 800870, Toccoa Falls GA 30598. Debora Gerl, ed.

+TOUCH PUBLICATIONS, PO Box 19888, Houston TX 77079. (281)497-7901. Fax (281)497-0904. E-mail: touchusa@domi.net. Touch Outreach Ministries. Jim Egli, dir. of new products. To awaken the church in North America to dynamic life and outreach so more brought to Christ through cell churches. Publishes 8 titles/yr. Receives 25 submissions annually. 40% of books from first-time authors. Reprints books. Prefers 75-200 pgs. Royalty 10-15% of net; no advance. Average first printing 2,000. Not in topical listings.

   Nonfiction: Query only."Must relate to cell church life. "

   Tips: "Our market is extremely focused. We publish books, resources and discipleship tools for churches, using a cell group strategy."

+TREASURE PUBLISHING, MSC 1000, 829 S. Shields, Fort Collins CO 80521. (970)484-8483. Fax (970)495-6700. Treasure Learning Systems. Mark Steiner, pres. To assist the church in fulfilling the Great Commission. Publishes 4 titles/yr. Receives 40-50 submissions annually. 0% of books from first-time authors. Prefers 26 pgs. Royalty; advance. Average first printing 2,500. Publication within 1 yr. Considers simultaneous submissions. Responds in 8 wks. Free guidelines.

   Nonfiction: Query only. Children's picture books or topical and exegetical Bible study resources for adults.

   Tips: "Most open to children's picture books with references."

THE TRINITY FOUNDATION, PO Box 1666, Hobbs NM 88240. Phone/fax (505)392-8584. Fax (505392-7274. John W. Robbins, pres. To promote the logical system of truth found in the Bible. Publishes 6 titles/yr. Receives 12 submissions annually. No books from first-time authors. No mss through agents. Reprints books. Prefers 200 pgs. Outright purchase; free books; no advance. Average first printing 3,000. Publication within 9 mos. No simultaneous submissions. Responds in 2 mos. Catalog for #10 SAE/1 stamp.

   Nonfiction: Query letter only. Most open to Calvinist/Clarkian books.

   Also Does: Booklets & tracts.

   Tips: "Most open to well-written, Calvinist, biblical books. Read Gordon Clark first."

*TRINITY PRESS INTERNATIONAL, PO Box 851, Valley Forge PA 19482. (610)768-2120. Fax (610)768-2441. Dr. Harold W. Rast, dir. A nondenominational, academic religious publisher. Publishes 25 titles/yr. Receives 150-200 submissions annually. 3% of books from first-time authors. Reprints books. Royalty 6-15% on retail (some net); advance $500 & up. Average first printing 2,000. Publication within 8-12 mos. Responds in 3-6 mos. Guidelines; free catalog.

   Nonfiction: Complete ms or proposal/3 chapters. "Religious material only in the area of Bible studies, theology, ethics, etc." No dissertations or essays.

   Tips: "Most open to a book that is academic, to be used in undergraduate biblical studies, theology or religious studies program."

TYNDALE HOUSE PUBLISHERS, 351 Executive Dr., Box 80, Wheaton IL 60189-0080. (630)668-8300. Fax (630)668-6885. Ronald Beers, VP editorial. Imprints: Living Books; Pocket Guides. Publishes 100 titles/yr. 5-10% of books from first-time authors. Reprints books. Royalty; outright purchase of some children's books. **SUBSIDY PUBLISHES 30%.** Average first printing 5,000-

10,000. Publication within 12-18 mos. No unsolicited mss. Guidelines (separate guidelines for children's books—request specifically); catalog for 9x12 SAE/9 stamps.

Note: This publisher serviced by The Writer's Edge.

UNITED CHURCH PRESS, 700 Prospect Ave. E., Cleveland OH 44115-1100. (216)736-3700. Fax (216)736-3703. E-mail: sadlerk@ucc.org. United Church of Christ/Board for Homeland Missions. Kim M. Sadler, ed. Publishes 12-15 titles/yr. Receives 60+ submissions annually. 50% of books from first-time authors. Royalty 8% of net; work for hire, one-time fee; advance negotiable. Average first printing 3,000. Publication within 9-12 mos. Rarely considers simultaneous submissions. Responds in 10-12 wks. Requires disk. Free guidelines/catalog.

> **Nonfiction:** Proposal/2 or more chapters or complete ms; e-mail query OK.
>
> **Special Needs:** Children's sermons, worship resources, youth materials, religious materials for ethnic groups.
>
> **Ethnic Books:** African-American, Native-American, Asian-American, Pacific Islanders, and Hispanic.
>
> **Tips:** "Most open to well-written mss that are United Church of Christ specific and/or religious topics that cross denominations. Use inclusive language and follow the Chicago Manual of Style."

THE UNITED CHURCH PUBLISHING HOUSE, 3250 Bloor St. W., 4th floor, Etobicoke ON M8X 2Y4 Canada. (416)231-5931. Fax (416)232-6004. E-mail: rbradley@uccan.org. Website: http://www.uccan.org. The United Church of Canada. Ruth Bradley-St-Cyr, mng. ed. Publishes 10-12 titles/yr. Receives 50-60 submissions annually. 30% of books from first-time authors. Prefers 200 pgs. Royalty 8-12% on retail; advance $100-300. Average first printing 1,500. Publication within 1yr. Responds in 4-8 wks. Disk required. Guidelines.

> **Nonfiction:** Query only; fax/e-mail query OK. Publishes Canadian authors only.
>
> **Tips:** "We publish books in the areas of Christian education; resources for church, worship, music; social issues; United Church History and leaders; and women and religion." No material returned without SASE.

UNITED METHODIST PUBLISHING HOUSE, Box 801, Nashville TN 37202-0801. (615)749-6301. Fax (615)748-6512. United Methodist. Imprints: Abingdon Press, Dimensions for Living, Kingswood Books, and Parthenon Press. Neil M. Alexander, pub. To provide resources that help others know, love and serve God and neighbor. Publishes 130 titles/yr. Receives 2,500 submissions annually. Few books from first-time authors. No mss through agents. Reprints books. Prefers 32-300 pgs. Negotiable royalty; advance 25% of expected first year royalty. Average first printing 4,000-5,000. Publication within 24 mos. Responds in 3 mos. Guidelines; free catalog.

> **Nonfiction:** Proposal/2 chapters; fax query OK.
>
> **Fiction:** Children's picture books.
>
> **Ethnic Books:** African-American, Korean, and Hispanic.
>
> **Also Does:** Booklets.
>
> **Tips:** "Most open to books different than similar books in the market. Include detailed information in the proposal regarding competitive books and what sets yours apart."

UNIVERSITY OF OTTAWA PRESS, 542 King Edward St., Ottawa ON K1N 6N5 Canada. (613)562-5246. Fax (613)562-5247. E-mail: press@uottawa.ca. Suzanne Bosse, ed-in-chief. Publishes 2 titles/yr. Receives 200+ submissions annually. Many books from first-time authors. Prefers 250 pgs. Royalty 8-10% on net; no advance. Average first printing 800. Publication within 8 mos. Doesn't like simultaneous submissions. Responds in 2-4 wks. Requires disk. Free guidelines/catalog.

   Nonfiction: Proposal/2 chapters; fax/e-mail query OK. Scholarly books only (peer reviewed).

UNIVERSITY PRESS OF AMERICA, 4720 Boston Way, Lanham MD 20706. (301)459-3366. Fax (301)459-2118. Academic press. Nancy J. Ulrich, acq. Ed. Publishes scholarly works in the social sciences and humanities. Publishes 50 religious titles/yr. Receives 200 submissions annually. 70% of books from first-time authors. Reprints books. Prefers 200 pgs. Royalty to 12.5% of net; no advances. Average first printing 500. Publication within 5 mos. Considers simultaneous submissions. Responds in 1-2 mos. Free guidelines/book flyer.

   Nonfiction: Complete ms/resume; phone/fax query OK. "Looking for scholarly manuscripts."

   Ethnic Books: African studies; Black studies.

   Tips: "We have a strong religious studies line. Most of our authors have good academic credentials."

UPPER ROOM BOOKS, 1908 Grand Ave., Box 189, Nashville TN 37202-0189. (615)340-7256. Fax (615)340-7006. Website: http://www.UPPERROOM.ORG. United Methodist. George Donigian, leadership & group resources; JoAnn Miller, laity & family resources. Provides resources for individuals and congregations to encourage and support spiritual growth. Publishes 25-30 titles/yr. Receives 150-200 submissions annually. 50% of books from first-time authors. Reprints books. Prefers 40,000-60,000 wds. Royalty on net; some work for hire; $1,000 advance. Average first printing 5,000. Publication within 1 yr. Responds in 6-8 wks. Free guidelines/catalog.

   Nonfiction: Query letter or proposal; fax query OK.

   Fiction: Query letter or proposal. They are investigating fiction possibilities.

   Tips: "Wants books that focus less on the intimate individual experience and more on that which relates to the concerns of all disciples."

*VESTA PUBLICATIONS, LTD., Box 1641, Cornwall ON K6H 5V6 Canada. (613)932-7721. Fax (613)932-7735. General trade publisher that does a few religious titles. Stephen Gill, ed. Publishes 4 titles/yr. Receives 350 submissions annually. 90% of books from first-time authors. No mss through agents. **SUBSIDY PUBLISHES 5%** (author pays about 50% of cost). Prefers 75,000 wds & up. Royalty 10% of net; no advance. Average first printing 1,500. Publication within 14 mos. Considers simultaneous submissions. Responds in 6 wks. Catalog for SAE/IRCs.

   Nonfiction & Fiction: Query/outline; phone query OK. Literary fiction.

   Ethnic Books: Ethnic fiction.

VICTOR BOOKS, 4050 Lee Vance View, Colorado Springs CO 80918. Chariot Victor Publishing/Cook Communications Ministries. Greg Clouse, ed. dir.; David Horton, sr. acq. ed. Publishes 35 titles/yr. Receives 2,500 submissions annually.

5-10% of books from first-time authors. Variable length. Royalty on net; occasional outright purchase; advance $2,000-3,000. Average first printing 7,500. Publication within 9-12 mos. Considers simultaneous submissions. Responds in 3 mos. Requires disk. Guidelines; no catalog.

Nonfiction: Query letter only; no phone query. "Most open to fresh, marketable concepts; well-thought-out and well-written books."

Fiction: Query letter only. Children/adult; picture books.

**Note: This publisher serviced by The Writer's Edge.

VICTORY HOUSE, INC., Box 700238, Tulsa OK 74170. (918)747-5009. Fax (918)747-1970. Lloyd B. Hildebrand, mng. ed. To edify the body of Christ. Publishes 4-5 titles/yr. Not accepting unsolicited mss at this time. No mss through agents. No guidelines; catalog for #10 SAE/1 stamp.

VISION HOUSE PUBLISHING, INC. Sold to Questar Publishers.

#VITAL ISSUES PRESS, (Formerly **HUNTINGTON HOUSE PUBLISHERS**), Box 53788, Lafayette LA 70505-3788. (319)237-7049. Mark Anthony, ed-in-chief. Focus is on educating readers on current events. Publishes 25-30 titles/yr. Receives 1,500 submissions annually. 25% of books from first-time authors. Reprints books. Prefers 50,000-60,000 wds or 208-224 pgs. Royalty 10% on net; negotiable advance. Average first printing 5,000-10,000. Publication within 1 yr. Considers simultaneous submissions. Responds in 4 mos. Free guidelines/catalog.

Nonfiction: Query/outline.

WADSWORTH PUBLISHING COMPANY, 10 Davis Dr., Belmont CA 94002. (415)595-2350. Fax (415)637-7544. E-mail: peter_adams@wadsworth.com. Website: http://www.thomson.com/wadsworth.html. Secular publisher that does some religious books. Mr. Robin Zwettler, ed. dir. Publishes 5-10 higher education religious textbooks/yr. Receives 200 submissions annually. 35% of books from first-time authors. No mss through agents. Reprints books. Royalty 5-15% on net; few advances. Average first printing 5,000. Publication within 1 yr. Considers simultaneous submissions. Responds in 1 mo. Free guidelines/catalog (by subject area).

Nonfiction: Query or proposal/chapters; fax/e-mail query OK. "Looking for college textbooks, especially on world religions; anthologies."

WALKER AND COMPANY, 435 Hudson St., New York NY 10014. (212)727-8300. Fax (212)727-0984. Walker Publishing Co., Inc. Beth Walker, VP. Publishes large-print reprints of already published books. Publishes 12 titles/yr. Royalty on net; advance. Free catalog. Not in topical listings.

*WARNER PRESS, Box 2499, Anderson IN 46018-2499. (317)644-7721. Church of God. David C. Schultz, ed-in-chief; Dan Harman, book ed. Publishes 10-15 titles/yr. Receives 200 submissions annually. 5% of books by first-time authors. Prefers 120 pgs. Royalty 15% of net; seldom makes advances. Average first printing 5,000. Publication within 8 mos. Responds in 2 wks. Free catalog.

Nonfiction: Query only.

+WATERBROOK PRESS, 220 Pine St., Ste 106, Sisters OR 97759 (this is a temporary address until a permanent location is found). (541)549-0773. Autonomous subsidiary of Bantam Doubleday Dell Publishing Group. Dan Rich, pres.; Thomas Womack, sr. ed; Lisa Bergren, exec. ed, fiction. New publisher; will publish a wide range of nonfiction and fiction for adult and young readers. Expects to release first titles in early 1998.

Note: This publisher serviced by The Writer's Edge.

WESTMINSTER/JOHN KNOX PRESS, 100 Witherspoon St., Louisville KY 40202-1396. (502)569-5043. Fax (502)569-5113. Presbyterian Church (USA). Richard E. Brown, dir.; Stephanie Egnotovich, mng. ed.; Jon L. Berquist, ed. Publishes 80-100 titles/yr. Prefers 200 pgs. Royalty 7-10%; negotiable advance. Responds in 2-3 mos. Requires disk. Guidelines; free catalog.

> **Nonfiction:** Proposal/chapters; phone/fax query OK. Emphasizes Bible, ethics, spirituality and theology.

WINSTON-DEREK PUBLISHERS, PO Box 90883, Nashville TN 37209. (615)321-0535. Fax (615)329-4824. E-mail: jillmerry@aol.com. Maggie Staton, ed. Imprints: Scythe Publications (cooperative publisher); James C. Winston (religious trade division); One Horn Press; Magpie Books. Publishes 70 titles/yr. Receives 500 submissions annually. 60% of books from first-time authors. **SUBSIDY PUBLISHES 10-15%.** Reprints books. Prefers 80,000-100,000 wds or 300-400 pgs. Royalty 10-15% of net; advance $5,000-10,000. Average first printing 4,000. Publication within 18 mos. Responds in 6-15 wks. Guidelines; catalog for 9x12 SAE/4 stamps.

> **Nonfiction:** Complete ms/synopsis/introductory author letter; no phone/fax/e-mail query. "We are looking for titles that are unique in any phase of religious studying. They must be theologically sound (Christian), well-researched, and written for the general market." Send hard copy of mss, with SASE.
>
> **Fiction:** Proposal or complete ms. Children, teen & adult. "No occult, science fiction or New Age."
>
> **Ethnic Books:** African-American; Native-American. Fiction & nonfiction; Black studies.

WOMAN'S MISSIONARY UNION, PO Box 830010, Birmingham AL 35283-0010. (205)991-8100. Fax (205)991-4990. Southern Baptist. Cindy McClain, ed. dir. A missions publisher. Publishes 15-25 titles/yr. (many are work for hire). Receives 20-30 submissions annually. 25% of books from first-time authors. Rarely reprints books. Prefers 150-250 pgs. Royalty on retail or outright purchase; no advance. Average first printing 5,000-10,000. Publication within 18 mos. Considers simultaneous submissions. Responds in 6 mos. Requires disk. Guidelines; copy for 9x12 SAE/4 stamps.

> **Nonfiction:** Complete ms or proposal/3-4 chapters; no phone/fax query. (Mss considered in the spring and fall only.) "All that we produce must have a missions/ministry emphasis."
>
> **Fiction:** Complete ms or proposal/3-4 chapters. Children's picture books or storybooks, particularly with a multicultural aspect.
>
> **Ethnic Books:** Hispanic.
>
> **Tips:** "Most open to how-to for missions involvement or books that address involvement in missions or lead persons into involvement."

WOOD LAKE BOOKS, INC., 10162 Newene Rd., Winfield BC V4V 1R2 Canada. (604)766-2778. Fax (604)766-2736. E-mail: info@woodlake.com. Northstone Productions, Inc./Ecumenical/mainline. James Taylor, ed.; submit to Alan Whitmore. Quality resources that respond to the needs of the ecumenical church and promote spiritual growth and commitment to God. Publishes 7-10 titles/yr. Receives 150-200 submissions annually. 25-30% of books from first-time authors. Prefers 50,000-70,000 wds or 128-196 pgs. Royalty 7-12% on net; some advances $1,000-1,500. Average first printing 4,000. Publication within 1 yr. Considers simultaneous submissions. Requires disk. Responds in 6 mos. Free guidelines/one-page flyer.

Nonfiction: Query, some proposals; fax/e-mail query OK.

Tips: "We publish Canadian authors only."

WORD PUBLISHING, 1501 LBJ Freeway Ste 650, Dallas TX 75234-6069. (214)488-9673. Fax (214)488-1311. Does not accept unsolicited manuscripts.

**Note: This publisher serviced by The Writer's Edge.

WORLD BIBLE PUBLISHERS, 2976 Ivanrest Ave., Grandville MI 49418. (616)531-9110. Fax (616)531-9120. Riverside/World. Shari TeSlaa. ed.; submit to Carol Ochs, pub. asst. Publishes Bibles and Bible-related products. Imprint: Riverside. Publishes 8-10 titles/yr. Receives 80-100 submissions annually. 2% of books from first-time authors. Reprints books. Prefers 100-300 pgs. Royalty 5-12% of net; advance $3,000. Average first printing 750. Publication within 24 mos. Considers simultaneous submissions. Responds in 2 mos. Free guidelines/catalog.

Nonfiction: Proposal/3 chapters; no phone/fax query. "Looking for devotional/inspirational books with a unique approach, and well-written."

Ethnic Books: African-American.

Tips: "Most open to books that are Bible-based; non-technical reference; devotional; apologetics; books that can incorporate God's Word translation."

**Note: This publisher serviced by The Writer's Edge.

*YALE UNIVERSITY PRESS, 92A Yale Station, New Haven CT 06520. (203)432-0900. Charles Grench, exec. ed. Publishes 10 religious titles/yr. Receives 175 submissions annually. 15% of books from first-time authors. Reprints books. Prefers up to 100,000 wds or 400 pgs. Royalty to 15% on retail; advances as needed. Average first printing 1,500. Publication within 1 yr. Responds in 2-13 wks. Free catalog.

Nonfiction: Query first. "Excellent and salable scholarly books."

*YOUNG READER'S CHRISTIAN LIBRARY, 1810 Barbour Dr., PO Box 719, Uhrichsville OH 44683. (614)922-6045. Fax (614)922-5948. Stephen Reginald, VP editorial. Children's imprint of Barbour & Co., Inc. 90% of books from first-time authors. No mss through agents. Reprints books. Prefers 16,000 wds. Royalty 5-10% of net; or outright purchases $500-2,500; advance $500. Publication within 10 mos. Considers simultaneous submissions. Responds in 10 wks. Guidelines; catalog for 9x12 SAE/4 stamps.

Nonfiction & Fiction: Proposal/3-4 chapters.

Tips: "We prefer action-oriented, fast-paced style at a sixth-grade reading level. The subject of the manuscript can be contemporary (post-World War II to today), a Bible character, or an historical figure."

ZONDERVAN PUBLISHING HOUSE, General Trade Books, 5300 Patterson SE, Grand Rapids MI 49530-0002. (616)698-6900. Web Site: http://www.zondervan. com. HarperCollins. Submit to Trade Manuscript Review Editor (A-1). Seeks to meet the needs of people with resources that glorify Jesus Christ and promote

Bible principles. Publishes 130 trade titles/yr. Receives 3,000 submissions annually. 20% of books from first-time authors. Reprints books. Royalty 12-14% of net; variable advance. Average first printing 5,000. Publication within 14 mos. Considers simultaneous submissions. Responds in 3 mos. Prefers NIV. Guidelines.

Nonfiction: Proposal/1-2 chapters (follow guidelines). If a previously published book, send copy in lieu of ms.

Fiction: Proposal/1 chapter. "Looking for series for adults and juveniles (8-12 years, series only)." Expanding their fiction line.

Ethnic Books: Vida Publishers division: Spanish, Portuguese, and French.

Tips: "Send something unique, distinctive in content. Proposal must show strong understanding of competition and audience." Does not acknowledge receipt of mss or give status reports.

**Note: This publisher serviced by The Writer's Edge.

ZONDERVAN PUBLISHING HOUSE, Academic and Professional Books, 5300 Patterson Ave. SE, Grand Rapids MI 49530. (616)698-6900. Division of Harper-Collins Publishers. Submit to Academic Manuscript Review Editor (A-1). Publishes 40-45 academic titles/yr. Seldom reprints books or dissertations. Royalty 14% of net; usually pays advance. Publication within 3 months. Free guidelines/catalog.

Nonfiction: Query or proposal/1-2 chapters. Academic books only.

Tips: "Includes college and seminary textbooks, books on preaching, counseling, discipleship, worship, and church renewal for pastors, professionals, and lay leaders in ministry." Wesleyan perspective.

**Note: This publisher serviced by The Writer's Edge.

BOOK PUBLISHERS NOT INCLUDED

Following is a list of book publishers who did not return a questionnaire, have gone out of business, or asked to be deleted for various reasons. Their inclusion on this list indicates a lack of interest in freelance submissions. The following codes indicate the reason for each: OB—Out of business, ABD—Asked to be deleted, NF—No freelance, NQ—Did not return questionnaire, or BA—Bad address.

Abbey Press (ABD)
A Beka Books (NF)
Affirmation Books (OB)
Aglow (OB)
Amherst Press (OB)
And Books (NF)
Arnold Publications (NF)
August House (NF)
Banner of Truth Trust (NF)
Bethesda Press (NF)
Bible Temple Publishing (NF)
Bookmates Intl., Inc. (NF for now)
Brethren Press (NF)
Brownlow Publishing Co. (NF)
Cantelon House (NF)
Canyonview Press (NF)
Center for Learning (ABD)
Chick Publications (NF)

Chosen People Ministries (NF)
Christian Schools Intl. (NF)
Collier-Macmillan (OB)
Covenant Publishers (OB)
Credo (BA)
Crystal Sea Books (NF)
Editorial Evangelica (NF)
End-Time Handmaidens (NF for now)
Engeltal Press (NF for now)
Gazelle Publications (NF for now)
Gibson Co., The C.R. (NF)
Greenlawn Press (ABD)
Guideposts Books (ABD)
Holman Bible Publishers (now Broadman & Holman)
Howard Publishing (ABD)

Ideals Publishing (NF)
Krieger Publishing (NF)
Ktisis Publishing (NF)
Life Books (NQ)
LifeCare Books (ABD)
Life Enrichment (bad phone #)
Living Flame (bad phone #)
Living Truth Publishers (NF)
Majestic Books (ABD)
Ministry Pub Co (OB)
Morse Press (BA)
Mott Media (NF)
Multi-Language Media (NF)
Mustard Seed Books (NF)
Nelson-Hall Publishers (ABD)
New Society Publishers (NF)
Northwest Publishing (bad phone #)
Novalis (bad phone #)

OMF Books (NF)
Pacific Theatre Press (OB)
Pastoral Fisherman (BA)
People of Destiny, Intl. (NF)
Peregrine Press (NF for now)
Pillar Books (OB)
Pine Mt Press (BA)
Polaris Press (NF)
Prometheus Books (NQ)
Provident Press (OB)
Quintessential Books (bad phone #)
Randall House Publications (NF)

Regency Press (NQ)
Russell House (BA)
Rutledge Hill Press (ABD)
William H. Sadlier (NF)
Scroll Publishing (NF for now)
Silver Burdett Ginn, Inc. (ABD)
Skipjack Press (NF)
Sophia Institute Press (NF)
Sparrow Press (NF)
Star Books (OB)
Storytime Ink (NF)
Sunday School Dynamics (ABD)

Sweetwater Publications (NF)
Today's Christian Woman Books (NF)
Triumph Books (NF)
Twenty-Third Publications (NF)
Union Gospel Press (NF)
Wesleyan Univ. Press (NF)
Westport Publishers (ABD)
Whitaker House (NF for now)
WRS Publishing (ABD)

SUBSIDY PUBLISHERS

WHAT YOU NEED TO KNOW ABOUT SUBSIDY PUBLISHERS

For the first time this year, I am listing any publishers who do 50% or more subsidy publishing in this separate listing. For our purposes here, I am calling any publisher that requires the author to pay for any part of the publishing costs as a subsidy publisher. They may call themselves by a variety of names, such as a book packager, a cooperative publisher, self-publisher, or simply someone who helps authors get their books published. Note that some of these also do at least some royalty publishing.

In the last couple of years, with the refinement of desk-top publishing, more subsidy publishers have sprung up and there has been an increase in confusion over who or what type of subsidy publishing is legitimate, and what publishers fall in with what we call "vanity publishers." As many of the legitimate publishers (and even some questionable ones) try to distance themselves from the notoriety of the vanity publisher, they have come up with a variety of names to try to form definite lines of distinction. Unfortunately, it has only served to confuse the authors who might use their services. It is my hope in offering this separate listing that I can help you understand what this side of publishing entails, what things to look for in a subsidy publisher, as well as what to look out for. Realize, too, that some of these publishers will publish any book, as long as the author can afford to pay for it. Others are as selective about what they publish as a royalty publisher would be, or they publish only certain types of books. Many will do only nonfiction, no novels or children's books. These distinctions will be important as you seek the right publisher for your project.

Because there is so much confusion about subsidy publishing, with many authors going into agreements with these publishers having little or no knowledge of what to expect, or even what is typical in this situation, many have come away unhappy or disillusioned. For that reason I frequently get complaints from authors who feel they have been cheated or taken advantage of (of course, I often get similar complaints about the royally publishers listed in this book). Each complaint brings with it an expectation that I should drop that publisher from the book. Although I am sensitive to their complaints, I also have come to the realization that I am not in a position to pass judgment on which publishers should be dropped. It has been my experience in publishing, that for every complaint I get on a publisher, I can usually find several other authors who will sing the praises of the same publishers. For that reason, I feel I can serve the needs of authors better by giving them some insight into what to expect from a subsidy publisher, and what kinds of terms should send up a red flag.

Because I am not an expert in this field, and because of space limitations, I will keep this brief and to the point. Let me clarify first that unless you know your book has a limited audience or you have your own method of distribution (such as being a speaker who can sell your own books when you speak), I recommend that you try all the appropriate royalty publishers first. If you are unsuccessful with the royalty publishers, but feel strongly about seeing your book published, and have the financial resources to do so (or do have your own distribution), one of the publishers listed below may be able to help you.

You can go to a local printer and take your book through all the necessary steps yourself, but a legitimate subsidy publisher has the contacts, know-how and resources to make the task easier and often less expensive. It is always good to get more than one bid to determine whether the terms you are being offered are fair and competitive with other such publishers.

There is not currently any kind of watchdog organization for subsidy publishers, but one is in the works. Until that group is in place, and since I do not have direct knowledge about all of the publishers listed below, I would recommend that no matter who makes you a first offer, that you get a second one from Wine Press Publishing, Longwood Communications, or ACW Press (ones I can personally recommend).

As with any contract, have someone review it before signing anything. I do such reviews, as do a number of others listed in the Editorial Services section of this book. Be sure that any terms agreed upon are IN WRITING. Verbal agreements won't be binding. A legitimate subsidy publisher will be happy to provide you with a list of former clients as references (if they aren't, watch out). Don't just ask for that list, follow through and contact more than one of those references. Get a catalog of their books, or a list of books they have published and try to find them or ask them to send you a review copy of one or two books they have published. Use those to check the quality of their work, the bindings, etc. Get answers to all your questions before you commit yourself to anything.

Keep in mind that the more copies of a book that are printed, the lower the cost per copy, but never let a publisher talk you into publishing more (or fewer) copies than you think is reasonable. Also find out up front, and have included in the contract, whether and how much promotion the publisher is going to do. Some will do as much as a royalty publisher, others do none at all. If they are not doing promotion, and you don't have any means of distribution yourself, it may not be a good idea to pursue publication. You don't want to end up with a garage full of books you can't sell. At the end of this section I am including the names and addresses of some of the main Christian book distributors. I don't know which ones will consider distributing a subsidy published book, so you will want to contact them to find out before you sign a contract.

LISTING OF SUBSIDY PUBLISHERS

Below is a listing of any publishers that do 50% or more subsidy publishing (where author pays some or all of the production costs). Before entering into dealings with any of these publishers, be sure to read the preceding section or what you need to know.

(*) An asterisk before a listing indicates no or unconfirmed information update.
(#) A number symbol before a listing indicates it was updated from their guidelines or other current sources.
(+) A plus sign before a listing indicates it is a new listing this year or was not included last year.

+ACW PRESS, 5501 N. 7th Ave., Ste. 502, Phoenix AZ 85013. (800)931-BOOK.

E-mail: ACWPress@aol.com. American Christian Writers. Steven R. Laube, exec. ed. Est. 1997. A self-publishing book packager. Reprints books. **SUBSIDY PUBLISHES 95%.** Average first printing 500 minimum. Responds in 1 wk. Guideline booklet. Not in topical listings; will consider any topic.

Tips: "We offer a high quality publishing alternative to help Christian authors get their material into print. High standards, high quality."

BLACK FOREST PRESS , 539 Telegraph Canyon Rd. #521, Chula Vista CA 91910. (619)656-8048. Fax (619)482-8704. Keith Pearson, acq. ed. A self-publishing company. Imprints: Kinder Books (children's); Dichter Books. Publishes 25-30 titles/yr. Receives 1,000+ submissions annually. 90% of books from first-time authors. **SUBSIDY PUBLISHES 90%** (helps people get published). Reprints books. Prefers 100-300 pgs. Average first printing 2,000-3,000. Publication within 4-6 months. Considers simultaneous submissions. Disk on request. Responds in 2 wks. Free guidelines/catalog.

Nonfiction: Query only/synopsis of book; phone/fax query OK. "Looking for true testimonials."

Fiction: Query only/synopsis. "Looking for Christian novels and prophecy novels; 150-350 pages."

Ethnic Books: Publishes in Spanish, Tagalog, Russian and Japanese.

Tips: "Most interested in good novels."

BRENTWOOD CHRISTIAN PRESS, 4000 Beallwood Ave., Columbus GA 31904. (404)576-5787. Mainline. Jerry L. Luquire, exec. ed. Publishes 267 titles/yr. Receives 2,000 submissions annually. Reprints books. **SUBSIDY PUBLISHES 95%.** Prefers 120 pgs. Average first printing 500. Publication within 2 mos. Considers simultaneous submissions. Responds in 2 days. Guidelines.

Nonfiction: Complete ms. "Collection of sermons on family topics; poetry; relation of Bible to current day."

Fiction: Complete ms. "Stories that show how faith helps overcome small, day-to-day problems. Prefer under 200 pgs."

Tips: "Keep it short; support facts with reference."

COMMENTS PUBLISHING, PO Box 819, Assonet MA 02702. David A. Reed, ed. A Christian outreach to Jehovah's Witnesses; cult exposé. Publishes 1-2 titles/yr. Receives 5 submissions annually. 75% of books from first-time authors. **SUBSIDY PUBLISHES 50%.** Prefers 40,000 wds or 150 pgs. In most cases author pays for books; average cost $2-4/bk. Average first printing 1,000. Publication within 6 mos. Considers simultaneous submissions. Responds in 1 mo. Guidelines; catalog for 8x10 SAE/2 stamps.

Nonfiction: Query.

Also Does: Pamphlets, booklets & tracts.

Tips: "Our marketing and distribution are limited; we sell mostly via direct mail-order to evangelicals in counter-cult work. Authors in other fields should plan to distribute most of their own books."

*DESTINY IMAGE PUBLISHERS, INC., 167 Walnut Bottom Rd., Shippenburg PA 17257. (717)532-3040. Fax (717)532-9291. E-mail: di@reapernet.com. Charismatic/Pentecostal. Submit to The Editor. Publishes 70 titles/yr. Receives 800 submissions annually. 85% of books from first-time authors. Reprints books. **SUBSIDY PUBLISHES 85%.** Prefers 60,000 wds. Royalty 4-8% on retail; for subsidy, purchase books at 70% of retail price; no advance. Average first printing 5,000. Publication within 3 mos. Considers simultaneous submissions. Responds in 2 wks. Free guidelines & catalog.

Nonfiction & Fiction: Complete ms; phone/fax query OK. All types/topics. Also videos.

+DRY BONES PRESS, PO Box 640345, San Francisco CA 94164. (415)292-7371. Fax (415)292-7314. Jim Rankin, ed/pub. Nursing and specialty books. Receives 10-20 submissions annually. 100% of books from first-time authors. **SUBSIDY PUBLISHES 80%.** Reprints books. Prefers about 50 pgs (unless poetry, special topic or tract). Royalty 6-10% on retail; no advance. Average first printing 200-1,000. Publication within 12-18 mos. Considers simultaneous submissions. Prefers disk. Responds in 1-2 mos. No guidelines; backlist for #10 SAE/2 stamps.

Nonfiction: Query (best) or proposal/1 or more chapters; fax query OK. "Looking for nursing, patient experiences, old Catholics, spirituality/psalter/liturgical. Guidelines not rigid. Will consider anything that is unique or interesting."

Fiction: Query or proposal/1 or more chapters. All ages.

Also Does: Pamphlets, booklets, tracts.

Tips: "Most open to good fiction or a significant work on key concepts of Christian tradition. However, will consider any good work ."

+ESSENCE PUBLISHING CO., INC., 103 Cannifton Rd., Belleville ON K8N 4V2 Canada. (613)962-2360. Fax (613)962-3055. E-mail: essence@intranet.on.ca. David Visser, ed. Provides affordable, short-run book publishing to the Christian community. Publishes 30 titles/yr. Receives 50+ submissions annually. 90% of books from first-time authors. **SUBSIDY PUBLISHES 95%.** Reprints books. Average first printing 500. Publication within 3 mos. Considers simultaneous submissions. Responds in 1-2 wks. Usually requires disk. Free guidelines/catalog. Not in topical listings; any topic.

Nonfiction & Fiction: Complete ms; phone/fax/e-mail query OK.

Also Does: Pamphlets, booklets and tracts.

FAIRWAY PRESS, Subsidy Division for C.S.S. Publishing Company, 517 S. Main St., Box 4503, Lima OH 45802-4503. (419)227-1818. Fax (419)228-9184. E-mail: csspub@bright.net. Teresa Rhoads, ed; submit to Ruth Ann Baker. Publishes 100 titles/yr. Receives 200-300 submissions annually. 80% of books from first-time authors. Reprints books. **SUBSIDY PUBLISHES 100%.** Royalty to 50%; no advance. Average first printing 500-1,000. Publication within 6-9 mos. Considers simultaneous submissions. Responds in up to 1 month. Prefers disk. Free guidelines/catalog for 9x12 SAE.

Nonfiction: Complete ms; phone/fax/e-mail query OK. "Looking for mss with a Christian theme, and seasonal material."

Fiction: Complete ms. For adults, teens, or children; all types.

+FAME PUBLISHING, INC., 820 S. MacArthur Blvd., Ste. 105-220, Coppell TX 75019. (214)393-1467. Fax (214)462-9350. Nondenominational. Margaret J. Kinney, pres. Publishes 3-5 titles/yr. **SUBSIDY PUBLISHER.** Not included in topical listings.

Nonfiction & Fiction: Proposal/chapters.

HARVARD HOUSE, PO Box 5172, Golden CO 80401. (303)378-3813. Fax

(707)434-0850. Donald Webster, ed. Publishes 1-2 titles/yr. Receives 30 submissions annually. All books from first-time authors. No mss through agents. **SUBSIDY PUBLISHES 100%.** Prefers 80-200 pgs. Average first printing 1,000. Publication within 6 mos. Considers simultaneous submissions. Responds in 1-2 mos. Guidelines; catalog $1.

Nonfiction: Proposal/up to 5 chapters or complete ms; fax query OK. "Looking for apologetics, prophecy, science/religion interface that appeals to both religious and secular. Must be marketable to secular talk shows."

Tips: "Author must be capable/willing to do radio/TV interviews."

LONGWOOD COMMUNICATIONS, 397 Kingslake Dr., DeBary FL 32713. (904)774-1991. Fax (904)774-8181. E-mail: longwood@totcon.com. Murray Fisher, VP. A service for authors who cannot get their books accepted by a traditional house. Publishes 8-10 titles/yr. Receives 100 submissions annually. 90% of books from first-time authors. No mss through agents. **100% SUBSIDY.** Reprints books. Average first printing 5,000. Publication within 4-6 mos. Considers simultaneous submissions. Responds in 1-2 wks. Prefers disk. No guidelines; free catalog.

Nonfiction: Complete ms; phone/fax /e-mail query OK. Any topic as long as it's Christian. Also does booklets. Not included in topical listings.

Fiction: Complete ms. For all ages. Any genre.

MOUNT OLIVE COLLEGE PRESS, 634 Henderson St., Mount Olive NC 28365. (919)658-2502. Dr. Pepper Worthington, ed. Publishes 4 titles/yr. Receives 500 submissions annually. 70% of books from first-time authors. No mss through agents. Prefers 64-280 pgs. **SUBSIDY PUBLISHES 65%.** Average first printing 500. Publication within 2 yrs. Considers simultaneous submissions. Sends postcard response. No disk. Free guidelines/catalog.

Nonfiction: Proposal/1-2 chapters; no phone query. Religion. For poetry submit 6 sample poems.

Fiction: Proposal/1-2 chapters. Religious.

+PARTNERSHIP BOOK SERVICES, 212 N. Ash, Hillsboro KS 67063. (800)844-1655 or (316)947-3966. Fax (316)947-3392. Hearth Publishing, Inc. Stan Thiessen, ed. Publishes 12 religious titles/yr. (70 total). Receives 200 submissions annually. 85% of books from first-time authors. No mss through agents. Reprints books. **92% SUBSIDY.** Reprints books. Prefers 20,000-150,000 wds or 96-352 pgs. Average first printing 500-20,000. Publication within 6 mos. Considers simultaneous submissions. Responds in 2-3 wks. Requires disk. Free guidelines/catalog. Not included in topical listings; considers any topic.

Nonfiction/Fiction: Proposal/4-6 chapters or complete ms; phone/fax query OK. Send $35/SASE for manuscript evaluation. "Response includes suggestions for improvement."

Also Does: Booklets and chapbooks.

Tips: "PBS services include evaluation, editing, cover design, formatting, disk to film, printing, promotions and marketing. "

PASTOR'S CHOICE PRESS, 4000 Beallwood Ave., Columbus GA 31904. (404/706)576-5787. Subsidiary of Brentwood Publishers Group. Jerry Luquire, exec. dir. **SUBSIDY OR CUSTOM PUBLISHES 100%.** Focus is on sermon notes, outlines, illustrations, plus news that pastors would find interesting. Publishes 300-500 copies. Cost of about $3-4/book. Publication in 45 days. Same day response.

POET'S COVE PRESS, 4000 Beallwood Ave., Columbus GA 31904. (404/706)576-5787. Subsidiary of Brentwood Publishers Group. Jerry Luquire, exec. dir. Publishes 125 titles/yr. **SUBSIDY OR CUSTOM PUBLISHES 100%.** Specializes in self-publishing books of religious or inspirational poetry, in small press runs of under 500 copies. Publication in 45 days. Same day response.

> **Tips:** "Type one poem per page; include short bio and photo with first submission."

PROMISE PUBLISHING, 2324 N. Batavia #105, Orange CA 92665. (714)282-1199. Fax (714)997-5545. E-mail: 105207.2262@compuserve.com. M.B. Steele, ed./V.P. Publishes 6 titles/yr. 50% of books from first-time authors. **100% CO-OPERATIVE PUBLISHING** in support of ministry organizations. Royalty 10% on retail (negotiable); no advance. Average first printing 5,000. Publication within 6 mos. Considers simultaneous submissions. Pre-acceptance talks determine acceptance. Prefers disk.

> **Nonfiction:** Proposal/3 chapters; phone/fax/e-mail query OK.

> **Special Needs:** "We are interested in whatever topics fall within the parameters of our 'cooperative publishing' approach, if it is not contradictory to the Bible. Not included in topical listings.

RAINBOW'S END CO., 354 Golden Grove Rd., Baden PA 15005. Phone/fax (412)266-4997. E-mail: btucker833@aol.com. Website: http://adpages.com/ REBOOKS. Wayne P. Brumagin, assoc. ed.; Bettie Tucker, poetry ed. Publishes 10-12 titles/yr. Receives 200+ submissions annually. 90% of books from first-time authors. **COOPERATIVE PUBLISHING (author pays half) for 90%.** Prefers 200 pgs. Author and publisher each pay the publishing costs, all moneys from first printing go to author, on second printing profits are shared equally; occasional advance $300. Average first printing 1,000. Publication within 3 mos. Considers simultaneous submissions. Responds in 4-12 wks. Prefers disk. Guidelines; catalog for 9x12 SAE; sample book $5. Also request guidelines for any profit-sharing anthologies they have in progress.

> **Nonfiction:** Complete ms; e-mail query OK. "Looking for recovery books, personal experience and poetry."

> **Fiction:** Complete ms. "Self-help fiction based on reality."

> **Tips:** "We are offering Christian writers a reputable way of getting their work into print through a reasonably-priced publishing program. Standards are high. Don't be too wordy. Make sure Scripture quotes are accurate. Stay within specified length."

*RECOVERY COMMUNICATIONS, INC., PO Box 19910, Baltimore MD 21211. Phone/fax (410)243-8558. Toby R. Drews, ed. Publishes 1-2 titles/yr. No mss through agents. **SUBSIDY PUBLISHER.** Prefers 110 pgs. Co-op projects; no royalty or advance. Average first printing 5,000. Publication within 11 mos.

> **Nonfiction:** Query only.

SELAH HOUSE PUBLISHING, 1300 Airport Rd. #E, North Brunswick NJ 08902-1700. (908)435-8700. Fax (908)435-8701. E-mail: BLOGOS@aol.com. Subsidy division of Bridge-Logos Publishers. Catherine J. Barrier, ed.; submit to Hollee Chadwick-Loney. Publishes up to 5 titles/yr. Receives 100 submissions annually.

80% of books from first-time authors. **SUBSIDY PUBLISHES 100%.** Reprints books. Prefers 200-280 pgs. Average first printing 5,000. Publication within 3-6 mos. Considers simultaneous submissions. Responds in 6-8 wks. Requires disk.

Nonfiction: Proposal/3 chapters; phone query OK. "Most open to evangelism, spiritual growth, self-help and education."

Fiction: "In general, we don't consider fiction."

Tips: "The Christian publishing market is saturated. Find a hole in the market that hasn't been written about. Then find a unique approach or perspective."

*SHEER JOY! PRESS/PROMOTIONS, Rt. 1 Box 110E, Pink Hill NC 28572. (919)568-6101. Fax (919)568-4171. Protestant. James R. Adams, pres.; submit to Patricia Adams, ed. Publishes 1-2 titles/yr. Receives 5-10 submissions annually. No mss through agents. **SUBSIDY PUBLISHES 85%.** Prefers 20,000-30,000 wds (200 pgs). Royalty on retail; no advance. Average first printing 1,000. Publication within 6 mos. Considers simultaneous submissions. Responds in 3-4 wks.

Nonfiction: Complete ms. "Need Bible-based dramatic readings."

Fiction: Complete ms. "Need Bible-based puppet skits."

Tips: "Be very illustrative and forceful in writing Christian drama."

SON-RISE PUBLICATIONS, 143 Greenfield Rd., New Wilmington PA 16142. (800)358-0777. Fax (412)946-8700. Florence W. Biros, acq. ed. Publishes 5-6 titles/yr. Receives 20 submissions annually. 50% of books from first-time authors. **SUBSIDY PUBLISHES 50%.** Prefers 25,000-40,000 wds or 90-196 pgs. Royalty 7.5-10% on retail; no advance. Average first printing 3,000. Publication within 8-9 mos. Responds ASAP.

Nonfiction: Query. "Most open to Christian teaching and testimony combined."

Fiction: Query only; overstocked.

SOUTHERN BAPTIST PRESS, 4000 Beallwood, Columbus GA 31904. (404)576-5787. Jerry L. Luquire, exec. ed. Publishes 42 books/yr. Receives 600 submissions annually. Reprints books. **SUBSIDY OR CUSTOM PUBLISHES 95%.** Prefers 120 pgs. Average first printing 500. Publication within 2 mos. Considers simultaneous submissions. Responds in 1 week. Guidelines.

Nonfiction: Complete ms. "Collections of sermons on family topics; poetry; relation of Bible to current day."

Fiction: Complete ms. "Stories that show how faith helps overcome small, day-to-day problems. Prefers under 200 wds."

Tips: "Keep it short; support facts with reference."

*TYLER PRESS, 1221 W.S.W. Loop 323, Tyler TX 75701. (903)581-2255. Fax (903)581-7841. J. A. Johnson, sr. ed. A self-publisher's service bureau that will lend its imprint to selected titles for copublished distribution. Publishes 20 titles/yr. Receives 250+ submissions annually. 98% of books from first-time authors. **SUBSIDY PUBLISHES 100%.** Reprints books. Prefers 204 pgs & up. Works on a joint publishing venture with the author; no advance. Average first printing 1,500-2,000. Publication within 2 mos. Considers simultaneous submissions. Responds in 3-4 wks.

Nonfiction: Query; fax query OK. "We enthusiastically promote self-help/how-to, historical, creation science, current social and political issues,

biographies, autobiographies, marriage and family, and women's issues."
Fiction: Query. For children only.
Also Does: Booklets.

WELLNESS PUBLICATIONS, Box 2397, Holland MI 49423. (616)335-5553 or (800)543-0815. Darrell Franken, pres. Specializes in health and faith books. Publishes 3 titles/yr. Receives 200 submissions annually. All books from first-time authors. **100% SUBSIDY.** Prefers 250 pgs. Royalty 10% on retail; no advance; minimum subsidy $3,000. Average first printing 2,000. Publication within 6 mos. Considers simultaneous submissions. Responds in 2-4 wks. Free catalog.
Nonfiction: Complete ms.
Tips: "Most open to health/healing, stress management and psychological concerns."

WINDFLOWER COMMUNICATIONS, 844-K McLeod Ave., Winnipeg MB R2G 2T7 Canada. (204)668-7475. Fax (204)661-8530. E-mail: windflower@brandt family.com. Website: http://www.infobahn.mb.ca/brandtfamily. Brandt Family Enterprises. Gilbert Brandt, pres. Publishes quality, wholesome literature for family reading, pleasure and learning. Publishes 4-6 titles/yr. Receives 200 submissions annually. 90% of books from first-time authors. **SUBSIDY PUBLISHES 80%.** Reprints books. Prefers 200 pgs. Royalty 10-20% on net; no advance. Average first printing 2,500. Publication within 10 mos. Considers simultaneous submissions. Responds in 6 mos. Prefers disk. Free guidelines/catalog.
Nonfiction: Query or proposal/1-2 chapters; fax/e-mail query OK.
Fiction: Proposal/1-2 chapters. All ages.
Tips: "We are currently focusing on historical fiction."

WINE PRESS PUBLISHING, PO Box 1406, Mukilteo WA 98275. (800)326-4674. Fax (206)353-4402. E-mail: BOOKS4HIM@aol.com. Chuck Dean, pub; submit to Athena Dean. Publishes 100+ titles/yr. Receives 200+ submissions annually. 85% of books from first-time authors. **BOOK PACKAGERS 95%.** Reprints books. All profits belong to the author. Average first printing 1,000-2,500. Publication in 3-4 mos. Considers simultaneous submissions. Responds in 1 wk. Free guidelines/catalog. Not included in topical listings because they consider any topic or genre.
Nonfiction: Complete ms; phone/fax/e-mail query OK. Publishes any topic as long as it's biblical or glorifies God.
Fiction: Complete ms. All ages and all genres.
Tips: "We offer professional, yet affordable, book packaging for Christian writers, with unique marketing, distribution and fulfillment services available for qualifying projects."

LISTING OF CHRISTIAN BOOK DISTRIBUTORS

APPALACHIAN, INC., PO Box 1573, 506 Princeton Rd., Johnson City TN 37601. (800)289-2772.

INGRAM BOOK COMPANY, 1125 Heil Quaker Rd., Nashville TN 37217. (615)793-5000.

R.G. MICHELL, 565 Gordon Baker Rd., Willowdale ON M2H 2W2, Canada.

NEW DAY CHRISTIAN DISTRIBUTORS, 126 Shivel Dr., Hendersonville TN 37075. (800)251-3633.

QUALITY BOOKS, 1003 W. Pines Rd., Oregon IL 61061. (815)732-4450. Distributes to secular libraries.

RIVERSIDE BOOK AND BIBLE, PO Box 370, Iowa Falls IA 50126-0370. (515)648-4271.

SLEEPER, DICK, DISTRIBUTION, 18680-B Langensand Rd., Sandy OR 97055-9427. (503)668-3454. Fax (503)668-5314. Represents small press authors.

SPRING ARBOR DISTRIBUTORS, 10885 Textile Rd., Belleville MI 48111. (313)481-0900.

STAR SONG DISTRIBUTION GROUP, PO Box 150009, Nashville TN 37215.

WARNER CHRISTIAN DISTRIBUTION, 24 Music Square East, Nashville TN 37203. (615)248-3300. Distributes records.

WHITAKER DISTRIBUTORS, 580 Pittsburgh St., Springdale PA 15144. (412)274-4440.

MARKET ANALYSIS

ALL PUBLISHERS IN ORDER OF MOST BOOKS PUBLISHED PER YEAR

Thomas Nelson 150-200
Standard Publishing 150
Wm. B. Eerdmans 140
Questar 134
United Methodist 130
Zondervan/Trade 130
Bethany House 125
Baker Books 120
HarperSanFrancisco 100
Liturgical Press 100
Tyndale House 100
Paulist Press 90-100
Westmin./John Knox 80-100
Christian Ed Publishers 80
Harvest House 80
Joshua Morris 75-100
Barbour & Co. 75-80
InterVarsity Press 75
Multnomah Press 75
Fleming H. Revell 75
Schocken Books 75
Honor Books 72
Crossroad Publishing 70
Winston-Derek 70
TEACH Services 68
Oxford University 60+
Concordia 60
CSS Publishing 60
Kregel 60
Heartsong Presents 52
Brown/ROA 50-100
Custom Commun. 50-75
Chariot Family Publishing 50-60
Orbis Books 50-55
Liguori Publications 50
Moody Press 50
Servant Publications 50
Univ. Press of America 50
Broadman & Holman 45-50
Crossway 45-50
Doubleday 45
Review and Herald 40-50
Harold Shaw 40-45
Zondervan/Academic 40-45
CEF Press 40+
Ignatius Press 40
Fortress Press 37
Harlequin 36

Harrison House 36
Augsburg Books 35
Meriwether 35 (plays)
Pacific Press 35
Pauline Book 35
Victor Books 35
Chariot Books 30-35
Garborg's 30-35
Alba House 30
Beacon Hill Press 30
College Press 30
Continuum 30
Discipleship Resources 30
Light and Life 30
Morehouse Publishing 30
Sheed & Ward 30
Bridge/Logos 25-35
Upper Room Books 25-30
Vital Issues Press 25-30
Mel Bay Publications 25
Christian Publications 25
Eldridge 25 (plays)
Element Books 25
Hunt and Thorpe 25
Liturgy Training 25
Pilgrim Press 25
Trinity Press Intl. 25
Group's Hands-On 24
Herald Press 24
GROUP Publishing 20-30
Our Sunday Visitor 20-30
Creation House 20+
Gold 'n' Honey 20
Lillenas 20
Resource Publications 20
Shining Star 20
Focus on the Family 18-20
St. Anthony Mess. Press 16-20
Pastoral Press 16
Woman's Mission. Union 15-25
Catholic Book Publishing 15-20
Catholic Univ of America 15-20
Chalice Press 15-20
Christian Univ Press 15-20
Hendrickson 15-20
Judson Press 15-20

New Leaf Press 15-20
Regal Books 15-20
Evangel Pub. House 15
Living the Good News 15
Loyola Press 15
Paraclete Press 15
Still Waters 15
Schoettle 14-28
Northstone Publishing 14-20
Palisades 14
Sword Of The Lord 12-18
Cornerstone Publishing 12-15
United Church Press 12-15
Albury Publishing 12
Dimension Books 12
Friendship Press 12
Libros Liguori 12
New City Press 12
Rainbow/Daybreak 12
Rainbow Publishers 12
Walker and Co. 12
Miracle Publishing 10-50
Carey Library, Wm. 10-15
Cross Cultural 10-15
Lydia Press 10-15
Pentecostal Publishing 10-15
Ragged Edge 10-15
Southern Methodist 10-15
Warner Press 10-15
Faith & Life Press 10-12
Howard Publishing 10-12
New Hope 10-12
United Church Publishing 10-12
ACTA Publications 10
ACU Press 10
Alban Institute 10
Church Growth Institute 10
Haworth Press 10
Loizeaux 10
Monument Press 10
St. Bede's Publications 10
Yale University Press 10
Cistercian Publications 8-14
Holy Cross Orthodox 8-10
Master Books 8-10
Presbyterian/Reformed 8-10
World Bible 8-10
Accent Publications 8

American Catholic Press 8
Appaloosa Press 8
Cameron Press 8
Chosen Books 8
Forward Movement 8
ICS Publications 8
Neibauer Press 8
Resurrection Press 8
Royal Productions 8
Touch Publications 8
Wood Lake Books 7-10
Kaleidoscope Press 7
MasterMedia 7
Faith Publishing 6-12
Riehle Foundation 6-12
Elder Books 6-10
Success Publishers 6-10
Bob Jones University Press 6-10
Gospel Folio Press 6-10
Thomas More Press 6-10
Christian Literature Crusade 6-8
Christopher Pub Hs 6-8
Cornell University Press 6-8
Innisfree Press 6-8
Christendom Press 6
Church & Synagogue Libraries 6
Read 'N Run Books 6
Trinity Foundation 6
Regina Press 5-10
Starburst Publishers 5-10
Stillpoint Publishing 5-10
Wadsworth Publishing 5-10
Blue Dolphin 5-7
FOG Publishing 5+
Christian Media 5
Conari Press 5
Wm. Morrow 5
Pelican Publishing 5
Rainbow Books 5 .
Rose Publishing 5

Hensley, Virgil 4-10
Hearth Publishing 4-8
Friends United Press 4-6
Hannibal Books 4-6
Roper Press 4-6
Franciscan Univ Press 4-5
Lion Publishing 4-5
Religious Education Press 4-5
Victory House 4-5
Bristol House 4
Cornerstone Press 4
Intl. Awakening Press 4
Langmarc Publishing 4
North Point Press 4
Open Court 4
Pansophic 4
Paradise Research 4
Treasure Publishing 4
VESTA Publications 4
PREP Publishing 3-7
Bethel Publishing 3-5
Cerdic Publications 3-5
Purple Pomegranate 3-5
Eden Publishing 3-4
Design Communications 3
Meriwether 3 (books)
Dabar Publishers 2-5
Lifetime Books 2-4
Regnery Publishing 2-4
Hi-Time Publishing 2-3
Kindred Productions 2-3
Probe Ministries 2-3
Sower's Press 2-3
Baldwin & Knowlton 2
Barclay Press 2
Good Book 2
Morning Star Press 2
Seaside Press 2
Univ. of Ottawa Press 2
Baker's Plays 1-5 (plays)
Life Cycle Books 1-3
Middle Atlantic 1-3
Shoestring Press 1-2

Aanvil Press 1
Baylor Univ. Press 1
Discus Press 1
Gilgal Publications 1
B.J. Goetz 1
Guernica Editions 1
Higley Publishing 1
Illumination Arts 1
Misty Hill Press 1
Renewal Press 1
Small Helm Press 1

SUBSIDY PUBLISHERS:

Brentwood 267
Poet's Cove 125
Wine Press 100+
Fairway Press 100
Destiny Image 70
Southern Baptist Press 42
Essence Publishing 30
Black Forest Press 25-30
Tyler Press 20
Partnership Book Services 12
Rainbow's End 10-12
Longwood Communications 8-10
Promise Publishing 6
Son-Rise 5-6
Selah House 5
Windflower Communications 4-6
Mt. Olive College Press 4
Fame Publishing 3-5
Wellness Publications 3
Comments Books 1-2
Harvard House 1-2
Recovery Communications 1-2
Sheer Joy! Press 1-2

BOOK PUBLISHERS WITH THE MOST BOOKS ON THE BEST SELLER LIST FOR THE LAST YEAR

Note: This tally is based on actual sales in Christian bookstores for December 1995-November 1996. The list is broken down by types of books, i.e., children's, teen, fiction, paperback and cloth, plus a new category this year, mass-market paperbacks. Numbers behind the names indicate the number of titles each publisher had on that best-seller list during the year. The combined list indicates the total number a particular publisher had on all the lists combined. It is interesting to note that each year the number of publishers appearing on the list increases: 26 publishers in 1993; 35 publishers in 1994; 43 in 1995, and 60 in 1996.

FICTION BOOKS
1. Bethany House 21

2. Tyndale House 11
3. Palisades/Questar 8

4. Multnomah/Questar 6
5. Harvest House 5

6. Word 4
7. Zondervan 4
8. Crossway 3
9. Lion Publishing 3
10. Thomas Nelson 3
11. Barbour Books 2
12. Moody Press 2
13. Simon & Schuster 2
14. Avon 1
15. Baker Books 2
16. Beacon Hill 1
17. Doubleday 1
18. Herald Press 1
19. Inspirational Press 1
20. Walker 1
21. Western Front 1

NONFICTION—CLOTH
1. Zondervan 14
2. Word 12
3. Thomas Nelson 8
4. Harvest House 6
5. Honor Books 5
6. Focus on the Family 3
7. Broadman & Holman 2
8. Crossway 2
9. Moody Press 2
10. Multnomah Press/Questar 2
11. Regal Books 2
12. Tyndale House 2
13. Baker Books 1
14. Barbour Books 1
15. Brownlow 1
16. Creation House 1
17. Harrison House 1
18. Revell 1
19. Vision House 1

NONFICTION—PAPERBACK
1. Harvest House 5
2. Honor Books 5
3. Multnomah/Questar 5
4. NavPress 4
5. Word 4
6. Barbour Books 3
7. Creation House 3
8. Thomas Nelson 3
9. Tyndale House 3
10. Western Front, Ltd. 3
11. Albury 2
12. Destiny Image 2
13. Focus on the Family 2
14. Frontier Research 2
15. Harrison House 2
16. Health Communications 2
17. Kregel 2

18. Regal Books 2
19. Starburst 2
20. Baker Books 1
21. Broadman & Holman 1
22. Discovery House 1
23. Fortress Press 1
24. Moody Press 1
25. Pneuma Life 1
26. Questar 1
27. Victor Books 1
28. Walker 1
29. Whitaker House 1
30. Zondervan 1

MASS-MARKET PAPERBACKS
1. Barbour Books 12
2. Tyndale House 8
3. Word 6
4. Zondervan 6
5. Whitaker House 2
6. Ave Maria 1
7. Avon 1
8. Baker Books 1
9. Bantam 1
10. Focus on the Family 1
11. Harvest House 1
12. Honor Books 1
13. Thomas Nelson 1
14. Paulist Press 1
15. Pocket Books 1
16. Regal Books 1
17. Revell 1
18. Simon Schuster 1
19. Walker 1
20. World Bible 1

CHILDREN'S BOOKS
1. Word 12
2. Chariot 9
3. Gold 'n' Honey/Questar 9
4. Tyndale House 8
5. Thomas Nelson 7
6. Concordia 5
7. Regina Press 5
8. Bethany House 4
9. Crossway Books 3
10. Zondervan 3
11. Catholic Book Pub 2
12. Standard Publishing 2
13. Baker Books 1
14. Barbour Books 1
15. Firefly 1
16. Harvest House 1
17. Honor Books 1
18. Lion 1
19. Sparrow 1
20. Star Song 1

21. Western Publishing 1
22. World Bible 1

YOUTH/TEEN BOOKS
1. Focus on the Family 4
2. Bethany House 3
3. Regal Books 3
4. Baker Books 2
5. Harvest House 2
6. Thomas Nelson 2
7. Word 2
8. Baptist SS Board 1
9. Chariot Books 1
10. Crossway Books 1
11. Harrison House 1
12. Honor Books 1
13. Servant 1
14. Standard 1
15. Tyndale House 1

Combined Best-Seller Lists (Combination of six lists above)
1. Word 40
2. Tyndale House 33
3. Questar (3 imprints*) 31
4. Zondervan 29
5. Bethany House 28
6. Thomas Nelson 24
7. Harvest House 20
8. Barbour Books 19
9. (*Multnomah Books 14)
10. Honor Books 13
11. Chariot 10
12. Focus on the Family 10
13. Crossway Books 9
14. (*Gold 'n' Honey 9)
15. (*Palisades 8)
16. Regal Books 8
17. Baker Books 7
18. Concordia 5
19. Moody Press 5
20. Regina Press 5
21. Creation House 4
22. Harrison House 4
23. Lion 4
24. NavPress 4
25. Western Front 4
26. Broadman & Holman 3
27. Simon & Schuster 3
28. Standard 3
29. Walker 3
30. Whitaker House 3
31. Albury 2
32. Avon 2
33. Catholic Book 2
34. Destiny Image 2
35. Frontier Research 2

36. Health Communications 2
37. Kregel 2
38. Revell 2
39. Starburst 2
40. World Bible 2
41. Ave Maria Press 1
42. Bantam 1
43. Baptist SS Board 1
44. Beacon Hill Press 1

45. Brownlow 1
46. Discovery House 1
47. Doubleday 1
48. Firefly 1
49. Fortress Press 1
50. Herald Press 1
51. Inspirational Press 1
52. Paulist Press 1
53. Pneuma Life 1

55. Pocket Books 1
55. Servant 1
56. Sparrow Press 1
57. Star Song 1
58. Vision House 1
59. Victor Books 1
60. Western Publishing 1

BOOK TOPICS MOST POPULAR WITH PUBLISHERS

Note: The numbers following the topics indicate how many publishers said they were interested in seeing a book on that topic. To find the list of publishers interested in each topic, go to the Topical Listings for books (see Table of Contents).

1. Christian Living 115
2. Prayer 112
3. Bible/Biblical 111
4. Family Life 109
5. Religion 106
6. Spirituality 106
7. Devotional Books 103
8. Women's Issues 103
9. Inspirational 101
10. Current/Social Issues 97
11. Marriage 93
12. Theological 93
13. Parenting 91
14. Evangelism/Witnessing 87
15. How-To 87
16. Christian Education 86
17. Ethics 83
18. Biography 78
19. Discipleship 77
20. Historical 76
21. Church Renewal 75
22. Youth Books (nonfiction) 74
23. Church Life 72
24. Pastor's Helps 68
25. Social Justice Issues 67
26. Psychology 64
27. Fiction: Adult/Religious 62
28. Healing 61
29. Health 61
31. Men's Books 61
30. Ethnic/Cultural 60
32. Doctrinal 58
33. Humor 58
34. Counseling Aids 57
35. Apologetics 55
36. Controversial Issues 55
37. Booklets 54
38. Fiction: Historical 54

39. Leadership 54
40. Group Study Books 53
41. Fiction: Contemporary 52
42. Gift Books 52
43. Philosophy 52
44. Reference Books 50
45. World Issues 49
46. Fiction: Juvenile 46
47. Liturgical Studies 46
48. Scholarly 46
49. Senior Adult Concerns 46
50. Worship Resources 46
51. Environmental Issues 45
52. Fiction: Adventure 45
53. Prophecy 44
54. Cults/Occult 43
55. Divorce 43
56. Fiction: Biblical 43
57. Children's Picture Books 42
58. Autobiography 41
59. Christian Home Schooling 40
60. Miracles 40
61. Missionary 40
62. Singles Issues 38
63. *Death/Dying 37
64. Money Management 37
65. *Self-Help 37
66. Archaeology 36
67. Pamphlets 36
68. Personal Experience 36
69. Personal Renewal 36
70. Music-Related Books 35
71. Fiction: Mystery 34
72. Sociology 34
73. Stewardship 34
74. Drama 33
75. Fiction: Historical/Romance 33

76. Fiction: Teen/Young Adult 33
77. Poetry 33
78. Political Theory 31
79. Recovery Books 31
80. Spiritual Warfare 31
81. Curriculum 30
82. Economics 30
83. Fiction: Humor 30
84. Retirement 29
85. Science 29
86. Sermons 29
87. Fiction: Frontier/Romance 28
88. Fiction: Frontier 27
89. Games/Crafts 26
90. Tracts 26
91. Fiction: Mystery/Romance 25
92. Fiction: Romance 24
93. Celebrity Profiles 23
94. Fiction: Short Story Collection 23
95. Youth Programs 23
96. Fiction: Allegory 21
97. Fiction: Literary 21
98. Plays 21
99. Christian School Books 19
100. Cookbooks 19
102. Creation Science 19
103. Exposes 19
104. Fiction: Science-Fiction 18
105. Sports/Recreation 17
106. Fiction: Fantasy 16
107. Travel 16
108. *Fiction: Ethnic 13
109. *Writing How-To 9

Comments:

If you are a fiction writer, you are more likely to sell adult fiction (62 possible publishers—3 less than last year), than you are juvenile fiction (46 publishers—5 less than last year) or teen fiction (33 publishers—3 less than last year). These figures indicate that fiction has leveled off after a significant increase last year for all ages.

The most popular genres with publishers are (1) Historical Fiction, 54 markets (went ahead of Contemporary fiction since last year), (2) Contemporary Fiction, 52 markets, (3) Adventure Fiction, 45 markets, (4) Biblical Fiction, 43 markets, (5) Mystery, 34 markets, and (6) Historical/Romance, 33 markets. Mystery has moved up two years in a row, showing a growing interest in that genre. Most of the other genres stayed about the same, with the exception of Frontier, Fantasy and Romance (second year in a row), which all dropped in interest.

Good news for poets again this year: While there were 32 book publishers who published poetry books last year, this year there are 33. That compares to only 14 in 1993, more than doubling the market in the last four years. Even though the market is improving, many will still want to consider self-publishing (look for subsidy publishers listed in a new section of this book), or sell to periodicals. Go to the periodical topical listings in this book to find 257 markets for poetry.

Compared to last year, Bible Study has dropped from 1st to 3rd. Christian Living has moved back to 1st and Prayer has jumped from 4th to 2nd. Religion jumped from 8th to 5th, with Family Life dropping from 3rd to 4th. Women's Issues dropped from 5th to 8th, and Spirituality stayed the same. Devotional Books moved up from 11th to 7th, Inspirational dropped from 7th to 9th, and Current/Social Issues stayed at 10th. That is more movement than we've had the last few years. However, we find the same topics among the top 10, except for Marriage that dropped out of the top 10 and Devotional Books that moved into it. Among the next 10 topics, the only significant changes were Evangelism/Witnessing moving up 6 places; and How-To and Discipleship both dropping 3 places.

In a general comparison to last year, the following topics showed a significant increase or decrease in interest among the publishers. The topics are listed under each heading with those making the greatest change in position at the top. The numbers indicate the number of places that topic moved up or down on the list since last year. An asterisk (*) before a topic indicates that the increase or decrease has continued from last year.

DECREASED IN INTEREST:
Cults/Occult—down 15
*Sermons—down 13
Fiction: Teen—down 12
Political Theory—down 10
Apologetics—down 9
*Divorce—down 9
Worship Resources—down 9
*Christian School Books—
   down 8
Group Study Books—down 8
*Cookbooks—down 7
Doctrinal—down 7

*Singles Issues—down 7
Autobiography—down 6
*Celebrity Profiles—down 6
Fiction: Frontier—down 6
*Missionary—down 6
*Money Management—down
   6
*Youth Programs—down 6

INCREASED IN INTEREST:
*Booklets—up 23
Scholarly—up 18
Curriculum—up 16

*Pamphlets—up 14
Drama—up 12
Environment—up 11
Fiction: Short Story Coll.—
   up 11
Sociology—up 11
Tracts—up 11
Leadership—up 9
Prophecy—up 9
Fiction: Romance—up 8
*Fiction: Historical—up 6
Health—up 6
Pastor's Helps—up 6

Comments:

Referring to the topics showing a decrease for more than one year, there are no significant trends, except that both Money Management and Single Issues are on the list for the third year in a row. Note that children's books are not on the list this year—they seem to be holding their own for now.

The only topics that were down last year, but up this year are Pastor's Helps, and Prophecy.

On the increased interest list, both Pamphlets and Booklets appear for the second year, but

Historical Fiction is the only topic appearing again. Drama, the Environment, and Health appear to be growing trends.

The only topic that was up last year, but down this year is Teen Fiction.

SUMMARY OF INFORMATION ON CHRISTIAN BOOK PUBLISHERS FOUND IN THE ALPHABETICAL LISTINGS

Note: The following numbers are based on the maximum total estimate for each company. For example, if a company gave a range of 5-10, the averages were based on the higher number, 10. This information will be valuable in determining if the contract offered by your publisher is in line with other publishers in some of these areas. For further help, check the section on editorial services to find those who offer contract evaluations, which are most valuable.

TOTAL MANUSCRIPTS RECEIVED:
Two hundred forty-eight publishers indicated they received a combined total of over 132,400 manuscripts during the year. That is an average of 534 manuscripts per editor, per year, a 14% drop from last year—20% drop over the last two years. The actual number of manuscripts received ranged from 1 to 10,000 per editor.

NUMBER OF BOOKS PUBLISHED:
Two hundred fifty-four publishers reported that they will publish a combined total of 6,943 titles during the coming year. That is an average of over 27 books per publisher (one less per publisher than last year). The actual number per publisher ranges from 1 to 267. Of those who responded to the question this year, 30% will publish more books than last, 39% will publish about the same number, and 31% will publish fewer. If each publisher actually publishes his maximum estimate of books for the year, about 5% of the manuscripts submitted will be published (about the same as last year).

AVERAGE FIRST PRINT RUN:
Based on 214 book publishers who indicated their average first print run, the average first printing of a book for a new author is about 5,800 books. That's a decrease of just over 3% from last year. Actual print runs ranged from 200 to 50,000 copies.

ROYALTIES:
Of the 216 publishers who reported that they paid royalties, 60 (28%) pay on the retail price; 107 (50%) pay on the wholesale price or net; and 49 (22%) didn't tell which. Many publishers are not telling what they pay, but of those who do, this year fewer are paying on retail (36%), and more on net (64%). The average royalty based on the retail price of the book was 7.6% to 11% (up from 7.5% to 10% last year). Actual royalties varied from 2% to 15%. The average royalty based on net varied from 10% to 14%, up slightly from the 9.5% to 14% last year. (Actual royalties varied from 5% to 50%.) The recommended royalty based on net is 18%, but only 14% of the Christian publishers counted here are paying 18% or higher (that is up 1% from last year).

ADVANCES:
Two hundred fourteen publishers responded to the question about whether or not they paid advances. Of those, 114 paid advances and 100 did not—which means those who do are moving ahead of those who don't for the first time (it's been half and half the last couple of years). Of those who pay advances, only 21% (44 publishers) gave a specific amount. The average advance for those 44 was $836–3,380 (about an 11% decrease from last year). The actual range was from $100 to $50,000. Of course, some publishers pay more for established authors or potentially best-selling books. It is not unusual for a first-time author to get no advance or a small one. Once you have one or more books published, feel free to ask for an advance, and raise the amount for each book. Don't be afraid to ask for an advance, even on a first book, if you need the money to support you while you finish the manuscript. Although more publishers are saying they don't give an advance or are reluctant to name an amount, the truth is many

publishers do give advances when warranted but are reluctant to advertise that fact or to divulge an amount.

REPORTING TIME:

Waiting for a response from an editor is often the hardest part of the writing business. Of the 237 editors who indicated how long you should have to wait for a response from them, the average time was just under 10 weeks (about the same as last year). However, since the times they actually gave ranged from 1 to 52 weeks, be sure to check the listing for the publisher you are interested in. Give them a 2-week grace period; then feel free to write a polite letter asking about the current status of your manuscript. Give them another month to respond, and if you don't hear anything, you can call as a last resort.

E-MAIL AND WEBSITES:

Last year we didn't even have enough information in this area to include this section. A lot has changed. Of the 266 book editors listed this year, 73 have e-mail addresses and 50 will accept e-mail queries; 30 have websites.

TOPICAL LISTINGS OF PERIODICALS

As soon as you have an article or story idea, look up that topic in the following topical listings (see Table of Contents for a full list of topics). Study the appropriate periodicals in the primary/alphabetical listings (as well as their writers' guidelines and sample copies), and select those that are most likely targets for the piece you are writing.

Note that most ideas can be written for more than one periodical if you slant them to the needs of different audiences; for example, current events for teens, or pastors, or women. Have a target periodical and audience in mind before you start writing. Each topic is divided by age group/audience, so you can pick appropriate markets for your particular slant.

If the magazine prefers or requires a query letter, be sure to write that letter first, and then follow any guidelines or suggestions they make if they give you a go-ahead.

R—Takes reprints.
(*)—Indicates new topic this year.

BIBLE STUDIES

ADULT/GENERAL
America
Annals of St. Anne
Arlington Catholic
Atlantic Baptist
Banner, The
Baptist Beacon—R
Baptist Informer
Believer, The—R
Bible Advocate—R
Bible Today
Biblical Reflections—R
Bread of Life—R
Brethren Evangelist
Canadian Catholic
Catholic Digest—R
Catholic Rural Life
Catholic Twin Circle—R
Celebrate Life—R
Christian Computing—R
Christian Info. Assoc.—R
Christian Ranchman
Christian Standard—R
Church Advocate—R
Church Herald/Holiness—R
Companions—R
Compass
Connecting Point—R
Emphasis/Faith & Living—R
Evangelical Baptist—R
Evangelical Friend

Fellowship Link—R
Family Network—R
Fidelity—R
Foursquare World—R
God's Revivalist
Good News Journal—R
Gospel Today
Hallelujah! (CAN)—R
Head to Head—R
Healing Inn—R
Hearing Hearts
Highway News—R
Indian Life—R
Inspirer, The—R
Island Christian—R
John Milton—R
Life Gate—R
Liguorian
Lutheran, The—R
Lutheran Digest—R
Lutheran Layman
Lutheran Witness—R
Mennonite, The—R
MESSAGE/Open Bible
Messenger/St. Anthony
Ministry Today—R
North American Voice
Our Family—R
Our Sunday Visitor
Pentecostal Homelife—R
Perspectives
Plain Truth—R
Pourastan—R

PrayerWorks—R
Presbyterian Outlook
Presbyterian Record—R
Presbyterians Today—R
St. Anthony Messenger
St. Willibrord Journal
Signs of the Times—R
Silver Wings—R
Social Justice—R
Sojourners
Spiritual Life
Stand Firm—R
Star of Zion
Today's Christian Senior—R
U.S. Catholic
War Cry—R
Watchman, The
Way of St. Francis—R
Weavings—R
Wesleyan Advocate—R
Witness, The

CHILDREN
Crusader—R
Discovery—R
Focus/Clubhouse

*CHRISTIAN
EDUCATION/LIBRARY*
CE Connection—R
Christian School
Church & Synagogue Lib.
Church Educator—R

GROUP
R-A-D-A-R—R
Religion Teacher's Journal
Shining Star
Teacher's Interaction

MISSIONS
Childlife
Missiology
Quiet Hour Echoes
Urban Mission—R

PASTORS/LEADERS
Celebration (Catholic)
Celebration (SDA)—R
Emmanuel
Five Stones, The—R
GROUP's Jr. High
Jour/Biblical Ethics—R
Journal/Christian Healing—R
Liturgy—R
Ministries Today
Preacher's Magazine—R
Priest, The
PROCLAIM—R
Pulpit Helps—R
Quarterly Review
Single Ad. Ministries Jour.
Today's Christian Preacher—
   R
Word & World

TEEN/YOUNG ADULT
Challenge (TN)—R
Conqueror—R
Cross Walk
Devo'Zine—R
On Course—R
Student Leadership—R
Teenage Christian—R
Teen Life (AG)—R
Teens on Target—R
Today's Christian Teen—R
Transcend
YOU!—R
Young Adult Today
Young Salvationist—R
Youth Challenge—R

WOMEN
Anna's Journal—R
Church Woman
CoLaborer
Horizons
Joyful Woman—R
Just Between Us—R
Lutheran Woman Today
Proverbs 31 Homemaker—R

Unique—R
Virtue—R
Wesleyan Woman—R
Woman's Touch—R

BOOK EXCERPTS

ADULT/GENERAL
African Amer. Heritage—R
AXIOS—R
Bible Advocate—R
Biblical Reflections—R
Canadian Catholic
Catholic Digest—R
Celebrate Life—R
Charisma/Christian Life
Christian Arts Review
Christian Chronicle (PA)—R
Christian Edge—R
Christian Reader—R
Christian Single—R
Christianity Today—R
Church Herald/Holiness—R
Columbia
Comments from the Friends—
   R
Covenant Companion—R
Door, The
Emphasis/Faith & Living—R
Evangelical Friend
Expression Christian
Family Network—R
Fellowship in Prayer—R
Fellowship Link—R
Fidelity—R
Good News Reporter—R
Gospel Today
Hearing Hearts
Indian Life—R
InterVarsity
Jewel Among Jewels—R
Kansas City Christian—R
Mennonite, The—R
MESSAGE
MESSAGE/Open Bible
Ministry Today—R
National Review
New Covenant
New Heart, A—R
Plain Truth—R
Plus—R
Presbyterian Outlook
Presbyterian Record—R
Prism—R
Religious Broadcasting—R
SCP Journal—R
Signs of the Times—R
Sojourners

Standard, The—R
Stand Firm—R
Star of Zion
Sunday Digest—R
TEAK Roundup—R
U.S. Catholic
War Cry—R
Watchman, The
Way of St. Francis—R
Weavings—R
Witness, The

*CHRISTIAN
EDUCATION/LIBRARY*
CE Connection—R
CE Leadership—R
Christian School
GROUP
Memos—R

MISSIONS
Areopagus—R
East-West Church—R
Intl. Journal/Frontier—R
Missiology

PASTORS/LEADERS
Celebration (SDA)—R
Christian Century
Diaconalogue—R
Five Stones, The—R
Ivy Jungle Report—R
Jour/Biblical Ethics—R
Journal/Christian Healing—R
Ministries Today
Modern Liturgy—R
Networks—R
Pastor's Family
Single Ad. Ministries Jour.
Voice of the Vineyard —R
Worldwide Challenge—R
Youthworker—R

TEEN/YOUNG ADULTS
Breakaway—R
Insight—R
On Course—R
Teens on Target—R
YOU!—R
Youth Challenge—R

WOMEN
Conscience—R
Journey—R
Joyful Woman—R
Link & Visitor—R
Wesleyan Woman—R
Woman's Touch—R

WRITERS
New Writing—R
Southwestern Writers—R
Writers Connection—R
Writer's Exchange—R
Writing Right—R

BOOK REVIEWS

ADULT/GENERAL
AGAIN—R
Anglican Journal—R
Arkansas Catholic
Arlington Catholic
AXIOS—R
Believer, The—R
Biblical Reflections—R
Burning Light—R
Canadian Catholic
Cathedral Age
Catholic Insight
Catholic Rural Life
Catholic Twin Circle—R
CBA Marketplace
Celebrate Life—R
Charisma/Christian Life
Christian Advocate—R
Christian Arts Review
Christian Century
Christian Chronicle (PA)—R
Christian Computing—R
Christian Courier (CAN)—R
Christian Edge—R
Christian Media—R
Christian Ranchman
Christian Renewal—R
Christian Research
Christian Retailing—R
Christianity/Arts
Christianity Today—R
Church Advocate—R
Comments /Friends—R
Commonweal
Compass
Connecting Point—R
Cornerstone—R
Cresset
Disciple's Journal—R
Discovery—R
Dovetail—R
Evangelical Baptist—R
Expression Christian
Family Network—R
Fellowship in Prayer—R
Fellowship Link—R
Fidelity—R
Good News Journal
Good News Reporter—R

Head to Head—R
Hearing Hearts
Home Times—R
Impact Magazine—R
Inland NW Christian
Interim—R
Island Christian—R
Jewel Among Jewels—R
John Milton—R
Joyful Noise
Life Gate—R
Living Light News—R
Mennonite Historian—R
MESSAGE
Methodist History
Minnesota Christian—R
MovieGuide
National Catholic
National Review
New Trumpet—R
Parent Paper, The
Perspectives
Plain Truth—R
Plowman, The—R
Poet's Park—R
Pourastan—R
Prairie Messenger—R
Presbyterian Layman
Presbyterian Outlook
Presbyterian Record—R
Presbyterians Today—R
Prism—R
Providence—R
Ratio
Religious Education
Role Model
Rutherford
Salt & The Light, The—R
SCP Journal—R
Smart Dads
Social Justice—R
Sojourners
Spiritual Life
Stand Firm—R
Star of Zion
TEAK Roundup—R
Today's Family Matters—R
Touchstone
United Church Observer
Upsouth—R
Watchman, The
Weavings—R

CHILDREN
Power & Light—R
Skipping Stones
Touch—R

CHRISTIAN EDUCATION/LIBRARY
Caravan
CE Counselor—R
Christian Librarian—R
Christian Library Jour.—R
Christian School
Church & Synagogue Lib.
Church Libraries—R
Journal/Adventist Educ.—R
Memos—R
Religion Teacher's Journal
Vision—R

MISSIONS
Areopagus—R
East-West Church—R
Intl. Journal/Frontier—R
Missiology
World Christian—R
World Vision—R

MUSIC
CCM Magazine
Gospel Music

PASTORS/LEADERS
Catechumenate
Celebration (SDA)—R
Christian Century
Christian Management—R
Christian Sentinel
Clergy Journal—R
Diocesan Dialogue—R
Enrichment—R
Five Stones, The—R
Ivy Jungle Report—R
Jour/Biblical Ethics—R
Journal/Christian Healing—R
Journal/Pastoral Care
Jour/Amer Soc/Chur Growth
Lutheran Partners—R
Ministries Today
Networks—R
Pastor's Family
Preacher, The
Preacher's Magazine—R
P.W. Religion BookLine
Resource—R
Sermon Notes
Single Ad. Ministries Jour.
Voice of the Vineyard —R
WCA Monthly—R
Word & World
Worship Leader

TEEN/YOUNG ADULT
Christteen—R

Student Leadership—R
Teen Power—R
Young Christian—R
Youth 97—R

WOMEN
Aspire
Conscience—R
Esprit—R
Horizons
Just Between Us—R
Proverbs 31 Homemaker—R
Tea and Sunshine
Wesleyan Woman
Woman's Touch—R

WRITERS
Canadian Writer's Jour—R
Cross & Quill—R
Gotta Write
Inklings
NW Christian Author—R
Writer's Ink—R
Salt & The Light, The—R
Southwestern Writers—R
Tickled by Thunder—R
VA Christian Writer—R
Writers Connection
Writer's Infor Network
Writer's News—R
Writer's Nook News
Writing Right—R

*CANADIAN/FOREIGN MARKETS

ADULT/GENERAL
Anglican Journal
Annals of St. Anne
Atlantic Baptist
Baptist Beacon
BC Catholic
Believer, The
Bread of Life
Canada Lutheran
Canadian Baptist
Canadian Catholic Review
Christian Courier
Companion
Compass
Crossway/Newsline
Dreams & Visions
Evangelical Baptist
Faith Today
Fellowship Link
Fellowship Today
Hallelujah!
Impact

Indian Life
Interim
Island Christian Info
Living Light News
Mennonite Brethren Herald
Mennonite Historian
Mennonite Reporter
Messenger of the Sacred
   Heart
Messenger of St. Anthony
Our Family
Pentecostal Testimony
Plowman, The
Pourastan
Prairie Messenger
Presbyterian Record
Revelation Post
Shantyman, The
TEAK Roundup
Time for Rhyme
United Church Observer

CHRISTIAN EDUCATION/LIBRARY
Caravan
Christian Librarian

MISSIONS
Areopagus

PASTORS/LEADERS
Cell Life FORUM
Technologies for Worship
Resource

WOMEN
Esprit
Link & Visitor

WRITERS
Canadian Writer's Journal
Exchange
Tickled by Thunder
Writer's Lifeline

CELEBRITY PIECES

ADULT/GENERAL
American Tract Soc.—R
Angels on Earth
Arlington Catholic
AXIOS—R
Banner News
Canada Lutheran—R
Canadian Catholic
Catholic Digest—R
Catholic Twin Circle—R
CBA Frontline

Celebrate Life—R
Charisma/Christian Life
Christian Advocate—R
Christian Arts Review
Christian Chronicle (PA)—R
Christian Edge—R
Christian Ranchman
Christian Reader—R
Christian Single—R
Christianity Today—R
Columbia
Companion
Door, The
Dovetail—R
Emphasis/Faith & Living—R
Expression Christian
Family Journal—R
Fellowship Link—R
Good News, Etc—R
Good News Journal—R
Good News Reporter—R
Guideposts
Head to Head—R
Hearing Hearts
Herald of Holiness—R
Home Life—R
Home Times—R
Indian Life—R
Inside Journal—R
Kansas City Christian—R
Life Gate—R
Living Light News—R
Lutheran Layman
Marriage Partnership
MESSAGE
Minnesota Christian—R
Ministry Today—R
MovieGuide
New Man—R
New Writing—R
Our Sunday Visitor
Plain Truth—R
Plus—R
Power for Living—R
PrayerWorks—R
Presbyterian Record—R
Prism—R
Pursuit—R
Religious Broadcasting—R
Revelation Post—R
Role Model
Signs of the Times—R
Sports Spectrum
Standard—R
Standard, The—R
Stand Firm—R
Sunday Digest—R
Table Talk—R

Upsouth—R
Vibrant Life—R

CHILDREN
Counselor—R
Crusader—R
Focus/Clubhouse
Guideposts for Kids
Touch—R

MISSIONS
Save Our World—R
Teachers in Focus—R
Worldwide Challenge—R

MUSIC
Christian Country—R
Gospel Industry Today
Gospel Music
Shout!

PASTORS/LEADERS
Five Stones, The—R
Journal/Christian Camping
P.W. Religion BookLine
   (author)

TEEN/YOUNG ADULT
Breakaway—R
Brio
Christteen—R
Insight—R
Listen—R
On Course—R
Sharing the VICTORY
   (sports)
Spirit
Straight—R
Teen Life (AG)—R
YOU!—R
Young Salvationist—R
Youth 97—R

WOMEN
Aspire
Journey—R
Today's Christian Woman
Wesleyan Woman—R

WRITERS
Christian Communicator—R
Gotta Write
New Writing—R
Once Upon a Time—R
Writer's Infor Network

CHRISTIAN BUSINESS

ADULT/GENERAL
Angels on Earth
Annals of St. Anne
AXIOS—R
Banner, The
Believer, The—R
Biblical Reflections—R
Canada Lutheran—R
Catholic Sentinel—R
Catholic Twin Circle—R
CBA Marketplace
Christian Advocate—R
Christian Chronicle (PA)—R
Christian Courier (CAN)—R
Christian Edge—R
Christian Living—R
Christian Ranchman
Christian Retailing—R
Christian Single—R
Christianity Today—R
Disciple's Journal—R
Discovery—R
Emphasis/Faith & Living—R
Evangel—R
Evangelical Visitor—R
Expression Christian
Faith Today
Family Network—R
Good News Journal—R
Good News Reporter—R
Guideposts
Herald of Holiness—R
Home Times—R
Indian Life—R
InterVarsity
Island Christian
John Milton—R
Kansas City Christian
Life Gate—R
Living Light News—R
Mennonite, The—R
MESSAGE
Ministry Today—R
Minnesota Christian—R
New Covenant
New Man—R
Pentecostal Homelife—R
PrayerWorks—R
Presbyterian Record—R
Prism—R
Providence—R
Religious Broadcasting—R
Social Justice—R
Standard, The—R
Stand Firm—R
Star of Zion

Today's Family Matters—R
United Church Observer
Upsouth—R
War Cry—R

MISSIONS
Childlife
Worldwide Challenge—R

PASTORS/LEADERS
Celebration (SDA)—R
Christian Management—R
Preacher's Magazine—R
Today's Christian Preacher—
   R
Today's Parish
Your Church—R

TEEN/YOUNG ADULT
Teenage Christian—R
Young Christian—R

WOMEN
Horizons—R
Lutheran Woman Today
Proverbs 31 Homemaker—R
Virtue—R
Wesleyan Woman—R

CHRISTIAN EDUCATION

ADULT/GENERAL
America
Anglican Journal—R
Annals of St. Anne
Arkansas Catholic
Arlington Catholic
Atlantic Baptist
AXIOS—R
Banner, The
Banner News
Baptist Informer
B.C. Catholic—R
Believer, The—R
Bible Advocate—R
Biblical Reflections—R
Canadian Baptist
Canada Lutheran—R
Canadian Catholic
Catholic Digest—R
Catholic Parent
Catholic Sentinel—R
Catholic Twin Circle—R
Christian Advocate—R
Christian C.L. RECORD—R
Christian Courier (CAN)—R
Christian Edge—R
Christian Home & School

Christian Living—R
Christian Parenting—R
Christian Ranchman
Christianity Today—R
Church Advocate—R
Church Herald/Holiness—R
Columbia
Compass
Covenant Companion—R
Disciple's Journal—R
Discovery—R
Emphasis/Faith & Living—R
Evangel—R
Evangelical Baptist—R
Evangelical Friend
Evangelical Visitor—R
Faith Today
Family Network—R
Fidelity—R
Foursquare World—R
God's Revivalist
Good News, Etc—R
Good News Reporter—R
Hearing Hearts
Herald of Holiness—R
Home Times—R
Inland NW Christian
Interchange
Island Christian—R
John Milton—R
Joyful Noise
Kansas City Christian—R
Life Gate—R
Liguorian
Living Church
Living Light News—R
Lutheran Digest—R
Mennonite, The—R
Mennonite Brethren—R
MESSAGE
Ministry Today—R
Minnesota Christian—R
National Review
New Covenant
North American Voice
NW Christian Journal—R
Our Family—R
Our Sunday Visitor
Pentecostal Homelife—R
Pentecostal Testimony—R
Perspectives
Plowman, The—R
Pourastan—R
PrayerWorks—R
Presbyterian Layman
Presbyterian Outlook
Presbyterian Record—R
Prism—R

Providence—R
Religious Education
SCP Journal—R
Social Justice—R
Something Better—R
Standard, The—R
Stand Firm—R
Star of Zion
Table Talk—R
United Church Observer
Upsouth—R
U.S. Catholic
War Cry—R
Way of St. Francis—R
Witness, The

CHILDREN
Discovery—R
My Friend
Together Time
Touch—R
(See Alphabetical listings)

MISSIONS
Compassion
East-West Church—R
Partners
Save Our World—R

PASTORS/LEADERS
Celebration (SDA)—R
Christian Ministry
Church Administration
Clergy Journal—R
Discipleship Training
Five Stones, The—R
Groups's Jr High
Liturgy—R
Lutheran Partners—R
Ministries Today
Modern Liturgy—R
Networks—R
Pastoral Life
Preacher's Magazine—R
Pulpit Helps—R
Resource—R
Today's Christian Preacher—R
Today's Parish
Word & World
Youthworker—R

TEEN/YOUNG ADULT
Challenge (TN)—R
Christteen—R
Conqueror—R
Cross Walk
On Course—R

Teenage Christian—R
Today's Christian Teen—R
Transcend
YOU!—R
Young Christian—R

WOMEN
Cottage Connections—R
Helping Hand—R
Horizons
Just Between Us—R
Lutheran Woman Today
Proverbs 31 Homemaker—R
Virtue—R

CHRISTIAN LIVING

ADULT/GENERAL
Advent Christian Witness—R
Alive!—R
alive now!
America
American Tract Soc.—R
Angels on Earth
Annals of St. Anne
Arkansas Catholic
Arlington Catholic
At Ease—R
AXIOS—R
Banner, The
Baptist Beacon—R
B.C. Catholic—R
Believer, The—R
Bible Advocate—R
Biblical Reflections—R
Bread of Life—R
Brethren Evangelist
Canadian Baptist
Canada Lutheran—R
Canadian Catholic
Catholic Digest—R
Catholic New York
Catholic Parent
Catholic Rural Life
Catholic Sentinel—R
Catholic Twin Circle—R
Charisma/Christian Life
Christian Advocate—R
Christian Century
Christian Chronicle (PA)—R
Christian Courier (WI)—R
Christian Courier (CAN)—R
Christian Edge—R
Christian Home & School
Christian Living—R
Christian Ranchman
Christian Reader—R
Christian Renewal—R

Christian Single—R
Christian Standard—R
Christianity Today—R
Church Advocate—R
Church Herald/Holiness—R
Church of God EVANGEL
Columbia
Commonweal
Companion
Companions—R
Connecting Point—R
Conquest
Cornerstone—R
Covenant Companion—R
Crossway/Newsline—R
Decision
Disciple's Journal—R
Discipleship Journal
Emphasis/Faith & Living—R
Evangel—R
Evangelical Baptist—R
Evangelical Friend
Evangelical Visitor—R
Explorer
Family Digest—R
Family Network—R
Fellowship in Prayer—R
Fellowship Link—R
Fellowship Today—R
Fidelity—R
Focus on the Family—R
Foursquare World—R
Gem, The—R
God's Revivalist
Good News—R
Good News, Etc—R
Good News Reporter—R
Gospel Tidings—R
Hallelujah! (CAN)—R
Head to Head—R
Healing Inn—R
Hearing Hearts
Herald of Holiness—R
Highway News—R
Home Life—R
Home Times—R
Impact Magazine—R
Indian Life—R
Inland NW Christian
Inspirer, The—R
Interim—R
InterVarsity
Island Christian—R
Jewel Among Jewels—R
John Milton—R
Jour/Christian Nursing—R
Kansas City Christian—R
Life Gate—R

Lifeglow—R
Light and Life
Liguorian
Live—R
Living—R
Living with Teenagers—R
Lookout—R
Lutheran, The—R
Lutheran Digest—R
Lutheran Journal—R
Lutheran Layman
Marian Helpers—R
Marriage Partnership
Mature Years—R
Mennonite, The—R
Mennonite Brethren—R
MESSAGE
MESSAGE/Open Bible
Messenger/St. Anthony
Messenger of the Sacred
   Heart
Ministry Today—R
Montana Catholic—R
Moody—R
New Covenant
New Man—R
New Oxford Review
No-Debt Living—R
North American Voice
Northwestern Lutheran—R
Our Family—R
Our Sunday Visitor
Pentecostal Evangel
Pentecostal Homelife—R
Perspectives
Plain Truth—R
Plus—R
Poet's Park—R
Pourastan—R
Power for Living—R
PrayerWorks—R
Presbyterian Layman
Presbyterian Record—R
Presbyterians Today—R
Progress—R
Purpose—R
Religious Broadcasting—R
Role Model
SCP Journal—R
Seek—R
Signs of the Times—R
Social Justice—R
Something Better—R
Spiritual Life
Standard—R
Standard, The—R
Stand Firm—R
Star of Zion

Sunday Digest—R
Table Talk—R
TEAK Roundup—R
Time of Singing—R
Today's Christian Senior—R
Today's Family Matters—R
United Church Observer
U.S. Catholic
Upsouth—R
Vibrant Life—R
Vision, The—R
Voice, The—R
War Cry—R
Way of St. Francis—R
Wesleyan Advocate—R
Witness, The

CHILDREN
BREAD/God's Children—R
Club Connection—R
CLUBHOUSE—R
Courage
Crusader (TN)
Discovery—R
Focus/Clubhouse
GUIDE—R
High Adventure—R
Junior Trails—R
Lad
My Friend
Partners—R
Power & Light—R
Touch—R
Wonder Time

CHRISTIAN
EDUCATION/LIBRARY
Brigade Leader—R
CE Counselor—R
Children's Ministry
Church & Synagogue Lib.
Church Educator—R
Religion Teacher's Journal
Resource—R
Shining Star
Teacher's Interaction

MISSIONS
American Horizon—R
Quiet Hour Echoes
Worldwide Challenge—R

MUSIC
Christian Country—R
Gospel Music

PASTORS/LEADERS
Cell Church—R

Cell Life FORUM
Christian Management—R
Diaconalogue—R
Discipleship Training
Eucharistic Minister—R
Five Stones, The—R
GROUP's Jr. High
Jour/Biblical Ethics—R
Journal/Christian Healing—R
Preacher, The
Preacher's Illus. Service—R
Preacher's Magazine—R
Pulpit Helps—R
Review for Religious
Today's Christian Preacher—
   R
Word & World

TEEN/YOUNG ADULT
Certainty
Challenge (IL)
Challenge (TN)—R
Christteen—R
Conqueror—R
Devo'Zine—R
On Course—R
Pathways—R
Straight—R
Student Leadership—R
Teenage Christian—R
Teen Life (AG)—R
Teen Power—R
Teens on Target—R
Today's Christian Teen—R
Transcend
With—R
YOU!—R
Young Adult Today
Young & Alive—R
Young Christian—R
Young Salvationist—R
Youth Challenge—R
Youth 97—R
Youth World—R
Zelos—R

WOMEN
Aspire
CoLaborer
Cottage Connections—R
DOMESTIQUE—R
Esprit—R
Horizons
Joyful Woman—R
Just Between Us—R
Link & Visitor—R
Lutheran Woman Today
Lutheran Woman's Quar.

Proverbs 31 Homemaker—R
Sisters Today
Tea and Sunshine
Today's Christian Woman
Unique—R
Virtue—R
Wesleyan Woman—R
Woman's Touch—R
Women Alive!—R

WRITERS
Southwestern Writers—R

CHURCH GROWTH

ADULT/GENERAL
Annals of St. Anne
Banner, The
Banner News
Believer, The—R
Bible Advocate—R
Canadian Baptist
Catholic Digest—R
Charisma/Christian Life
Christian Advocate—R
Christian Edge—R
Church Advocate—R
Covenant Companion—R
Disciple's Journal—R
Faith Today
Fellowship Link—R
Fidelity—R
Focus on the Family—R
Good News, Etc—R
Gospel Today
Hallelujah! (CAN)—R
Inside Journal—R
Interchange
Island Christian—R
John Milton—R
Liguorian
Living Light News—R
Lutheran Journal—R
Mennonite, The—R
Mennonite Brethren—R
MESSAGE/Open Bible
Pentecostal Evangel
Plain Truth—R
Power for Living—R
Presbyterian Layman
Presbyterian Outlook
Presbyterian Record—R
United Church Observer
Upsouth—R
War Cry—R
Watchman, The
Way of St. Francis—R

CHRISTIAN EDUCATION/LIBRARY
CE Counselor—R
CE Leadership—R
Children's Ministry
Church & Synagogue Lib.
Church Educator—R
Resource—R
Teacher's Interaction

MISSIONS
Missiology
P.I.M.E. World

PASTORS/LEADERS
Cell Life FORUM—R
Christian Ministry
Church Growth Network—R
Clergy Journal—R
Creator—R
Enrichment—R
Jour/Amer Soc/Chur Growth
Five Stones, The—R
Leadership Journal—R
Lutheran Forum—R
Ministries Today
Ministry
Modern Liturgy—R
Preacher's Magazine—R
Pulpit Helps—R
Sermon Notes
Today's Christian Preacher—
   R
Voice of the Vineyard —R
WCA Monthly—R
Worship Leader

WOMEN
DOMESTIQUE—R
Just Between Us—R
Sisters Today
Virtue—R

*CHURCH LIFE

ADULT/GENERAL
Annals of St. Anne
Arkansas Catholic
Banner, The
Believer, The—R
Bible Advocate—R
Bread of Life—R
Catholic Courier
Christian Advocate—R
Christian Edge—R
Christian Living—R
Companion
Conquest

Covenant Companion—R
Decision
Disciple's Journal—R
Discovery—R
Evangel—R
Faith Today
Family Digest—R
Family Journal—R
Family Network—R
Good News Reporter—R
Gospel Today
Island Christian—R
John Milton—R
Living Church
Lookout—R
Lutheran Digest—R
Lutheran Journal—R
Marriage Partnership
Mennonite, The—R
Mennonite Brethren—R
Moody—R
Our Family—R
Plain Truth—R
Power for Living—R
Presbyterian Outlook
Today's Christian Senior—R
United Church Observer
Upsouth—R
War Cry—R
Watchman, The
Weavings—R

CHILDREN
Touch—R

*CHRISTIAN
EDUCATION/LIBRARY*
CE Leadership—R
Church Educator—R
Leader/Church School To-
    day—R

MISSIONS
Quiet Hour Echoes

PASTORS/LEADERS
Cell Church—R
Emmanuel
Five Stones, The—R
Leadership Journal—R
Ministry
Modern Liturgy—R
Pastoral Life
Preacher, The
Preacher's Magazine—R
Pulpit Helps—R
Review for Religious
Technologies/Worship—R

Today's Christian Preacher—
    R
Voice of the Vineyard —R

TEEN/YOUNG ADULT
Challenge (TN)—R
Pathways—R
Teen Life (AG)—R
Young Salvationist—R

WOMEN
Cottage Connections—R
Virtue—R

CHURCH MANAGEMENT

ADULT/GENERAL
AXIOS—R
Banner, The
Believer, The—R
Biblical Reflections—R
Brethren Evangelist
Canada Lutheran—R
Canadian Catholic
Christian Advocate—R
Christian Computing—R
Christian Edge—R
Church of God EVANGEL
Covenant Companion—R
Disciple's Journal—R
Emphasis/Faith & Living—R
Evangelical Baptist—R
Faith Today
Fidelity—R
Good News, Etc—R
Hearing Hearts
Island Christian—R
John Milton—R
Joyful Noise
Kansas City Christian—R
Living Church
Lutheran Digest—R
MESSAGE/Open Bible
Ministry Today—R
Star of Zion
U.S. Catholic
Our Sunday Visitor
Presbyterian Layman
Presbyterian Outlook
Way of St. Francis—R
Wesleyan Advocate—R

*CHRISTIAN
EDUCATION/LIBRARY*
CE Connection—R
CE Counselor—R
CE Leadership—R
Children's Ministry

Church Educator—R
Resource—R
Teacher's Interaction

PASTORS/LEADERS
Celebration (Catholic)
Celebration (SDA)—R
Christian Management—R
Christian Ministry
Church Growth Network—R
Clergy Journal—R
Enrichment—R
Five Stones, The—R
GROUP's Jr. High
Leadership Journal—R
Lutheran Forum—R
Lutheran Partners—R
Ministries Today
Ministry
Preacher, The
Preacher's Magazine—R
Priest, The
Pulpit Helps—R
Resource—R
Today's Christian Preacher—
    R
Voice of the Vineyard —R
WCA Monthly—R
Word & World
Worship Leader
Your Church—R
Youthworker—R

WOMEN
Horizons—R
Just Between Us—R
Virtue—R

CHURCH OUTREACH

ADULT/GENERAL
Alive!—R
America
Annals of St. Anne
Arkansas Catholic
At Ease—R
AXIOS—R
Banner, The
Baptist Beacon—R
Baptist Informer
Believer, The—R
Bible Advocate—R
Bread of Life—R
Canada Lutheran—R
Canadian Baptist
Canadian Catholic
Cathedral Age
Catholic Digest—R

Catholic Rural Life
Catholic Sentinel—R
Catholic Twin Circle—R
Charisma/Christian Life
Christian Advocate—R
Christian Edge—R
Christian Reader—R
Christianity Today—R
Church Advocate—R
Church Herald/Holiness—R
Columbia
Companion
Companions—R
Conquest
Covenant Companion—R
Decision
Disciple's Journal—R
Emphasis/Faith & Living—R
Episcopal Life—R
Evangel—R
Evangelical Baptist—R
Evangelical Friend
Evangelical Visitor—R
Expression Christian
Faith Today
Family Network—R
Fellowship Today—R
Fidelity—R
God's Revivalist
Good News—R
Good News, Etc—R
Good News Reporter—R
Indian Life—R
Inspirer, The—R
Island Christian—R
John Milton—R
Kansas City Christian—R
Liguorian
Living Church
Living Light News—R
Lookout—R
Lutheran, The—R
Lutheran Digest—R
Lutheran Journal—R
Lutheran Layman
Mature Years—R
Mennonite Reporter
MESSAGE
MESSAGE/Open Bible
Ministry Today—R
Moody—R
New Covenant
New Oxford Review
North American Voice
Northwestern Lutheran—
  R
Our Family—R
Our Sunday Visitor

Pentecostal Evangel
Plain Truth—R
Presbyterian Layman
Presbyterian Outlook
Presbyterian Record—R
Presbyterians Today—R
Prism—R
Purpose—R
Religious Education
Revelation Post—R
St. Joseph's Messenger—R
SCP Journal—R
Seek—R
Social Justice—R
Standard, The—R
Stand Firm—R
Star of Zion
TEAK Roundup—R
Today's Christian Senior—R
United Church Observer
Upsouth—R
U.S. Catholic
War Cry—R
Watchman, The
Way of St. Francis—R
Wesleyan Advocate—R

CHILDREN
Focus/Clubhouse
Kids' Stuff—R

*CHRISTIAN
EDUCATION/LIBRARY*
Caravan
CE Connection—R
CE Counselor—R
CE Leadership—R
Children's Ministry
Church Educator—R
Insight—R
Journal/Adventist Educ.—R
Perspective—R
Teacher's Interaction
Religion Teacher's Journal
Resource—R

MISSIONS
American Horizon—R
Catholic Near East
Childlife
Compassion
East-West Church—R
Great Commission—R
Mission Today—R
Urban Mission—R
World Vision—R
Worldwide Challenge—R

PASTORS/LEADERS
Celebration (SDA)—R
Cell Church—R
Cell Life FORUM—R
Christian Management—R
Christian Ministry
Church Administration
Church Growth Network—R
Clergy Journal—R
Enrichment—R
Evangelism USA
Five Stones, The—R
GROUP's Jr. High
Jour/Amer Soc/Chur Growth
Liturgy—R
Lutheran Forum—R
Lutheran Partners—R
Ministries Today
Ministry
Modern Liturgy—R
Pastoral Life
Preacher's Magazine—R
Priest, The
Pulpit Helps—R
Resource—R
Single Ad. Ministries Jour.
Today's Christian Preacher—
  R
Today's Parish
Word & World
Worship Leader

TEEN/YOUNG ADULT
Pathways—R
Young Adult Today
Young Christian—R

WOMEN
CoLaborer
Cottage Connections—R
Helping Hand—R
Just Between Us—R
Lutheran Woman Today
Virtue—R
Wesleyan Woman

CONTESTS

Byline
Cameron Press
Canadian Writer's Jour
CEHUC Spanish Group (CA)
Celebration (Catholic)
Christian Arts Review
Christian Ministry
Christian Reader
CoLaborer
Columbus Christian Writers

(OH)
Common Boundary
CWI Florida Conference
Explorer
Faith Today
Fatted Calf Forum
Feelings Quarterly
Felicity
Insight (teen)
Intl. Network (conf./ID)
It's Your Choice
Jour/Christian Nursing
MESSAGE
New Writing
Plowman, The
Pockets
Poetry Connection
Poetry Forum
Read 'N Run Books
Skipping Stones
Smile
Southwest Writers Wkshp
  (NM)
Tickled by Thunder
Time of Singing
United Church Observer (sel-
  dom)
With (for teens)
Writer's Digest
Writer's Exchange
Writer's Ink
Writer's Journal
Young Christian
Young Salvationist

CONTROVERSIAL ISSUES

ADULT/GENERAL
American Tract Soc.—R
At Ease—R
AXIOS—R
Banner News
Believer, The—R
Bible Advocate—R
Biblical Reflections—R
Canada Lutheran—R
Canadian Baptist
Canadian Catholic
Catholic Insight
Catholic Rural Life
Celebrate Life—R
Charisma/Christian Life
Christian Advocate—R
Christian Arts Review
Christian Century
Christian Chronicle (PA)—R
Christian Courier (CAN)—R

Christian Living—R
Christian Media—R
Christian Reader—R
Christian Research
Christian Single—R
Christian Social Action—R
Christianity Today—R
Church Advocate—R
Columbia
Comments/Friends—R
Commonweal
Compass
Cornerstone—R
Covenant Companion—R
Cresset
Disciple's Journal—R
Discipleship Journal
Door, The
Dovetail—R
Episcopal Life—R
Evangel—R
Evangelical Baptist—R
Evangelical Friend
Expression Christian
Faith Today
Family Network—R
Fatted Calf Forum—R
Fellowship in Prayer—R
Fidelity—R
Friends Journal—R
Good News, Etc—R
Good News Journal—R
Good News Reporter—R
Hallelujah! (CAN)—R
Head to Head—R
Healing Inn—R
Hearing Hearts
Home Times—R
Indian Life—R
Island Christian—R
It's Your Choice—R
John Milton—R
Jour/Christian Nursing—R
Joyful Noise
Kansas City Christian—R
Light and Life
Living Church
Lutheran, The—R
Lutheran Witness—R
MESSAGE (limited)
Messenger/St. Anthony
Minnesota Christian—R
Moody—R
MovieGuide
National Review
New Man—R
New Oxford Review
Newsline—R

New Thought—R
New Trumpet—R
New Writing—R
Our Family—R
Pentecostal Homelife—R
Perspectives
Plain Truth—R
Prairie Messenger—R
Presbyterian Layman
Presbyterian Outlook
Presbyterian Record—R
Presbyterians Today—R
Prism—R
Providence—R
Religious Education
Religious Broadcasting—R
Rutherford
St. Anthony Messenger
Salt of the Earth—R
SCP Journal—R
Seek—R
Social Justice—R
Something Better—R
Standard, The—R
Stand Firm—R
Star of Zion
Table Talk—R
TEAK Roundup—R
United Church Observer
U.S. Catholic
Upsouth—R
War Cry—R
Watchman, The
Way of St. Francis—R
Wesleyan Advocate—R
Witness, The

CHILDREN
Discovery—R

CHRISTIAN EDUCATION/LIBRARY
CE Connection—R
CE Counselor—R
Today's Catholic Teacher—R

MISSIONS
American Horizon—R
Save Our World—R
Worldwide Challenge—R

MUSIC
Gospel Music

PASTORS/LEADERS
Christian Century
Christian Ministry
Christian Sentinel

Cross Currents—R
Diaconalogue—R
GROUP's Jr. High
Jour/Biblical Ethics—R
Journal/Christian Camping
Lutheran Forum—R
Lutheran Partners—R
Ministries Today
Modern Liturgy—R
Networks—R
Single Ad. Ministries Jour.
Word & World
Youthworker—R

TEEN/YOUNG ADULT
Brio
Caleb Issues & Answers
Christteen—R
Conqueror—R
Insight—R
On Course—R
Pathways—R
Student Leadership—R
Teen Life (AG)—R
YOU!—R
Young Adult Today
Young Christian—R
Young Salvationist—R

WOMEN
Anna's Journal—R
Aspire
Conscience—R
Cottage Connections—R
Horizons
Virtue—R

WRITERS
Christian Response—R

*CREATION SCIENCE

ADULT/GENERAL
Banner, The
Bible Advocate—R
Christian Advocate—R
Christian Chronicle (PA)—R
Companions—R
Conquest
Cornerstone—R
Chrysalis Reader
Faith Today
Fatted Calf Forum—R
Good News Reporter—R
Gospel Today
Hallelujah! (CAN)—R
Live—R
Living—R

MESSAGE/Open Bible
MovieGuide
National Review
New Thought—R
Pentecostal Evangel
Plain Truth—R
PrayerWorks—R
Providence—R
Something Better—R
Upsouth—R
War Cry—R

CHILDREN
Courage
Nature Friend
Partners—R
Primary Pal
R-A-D-A-R—R

*CHRISTIAN
EDUCATION/LIBRARY*
Journal/Adventist Educ.—R

PASTORS/LEADERS
Pulpit Helps—R

TEEN/YOUNG ADULT
Certainty
Challenge (IL)
Straight—R
Teen Life (AG)—R
Teens on Target—R
Youth Challenge—R

CULTS/OCCULT

ADULT/GENERAL
America
American Tract Soc.—R
AXIOS—R
Banner, The
Baptist Beacon—R
Bible Advocate—R
Biblical Reflections—R
Canada Lutheran—R
Catholic Digest—R
Catholic Twin Circle—R
CBA Marketplace
Charisma/Christian Life
Christian Advocate—R
Christian Chronicle (PA)—R
Christian Edge—R
Christian Ranchman
Christian Research
Christianity Today—R
Church Advocate—R
Church Herald/Holiness—R
Comments from the Friends—

R
Companions—R
Conquest
Evangelical Baptist—R
Evangelical Friend
Faith Today
Fidelity—R
God's Revivalist
Good News, Etc—R
Good News Journal—R
Good News Reporter—R
Gospel Today
Healing Inn—R
Indian Life—R
Jour/Christian Nursing—R
Kansas City Christian—R
Liguorian
Live—R
Lutheran Digest—R
MESSAGE/Open Bible
Minnesota Christian—R
MovieGuide
New Heart, A—R
New Oxford Review
New Trumpet—R
Our Sunday Visitor
Plain Truth—R
Providence—R
Rutherford
SCP Journal—R
Something Better—R
Table Talk—R
United Church Observer
VISION (CA)—R
War Cry—R
Watchman, The

CHILDREN
Crusader—R
High Adventure—R

*CHRISTIAN
EDUCATION/LIBRARY*
Team—R

MISSIONS
American Horizon—R
Areopagus—R
East-West Church—R
World Christian—R

PASTORS/LEADERS
Christian Sentinel
Discipleship Training
Jour/Biblical Ethics—R
Journal/Christian Healing—R
Ministries Today
Today's Christian Preacher—

R
Word & World

TEEN/YOUNG ADULT
Brio
Caleb Issues & Answers
Certainty
Christteen—R
On Course—R
Straight—R
Teen Life (AG)—R
Teens on Target—R
YOU!—R
Young Adult Today
Young Christian—R
Youth Challenge—R
Youth Update

WRITERS
New Writing—R

CURRENT/SOCIAL ISSUES

ADULT/GENERAL
AGAIN—R
Alive!—R
alive now!
America
American Tract Soc.—R
Anglican Journal—R
Arlington Catholic
Atlantic Baptist
AXIOS—R
Banner, The
Banner News
Baptist Informer
B.C. Catholic—R
Believer, The—R
Bible Advocate—R
Biblical Reflections—R
Brethren Evangelist
Canada Lutheran—R
Canadian Catholic
Catholic Courier
Catholic Digest—R
Catholic Forester—R
Catholic Insight
Catholic New York
Catholic Rural Life
Catholic Sentinel—R
Catholic Twin Circle—R
CBA Marketplace
Celebrate Life—R
Changes
Charisma/Christian Life
Christian Advocate—R
Christian American

Christian Arts Review
Christian Chronicle (PA)—R
Christian Courier (WI)—R
Christian Courier (CAN)—R
Christian Crusade
Christian Edge—R
Christian Home & School
Christian Living—R
Christian Ranchman
Christian Reader—R
Christian Renewal—R
Christian Single—R
Christian Social Action—R
Christian Standard—R
Christianity Today—R
Church Advocate—R
Church & State—R
Church Herald/Holiness—R
Church of God EVANGEL
Columbia
Commonweal
Compass
Cornerstone—R
Covenant Companion—R
Cresset
Disciple's Journal—R
Discipleship Journal
Door, The
Dovetail—R
Emphasis/Faith & Living—R
Episcopal Life—R
Evangel—R
Evangelical Baptist—R
Evangelical Friend
Evangelical Visitor—R
Faith Today
Fellowship Link—R
Fellowship Today—R
Fidelity—R
First Things
Foursquare World—R
Good News—R
Good News, Etc—R
Good News Journal—R
Good News Reporter—R
Gospel Tidings—R
Hallelujah! (CAN)—R
Head to Head—R
Healing Inn—R
Hearing Hearts
Herald of Holiness—R
Highway News—R
Home Life—R
Home Times—R
Impact Magazine—R
Indian Life—R
Inland NW Christian
Interim—R

InterVarsity
Island Christian—R
It's Your Choice—R
Jewel Among Jewels—R
John Milton—R
Jour/Christian Nursing—R
Journal of Church & State
Kansas City Christian—R
Liberty—R
Life Gate—R
Light and Life
Liguorian
Live—R
Living Church
Living with Teenagers—R
Lookout—R
Lutheran, The—R
Lutheran Layman
Marian Helpers Bulletin
Marriage Partnership
Mature Living
Mennonite Brethren—R
Mennonite Reporter
MESSAGE
MESSAGE/Open Bible
Messenger/St. Anthony
Ministry Today—R
Minnesota Christian—R
Moody—R
MovieGuide
National Review
New Covenant
New Heart, A—R
New Man—R
New Oxford Review
New Thought—R
New Trumpet—R
North American Voice
Our Family—R
Our Sunday Visitor
Pentecostal Evangel
Perspectives
Physician
Plain Truth—R
PrayerWorks—R
Presbyterian Layman
Presbyterian Outlook
Presbyterian Record—R
Presbyterians Today—R
Prism—R
Providence—R
Purpose—R
Quiet Revolution—R
Religious Broadcasting—R
Religious Education
Rutherford
St. Joseph's Messenger—R
Salt of the Earth—R

SCP Journal—R
Seek—R
Signs of the Times—R
Social Justice—R
Sojourners
Something Better—R
Standard—R
Stand Firm—R
Star of Zion
TEAK Roundup—R
Today's Christian Senior—R
Touchstone
United Church Observer
Upsouth—R
War Cry—R
Watchman, The
Way of St. Francis—R
Wesleyan Advocate—R
Witness, The

CHILDREN
BREAD/God's Children—R
Club Connection—R
Crusader—R
Discovery—R
Focus/Clubhouse
God's World Today
GUIDE—R
High Adventure—R
Power & Light—R
Skipping Stones
Touch—R

*CHRISTIAN
EDUCATION/LIBRARY*
Brigade Leader—R
CE Connection—R
CE Counselor—R
CE Leadership—R
Children's Ministry
Memos—R
Team—R
Today's Catholic Teacher—R
Vision—R

MISSIONS
American Horizon—R
Areopagus—R
Childlife—R
Compassion
East-West Church—R
New World Outlook
Urban Mission—R
World Christian—R
World Vision—R
Worldwide Challenge—R

MUSIC
CCM Magazine

PASTORS/LEADERS
Celebration (SDA)—R
Christian Century
Christian Ministry
Cross Currents—R
Diaconalogue—R
Discipleship Training
GROUP's Jr. High
Ivy Jungle Report—R
Jour/Biblical Ethics—R
Liturgy
Lutheran Forum—R
Lutheran Partners—R
Ministries Today
Quarterly Review
Resource—R
Single Ad. Ministries Jour.
Word & World
Youthworker—R

TEEN/YOUNG ADULT
Brio
Caleb Issues & Answers
Challenge (TN)—R
Christteen—R
Conqueror—R
Devo'Zine—R
Insight—R
Listen—R
On Course—R
Pathways—R
Straight—R
Student Leadership—R
Teenage Christian—R
Teen Power—R
Teens on Target—R
Today's Christian Teen—R
Transcend
With—R
YOU!—R
Young Adult Today
Young Christian—R
Young Salvationist—R
Youth Challenge—R
Youth 97—R
Youth Update

WOMEN
CoLaborer
Conscience—R
Cottage Connections—R
DOMESTIQUE—R
Esprit—R
Horizons
Jour/Women's Ministries

Link & Visitor—R
Lutheran Woman Today
Sisters Today
Today's Christian Woman
Virtue—R
Wesleyan Woman
Woman's Touch—R

DEATH/DYING

ADULT/GENERAL
Arlington Catholic
Banner, The
Bible Advocate—R
Bread of Life—R
Brethren Evangelist
Catholic Courier
Christian Advocate—R
Christian Living—R
Companions—R
Covenant Companion—R
Dovetail—R
Evangel—R
Faith Today
Family Digest—R
Family Network—R
Fellowship Link—R
Friends Journal—R
John Milton—R
Jour/Christian Nursing—R
Live—R
Living—R
Lutheran Journal—R
Mennonite, The—R
Pentecostal Evangel
Presbyterian Outlook
Prism—R
Remembrance—R
St. Anthony Messenger
Table Talk—R
Today's Christian Senior—R
United Church Observer
Upsouth—R
War Cry—R

CHILDREN
Skipping Stones

*CHRISTIAN
EDUCATION/LIBRARY*
Church Educator—R

PASTORS/LEADERS
Celebration (Catholic)
Christian Ministry
Lutheran Partners—R
Preacher's Magazine—R
Pulpit Helps—R

Today's Christian Preacher—
R

TEEN/YOUNG ADULT
Challenge (TN)—R
Devo'Zine—R
On Course—R
Straight—R
Teen Life (AG)—R
Today's Christian Teen—R
YOU!—R
Youth 97—R
With—R

WOMEN
Horizons—R
Virtue—R

DEVOTIONALS/ MEDITATIONS

ADULT/GENERAL
alive now!
Arlington Catholic
At Ease—R
Banner, The
Baptist Beacon—R
Baptist Informer
Believer, The—R
Bible Advocate—R
Bread of Life—R
Broken Streets
Canadian Catholic
Catholic Digest—R
Catholic Forester—R
Catholic Rural Life
Catholic Twin Circle—R
Celebrate Life—R
Charisma/Christian Life
Christian Advocate—R
Christian Century
Christian Renewal—R
Christianity Today—R
Church Advocate—R
Companion
Companions—R
Conquest (meditations)
Covenant Companion—R
Emphasis/Faith & Living—R
Evangel—R
Evangelical Baptist—R
Evangelical Friend
Explorer
Family Digest—R
Family Network—R
Fellowship Link—R
Fellowship Today—R
Foursquare World—R

God's Revivalist
Good News Journal—R
Green Cross—R
Head to Head—R
Healing Inn—R
Hearing Hearts
Highway News—R
Ideals—R
Indian Life—R
Inspirer, The—R
Island Christian—R
Jewel Among Jewels—R
John Milton—R
Kansas City Christian—R
Life Gate—R
Lifeglow—R
Light and Life
Liguorian
Living Church
Lutheran Journal—R
Lutheran Witness—R
Mature Years—R
Mennonite Brethren—R
MESSAGE
MESSAGE/Open Bible
Messenger/Sacred Heart
Montana Catholic—R
New Covenant
New Heart, A—R
New Trumpet—R
North American Voice
Our Sunday Visitor
Pentecostal Homelife—R
Perspectives
Plain Truth—R
Plowman, The—R
Pourastan—R
PrayerWorks—R
Presbyterian Outlook
Presbyterian Record—R
Presbyterians Today—R
Prism—R
Revelation Post—R
Seek—R
Silver Wings—R
Sojourners
Standard—R
Stand Firm—R
Star of Zion
TEAK Roundup—R
Today's Christian Senior—R
Today's Single—R
Upsouth—R
U.S. Catholic
Way of St. Francis—R
Weavings—R

CHILDREN
Club Connection—R
Courage
Discovery—R
High Adventure—R
Keys for Kids—R
Partners—R
Pockets—R
Power & Light—R
Primary Pal
Touch—R

CHRISTIAN EDUCATION/LIBRARY
Church & Synagogue Lib.
Church Worship
Religion Teacher's Journal
Shining Star
Teacher's Interaction
Today's Catholic Teacher—R

DAILY DEVOTIONAL
(See alphabetical list)

MISSIONS
Areopagus—R
Quiet Hour Echoes
Save Our World—R

PASTORS/LEADERS
Celebration (SDA)—R
Christian Century
Diaconalogue—R
Emmanuel
Five Stones, The—R
GROUP's Jr. High
Journal/Christian Healing—R
Preacher, The
Priest, The
Today's Christian Preacher—
R
Voice of the Vineyard —R

TEEN/YOUNG ADULT
Breakaway—R
Brio
Certainty
Challenge (IL)
Challenge (TN)—R
Conqueror—R
Cross Walk
Devo'Zine—R
Insight—R
Pathways—R
Take Five
Teenage Christian—R
Teen Life (AG)—R
Teens on Target—R

Today's Christian Teen—R
With—R
YOU!—R
Young Adult Today
Young Christian—R
Youth Challenge—R

WOMEN
Cottage Connections—R
DOMESTIQUE—R
Helping Hand—R
Horizons—R
Jour/Women's Ministries
Journey—R
Just Between Us—R
Lutheran Woman Today
Proverbs 31 Homemaker—R
Tea and Sunshine
Unique—R
Virtue—R
Wesleyan Woman—R
Woman's Touch—R
Women Alive!—R

WRITERS
Cross & Quill—R
Southwestern Writers—R

DISCIPLESHIP

ADULT/GENERAL
Advent Christian Witness—R
American Tract Soc.—R
At Ease—R
Arlington Catholic
Atlantic Baptist
Banner, The
Baptist Beacon—R
Bible Advocate—R
Bread of Life—R
Brethren Evangelist
Canada Lutheran—R
Canadian Baptist
Canadian Catholic
Catholic Digest—R
Charisma/Christian Life
Christian Advocate—R
Christian Century
Christian Living—R
Christian Parenting—R
Christian Ranchman
Christian Reader—R
Christianity Today—R
Church Advocate—R
Church Herald/Holiness—R
Companion
Companions—R
Conquest

Cornerstone—R
Covenant Companion—R
Cresset
Decision
Discipleship Journal
Emphasis/Faith & Living—R
Evangel—R
Evangelical Baptist—R
Family Network—R
Friends Journal—R
Good News, Etc—R
Green Cross—R
Hallelujah! (CAN)—R
Head to Head—R
Healing Inn—R
Hearing Hearts
Herald of Holiness—R
Highway News—R
Inland NW Christian
Inspirer, The—R
Island Christian—R
John Milton—R
Kansas City Christian—R
Life Gate—R
Light and Life
Liguorian
Live—R
Lookout—R
Lutheran Digest—R
Lutheran Journal—R
Mature Years—R
Mennonite, The—R
Mennonite Brethren—R
Ministry Today—R
Montana Catholic—R
Moody—R
New Covenant
New Man—R
New Oxford Review
New Trumpet—R
Our Family—R
Pentecostal Evangel
Pentecostal Testimony—R
Plain Truth—R
Plowman, The—R
PrayerWorks—R
Presbyterian Layman
Presbyterian Outlook
Prism—R
Purpose—R
Religious Education
St. Joseph's Messenger—R
Seek—R
Silver Wings—R
Sojourners
Standard—R
Standard, The—R
Stand Firm—R

Star of Zion
Sunday Digest—R
Today's Christian Senior—R
Upsouth—R
U.S. Catholic
Vision, The—R
War Cry—R
Watchman, The
Way of St. Francis—R
Wesleyan Advocate—R
Witness, The

CHILDREN
BREAD/God's Children—R
Club Connection—R
Courage
Discovery—R
Power & Light—R

*CHRISTIAN
EDUCATION/LIBRARY*
Brigade Leader—R
Caravan
CE Connection—R
CE Counselor—R
CE Leadership—R
Christian School
Church Educator—R
Evangelizing Today's Child—
R
Team—R

MISSIONS
American Horizon—R
Urban Mission—R
Worldwide Challenge—R

PASTORS/LEADERS
Celebration (SDA)—R
Cell Church—R
Cell Life FORUM—R
Christian Century
Christian Management—R
Five Stones, The—R
Ivy Jungle Report—R
Journal/Christian Camping
Journal/Christian Healing—R
Jour/Amer Soc/Chur Growth
Lutheran Forum—R
Lutheran Partners—R
Ministries Today
Ministry
Modern Liturgy—R
Preacher's Magazine—R
PROCLAIM—R
Review for Religious
Today's Christian Preacher—
R

Word & World
Youthworker—R

TEEN/YOUNG ADULT
Certainty
Challenge (IL)
Challenge (TN)—R
Conqueror—R
Devo'Zine—R
On Course—R
Pathways—R
Student Leadership—R
Teenage Christian—R
Teen Life (AG)—R
Teen Power—R
Teens on Target—R
Today's Christian Teen—R
With—R
YOU!—R
Young Salvationist—R
Youth Challenge—R
Zelos—R

WOMEN
CoLaborer—R
Cottage Connections—R
Esprit—R
Helping Hand—R
Horizons
Journey—R
Just Between Us—R
Link & Visitor—R
Sisters Today
Today's Christian Woman
Unique—R
Virtue—R
Wesleyan Woman—R
Woman's Touch—R
Women Alive!—R

DIVORCE

ADULT/GENERAL
America
Angels on Earth
Arlington Catholic
At Ease—R
Banner, The
Believer, The—R
Bible Advocate—R
Canada Lutheran—R
Canadian Baptist
Catholic Digest—R
Catholic Twin Circle—R
Charisma/Christian Life
Christian Chronicle—R
Christian Edge—R
Christian Home & School

Christian Parenting—R
Christian Ranchman
Christian Single—R
Church Advocate—R
Church Herald/Holiness—R
Dovetail—R
Evangel—R
Evangelical Baptist—R
Faith Today
Fidelity—R
Focus on the Family—R
Good News, Etc—R
Good News Journal—R
Home Times—R
Impact Magazine—R
Island Christian—R
John Milton—R
Kansas City Christian—R
Life Gate—R
Liguorian
Lutheran Digest—R
MESSAGE
MESSAGE/Open Bible
Minnesota Christian—R
National Review
New Covenant
New Heart, A—R
New Man—R
New Trumpet—R
Our Family—R
Pentecostal Homelife—R
Plain Truth—R
PrayerWorks—R
Presbyterian Outlook
Presbyterian Record—R
Presbyterians Today—R
Prism—R
Purpose—R
Seek—R
Signs of the Times—R
Single-Parent Family
Standard—R
Standard, The—R
Stand Firm—R
Star of Zion
Table Talk—R
Today's Single—R
United Church Observer
Upsouth—R
U.S. Catholic
VISION (CA)—R
War Cry—R

CHILDREN
Power & Light—R
Touch—R

*CHRISTIAN
EDUCATION/LIBRARY*
CE Counselor—R

MISSIONS
Worldwide Challenge—R

PASTORS/LEADERS
Celebration (SDA)—R
Chicago Studies
Journal/Pastoral Care
Lutheran Partners—R
Ministries Today
Pastoral Life
Ministries Today
Ministry
Pastor's Family
PROCLAIM—R
Single Ad. Ministries Jour.
Word & World

TEEN/YOUNG ADULT
Pathways—R
Straight—R
Teen Life (AG)—R
Young Adult Today
Young Christian—R
Youth 97—R
Youth Update

WOMEN
Aspire
Helping Hand—R
Horizons
Journey—R
Joyful Woman—R
Lutheran Woman Today
Unique—R
Virtue—R
Wesleyan Woman—R
Woman's Touch—R
Women Alive—R

DOCTRINAL

ADULT/GENERAL
America
Anglican Journal—R
At Ease—R
Banner, The
Baptist Beacon—R
Baptist Informer
B.C. Catholic—R
Bible Advocate—R
Biblical Reflections—R
Bread of Life—R
Canadian Baptist
Canadian Catholic

Catholic Digest—R
Catholic Insight
Charisma/Christian Life
Christian Century
Christian Media—R
Christian Renewal—R
Christianity Today—R
Church Herald/Holiness—R
Church of God EVANGEL
Comments/Friends—R
Companions—R
Compass
Conquest
Cornerstone—R
Cresset
Emphasis/Faith & Living—R
Evangelical Baptist—R
Evangelical Friend
Evangelical Visitor—R
Fellowship Link—R
Fidelity—R
First Things
Good News—R
Gospel Today
Hallelujah! (CAN)—R
Hearing Hearts
Indian Life—R
Interim—R
John Milton—R
Kansas City Christian—R
Lutheran Layman
Lutheran Witness—R
MESSAGE
Ministry Today—R
MovieGuide
North American Voice
Our Family—R
Our Sunday Visitor
Perspectives
PrayerWorks—R
Presbyterian Layman
Presbyterian Outlook
Presbyterian Record—R
Presbyterians Today—R
Queen of All Hearts
St. Willibrord Journal
SCP Journal—R
Signs of the Times—R
Silver Wings—R
Social Justice—R
Standard, The—R
Star of Zion
Sunday Digest—R
This Rock
United Church Observer
U.S. Catholic
Upsouth—R
Watchman, The

Way of St. Francis—R

CHILDREN
R-A-D-A-R—R

*CHRISTIAN
EDUCATION/LIBRARY*
CE Counselor—R

MISSION
Intl Jour/Frontier—R
Quiet Hour Echoes
Urban Mission—R
Worldwide Challenge—R

PASTORS/LEADERS
Celebration (SDA)—R
Chicago Studies
Christian Century
Discipleship Training
Homiletic & Pastoral Review
Jour/Biblical Ethics—R
Lutheran Partners—R
Ministries Today
Ministry
Preacher's Magazine—R
Priest, The
PROCLAIM—R
Quarterly Review
Today's Christian Preacher—
   R
Word & World

TEEN/YOUNG ADULT
Certainty
Teenage Christian—R
Today's Christian Teen—R
YOU!—R
Young Adult Today
Youth Update

WOMEN
Lutheran Woman Today
Wesleyan Woman—R

ECONOMICS

ADULT/GENERAL
America
AXIOS—R
Banner, The
Believer, The—R
Biblical Reflections—R
Canadian Catholic
Catholic Forester—R
Catholic Rural Life
Catholic Twin Circle—R
CBA Marketplace

Christian C.L. RECORD—R
Christian Century
Christian Courier (CAN)—R
Christian Ranchman
Christian Retailing—R
Christian Social Action—R
Christianity Today—R
Compass
Covenant Companion—R
Cresset
Disciple's Journal—R
Discovery—R
Evangelical Friend
Expression Christian
Faith Today
Family Network—R
Fidelity—R
First Things
Friends Journal—R
Good News, Etc—R
Good News Journal—R
Home Times—R
Island Christian—R
It's Your Choice—R
Kansas City Christian—R
Life Gate—R
Minnesota Christian—R
MovieGuide
National Review
New Man—R
No-Debt Living—R
Our Sunday Visitor
Pentecostal Homelife—R
Perspectives
Prairie Messenger—R
Presbyterian Layman
Prism—R
Providence—R
Quiet Revolution—R
Salt of the Earth—R
SCP Journal—R
Single-Parent Family
Social Justice—R
Sojourners
Standard, The—R
Stand Firm—R
Star of Zion
Table Talk—R
Today's Christian Senior—R
U.S. Catholic
War Cry—R
Witness, The

MISSIONS
Urban Mission—R
World Vision—R

PASTORS/LEADERS
Celebration (SDA)—R
Christian Century
Christian Ministry
Five Stones, The—R
Jour/Biblical Ethics—R
Today's Christian Preacher—
R
Today's Parish
Word & World

TEEN/YOUNG ADULT
Caleb Issues & Answers
Christteen—R
Today's Christian Teen—R
Young Adult Today
Youth Update

WOMEN
Horizons—R

WRITERS
Writer's Nook News

ENVIRONMENTAL
ISSUES

ADULT/GENERAL
Anglican Journal—R
AXIOS—R
Banner, The
Banner News
Bible Advocate—R
Biblical Reflections—R
Canada Lutheran—R
Canadian Catholic
Catholic Forester—R
Catholic Rural Life
Catholic Sentinel—R
Celebrate Life—R
Christian Century
Christian Courier (CAN)—R
Christian Living—R
Christian Single—R
Christian Social Action—R
Christianity Today—R
Chrysalis Reader
Commonweal
Companion
Compass
Cornerstone—R
Covenant Companion—R
Cresset
Disciple's Journal—R
Emphasis/Faith & Living—R
Evangelical Friend
Faith Today
Fellowship Link—R

Friends Journal—R
Good News Journal—R
Green Cross—R
Herald of Holiness—R
It's Your Choice—R
John Milton—R
Kansas City Christian—R
Liguorian
Lutheran, The—R
Lutheran Digest—R
Mennonite, The—R
Messenger/St. Anthony
Ministry Today—R
Minnesota Christian—R
MovieGuide
National Review
New Thought—R
NW Christian Journal—R
Our Family—R
Our Sunday Visitor
Pegasus Review—R
Plain Truth—R
PrayerWorks—R
Presbyterian Layman
Presbyterian Outlook
Presbyterian Record—R
Presbyterians Today—R
Prism—R
Providence—R
Purpose—R
Salt of the Earth—R
SCP Journal—R
Signs of the Times—R
Sojourners
Standard, The—R
Star of Zion
Table Talk—R
TEAK Roundup—R
Time of Singing—R
Total Health
United Church Observer
Upsouth—R
War Cry—R
Way of St. Francis—R
Witness, The

CHILDREN
Crusader—R
Discovery—R
Focus/Clubhouse
GUIDE—R
My Friend
On the Line—R
Pockets—R
Power & Light—R
Primary Days—R
R-A-D-A-R—R
Skipping Stones

CHRISTIAN
EDUCATION/LIBRARY
Christian School

MISSIONS
World Vision—R

PASTORS/LEADERS
Celebration (SDA)—R
Christian Century
Christian Ministry
Cross Currents—R
Five Stones, The—R
Jour/Biblical Ethics—R
Journal/Christian Camping
Lutheran Partners—R
Word & World
World Vision—R

TEEN/YOUNG ADULT
Caleb Issues & Answers
Challenge (TN)—R
Devo'Zine—R
Listen—R
Pathways—R
Student Leadership—R
Teen Power—R
Transcend
With—R
YOU!—R
Young Adult Today
Young Christian—R
Youth Update

WOMEN
Horizons
Sisters Today

ESSAYS

ADULT/GENERAL
African Amer. Heritage—R
alive now!
Arlington Catholic
AXIOS—R
Banner, The
Biblical Reflections—R
Burning Light—R
Catholic Answer
Catholic Insight
Catholic Parent
Catholic Twin Circle
Christian Advocate—R
Christian Arts Review
Christian Century
Christianity/Arts
Christianity Today—R
Chrysalis Reader

Church & State—R
Church Herald/Holiness—R
Columbia
Commonweal
Companions—R
Compass
Covenant Companion—R
Cresset
Door, The—R
Emphasis/Faith & Living—R
Evangelical Friend
Evangelical Visitor—R
Explorer
Faith Today
Family Journal—R
Fatted Calf Forum—R
Fellowship in Prayer—R
Fidelity—R
First Things
Friends Journal—R
Good News Reporter—R
Green Cross—R
Head to Head—R
Healing Inn—R
Highway News—R
Home Times—R
Inspirer, The—R
It's Your Choice—R
Kansas City Christian—R
Liguorian
Marriage Partnership
Messenger/St. Anthony
Ministry Today—R
MovieGuide
National Catholic
National Review
New Oxford Review
New Thought—R
New Writing—R
Pegasus Review—R
Perspectives
Plenty Good Room
Poetry Forum
Poet's Park—R
PrayerWorks—R
Presbyterian Outlook
Presbyterians Today—R
Prism—R
Ratio
Religious Education
Remembrance—R
Rutherford
SCP Journal—R
Smile
Sojourners
Spiritual Life
TEAK Roundup—R
Touchstone

Upsouth—R
War Cry—R
Way of St. Francis—R
Weavings—R

CHILDREN
Discovery—R
Nature Friend—R

MISSIONS
Areopagus—R
Catholic Near East
PFI World Report—R

MUSIC
Creator—R
Gospel Music

PASTORS/LEADERS
Christian Century
Homiletic & Pastoral Review
Liturgy—R
Pulpit Helps—R
Word & World
Youthworker—R

TEEN/YOUNG ADULT
Christteen—R
Student Leadership—R
Transcend
YOU!—R
Young Adult Today
Youth Focus—R

WOMEN
Cottage Connections—R
DOMESTIQUE—R
Lutheran Woman Today
Proverbs 31 Homemaker—R
Tea and Sunshine
Virtue—R

WRITERS
Byline
Canadian Writer's Jour—R
Inklings
New Writing—R
Once Upon a Time—R
Salt & The Light, The—R
Southwestern Writers—R
Writer's Digest
Writer's Exchange—R
Writer's Infor Network
Writer's Ink—R
Writer's News—R
Writer's Nook News
Writer's World—R

ETHICS

ADULT/GENERAL
Angels on Earth
At Ease—R
Atlantic Baptist
AXIOS—R
Banner, The
Bible Advocate—R
Biblical Reflections—R
Brethren Evangelist
Canadian Catholic
Catholic Digest—R
Catholic Insight
Catholic Parent
Catholic Rural Life
Celebrate Life—R
Christian Advocate—R
Christian Century
Christian Courier (CAN)—R
Christian Edge—R
Christian Media—R
Christian Research
Christianity Today—R
Chrysalis Reader
Church Advocate—R
Church Herald/Holiness—R
Columbia
Commonweal
Companions—R
Compass
Conquest
Covenant Companion—R
Emphasis/Faith & Living—R
Evangelical Baptist—R
Faith Today
Family Journal—R
Fellowship Link—R
Fidelity—R
First Things
Friends Journal—R
Good News, Etc—R
Good News Reporter—R
Head to Head—R
Herald of Holiness—R
Home Times—R
Impact Magazine—R
Indian Life—R
It's Your Choice—R
John Milton—R
Jour/Christian Nursing—R
Journal of Church & State
Kansas City Christian—R
Liguorian
Messenger/St. Anthony
Ministry Today—R
Minnesota Christian—R
Moody—R

MovieGuide
National Review
New Covenant
New Heart, A—R
New Man—R
New Oxford Review
New Thought—R
Our Family—R
Our Sunday Visitor
Pegasus Review—R
Perspectives
Plain Truth—R
Pourastan—R
Prairie Messenger—R
PrayerWorks—R
Presbyterian Layman
Presbyterian Outlook
Prism—R
Purpose—R
Religious Broadcasting—R
Religious Education
Rutherford
St. Anthony Messenger
Seek—R
Social Justice—R
Sojourners
Standard, The—R
Stand Firm—R
United Church Observer
War Cry—R
Way of St. Francis—R
Witness, The

CHILDREN
CLUBHOUSE—R
Discovery—R
High Adventure—R
Skipping Stones
Wonder Time

CHRISTIAN EDUCATION/LIBRARY
CE Connection—R
Vision—R

MISSIONS
Areopagus—R
East-West Church—R
Urban Mission—R
Worldwide Challenge—R

PASTORS/LEADERS
Celebration (SDA)—R
Christian Century
Christian Management—R
Christian Ministry
Cross Currents—R
Ivy Jungle Report—R

Jour/Biblical Ethics—R
Journal/Christian Healing—R
Journal/Pastoral Care
Lutheran Partners—R
Priest, The
PROCLAIM—R
Pulpit Helps—R
Resource—R
Today's Christian Preacher—
   R
Word & World
Youthworker—R

TEEN/YOUNG ADULT
Certainty
Christteen—R
Conqueror—R
Pathways—R
Student Leadership—R
Teen Life (AG)—R
Today's Christian Teen—R
Transcend
With—R
YOU!—R
Youth Update

WOMEN
Conscience—R
Esprit—R
Horizons
Unique—R
Virtue—R
Wesleyan Woman—R

WRITERS
Canadian Writer's Jour—R
Exchange—R
Inklings

ETHNIC/CULTURAL PIECES

ADULT/GENERAL
African Amer. Heritage—R
Arlington Catholic
Banner, The
Baptist Informer
Canadian Baptist
Catholic Digest—R
Catholic Insight
CBA Marketplace
Christian Advocate—R
Christian Century
Christian Edge—R
Christian Living—R
Christian Ranchman
Christian Single—R
Christian Social Action—R

Common Boundary
Cornerstone—R
Discipleship Journal
Dovetail—R
Evangelical Baptist
Faith Today
Fellowship Link—R
First Things
Foursquare World—R
Friends Journal—R
Good News, Etc.—R
Good News Reporter—R
Gospel Today
Green Cross—R
Guideposts
Hallelujah! (CAN)—R
Healing Inn—R
Home Times—R
Impact Magazine—R
Indian Life—R
John Milton—R
Jour/Christian Nursing—R
Journal of Church & State
Lookout—R
Joyful Noise
Lutheran Journal—R
Mennonite Historian—R
MESSAGE
Moody—R
MovieGuide
New Man—R
New Trumpet—R
Northwestern Lutheran—R
Pentecostal Homelife—R
Plenty Good Room
PrayerWorks—R
Presbyterian Outlook
Prism—R
Purpose—R
Religious Broadcasting—R
Rutherford
Salt of the Earth—R
Sojourners
Standard, The—R
Star of Zion
Table Talk—R
TEAK Roundup—R
United Church Observer
Upsouth—R
War Cry—R
Watchman, The

CHILDREN
Discovery—R
Focus/Clubhouse
GUIDE—R
On the Line—R
Power & Light—R

R-A-D-A-R—R
Skipping Stones
Story Friends—R

CHRISTIAN EDUCATION/LIBRARY
CE Counselor—R
Vision—R

MISSIONS
Urban Mission
World Vision—R

PASTORS/LEADERS
Celebration (SDA)—R
Cell Life FORUM—R
Christian Ministry
Five Stones, The—R
Journal/Pastoral Care—R
Liturgy—R
Lutheran Partners—R
Ministries Today
Pastoral Life
Quarterly Review

TEEN/YOUNG ADULT
Certainty
Challenge (TN)—R
Christteen—R
Devo'Zine—R
Insight—R
On Course—R
Pathways—R
Rock, The
Student Leadership—R
Take Five (photos)
Teen Life (AG)—R
With—R
Young Adult Today
Young Christian—R
Young Salvationist—R
Youth Focus—R

WOMEN
Horizons
Link & Visitor—R
Sisters Today
Today's Christian Woman
Virtue—R

WRITERS
Inklings

EVANGELISM/ WITNESSING

ADULT/GENERAL
American Tract Soc.—R

Anglican Journal—R
Annals of St. Anne
At Ease—R
Atlantic Baptist
Banner, The
Banner News
Baptist Beacon—R
Baptist Informer
Bible Advocate—R
Bread of Life—R
Brethren Evangelist
Canadian Baptist
Canadian Catholic
Canadian Lutheran—R
Catholic Digest—R
Catholic Insight
Charisma/Christian Life
Christian Advocate—R
Christian Century
Christian Chronicle (OK)
Christian Courier (WI)—R
Christian Edge—R
Christian Ranchman
Christian Reader—R
Christian Research
Christian Single—R
Church Advocate—R
Church Herald/Holiness—R
Church of God EVANGEL
Comments/Friends—R
Companion
Companions—R
Conquest
Cornerstone—R
Covenant Companion—R
Crossway/Newsline—R
Decision
Discipleship Journal
Emphasis/Faith & Living—R
Evangel—R
Evangelical Baptist—R
Evangelical Friend
Evangelical Visitor—R
Faith Today
Fellowship Link—R
God's Revivalist
Good News, Etc—R
Good News Journal—R
Good News Reporter—R
Gospel Today
Green Cross—R
Hallelujah! (CAN)—R
Healing Inn—R
Hearing Hearts
Herald of Holiness—R
Highway News—R
Indian Life—R
Inland NW Christian

Inspirer, The—R
InterVarsity
Island Christian—R
John Milton—R
Journal/Christian Nursing—R
Kansas City Christian—R
Life Gate—R
Light and Life
Liguorian
Live—R
Living Light News—R
Lutheran, The—R
Lutheran Digest—R
Lutheran Layman
Lutheran Witness—R
Marriage Partnership
MESSAGE/Open Bible
Ministry Today—R
Moody—R
New Covenant
New Heart, A—R
New Man—R
New Oxford Review
New Trumpet—R
New Writing—R
Northwestern Lutheran—R
Our Family—R
Pentecostal Evangel
Pentecostal Testimony—R
Plain Truth—R
Poet's Park—R
Power for Living—R
PrayerWorks—R
Presbyterian Layman
Presbyterian Record—R
Presbyterians Today—R
Prism—R
Purpose—R
Pursuit—R
Queen of All Hearts
Religious Education
Revelation Post—R
SCP Journal—R
Seek—R
Shantyman, The—R
Sharing—R
Silver Wings—R
Sojourners
Something Better—R
Standard—R
Standard, The—R
Stand Firm—R
Star of Zion
Sunday Digest—R
This Rock
Today's Christian Senior—R
United Church Observer
Upsouth—R

U.S. Catholic
Vision—R
Vision, The—R
Voice, The—R
War Cry—R
Watchman, The
Way of St. Francis—R
Wesleyan Advocate—R

CHILDREN
BREAD/God's Children—R
Club Connection—R
Counselor—R
Courage
Discovery—R
Focus/Clubhouse
GUIDE—R
Kids' Stuff—R
Power & Light—R
Primary Days—R
Primary Pal
R-A-D-A-R—R
Touch—R

CHRISTIAN EDUCATION/LIBRARY
Brigade Leader—R
CE Connection—R
CE Counselor—R
Church Educator—R
Church Media Library—R
Evangelizing Today's Child—R
Resource—R
Shining Star—R
Teacher's Interaction

MISSIONS
American Horizon—R
Great Commission—R
Intl Jour/Frontier—R
Leaders for Today
Message of the Cross—R
Missiology
Mission Today—R
Partners
Quiet Hour Echoes
Save Our World—R
Urban Mission—R
World Christian—R
World Mission People—R
World Vision—R
Worldwide Challenge—R

MUSIC
Quest—R

PASTORS/LEADERS
Celebration (SDA)—R
Cell Church—R
Cell Life FORUM—R
Christian Recreation
Church Administration
Church Growth Network—R
Discipleship Training
Eucharistic Minister—R
Evangelism—R
Evangelism USA
Five Stones, The—R
Jour/Amer Soc/Chur Growth
Journal/Christian Healing—R
Lutheran Forum—R
Lutheran Partners—R
Ministries Today
Networks—R
Preacher's Magazine—R
Priest, The
PROCLAIM—R
Pulpit Helps—R
Resource—R
Review for Religious
Sermon Notes
Today's Christian Preacher—R
Voice of the Vineyard —R
Youthworker—R

TEEN/YOUNG ADULT
Certainty
Challenge (IL)
Christteen—R
Conqueror—R
Devo'Zine—R
On Course—R
Pathways—R
Straight—R
Student Leadership—R
Teenage Christian—R
Teen Life (AG)—R
Teen Power—R
Teens on Target—R
Today's Christian Teen—R
With—R
YOU!—R
Young Adult Today
Young Christian—R
Youth Challenge—R
Zelos—R

WOMEN
CoLaborer
Cottage Connections—R
Helping Hand—R
Horizons—R
Journey—R

Joyful Woman—R
Just Between Us—R
Link & Visitor—R
Lutheran Woman Today
Proverbs 31 Homemaker—R
Sisters Today
Today's Christian Woman
Virtue—R
Wesleyan Woman—R
Woman's Touch—R

WRITERS
Southwestern Writers—R

FAMILY LIFE

ADULT/GENERAL
Alive!—R (grandparenting)
America
American Tract Soc.—R
Angels on Earth
Annals of St. Anne
Arlington Catholic
At Ease—R
Atlantic Baptist
AXIOS—R
Banner, The
Baptist Beacon—R
Baptist Informer
B.C. Catholic—R
Bible Advocate—R
Biblical Reflections—R
Bread of Life—R
Brethren Evangelist
Canada Lutheran—R
Canadian Baptist
Canadian Catholic
Catholic Digest—R
Catholic Forester—R
Catholic Insight
Catholic Parent
Catholic Twin Circle—R
Celebrate Life—R
Changes
Charisma/Christian Life
Chesapeake Citizen
Christian Advocate—R
Christian C.L. RECORD—R
Christian Courier (WI)—R
Christian Courier (CAN)—R
Christian Edge—R
Christian Home & School
Christian Living—R
Christian Parenting—R
Christian Ranchman
Christian Reader—R
Christian Renewal—R
Christian Social Action—R

Church Advocate—R
Church Herald/Holiness—R
Church of God EVANGEL
Columbia
Companion
Companions—R
Connecting Point—R
Conquest
Covenant Companion—R
Disciple's Journal—R
Decision
Dovetail—R
Emphasis/Faith & Living—R
Evangel—R
Evangelical Baptist—R
Evangelical Friend
Evangelical Visitor—R
Explorer
Expression Christian
Faith Today
Family Digest—R
Family Journal—R
Family Network—R
Fellowship in Prayer—R
Fellowship Link—R
Fellowship Today—R
Fidelity—R
Focus on the Family—R
Foursquare World—R
Gem, The—R
God's Revivalist
Good News, Etc—R
Good News Journal
Good News Reporter—R
Gospel Tidings—R
Head to Head—R
Healing Inn—R
Hearing Hearts
Herald of Holiness—R
Highway News—R
Home Life—R
Homeschooling Today
Home Times—R
Ideals—R
Impact Magazine—R
Indian Life—R
Inland NW Christian
Interim—R
Island Christian—R
It's Your Choice—R
John Milton—R
Kansas City Christian—R
LA Catholic Agitator
Life Gate—R
Light and Life
Liguorian
Live—R
Living—R

Living with Teenagers—R
Lookout—R
Lutheran, The—R
Lutheran Digest—R
Lutheran Journal—R
Lutheran Layman
Lutheran Witness—R
Marriage Partnership
Mature Years—R
Mennonite, The—R
Mennonite Brethren—R
MESSAGE
MESSAGE/Open Bible
Messenger
Messenger/St. Anthony
Ministry Today—R
Minnesota Christian—R
Moody—R
New Man—R
New Oxford Review
Northwestern Lutheran—R
Our Family—R
Our Sunday Visitor
ParentLife—R
Parent Paper, The
Pegasus Review—R
Pentecostal Evangel
Pentecostal Homelife—R
Pentecostal Testimony—R
Plain Truth—R
Plus—R
Positive Living—R
Pourastan—R
Power for Living—R
Prairie Messenger—R
PrayerWorks—R
Presbyterian Layman
Presbyterian Record—R
Presbyterians Today—R
Progress—R
Purpose—R
Religious Education
  Remembrance—R
St. Anthony Messenger
Seek—R
Signs of the Times—R
Smart Dads
Social Justice—R
Sojourners
Standard—R
Standard, The—R
Stand Firm—R
Star of Zion
Sunday Digest—R
Table Talk—R
TEAK Roundup—R
Time of Singing—R
Today's Christian Senior—

R(grandparenting)
Today's Family Matters—R
United Church Observer
Upsouth—R
U.S. Catholic
Vibrant Life—R
VISION (CA)—R
Vision, The—R
War Cry—R
Way of St. Francis—R
Wesleyan Advocate—R

CHILDREN
BREAD/God's Children—R
Club Connection—R
CLUBHOUSE—R
Courage
Discovery—R
Focus/Clubhouse
GUIDE—R
Guideposts for Kids
High Adventure—R
Junior Trails—R
My Friend
On the Line—R
Power & Light—R
R-A-D-A-R—R
Skipping Stones
Story Friends—R
Touch—R
Wonder Time

CHRISTIAN
EDUCATION/LIBRARY
Brigade Leader—R
Caravan
CE Connection—R
CE Counselor—R
Church Educator—R
GROUP
Shining Star
Teacher's Interaction

MISSIONS
American Horizon—R
Childlife—R
Quiet Hour Echoes
World Christian—R
Worldwide Challenge—R

MUSIC
Tradition—R

PASTORS/LEADERS
Celebration (SDA)—R
Cell Life FORUM—R
Chicago Studies
Christian Recreation

Diaconalogue—R
Five Stones, The—R
GROUP's Jr. High
Journal/Christian Healing—R
Leadership Journal—R
Lutheran Partners—R
Ministries Today
Networks—R
Pastor's Family
Preacher's Illus. Service—R
PROCLAIM—R
Pulpit Helps—R
Sunday School Leader
Today's Christian Preacher—R
Today's Parish
Voice of the Vineyard —R
Word & World
Youthworker—R

TEEN/YOUNG ADULT
Breakaway—R
Certainty
Challenge (IL)
Christteen—R
Conqueror—R
Devo'Zine—R
On Course—R
Pathways—R
Straight—R
Teen Life (AG)—R
Teens on Target—R
Today's Christian Teen—R
Transcend
With—R
YOU!—R
Young Adult Today
Young Christian—R
Youth Challenge—R
Youth 97—R

WOMEN
Aspire
CoLaborer
DOMESTIQUE—R
Esprit—R
Helping Hand—R
Horizons
Journey—R
Just Between Us—R
Link & Visitor—R
Lutheran Woman's Quar.
Lutheran Woman Today
Proverbs 31 Homemaker—R
Tea and Sunshine
Today's Christian Woman
Unique—R
Virtue—R

Welcome Home
Wesleyan Woman—R
Woman's Touch—R
Women Alive!—R

WRITERS
Housewife-Writer—R
Southwestern Writers—R
Writer's World—R

FILLERS: ANECDOTES

ADULT/GENERAL
African Amer. Heritage—R
Alive!—R
Angels on Earth
AXIOS—R
Catholic Digest—R
Christian Advocate—R
CBA Frontline
CBA Marketplace
Christian Arts Review
Christian Chronicle (PA)—R
Christian Courier (WI)—R
Christian Edge—R
Christian Info. Assoc.—R
Christian Ranchman
Christian Reader—R
Church Herald/Holiness—R
Church of God EVANGEL
Companion
Companions—R
Conquest
Decision
Disciple's Journal—R
Dovetail—R
Explorer
Family Digest—R
Family Network—R
Foursquare World—R
Good News Reporter—R
Guideposts
Head to Head—R
Healing Inn—R
Home Times—R
Impact Magazine—R
Inspirer, The—R
Island Christian—R
Jewel Among Jewels—R
John Milton—R
Kansas City Christian—R
Life Gate—R
Liguorian
Live—R
Living—R
Living with Teenagers—R
Lutheran Digest—R
Lutheran Journal—R

Mature Living
Mennonite, The—R
New Heart, A—R
New Trumpet—R
Our Family—R
ParentLife—R
Plowman, The—R
Pourastan—R
Presbyterian Record—R
Presbyterians Today—R
Purpose—R
Sunday Digest—R
Table Talk—R
TEAK Roundup—R
Today's Family Matters—R

CHILDREN
Club Connection—R
CLUBHOUSE—R
Discovery—R
High Adventure—R
Skipping Stones

*CHRISTIAN
EDUCATION/LIBRARY*
Christian School
Christian Librarian—R
Religion Teacher's Journal
Shining Star
Teachers in Focus—R
Vision—R

MUSIC
Church Pianist, etc.
Creator—R
Gospel Music
Tradition

PASTORS/LEADERS
Art+Plus
Cell Life FORUM—R
Christian Management—R
Christian Ministry
Eucharistic Minister—R
Five Stones, The—R
Ivy Jungle Report—R
Journal/Christian Healing—R
Leadership Journal—R
Pastor's Family
Preacher's Magazine—R
Pulpit Helps—R
Resource—R
Voice of the Vineyard —R
Worship Leader—R

TEEN/YOUNG ADULT
Christteen—R
Pathways—R

YOU!—R
Young Christian—R
Young Salvationist—R
Youth 97—R

WOMEN
CoLaborer
Cottage Connections—R
DOMESTIQUE—R
Esprit—R
Just Between Us—R
Proverbs 31 Homemaker—R
Today's Christian Woman
Woman's Touch—R

WRITERS
Byline
Cross & Quill—R
Canadian Writer's Jour—R
Christian Response—R
Felicity—R
Housewife-Writer—R
Once Upon a Time—R
Southwestern Writers—R
Tickled by Thunder—R
Writer's Digest
Writer's Exchange—R
Writer's Resource—R
Write Touch—R

FILLERS: CARTOONS

ADULT/GENERAL
Alive!—R
alive now!
Angels on Earth
At Ease—R
AXIOS—R
Banner, The
Catholic Forester—R
CBA Frontline
CBA Marketplace
Christian Advocate—R
Christian Chronicle (PA)—R
Christian Computing—R
Christian Edge—R
Christian Information
Christian Ranchman
Commonweal
Companion
Connecting Point—R
Covenant Companion—R
Dawn & Dusk
Disciple's Journal—R
Door, The
Dovetail—R
Evangel—R
Faith Today

Family Network—R
Fidelity—R
Foursquare World—R
Good News Journal—R
Good News Reporter—R
Green Cross—R
Head to Head—R
Hearing Hearts
Herald of Holiness—R
Highway News—R
Home Life—R
Home Times—R
Impact Magazine—R
Inside Journal
Inspirer, The—R
Jewel Among Jewels—R
Kansas City Christian—R
Living—R
Living with Teenagers—R
Lookout—R
Lutheran, The—R
Lutheran Digest—R
Lutheran Journal—R
Lutheran Witness—R
Marriage Partnership
Mature Living
Mature Years—R
Mennonite, The—R
National Review
New Heart, A—R
New Trumpet—R
Our Family—R
ParentLife—R
Pegasus Review—R
Pentecostal Testimony—R
Physician
Power for Living—R
Presbyterian Record—R
Presbyterians Today—R
Providence—R
Purpose—R
Pursuit—R
Rutherford
Sojourners
Standard—R
Standard, The—R
Table Talk—R
TEAK Roundup—R
Today's Family Matters—R
Touchstone

CHILDREN
Club Connection—R
CLUBHOUSE—R
Crusader—R
Discoveries—R
Focus/Clubhouse Jr
GUIDE—R

High Adventure—R
My Friend
On the Line—R
Power & Light—R
R-A-D-A-R—R
Skipping Stones
Touch—R

*CHRISTIAN
EDUCATION/LIBRARY*
Baptist Leader—R
CE Counselor—R
Christian Librarian—R
Journal/Adventist Educ.—R
Leader/Church School To-
    day—R
Team—R
Today's Catholic Teacher—R
Vision—R

MUSIC
Christian Country—R
Church Pianist, etc.
Creator—R
Glory Songs—R
Gospel Music
Senior Musician—R

PASTORS/LEADERS
Art+Plus
Celebration (SDA)—R
Cell Life FORUM—R
Christian Century
Christian Management—R
Christian Ministry
Christian Sentinel
Clergy Journal—R
Diocesan Dialogue—R
Eucharistic Minister—R
Five Stones, The—R
Ivy Jungle Report—R
Journal/Christian Camping
Leadership Journal—R
Pastor's Family
Preacher's Magazine—R
Preaching
Priest, The
Reformed Worship
Resource—R
Sermon Notes
Voice of the Vineyard —R
WCA Monthly—R

TEEN/YOUNG ADULT
Breakaway—R
Brio
Campus Life—R
Christteen—R

Insight—R
Listen—R
On Course—R
Pathways—R
Teenage Christian—R
Teen Life (AG)—R
Teen Power—R
With—R
YOU!—R
Young Christian—R
Young Salvationist—R

WOMEN
Esprit—R
Horizons
Joyful Woman—R
Just Between Us—R
Proverbs 31 Homemaker—R
Today's Christian Woman
Wesleyan Woman—R
Women Alive!—R

WRITERS
Byline
Canadian Writer's Jour—R
Cross & Quill—R
Felicity—R
Heaven—R
Housewife-Writer—R
New Writing—R
NW Christian Author—R
Once Upon a Time—R
Writer's Exchange—R

FILLERS: FACTS

ADULT/GENERAL
African Amer. Heritage—R
Alive!—R
Angels on Earth
AXIOS—R
Bible Advocate—R
Bread of Life—R
CBA Frontline
CBA Marketplace
Christian Advocate—R
Christian Arts Review
Christian Chronicle (PA)—R
Christian Courier (WI)—R
Christian Edge—R
Christian Information
Christian Ranchman
Christian Reader—R
Christian Single—R
Church Herald/Holiness—R
Companions—R
Cornerstone—R
Disciple's Journal—R

Family Network—R
God's Revivalist
Good News Reporter—R
Hallelujah! (CAN)—R
Head to Head—R
Healing Inn—R
Inspirer, The—R
It's Your Choice—R
Jewel Among Jewels—R
Life Gate—R
Live—R
Lutheran Digest—R
Lutheran Journal—R
Mature Living
Mennonite, The—R
MESSAGE
New Man—R
New Trumpet—R
PrayerWorks—R
Presbyterian Record—R
Revelation Post—R
Standard, The—R

CHILDREN
Club Connection—R
Focus/Clubhouse
GUIDE—R
Guideposts for Kids
High Adventure—R
Junior Trails—R
On the Line—R
R-A-D-A-R—R
Skipping Stones
Story Friends—R

*CHRISTIAN
EDUCATION/LIBRARY*
Shining Star
Today's Catholic Teacher—R
Vision—R

MISSIONS
Save Our World—R

PASTORS/LEADERS
Christian Ministry
Church Management—R
Ivy Jungle Report—R
Journal/Christian Healing—R
Single Ad. Ministries Jour.
Voice of the Vineyard —R

TEEN/YOUNG ADULT
Breakaway—R
Brio
Campus Life—R
Certainty
Christteen—R

Insight—R
Student Leadership—R
Teen Life (AG)—R
YOU!—R
Young Christian—R
Young Salvationist—R
Youth 97—R

WOMEN
Cottage Connections—R
DOMESTIQUE—R
Wesleyan Woman—R

WRITERS
Christian Response—R
Cross & Quill—R
Gotta Write
Once Upon a Time—R
Southwestern Writers—R
Writers Connection
Writer's Exchange—R
Writer's Nook News
Writer's Resource—R
Write Touch—R

FILLERS: GAMES

ADULT/GENERAL
Alive!—R
Angels on Earth
Banner News
Catholic Digest—R
Catholic Forester—R
Christian Edge—R
Christian Ranchman
Christian Recreation
Connecting Point—R
Disciple's Journal—R
Family Network—R
Good News Journal—R
Good News Reporter—R
Head to Head—R
Healing Inn—R
Hearing Hearts
Inspirer, The—R
Living—R
Mature Living
Smart Dads
Table Talk—R

CHILDREN
Club Connection—R
CLUBHOUSE—R
Counselor—R
Courage
Crusader—R
Discoveries—R
Discovery—R

Focus/Clubhouse
Focus/Clubhouse Jr
GUIDE—R
Guideposts for Kids
High Adventure—R
Listen
On the Line—R
Pockets—R
Power & Light—R
Primary Days—R
Primary Pal
R-A-D-A-R—R
Skipping Stones
Story Friends—R
Together Time
Touch—R

CHRISTIAN EDUCATION/LIBRARY
CE Counselor—R
Perspective—R
Religion Teacher's Journal
Shining Star
Voice of the Vineyard —R

TEEN/YOUNG ADULT
Challenge (IL)
Conqueror—R
Listen—R
Pathways—R
Student Leadership—R
YOU!—R
Young Salvationist—R

FILLERS: IDEAS

ADULT/GENERAL
Alive!—R
Angels on Earth
Catholic Parent
CBA Frontline
CBA Marketplace
Christian Chronicle (PA)—R
Christian Edge—R
Christian Info. Assoc. —R
Christian Ranchman
Church of God EVANGEL
Conquest
Disciple's Journal—R
Dovetail—R
Family Network—R
God's Revivalist
Good News Reporter—R
Head to Head—R
Healing Inn—R
Hearing Hearts
Inspirer, The—R
It's Your Choice—R

Jewel Among Jewels—R
Kansas City Christian—R
New Man—R
New Thought—R
New Trumpet—R
ParentLife—R
Pourastan—R
Presbyterian Record—R
St. Joseph's Messenger—R
Seek—R
Smart Dads
Standard, The—R
Table Talk—R
TEAK Roundup—R

CHILDREN
Club Connection—R
Discovery—R
Focus/Clubhouse
High Adventure—R
Listen
Pockets—R
Skipping Stones
Together Time
Touch—R

CHRISTIAN EDUCATION/LIBRARY
CE Counselor—R
Church Worship
Parish Teacher—R
Religion Teacher's Journal
Shining Star
Teacher's Interaction
Team—R
Vision—R

MUSIC
Creator—R
Glory Songs—R
Senior Musician—R

PASTORS/LEADERS
Cell Life FORUM—R
Five Stones, The—R
Journal/Christian Healing—R
Leadership Journal—R
Lutheran Partners—R
Preacher's Illus. Service—R
Preacher's Magazine—R
Single Ad. Ministries Jour.
Voice of the Vineyard —R
WCA Monthly—R

TEEN/YOUNG ADULT
Brio
Campus Life—R
Certainty

Challenge (TN)—R
Christteen—R
YOU!—R
Young Christian—R

WOMEN
CoLaborer
Proverbs 31 Homemaker—R
Woman's Touch—R

WRITERS
Canadian Writer's Jour—R
Felicity—R
Just Between Us—R
Housewife-Writer—R
New Writing—R
Southwestern Writers—R
Tickled by Thunder—R
VA Christian Writer—R
Writers Connection (tips)
Writer's Exchange—R
Writer's Ink—R
Write Touch—R
Writing Right—R

FILLERS: JOKES

ADULT/GENERAL
Alive!—R
Angels on Earth
Catholic Digest—R
Christian Ranchman
Disciple's Journal—R
Family Network—R
Good News Reporter—R
Healing Inn—R
Home Times—R
Impact Magazine—R
Inspirer, The—R
Liguorian
Lutheran, The—R
Lutheran Digest—R
Lutheran Journal—R
Mature Years—R
New Heart, A—R
New Trumpet—R
Our Family—R
PrayerWorks—R
Seek—R
Standard, The—R

CHILDREN
Club Connection—R
CLUBHOUSE—R
Discovery—R
Guideposts for Kids
High Adventure—R
My Friend

On the Line—R
Pockets—R (& riddles)
Power & Light—R
R-A-D-A-R—R
Skipping Stones

CHRISTIAN
EDUCATION/LIBRARY
Baptist Leader—R

MUSIC
Creator—R
Tradition

PASTORS/LEADERS
Art+Plus
Cell Life FORUM—R
Five Stones, The—R
Ivy Jungle Report—R
Journal/Christian Healing—R
Preacher's Illus. Service—R
Voice of the Vineyard—R

TEEN/YOUNG ADULT
Christteen—R
Pathways—R
Teen Power—R
YOU!—R

WOMEN
DOMESTIQUE—R
Horizons
Joyful Woman—R

WRITERS
Felicity—R
Housewife-Writer—R
Writer's Exchange—R
Writer's News—R

FILLERS: NEWSBREAKS

ADULT/GENERAL
Angels on Earth
Anglican Journal—R
Arkansas Catholic
B.C. Catholic—R
Canada Lutheran—R
Catholic Telegraph
CBA Frontline
CBA Marketplace
Celebrate Life—R
Christian Arts Review
Christian Courier (WI)—R
Christian Edge—R
Christian Information
Christian Living—R
Christian Ranchman

Christian Renewal—R
Christian Single—R
Common Boundary
Disciple's Journal—R
Family Network—R
Good News Reporter—R
Green Cross—R
Hallelujah! (CAN)—R
Head to Head—R
Healing Inn—R
Home Times—R
Indian Life—R
Inspirer, The—R
Interim—R
Jewel Among Jewels—R
Kansas City Christian—R
Mennonite Weekly
Religious Broadcasting—R
Standard, The—R
TEAK Roundup—R

CHILDREN
Club Connection—R
GUIDE—R
Skipping Stones

CHRISTIAN
EDUCATION/LIBRARY
Christian Librarian—R
Vision—R

MISSIONS
Save Our World—R

PASTORS/LEADERS
Christian Management—R
Christian Ministry, The
Ivy Jungle Report—R
Journal/Christian Healing—R
Preacher's Illus. Service—R
Single Ad. Ministries Jour.
Voice of the Vineyard—R

TEEN/YOUNG ADULT
Certainty
YOU!—R
Young Christian—R

WOMEN
Conscience—R
Joyful Woman—R
Wesleyan Woman—R

WRITERS
Gotta Write
Southwestern Writers—R
Writers Connection
Writer's Exchange—R

Writer's Ink—R
Writer's Nook News
Writer's Resource—R
Writing Right—R

FILLERS: PARTY IDEAS

ADULT/GENERAL
Christian Ranchman
Family Network—R
Good News Reporter—R
Head to Head—R
Hearing Hearts
Living with Teenagers—R
ParentLife—R
Standard, The—R
TEAK Roundup—R

CHILDREN
Club Connection—R
Focus/Clubhouse
On the Line—R
Story Friends—R
Young Christian—R

CHRISTIAN
EDUCATION/LIBRARY
Perspective—R
Team—R

MUSIC
Creator—R
Glory Songs
Senior Musician—R

TEEN/YOUNG ADULT
Conqueror—R
Student Leadership—R
YOU!—R
Young Christian—R

WOMEN
CoLaborer
Proverbs 31 Homemaker—R

FILLERS: PRAYERS

ADULT/GENERAL
alive now!
Angels on Earth
Bible Advocate—R
Catholic Digest—R
Christian Living—R
Christian Ranchman
Disciple's Journal—R
Explorer
Family Network—R
Good News Reporter—R

Green Cross—R
Head to Head—R
Healing Inn—R
Inspirer, The—R
Jewel Among Jewels—R
John Milton—R
Liguorian
Mature Years—R
New Trumpet—R
Plowman, The—R
Pourastan—R
PrayerWorks—R
Presbyterian Record—R

CHILDREN
On the Line—R
Pockets—R
Primary Pal
R-A-D-A-R—R

CHRISTIAN
EDUCATION/LIBRARY
Baptist Leader—R
Religion Teacher's Journal
Teacher's Interaction
Vision—R

PASTORS/LEADERS
Art+Plus
Church Management—R
Preacher, The
Reformed Worship

TEEN/YOUNG ADULT
Christteen—R
Pathways—R
Straight—R
Teenage Christian—R
YOU!—R
Young Christian—R
Young Salvationist—R

WOMEN
Anna's Journal—R
CoLaborer
Cottage Connections—R
Esprit—R
Horizons
Journey—R
Joyful Woman—R
Just Between Us—R
Proverbs 31 Homemaker—R
Unique—R

WRITERS
Cross & Quill—R
Southwestern Writers—R
Writer's Infor Network

FILLERS: PROSE

ADULT/GENERAL
Angels on Earth
Bible Advocate—R
Bread of Life—R
Broken Streets—R
Christian Ranchman
Christian Single—R
Church Herald/Holiness—R
Companions—R
Conquest
Decision
Discovery—R
Explorer
Family Network—R
God's Revivalist
Good News Reporter—R
Hallelujah! (CAN)—R
Head to Head—R
Healing Inn—R
Inspirer, The—R
Jewel Among Jewels—R
Liguorian
Live—R
New Man—R
New Thought—R
New Trumpet—R
Plowman, The—R
Presbyterian Record—R
Presbyterians Today—R
Standard, The—R
Sunday Digest—R
TEAK Roundup—R
Wesleyan Advocate—R

CHILDREN
CLUBHOUSE—R
Courage

CHRISTIAN
EDUCATION/LIBRARY
Vision—R

PASTORS/LEADERS
Church Management—R
Preacher's Illus. Service—R
Pulpit Helps—R

TEEN/YOUNG ADULT
Brio
Certainty
Christteen—R
Conqueror—R
Pathways—R
Teen Power—R
YOU!—R

WOMEN
Anna's Journal—R
Cottage Connections—R
DOMESTIQUE—R
Esprit—R
Proverbs 31 Homemaker—R
Tea and Sunshine
Today's Christian Woman

WRITERS
Chip Off Writer's Block—R
Southwestern Writers—R
Writer's Exchange—R
Write Touch—R

FILLERS: QUIZZES

ADULT/GENERAL
Alive!—R
Angels on Earth
Catholic Digest—R
Catholic Forester—R
Christian Ranchman
Companions—R
Door, The
Family Network—R
Good News Journal—R
Good News Reporter—R
Healing Inn—R
Hearing Hearts
Impact Magazine—R
Inspirer, The—R
Jewel Among Jewels—R
Living—R
Mature Living
MESSAGE
New Man—R
New Trumpet—R
St. Willibrord Journal

CHILDREN
Club Connection—R
Discoveries—R
Discovery—R
Focus/Clubhouse
GUIDE—R
Guideposts for Kids
High Adventure—R
On the Line—R
Partners—R
R-A-D-A-R—R
Skipping Stones
Story Mates—R
Touch—R
Young Christian—R

CHRISTIAN EDUCATION/LIBRARY
CE Counselor—R

MUSIC
Glory Songs—R
Senior Musician—R

PASTORS/LEADERS
Art+Plus
Ivy Jungle Report—R
Voice of the Vineyard —R

TEEN/YOUNG ADULT
Breakaway—R
Brio
Certainty
Conqueror—R
Insight—R
Listen—R
Student Leadership—R
Teenage Christian—R
Teen Power—R
Teens on Target—R
YOU!—R
Young Christian—R
Young Salvationist—R
Youth Challenge—R

WOMEN
Esprit—R

WRITERS
Felicity—R
Southwestern Writers—R
Writer's Infor Network
Writer's Ink—R

FILLERS: QUOTES

ADULT/GENERAL
Angels on Earth
Bible Advocate—R
Bread of Life—R
Catholic Digest—R
Christian Arts Review
Christian Chronicle (PA)—R
Christian Edge—R
Christian Information
Christian Ranchman
Christian Single—R
Church Herald/Holiness—R
Companion
Disciple's Journal—R
Family Network—R
Feelings Quarterly—R
Fidelity—R
Good News Journal—R

Good News Reporter—R
Guideposts
Hallelujah! (CAN)—R
Head to Head—R
Healing Inn—R
Home Times—R
Inspirer, The—R
It's Your Choice—R
Jewel Among Jewels—R
Kansas City Christian—R
Lutheran Journal—R
New Man—R
New Thought—R
New Trumpet—R
Pourastan—R
PrayerWorks—R
Revelation Post—R
Seek—R
Smart Dads
Smile

CHILDREN
Skipping Stones

CHRISTIAN EDUCATION/LIBRARY
Christian Library Jour.—R
Shining Star

PASTORS/LEADERS
Christian Management—R
Ivy Jungle Report—R
Journal/Christian Healing—R
Pastor's Family
Pulpit Helps—R
Single Adult Min Journal
Voice of the Vineyard —R
Worship Leader

TEENS/YOUNG ADULTS
Christteen—R
Insight—R
YOU!—R
Young Christian—R

WOMEN
Anna's Journal—R
Cottage Connections—R
Joyful Woman—R
Just Between Us—R
Proverbs 31 Homemaker—R

WRITERS
Christian Response—R
Southwestern Writers—R
Writer's Exchange—R
Writer's Infor Network
Writer's Ink—R

FILLERS: SHORT HUMOR

ADULT/GENERAL
Alive!—R
Angels on Earth
Catholic Digest—R
CBA Frontline
CBA Marketplace
Christian Chronicle (PA)—R
Christian Edge—R
Christian Ranchman
Christian Reader—R
Companion
Covenant Companion—R
Disciple's Journal—R
Door, The
Dovetail—R
Evangel—R
Evangelical Baptist
Family Network—R
Friends Journal—R
Gem, The
God's Revivalist
Good News Reporter—R
Guideposts
Head to Head—R
Healing Inn—R
Home Life—R
Home Times—R
Impact Magazine—R
Inspirer, The—R
Jewel Among Jewels—R
John Milton—R
Kansas City Christian—R
Liguorian
Live—R
Living—R
Living with Teenagers—R
Lutheran, The—R
Lutheran Digest—R
Lutheran Journal—R
Lutheran Witness—R
Mature Living
New Heart, A—R
New Trumpet—R
Our Family—R
Pourastan—R
PrayerWorks—R
Presbyterian Record—R
Presbyterians Today—R
Purpose—R
St. Willibrord Journal
Seek—R
Smile
Standard, The—R
Star of Zion
TEAK Roundup—R

Today's Family Matters—R

CHILDREN
Club Connection—R
Crusader Magazine (MI)
Discovery—R
Focus/Clubhouse
GUIDE—R
Guideposts for Kids
Junior Trails—R
Power & Light—R
Touch—R

CHRISTIAN EDUCATION/LIBRARY
Christian Librarian—R
Teachers in Focus
Team—R

MUSIC
Christian Country—R
Creator—R
Glory Songs—R
Senior Musician—R

PASTORS/LEADERS
Art+Plus
Celebration (SDA)—R
Christian Management—R
Eucharistic Minister—R
Five Stones, The—R
Ivy Jungle Report—R
Journal/Christian Healing—R
Leadership Journal—R
Preacher's Illus. Service—R
Pulpit Helps—R
Resource—R
Sermon Notes
Voice of the Vineyard —R

TEEN/YOUNG ADULT
Brio
Campus Life—R
Certainty
Christteen—R
Insight—R
Pathways—R
Straight—R
Teen Life (AG)—R
Teen Power—R
YOU!—R
Young Christian—R
Young Salvationist—R

WOMEN
CoLaborer
Cottage Connections—R
DOMESTIQUE—R

Esprit—R
Horizons
Journey—R
Joyful Woman—R
Just Between Us—R
Proverbs 31 Homemaker—R
Tea and Sunshine
Unique—R

WRITERS
Byline
Canadian Writer's Jour—R
Housewife-Writer—R
Once Upon a Time
Southwestern Writers—R
Tickled by Thunder—R
Writer's Digest
Writer's Exchange—R
Writer's World—R
Write Touch—R

FILLERS: WORD PUZZLES

ADULT/GENERAL
Alive!—R
Catholic Forester—R
Christian Edge—R
Christian Ranchman
Companion
Connecting Point—R
Conquest
Covenant Companion—R
Disciple's Journal—R
Evangel—R
Family Network—R
Friends Journal—R
Good News Journal—R
Good News Reporter—R
Head to Head—R
Healing Inn—R
Hearing Hearts
Impact Magazine—R
Inspirer, The—R
Jewel Among Jewels—R
Living—R
Mature Living
Mature Years—R
Power for Living—R
Standard—R
Today's Single

CHILDREN
Club Connection—R
CLUBHOUSE—R
Counselor—R
Courage
Crusader—R

Focus/Clubhouse
Focus/Clubhouse Jr
GUIDE—R
Guideposts for Kids
High Adventure—R
On the Line—R
Our Little Friend—R
Partners—R
Pockets—R
Power & Light—R
Primary Days—R
Primary Pal
R-A-D-A-R—R
Skipping Stones
Story Friends—R
Story Mates—R
Touch—R
Young Christian—R

CHRISTIAN EDUCATION/LIBRARY
Parish Teacher—R
Shining Star
Voice of the Vineyard —R

MUSIC
Young Musicians

TEEN/YOUNG ADULT
Certainty
Challenge (IL)
Challenge (TN)—R
Conqueror—R
Listen—R
Pathways—R
Teenage Christian—R
Teen Power—R
Teens on Target—R
YOU!—R
Young Christian—R
Young Salvationist—R
Youth Challenge—R

WOMEN
Esprit—R
Horizons

WRITERS
Felicity—R
Heaven—R
Southwestern Writers—R

FOOD/RECIPES

ADULT/GENERAL
AXIOS—R
Catholic Forester—R
Catholic Parent

Christian C.L. RECORD—R
Christian Single—R
Disciple's Journal—R
Dovetail—R
Family Network—R
Fellowship Link—R
Good News Reporter—R
Healing Inn—R
Home Life—R
Home Times—R
Ideals—R
John Milton—R
Living—R
Living with Teenagers—R
Lutheran Digest—R
Lutheran Journal—R
Mature Living
MESSAGE
National Review
ParentLife—R
Parent Paper, The
Progress—R
Providence—R
Standard, The—R
Table Talk—R
Today's Christian Senior—R
Today's Family Matters—R
Vibrant Life—R

CHILDREN
Club Connection—R
CLUBHOUSE—R
Discovery—R
Focus/Clubhouse
Focus/Clubhouse Jr.
Listen
On the Line—R
Pockets—R (recipes)
Skipping Stones
Together Time

MISSIONS
World Mission People—R
Young Christian—R

MUSIC
Gospel Music

WOMEN
Aspire
DOMESTIQUE—R
Helping Hand—R
Proverbs 31 Homemaker—R
Unique—R
Virtue—R
Welcome Home
Wesleyan Woman—R

WRITERS
New Writing—R

HEALING

ADULT/GENERAL
Angels on Earth
At Ease—R
Banner, The
Biblical Reflections—R
Bread of Life—R
Canadian Baptist
Catholic Digest—R
Catholic Twin Circle—R
Changes
Charisma/Christian Life
Christian Chronicle (PA)—R
Christian Ranchman
Christian Single—R
Chrysalis Reader
Church Herald/Holiness—R
Common Boundary
Connecting Point—R
Covenant Companion—R
Disciple's Journal—R
Evangelical Baptist—R
Explorer
Faith Today
Family Network—R
Fellowship in Prayer—R
Foursquare World—R
Friends Journal—R
Good News, Etc—R
Good News Journal—R
Guideposts
Head to Head—R
Healing Inn—R
Home Times—R
Island Christian—R
It's Your Choice
John Milton—R
Jour/Christian Nursing—R
Kansas City Christian—R
Life Gate—R
Liguorian
Live—R
Lutheran Digest—R
Mennonite, The—R
MESSAGE
MESSAGE/Open Bible
New Covenant
New Heart, A—R
New Oxford Review
Our Family—R
Pentecostal Testimony—R
PrayerWorks—R
Presbyterian Record—R
Presbyterians Today—R

Purpose—R
Remembrance—R
SCP Journal—R
Sharing—R
Sojourners
Spiritual Life
Today's Christian Senior—R
Total Health
United Church Observer
Upsouth—R
VISION (CA)—R
Vision, The—R
Voice, The—R
War Cry—R
Watchman, The
Way of St. Francis—R

CHILDREN
BREAD/God's Children
  —R
Discovery—R
High Adventure—R

MISSIONS
American Horizon—R
Areopagus—R

PASTORS/LEADERS
Diaconalogue—R
Eucharistic Minister—R
Jour/Biblical Ethics—R
Journal/Christian Healing—R
Journal/Pastoral Care
Lutheran Partners—R
Ministries Today
Ministry
Networks—R
Priest, The
Voice of the Vineyard —R
Word & World

TEEN/YOUNG ADULT
Conqueror—R
Devo'Zine—R
Young Adult Today
Young Christian—R

WOMEN
Helping Hand—R
Horizons
Lutheran Woman Today
Unique—R
Woman's Touch—R

WRITERS
New Writing—R

HEALTH

ADULT/GENERAL
Alive!—R
Angels on Earth
Anglican Journal—R
Banner, The
B.C. Catholic—R
Bible Advocate—R
Biblical Reflections—R
Canada Lutheran—R
Catholic Digest—R
Catholic Forester—R
Catholic Twin Circle—R
Changes
Charisma/Christian Life
Christian Chronicle (PA)—R
Christian Courier (WI)—R
Christian Courier (CAN)—R
Christian Ranchman
Christian Single—R
Christian Social Action—R
Church Herald/Holiness—R
Companion
Covenant Companion—R
Disciple's Journal—R
Discovery—R
Evangelical Friend
Family Network—R
Fellowship in Prayer—R
Fellowship Link—R
Friends Journal—R
Good News Journal—R
Good News Reporter—R
Green Cross—R
Head to Head—R
Healing Inn—R
Home Times—R
Inland NW Christian
Inside Journal—R
Interim—R
Island Christian—R
It's Your Choice—R
John Milton—R
Jour/Christian Nursing—R
Kansas City Christian—R
Lifeglow—R
Living with Teenagers—R
Lutheran Digest—R
Lutheran Journal—R
Lutheran Witness—R
Marriage Partnership
MESSAGE
MESSAGE/Open Bible
Montana Catholic—R
National Review
New Heart, A—R
New Man—R

New Thought—R
ParentLife—R
Parent Paper, The
Physician
Plain Truth—R
Plus—R
Poetry Forum
Pourastan—R
PrayerWorks—R
Salt of the Earth—R
SCP Journal—R
Single-Parent Family
Standard, The—R
Stand Firm—R
Star of Zion
Table Talk—R
TEAK Roundup—R
Today's Christian Senior—R
Today's Family Matters—R
Today's Single—R
Total Health
Upsouth—R
Vibrant Life—R
War Cry—R

CHILDREN
BREAD/God's Children—R
Club Connection—R
Focus/Clubhouse Jr
GUIDE—R
High Adventure—R
Young Christian—R

CHRISTIAN EDUCATION/LIBRARY
CE Connection—R

MISSIONS
Areopagus—R
Childlife—R
Compassion
Missiology
Quiet Hour Echoes

MUSIC
Gospel Music

PASTORS/LEADERS
Celebration (SDA)—R
Chicago Studies
Christian Recreation
Jour/Biblical Ethics—R
Journal/Christian Camping
Journal/Christian Healing—R
Journal/Pastoral Care
Lutheran Partners—R
Ministries Today
Pastor's Family

Word & World

TEEN/YOUNG ADULT
Challenge (TN)—R
Christteen—R
Conqueror—R
Insight—R
Straight—R
Young Adult Today
Young & Alive—R
Young Christian—R

WOMEN
Aspire
Esprit—R
Helping Hand—R
Horizons
Journey—R
Lutheran Woman's Quar.
Lutheran Woman Today
Proverbs 31 Homemaker—R
Today's Christian Woman
Virtue—R
Welcome Home
Wesleyan Woman—R
Woman's Touch—R

WRITERS
New Writing—R

HISTORICAL

ADULT/GENERAL
African Amer. Heritage—R
AGAIN—R
America
Angels on Earth
Arlington Catholic
At Ease—R
AXIOS—R
Banner, The
Banner News
Baptist History
Canadian Catholic
Cathedral Age
Catholic Answer
Catholic Digest—R
Catholic Heritage—R
Catholic Insight
Catholic Sentinel—R
Catholic Twin Circle—R
Celebrate Life—R
Christian C.L. RECORD—R
Christian Courier (CAN)—R
Christian History—R
Christian Ranchman
Christian Reader—R
Christian Renewal—R

Christianity Today—R
Chrysalis Reader
Church & State—R
Comments/Friends—R
Companions—R (church)
Compass
Conquest
Covenant Companion—R
Cresset
Dallas/Ft. Worth Heritage
Decision
Dovetail—R
Evangelical Baptist—R
Evangelical Friend
Faith Today
Family Digest—R
Fellowship in Prayer—R
Fellowship Link—R
First Things
Good News, Etc—R
Good News Reporter—R
Gospel Today
Healing Inn—R
Herald of Holiness—R
Home Times—R
Indian Life—R
InterVarsity
Island Christian—R
It's Your Choice—R
John Milton—R
Jour/Christian Nursing—R
Journal of Church & State
Lifeglow—R
Live—R
Lutheran Digest—R
Lutheran Journal—R
Lutheran Layman
Lutheran Witness—R
Mennonite Historian—R
MESSAGE
Messenger/St. Anthony
Methodist History
Minnesota Christian—R
MovieGuide
National Review
Our Sunday Visitor
Presbyterian Layman
Presbyterian Outlook
Presbyterian Record—R
Presbyterians Today—R
Pourastan—R
Power for Living—R
PrayerWorks—R
Purpose—R
Religious Education
SCP Journal—R
Sharing—R
Social Justice—R

Something Better—R
Standard, The—R
Star of Zion
TEAK Roundup—R
Today's Christian Senior—R
Upsouth—R
Way of St. Francis—R

CHILDREN
Courage
Focus/Clubhouse
Junior Trails—R
My Friend
On the Line—R
Partners—R
Young Christian—R

*CHRISTIAN
EDUCATION/LIBRARY*
Vision—R

MISSIONS
American Horizon—R
Areopagus—R
Catholic Near East
East-West Church—R
Missiology
Save Our World—R
Urban Mission—R
Worldwide Challenge—R

MUSIC
Church Pianist, etc.
Creator—R
Tradition—R

PASTORS/LEADERS
Five Stones, The—R
Jour/Biblical Ethics—R
Journal/Christian Healing—R
Lutheran Partners—R
Ministry
Preacher's Magazine—R
Today's Parish—R
Word & World

TEEN/YOUNG ADULT
Caleb Issues & Answers
Certainty
Challenge (IL)
Listen—R
Student Leadership—R
Young Adult Today
Young & Alive—R
Young Christian—R
Youth Focus—R

WOMEN
Horizons
Just Between Us—R
Virtue—R
Wesleyan Woman—R

WRITERS
Southwestern Writers—R

HOLIDAY/SEASONAL

ADULT/GENERAL
Advent Christian Witness—R
Alive!—R
alive now!
American Tract Soc.—R
Angels on Earth
Arlington Catholic
At Ease—R
AXIOS—R
Banner, The
Baptist Beacon—R
Bible Advocate—R
Bread of Life—R
Canada Lutheran—R
Canadian Baptist
Canadian Catholic
Cathedral Age
Catholic Digest—R
Catholic Forester—R
Catholic New York
Catholic Parent
Catholic Sentinel—R
Catholic Twin Circle—R
Charisma/Christian Life
Christian Century
Christian Chronicle (PA)—R
Christian C.L. RECORD—R
Christian Courier (WI)—R
Christian Edge—R
Christian Home & School
Christian Living—R
Christian Parenting—R
Christian Ranchman
Christian Reader—R
Christian Single—R
Christian Standard—R
Christianity Today—R
Christmas—R
Church Advocate—R
Church Herald/Holiness—R
Church of God EVANGEL
Companions—R
Connecting Point—R
Conquest
Covenant Companion—R
Decision
Disciple's Journal—R

Discovery—R
Dovetail—R
Emphasis/Faith & Living—R
Evangel—R
Evangelical Baptist—R
Evangelical Friend
Evangelical Visitor—R
Explorer
Expression Christian
Family Digest—R
Family Network—R
Fellowship in Prayer—R
Fellowship Link—R
Fellowship Today—R
Foursquare World—R
Gem, The—R
God's Revivalist
Good News, Etc—R
Good News Journal—R
Good News Reporter—R
Gospel Tidings—R
Gospel Today
Guideposts
Healing Inn—R
Hearing Hearts
Herald of Holiness—R
Home Life—R
Home Times—R
Ideals—R
Indian Life—R
Inside Journal—R
Inspirer, The—R
Island Christian—R
John Milton—R
Jour/Christian Nursing—R
Life Gate—R
Lifeglow—R
Light and Life
Liguorian
Live—R
Living Church, The
Living Light News—R
Living with Teenagers—R
Lutheran Digest—R
Lutheran Journal—R
Lutheran Witness—R
Marriage Partnership
Mature Years—R
Mennonite, The—R
Mennonite Brethren—R
MESSAGE
MESSAGE/Open Bible
Messenger
Messenger/St. Anthony
Minnesota Christian—R
Ministry Today—R
Montana Catholic—R
MovieGuide

New Man—R
NW Christian Journal—R
Oblates
Our Sunday Visitor
ParentLife—R
Pegasus Review—R
Pentecostal Homelife—R
Plenty Good Room
Plus—R
Power for Living—R
PrayerWorks—R
Presbyterian Outlook
Presbyterian Record—R
Presbyterians Today—R
Progress—R
Purpose—R
Religious Broadcasting—R
Role Model
St. Joseph's Messenger—R
Seek—R
Sharing—R
Sojourners
Something Better—R
Standard—R
Standard, The—R
Stand Firm—R
Star of Zion
Sunday Digest—R
Table Talk—R
TEAK Roundup—R
Time of Singing—R
Today's Single—R
United Church Observer
Upsouth—R
U.S. Catholic
Voice, The—R
War Cry—R
Way of St. Francis—R
Wesleyan Advocate—R

CHILDREN
Club Connection—R
CLUBHOUSE—R
Counselor—R
Courage
Discovery—R
Focus/Clubhouse
Focus/Clubhouse Jr
Guideposts for Kids
Junior Trails—R
On the Line—R
Pockets—R
Power & Light—R
Primary Pal
R-A-D-A-R—R
Skipping Stones
Together Time
Wonder Time

Young Christian—R

*CHRISTIAN
EDUCATION/LIBRARY*
Baptist Leader—R
CE Connection—R
CE Counselor—R
CE Leadership—R
Church Educator—R
Evangelizing Today's Child—R
GROUP
Leader/Church School Today—R
Parish Teacher—R
Shining Star
Teacher's Interaction
Vision—R

MISSIONS
Catholic Near East
World Vision—R
Worldwide Challenge—R

MUSIC
Church Pianist
Creator—R
Music Leader
Quest—R

PASTORS/LEADERS
Celebration (Catholic)
Celebration (SDA)—R
Christian Management—R
Five Stones, The—R
GROUP's Jr. High
Lutheran Forum—R
Lutheran Partners—R
Modern Liturgy—R
Preacher's Magazine—R
Proclaim

TEEN/YOUNG ADULT
Breakaway—R
Certainty
Challenge (IL)
Challenge (TN)—R
Christteen—R
Conqueror—R
Cornerstone—R
Devo'Zine—R
Listen—R
On Course—R
Pathways—R
Straight—R
Teen Life (AG)—R
Teen Power—R
With—R

YOU!—R
Young & Alive—R
Young Christian—R
Young Salvationist—R
Youth 97—R

WOMEN
Anna's Journal—R
Aspire
CoLaborer
DOMESTIQUE—R
Esprit—R
Helping Hand—R
Horizons
Journey—R
Joyful Woman—R
Lutheran Woman's Quar.
Probe
Proverbs 31 Homemaker—R
Tea and Sunshine
Today's Christian Woman
Unique—R
Virtue—R
Wesleyan Woman—R
Woman's Touch—R

WRITERS
Tickled by Thunder—R

HOME SCHOOLING

ADULT/GENERAL
Anglican Journal—R
Arlington Catholic
AXIOS—R
Banner, The
Banner News
Catholic Insight
CBA Marketplace
Charisma/Christian Life
Christian Chronicle (PA)—R
Christian C.L. RECORD—R
Christian Computing—R
Christian Edge—R
Christian Parenting—R
Christian Ranchman
Church Advocate—R
Disciple's Journal—R
Dovetail—R
Evangelical Baptist—R
Expression Christian
Faith Today
Family Journal—R
Family Network—R
Good News, Etc—R
Good News Journal—R
Good News Reporter—R
Gospel Today

Green Cross—R
Home Life—R
Homeschooling Today
Home Times—R
Inspirer, The—R
Island Christian—R
It's Your Choice—R
Kansas City Christian—R
Life Gate—R
Liguorian
Living Light News—R
Living with Teenagers—R
Lutheran Life—R
MESSAGE/Open Bible
Minnesota Christian—R
National Review
No-Debt Living—R
NW Christian Journal—R
ParentLife—R
Pentecostal Homelife—R
Providence—R
Religious Education
Rutherford
Social Justice—R
Something Better—R
Table Talk—R
Watchman, The
Wesleyan Advocate—R

CHILDREN
BREAD/God's Children—R
GUIDE—R
Power & Light—R
Skipping Stones
Touch—R
Young Christian—R

CHRISTIAN
EDUCATION/LIBRARY
CE Connection—R
CE Counselor—R
Christian Educators Jour—R
Christian School

PASTORS/LEADERS
Journal/Christian Camping
Today's Christian Preacher—
   R

TEEN/YOUNG ADULT
Christteen—R
Conqueror—R
Teen Life (AG)—R
YOU!—R
Young Christian—R

WOMEN
Aspire

Cottage Connections—R
Esprit—R
Helping Hand—R
Horizons
Proverbs 31 Homemaker—R
Tea and Sunshine
Virtue—R
Wesleyan Woman—R

HOW-TO ACTIVITIES (JUV.)

ADULT/GENERAL
Catholic Forester—R
Christian Edge—R
Christian Living—R
Christian Ranchman
Family Network—R
Good News Reporter—R
Gospel Today
Green Cross—R
Living—R
Living with Teenagers—R
Lutheran Life—R
Ministry Today—R
MovieGuide
ParentLife—R
Pentecostal Homelife—R
Table Talk—R

CHILDREN
BREAD/God's Children—R
Club Connection—R
Counselor—R
Courage
Discovery—R
Focus/Clubhouse
Focus/Clubhouse Jr.
God's World Today
High Adventure—R
Junior Trails—R
Kids' Stuff—R
Listen
My Friend
Nature Friend—R
On the Line—R
Partners—R
Pockets—R
Power & Light—R
Primary Days—R
Primary Pal
R-A-D-A-R—R
Together Time (3-4)
Touch—R
Wonder Time
Young Christian—R

*CHRISTIAN
EDUCATION/LIBRARY*
CE Counselor—R
Church Educator—R
Evangelizing Today's Child—
R
Junior Teacher—R
Memos—R
Perspective—R
Shining Star
Today's Catholic Teacher—R

PASTORS/LEADERS
Networks—R

TEEN/YOUNG ADULT
Breakaway—R
Challenge (TN)—R
Listen—R
Teen Life (AG)—R
Teen Power—R
Young Christian—R
Young Salvationist—R
Youth 97—R

WOMEN
Proverbs 31 Homemaker—R

HOW-TO

Note: See Self-Help, now listed
separately.

ADULT/GENERAL
African Amer. Heritage—R
Alive!—R
At Ease—R
Baptist Informer
Believer, The—R
Biblical Reflections—R
Canada Lutheran—R
Catholic Digest—R
Catholic Twin Circle—R
CBA Frontline
CBA Marketplace
Changes
Charisma/Christian Life
Christian Arts Review
Christian Chronicle (PA)—R
Christian Edge—R
Christian Home & School
Christian Living—R
Christian Parenting—R
Christian Ranchman
Christian Reader—R
Christian Single—R
Christian Standard—R
Columbia

Companion
Companions—R
Connecting Point—R
Conquest
Cornerstone—R
Discovery—R
Emphasis/Faith & Living—R
Expression Christian
Family Digest—R
Family Network—R
Fellowship Link—R
Focus on the Family—R
Good News, Etc.—R
Good News Reporter—R
Gospel Today
Green Cross—R
Hallelujah! (CAN)—R
Head to Head—R
Healing Inn—R
Hearing Hearts
Home Times—R
Inland NW Christian
Island Christian—R
John Milton—R
Jour/Christian Nursing—R
Light and Life
Liguorian
Living—R
Living with Teenagers—R
Lutheran Digest—R
Lutheran Layman
Marriage Partnership
Mature Living
Mature Years—R
Mennonite, The—R
MESSAGE
MESSAGE/Open Bible
Ministry Today—R
MovieGuide
New Writing—R
No-Debt Living—R
Northwestern Lutheran—R
Our Sunday Visitor
ParentLife—R
Plus—R
Positive Living—R
PrayerWorks—R
Pursuit—R
Quiet Revolution—R
Religious Broadcasting—R
Role Model
Salt of the Earth—R
Smart Dads
Standard—R
Standard, The—R
Star of Zion
Sunday Digest—R
TEAK Roundup—R

Today's Family Matters—R
Today's Single—R
Total Health
Vibrant Life—R
War Cry—R

CHILDREN
High Adventure—R
Kids' Stuff—R
Power & Light—R

*CHRISTIAN
EDUCATION/LIBRARY*
CE Connection—R
CE Connection Communi-
que—R
CE Counselor—R
CE Leadership—R
Children's Ministry
Christian School
Church & Synagogue Lib.—R
Church Educator—R
Church Libraries—R
GROUP
Leader/Church School To-
day—R
Lollipops
Shining Star
Vision—R

MISSIONS
Great Commission—R
Mission Today—R
PFI World Report—R
Quiet Hour Echoes

MUSIC
Church Music Report
Gospel Industry Today
Music Leader

PASTORS/LEADERS
Church Administration
Five Stones, The—R
GROUP's Jr. High
Ivy Jungle Report—R
Jour/Biblical Ethics—R
Journal/Christian Camping
Journal/Christian Healing—R
Modern Liturgy—R
Newsletter Newsletter
Networks—R
Pastor's Family
Priest, The
Resource—R
Sunday School Leader
Technologies/Worship—R
Youthworker—R

TEEN/YOUNG ADULT
Breakaway—R
Certainty
Challenge (IL)
Challenge (TN)—R
Christteen—R
Insight—R
Student Leadership—R
Teen Power—R
Teens on Target—R
Transcend
With—R
YOU!—R
Young Christian—R
Youth Challenge—R

WOMEN
Aspire
DOMESTIQUE—R
Helping Hand—R
Horizons
Journey—R
Just Between Us—R
Lutheran Woman Today
Probe
Today's Christian Woman
Unique—R
Virtue—R
Wesleyan Woman—R
Women Alive!—R

WRITERS
Byline
Canadian Writer's Jour—R
Chips Off Writer's Block—R
Christian Communicator—R
Cross & Quill—R
Exchange—R
Housewife-Writer—R
New Writing—R
NW Christian Author
Once Upon a Time
Southwestern Writers—R
Tickled by Thunder—R
VA Christian Writer—R
Writers Connection—R
Writer's Digest
Writer's Exchange—R
Writer's Forum (OH)—R
Writer's Infor Network
Writer's Ink—R
Writer's World—R

HUMOR

ADULT/GENERAL
African Amer. Heritage—R
Alive!—R

alive now!
Angels on Earth
At Ease—R
AXIOS—R
Biblical Reflections—R
Canada Lutheran—R
Canadian Baptist
Catholic Digest—R
Catholic Forester—R
Catholic Parent
Catholic Twin Circle—R
CBA Frontline
Charisma/Christian Life
Christian Chronicle (PA)—R
Christian C.L. RECORD—R
Christian Computing—R
Christian Edge—R
Christian Living—R
Christian Parenting—R
Christian Ranchman
Christian Reader—R
Christian Single—R
Church of God EVANGEL
Companion
Connecting Point—R
Covenant Companion—R
Disciple's Journal—R
Door, The—R(satire)
Dovetail—R
Emphasis/Faith & Living—R
Evangelical Visitor—R
Faith Today
Family Journal—R
Family Network—R
Fellowship Link—R
Focus on the Family—R
Good News, Etc.—R
Good News Journal—R
Good News Reporter—R
Gospel Today
Head to Head—R
Healing Inn—R
Hearing Hearts
Highway News—R
Home Life—R
Home Times—R
Impact Magazine—R
Indian Life—R
Inland NW Christian
Island Christian—R
John Milton—R
Jour/Christian Nursing—R
Life Gate—R
Light and Life
Liguorian
Live—R
Living with Teenagers—R
Lookout—R

Lutheran, The—R
Lutheran Digest—R
Lutheran Journal—R
Lutheran Layman
Lutheran Witness—R
Marriage Partnership
Mature Living
Mature Years—R
Mennonite Brethren—R
MESSAGE
MESSAGE/Open Bible
Ministry Today—R
Minnesota Christian—R
National Review
New Man—R
New Trumpet—R
New Writing—R
Our Family—R
ParentLife—R
Pegasus Review—R
Pentecostal Homelife—R
Pentecostal Testimony—R
Power for Living—R
PrayerWorks—R
Presbyterian Record—R
Presbyterians Today—R
Progress—R
Providence—R
Pursuit—R
Religious Broadcasting—R
Salt of the Earth—R
Single-Parent Family
Sojourners
Something Better—R
Standard—R
Standard, The—R
Stand Firm—R
Star of Zion
Sunday Digest—R
Table Talk—R
Today's Family Matters—R
Today's Single—R
Upsouth—R
Voice, The—R
War Cry—R
Way of St. Francis—R

CHILDREN
Club Connection—R
Courage
Crusader—R
Discovery—R
Focus/Clubhouse
Focus/Clubhouse Jr
GUIDE—R
Guideposts for Kids
High Adventure—R
My Friend

On the Line—R
Power & Light—R
R-A-D-A-R—R
Touch—R
Wonder Time

*CHRISTIAN
EDUCATION/LIBRARY*
CE Counselor—R
CE Leadership—R
Christian School
Teachers in Focus—R
Team—R
Vision—R

MISSIONS
Areopagus—R
Great Commission—R
Mission Today—R
World Christian—R
Worldwide Challenge—R

MUSIC
Church Pianist, etc.
Creator—R
Gospel Music
Quest—R

PASTORS/LEADERS
Celebration (SDA)—R
Cell Life FORUM—R
Christian Ministry
Five Stones, The—R
GROUP's Jr. High
Journal/Christian Healing—R
Ministries Today
Modern Liturgy—R
Networks—R
Pastor's Family
Preacher's Illus. Service—R
Priest, The
Resource—R
Sermon Notes
Sunday School Leader
Today's Parish
WCA Monthly—R

TEEN/YOUNG ADULT
Breakaway—R
Brio
Certainty
Challenge (IL)
Christteen—R
Conqueror—R
Devo'Zine—R
Insight—R
On Course—R
Pathways—R

Straight—R
Teenage Christian—R
Teen Life (AG)—R
Teen Power—R
Transcend
With—R
YOU!—R
Young Adult Today
Youth Focus—R
Zelos—R

WOMEN
CoLaborer
Cottage Connections—R
DOMESTIQUE—R
Esprit—R
Helping Hand—R
Horizons
Joyful Woman—R
Just Between Us—R
Lutheran Woman's Quar.
Lutheran Woman Today
Proverbs 31 Homemaker—R
Today's Christian Woman
Unique—R
Virtue—R
Wesleyan Woman—R
Woman's Touch—R

WRITERS
Byline
Canadian Writer's Jour—R
Exchange—R
Felicity—R
Housewife-Writer—R
Inklings
New Writing—R
Once Upon a Time—R
Southwestern Writers—R
Tickled by Thunder—R
Writer's Exchange—R
Writers Infor Network
Writer's World—R

INSPIRATIONAL

ADULT/GENERAL
African Amer. Heritage—R
Angels on Earth
Annals of St. Anne
Arlington Catholic
At Ease—R
Banner, The
Baptist Beacon—R
Bible Advocate—R
Bread of Life—R
Brethren Evangelist
Broken Streets

Canada Lutheran—R
Catholic Answer
Catholic Digest—R
Catholic Forester—R
Catholic Parent
Catholic Twin Circle—R
CBA Frontline
Celebrate Life—R
Changes
Charisma/Christian Life
Christian Arts Review
Christian Chronicle (PA)—R
Christian Edge—R
Christian Living—R
Christian Parenting—R
Christian Reader—R
Christian Single—R
Church Advocate—R
Church Herald/Holiness—R
Church of God EVANGEL
Columbia
Companion
Companions—R
Connecting Point—R
Covenant Companion—R
Disciple's Journal—R
Emphasis/Faith & Living—R
Evangel—R
Evangelical Baptist—R
Evangelical Friend
Evangelical Visitor—R
Explorer
Family Digest—R
Fellowship in Prayer—R
Fellowship Link—R
Fellowship Today—R
Family Network—R
Focus on the Family—R
Foursquare World—R
Friends Journal—R
Gem, The—R
God's Revivalist
Good News—R
Good News Reporter—R
Gospel Tidings—R
Gospel Today
Guideposts
Head to Head—R
Healing Inn—R
Hearing Hearts
Herald of Holiness—R
Highway News—R
Home Life—R
Home Times—R
Ideals—R
Indian Life—R
Inland NW Christian
Inspirer, The—R

Island Christian—R
Jewel Among Jewels—R
John Milton—R
Jour/Christian Nursing—R
Life Gate—R
Lifeglow—R
Light and Life
Liguorian
Live—R
Living—R
Living Light News—R
Living with Teenagers—R
Lutheran, The—R
Lutheran Digest—R
Lutheran Journal—R
Lutheran Layman
Lutheran Witness—R
Marian Helpers—R
Marriage Partnership
Mature Living
Mature Years—R
Mennonite Brethren—R
MESSAGE
MESSAGE/Open Bible
Messenger/Sacred Heart
Ministry Today—R
New Covenant
New Heart, A—R
New Man—R
New Thought—R
New Trumpet—R
Northwestern Lutheran—R
Oblates
Our Sunday Visitor
ParentLife—R
Pegasus Review—R
Pentecostal Evangel
Pentecostal Homelife—R
Plain Truth—R
Plenty Good Room
Plowman, The—R
Plus—R
Pourastan—R
Power for Living—R
PrayerWorks—R
Presbyterian Outlook
Presbyterian Record—R
Presbyterians Today—R
Progress—R
Purpose—R
Queen of All Hearts
  Remembrance—R
Role Model
St. Anthony Messenger
St. Joseph's Messenger—R
Seek—R
Shantyman, The—R
Social Justice—R

Sojourners
Standard—R
Standard, The—R
Stand Firm—R
Sunday Digest—R
TEAK Roundup—R
Time of Singing—R
Today's Christian Senior—R
Today's Single—R
Total Health
Upsouth—R
U.S. Catholic
VISION (CA)—R
Vision, The—R
Voice, The—R
War Cry—R
Watchman, The
Way of St. Francis—R
Weavings—R
Wesleyan Advocate—R
Worldwide Challenge—R

CHILDREN
Club Connection—R
CLUBHOUSE—R
Counselor—R
Discovery—R
Focus/Clubhouse
GUIDE—R
High Adventure—R
Partners—R
Power & Light—R
Primary Days—R
Touch—R
Wonder Time

CHRISTIAN EDUCATION/LIBRARY
Brigade Leader—R
CE Connection—R
CE Counselor—R
Christian School
Church & Synagogue Lib.
Journal/Adventist Educ.—R
Junior Teacher—R
Shining Star
Teacher's Interaction
Vision—R

MISSIONS
American Horizon—R
Areopagus—R
Message of the Cross—R
Quiet Hour Echoes
World Vision—R

MUSIC
Creator—R

Quest—R
Senior Musician—R

PASTORS/LEADERS
Celebration (SDA)—R
Cell Church—R
Cell Life FORUM—R
Christian Management—R
Christian Ministry
Eucharistic Minister—R
Evangelism USA
Five Stones, The—R
GROUP's Jr. High
Journal/Christian Healing—R
Journal/Pastoral Care
Ministry
Networks—R
Preacher's Magazine—R
Priest, The
PROCLAIM—R
Sunday School Leader
Today's Christian Preacher—R
Voice of the Vineyard —R

TEEN/YOUNG ADULT
Breakaway—R
Challenge (TN)—R
Christteen—R
Conqueror—R
Devo'Zine—R
On Course—R
Pathways—R
Straight—R
Teen Life (AG)—R
Teen Power—R
Teens on Target—R
Today's Christian Teen—R
Transcend
With—R
YOU!—R
Young Adult Today
Young & Alive—R
Young Christian—R
Youth Challenge—R
Zelos—R

WOMEN
CoLaborer
Cottage Connections—R
DOMESTIQUE—R
Esprit—R
Helping Hand—R
Horizons
Journey—R
Joyful Woman—R
Just Between Us
Lutheran Woman's Quar.

Lutheran Woman Today
Proverbs 31 Homemaker—R
Sisters Today
Tea and Sunshine
Today's Christian Woman
Unique—R
Virtue—R
Wesleyan Woman—R
Woman's Touch—R
Women Alive!—R

WRITERS
Byline
Canadian Writer's Jour—R
Felicity—R
Once Upon a Time—R
Southwestern Writers—R
VA Christian Writer—R
Writer's Digest—R
Writer's Forum (OH)—R
Writer's Infor Network
Writer's World—R

INTERVIEWS/PROFILES

ADULT/GENERAL
African Amer. Heritage—R
AGAIN—R
Alive!—R
Anglican Journal—R
Arkansas Catholic
Arlington Catholic
At Ease—R
AXIOS—R
Biblical Reflections—R
Canadian Baptist
Canadian Catholic
Catholic Digest—R
Catholic Forester—R
Catholic New York
Catholic Parent
Catholic Sentinel—R
Catholic Twin Circle—R
Charisma/Christian Life
Christian Arts Review
Christian Chronicle (PA)—R
Christian C.L. RECORD—R
Christian Courier (WI)—R
Christian Courier (CAN)—R
Christian Edge—R
Christian Parenting—R
Christian Ranchman
Christian Reader—R
Christian Renewal—R
Christian Single—R
Christianity Today—R
Church Advocate—R
Church & State—R

Church Herald/Holiness—R
Church of God EVANGEL
Columbia
Companion
Cornerstone—R (music)
Covenant Companion—R
Disciple's Journal—R
Discipleship Journal
Door, The
Dovetail—R
Emphasis/Faith & Living—R
Episcopal Life—R
Evangelical Baptist—R
Evangelical Friend
Expression Christian
Faith Today
Family Digest—R
Family Journal—R
Fellowship in Prayer—R
Fidelity—R
Good News, Etc—R
Good News Reporter—R
Gospel Today
Green Cross—R
Guideposts
Head to Head—R
Healing Inn—R
Hearing Hearts
Herald of Holiness—R
Home Life—R
Home Times—R
Impact Magazine—R
Indian Life—R
Inside Journal—R
Interim—R
InterVarsity
Island Christian—R
Jewel Among Jewels—R
John Milton—R
Jour/Christian Nursing—R
Joyful Noise
Kansas City Christian—R
Lifeglow—R
Liguorian
Living—R
Living Church
Living Light News—R
Living with Teenagers—R
Lutheran, The—R
Lutheran Layman
Lutheran Witness—R
Marriage Partnership
Mature Living
Mature Years—R
Mennonite, The—R
Mennonite Historian—R
Mennonite Reporter
MESSAGE

Messenger
Minnesota Christian—R
National Review
New Covenant
New Heart, A—R
New Man—R
New Thought—R
New Trumpet—R
New Writing—R
NW Christian Journal—R
Our Sunday Visitor
ParentLife—R
Pentecostal Evangel
Plain Truth—R
Plenty Good Room
Positive Living—R
Power for Living—R
Presbyterian Layman
Presbyterian Outlook
Presbyterian Record—R
Presbyterians Today—R
Prism—R
Providence—R
Pursuit—R
Quiet Revolution—R
Religious Broadcasting—R
Rutherford
St. Anthony Messenger
Salt of the Earth—R
SCP Journal—R
Signs of the Times—R
Single-Parent Family
Sojourners
Something Better—R
Standard—R
Standard, The—R
Stand Firm—R
Stewardship
Sunday Digest—R
Table Talk—R
TEAK Roundup—R
Touchstone
United Church Observer
Upsouth—R
U.S. Catholic
War Cry—R
Way of St. Francis—R
Witness, The

CHILDREN
Counselor—R
Crusader—R
Discovery—R
Guideposts for Kids
Pockets—R
Primary Days—R
Skipping Stones

CHRISTIAN EDUCATION/LIBRARY
Brigade Leader—R
CE Counselor—R
Christian Educators Jour—R
Christian Library Jour—R
Christian School
Church Libraries—R
GUIDE—R
Perspective—R
Teachers in Focus—R
Teacher's Interaction
Vision—R

MISSIONS
American Horizon—R
Childlife—R
Compassion
East-West Church—R
Leaders for Today
Partners
PFI World Report—R
Save Our World—R
Urban Mission—R
World Christian—R
Worldwide Challenge—R

MUSIC
Church Music World
Gospel Industry Today
Gospel Music
Quest—R

PASTORS/LEADERS
Celebration (SDA)—R
Cell Church—R
Christian Management—R
Christian Ministry
Cross Currents—R
Diaconalogue—R
Evangelism USA
Five Stones, The—R
Ivy Jungle Report—R
Journal/Christian Camping
Journal/Christian Healing—R
Ministries Today
Modern Liturgy—R
Networks—R
Pastor's Family
Preacher, The
Preacher's Magazine—R
PROCLAIM—R
Sermon Notes
Single Ad. Ministries Jour.
Technologies/Worship—R
Voice of the Vineyard —R
WCA Monthly—R
Youthworker—R

TEEN/YOUNG ADULT
Breakaway—R
Caleb Issues & Answers
Christteen—R
Devo'Zine—R
Insight—R
On Course—R
Pathways—R
Sharing the VICTORY
Spirit
Straight—R
Teen Life (AG)—R
Teen Power—R
Transcend
YOU!—R
Young Adult Today
Young & Alive—R
Youth Focus—R
Youth 97—R
Zelos—R

WOMEN
Aspire
Church Woman
Cottage Connections—R
Horizons
Jour/Women's Ministries
Lutheran Woman Today
Probe
Proverbs 31 Homemaker—R
Today's Christian Woman
Virtue—R
Wesleyan Woman—R

WRITERS
Canadian Writer's Jour—R
Christian Communicator, The—R
Cross & Quill—R
Housewife-Writer—R
Inklings
NW Christian Author—R
Once Upon a Time—R
Writers Connection—R
Writer's Exchange—R
Writer's Info
Writer's Infor Network
Writer's Ink—R
Writer's World—R

LEADERSHIP

ADULT/GENERAL
Angels on Earth
At Ease—R
Atlantic Baptist
Banner, The
Baptist Beacon—R

Biblical Reflections—R
Canada Lutheran—R
Canadian Baptist
Catholic Digest—R
Christian Century
Christian Chronicle (PA)—R
Christian Edge—R
Christian Ranchman
Christianity Today—R
Church Advocate—R
Church Herald/Holiness—R
Columbia
Companion
Covenant Companion—R
Discipleship Journal
Emphasis/Faith & Living—R
Evangelical Baptist—R
Faith Today
Family Network—R
Fidelity—R
Foursquare World—R
Friends Journal—R
Good News, Etc—R
Good News Reporter—R
Gospel Today
Hearing Hearts
Inland NW Christian
Island Christian—R
It's Your Choice—R
John Milton—R
Jour/Christian Nursing—R
Living Church
Living Light News—R
Lutheran Digest—R
Lutheran Journal—R
MESSAGE
Ministry Today—R
New Man—R
NW Christian Journal—R
Our Family—R
Our Sunday Visitor
Pentecostal Testimony—R
Pourastan—R
Presbyterian Layman
Presbyterian Outlook
Prism—R
Purpose—R
Religious Broadcasting—R
Religious Education
Standard, The—R
Stand Firm—R
Star of Zion
Today's Christian Senior—R
United Church Observer
Upsouth—R
War Cry—R
Watchman, The

CHILDREN
Club Connection—R
Skipping Stones

*CHRISTIAN
EDUCATION/LIBRARY*
Baptist Leader—R
Brigade Leader—R
CE Connection—R
CE Connection Communi-
que—R
CE Counselor—R
CE Leadership—R
Church Educator—R
Church Worship
GROUP
Leader/Church School To-
day—R
Memos—R
Perspective—R
Resource—R
Teacher's Interaction
Team—R
Vision—R

MISSIONS
American Horizon—R
East-West Church—R
Leaders for Today
Missiology
Mission Today—R
Urban Mission—R
Worldwide Challenge—R

PASTORS/LEADERS
Celebration (SDA)—R
Cell Church—R
Cell Life FORUM—R
Christian Century
Christian Management—R
Christian Ministry
Church Growth Network—R
Church Management—R
Clergy Journal—R
Emmanuel
Enrichment—R
Evangelism USA
Five Stones, The—R
GROUP's Jr. High
Ivy Jungle Report—R
Jour/Biblical Ethics—R
Journal/Christian Healing—R
Jour/Amer Soc/Chur Growth
Leadership Journal—R
Lutheran Partners—R
Ministries Today
Ministry
Pastor's Family

Preacher's Magazine—R
Priest, The
Resource—R
Sermon Notes
Sunday School Leader
Today's Christian Preacher—
R
Voice of the Vineyard —R
WCA Monthly—R
Word & World
Worship Leader
Youthworker—R

TEEN/YOUNG ADULT
Challenge (TN)—R
Student Leadership—R
Today's Christian Teen—R
Transcend
YOU!—R
Youth 97—R

WOMEN
Horizons
Just Between Us—R
Sisters Today
Unique—R
Virtue—R
Wesleyan Woman—R
Woman's Touch—R

LITURGICAL

ADULT/GENERAL
AGAIN—R
alive now!
Annals of St. Anne
Arkansas Catholic
Arlington Catholic
Banner, The
Canada Lutheran—R
Canadian Catholic
Catholic Digest—R
Catholic Insight
Catholic Parent
Christian Century
Church Herald/Holiness—R
Commonweal
Companion
Cresset
Episcopal Life—R
Family Digest—R
Fidelity—R
Gospel Today
John Milton—R
Liguorian
Living Church
Messenger (KY)
North American Voice

Our Family—R
Our Sunday Visitor
Perspectives
Prairie Messenger—R
Presbyterian Record—R
St. Anthony Messenger
Silver Wings—R
Star of Zion
United Church Observer
U.S. Catholic
Way of St. Francis—R

*CHRISTIAN
EDUCATION/LIBRARY*
Church Educator—R
Church Worship
Parish Teacher—R
Religion Teacher's Journal

MISSIONS
Areopagus—R
Catholic Near East

MUSIC
Church Pianist, etc.
Gospel Industry Today
Hymn, The

PASTORS/LEADERS
Catechumenate
Celebration (Catholic)
Celebration (SDA)—R
Chicago Studies
Christian Century
Christian Ministry
Church Administration
Clergy Journal—R
Diocesan Dialogue—R
Emmanuel
Eucharistic Minister—R
Five Stones, The—R
Journal/Christian Healing—R
Liturgy
Lutheran Forum—R
Lutheran Partners—R
Ministries Today
Modern Liturgy—R
Parish Liturgy
Pastoral Life
Preacher's Illus. Service—R
Preacher's Magazine—R
Priest, The
PROCLAIM—R
Reformed Worship
Today's Parish
Word & World
Worship Leader

TEENS/YOUNG ADULT
Pathways—R
Youth Update

WOMEN
Horizons
Lutheran Woman Today
Sisters Today
Virtue—R

MARRIAGE

ADULT/GENERAL
Alive!—R
America
American Tract Soc.—R
Angels on Earth
Annals of St. Anne
Arkansas Catholic
Arlington Catholic
At Ease—R
Atlantic Baptist
AXIOS—R
Banner, The
Bible Advocate—R
Biblical Reflections—R
Bread of Life—R
Canada Lutheran—R
Canadian Baptist
Canadian Catholic
Catholic Digest—R
Catholic Forester—R
Catholic Parent
Catholic Twin Circle—R
Celebrate Life—R
Charisma/Christian Life
Christian C.L. RECORD—R
Christian Courier (CAN)—R
Christian Edge—R
Christian Home & School
Christian Living—R
Christian Parenting—R
Christian Ranchman
Christian Reader—R
Church Advocate—R
Church Herald/Holiness—R
Church of God EVANGEL
Columbia
Companion
Companions—R
Covenant Companion—R
Disciple's Journal—R
Discipleship Journal
Dovetail—R
Emphasis/Faith & Living—R
Evangel—R
Evangelical Baptist—R
Evangelical Friend

Evangelical Visitor—R
Expression Christian
Faith Today
Family Digest—R
Family Network—R
Fellowship Today—R
Fidelity—R
Focus on the Family—R
Foursquare World—R
Good News, Etc—R
Good News Journal—R
Gospel Today
Head to Head—R
Hearing Hearts
Highway News—R
Home Life—R
Home Times—R
Impact Magazine—R
Indian Life—R
Inside Journal—R
Island Christian—R
It's Your Choice—R
John Milton—R
Joyful Noise
Kansas City Christian—R
Life Gate—R
Lifeglow—R
Light and Life
Liguorian
Live—R
Living—R
Lookout—R
Lutheran, The—R
Lutheran Digest—R
Lutheran Journal—R
Lutheran Witness—R
Marriage Partnership
Mennonite, The—R
Mennonite Brethren—R
MESSAGE
MESSAGE/Open Bible
Messenger/St. Anthony
Ministry Today—R
Minnesota Christian—R
Montana Catholic—R
Moody—R
National Review
New Covenant
New Man—R
New Oxford Review
New Trumpet—R
North American Voice
NW Christian Journal—R
Our Family—R
Our Sunday Visitor
Pegasus Review—R
Pentecostal Homelife—R
Pentecostal Testimony—R

Perspectives
Physician
Plain Truth—R
Plus—R
Pourastan—R
Prairie Messenger—R
PrayerWorks—R
Presbyterian Layman
Presbyterian Record—R
Presbyterians Today—R
Prism—R
Progress—R
Purpose—R
St. Anthony Messenger
Seek—R
Signs of the Times—R
Smart Dads
Social Justice—R
Standard—R
Standard, The—R
Stand Firm—R
Table Talk—R
Today's Christian Senior—R
United Church Observer
Upsouth—R
U.S. Catholic
VISION (CA)—R
Vision, The—R
Voice, The—R
War Cry—R
Wesleyan Advocate—R

CHRISTIAN EDUCATION/LIBRARY
Brigade Leader—R
CE Connection—R
CE Counselor—R
Children's Ministry

MISSIONS
Quiet Hour Echoes
Worldwide Challenge—R

PASTORS/LEADERS
Celebration (SDA)—R
Cell Church—R
Chicago Studies
Five Stones, The—R
GROUP's Jr. High
Jour/Biblical Ethics—R
Journal/Christian Healing—R
Journal/Pastoral Care
Lutheran Forum—R
Lutheran Partners—R
Ministries Today
Networks—R
Pastor's Family
Preacher, The

Preacher's Illus. Service—R
PROCLAIM—R
Today's Christian Preacher—R
Today's Parish
Voice of the Vineyard —R
Word & World

TEEN/YOUNG ADULT
YOU!—R
Young Adult Today
Young & Alive—R
Young Christian—R
Youth Update

WOMEN
Aspire
Anna's Journal—R
CoLaborer
DOMESTIQUE—R
Esprit—R
Helping Hand—R
Horizons
Journey—R
Joyful Woman—R
Just Between Us—R
Lutheran Woman's Quar.
Lutheran Woman Today
Proverbs 31 Homemaker—R
Tea and Sunshine
Today's Christian Woman
Unique—R
Virtue—R
Welcome Home
Wesleyan Woman—R
Woman's Touch—R
Women Alive!—R

MEN'S ISSUES

ADULT/GENERAL
Advent Christian Witness—R
Annals of St. Anne
Arlington Catholic
At Ease—R
Atlantic Baptist
AXIOS—R
Banner, The
Biblical Reflections—R
Bread of Life—R
Brethren Evangelist
Canada Lutheran—R
Canadian Baptist
Catholic Forester—R
Catholic Parent
CBA Marketplace
Celebrate Life—R
Charisma/Christian Life

Christian Edge—R
Christian Living—R
Christian Ranchman
Christian Reader—R
Christian Single—R
Christian Social Action—R
Christianity Today—R
Chrysalis Reader
Church of God EVANGEL
Companion
Covenant Companion—R
Disciple's Journal—R
Emphasis/Faith & Living—R
Evangel—R
Evangelical Baptist—R
Expression Christian
Faith Today
Family Journal—R
Family Network—R
Fatted Calf Forum—R
Foursquare World—R
Good News, Etc—R
Good News Journal—R
Gospel Today
Healing Inn—R
Hearing Hearts
Herald of Holiness—R
Highway News—R
Home Life—R
Home Times—R
Indian Life—R
Inland NW Christian
Inside Journal—R
Island Christian—R
It's Your Choice—R
Jour/Christian Nursing—R
Joyful Noise
Kansas City Christian—R
Life Gate—R
Liguorian
Light and Life
Live—R
Living—R
Lookout—R
Marriage Partnership
Mennonite, The—R
MESSAGE/Open Bible
Ministry Today—R
Moody—R
National Review
New Man—R
Newsline—R
New Thought—R
New Trumpet—R
Our Family—R
Pentecostal Homelife—R
Plain Truth—R
Plus—R

PrayerWorks—R
Presbyterian Outlook
Prism—R
Purpose—R
St. Anthony Messenger
Smart Dads
Standard, The—R
Stand Firm—R
Star of Zion
Table Talk—R
Today's Christian Senior—R
United Church Observer
Vibrant Life—R (health)
Voice, The—R
War Cry—R
Way of St. Francis—R
Witness, The

*CHRISTIAN
EDUCATION/LIBRARY*
Brigade Leader—R

MISSIONS
American Horizon—R
Brigade Leader—R
World Mission People—R
Worldwide Challenge—R

MUSIC
Quest—R

PASTORS/LEADERS
Celebration (SDA)—R
Christian Ministry
Jour/Biblical Ethics—R
Journal/Pastoral Care
Leadership Journal—R
Lutheran Partners—R
Ministries Today
Pastor's Family
Preacher, The
Preacher's Magazine—R
Pulpit Helps—R
Today's Christian Preacher—R
Voice of the Vineyard —R
Word & World

TEEN/YOUNG ADULT
Challenge (TN)—R
YOU!—R

WOMEN
Anna's Journal—R
Virtue—R

MIRACLES

ADULT/GENERAL
America
Angels on Earth
At Ease—R
Biblical Reflections—R
Bread of Life—R
Canadian Baptist
Canadian Catholic
Catholic Digest—R
Catholic Twin Circle—R
Charisma/Christian Life
Christian Chronicle (PA)—R
Christian Edge—R
Christian Ranchman
Christian Single—R
Church Advocate—R
Church Herald/Holiness—R
Companion
Connecting Point—R
Explorer
Family Network—R
Fellowship in Prayer—R
Fidelity—R
Friends Journal—R
God's Revivalist
Good News, Etc—R
Good News Journal—R
Gospel Today
Guideposts
Hallelujah! (CAN)—R
Healing Inn—R
Home Times—R
Impact Magazine—R
Island Christian—R
John Milton—R
Live—R
Lutheran Digest—R
MESSAGE
MESSAGE/Open Bible
New Oxford Review
Pegasus Review—R
PrayerWorks—R
Queen of All Hearts
Standard—R
Sunday Digest—R
Total Health
Upsouth—R
VISION (CA)—R
Vision, The—R
War Cry—R
Watchman, The
Way of St. Francis—R

CHILDREN
Focus/Clubhouse
GUIDE—R

Touch—R

MISSIONS
American Horizon—R
Areopagus—R
Save Our World—R

PASTORS/LEADERS
Journal/Christian Healing—R
Ministries Today
Networks—R
Voice of the Vineyard —R
Word & World

TEEN/YOUNG ADULT
Conqueror—R
Insight—R
On Course—R
Teen Life (AG)—R
YOU!—R
Young Adult Today
Young Christian—R

WOMEN
Cottage Connections—R
Helping Hand—R
Horizons—R
Joyful Woman—R
Lutheran Woman Today
Unique—R
Virtue—R
Woman's Touch—R

MISSIONS

ADULT/GENERAL
Alive!—R
Anglican Journal—R
At Ease—R
Banner, The
Banner News
Baptist Informer
B.C. Catholic—R
Bible Advocate—R
Biblical Reflections—R
Canada Lutheran—R
Canadian Baptist
Canadian Catholic
Catholic Digest—R
Catholic Twin Circle—R
Charisma/Christian Life
Christian Chronicle (PA)—R
Christian Edge—R
Christian Ranchman
Christian Reader—R
Christian Renewal—R
Christian Single—R
Christianity Today—R

Church Advocate—R
Church Herald/Holiness—R
Columbia
Companion
Companions—R
Connecting Point—R
Conquest
Covenant Companion—R
Disciple's Journal—R
Discipleship Journal
Decision
Episcopal Life—R
Evangel—R
Evangelical Baptist—R
Evangelical Friend
Faith Today
Family Network—R
Fidelity—R
Good News, Etc—R
Gospel Today
Hallelujah! (CAN)—R
Healing Inn—R
Indian Life—R
InterVarsity
Island Christian—R
John Milton—R
Jour/Christian Nursing—R
Life Gate—R
Live—R
Living Church
Lutheran, The—R
Lutheran Journal—R
Lutheran Witness—R
Mennonite Reporter
MESSAGE
MESSAGE/Open Bible
New Heart, A—R (medical)
New Man—R
New Oxford Review
New Trumpet—R
North American Voice
Our Family—R
Our Sunday Visitor
Pentecostal Testimony—R
Perspectives
Power for Living—R
PrayerWorks—R
Presbyterian Layman
Presbyterian Outlook
Presbyterian Record—R
Presbyterians Today—R
Prism—R
Purpose—R
Queen of All Hearts
Seek—R
Something Better—R
Standard—R
Standard, The—R

Stand Firm—R
Star of Zion
TEAK Roundup—R
Upsouth—R
Vision, The—R
War Cry—R
Way of St. Francis—R

CHILDREN
BREAD/God's Children—R
Crusader (TN)
Focus/Clubhouse
GUIDE—R
Lad
Partners—R
Power & Light—R
R-A-D-A-R—R

CHRISTIAN
EDUCATION/LIBRARY
Brigade Leader—R
CE Counselor—R
Church Educator—R
Courage
Evangelizing Today's Child—
R
Shining Star
Teacher's Interaction

MISSIONS
(see alphabetical listings)

MUSIC
Quest—R

PASTORS/LEADERS
Christian Management—R
Church Administration
Clergy Journal—R
Discipleship Training
Evangelism—R
Five Stones, The—R
Journal/Christian Healing—R
Lutheran Partners—R
Ministries Today
Networks—R
Preacher's Magazine—R
PROCLAIM—R
Today's Christian Preacher—
R
Voice of the Vineyard —R
Word & World
Youthworker—R

TEEN/YOUNG ADULT
Certainty
Challenge (IL)
Challenge (TN)—R

Christteen—R
Conqueror—R
Devo'Zine—R
Insight—R
On Course—R
Pathways—R
Priest, The
Straight—R
Student Leadership—R
Teenage Christian—R
Teen Life (AG)—R
Teen Power—R
Today's Christian Teen—R
Transcend
YOU!—R
Young Adult Today

WOMEN
CoLaborer
Cottage Connections—R
Horizons
Joyful Woman—R
Just Between Us—R
Lutheran Woman Today
Unique—R
Virtue—R
Wesleyan Woman

MONEY MANAGEMENT

ADULT/GENERAL
Anglican Journal—R
At Ease—R
AXIOS—R
Banner, The
Biblical Reflections—R
Brethren Evangelist
Catholic Digest—R
Catholic Forester—R
Catholic Parent
Catholic Twin Circle—R
CBA Marketplace
Christian C.L. RECORD—R
Christian Edge—R
Christian Living—R
Christian Parenting—R
Christian Ranchman
Christian Single—R
Church Advocate—R
Church Herald/Holiness—R
Connecting Point—R
Conquest
Covenant Companion—R
Disciple's Journal—R
Discovery—R
Emphasis/Faith & Living—R
Evangel—R
Evangelical Baptist—R

Evangelical Friend
Evangelical Visitor—R
Expression Christian
Family Network—R
Gospel Today
Head to Head—R
Healing Inn—R
Herald of Holiness—R
Home Times—R
Indian Life—R
Inland NW Christian
Island Christian—R
It's Your Choice—R
Life Gate—R
Living with Teenagers—R
Lutheran Digest—R
Marriage Partnership
Mennonite, The—R
MESSAGE
MESSAGE/Open Bible
Ministry Today—R
New Man—R
No-Debt Living—R
ParentLife—R
Parent Paper, The
Pentecostal Homelife—R
Presbyterian Layman
Providence—R
Religious Broadcasting—R
Signs of the Times—R
Smart Dads
Standard, The—R
Stand Firm—R
Star of Zion
Stewardship
Table Talk—R
Today's Christian Senior—R
Today's Family Matters—R
War Cry—R

CHILDREN
Courage
Crusader—R
Power & Light—R
Touch—R
Young Christian—R

CHRISTIAN
EDUCATION/LIBRARY
CE Connection—R
Christian School

MISSIONS
Quiet Hour Echoes
World Christian—R

PASTORS/LEADERS
Celebration (SDA)—R

Cell Church—R
Christian Ministry
GROUP's Jr. High
Journal/Christian Camping
Journal/Christian Healing—R
Leadership Journal—R
Ministries Today
Networks—R
Pastoral Life
Pastor's Family
Pastor's Tax & Money
Today's Christian Preacher—R
Today's Parish
Your Church—R
Youthworker—R

TEEN/YOUNG ADULT
Certainty
Challenge (IL)
Challenge (TN)—R
Christteen—R
Today's Christian Teen—R
Young Adult Today
Young Christian—R

WOMEN
Aspire
DOMESTIQUE—R
Esprit—R
Helping Hand—R
Horizons
Just Between Us—R
Lutheran Woman Today
Proverbs 31 Homemaker—R
Today's Christian Woman
Virtue—R
Wesleyan Woman—R
Woman's Touch—R

MUSIC REVIEWS

ADULT/GENERAL
Arlington Catholic
Atlantic Baptist
Banner, The
Canadian Catholic
CBA Marketplace
Charisma/Christian Life
Christian Arts Review
Christian Edge—R
Christian Media—R
Christian Parenting—R
Christian Retailing—R
Christian Single—R
Christianity/Arts
Commonweal
Cornerstone—R

Disciple's Journal—R
Expression Christian
Fatted Calf Forum—R
Good News Journal—R
Good News Reporter—R
Head to Head—R
Home Life—R
Home Times—R
Impact Magazine—R
Island Christian—R
John Milton—R
Life Gate—R
Living Light News—R
Living with Teenagers—R
New Thought—R
ParentLife—R
Plain Truth—R
Plowman, The—R
Presbyterian Record—R
Prism—R
Rutherford
Sojourners
Something Better—R
Stand Firm—R
TEAK Roundup—R
United Church Observer
Upsouth—R
War Cry—R

CHILDREN
Club Connection—R
Discovery—R
Power & Light—R
Touch—R

CHRISTIAN EDUCATION/LIBRARY
CE Counselor—R
Church Libraries—R

MUSIC
CCM Magazine
Christian Country—R
Creator—R
Gospel Industry Today
Gospel Music
Hymn, The
Quest—R
Shout!

PASTORS/LEADERS
Ivy Jungle Report—R
Ministries Today
WCA Monthly—R
Reformed Worship

TEEN/YOUNG ADULT
Christteen—R

Devo'Zine—R
Teenage Christian—R
Teen Power—R
Transcend
With—R
Young Christian—R
Young Salvationist—R
Youth 97—R

WOMEN
Aspire
Joyful Woman—R

WRITERS
Inklings
New Writing—R

NATURE

ADULT/GENERAL
Alive!—R
AXIOS—R
Canadian Catholic
Catholic Digest—R
Catholic Forester—R
Chrysalis Reader
Companion
Covenant Companion—R
Fellowship Link—R
Friends Journal—R
Gospel Today
Green Cross—R
Ideals—R
It's Your Choice—R
Lifeglow—R
Lutheran Digest—R
New Thought—R
Pegasus Review—R
Pourastan—R
PrayerWorks—R
Seek—R
Standard, The—R
TEAK Roundup—R
Time of Singing—R
Upsouth—R
War Cry—R

CHILDREN
Club Connection—R
Courage
Crusader—R
Discovery—R
Focus/Clubhouse
Junior Trails—R
My Friend
Nature Friend
On the Line
Partners—R

R-A-D-A-R—R
Skipping Stones
Story Friends—R
Touch—R
Young Christian—R

*CHRISTIAN
EDUCATION/LIBRARY*
Shining Star

PASTORS/LEADERS
Journal/Christian Healing—R
Word & World

TEEN/YOUNG ADULT
Challenge (TN)—R
Pathways—R
Teenage Christian—R
YOU!—R
Young & Alive—R
Young Christian—R

WOMEN
Cottage Connections—R
Esprit—R
Helping Hand—R
Horizons
Proverbs 31 Homemaker—R
Virtue—R

WRITERS
Southwestern Writers—R

NEWSPAPERS

Alabama Baptist
Alive
Anglican Journal
Arkansas Catholic
Arlington Catholic
Awareness TN Christian
B.C. Catholic
Caleb Issues & Answers
   (teen)
Catholic Courier
Catholic New York
Catholic Peace Voice
Catholic Sentinel
Catholic Telegraph
Catholic Twin Circle
Christian Advocate
Christian American
Christian Chronicle (OK)
Christian Courier (WI)
Christian Courier (CAN)
Christian Crusade
Christian Edge
Christian Focus

Christian Observer
Christian Renewal
Dallas/Ft.Worth Heritage
Disciple's Journal
Discovery
Episcopal Life
Expression Christian
Family Journal, The
Fatted Calf Forum
Good News, Etc.
Good News Journal
Harvest Times
Home Times
Indian Life
Inland NW Christian
Inside Journal
Interchange
Interim
Kansas City Christian
Kentucky Christian News
Living Light News
Mennonite Reporter
Mennonite Weekly
Messenger
Minnesota Christian Chronicle
Montana Catholic
National Catholic Reporter
Northstate Christian Times
NW Christian Journal—R
Oblate World
Our Sunday Visitor
Parent Paper
Plowman, The
Prayerworks
Probe
Presbyterian Layman
Providence
Pulpit Helps
Revelation Post
Something Better News
Texas Messenger
Today's Single
United Voice
YOU! (teen)

OPINION PIECES

ADULT/GENERAL
African Amer. Heritage—R
Arlington Catholic
At Ease—R
AXIOS—R
Banner, The
B.C. Catholic—R
Bible Advocate—R
Biblical Reflections—R
Canadian Catholic
Catholic New York

Celebrate Life—R
Changes
Charisma/Christian Life
Christian Arts Review
Christian Chronicle (OK)
Christian Chronicle (PA)—R
Christian Edge—R
Christian Renewal—R
Christian Social Action—R
Christianity Today—R
Commonweal
Compass
Cornerstone—R
Covenant Companion—R
Door, The
Dovetail—R
Episcopal Life—R
Evangelical Baptist—R
Evangelical Friend
Expression Christian
Faith Today
Family Journal—R
Family Network—R
Fellowship Today—R
Fidelity—R
First Things
Good News, Etc—R
Good News Reporter—R
Gospel Today
Head to Head—R
Healing Inn—R
Home Times—R
Indian Life—R
Inland NW Christian
Interim—R
It's Your Choice—R
John Milton—R
Jour/Christian Nursing—R
Kansas City Christian—R
Light and Life (600 wds)
Lutheran, The—R
Mennonite Brethren—R
Mennonite Reporter
Mennonite Weekly
MESSAGE/Open Bible
Messenger
Minnesota Christian—R
National Review
New Oxford Review
PrayerWorks—R
Presbyterian Outlook
Presbyterian Record—R
Presbyterians Today—R
Quiet Revolution—R
Role Model
Salt of the Earth—R
Social Justice—R
Sojourners

Standard, The—R
Star of Zion
United Church Observer
Upsouth—R
U.S. Catholic
Way of St. Francis—R

CHILDREN
Discovery—R

CHRISTIAN EDUCATION/LIBRARY
CE Connection—R
Today's Catholic Teacher—R

MISSIONS
American Horizon—R
Areopagus—R
East-West Church—R
Mission Today—R
Save Our World—R

PASTORS/LEADERS
Cell Life FORUM—R
Christian Century
Jour/Biblical Ethics—R
Journal/Christian Healing—R
Lutheran Forum—R
Priest, The
Single Ad. Ministries Jour.
Word & World
Worship Leader

TEEN/YOUNG ADULT
Christteen—R
Insight—R
Teen Life (AG)—R
Transcend
YOU!—R
Young Adult Today
Young Christian—R
Youth Focus—R

WOMEN
Anna's Journal—R
Conscience—R
Cottage Connections—R
DOMESTIQUE—R
Horizons
Lutheran Woman Today
Virtue—R

WRITERS
Canadian Writer's Jour—R
Exchange—R
Once Upon a Time—R
Southwestern Writers—R
Writer's Exchange—R

Writers Infor Network
Writer's Ink—R
Writer's News—R

PARENTING

ADULT/GENERAL
American Tract Soc.—R
Angels on Earth
Annals of St. Anne
Arkansas Catholic
Arlington Catholic
Atlantic Baptist
AXIOS—R
Banner, The
Baptist Beacon—R
Bible Advocate—R
Biblical Reflections—R
Bread of Life—R
Canada Lutheran—R
Canadian Baptist
Catholic Digest—R
Catholic Forester—R
Catholic Parent
Catholic Sentinel—R
Charisma/Christian Life
Christian Courier (CAN)—R
Christian Home & School
Christian Living—R
Christian Parenting—R
Christian Ranchman
Christian Reader—R
Christian Single—R
Church Advocate—R
Church Herald/Holiness—R
Columbia
Companion
Covenant Companion—R
Disciple's Journal—R
Dovetail—R
Emphasis/Faith & Living—R
Evangel—R
Evangelical Baptist—R
Evangelical Friend
Evangelical Visitor—R
Expression Christian
Faith Today
Family Digest—R
Family Network—R
Fellowship Today—R
Fidelity—R
Focus on the Family—R
Foursquare World—R
Friends Journal—R
God's Revivalist
Good News, Etc—R
Good News Journal—R
Gospel Tidings—R

Gospel Today
Hearing Hearts
Herald of Holiness—R
Home Life—R
Home Times—R
Impact Magazine—R
Indian Life—R
Inside Journal—R
Island Christian—R
It's Your Choice—R
Kansas City Christian—R
Life Gate—R
Light and Life
Liguorian
Live—R
Living—R
Living with Teenagers—R
Lookout—R
Lutheran, The—R
Marriage Partnership
Lutheran Digest—R
Lutheran Journal—R
Mennonite, The—R
Mennonite Brethren—R
MESSAGE
MESSAGE/Open Bible
Messenger/St. Anthony
Ministry Today—R
Moody—R
MovieGuide
National Review
New Covenant
New Man—R
New Oxford Review
Our Family—R
Our Sunday Visitor
ParentLife—R
Parent Paper, The
Pegasus Review—R
Pentecostal Evangel
Pentecostal Homelife—R
Plain Truth—R
Plus—R
Pourastan—R
PrayerWorks—R
Presbyterians Today—R
Progress—R
Purpose—R
Religious Education
St. Anthony Messenger
St. Joseph's Messenger—R
Seek—R
Single-Parent Family
Smart Dads
Social Justice—R
Sojourners
Standard—R
Standard, The—R

Stand Firm—R
Table Talk—R
Today's Family Matters—R
Today's Single—R
U.S. Catholic
Vibrant Life—R
Vision, The—R
War Cry—R
Wesleyan Advocate—R

CHRISTIAN EDUCATION/LIBRARY
Brigade Leader—R
CE Connection—R
CE Counselor—R
Children's Ministry
Christian School
Church Educator—R
GROUP

MISSIONS
Quiet Hour Echoes
Worldwide Challenge—R

MUSIC
Gospel Music

PASTORS/LEADERS
Celebration (SDA)—R
Diaconalogue—R
Discipleship Training
GROUP's Jr. High
Journal/Christian Healing—R
Journal/Pastoral Care
Lutheran Partners—R
Networks—R
Pastor's Family
Preacher's Illus. Service—R
Pulpit Helps—R
Single Ad. Ministries Jour.
Today's Christian Preacher—R
Youthworker—R

WOMEN
Aspire
DOMESTIQUE—R
Esprit—R
Helping Hand—R
Horizons
Joyful Woman—R
Just Between Us—R
Link & Visitor—R
Lutheran Woman's Quar.
Lutheran Woman Today
Proverbs 31 Homemaker—R
Tea and Sunshine
Today's Christian Woman

Virtue—R
Welcome Home
Wesleyan Woman—R
Woman's Touch—R

PERSONAL EXPERIENCE

ADULT/GENERAL
African Amer. Heritage—R
AGAIN—R
alive now!
Angels on Earth
Annals of St. Anne
At Ease—R
Banner, The
B.C. Catholic—R
Bible Advocate—R
Biblical Reflections—R
Canada Lutheran—R
Canadian Baptist
Catholic Digest—R
Catholic Forester—R
Catholic New York
Catholic Sentinel—R
Catholic Twin Circle—R
Celebrate Life—R
Christian Chronicle (PA)—R
Christian Courier (CAN)—R
Christian Edge—R
Christian Ranchman
Christian Reader—R
Christian Renewal—R
Christian Single—R
Chrysalis Reader
Church Advocate—R
Church Herald/Holiness—R
Comments/Friends—R
Commonweal
Companion
Companions—R
Compass
Conquest
Covenant Companion—R
Crossway/Newsline—R
Door, The
Dovetail—R
Evangel—R
Evangelical Baptist—R
Evangelical Friend
Evangelical Visitor—R
Explorer
Family Digest—R
Family Journal—R
Family Network—R
Fellowship in Prayer—R
Fellowship Today—R
Friends Journal—R

Gem, The—R
God's Revivalist
Good News—R
Good News, Etc—R
Good News Journal
Good News Reporter—R
Gospel Tidings—R
Gospel Today
Guideposts
Hallelujah! (CAN)—R
Head to Head—R
Healing Inn—R
Hearing Heart—R
Herald of Holiness—R
Highway News—R
Home Life—R
Home Times—R
Ideals
Impact Magazine—R
Indian Life—R
Inland NW Christian
Inspirer, The—R
Inside Journal—R
Interim—R
InterVarsity
Island Christian—R
It's Your Choice—R
John Milton—R
Jour/Christian Nursing—R
Light and Life
Liguorian
Live—R
Living—R
Lutheran, The—R
Lutheran Digest—R
Lutheran Journal—R
Lutheran Layman
Marian Helpers—R
Marriage Partnership
Mennonite, The—R
Mennonite Brethren—R
Mennonite Reporter
MESSAGE
MESSAGE/Open Bible
Minnesota Christian—R
Moody—R
New Covenant
New Heart, A—R
New Man—R
Newsline—R
New Thought—R
New Trumpet—R
New Writing—R
No-Debt Living—R
Northwestern Lutheran—R
Oblates
Our Family—R
Pentecostal Evangel

Pentecostal Homelife—R
Plain Truth—R
Plenty Good Room
Plus—R
Power for Living—R
PrayerWorks—R
Presbyterian Record—R
Presbyterians Today—R
Progress—R
Purpose—R
Pursuit—R
Religious Broadcasting—R
Remembrance—R
Role Model
St. Anthony Messenger
SCP Journal—R
Seek—R
Shantyman, The—R
Sharing—R
Single-Parent Family
Smile
Sojourners
Spiritual Life
Standard—R
Standard, The—R
Stand Firm—R
Stewardship
Sunday Digest—R
Table Talk—R
Time of Singing—R
Today's Family Matters—R
Today's Single—R
Touchstone
United Church Observer
Upsouth—R
VISION—R
Vision, The—R
Voice, The—R
Way of St. Francis—R
Weavings—R
Wesleyan Advocate—R

CHILDREN
Club Connection—R
Counselor—R
Courage
Discovery—R
Focus/Clubhouse
GUIDE—R
Power & Light—R
R-A-D-A-R—R
Skipping Stones
Venture

CHRISTIAN
EDUCATION/LIBRARY
Brigade Leader—R
CE Connection—R

CE Counselor—R
Journal/Adventist Educ.—R
Perspective—R
Religion Teacher's Journal
Today's Catholic Teacher—R

MISSIONS
American Horizon—R
Areopagus—R
Great Commission—R
Heartbeat—R
Mission Today—R
P.I.M.E. World
Quiet Hour Echoes
Save Our World—R
World Christian—R
Worldwide Challenge—R

MUSIC
Music Leader

PASTORS/LEADERS
Celebration (SDA)—R
Cell Church—R
Cell Life FORUM—R
Christian Century
Christian Ministry
Christian Recreation
Diaconalogue—R
Discipleship Training
Eucharistic Minister—R
Five Stones, The—R
Journal/Christian Healing—R
Journal/Pastoral Care
Leadership Journal—R
Networks—R
Pastor's Family
Preacher's Illus. Service—R
Preacher's Magazine—R
Sunday School Leader
Today's Parish
Youthworker—R

TEEN/YOUNG ADULT
Breakaway—R
Campus Life—R
Certainty
Challenge (IL)
Challenge (TN)—R
Christteen—R
Conqueror—R
Devo'Zine—R
Insight—R
Listen—R
On Course—R
Pathways—R
Sharing the VICTORY
Spirit

Straight—R
Teenage Christian—R
Teen Life (AG)—R
Teen Power—R
Teens on Target—R
Transcend
With—R (1st person teen)
YOU!—R
Young Adult Today
Young Christian—R
Young Salvationist—R
Youth Challenge—R
Youth Focus—R
Youth 97—R
Youth World—R
Zelos—R

WOMEN
Aspire
Cottage Connections—R
DOMESTIQUE—R
Esprit—R
Helping Hand—R
Horizons
Journey—R
Jour/Women's Ministries
Joyful Woman—R
Just Between Us—R
Link & Visitor—R
Lutheran Woman Today
Probe
Proverbs 31 Homemaker—R
Tea and Sunshine
Today's Christian Woman
Unique—R
Virtue—R
Welcome Home
Wesleyan Woman—R
Woman's Touch—R

WRITERS
Byline
Chips Off Writer's Block—R
Exchange—R
Housewife-Writer—R
Inklings
New Writing—R
Once Upon a Time—R
Southwestern Writers—R
Tickled by Thunder—R
Writer's Infor Network
Writer's Ink—R
Writer's News—R
Writer's Nook News

PHOTOGRAPHS

Note: "Reprint" indicators (R)

have been deleted from this section, and "B" for black & white glossy prints or "C" for color transparencies inserted. An asterisk (*) before a listing indicates they buy photos with articles only.

ADULT/GENERAL
ABS RECORD
African-Amer Heritage—B
Alive!—B
alive now!—B
American Tract Soc.
Anglican Journal—B/C
*Annals of St. Anne—B/C
Arlington Catholic—B
At Ease—B/C
Banner, The
Bible Advocate—B/C
Bible Today—B
Calvinist Contact—B/C
Canada Lutheran—B
*Cathedral Age—B
Catholic Courier—B
Catholic Digest—B/C
Catholic Forester—B/C
Catholic Heritage
Catholic New York—B
Catholic Parent
Catholic Rural Life—B
*Catholic Sentinel—B/C
Catholic Telegraph—B
Catholic Twin Circle—B
CBA Frontline—C
CBA Marketplace—C
Celebrate Life—B/C
Changes—B
Charisma/Christian Life—C
Christian Advocate—B/C
Christian Century—B
Christian Chronicle (OK)—B
Christian Courier—B
Christian Crusade—B
*Christian Edge—B
*Christian History—B/C
Christian Home & School—
   B/C
*Christian Information
Christian Living—B
Christian Parenting Today—
   B/C
*Christian Reader—B/C
Christian Retailing—C
*Christian Single—C
Christian Social Action—B
Christian Standard—B/C
Christianity Today—B/C

*Christmas—C
Church Advocate
Church & State
Church of God EVANGEL—
   C
Columbia—C/prints
Comments/Friends—B
*Commonweal—B/C
Companion—B
Connecting Point—B
*Conquest—B/C
Cornerstone—B/C
Covenant Companion—B/C
Disciple's Journal—B
Episcopal Life—B
*Evangel—B
Evangelical Baptist—B/C
Evangelical Beacon—B/C
Evangelical Friend—B
Evangelical Visitor—B
Expression Christian—B
Faith Today—B
Feelings Quarterly
Fellowship in Prayer—B
Fellowship Today—B
Fidelity—B/C
Focus on the Family—B/C
Foursquare World—C
Good News, Etc—C
Good News Journal—B
Gospel Tidings—B
Gospel Today—C
*Green Cross
*Guideposts—B/C
Hallelujah—B
Head to Head—B/C
Herald of Holiness—B/C
Highway News—B
*Home Life—C
*Home Times—B
Impact Magazine—C
Inland NW Christian—B
*Inside Journal—B
Inspirer, The—B
Interchange—B
Interim
InterVarsity—B
*Journal/Christian Nursing—
   B/C
Joyful Noise
Liberty—B/C
*Lifeglow—B/C
Light and Life—B/C
*Liguorian—B/C
Live—B/C
Living—B/C
Living Church—B/C
Living Light News—B/C

Lookout—B/C
Lutheran, The—B
Lutheran Journal—B/C
Lutheran Witness—B/C
Marian Helpers—B/C
Mature Living
*Mature Years—C
Mennonite, The—B/C
Mennonite Brethren—B
Mennonite Reporter—B/C
Mennonite Weekly—B
MESSAGE—B/C
Messenger—B
*Montana Catholic—B
Nat. Christian Reporter—
   B/C/prints
*New Heart, A—B
*New Man—C
New Thought—B/C
*New Trumpet—B
Northwestern Lutheran
Our Family—B/C
Our Sunday Visitor—B/C
Pentecostal Evangel—B/C
*Pentecostal Testimony—B/C
*Plain Truth—B/C
Plenty Good Room—B
*Power for Living—B
*Prairie Messenger—C
*Presbyterian Layman—B
Presbyterian Outlook—B/C
Presbyterian Record—B/C
Presbyterians Today—B/C
Prism—B/C
*Purpose—B
Pursuit—B
Quiet Revolution—B
Revelation Post—B/C
Role Model—B/C
Rutherford—B/C
*St. Anthony Messenger—
   B/C
Salt of the Earth—B
SCP Journal—B/C
Seek—B
Signs of the Times—C
Sojourners—B/C
Something Better
Spiritual Life—B
Sports Spectrum—C
Standard—B
Standard, The
Stand Firm—C
Sunday Digest—C
*Today's Family Matters—C
Today's Single—B
Total Health—B/C
Twin Cities Christian—B

*United Church Observer—
  B/C
*Vibrant Life—B/C
VISION—B/C
War Cry—C
Wesleyan Advocate—C
Witness, The

CHILDREN
*Counselor—B/C
*Courage
*Focus/Clubhouse—C
*Focus/Clubhouse Jr.—C
God's World Today—C
Guideposts for Kids—C
Junior Trails—C
Listen—C
Nature Friend—B/C
My Friend
On the Line—B
*Pockets—B/C
Power & Light—B/C
*Primary Days—B/C
*Primary Pal
R-A-D-A-R—C
*Skipping Stones—B
Story Friends—B
Together Time—C
Touch—C
Venture—C
Wonder Time—B/C

CHRISTIAN
EDUCATION/LIBRARY
Baptist Leader—B/C
*Brigade Leader—B
CE Counselor—B/C
CE Leadership—B/C
Children's Ministry—B/C
Christian Librarian—B
Christian School—C
*Church Educator—B
*Church Libraries—B/C
  prints
Evangelizing Today's Child—
  B/C
GROUP—B
Journal/Adventist Educa-
  tion—B
Junior Teacher—B/C
*Leader/Church School To-
  day—B
Level C Teacher—B
Lollipops
Parish Teacher—B
Religion Teacher's Journal—
  B/C
Teachers in Focus—C

Teachers Interaction—B
Team—B/C
*Today's Catholic Teacher—C

DAILY DEVOTIONALS
Daily Dev for Deaf—C
Light from the Word—C
Secret Place—B/C

MISSIONS
American Horizon
Areopagus—B/C
Catholic Near East—C
Great Commission—B/C
 PFI World Report
*P.I.M.E. World—C
Childlife
Intl Jour/Frontier—R
Message of the Cross—B/C
Mission Today—B/C
New World Outlook—C
Partners—C
*Wherever—B
World Christian—B/C
*World Vision—C
Worldwide Challenge—C

MUSIC
Christian Country—B
Church Musician—B
*Creator—B/C
*Gospel Music—C
Music Leader—B/C
Shout!—C

PASTORS/LEADERS
Celebration (SDA)—B/C
*Cell Life FORUM)—B/C
Christian Century—B/C
Christian Ministry—B
Discipleship Training—B
Environment & Art—B/C
GROUP's Jr. High—B/C
*Journal/Christian Camping—
  B/C
Leadership Journal—B
Liturgy—B
Lutheran Forum—B
*Lutheran Partners—B
Ministry—B
Networks—B
Preacher, The—B
Preacher's Magazine—B/C
Resource—B/C
Today's Parish—B/C
WCA Monthly—C
*Worship Leader—C
*Your Church—B/C

TEEN/YOUNG ADULT
Breakaway—C
Brio—C
Campus Life—C
*Certainty—B
*Challenge (IL)
*Challenge (TN)—B/C
*Christteen—B/C
The Conqueror—B/C
*Insight—B/C
Lighted Pathway—B/C
*Listen—B/C
On Course—C
Pathways—B/C
*Sharing the VICTORY—C
Spirit—B/C
Straight—C
Student Leadership—B/C
Take Five—B/C
Teenage Christian—B/C
Teen Life—B
*Teen Power—B
Teen Quest—B/C
Venture—B
With—B
Young Adult Today—B
Young & Alive—B(prefer)/C
Young Christian—B/C
*Youth Focus
Youth 97—C
*Zelos

WOMEN
Anna's Journal—B
Conscience—B
Esprit—B
Helping Hand—B
*Horizons—B/C
Jour/Women's Ministries—B
Joyful Woman—C
*Link & Visitor—B
Lutheran Woman Today—B
Probe—B/C
*Sisters Today—B
Today's Christian Woman—C
*Virtue—B/C
Wesleyan Woman
Women Alive!—B

WRITERS
*Byline
Gotta Write—B
*Housewife-Writer—B
Tickled by Thunder—B
Virginia Christian Writer
*Writer's Digest
Writer's World

POETRY

ADULT/GENERAL
African Amer. Heritage—R
alive now!
America
AXIOS—R
Banner, The
Baptist Beacon—R
Bible Advocate—R
Bread of Life—R
Broken Streets—R
Burning Light—R
Changes
Christian Century
Christian Courier (CAN)—R
Christian Living—R
Christian Ranchman
Christian Reader—R
Christian Single—R
Christianity/Arts
Christmas—R
Church Herald/Holiness—R
Commonweal
Companion
Companions—R
Connecting Point—R
Cornerstone—R
Covenant Companion—R
Creatively Yours
Cresset
Dawn & Dusk
Decision
Door, The
Evangel—R
Explorer
Family Journal—R
Family Network—R
Fatted Calf Forum—R
Feelings Quarterly—R
Fellowship in Prayer—R
Fidelity—R
First Things
Foursquare World—R
Friends Journal—R
God's Revivalist
Gospel Today
Green Cross—R
Guideposts
Hallelujah! (CAN)—R
Head to Head—R
Healing Inn—R
Hearing Hearts
Herald of Holiness—R
Home Life—R
Home Times—R
Ideals—R
Impact Magazine—R

Inspirer, The—R
Island Christian—R
Jewel Among Jewels—R
John Milton—R
Jour/Christian Nursing—R
Joyful Noise (KY)
Liberty (little)—R
Life Gate—R
Light and Life
Lighthouse Fiction
Live—R
Living Church
Lutheran Digest—R
Manna
Mature Living
Mature Years—R
Mennonite, The—R
Mennonite Brethren—R
Messenger of St. Anthony
Miraculous Medal
New Heart, A—R
New Thought—R
New Trumpet—R
New Writing—R
North American Voice
Oblates
Our Family—R
Parent Paper, The
Pegasus Review—R
Pentecostal Testimony—R
Perspectives
Plowman, The—R
Poetry Forum
Poet's Park—R
Pourastan—R
Prairie Messenger—R
PrayerWorks—R
Presbyterian Layman
Presbyterian Record—R
Presbyterians Today—R
Purpose—R
Queen of All Hearts
Ratio
Remembrance—R
Revelation Post—R
Role Model
St. Anthony Messenger
St. Joseph's Messenger—R
San Diego Co. Christian
Sharing—R
Silver Wings—R
Smile
Sojourners
Standard—R
Star of Zion
Sunday Digest—R
Table Talk—R
TEAK Roundup—R

Time for Rhyme
Time of Singing—R
Today's Single—R
Touchstone
Upsouth—R
Vision, The—R
Voice, The—R
War Cry—R
Weavings—R
Wesleyan Advocate—R
Witness, The

CHILDREN
Club Connection—R
CLUBHOUSE—R
Creatively Yours
Discovery—R
Focus/Clubhouse Jr
Guideposts for Kids
Junior Trails—R
Listen
Mission
Nature Friend—R
On the Line—R
Our Little Friend—R
Partners—R
Pockets—R
Primary Treasure—R
R-A-D-A-R—R
Skipping Stones
Story Friends—R
Story Mates—R
Together Time
Touch—R
Young Christian—R

CHRISTIAN EDUCATION/LIBRARY
Baptist Leader—R
Christian Educators Jour—R
Christian School
Church Educator—R
Church Worship
Level C Teacher—R
Lollipops
Resource—R
Shining Star
Teacher Interaction
Today's Catholic Teacher—R
Vision—R

DAILY DEVOTIONALS
Living Words—R
Secret Place

MISSIONS
Quiet Hour Echoes

MUSIC
Choir Herald, etc.
Church Musician—R
Church Pianist, etc.
Glory Songs—R
Gospel Music
Hymn, The (hymns only)
Music Leader
Quest—R
Senior Musician—R
Tradition

PASTORS/LEADERS
Art+Plus
Catechumenate
Cell Life FORUM—R
Christian Century
Cross Currents—R
Diaconalogue—R
Emmanuel
Journal/Christian Camping
Journal/Christian Healing—R
Journal/Pastoral Care
Liturgy
Lutheran Forum—R
Lutheran Partners—R
Networks—R
Preacher, The
Preacher's Illus. Service—R
Pulpit Helps—R
Review for Religious
Today's Parish

TEEN/YOUNG ADULT
Campus Life
Christteen—R
Devo'Zine—R
Insight—R
On Course—R
Pathways—R
Sharing the VICTORY
Straight—R
Student Leadership—R
Take Five—R
Teenage Christian—R
Teen Life (AG)—R
Teen Power—R (by teens)
Teen Quest—R (by teens)
Transcend
With—R
YOU!—R
Young Christian—R
Young Salvationist—R
Youth Focus—R
Youth 97—R (by teens)
Youth World—R
Zelos—R

WOMEN
Anna's Journal—R
Conscience—R
Cottage Connections—R
DOMESTIQUE—R
Esprit—R
Horizons
Jour/Women's Ministries
Journey—R
Joyful Woman—R
Link & Visitor—R
Lutheran Woman Today
Probe
Proverbs 31 Homemaker—R
Sisters Today
Tea and Sunshine
Unique—R
Virtue—R
Welcome Home
Wesleyan Woman—R
Woman's Touch—R
Women Alive!—R

WRITERS
Byline
Canadian Writer's Jour—R
Christian Communicator—R
Cross & Quill—R
Felicity—R
Gotta Write
Heaven—R
Housewife-Writer—R
Inklings
My Legacy—R
Omnific—R
Once Upon a Time—R
Poetry Connection
Salt & The Light, The—R
Southwestern Writers—R
Tickled by Thunder—R
Today's $85,000 Freelance
Writer's Digest
Writer's Exchange—R
Writer's Infor Network
Writer's Ink—R
Writer's World—R
Write Touch—R

POLITICAL

ADULT/GENERAL
Anglican Journal—R
Arkansas Catholic
Arlington Catholic
AXIOS—R
Banner, The
Banner News
Bible Advocate—R

Biblical Reflections—R
Canadian Catholic
Catholic Courier
Catholic Insight
Celebrate Life—R
Christian American
Christian Chronicle (PA)—R
Christian C.L. RECORD—R
Christian Courier (WI)—R
Christian Courier (CAN)—R
Christian Crusade
Christian Edge—R
Christian Renewal—R
Christian Single—R
Christian Social Action—R
Christianity Today—R
Commonweal
Compass
Cornerstone—R
Cresset
Evangelical Baptist—R
Evangelical Friend
Expression Christian
Fatted Calf Forum—R
First Things
Good News, Etc—R
Good News Reporter—R
Gospel Today
Head to Head—R
Home Times—R
Indian Life—R
Inland NW Christian
Interim—R
It's Your Choice—R
Journal of Church & State
Kansas City Christian—R
MESSAGE
Minnesota Christian—R
National Review
Presbyterian Outlook
Presbyterians Today—R
Prism—R
Providence—R
Religious Broadcasting—R
Religious Education
Rutherford
Salt of the Earth—R
SCP Journal—R
Social Justice—R
Sojourners
Standard, The—R
Stand Firm—R
Upsouth—R
Way of St. Francis—R
Witness, The

CHRISTIAN EDUCATION/LIBRARY
Today's Catholic Teacher—R

MISSIONS
Areopagus—R
East-West Church—R

PASTORS/LEADERS
Christian Century
Networks—R
Preacher's Illus. Service—R
Word & World

TEEN/YOUNG ADULT
Caleb Issues & Answers
Transcend
With—R
Young Adult Today
Young Christian—R

WOMEN
Conscience—R
Cottage Connections—R
Horizons
Virtue—R
Wesleyan Woman—R

PRAYER

ADULT/GENERAL
alive now!
Angels on Earth
Annals of St. Anne
At Ease—R
Atlantic Baptist
Banner, The
Baptist Beacon—R
Baptist Informer
Bible Advocate—R
Bread of Life—R
Brethren Evangelist
Broken Streets
Canadian Baptist
Canadian Catholic
Catholic Digest—R
Celebrate Life—R
Charisma/Christian Life
Christian Chronicle (PA)—R
Christian Edge—R
Christianity Today—R
Christian Living—R
Christian Ranchman
Christian Reader—R
Christian Single—R
Church Advocate—R
Church Herald/Holiness—R
Church of God EVANGEL

Companion
Companions—R
Compass
Connecting Point—R
Conquest
Cornerstone—R
Covenant Companion—R
Decision
Disciple's Journal—R
Discipleship Journal
Emphasis/Faith & Living—R
Episcopal life—R
Evangel—R
Evangelical Baptist—R
Evangelical Friend
Evangelical Visitor—R
Explorer
Family Digest—R
Family Journal—R
Family Network—R
Fellowship in Prayer—R
Fellowship Link—R
Fellowship Today—R
Fidelity—R
Foursquare World—R
Friends Journal—R
God's Revivalist
Good News, Etc—R
Good News Journal—R
Good News Reporter—R
Gospel Today
Head to Head—R
Healing Inn—R
Hearing Hearts
Herald of Holiness—R
Home Times—R
Indian Life—R
Inland NW Christian
Inspirer, The—R
Island Christian—R
John Milton—R
Jour/Christian Nursing—R
Kansas City Christian—R
Life Gate—R
Light and Life
Liguorian
Live—R
Living Church
Lookout—R
Lutheran, The—R
Lutheran Digest—R
Lutheran Journal—R
Lutheran Layman
Lutheran Witness—R
Marian Helpers—R
Marriage Partnership
Mennonite, The—R
Mennonite Brethren—R

MESSAGE
MESSAGE/Open Bible
Messenger/St. Anthony
Messenger of the Sacred
    Heart
Ministry Today—R
Moody—R
New Covenant
New Man—R
New Oxford Review
North American Voice
Northwestern Lutheran—R
Our Family—R
Our Sunday Visitor
Pegasus Review—R
Pentecostal Homelife—R
Perspectives
Plain Truth—R
Plowman, The—R
Plus—R
Poet's Park—R
Pourastan—R
Power for Living—R
Prairie Messenger—R
PrayerWorks—R
Presbyterian Outlook
Presbyterian Record—R
Presbyterians Today—R
Purpose—R
Queen of All Hearts
St. Anthony Messenger
Salt of the Earth—R
Seek—R
Silver Wings—R
Sojourners
Spiritual Life
Standard—R
Standard, The—R
Stand Firm—R
Star of Zion
Sunday Digest—R
Table Talk—R
Time of Singing—R
Today's Christian Senior—R
Upsouth—R
U.S. Catholic
Vision, The—R
War Cry—R
Watchman, The
Way of St. Francis—R
Weavings—R
Wesleyan Advocate—R

CHILDREN
BREAD/God's Children—R
Club Connection—R
Counselor—R
Courage

Discovery—R
Focus/Clubhouse
GUIDE—R
High Adventure—R
Power & Light—R
R-A-D-A-R—R
Touch—R
Wonder Time
Young Christian—R

*CHRISTIAN
EDUCATION/LIBRARY*
Brigade Leader—R
CE Connection—R
CE Counselor—R
Church Educator—R
Church Worship
Evangelizing Today's Child—R
Religion Teacher's Journal
Shining Star
Vision—R

MISSIONS
American Horizon—R
Areopagus—R
Childlife—R
Intl Jour/Frontier—R
Message of the Cross—R
Mission Today—R
PFI World Report—R
Save Our World—R
World Mission People—R
Worldwide Challenge—R

MUSIC
Creator—R
Quest—R
Quiet Hour Echoes

PASTORS/LEADERS
Celebration (Catholic)
Celebration (SDA)—R
Cell Life FORUM—R
Chicago Studies
Christian Ministry
Emmanuel
Evangelism USA
Five Stones, The—R
Journal/Christian Healing—R
Jour/Amer Soc/Chur Growth
Leadership Journal—R
Liturgy—R
Lutheran Partners—R
Ministries Today
Ministry
Modern Liturgy—R
Networks—R

Pastoral Life
Preacher, The
Preacher's Illus. Service—R
Preacher's Magazine—R
Priest, The
PROCLAIM—R
Reformed Worship
Resource—R
Today's Christian Preacher—R
Today's Parish
Word & World
Worship Leader

TEEN/YOUNG ADULT
Certainty
Challenge (IL)
Challenge (TN)—R
Conqueror—R
Devo'Zine—R
Insight—R
On Course—R
Pathways—R
Straight—R
Student Leadership—R
Teenage Christian—R
Teen Life (AG)—R
Teen Power—R
Teens on Target—R
Today's Christian Teen—R
Transcend
Vision—R
With—R
YOU!—R
Young Adult Today
Young Christian—R
Young Salvationist—R
Youth Challenge—R
Youth 97—R
Youth Update

WOMEN
CoLaborer
Cottage Connections—R
Esprit—R
Helping Hand—R
Horizons
Journey—R
Joyful Woman—R
Just Between Us—R
Lutheran Woman's Quar.
Lutheran Woman Today
Proverbs 31 Homemaker—R
Sisters Today
Today's Christian Woman
Unique—R
Virtue—R
Wesleyan Woman—R

Women Alive!—R

WRITERS
Southwestern Writers—R

PROPHECY

ADULT/GENERAL
Apocalypse Chronicles—R
Banner, The
Baptist Beacon—R
Bible Advocate—R
Bread of Life—R
Catholic Digest—R
Charisma/Christian Life
Christian Edge—R
Christian Info. Assoc. —R
Church Herald/Holiness—R
Conquest
Evangelical Baptist—R
Evangelical Friend
Faith Today
Fellowship Link—R
Foursquare World—R
God's Revivalist
Good News, Etc—R
Gospel Today
Hallelujah! (CAN)—R
Kansas City Christian—R
MESSAGE
MESSAGE/Open Bible
New Thought—R
Our Family—R
Pentecostal Testimony—R
Queen of All Hearts
Revelation Post—R
SCP Journal—R
Signs of the Times—R
Silver Wings—R
Today's Christian Senior—R
Watchman, The
Way of St. Francis—R

MISSIONS
Quiet Hour Echoes

PASTORS/LEADERS
Journal/Christian Healing—R
Ministries Today
PROCLAIM—R
Today's Christian Preacher—R
Voice of the Vineyard —R
Word & World

TEEN/YOUNG ADULT
Caleb Issues & Answers
Certainty

Young Adult Today

WOMEN
Virtue—R
Woman's Touch—R

WRITERS
New Writing—R

PSYCHOLOGY

ADULT/GENERAL
AXIOS—R
Banner, The
Biblical Reflections—R
Catholic Digest—R
Catholic Twin Circle—R
Christian Chronicle (PA)—R
Chrysalis Reader
Church Advocate—R
Common Boundary
Companion
Cornerstone—R
Evangelical Friend
Faith Today
Good News, Etc—R
Island Christian—R (maybe)
It's Your Choice—R
Jewel Among Jewels—R
John Milton—R
Jour/Christian Nursing—R
Lutheran Layman
MESSAGE
MESSAGE/Open Bible
MovieGuide
New Covenant
New Thought—R
New Writing—R
Our Family—R
Perspectives
Ratio
Religious Education
St. Anthony Messenger
SCP Journal—R
Social Justice—R
Spiritual Life
Standard, The—R
Star of Zion
Total Health
Upsouth—R

CHILDREN
Discovery—R

CHRISTIAN
EDUCATION/LIBRARY
Church Educator—R

PASTORAL/LEADERS
Cell Church—R
Christian Counseling Today
Christian Ministry
Eucharistic Minister—R
Five Stones, The—R
Jour/Biblical Ethics—R
Journal/Christian Healing—R
Journal/Pastoral Care
Ministries Today
Priest, The
Single Ad. Ministries Jour.
Word & World

WOMEN
Esprit—R
Horizons
Virtue—R

WRITERS
Inklings

PUPPET PLAYS

CE Counselor—R
Children's Ministry
Christian Recreation
Christianity/Arts
Church Educator—R
Church Street Press
Club Connection—R
Creatively Yours
Evangelizing Today's Child—
  R
Focus/Clubhouse
Focus/Clubhouse Jr
Kids' Stuff—R
Lillenas
Sheer Joy! Press
Shining Star
Teacher's Interaction
Touch—R

RELATIONSHIPS

ADULT/GENERAL
Angels on Earth
Annals of St. Anne
At Ease—R
AXIOS—R
Banner, The
Bible Advocate—R
Biblical Reflections—R
Canada Lutheran—R
Catholic Digest—R
Charisma/Christian Life
Christian Edge—R
Christian Living—R

Christian Parenting—R
Christian Ranchman
Christian Reader—R
Christian Single—R
Chrysalis Reader
Church Advocate—R
Columbia
Companion
Conquest
Covenant Companion—R
Decision
Disciple's Journal—R
Discipleship Journal
Dovetail—R
Evangel—R
Evangelical Baptist—R
Explorer
Faith Today
Family Network—R
Fellowship Link—R
Foursquare World—R
Good News, Etc—R
Good News Journal—R
Gospel Tidings—R
Gospel Today
Guideposts
Head to Head—R
Healing Inn—R
Hearing Hearts
Herald of Holiness—R
Highway News—R
Home Times—R
Island Christian—R
Inside Journal—R
It's Your Choice—R
Jewel Among Jewels—R
John Milton—R
Jour/Christian Nursing—R
Kansas City Christian—R
Life Gate—R
Lifeglow—R
Liguorian
Live—R
Lookout—R
Lutheran Digest—R
Lutheran Journal—R
Marriage Partnership
MESSAGE
Ministry Today—R
Moody—R
MovieGuide
New Man—R
New Thought—R
Pegasus Review—R
Pentecostal Homelife—R
Plus—R
Positive Living—R
Pourastan—R

PrayerWorks—R
Progress—R
Purpose—R
Pursuit—R
Remembrance—R
Silver Wings—R
Single-Parent Family
Standard, The—R
Stand Firm—R
Sunday Digest—R
Table Talk—R
TEAK Roundup—R
Time of Singing—R
Today's Christian Senior—R
Upsouth—R
U.S. Catholic
Voice, The—R
War Cry—R
Way of St. Francis—R

CHILDREN
BREAD for God's Children
Club Connection—R
Discovery—R
Focus/Clubhouse Jr
GUIDE—R
High Adventure—R
On the Line—R
Power & Light—R
R-A-D-A-R—R
Touch—R
Young Christian—R

*CHRISTIAN
EDUCATION/LIBRARY*
Brigade Leader—R
CE Counselor—R
Perspective—R

MISSIONS
American Horizon—R
Message of the Cross—R
Quiet Hour Echoes
Worldwide Challenge—R

PASTORS/LEADERS
Celebration (SDA)—R
Cell Church—R
Cell Life FORUM—R
Five Stones, The—R
Journal/Pastoral Care
Leadership Journal—R
Lutheran Partners—R
Ministries Today
Ministry
Pastor's Family
Preacher's Magazine—R
Today's Christian Preacher—

R
Youthworker—R
Voice of the Vineyard —R
Word & World

TEEN/YOUNG ADULT
Certainty
Challenge (IL)
Challenge (TN)—R
Christteen—R
Devo'Zine—R
Insight—R
Listen—R
On Course—R
Straight—R
Student Leadership—R
Teenage Christian—R
Teen Life (AG)—R
Teen Power—R
Teens on Target—R
Today's Christian Teen—R
With—R
YOU!—R
Young Christian—R
Young Salvationist—R
Youth Challenge—R
Youth 97—R
Youth Update
Zelos—R

WOMEN
Anna's Journal—R
Aspire
Esprit—R
Helping Hand—R
Horizons
Journey—R
Joyful Woman—R
Just Between Us—R
Link & Visitor—R
Lutheran Woman's Quar.
Proverbs 31 Homemaker—R
Tea and Sunshine
Today's Christian Woman
Unique—R
Virtue—R
Welcome Home
Wesleyan Woman—R
Woman's Touch—R

WRITERS
Southwestern Writers—R

RELIGIOUS FREEDOM

ADULT/GENERAL
AGAIN—R
America

Annals of St. Anne
Arlington Catholic
AXIOS—R
Banner, The
Banner News
Bible Advocate—R
Biblical Reflections—R
Bread of Life—R
Catholic Twin Circle—R
Charisma/Christian Life
Christian Advocate—R
Christian Arts Review
Christian Chronicle (PA)—R
Christian C.L. RECORD—R
Christian Courier (WI)—R
Christian Courier (CAN)—R
Christian Edge—R
Christian Info. Assoc. —R
Christian Ranchman
Christianity Today—R
Church & State—R
Church Herald/Holiness—R
Columbia
Comments/Friends—R
Connecting Point—R
Cornerstone—R
Covenant Companion—R
Cresset
Disciple's Journal—R
Dovetail—R
Episcopal Life—R
Evangelical Friend
Family Journal—R
Faith Today
Fatted Calf Forum—R
First Things
Friends Journal—R
God's Revivalist
Good News, Etc—R
Good News Journal—R
Good News Reporter—R
Gospel Today
Hallelujah! (CAN)—R
Herald of Holiness—R
Home Times—R
It's Your Choice—R
John Milton—R
Journal of Church & State
Kansas City Christian—R
Liberty—R
Life Gate—R
MESSAGE
MESSAGE/Open Bible
Minnesota Christian—R
Moody—R
National Review
New Thought—R
Our Family—R

Our Sunday Visitor
Pegasus Review—R
Pourastan—R
Presbyterian Layman
Presbyterian Outlook
Presbyterians Today—R
Prism—R
Providence—R
Religious Broadcasting—R
Religious Education
Rutherford
SCP Journal—R
Social Justice—R
Something Better—R
Spiritual Life
Stand Firm—R
Star of Zion
Today's Christian Senior—R
United Church Observer
U.S. Catholic
Upsouth—R
War Cry—R
Way of St. Francis—R

CHILDREN
GUIDE—R
High Adventure—R
Skipping Stones

CHRISTIAN EDUCATION/LIBRARY
CE Connection—R
Church Worship
Vision—R

MISSIONS
Areopagus—R
East-West Church—R
Quiet Hour Echoes
Worldwide Challenge—R

MUSIC
Quest—R

PASTORS/LEADERS
Cell Church—R
Christian Century
Christian Ministry
Discipleship Training
Five Stones, The—R
Jour/Biblical Ethics—R
Journal/Christian Healing—R
Ministry
Networks—R
Today's Christian Preacher—R
Word & World

TEEN/YOUNG ADULT
Caleb Issues & Answers
Conqueror—R
Young Adult Today
Young Christian—R

WOMEN
Esprit—R
Horizons
Virtue—R

WRITERS
Christian Response—R

SALVATION TESTIMONIES

ADULT/GENERAL
AGAIN—R
American Tract Soc.—R
At Ease—R
Banner, The
Bible Advocate—R
Broken Streets
Christian Chronicle (PA)—R
Christian Ranchman
Church Herald/Holiness—R
Companions—R
Connecting Point—R
Conquest
Covenant Companion—R
Crossway/Newsline—R
Decision
Emphasis/Faith & Living—R
Evangel—R
Evangelical Baptist—R
Evangelical Friend
Explorer
Family Network—R
Fellowship Link—R
God's Revivalist
Good News—R
Good News, Etc—R
Good News Journal
Good News Reporter—R
Gospel Today
Hallelujah! (CAN)—R
Head to Head—R
Healing Inn—R
Hearing Hearts
Herald of Holiness—R
Highway News—R
Home Times—R
Indian Life—R
Inside Journal—R
Inspirer, The—R
Island Christian—R
John Milton—R

Light and Life
Live—R
Living Light News—R
Lutheran Journal—R
Mennonite Brethren—R
MESSAGE
MESSAGE/Open Bible
Ministry Today—R
Moody—R
New Covenant
New Heart, A—R
New Man—R
New Oxford Review
New Trumpet—R
Pentecostal Testimony—R
Power for Living—R
PrayerWorks—R
Progress—R
Pursuit—R
Revelation Post—R
Salt & The Light, The—R
SCP Journal—R
Shantyman, The—R
Silver Wings—R
Something Better—R
Standard—R
Stand Firm—R
Sunday Digest—R
Upsouth—R
VISION (CA)—R
Voice, The—R
War Cry—R
Watchman, The
Wesleyan Advocate—R

CHILDREN
Club Connection—R
Counselor—R
Courage
Discovery—R
GUIDE—R
Primary Days—R

CHRISTIAN EDUCATION/LIBRARY
Evangelizing Today's Child—R

MISSIONS
American Horizon—R
Childlife—R
Save Our World—R
Worldwide Challenge—R

PASTORS/LEADERS
Cell Church—R
Journal/Christian Healing—R
Ministry

Networks—R
Preacher's Magazine—R

TEEN/YOUNG ADULT
Challenge (IL)
Challenge (TN)—R
Christteen—R
Conqueror—R
On Course—R
Teen Life (AG)—R
Teen Power—R
With—R
Young Adult Today

WOMEN
Esprit—R
Helping Hand—R
Journey—R
Joyful Woman—R
Unique—R
Virtue—R
Wesleyan Woman—R
Woman's Touch—R

SCIENCE

ADULT/GENERAL
AXIOS—R
Banner, The
Banner News
Biblical Reflections—R
Canadian Catholic
Catholic Digest—R
Catholic Twin Circle—R
Christian C.L. RECORD—R
Christian Courier (CAN)—R
Christian Reader—R
Companions—R
Compass
Disciple's Journal—R
Faith Today
Family Journal—R
Home Times—R
John Milton—R
Kansas City Christian—R
MovieGuide
National Review
Perspectives
PrayerWorks—R
Religious Education
SCP Journal—R
Something Better—R
Standard, The—R
Upsouth—R
War Cry—R

CHILDREN
My Friend

Nature Friend—R
Power & Light—R
Primary Days—R
R-A-D-A-R—R

*CHRISTIAN
EDUCATION/LIBRARY*
Vision—R

PASTORS/LEADERS
Jour/Biblical Ethics—R
Journal/Christian Healing—R
Lutheran Partners—R
Word & World

TEEN/YOUNG ADULT
Caleb Issues & Answers
Challenge (TN)—R
Young Adult Today

WOMEN
Esprit—R

WRITERS
New Writing—R

*SELF-HELP

Note: This year, How-To and Self-Help are listed separately. All markets listed when they were combined are still under How-to, so check that topic.

ADULT/GENERAL
Believer, The—R
Catholic Forester—R
Christian Edge—R
Christian Living—R
Christian Ranchman
Christian Single—R
Companion
Disciple's Journal—R
Discovery—R
Dovetail—R
Expression Christian
Family Digest—R
Fellowship Link—R
Gospel Today
Island Christian—R
John Milton—R
Lutheran Journal—R
Marriage Partnership
Mennonite, The—R
New Thought—R
New Writing—R
Our Family—R
Stand Firm—R

TEAK Roundup—R
Upsouth—R
War Cry—R

CHILDREN
Discovery—R
Skipping Stones

*CHRISTIAN
EDUCATION/LIBRARY*
Brigade Leader—R

PASTORS/LEADERS
Cell Church—R

TEEN/YOUNG ADULT
Challenge (TN)—R
Straight—R
Teen Life (AG)—R
With—R
Youth 97—R

WOMEN
DOMESTIQUE—R
Esprit—R
Horizons—R
Today's Christian Woman

SENIOR ADULT ISSUES

ADULT/GENERAL
Alive!—R
Angels on Earth
Anglican Journal—R
Annals of St. Anne
Atlantic Baptist
AXIOS—R
Banner, The
B.C. Catholic—R
Bible Advocate
Biblical Reflections—R
Brethren Evangelist
Canada Lutheran—R
Canadian Baptist
Catholic Digest—R
Catholic Forester—R
Christian Courier (CAN)—R
Christian Edge—R
Christian Home & School
Christian Living—R
Church Advocate—R
Church Herald/Holiness—R
Church of God EVANGEL
Columbia
Companion
Conquest
Covenant Companion—R
Disciple's Journal—R

Discovery—R
Emphasis/Faith & Living—R
Evangel—R
Evangelical Baptist—R
Evangelical Friend
Expression Christian
Family Network—R
Fellowship Link—R
Good News, Etc—R
Good News Journal—R
Gospel Today
Hearing Hearts
Herald of Holiness—R
Home Times—R
Inspirer, The—R
Island Christian—R
John Milton—R
Jour/Christian Nursing—R
Kansas City Christian—R
Life Gate—R
Light and Life
Liguorian
Lutheran, The—R
Lutheran Digest—R
Lutheran Journal—R
Mature Years—R
MESSAGE/Open Bible
Minnesota Christian—R
Montana Catholic—R
Moody—R
NW Christian Journal—R
Our Family—R
Our Sunday Visitor
Pentecostal Evangel
Plus—R
Power for Living—R
PrayerWorks—R
Presbyterian Record—R
Presbyterians Today—R
Purpose—R
Resource—R
Sojourners
Standard—R
Standard, The—R
Star of Zion
Sunday Digest—R
Today's Christian Senior—R
Upsouth—R
U.S. Catholic
Voice, The—R
War Cry—R
Wesleyan Advocate—R
Witness, The

*CHRISTIAN
EDUCATION/LIBRARY*
CE Connection—R
CE Counselor—R

CE Leadership—R
Church Educator—R

MISSIONS
Worldwide Challenge—R

MUSIC
Senior Musician—R

PASTORS/LEADERS
Celebration (SDA)—R
Christian Ministry
Diocesan Dialogue—R
Diaconalogue—R
Five Stones, The—R
Jour/Biblical Ethics—R
Journal/Christian Healing
  —R
Lutheran Partners—R
Pastoral Life
Pulpit Helps—R
Single Ad. Ministries Jour.
Word & World

WOMEN
Cottage Connections—R
Esprit—R
Horizons
Today's Christian Woman
Virtue—R
Wesleyan Woman—R
Woman's Touch—R

SERMONS

ADULT/GENERAL
Arlington Catholic
Banner, The
Baptist Beacon—R
Bible Advocate—R
Cathedral Age
Christian Chronicle (PA)—R
Church Herald/Holiness—R
Cresset
Evangelical Baptist—R
God's Revivalist
Good News, Etc—R
Gospel Today
Green Cross—R
Hallelujah! (CAN)—R
Healing Inn—R
Inspirer, The—R
Joyful Noise
Presbyterians Today—R
Sojourners
Standard, The—R
Star of Zion
Upsouth—R

Way of St. Francis—R
Weavings—R

*CHRISTIAN
EDUCATION/LIBRARY*
Church Educator—R
Church Worship

MISSIONS
Quiet Hour Echoes

PASTORS/LEADERS
Celebration (Catholic)
Christian Ministry
Clergy Journal—R
Enrichment—R
In Season
Journal/Christian Healing—R
Leadership Journal—R
Preacher's Illus. Service—R
Preacher's Magazine—R
Preaching
PROCLAIM—R
Pulpit Helps—R
Sermon Notes
Today's Parish

WOMEN
Virtue—R

SHORT STORY:
ADULT/RELIGIOUS

African Amer. Heritage—R
Alive!—R
alive now!
Annals of St. Anne
Anna's Journal—R
Baptist Informer
Burning Light—R
Canadian Writer's Jour—R
Catholic Forester—R
Changes
Chip Off Writer's Block—R
Christian Advocate—R
Christian Century
Christian Chronicle (PA)—R
Christian Courier (CAN)—R
Christian Educators Journal
Christian Living—R
Christian Reader—R
Christian Renewal—R
Christian School
Christian Single—R
Christianity/Arts
Christmas—R
Church & Synagogue Lib.
Church Musician

CoLaborer
Companion
Connecting Point—R
Conquest
Cornerstone—R
Cottage Connections—R
Covenant Companion—R
Dawn & Dusk
Discipleship Journal
Discovery—R
Dreams & Visions—R
Emphasis/Faith & Living—R
Esprit—R
Evangel—R
Evangelical Baptist
Evangelical Visitor—R
Explorer
Family Network—R
Fatted Calf Forum—R
Felicity—R
Fellowship Link—R
Five Stones, The—R
Friends Journal—R
Gem, The
God's Revivalist
Gospel Tidings—R
Head to Head—R
Healing Inn—R
Hearing Hearts
Helping Hand—R
Home Life—R
Home Times—R
Horizons
Housewife-Writer—R
Impact Magazine—R
Inklings
Inspirer, The—R
It's Your Choice—R
John Milton—R
Journal/Christian Healing—R
Journal/Pastoral Care
Joyful Woman—R
Lighthouse Fiction
Liguorian
Live—R
Living Light News—R
Living with Teenagers—R
Lookout—R
Lutheran Digest
Lutheran Partners—R
Lutheran Witness—R
Lutheran Woman's Quar.
Lutheran Woman Today
Mature Living
Mature Years—R
Mennonite Brethren—R
Messenger/Sacred Heart
Ministry Today—R

Miraculous Medal
Moody—R
My Legacy—R
New Trumpet—R
New Writing—R
North American Voice
Pegasus Review—R
Pentecostal Homelife—R
Pentecostal Testimony—R
Perspectives
Place to Enter, A
Plowman, The—R
Poetry Forum
PrayerWorks—R
Presbyterian Record—R
Probe
Queen of All Hearts
Quest—R
Ratio
St. Anthony Messenger
St. Joseph's Messenger—R
Salt & The Light, The—R
San Diego Co. Christian
Seek—R
Sojourners
Standard—R
Sunday Digest—R
TEAK Roundup—R
Tickled by Thunder—R
Today's Christian Woman
Today's Single—R
Touchstone
Upsouth—R
U.S. Catholic
Virtue—R
Vision—R
Way of St. Francis—R
Weavings—R
Wherever
Women Alive!—R
Write Touch—R
Writing Right—R

SHORT STORY: ADVENTURE

CHILDREN
Annals of St. Anne
BREAD/God's Children—R
CLUBHOUSE—R
Connecting Point—R
Counselor—R
Courage
Crusader—R
Discoveries—R
Discovery—R
Focus/Clubhouse
Focus/Clubhouse Jr

GUIDE—R
Guideposts for Kids
Junior Trails—R
Lighthouse Fiction
Listen
Lollipops (young)
My Friend
Power & Light—R
Primary Days—R
Primary Pal
R-A-D-A-R—R
Touch—R
Young Christian—R

TEEN/YOUNG ADULT
Annals of St. Anne
Breakaway—R
Challenge (IL)
Christteen—R
Discovery—R
Insight—R
It's Your Choice—R
Lighthouse Fiction
Pathways—R
Straight—R
Teenage Christian—R
Teen Life (AG)—R
Teen Life (AG)—R
Teen Quest—R
Teens on Target—R
Teens Today—R
Young Adult Today
Young Christian—R
Youth Challenge—R
Youth World—R

ADULT
African Amer. Heritage—R
Alive!—R
Annals of St. Anne
Byline
Chip Off Writer's Block—R
Christian Courier (CAN)—R
Christianity/Arts
Dawn & Dusk
Dreams & Visions—R
Emphasis/Faith & Living—R
Felicity—R
Healing Inn—R
Home Life—R
Inklings
It's Your Choice—R
Lighthouse Fiction
Liguorian
Live—R
Miraculous Medal
My Legacy—R
New Thought—R

New Trumpet—R
New Writing—R
Pentecostal Testimony—R
Place to Enter, A
Standard—R
TEAK Roundup—R
Upsouth—R
Virtue—R
Vision, The—R

SHORT STORY: ALLEGORY

CHILDREN
Discovery—R
Focus/Clubhouse
GUIDE—R
Head to Head—R
Pockets—R
Touch—R

TEENS/YOUNG ADULT
Conqueror—R
Discovery—R
Head to Head—R
I.D.
It's Your Choice—R
John Milton—R
Student Leadership—R
Teen Life (AG)—R
Teen Quest—R
With—R
YOU!—R
Youth World—R

ADULT
Byline
Burning Light—R
Chip Off Writer's Block—R
Christianity/Arts
Christian Living—R
Christian Single—R
Cottage Connections—R
Covenant Companion—R
Dawn & Dusk
Discipleship Journal
Discovery—R
Dreams & Visions—R
Esprit—R
Family Network—R
Fatted Calf Forum—R
Felicity—R
Head to Head—R
Healing Inn—R
Hearing Hearts
Highway News—R
Home Times—R
Inklings

Inspirer, The—R
It's Your Choice—R
Mennonite Brethren—R
My Legacy—R
New Trumpet—R
New Writing—R
Pentecostal Testimony—R
Perspectives
Place to Enter, A
Prism—R
Ratio
Salt & The Light, The—R
Tea and Sunshine
Virtue—R
Vision, The—R
Way of St. Francis—R
Weavings—R

SHORT STORY: BIBLICAL

CHILDREN
Annals of St. Anne
BREAD/God's Children—R
Church Educator—R
Discoveries—R
Discovery—R
Focus/Clubhouse
Focus/Clubhouse Jr
Gospel Tidings—R
Head to Head—R
MESSAGE
John Milton—R
Pockets—R
Power & Light—R
Preacher's Illus. Service—R
R-A-D-A-R—R
Young Christian—R

TEEN/YOUNG ADULT
Annals of St. Anne
Christteen—R
Church Educator—R
Conqueror—R
Discovery—R
Gospel Tidings—R
Head to Head—R
John Milton—R
On Course—R
Preacher's Illus. Service—R
Student Leadership—R
Teenage Christian—R
Teen Life (AG)—R
Teen Power—R
Teens on Target—R
Teen Quest—R
YOU!—R
Young Adult Today

Young Christian—R
Youth Challenge—R

ADULT
Annals of St. Anne
Christian Advocate—R
Christian Courier (CAN)—R
Christianity/Arts
Church & Synagogue Lib.
Church Herald/Holiness—R
Church Worship
CoLaborer
Connecting Point—R
Cottage Connections—R
Dawn & Dusk
Discovery—R
Dreams & Visions—R
Esprit—R
Emphasis/Faith & Living—R
Evangel—R
Explorer
Family Network—R
Fatted Calf Forum—R
Fellowship Link—R
Five Stones, The—R
Head to Head—R
Healing Inn—R
Hearing Hearts
Highway News—R
Helping Hand—R
Impact Magazine—R
Inspirer, The—R
Lutheran Woman's Quar.
Lutheran Woman Today
Mature Years—R
Mennonite Brethren—R
Ministry Today—R
Miraculous Medal
My Legacy—R
New Writing—R
Pentecostal Homelife—R
Perspectives
Preacher, The
Preacher's Illus. Service—R
Presbyterian Record—R
Ratio
Sojourners
Standard—R
TEAK Roundup—R
U.S. Catholic
Virtue—R
Way of St. Francis—R
Weavings—R

SHORT STORY: CONTEMPORARY

CHILDREN
Annals of St. Anne
BREAD/God's Children—R
Canada Lutheran—R
Discoveries—R
Discovery—R
Focus/Clubhouse
Focus/Clubhouse Jr
Guideposts for Kids
Head to Head—R
Junior Trails—R
Lighthouse Fiction
Listen
Partners—R
Pockets—R
Power & Light—R
R-A-D-A-R—R
Story Friends—R
Together Time (3-4)
Young Christian—R

TEEN/YOUNG ADULT
Annals of St. Anne
BREAD/God's Children—R
Certainty
Challenge (IL)
Christteen—R
Discovery—R
Head to Head—R
Insight—R
It's Your Choice—R
Lighthouse Fiction
Listen—R
Pathways—R
Spirit
Straight—R
Teenage Christian—R
Teen Life (AG)—R
Teen Power—R
Teen Quest—R
Tradition—R
Young Christian—R

ADULT
Annals of St. Anne
Burning Light
Byline
Canadian Lutheran—R
Chip Off Writer's Block—R
Christian Century
Christian Living—R
Christian Single—R
Christianity/Arts
Companion
Connecting Point—R

Conquest
Cornerstone—R
Covenant Companion—R
Dawn & Dusk
Discipleship Journal
Dreams & Visions—R
Esprit—R
Evangel—R
Felicity—R
Head to Head—R
Healing Inn—R
Hearing Hearts
Home Life—R
Housewife-Writer—R
Inklings
Inspirer, The—R
It's Your Choice—R
Lighthouse Fiction
Liguorian
Live—R
Living Light News—R
Lookout—R
Messenger/St. Anthony
Miraculous Medal
Moody—R
My Legacy—R
New Trumpet—R
New Writing—R
Pentecostal Testimony—R
Perspectives
Place to Enter, A
St. Anthony Messenger
St. Joseph's Messenger—R
Salt & The Light, The—R
Standard—R
Sunday Digest—R
TEAK Roundup—R
Tickled by Thunder—R
Tradition—R
Upsouth—R
U.S. Catholic
Virtue—R

*SHORT STORY: ETHNIC

CHILDREN
Counselor—R
Discovery—R
Primary Days—R
Skipping Stones
Touch—R

TEEN/YOUNG ADULT
Discovery—R
Pathways—R
Straight—R
Teen Life (AG)—R
Young Salvationist—R

ADULT
Byline
Christian Living—R
Dreams & Visions—R
Fellowship Link—R
Inklings
Upsouth—R
Virtue—R

SHORT STORY: FANTASY

CHILDREN
Discovery—R
Focus/Clubhouse
Guideposts for Kids
Lollipops (young)
Touch—R
Venture
Young Christian—R

TEEN/YOUNG ADULT
Discovery—R
It's Your Choice—R
Spirit
Teen Quest—R
With—R
Young Adult Today
Young Christian—R
Young Salvationist—R

ADULT
Burning Light
Byline
Chip Off Writer's Block—R
Christian Courier (CAN)—R
Christianity/Arts
Connecting Point—R
Dawn & Dusk
Dreams & Visions—R
Esprit—R
Felicity—R
Inklings
It's Your Choice—R
My Legacy—R
New Thought—R
Place to Enter, A
Presbyterian Record—R
Ratio
Salt & The Light, The—R
Tickled by Thunder—R
Virtue—R
Writer's World—R

SHORT STORY: FRONTIER

CHILDREN
Focus/Clubhouse

Focus/Clubhouse Jr
Guideposts for Kids
High Adventure—R
Lighthouse Fiction
Young Christian—R

TEEN/YOUNG ADULT
Lighthouse Fiction
Teen Quest—R
Young Christian—R

ADULT
Byline
Chip Off Writer's Block—R
Christianity/Arts
Connecting Point—R
Dawn & Dusk
Dreams & Visions—R
Explorer
Felicity—R
Inklings
Inspirer, The—R
Lighthouse Fiction
Miraculous Medal
My Legacy—R
New Writing—R
Upsouth—R
Virtue—R

SHORT STORY: FRONTIER/ROMANCE

Byline
Chip Off Writer's Block—R
Christianity/Arts
Connecting Point—R
Dreams & Visions—R
Felicity—R
Healing Inn—R
Helping Hand—R
Lighthouse Fiction
Miraculous Medal
My Legacy—R
Teen Quest—R
Young Christian—R

SHORT STORY: HISTORICAL

CHILDREN
CLUBHOUSE—R
Counselor—R
Courage
Discovery—R
Focus/Clubhouse
Focus/Clubhouse Jr
Guideposts for Kids
High Adventure—R

Lighthouse Fiction
Friend
On the Line—R
R-A-D-A-R—R
Young Christian—R

TEEN/YOUNG ADULT
BREAD/God's Children—R
Challenge (IL)
Discovery—R
It's Your Choice—R
John Milton—R
Lighthouse Fiction
Teen Quest—R
Tradition—R
Young Adult Today
Young Christian—R
Youth—R

ADULT
African Amer. Heritage—R
Alive!—R
Byline
Chip Off Writer's Block—R
Christian Courier (CAN)—R
Christianity/Arts
Connecting Point—R
Conquest
Dawn & Dusk
Dreams & Visions—R
Esprit—R
Explorer
Family Network—R
Felicity—R
Fellowship Link—R
Healing Inn—R
Home Times—R
Inklings
It's Your Choice—R
Lighthouse Fiction
Lutheran Woman's Quar.
Miraculous Medal
My Legacy—R
New Writing—R
North American Voice
Perspectives
Presbyterian Record—R
Ratio
Seek—R
TEAK Roundup—R
Tradition—R
Upsouth—R
Virtue—R

SHORT STORY: HISTORICAL/ROMANCE

Byline

Chip Off Writer's Block—R
Christianity/Arts
Connecting Point—R
Dreams & Visions—R
Felicity—R
Healing Inn—R
Lighthouse Fiction
Miraculous Medal
My Legacy—R
New Trumpet—R
Teen Quest—R
Young Christian—R
Writer's World—R

SHORT STORY: HUMOROUS

CHILDREN
Crusader—R
Discovery—R
Focus/Clubhouse
Focus/Clubhouse Jr
GUIDE—R
Guideposts for Kids
High Adventure—R
Junior Trails—R
Lighthouse Fiction
My Friend
On the Line—R
Preacher's Illus. Service—R
R-A-D-A-R—R
Touch—R
Wonder Time

TEEN/YOUNG ADULT
Breakaway—R
Brio—R
Campus Life—R
Challenge (IL)
Discovery—R
Insight—R
It's Your Choice—R
Lighthouse Fiction
On Course—R
Pathways—R
Preacher's Illus. Service—R
Straight—R
Student Leadership—R
Teenage Christian—R
Teen Life (AG)—R
Teen Power—R
Teen Quest—R
Teens Today—R
Tradition—R
With—R
YOU!—R
Young Adult Today

ADULT

African Amer. Heritage—R
Alive!—R
Byline
Canada Lutheran—R
Catholic Forester—R
Chip Off Writer's Block—R
Christian Chronicle (PA)—R
Christian Courier (CAN)—R
Christian Living—R
Christian Single—R
Christianity/Arts
Church & Synagogue Lib.
Companion
Connecting Point—R
Conquest
Cottage Connections—R
Covenant Companion—R
Dawn & Dusk
Dreams & Visions—R
Esprit—R
Fatted Calf Forum—R
Felicity—R
Five Stones, The—R
Healing Inn—R
Helping Hand—R
Highway News—R
Home Life—R
Home Times—R
Horizons
Housewife-Writer—R
Impact—R
Inklings
Inspirer, The—R
It's Your Choice—R
John Milton—R
Lighthouse Fiction
Liguorian
Live—R
Living Light News—R
Mature Years—R
Miraculous Medal
My Legacy—R
New Writing—R
ParentLife—R
Pentecostal Homelife—R
Pentecostal Testimony—R
Place to Enter, A
Preacher's Illus. Service—R
Presbyterian Record—R
St. Joseph's Messenger—R
Salt & The Light, The—R
Seek—R
Sojourners
Standard—R
Table Talk—R
TEAK Roundup—R
Tickled by Thunder—R

Tradition—R
Upsouth—R
Virtue—R
Writer's World—R

SHORT STORY: JUVENILE

Annals of St. Anne
BREAD/God's Children—R
Catholic Forester—R
Children's Church—R (6-8)
Christian Home & School
  (few)
Christmas—R
Church Educator—R
Church & Synagogue Lib.
Counselor—R
Courage
Crusader—R
Discoveries—R
Discovery—R
Evangelizing Today's Child—
  R
Felicity—R
Focus/Clubhouse
Focus/Clubhouse Jr
Good News Journal—R
Gospel Tidings—R
GUIDE—R
Guideposts for Kids
Head to Head—R
High Adventure—R
It's Your Choice—R (by kids)
MESSAGE
Junior Trails—R
Lighthouse Fiction
Listen (4-6)
Lollipops
Lutheran Woman Today
My Friend
My Legacy—R
On the Line—R
Partners—R
Pockets—R
Power & Light—R
Presbyterian Record—R
Primary Days—R (6-8)
Primary Pal
R-A-D-A-R—R
Skipping Stones
Story Friends—R
Today's Catholic Teacher—R
Together Time (3-4)
Touch—R
United Church Observer
Venture
Wonder Time

Write Touch
Young Christian—R
Young Musicians

SHORT STORY: LITERARY

CHILDREN
Focus/Clubhouse

TEEN/YOUNG ADULT
Teen Life (AG)—R
Teen Quest—R

ADULT
Burning Light—R
Byline
Chip Off Writer's Block—R
Christian Century
Christian Courier (CAN)—R
Christianity/Arts
Compass
Conquest
Cornerstone—R
Covenant Companion—R
Dreams & Visions—R
Esprit—R
Fatted Calf Forum—R
Felicity—R
Healing Inn—R
Housewife-Writer—R
Inklings
Mennonite Brethren Herald—
  R
Miraculous Medal
My Legacy—R
New Thought—R
New Writing—R
Perspectives
Place to Enter, A
Ratio
Salt & The Light, The—R
Sojourners
Tea and Sunshine
TEAK Roundup—R
Tickled by Thunder—R
Upsouth—R
Virtue—R
Weavings—R

SHORT STORY: MYSTERY

CHILDREN
Courage
Discovery—R
Focus/Clubhouse
Focus/Clubhouse Jr

Guideposts for Kids
Junior Trails—R
Lighthouse Fiction
On the Line—R
Power & Light—R
R-A-D-A-R—R
Touch—R
Young Christian—R

TEEN/YOUNG ADULT
Challenge (IL)
Discovery—R
It's Your Choice—R
Lighthouse Fiction
Straight—R
Teen Life (AG)—R
Teen Quest—R
Young Adult Today
Young Christian—R

ADULT
African Amer. Heritage—R
Byline
Chip Off Writer's Block—R
Christian Courier (CAN)—R
Christianity/Arts
Connecting Point—R
Cottage Connections—R
Dawn & Dusk
Dreams & Visions—R
Felicity—R
Healing Inn—R
Housewife-Writer—R
Inklings
It's Your Choice—R
Lighthouse Fiction
Miraculous Medal
My Legacy—R
New Writing—R
Place to Enter, A
Quest
TEAK Roundup—R
Virtue—R
Writer's World—R

SHORT STORY: MYSTERY/ROMANCE

Byline
Chip Off Writer's Block—R
Christianity/Arts
Connecting Point—R
Cottage Connections—R
Dreams & Visions—R
Healing Inn—R
Helping Hand—R
Lighthouse Fiction
Miraculous Medal

Place to Enter, A
Standard—R
Teen Life (AG)—R
Teen Quest—R
Young Christian—R

SHORT STORY: PARABLES

CHILDREN
Annals of St. Anne
Church Educator—R
Courage
Discovery—R
Focus/Clubhouse
GUIDE—R
High Adventure—R
MESSAGE
John Milton—R
Pockets—R
Preacher's Illus. Service—R
R-A-D-A-R—R
Touch—R
Young Christian—R

TEEN/YOUNG ADULT
Annals of St. Anne
Church Educator—R
Discovery—R
Insight—R
John Milton—R
Pathways—R
Preacher's Illus. Service—R
Student Leadership—R
Teen Life (AG)—R
Teen Quest—R
With—R
YOU!—R
Young Adult Today
Young Christian—R

ADULT
alive now!
America
Annals of St. Anne
Catholic Twin Circle—R
Christian Advocate—R
Christian Chronicle (PA)—R
Christian Courier (CAN)—R
Christian Living—R
Christianity/Arts
Church Worship
Companion
Cottage Connections—R
Covenant Companion—R
Dawn & Dusk
Discipleship Journal
Discovery—R

Dreams & Visions—R
Emphasis/Faith & Living—R
Esprit—R
Explorer
Family Network—R
Fellowship Link—R
Five Stones, The—R
God's Revivalist
Healing Inn—R
Hearing Hearts
Helping Hand—R
Highway News—R
Home Times—R
Impact Magazine—R
Inklings
Inspirer, The—R
LA Catholic
Lutheran
Mennonite Brethren—R
MESSAGE
Messenger/St. Anthony
Ministry Today—R
New Thought—R
New Writing—R
Perspectives
Preacher's Illus. Service—R
Presbyterian Record—R
Ratio
Salt & The Light, The—R
Sojourners
Sunday Digest—R
Upsouth—R
U.S. Catholic
Virtue—R
Way of St. Francis—R
Weavings—R

SHORT STORY: PLAYS

Baptist Leader—R
Burning Light—R
Challenge (IL)
Christian Recreation
Church Worship
CoLaborer
Courage (short short)
Creatively Yours
Discovery (NY)—R
Esprit—R
Fellowship Link—R
Five Stones, The—R
Focus/Clubhouse
Focus/Clubhouse Jr
Guideposts for Kids
Head to Head—R
Horizons
Inklings
Lutheran Digest

Music Leader
National Drama Service
New Writing—R
Ratio
Shining Star
Touch—R
Way of St. Francis—R
YOU!—R
Young Christian—R

SHORT STORY: ROMANCE

TEEN/YOUNG ADULT
Brio
Discovery—R
Healing Inn—R
Lighthouse Fiction
Straight—R
Teen Life (AG)—R
Teen Quest—R
Teens Today—R
With—R
Young Christian—R
Young Salvationist—R

ADULT
African Amer. Heritage—R
Alive!—R
Byline
Chip Off Writer's Block—R
Christianity/Arts
Connecting Point—R
Dawn & Dusk
Dreams & Visions—R
Helping Hand—R
Housewife-Writer—R
Lighthouse Fiction
Miraculous Medal
New Writing—R
Pentecostal Homelife—R
Place to Enter, A
Ratio
St. Joseph's Messenger—R
Writer's World—R

SHORT STORY: SCIENCE FICTION

CHILDREN
Focus/Clubhouse Jr

TEEN/YOUNG ADULT
Breakaway—R
It's Your Choice—R
Teen Quest—R
With—R
Young Adult Today

Young Salvationist—R

ADULT
Byline
Chip Off Writer's Block—R
Christian Courier (CAN)—R
Christianity/Arts
Connecting Point—R
Dawn & Dusk
Dreams & Visions—R
Explorer
Fatted Calf Forum—R
Impact Magazine—R
Inklings
It's Your Choice—R
New Writing—R
Place to Enter, A
Ratio
Tickled by Thunder—R

SHORT STORY: SKITS

CHILDREN
Christian Recreation
Discovery—R
Focus/Clubhouse
Head to Head—R
Shining Star
Touch—R

TEEN/YOUNG ADULT
Christian Recreation
Discovery—R
Head to Head—R
Student Leadership—R
YOU!—R

ADULT
Baptist Leader—R
Christian Recreation
Church Worship
Esprit—R
Five Stones, The—R
Head to Head—R
Horizons
New Writing—R
Virtue—R
Wesleyan Woman—R

SHORT STORY: TEEN/YOUNG ADULT

Annals of St. Anne
BREAD/God's Children—R
Breakaway—R
Brio
Campus Life—R
Canada Lutheran—R

Catholic Forester—R
Certainty
Challenge (IL)
Church & Synagogue Lib.
Church Educator—R
Christteen—R
CLUBHOUSE—R
CoLaborer—R
Conqueror—R
Dawn & Dusk
Discovery—R
Evangel—R
Explorer
Five Stones, The—R
Gospel Tidings—R
Head to Head—R
High Adventure—R
Insight—R
It's Your Choice—R
Lighthouse Fiction
Liguorian
Listen—R
On Course—R
Parent Paper, The
Partners—R
Pentecostal Testimony—R
Presbyterian Record—R
Quest—R
Skipping Stones
Sojourners
Spirit
Straight—R
Student Leadership
Teenage Christian—R
Teen Life (AG)—R
Teen Power—R
Teen Quest—R
Teens on Target—R
Touch—R
Transcend
With—R
Write Touch—R
YOU!—R
Young Adult Today
Young Christian—R
Young Salvationist—R
Youth Challenge—R
Youth World—R
Zelos—R

SINGLES ISSUES

ADULT/GENERAL
American Tract Soc.—R
Annals of St. Anne
At Ease—R
Banner, The
Biblical Reflections—R

Canadian Baptist
Catholic Digest—R
Catholic Forester—R
Christian Advocate—R
Christian Courier (CAN)—R
Christian Living—R
Christian Parenting—R
Christian Reader—R
Christian Single—R
Church Advocate—R
Church Herald/Holiness—R
Church of God EVANGEL
Columbia
Companion
Conquest
Covenant Companion—R
Disciple's Journal—R
Discipleship Journal
Emphasis/Faith & Living—R
Evangel—R
Evangelical Baptist—R
Evangelical Friend
Expression Christian
Faith Today
Family Journal—R
Family Network—R
Fatted Calf Forum—R
Foursquare World—R
Good News, Etc.—R
Good News Journal—R
Gospel Today
Hearing Hearts
Herald of Holiness—R
Highway News—R
Home Times—R
Indian Life—R
Island Christian—R
It's Your Choice—R
Kansas City Christian—R
Light and Life
Liguorian
Live—R
Lookout—R
Lutheran, The—R
Lutheran Digest—R
Mennonite, The—R
MESSAGE/Open Bible
Ministry Today—R
Minnesota Christian—R
Moody—R
Newsline—R
NW Christian Journal—R
Plain Truth—R
Presbyterian Layman
Presbyterian Record—R
Presbyterians Today—R
Purpose—R
Signs of the Times—R

Single-Parent Family
Sojourners
Something Better—R
Standard—R
Upsouth—R
U.S. Catholic
War Cry—R
Wesleyan Advocate—R

*CHRISTIAN
EDUCATION/LIBRARY*
CE Connection—R
CE Counselor—R
CE Leadership—R

MISSIONS
Worldwide Challenge—R

MUSIC
Quest—R

PASTORS/LEADERS
Celebration (SDA)—R
Church Administration
Five Stones, The—R
Journal/Christian Healing—R
Lutheran Partners—R
Ministries Today
Pastoral Life
Resource—R
Single Ad. Ministries Jour.
Word & World

TEEN/YOUNG ADULT
Christteen—R
Conqueror—R
YOU!—R
Young Adult Today
Young Christian—R
Young Salvationist—R

WOMEN
Helping Hand—R
Horizons
Joyful Woman—R
Today's Christian Woman
Virtue—R
Wesleyan Woman—R

SOCIAL JUSTICE

ADULT/GENERAL
Arkansas Catholic
Arlington Catholic
Banner, The
Banner News
Bible Advocate—R
Biblical Reflections—R

Brethren Evangelist
Canadian Baptist
Canadian Catholic
Catholic Digest—R
Catholic Insight
Catholic Rural Life
Catholic Sentinel—R
Charisma/Christian Life
Christian Advocate—R
Christian Century
Christian Chronicle (PA)—R
Christian Edge—R
Christian Living—R
Christian Reader—R
Christian Social Action—R
Church Advocate—R
Commonweal
Cornerstone—R
Covenant Companion—R
Cresset
Discipleship Journal
Faith Today
Family Network—R
Fellowship in Prayer—R
Fidelity—R
Foursquare World—R
Good News, Etc—R
Gospel Today
Hallelujah! (CAN)—R
Head to Head—R
Home Times—R
Indian Life—R
Inland NW Christian
It's Your Choice—R
Jour/Christian Nursing—R
Liguorian
Lookout—R
Mennonite, The—R
Mennonite Brethren—R
Messenger/St. Anthony
Moody—R
New Thought—R
Our Family—R
Perspectives
Pourastan—R
Prairie Messenger—R
Presbyterian Layman
Prism—R
Purpose—R
Religious Broadcasting—R
Rutherford
Salt of the Earth—R
Social Justice—R
Sojourners
Spiritual Life
Star of Zion
United Church Observer
Upsouth—R

Voice, The—R
War Cry—R
Way of St. Francis—R

CHILDREN
Skipping Stones

**CHRISTIAN
EDUCATION/LIBRARY**
Journal/Adventist Educ.—R
Religion Teacher's Journal

PASTORS/LEADERS
Celebration (Catholic)
Jour/Biblical Ethics—R
Lutheran Partners—R
Ministries Today
Voice of the Vineyard —R

TEEN/YOUNG ADULT
Christteen—R
Devo'Zine—R
Pathways—R
Transcend
Young Christian—R

WOMEN
Horizons
Link & Visitor—R
Woman's Touch—R

WRITERS
Inklings

SOCIOLOGY

ADULT/GENERAL
Anglican Journal—R
Biblical Reflections—R
Catholic Rural Life
Christian Advocate—R
Christian Courier (CAN)—R
Christian Edge—R
Commonweal
Compass
Covenant Companion—R
Evangelical Friend
Faith Today
Family Network—R
Fellowship Link—R
Fidelity—R
Good News, Etc—R
Herald of Holiness—R
It's Your Choice—R
Journal of Church & State
MovieGuide
New Oxford Review
New Thought—R

Perspectives
Quiet Revolution—R
SCP Journal—R
Seek—R
Social Justice—R
Standard, The—R
Upsouth—R
War Cry—R
Witness, The

**CHRISTIAN
EDUCATION/LIBRARY**
CE Connection—R
CE Counselor—R
Church Educator—R

MISSIONS
Areopagus—R
Missiology
Urban Mission—R

PASTORS/LEADERS
Eucharistic Minister—R
Five Stones, The—R
Jour/Biblical Ethics—R
Journal/Christian Healing—R
Single Ad. Ministries Jour.
Word & World

TEEN/YOUNG ADULT
Christteen—R
Young Adult Today

WOMEN
Horizons
Virtue—R
Wesleyan Woman—R

WRITERS
Inklings

SPIRITUALITY

ADULT/GENERAL
Acts 2
Advent Christian Witness—R
alive now!
American Tract Soc.—R
Angels on Earth
Annals of St. Anne
Arlington Catholic
At Ease—R
Banner, The
Baptist Beacon—R
Bible Advocate—R
Bible Today
Biblical Reflections—R
Bread of Life—R

Canada Lutheran—R
Canadian Catholic
Cathedral Age
Catholic Digest—R
Catholic Insight
Catholic Parent
Catholic Rural Life
Changes
Charisma/Christian Life
Christian Advocate—R
Christian Century
Christian Chronicle (OK)
Christian Chronicle (PA)—R
Christian Home & School
Christian Living—R
Christian Reader—R
Christian Single—R
Christianity Today—R
Chrysalis Reader
Church Advocate—R
Church Herald/Holiness—R
Church of God EVANGEL
Columbia
Common Boundary
Commonweal
Companion
Companions—R
Compass
Conquest
Covenant Companion—R
Cresset
Disciple's Journal—R
Discipleship Journal
Door, The
Dovetail—R
Emphasis/Faith & Living—R
Episcopal Life—R
Evangelical Baptist—R
Evangelical Friend
Explorer
Faith Today
Family Digest—R
Family Network—R
Fellowship in Prayer—R
Fellowship Link—R
Fellowship Today—R
Fidelity—R
Friends Journal—R
God's Revivalist
Good News, Etc—R
Good News Journal—R
Gospel Today
Healing Inn—R
Hearing Hearts
Herald of Holiness—R
Highway News—R
Home Life—R
Inland NW Christian

Island Christian—R
Jewel Among Jewels—R
John Milton—R
Jour/Christian Nursing—R
Life Gate—R
Liguorian
Living Church
Lutheran, The—R
Lutheran Digest—R
Marriage Partnership
Mennonite, The—R
Mennonite Brethren—R
MESSAGE
Messenger/St. Anthony
Ministry Today—R
Montana Catholic—R
MovieGuide
New Covenant
New Man—R
New Oxford Review
Newsline—R
New Thought—R
North American Voice
Oblates
Our Family—R
Our Sunday Visitor
Pegasus Review—R
Pentecostal Homelife—R
Perspectives
Plowman, The—R
Poet's Park—R
Prairie Messenger—R
Presbyterian Outlook
Presbyterian Record—R
Presbyterians Today—R
Prism—R
Purpose—R
Queen of All Hearts
Religious Education
St. Willibrord Journal
Salt of the Earth—R
SCP Journal—R
Signs of the Times—R
Social Justice—R
Sojourners
Spiritual Life
Standard—R
Standard, The—R
Stand Firm—R
Star of Zion
Sunday Digest—R
TEAK Roundup—R
Today's Christian Senior—R
United Church Observer
Upsouth—R
U.S. Catholic
Vision, The—R
Voice, The—R

War Cry—R
Way of St. Francis—R
Weavings—R
Wesleyan Advocate—R
Witness, The

CHILDREN
BREAD/God's Children—R
GUIDE—R
Skipping Stones
Wonder Time

CHRISTIAN EDUCATION/LIBRARY
CE Connection—R
CE Counselor—R
Christian School
Church Educator—R
Church Worship
Religion Teacher's Journal
Vision—R

MISSIONS
Areopagus—R
Message of the Cross—R
Missiology
Quiet Hour Echoes
World Vision—R
Worldwide Challenge—R

MUSIC
Quest—R

PASTORS/LEADERS
Celebration (Catholic)
Chicago Studies
Christian Century
Christian Ministry
Cross Currents—R
Diaconalogue—R
Emmanuel
Eucharistic Minister—R
Five Stones, The—R
Homiletic & Pastoral Review
Jour/Biblical Ethics—R
Journal/Christian Healing—R
Journal/Pastoral Care
Lutheran Partners—R
Ministries Today
Ministry
Pastoral Life
Preacher, The
Preacher's Illus. Service—R
Priest, The
PROCLAIM—R
Pulpit Helps—R
Reformed Worship
Review for Religious

Today's Christian Preacher—R
Today's Parish
Word & World
Youthworker—R

TEEN/YOUNG ADULT
Challenge (TN)—R
Christteen—R
Conqueror—R
Devo'Zine—R
On Course—R
Pathways—R
Student Leadership—R
Teenage Christian—R
Teen Life (AG)—R
Today's Christian Teen—R
Transcend
With—R
YOU!—R
Young Adult Today
Young Christian—R
Young Salvationist—R
Youth Update

WOMEN
Esprit—R
Horizons
Joyful Woman—R
Just Between Us—R
Lutheran Woman's Quar.
Lutheran Woman Today
Sisters Today
Today's Christian Woman
Unique—R
Virtue—R
Wesleyan Woman—R
Women Alive!—R

WRITERS
Inklings

SPIRITUAL WARFARE

ADULT/GENERAL
Angels on Earth
Banner, The
Bible Advocate—R
Bread of Life—R
Charisma/Christian Life
Christian Advocate—R
Christian Chronicle (PA)—R
Christian Edge—R
Christian Info. Assoc.—R
Christian Ranchman
Common Boundary
Companions—R
Disciple's Journal—R

Discipleship Journal
Family Network—R
Fellowship Link—R
Good News, Etc—R
Gospel Today
Hallelujah! (CAN)—R
Healing Inn—R
Hearing Hearts
Indian Life—R
Island Christian—R
John Milton—R
Life Gate—R
MESSAGE
MESSAGE/Open Bible
MovieGuide
Pentecostal Evangel
PrayerWorks—R
Something Better—R
Standard, The—R
Stand Firm—R
Sunday Digest—R
Table Talk—R
Upsouth—R
Voice, The—R
War Cry—R
Watchman, The

CHILDREN
BREAD/God's Children—R
High Adventure—R

MISSIONS
Quiet Hour Echoes
World Mission People—R

PASTORS/LEADERS
Cell Church—R
Cell Life FORUM—R
Jour/Amer Soc/Chur Growth
Ministries Today
Preacher, The
Pulpit Helps—R
Today's Christian Preacher—R

TEEN/YOUNG ADULT
Challenge (TN)—R
Christteen—R
On Course—R
Teenage Christian—R
Teen Life (AG)—R
Teen Power—R
Zelos—R

WOMEN
Helping Hand—R
Horizons
Just Between Us—R

Tea and Sunshine
Unique—R
Virtue—R

SPORTS/RECREATION

ADULT/GENERAL
American Tract Soc.—R
Angels on Earth
Arlington Catholic
AXIOS—R
Banner, The
Catholic Forester—R
Christian Courier (WI)—R
Christian Courier (CAN)—R
Christian Ranchman
Christian Single—R
Columbia
Connecting Point—R
   (Special Olympics)
Covenant Companion—R
Disciple's Journal—R
Expression Christian
Faith Today
Good News, Etc—R
Good News Reporter—R
Gospel Today
Guideposts
Home Times—R
Indian Life—R
Kansas City Christian—R
Lifeglow—R
Living Light News—R
Living with Teenagers—R
Lutheran Layman
Lutheran Witness—R
MESSAGE
Minnesota Christian—R
MovieGuide
New Man—R
New Thought—R
New Writing—R
NW Christian Journal—R
Role Model
Something Better—R
Sports Spectrum
Standard, The—R
Stand Firm—R
Table Talk—R
TEAK Roundup—R
Vibrant Life—R

CHILDREN
Club Connection—R
Counselor—R
Courage
Crusader—R
Focus/Clubhouse

GUIDE—R
Guideposts for Kids
High Adventure—R
On the Line—R
Power & Light—R
Primary Days—R
R-A-D-A-R—R
Touch—R
Young Christian—R

*CHRISTIAN
EDUCATION/LIBRARY*
Christian School

MISSIONS
Worldwide Challenge—R

MUSIC
Quest—R

PASTORS/LEADERS
Christian Recreation
Preacher's Illus. Service—R

TEEN/YOUNG ADULT
Breakaway—R
Caleb Issues & Answers
Certainty
Challenge (IL)
Challenge (TN)—R
Christteen—R
Devo'Zine—R
Insight—R
On Course—R
Pathways—R
Sharing the VICTORY
Straight—R
Teenage Christian—R
Teen Life (AG)—R
Teen Power—R
Today's Christian Teen—R
With—R
YOU!—R
Young Adult Today
Young & Alive—R
Young Christian—R
Young Salvationist—R
Youth 97—R

WOMEN
Esprit—R
Virtue—R

STEWARDSHIP

ADULT/GENERAL
Angels on Earth
Banner, The

Bible Advocate—R
Biblical Reflections—R
Canadian Baptist
Canadian Catholic
Catholic Digest—R
Catholic Rural Life
Christian Edge—R
Christian Living—R
Christian Ranchman
Church Advocate—R
Church of God EVANGEL
Companions—R
Covenant Companion—R
Disciple's Journal—R
Discipleship Journal
Evangel—R
Faith Today
Family Network—R
Good News, Etc—R
Gospel Today
Green Cross—R
Healing Inn—R
Island Christian—R
John Milton—R
Life Gate—R
Liguorian
Live—R
Lutheran Journal—R
Mennonite, The—R
Mennonite Brethren—R
MESSAGE
Moody—R
New Thought—R
Pentecostal Homelife—R
Plain Truth—R
Power for Living—R
Presbyterian Layman
Presbyterian Outlook
Prism—R
Religious Broadcasting—R
Standard, The—R
Stand Firm—R
Star of Zion
Stewardship
Today's Christian Senior—R
United Church Observer
U.S. Catholic
Upsouth—R
War Cry—R
Watchman, The
Way of St. Francis—R

CHILDREN
BREAD/God's Children—R
Crusader (TN)
Focus/Clubhouse
Lad
Power & Light—R

R-A-D-A-R—R
Skipping Stones

*CHRISTIAN
EDUCATION/LIBRARY*
Brigade Leader—R
CE Leadership—R
Church Educator—R
Teacher's Interaction

MISSIONS
Quiet Hour Echoes
Save Our World—R
World Mission People—R

PASTORS/LEADERS
Celebration (SDA)—R
Cell Church—R
Christian Ministry
Clergy Journal—R
Five Stones, The—R
Jour/Biblical Ethics—R
Lutheran Partners—R
Ministries Today
Ministry
Preacher's Magazine—R
Resource—R
Today's Christian Preacher—
   R
Your Church—R

TEEN/YOUNG ADULT
Challenge (TN)—R
Christteen—R
Pathways—R
Teens on Target—R
With—R
Youth Challenge—R

WOMEN
Horizons
Today's Christian Woman
Unique—R
Virtue—R
Wesleyan Woman—R

TAKE-HOME PAPERS

ADULT/GENERAL
Companions—R
Conquest
Evangel—R
Gem, The—R
Live—R
Lookout—R
Power for Living—R
Purpose
Seek—R

Standard—R
Sunday Digest—R
Vision—R

CHILDREN
Bible-in-Life Pix
Counselor—R
Courage
Discoveries—R
Good News for Children
GUIDE—R
Junior Trails—R
On the Line—R
Our Little Friend—R
Partners
Power & Light—R
Primary Days—R
Primary Pal
Primary Treasure
Promise
R-A-D-A-R—R
Story Friends—R
Story Mates—R
Together Time
Venture
Wonder Time

TEEN/YOUNG ADULT
Certainty
Challenge
Cross Walk
Essential Connections
Insight
Rock, The
Straight—R
Teen Life (AG)—R
Teen Life (UPC)—R
Teen Power—R
Teens on Target
Visions
Youth Challenge
Youth World—R

THEOLOGICAL

ADULT/GENERAL
AGAIN—R
America
Anglican Journal—R
Annals of St. Anne
Arlington Catholic
At Ease—R
Banner, The
Banner News
Baptist Beacon—R
Baptist Informer
B.C. Catholic—R
Bible Advocate—R

Biblical Reflections—R
Canadian Baptist
Canadian Catholic
Catholic Digest—R
Catholic Insight
Catholic Rural Life
Catholic Twin Circle—R
Charisma/Christian Life
Christian Century
Christian Living—R
Christian Renewal—R
Christian Research
Christian Social Action—R
Christianity Today—R
Church Herald/Holiness—R
Columbia
Commonweal
Companion
Companions—R
Compass
Conquest
Covenant Companion—R
Cresset
Emphasis/Faith & Living—R
Episcopal Life—R
Evangelical Baptist—R
Evangelical Friend
Evangelical Visitor—R
Fellowship Link—R
Fidelity—R
First Things
Good News—R
Green Cross—R
Interim—R
John Milton—R
Journal of Church & State
Liguorian
Living Church
Lutheran, The—R
Lutheran Digest—R
Lutheran Layman
Mennonite Brethren—R
Messenger/St. Anthony
Ministry Today—R
National Review
New Man—R
New Oxford Review
New Thought—R
North American Voice
Our Family—R
Our Sunday Visitor
Perspectives
Prairie Messenger—R
Presbyterian Layman
Presbyterian Outlook
Presbyterian Record—R
Presbyterians Today—R
Queen of All Hearts

Ratio
Religious Education
St. Anthony Messenger
St.Willibrord Journal
SCP Journal—R
Silver Wings—R
Social Justice—R
Sojourners
Spiritual Life
Standard, The—R
Star of Zion
Sunday Digest—R
Today's Christian Senior—R
United Church Observer
U.S. Catholic
Upsouth—R
Watchman, The
Way of St. Francis—R
Weavings—R
Witness, The

CHRISTIAN EDUCATION/LIBRARY
CE Connection—R
CE Counselor—R
Church Educator—R
Church Worship

MISSIONS
Areopagus—R
East-West Church—R
Missiology
Quiet Hour Echoes
Urban Mission—R
Worldwide Challenge—R

PASTORS/LEADERS
Catechumenate
Celebration (Catholic)
Chicago Studies
Christian Century
Clergy Journal—R
Cross Currents—R
Diocesan Dialogue—R
Eucharistic Minister—R
Five Stones, The—R
Homiletic & Pastoral Review
Jour/Biblical Ethics—R
Journal/Christian Healing—R
Journal/Pastoral Care
Jour/Amer Soc/Chur Growth
Lutheran Forum—R
Lutheran Partners—R
Ministries Today
Ministry
Modern Liturgy—R
Networks—R
Preacher, The

Preacher's Illus. Service—R
Preacher's Magazine—R
Priest, The
PROCLAIM—R
Pulpit Helps—R
Quarterly Review
Review for Religious
Theology Today
Today's Christian Preacher—R
Today's Parish
Word & World
Youthworker—R

TEEN/YOUNG ADULT
Pathways—R
With—R
YOU!—R
Young Adult Today
Youth Update

WOMEN
Conscience—R
Esprit—R
Horizons
Jour/Women's Ministries
Lutheran Woman Today
Sisters Today
Virtue—R
Wesleyan Woman—R

WRITERS
Inklings

THINK PIECES

ADULT/GENERAL
American Tract Soc.—R
Annals of St. Anne
AXIOS—R
Banner, The
Bible Advocate—R
Biblical Reflections—R
Canada Lutheran—R
Canadian Catholic
Catholic Digest—R
Catholic Forester—R
Catholic Rural Life
Catholic Twin Circle—R
Christian Chronicle (PA)—R
Christian C.L. RECORD—R
Christian Courier (CAN)—R
Christian Edge—R
Christian Living—R
Christian Single—R
Christian Social Action—R
Christianity Today—R
Commonweal

Companion
Compass
Conquest
Covenant Companion—R
Disciple's Journal—R
Door, The
Dovetail—R
Episcopal Life—R
Evangelical Baptist—R
Evangelical Friend
Evangelical Visitor—R
Explorer
Family Journal—R
Good News, Etc—R
Gospel Today
Green Cross—R
Head to Head—R
Healing Inn—R
Hearing Hearts
Herald of Holiness—R
Home Times—R
Inspirer, The—R
Island Christian—R
It's Your Choice—R
John Milton—R
Kansas City Christian—R
Lutheran, The—R
Lutheran Digest—R
Lutheran Journal—R
Mennonite Brethren—R
MESSAGE
MESSAGE/Open Bible
Minnesota Christian—R
National Review
New Man—R
New Oxford Review
New Thought—R
New Writing—R
Pegasus Review—R
Pentecostal Homelife—R
Perspectives
Poet's Park—R
PrayerWorks—R
Presbyterian Layman
Presbyterian Outlook
Presbyterian Record—R
Presbyterians Today—R
Purpose—R
Ratio
Religious Broadcasting—R
Religious Education
Rutherford
San Diego Co. Christian
Seek—R
Sojourners
Standard, The—R
Stand Firm—R
Star of Zion

Table Talk—R
TEAK Roundup—R
Upsouth—R
War Cry—R
Way of St. Francis—R
Wesleyan Advocate—R

CHILDREN
Discovery—R
Power & Light—R
Skipping Stones

*CHRISTIAN
EDUCATION/LIBRARY*
CE Connection—R
Resource—R
Vision—R

MISSIONS
Areopagus—R
Catholic Near East
World Vision—R

MUSIC
Quest—R
Tradition—R

PASTORS/LEADERS
Celebration (Catholic)
Celebration (SDA)—R
Eucharistic Minister—R
Jour/Biblical Ethics—R
Journal/Christian Healing—R
Journal/Pastoral Care
Ministries Today
Networks—R
Priest, The
Word & World

TEEN/YOUNG ADULT
Certainty
Challenge (TN)—R
Christteen—R
Conqueror—R
Teenage Christian—R
Teen Life (AG)—R
Vision—R
YOU!—R
Young Adult Today
Young Christian—R
Young Salvationist—R

WOMEN
DOMESTIQUE—R
Esprit—R
Horizons
Lutheran Woman Today
Tea and Sunshine

Virtue—R
Wesleyan Woman—R

WRITERS
Inklings
Southwestern Writers—R
Writer's Exchange—R

TRAVEL

ADULT/GENERAL
African Amer. Heritage—R
Alive!—R
Angels on Earth
Arlington Catholic
Banner News
Catholic Digest—R
Catholic Twin Circle—R
Charisma/Christian Life
Christian Courier (CAN)—R
Christian Ranchman
Christian Single—R
Columbia
Companion
Disciple's Journal—R
Explorer
Family Digest—R
Fellowship in Prayer—R
Fellowship Link—R
Home Times—R
It's Your Choice—R
John Milton—R
Joyful Noise
Living with Teenagers—R
Lutheran Journal—R
Lutheran Layman
Mature Living
Mennonite Historian—R
MovieGuide
National Review
New Man—R
New Thought—R
ParentLife—R
Role Model
Seek—R
Smart Dads
Standard, The—R
Star of Zion
TEAK Roundup—R
Time of Singing—R
Today's Christian Senior—R
Upsouth—R
War Cry—R

CHILDREN
Focus/Clubhouse
High Adventure—R
R-A-D-A-R—R

Skipping Stones

MISSIONS
Areopagus—R
Childlife—R
East-West Church—R
Great Commission—R
World Mission People—R

MUSIC
Gospel Music

PASTORS/LEADERS
Preacher's Illus. Service—R

TEEN/YOUNG ADULT
Challenge (TN)—R
Conqueror—R
Pathways—R
Teenage Christian—R
Young Adult Today
Young & Alive—R
Young Christian—R
Youth Focus—R

WOMEN
Aspire
Horizons
Wesleyan Woman—R

WRITERS
Southwestern Writers—R

TRUE STORIES

ADULT/GENERAL
AGAIN—R
Angels on Earth
At Ease—R
Banner News
Baptist Beacon—R
Bible Advocate—R
Canada Lutheran—R
Canadian Baptist
Catholic Digest—R
Catholic Twin Circle—R
CBA Frontline
Christian Chronicle (PA)—R
Christian Edge—R
Christian Living—R
Christian Ranchman
Christian Reader—R
Christian Single—R
Church Advocate—R
Church Herald/Holiness—R
Companion
Conquest
Covenant Companion—R

Crossway/Newsline—R
Decision
Disciple's Journal—R
Emphasis/Faith & Living—R
Evangelical Friend
Evangelical Visitor—R
Family Network—R
Fellowship in Prayer—R
Fellowship Link—R
Fidelity—R
Foursquare World—R
Gem, The—R
God's Revivalist
Good News, Etc—R
Good News Journal
Gospel Tidings—R
Gospel Today
Green Cross—R
Guideposts
Head to Head—R
Healing Inn—R
Hearing Hearts
Herald of Holiness—R
Highway News—R
Home Times—R
Impact Magazine—R
Indian Life—R
Inspirer, The—R
InterVarsity
Island Christian—R
It's Your Choice—R
Jewel Among Jewels—R
John Milton—R
Jour/Christian Nursing—R
Kansas City Christian—R
Lifeglow—R
Light and Life
Liguorian
Live—R
Lutheran, The—R
Lutheran Digest—R
Lutheran Journal—R
Lutheran Layman
Lutheran Witness—R
Mennonite, The—R
Mennonite Brethren—R
MESSAGE
MESSAGE/Open Bible
Ministry Today—R
Minnesota Christian—R
Moody—R
New Heart, A—R
New Thought—R
New Trumpet—R
New Writing—R
Our Family—R
Pentecostal Evangel
Pentecostal Homelife—R

Plus—R
Power for Living—R
PrayerWorks—R
Presbyterian Record—R
Pursuit—R
Quiet Revolution—R
Religious Broadcasting—R
SCP Journal—R
Seek—R
Signs of the Times—R
Standard—R
Standard, The—R
Stand Firm—R
Sunday Digest—R
Table Talk—R
TEAK Roundup—R
Upsouth—R
Vision, The—R
War Cry—R
Wesleyan Advocate—R

CHILDREN
Club Connection—R
CLUBHOUSE—R
Counselor—R
Courage
Crusader—R
Discovery—R
Focus/Clubhouse
Focus/Clubhouse Jr
GUIDE—R
Guideposts for Kids
High Adventure—R
Junior Trails—R
Listen
Mission
Nature Friend—R
On the Line—R
Our Little Friend—R
Partners—R
Pockets—R
Primary Days—R
Primary Treasure—R
R-A-D-A-R—R
Skipping Stones
Story Friends—R
Touch—R

CHRISTIAN EDUCATION/LIBRARY
CE Connection—R
Church Media Library—R
Perspective—R
Shining Star

MISSIONS
American Horizon—R
Areopagus—R

Childlife
Heartbeat—R
Leaders for Today
Quiet Hour Echoes
Save Our World—R
Urban Mission—R
World Christian—R
World Mission People—R
World Vision—R
Worldwide Challenge—R

MUSIC
Quest—R

PASTORS/LEADERS
Cell Church—R
Cell Life FORUM—R
Eucharistic Minister—R
Five Stones, The—R
Leadership Journal—R
Networks—R
Preacher's Illus. Service—R

TEEN/YOUNG ADULT
Certainty
Challenge (IL)
Challenge (TN)—R
Christteen—R
Conqueror—R
Insight—R
On Course—R
Pathways—R
Straight—R
Teenage Christian—R
Teen Life (AG)—R
Teen Power—R
Teens on Target—R
With—R
YOU!—R
Young Adult Today
Young & Alive—R
Young Christian—R
Youth Challenge—R
Youth 97—R
Youth World—R
Zelos—R

WOMEN
Cottage Connections—R
DOMESTIQUE—R
Helping Hand—R
Joyful Woman—R
Just Between Us—R
Lutheran Woman Today
Proverbs 31 Homemaker—R
Today's Christian Woman
Unique—R
Virtue—R

Wesleyan Woman—R
Woman's Touch—R

WRITERS
Inklings
New Writing—R
Southwestern Writers—R
Writer's Nook News

*VIDEO REVIEWS

ADULT/GENERAL
Arlington Catholic
Believer, The—R
CBA Marketplace
Christian Arts Review
Christian Edge—R
Companion
Disciple's Journal—R
Discovery—R
Expression Christian
Fatted Calf Forum—R
Gospel Today
Home Times—R
Island Christian—R
Living Light News—R
MovieGuide
New Trumpet—R
Rutherford
Something Better—R
Stand Firm—R
Upsouth—R
War Cry—R

CHILDREN
Club Connection—R

CHRISTIAN EDUCATION/LIBRARY
Church Libraries—R
Leader/Church School
   Today—R

PASTORS/LEADERS
Five Stones, The—R
Lutheran Partners—R
Ministries Today
Technologies/Worship—R

TEEN/YOUNG ADULT
Devo'Zine—R
With—R
Youth 97—R

WOMEN'S ISSUES

ADULT/GENERAL
Advent Christian Witness—R

Anglican Journal—R
Annals of St. Anne
Arlington Catholic
At Ease—R
Atlantic Baptist
Banner, The
Banner News
Bread of Life—R
Brethren Evangelist
Canada Lutheran—R
Canadian Baptist
Canadian Catholic
Catholic Forester—R
Catholic Insight
Catholic Parent
Catholic Rural Life
Catholic Twin Circle—R
CBA Marketplace
Celebrate Life—R
Changes
Charisma/Christian Life
Christian C.L. RECORD—R
Christian Courier (CAN)—R
Christian Edge—R
Christian Living—R
Christian Ranchman
Christian Single—R
Christian Social Action—R
Chrysalis Reader
Church Advocate—R
Church of God EVANGEL
Columbia
Companion
Compass
Cornerstone—R
Covenant Companion—R
Disciple's Journal—R
Emphasis/Faith & Living—R
Episcopal Life—R
Evangel—R
Evangelical Baptist—R
Evangelical Friend
Expression Christian
Faith Today
Family Network—R
Fatted Calf Forum—R
Foursquare World—R
Good News, Etc—R
Good News Journal—R
Gospel Tidings—R
Gospel Today
Hallelujah! (CAN)—R
Healing Inn—R
Herald of Holiness—R
Home Life—R
Home Times—R
Indian Life—R
Interim—R

Island Christian—R
It's Your Choice—R
John Milton—R
Jour/Christian Nursing—R
Joyful Noise
Kansas City Christian—R
Life Gate—R
Light and Life
Liguorian
Living Light News—R
Lookout—R
Lutheran, The—R
Marriage Partnership
MESSAGE
Ministry Today—R
Minnesota Christian—R
Moody—R
National Review
Newsline—R
Our Sunday Visitor
ParentLife—R
Pentecostal Evangel
Plain Truth—R
Plus—R
Presbyterian Layman
Presbyterian Outlook
Presbyterians Today—R
Progress—R
Purpose—R
Role Model
St. Joseph's Messenger—R
Salt of the Earth—R
Signs of the Times—R
Sojourners
Standard—R
Standard, The—R
Star of Zion
Sunday Digest—R
Table Talk—R
Today's Christian Senior—R
Total Health
United Church Observer
Upsouth—R
Vibrant Life—R
Voice, The—R
War Cry—R
Way of St. Francis—R
Witness, The

CHRISTIAN EDUCATION/LIBRARY
Resource—R

MISSIONS
American Horizon—R
East-West Church—R
Urban Mission—R
World Mission People—R

Worldwide Challenge—R

PASTORS/LEADERS
Celebration (SDA)—R
Cell Church—R
Christian Century
Christian Ministry (feminist)
Diaconalogue—R
Journal/Christian Healing—R
Journal/Pastoral Care
Leadership Journal—R
Lutheran Partners—R
Ministries Today (little)
Ministry
Pastor's Family
Preacher, The
Preacher's Magazine—R
Pulpit Helps—R
Single Ad. Ministries Jour.
Youthworker—R
Word & World

TEEN/YOUNG ADULT
Brio
Christteen—R
Vision—R
YOU!—R
Young Adult Today
Young Christian—R

WOMEN
(See alphabetical listing)

WRITERS
Inklings

WORLD ISSUES

ADULT/GENERAL
Alive!
America
Annals of St. Anne
Arlington Catholic
At Ease—R
Atlantic Baptist
AXIOS—R
Banner, The
Banner News
Baptist Informer
Bible Advocate—R
Biblical Reflections—R
Canada Lutheran—R
Canadian Baptist
Canadian Catholic
Catholic Twin Circle—R
Charisma/Christian Life
Christian Century
Christian Courier (CAN)—R

Christian Crusade
Christian Edge—R
Christian Living—R
Christian Ranchman
Christian Single—R
Christian Social Action—R
Church Herald/Holiness—R
Columbia
Commonweal
Companion
Compass
Cornerstone—R
Covenant Companion—R
Disciple's Journal—R
Emphasis/Faith & Living—R
Evangel—R
Evangelical Baptist—R
Evangelical Friend
Evangelical Visitor—R
Expression Christian
Faith Today
Family Network—R
Fatted Calf Forum—R
Fellowship in Prayer—R
Fidelity—R
God's Revivalist
Good News, Etc.—R
Good News Reporter—R
Gotta Write
Gospel Today
Green Cross—R
Hallelujah! (CAN)—R
Healing Inn—R
Home Times—R
Inland NW Christian
Interchange
InterVarsity
Island Christian—R
It's Your Choice—R
John Milton—R
Journal of Church & State
Kansas City Christian—R
Liberty—R
Living Light News—R
Lutheran, The—R
Lutheran Layman
MESSAGE
MESSAGE/Open Bible
Messenger
Messenger/St. Anthony
Ministry Today—R
Minnesota Christian—R
Moody—R
National Review
New Man—R
New Thought—R
Our Sunday Visitor
Presbyterian Layman

Presbyterian Outlook
Presbyterian Record—R
Presbyterians Today—R
Quiet Revolution—R
Religious Broadcasting—R
SCP Journal—R
Sojourners
Something Better—R
Standard, The—R
Stand Firm—R
Table Talk—R
TEAK Roundup—R
United Church Observer
Upsouth—R
Vision, The—R
War Cry—R
Watchman, The
Witness, The

CHILDREN
Counselor—R
Focus/Clubhouse
God's World Today
Power & Light—R
Skipping Stones

MISSIONS
Areopagus—R
Catholic Near East
Childlife
Compassion
East-West Church—R
Missiology
Mission Today—R
New World Outlook
P.I.M.E. World
Save Our World—R
Urban Mission—R
World Christian—R
World Mission People—R
World Vision—R
Worldwide Challenge—R

PASTORS/LEADERS
Cell Church—R
Christian Century
Ministries Today
Networks—R
Preacher's Illus. Service—R
Preacher's Magazine—R
Word & World
Youthworker—R

TEEN/YOUNG ADULT
Caleb Issues & Answers
Christteen—R
Conqueror—R
Pathways—R

Student Leadership—R
Transcend
YOU!—R
Young Adult Today
Young Christian—R
Young Salvationist—R

WOMEN
Cottage Connections—R
Esprit—R
Helping Hand—R
Horizons
Link & Visitor—R
Lutheran Woman Today
Virtue—R
Wesleyan Woman—R

WRITERS
Inklings

WORSHIP

ADULT/GENERAL
Advent Christian Witness—R
alive now!
Angels on Earth
Annals of St. Anne
Arlington Catholic
At Ease—R
Atlantic Baptist
Baptist Beacon—R
Baptist Informer
Bible Advocate—R
Bread of Life—R
Brethren Evangelist
Canada Lutheran—R
Canadian Baptist
Canadian Catholic
Cathedral Age
Catholic Digest—R
Charisma/Christian Life
Christian Century
Christian Edge—R
Church Herald/Holiness—R
Commonweal
Companion
Companions—R
Conquest
Covenant Companion—R
Cresset
Disciple's Journal—R
Discipleship Journal
Emphasis/Faith & Living—R
Evangel—R
Evangelical Baptist—R
Evangelical Friend
Evangelical Visitor—R
Faith Today

Family Network—R
Fellowship Link—R
Fellowship Today—R
Fidelity—R
Foursquare World—R
Good News—R
Good News, Etc—R
Good News Journal—R
Gospel Today
Green Cross—R
Healing Inn—R
Herald of Holiness—R
Inspirer, The—R
Island Christian—R
John Milton—R
Joyful Noise
Life Gate—R
Liguorian
Living Church
Lookout—R
Lutheran, The—R
Lutheran Journal—R
Mennonite, The—R
Mennonite Brethren—R
Mennonite Reporter
MESSAGE
MESSAGE/Open Bible
Ministry Today—R
Moody—R
New Man—R
North American Voice
NW Christian Journal—R
Our Family—R
Our Sunday Visitor
Perspectives
Plain Truth—R
Plenty Good Room
Power for Living—R
Prairie Messenger—R
PrayerWorks—R
Presbyterian Outlook
Presbyterian Record—R
Presbyterians Today—R
St. Willibrord Journal
Seek—R
Silver Wings—R
Spiritual Life
Standard, The—R
Star of Zion
Sunday Digest—R
Time of Singing—R
Today's Christian Senior—R
United Church Observer
Upsouth—R
U.S. Catholic
Voice, The—R
War Cry—R
Watchman, The

Way of St. Francis—R
Weavings—R
Wesleyan Advocate—R

CHILDREN
R-A-D-A-R—R
Wonder Time

CHRISTIAN EDUCATION/LIBRARY
CE Connection—R
CE Counselor—R
Christian Ed Journal—R
CE Leadership—R
Church Educator—R
Church Media Library—R
Church Worship
Evangelizing Today's Child—R
Shining Star

MISSIONS
American Horizon—R
Areopagus—R
Catholic Near East
Quiet Hour Echoes
Worldwide Challenge—R

MUSIC
Church Pianist, etc.
Creator—R
Glory Songs—R
Gospel Industry Today
Hymn, The

PASTORS/LEADERS
Celebration (Catholic)
Celebration (SDA)—R
Cell Church—R
Cell Life FORUM—R
Chicago Studies
Christian Century
Christian Management—R
Christian Ministry
Clergy Journal—R
Environment & Art
Five Stones, The—R
Journal/Christian Healing—R
Jour/Amer Soc/Chur Growth
Leadership Journal—R
Liturgy
Lutheran Forum—R
Lutheran Partners—R
Ministries Today
Ministry
Modern Liturgy—R
Networks—R
Preacher's Illus. Service—R

Preacher's Magazine—R
Preaching
Priest, The
PROCLAIM—R
Reformed Worship
Today's Christian Preacher—R
Today's Parish
WCA Monthly—R
Word & World
Worship Leader
Youthworker—R

TEEN/YOUNG ADULT
Challenge (TN)—R
Conqueror—R
On Course—R
Pathways—R
Student Leadership—R
Teenage Christian—R
Teen Life (AG)—R
Teen Power—R
Teens on Target—R
Today's Christian Teen—R
Young Adult Today
Young Salvationist—R
Youth Challenge—R
Youth Update

WOMEN
Esprit—R
Horizons
Joyful Woman—R
Lutheran Woman Today
Proverbs 31 Homemakers—R
Sisters Today
Unique—R
Virtue—R
Wesleyan Woman—R

*WRITING HOW-TO

ADULT/GENERAL
Believer, The—R
CBA Marketplace
Christian Edge—R
Expression Christian
Feelings Quarterly—R
Home Times—R
TEAK Roundup—R
Upsouth—R

CHILDREN
Discovery—R
Skipping Stones

PASTORS/LEADERS
Newsletter Newsletter

WRITERS
Byline
Cross & Quill—R
Exchange—R
NW Christian Author—R
Once Upon a Time—R
Tickled by Thunder—R
Today's $85,000 Freelance
Virginia Christian Writer—R
Writer, The
Writer's Digest
Writer's Exchange—R
Writer's Forum—R
Writer's Infor Network
Writer's News—R

YOUTH ISSUES

ADULT/GENERAL
American Tract Soc.—R
Annals of St. Anne
Arlington Catholic
AXIOS—R
Banner, The
Canada Lutheran—R
Canadian Baptist
Canadian Catholic
Catholic Digest—R
Catholic Forester—R
Catholic Rural Life
Charisma/Christian Life
Christian Courier (CAN)—R
Christian Edge—R
Christian Living—R
Christian Ranchman
Christian Social Action—R
Church Herald/Holiness—R
Columbia
Companion
Covenant Companion—R
Disciple's Journal—R
Decision
Emphasis/Faith & Living—R
Evangel—R
Evangelical Baptist—R
Evangelical Friend
Expression Christian
Faith Today
Fidelity—R
Foursquare World—R
Good News, Etc—R
Good News Journal—R
Gospel Tidings—R
Gospel Today
Hallelujah! (CAN)—R
Herald of Holiness—R
Home Times—R
Indian Life—R

Island Christian—R
It's Your Choice—R
Kansas City Christian—R
Life Gate—R
Light and Life
Liguorian
Living—R
Living with Teenagers—R
Lutheran, The—R
Lutheran Digest—R
Mennonite Brethren—R
MESSAGE
Ministry Today—R
New Oxford Review
Our Family—R
Prairie Messenger—R
Presbyterian Outlook
Presbyterian Record—R
Presbyterians Today—R
Prism—R
Religious Education
Role Model
Rutherford
Smart Dads
Sojourners
Something Better—R
Standard, The—R
Table Talk—R
U.S. Catholic
Voice, The—R
Witness, The

CHILDREN
Club Connection—R
CLUBHOUSE—R
Courage
Crusader—R
Discovery—R
Focus/Clubhouse
Focus/Clubhouse Jr
GUIDE—R
My Friend
Power & Light—R
R-A-D-A-R—R
Skipping Stones
Touch—R

*CHRISTIAN
EDUCATION/LIBRARY*
Brigade Leader—R
CE Connection—R
CE Counselor—R
CE Leadership—R
Church Educator—R
GROUP
Journal/Adventist Educ.—R
Parish Teacher—R
Perspective—R
Resource—R
Team—R
Vision—R

MISSIONS
American Horizon—R
Quiet Hour Echoes
Worldwide Challenge—R

MUSIC
Quest—R

PASTORS/LEADERS
Cell Church—R
Cell Life FORUM—R
Clergy Journal—R
Five Stones, The—R
Ivy Jungle Report—R
Journal/Christian Healing
Lutheran Partners—R
Ministries Today
Pastoral Life
Pulpit Helps—R
Word & World
Youthworker—R

TEEN/YOUNG ADULT
(See alphabetical listing)

WOMEN
Cottage Connections—R
Horizons
Proverbs 31 Homemaker—R
Virtue—R
Wesleyan Woman—R

ALPHABETICAL LISTINGS OF PERIODICALS

Following are the listings of periodicals. They are arranged alphabetically by type of periodical (see Table of Contents for a list of types). Nonpaying markets are indicated in bold letters within those listings, e.g., **NO PAYMENT**.

If a listing is preceded by an asterisk (*), it indicates that publisher did not send updated information. If it is preceded by a number symbol (#) it was updated from available sources or by phone. If it is preceded by a (+) it is a new listing. It is important that freelance writers request writer's guidelines and a recent sample copy before submitting to any of these publications, but especially to those with the * and # symbols.

If you do not find the publication you are looking for, check the supplementary listings following this section for those periodicals that have ceased publication, changed names, or are not open to freelance submissions.

For a detailed explanation of how to understand and get the most out of these listings, as well as solid marketing tips, see the "How to Use This Book" section at the front of the book. Unfamiliar terms are explained in the Glossary at the back of the book.

(*) An asterisk before a listing indicates no or unconfirmed information update.
(#) A number symbol before a listing means it was updated from their current writer's guidelines or other sources.
(+) A plus sign means it is a new listing.

ADULT/GENERAL MARKETS

ADVENT CHRISTIAN WITNESS, PO Box 23152, Charlotte NC 28227. (704)545-6161. Fax (704)573-0712. E-mail: Mayerpub@aol.com. Advent Christian General Conference. Robert J. Mayer, ed. Denominational. Monthly (10X) mag; 20 pgs; circ 3,200. Subscription $11. 10-15% freelance. Complete ms/cover letter; no phone/fax/e-mail query. Pays $15-25 on publication for one-time rts. Articles 1,500-2,000 wds (3-4/yr). Responds in 6-10 wks. Seasonal 7 mos ahead. Accepts simultaneous submissions & reprints. Accepts disk. Sidebars OK. Prefers NIV. Guidelines; copy for 9x12 SAE/4 stamps.

***AFRICAN-AMERICAN HERITAGE**, 8443 S. Crenshaw Blvd., Ste. 103, Inglewood CA 90305. (213)752-3706. General publication that includes inspirational and religious articles. Dennis DeLoach, ed. To cultivate self-esteem, pride and appreciation for ethnic heritage. Quarterly mag; circ 25,000. 30% freelance. Query. Pays $25-300 on publication for 1st, one-time, or simultaneous rts. Articles 200-2,000 wds (6/yr); fiction 200-2,000 wds (6/yr). Responds in 4-9 wks. Seasonal 6 mos ahead. Accepts simultaneous submissions & reprints. Kill fee 25%. Guidelines; copy for 9x12 SAE/4 stamps.

    Poetry: Buys 60/yr. Any type; 4-36 lines; $10-25. Submit max. 5 poems.
    Fillers: Buys 12/yr. Anecdotes, facts; 10-200 wds; $25-100.

Special Needs: February is Black History Month.

AGAIN MAGAZINE, PO Box 76, Ben Lomond CA 95005. (408)338-3644. Fax (408)336-8882. E-mail: shouston@conciliarpress.com. Website: http://www. conciliarpress.com. Orthodox/Conciliar Press. Raymond Zell, mng ed. A call to the people of God to return to their roots of historical orthodoxy once AGAIN. Quarterly mag; 32 pgs; circ 5,000. Subscription $14.50. 1% freelance. Query. **PAYS IN COPIES.** Accepts simultaneous submissions & reprints. Articles 1,500-2,500 wds; fiction 1,500-2,500 wds; book reviews 500-700 wds. Responds in 16 wks. Seasonal 2 mos ahead. Serials 2 parts. Prefers disk. Copy $2.50/9x12 SAE/5 stamps.

+THE ALABAMA BAPTIST, 3310 Independence Dr., Birmingham AL 35209-5602. (205)870-4720. Fax (205)870-8957. E-mail: 70420.127@compuserve.com. Dr. Bob Terry, ed. Shares news and information relevant to members of Baptist churches in Alabama. Weekly newspaper; circ 117,000. Subscription $9. Open to freelance. Not in topical listings. (Ads)

+ALIVE, 1649 Cowling Ave., Ste. 100, Louisville KY 40205. Jim Mishler, ed. Christian Newspaper. Not in topical listings.

#ALIVE! A MAGAZINE FOR CHRISTIAN SENIOR ADULTS, PO Box 46464, Cincinnati OH 45246-0464. (513)825-3681. Christian Seniors Fellowship. June Lang, office ed. Focuses on activities and opportunities for active, Christian senior adults, 55 and older; upbeat rather than nostalgic. Quarterly mag; 12-16 pgs; circ 6,000. Subscription/membership $10. 60% freelance. Complete ms/cover letter. Pays .03-.05/wd ($18-75) on publication for 1st or reprint rts. Articles 600-1,200 wds (25/yr); fiction 600-1,200 wds (12/yr, pays $20-60). Responds in 6 wks. Seasonal 6 mos ahead. Accepts simultaneous submissions & reprints (pays less). Guidelines; copy for 9x12 SAE/3 stamps.

> **Poetry:** Buys 6/yr. Free verse, light verse, traditional; $3-10. Submit max. 3 poems.
>
> **Fillers:** Buys 15/yr. Anecdotes, cartoons, ideas, jokes, short humor, and word puzzles; 50-500 wds; $2-15.
>
> **Columns/Departments:** Buys 50/yr. Heart Medicine (humor, grandparent/grandchild anecdotes), to 100 wds, $2.50-5; Games 'n Stuff (word puzzles/games), $2-25.
>
> **Tips:** "No mss returned without SASE. Language must be consistent with Christian ethics. Need some articles/fiction from male point of view."

ALIVE NOW! 1908 Grand Ave., Box 189, Nashville TN 37202-0189. (615)340-7218. Fax (615)340-7006. E-mail: 102615.3122@compuserve.com. United Methodist/The Upper Room. George R. Graham, ed. Short theme-based writings in attractive graphic setting for reflection and meditation. Bimonthly mag; 64 pgs; circ 65,000. 30% freelance. Complete ms/cover letter. Pays $25 or more on acceptance for newspaper, periodical & electronic rts. Articles 250-500 wds; fiction 250-750 wds. Responds 13 wks before issue date. Seasonal 6-8 mos ahead. Accepts disk. Guidelines/theme list; free copy.

> **Poetry:** Free verse, traditional; to 25 lines.
>
> **Fillers:** Cartoons, prayers.

#AMERICA, 106 W. 56th St., New York NY 10019-3893. (212)581-4640. Fax (212)399-3596. Catholic. Rev. George W. Hunt, S.J., ed. A national journal of opinion. Weekly mag; 24-32 pgs; circ 36,000. 100% freelance. Query or complete ms/cover letter; fax query OK. Pays $75-150 on acceptance for all rts. Articles 1,000-2,500 wds. Responds in 3 wks. Seasonal 3 mos ahead. Guidelines; copy $1.50.

Poetry: Patrick Samway, S.J. Light verse, serious poetry, unrhymed; 15-30 lines; $7.50-25 or $1.40/line (on publication). Submit max. 3 poems.

*THE AMERICAN BAPTIST, Box 851, Valley Forge PA 19482. American Baptist Church. Philip E. Jenks, ed. Denominational. Little freelance. Not in topical listings.

Tips: "Interested in denominational-oriented news and issues stories."

AMERICAN BIBLE SOCIETY RECORD, 1865 Broadway, New York NY 10023. (212)408-1419. Fax (212)408-1456. E-mail: mmaus@americanbible.org. Website: www.americanbible.org. Mike Maus, ed. Report of stewardship for ABS members. Bimonthly mag; 32 pgs; circ 275,000. 2% freelance. Query; fax/e-mail query OK. Negotiable payment on acceptance for all rts. Prefers disk. Not copyrighted. Articles 500-600 wds (1/yr). Accepts simultaneous submission & reprints. Prefers disks. Not in topical listings. Free copy.

Tips: "Only articles concerning the Bible or the work and mission of the ABS."

*AMERICAN TRACT SOCIETY, Box 462008, Garland TX 75046. (214)276-9408. Perry Brown, tract ed. Majority of tracts written to win unbeliever. Bimonthly tracts; 25 million produced annually. 10% freelance. Query or complete ms/cover letter; phone query OK. Pays $100-150 on publication for simultaneous rts. Tracts 800-1,200 wds (3-6/yr). Responds in 4-6 wks. Seasonal 8-9 mos ahead. Accepts reprints. Guidelines; free samples.

Special Needs: Youth issues.

Tips: "Choose a subject that is very relevant and evident to potential readers."

ANGELS ON EARTH, 16 E. 34th St., New York NY 10016. (212)251-8100. Fax (212)684-0679. Guideposts. Colleen Hughes, mng. ed.; Celeste McCauley, ed. for columns & fillers. Presents true stories about God's angels and humans who have played angelic roles on earth. Bimonthly mag.; circ 500,000. Subscription $15.95. Est. 1995. 90% freelance. Complete ms/cover letter. Pays to $400 on publication for all rts. Articles to 1,500 wds (all stories must be true). Responds in 12 wks. Seasonal 6 mos ahead. Sidebars OK. No disk. Guidelines; copy for 7x10 SAE/4 stamps.

Fillers: Buys many. Any type except party ideas or word puzzles; to 250 wds; $25-150.

Columns/Departments: Accepts many. Earning Their Wings (good ideas, good deeds), 150 wds; Only Human? (human or angel?/mystery), 250 wds; $50-150.

#ANGLICAN JOURNAL, 600 Jarvis St., Toronto ON M4Y 2J6 Canada. (416)924-9192. Anglican Church of Canada. Carolyn Purden, ed; submit to Vianney Carriere, news ed. Informs Canadian Anglicans about the church at home and overseas. Newspaper (10x/yr); 24 pgs; circ 272,000. 25% freelance. Query; phone query OK. Pays $50-300 CAN, on acceptance for 1st rts. Articles to 1,000 wds. Responds in 2 wks. Seasonal 2 mos ahead. Accepts reprints. Guidelines.

THE ANNALS OF SAINT ANNE DE BEAUPRE, PO Box 1000, St. Anne de Beaupre QC G0A 3C0 Canada. (418)827-4538. Fax (418)827-4530. Catholic/Redemptorist Fathers. Father Roch Achard, C.Ss.R., ed. Promotes Catholic family values. Monthly mag; 32 pgs; circ 45,000. Subscription $8.75 US, $9.25 CAN. 40% freelance. Complete ms/cover letter. Pays .03-.04/wd on acceptance for 1st rts. Articles (200/yr) & fiction (200/yr); 500-1,500 wds. Responds in 3-4 wks. Seasonal 4-5 mos ahead. No disk. No sidebars. Guidelines; copy for 9x12 SAE/IRC.

> **Tips:** "Writing must be uplifting and inspirational; clearly written, not filled with long quotations. We tend to stay away from extreme controversy and focus on the family, good family values, devotion and Christianity."

THE APOCALYPSE CHRONICLES, Box 448, Jacksonville OR 97530. (541)899-8888. Christian Media. James Lloyd, ed/pub. Deals with the apocalypse exclusively. Quarterly newsletter; circ 2,000-3,000. Query; prefers phone query. Payment negotiable for reprint rts. Articles. Responds in 3 wks. KJV only. Copy for #10 SAE/2 stamps.

> **Tips:** "It's helpful if you understand your own prophetic position and are aware of its name, i.e., Futurist, Historicist, etc."

ARKANSAS CATHOLIC, PO Box 7417, Little Rock AR 72217. (501)664-0125. Fax (501)664-9075. Catholic—diocese of Little Rock. Malea Walters, ed. Regional newspaper for the local Diocese. Weekly tabloid; 12 pgs; circ 7,000. Subscription $15. 10% freelance. Query/clips; fax query OK. Pays to $100 on acceptance or publication for 1st rts. Articles (2/yr) 400-800 wds; book reviews 600 wds. Accepts simultaneous submissions. Accepts disk. Sidebars OK. Prefers Catholic Bible. Guidelines; copy for 7x10 SAE/2 stamps. (Ads)

> **Columns/Departments:** Leslie O'Malley. Accepts 2/yr. Seeds of Faith (education).
>
> **Tips:** "Make stories as localized as possible."

ARLINGTON CATHOLIC HERALD, 200 N. Glebe Rd., Ste. 607, Arlington VA 22203. (703)841-2590. Fax (703)524-2782. E-mail: ACHFLACH@aol.com. Catholic Diocese of Arlington. Michael Flach, ed. Regional newspaper for the local Diocese. Weekly newspaper; 28 pgs; circ 53,000. Subscription $14. 10% freelance. Query; phone/fax/e-mail query OK. Pays $50-150 on publication for one-time rts. Articles 500-1,500 wds. Responds in 2 wks. Seasonal 3 mos ahead. Accepts simultaneous submissions. Prefers disk. Sidebars OK. Guidelines; copy for 11x17 SAE. (Ads)

> **Columns/Departments:** Sports; School News; Local Entertainment; 500 wds.
>
> **Tips:** "All submissions must be Catholic-related. Avoid controversial issues within the Church."

AT EASE, 1445 Boonville Ave., Springfield MO 65802-1894. (417)862-2781. Fax (417)863-7276. Assemblies of God. Lemuel D. McElyea, ed. Devotional articles for military personnel. Bimonthly mag; 4 pgs; circ 28,000. Free to military. 90% freelance. Complete ms/cover letter; phone/fax query OK. Pays .03/wd on publication for 1st rts. Articles 400 wds (20/yr). Responds in 6 wks. Seasonal 6 mos ahead. Accepts simultaneous submissions & reprints. Accepts disk. Guidelines/copy for #10 SAE/1 stamp.

Fillers: Buys 5/yr. Cartoons; $20-40.

Tips: "Strong human interest; talk about real life. Make subject inspiring and uplifting. We want to win souls."

*ATLANTIC BAPTIST, PO Box 756, Kentville NS B4N 3X9 Canada. (902)681-6868. Fax (902)681-0315. Atlantic Baptist Convention. Michael A. Lipe, ed. Denominational. Monthly; 32-48 pgs; circ. 7,500. Subscription $27.50. 25% freelance. Query or complete ms; fax query OK. Pays $15-30 on publication for one-time rts. Articles 750-1,500 wds. Responds in 2-5 wks. Guidelines.

+AWARENESS TENNESSEE CHRISTIAN COMMUNICATOR, PO Box 100415, Nashville TN 37224. Phone/fax (615)889-1791. Non-denominational. Karynthia Phillips, pub/ed. Provides national, international and local news. Monthly newspaper; 8 pgs; circ 10,000. Free subscription. 100% freelance. Query/clips. **PAYS IN COPIES.**

*AXIOS, 1501 E. Chapman Ave. #345, Fullerton CA 92631-4000. Orthodox Christian. Fr. Daniel John Gorham, ed. Review of public affairs, religion, literature and the arts, and is especially interested in the Orthodox Catholic Church and its world view. Bimonthly newsletter; 32 pgs; circ 15,672. Subscription $25. 90% freelance. Complete ms/cover letter. Pays .04/wd & up ($25-500) on publication for 1st rts. Articles, any length (29/yr); book reviews 2,000 wds. Responds in 4-8 wks. Seasonal 4 mos ahead. Accepts simultaneous submissions & reprints. Kill fee 25%. Copy $4.20/9x12 SAE/$1.20 currency.

Poetry: Buys 6/yr. Traditional; any length; $5-25. Submit max. 3 poems.

Fillers: Buys 25/yr. Anecdotes, cartoons, facts.

Columns/Departments: Buys 80 religious book and film reviews/yr. Query.

Tips: "Most open to articles. Be sure you have an idea of who and what an orthodox Christian is."

** Axios was #58 on the 1994 Top 50 Christian Publishers list.

THE BANNER, 2850 Kalamazoo Ave. SE, Grand Rapids MI 49560. (616)224-0732. Fax (616)224-0834. E-mail: banner@crcna.org. Christian Reformed Church. Malcolm McBryde, assoc. ed. Denominational. Biweekly mag; 31 pgs; circ. 30,000. Subscription $41.95. 10% freelance. Complete ms/cover letter; phone/fax/e-mail query OK. Pays $100-125 on acceptance for all rts. Articles 850 or 1,200 wds (5/yr); book/music/video reviews, 850 wds, $50. Responds in 4 wks. Seasonal 6-8 mos ahead. Requires disk. Kill fee 50%. Sidebars OK. Prefers NIV. Guidelines/theme list; copy for 9x12 SAE/4 stamps. (Ads)

Poetry: Buys 10/yr. Any type; 5-10 lines; $32. Submit max. 5 poems.

Fillers: Buys 48/yr. Church related cartoons; $40.

Columns/Departments: Tuned In (critical critiques of movies, music, TV, etc), 800 wds; $50.

Tips: "One must really get to know the Christian Reformed Church. All of our articles are geared to this expression of faith."

BANNER NEWS SERVICE, 7127 Little River Turnpike, 2nd Floor, Ste. 206, Annandale VA 22003. (703)642-9416. Fax (703)642-0832. World-wide, non-denominational news organization. Fidelis Iyebote, ed. Provides companies, church organizations and individuals with news, information, ideas, innovations and facts to promote business and individual growth. Subscription $150. Buys 20 articles/day; 2 typed, double-spaced pages. Query/clips or complete ms; fax query

OK (prefers mail). Payment is attractive, but depends on quality. Responds in 4 wks. House style book available to accredited contributors & correspondents.

Tips: "Most open to exclusive, authentic, well-researched stories on topical current issues."

*THE BAPTIST BEACON, RR 1, Waterford ON N0E 1Y0 Canada. (519)443-8525. Baptist. Sterling Clark, ed. For adults, emphasizing biblical doctrine, evangelism, prophesy, and inspirational articles. Monthly mag; 20 pgs; circ 300. Subscription $12. 15% freelance. Complete ms/cover letter; phone query OK. **NO PAYMENT** for one-time use. Articles any length. Seasonal 3 mos ahead. Accepts reprints. Free copy.

Poetry: Accepts 24+/yr. Traditional; any length. Submit any number.

Tips: "Most open to devotional, inspirational and biblical teaching."

*BAPTIST HISTORY AND HERITAGE, 901 Commerce St., Ste. 400, Nashville TN 37203-3630. (615)244-0344. Southern Baptist. Lynn E. May, Jr., ed. A scholarly journal focusing on Baptist history. Quarterly journal; 64 pgs; circ 2,000. 15-20% freelance. Query. Pays $192 (for assigned only) for all rts. Articles to 4,000 wds. Responds in 9 wks. Prefers disk. Guidelines.

Tips: "Most open to lesser known aspects of Baptist history based on primary sources."

*THE BAPTIST INFORMER, 603 S. Wilmington St., Raleigh NC 27601. (919)821-7466. Fax (919)836-0061. General Baptist. Archie D. Logan, ed. Regional African-American publication. Monthly tabloid; 16 pgs; circ 10,000. 10% freelance. Query or complete ms/cover letter; fax query OK. **PAYS IN COPIES** for one-time rts. Articles & fiction. Responds in 13 wks. Accepts simultaneous submissions. Prefers disk. Free copy.

*THE B.C. CATHOLIC, 150 Robson St., Vancouver BC V6B 2A7 Canada. (604)683-0281. Fax (604)683-8117. Catholic. Rev. Vincent Hawkswell, ed. News, education and inspiration for Canadian Catholics. Weekly (47X) newspaper; 16 pgs; circ 20,000. 70% freelance. Query; phone query OK. Pays variable rate on publication for 1st rts. Articles 400-500 wds. Responds in 6 wks. Seasonal 4 wks ahead. Accepts simultaneous submissions & reprints.

Tips: "We prefer to use Catholic writers."

+THE BELIEVER, 5375 Alderley Rd., Victoria BC V8Y 1X9 Canada. (250)658-2644. Fax (250)658-8481. E-mail: msbowes@islandnet.com or believer@islandnet.com. Website: http://www.islandnet.com/believer. Tidewater Publishing Co. Madge S. Bowes, ed. Easy-to-read local news and inspiration for churches and businesses on Vancouver Island. Query; fax/e-mail query OK. Not copyrighted. **NO PAYMENT.** Articles 300-750 wds; little fiction; a few book/music reviews, 400 wds. Seasonal 2 mos ahead. Accepts simultaneous submissions and reprints. Accepts disk (Mac only). Copy for 9x12 SAE/IRCs or $1.

Poetry: Accepts 24-36/yr.

Fillers: Anecdotes; accepts few.

Tips: "I want a 'diet' for our readers of Christian growth, how-to's for church, individual and family needs with a Christian perspective." Prefers not to have to return mss.

BIBLE ADVOCATE, Box 33677, Denver CO 80233. (303)452-7973. Fax (303)452-0657. E-mail: cofgsd@denver.net. Church of God (Seventh Day). Roy Marrs, ed;

Sherri Langton, asst ed. Mostly older adult readers; 50% not members of the denomination. Monthly mag; 20-28 pgs; circ 13,500. Free subscription. 25% freelance. Complete ms/cover letter; no phone/fax/e-mail query. Pays $15-35 on publication for 1st, one-time, reprint & simultaneous rts. Articles 1,000-2,000 wds (25/yr). Responds in 4-6 wks. Seasonal 6 mos ahead. Accepts simultaneous submissions & reprints (tell when/where appeared). Accepts disk. Kill fee up to 50%. Sidebars OK. Guidelines; copy for 9x12 SAE/4 stamps.

Poetry: Accepts 10-20/yr. Free verse, traditional; 5-25 lines; $10. Submit max. 5 poems.

Fillers: Buys 5-10/yr. Facts, prayers, prose, quotes; 50-200 wds; $5-10.

Columns/Departments: Accepts 6/yr. Viewpoint (social or religious issues), to 700 wds, pays copies; Pastor's Corner (devotional by pastors only), 300-350 wds; $10.

Tips: "Viewpoint column and poetry most open. Keep your writing fresh. Have something different to say that is biblically sound and insightful, and stick to your focus."

THE BIBLE TODAY, Saint John's Abbey, Collegeville MN 56321-7500. (320)363-2213 or (800)858-5450. Fax (800)445-5899. Catholic/Benedictine Monks. Mss to: Rev. Donald Senior, C.P., ed., 5401 S. Cornell Ave., Chicago IL 60615. Explains the meaning and context of particular biblical passages and books and encourages a regular, prayerful reading of the Bible. Bimonthly mag; 64 pgs; circ 7,000. Subscription $24. 20% freelance. Complete ms/cover letter; phone/fax query OK. **PAYS 5 COPIES & 1 YR SUBSCRIPTION.** Articles to 2,000 wds (6/yr). Responds in 9 wks. Seasonal 6 mos ahead. No disk. No sidebars. Prefers NAB. Free guidelines/copy. (Ads)

Tips: "Most open to general articles on the Bible or biblical themes, biblical archaeology, biblical spirituality."

*BIBLICAL REFLECTIONS ON MODERN MEDICINE, PO Box 14488, Augusta GA 30919. (706)736-0161. Dr. Ed Payne, ed. For all Christians interested in medical-ethical issues. Bimonthly newsletter; circ 1,100. Subscription $19. 20% freelance. Complete ms/cover letter. **PAYS IN COPIES & SUBSCRIPTION**, for 1st rts. Articles to 1,500 wds (5/yr). Responds in 1-4 wks. Accepts simultaneous submissions & reprints. No sidebars. Guidelines/copy for #10 SAE/1 stamp.

+THE BREAD OF LIFE, 209 Macnab St. N., Box 395, Hamilton ON L8N 3H8 Canada. (905)529-4496. Fax (905)529-5373. Catholic. Fr. Peter Coughlin, ed. Catholic Charismatic; to encourage spiritual growth in areas of renewal in the catholic church today. Bimonthly mag; 32pgs; circ 5,200. Subscription $30. 10% freelance. Complete ms/cover letter; fax query OK. **PAYS IN COPIES.** Articles 1,200-1,400 wds; book reviews 250 wds. Responds in 2-3 wks. Seasonal 6 mos ahead. Accepts reprints (tell when/where appeared). No disk. No sidebars. Prefers NAB or NJB. Guidelines; copy for 9x12 SAE/6 stamps. (Ads)

Poetry: Accepts 12-15/yr. Traditional; 10-25 lines. Submit max. 2 poems.

Fillers: Accepts 10-12/yr. Facts, prose, quotes; to 250 wds.

+THE BRETHREN EVANGELIST, 524 College Ave., Ashland OH 44805. (419)289-1708. E-mail: Brethrench@aol.com. The Brethren Church. Richard C. Winfield, ed. Denominational. Monthly newsletter; 12 pgs; circ 7,325. Free to members. 5% freelance. Complete ms/cover letter. Pays .04/wd on publication for 1st rts. Not copyrighted. Articles 800 wds (6/yr). Responds in 8 wks. Accepts simultaneous submissions. Prefers disk. Sidebars OK. Prefers NIV. Copy for 9x12 SAE/3 stamps.

*BROKEN STREETS, 57 Morningside Dr. E., Bristol CT 06010. (203)582-2943. Ron Grossman, ed. For Christian writers of poetry, especially new writers. Semi-annual journal; 40-50 pgs; circ 500-1,000. Subscription $10. 99% freelance. Complete ms/cover letter. **PAYS IN COPIES**, for one-time rts. Articles 100-500 wds (5-10/yr). Responds in 1 wk. Accepts reprints. Guidelines; copy $2.50.

> **Poetry:** Accepts 200/yr. All types; no length limit (prefers 5-15 lines). Submit max. 5 poems.
>
> **Fillers:** Accepts 50/yr. Prose, devotionals, prayers, journal entries; to 500 wds.
>
> **Tips:** "Buy a sample, write a good cover letter, and pray for guidance."

BURNING LIGHT: A Journal of Christian Literature, 59 Treetop Ct., Bloomingdale NJ 07403-1016. (201)283-9516. Burning Light Press. Carl Simmons, ed/pub. A literary journal devoted to today's writer who is Christian. Quarterly jour; 32-48 pgs; circ 400. Subscription $14. Est. 1993. 100% freelance. Complete ms/cover letter; phone query OK. **PAYS IN COPIES/SUBSCRIPTION** for negotiable rts. Essays 1,000-3,000 wds (3-4/yr); fiction 1,000-10,000 wds (10/yr); book reviews, 200-400 wds. Responds in 3-4 wks. Seasonal 3-4 mos ahead. Accepts simultaneous submissions & reprints (rarely—tell when/where appeared). Accepts disk. No sidebars. Guidelines; copy $4.

> **Poetry:** Buys 50-80/yr. Avant-garde, free verse, haiku, traditional; to 600 lines. Submit any number.
>
> **Tips:** "Be real—don't say what you think God wants to hear; say what he's moved you to say. Prophetic voices are never pretty, but they're a lot more useful."

*CANADA LUTHERAN, 1512 St. James St., Winnipeg MB R3H 0L2 Canada. (204)786-6707. Fax (204)783-7548. Evangelical Lutheran Church in Canada. Kenn Ward, ed. Denominational. Monthly (11X) mag; 40 pgs; circ 23,000. Subscription $17 US Up to 50% freelance. Query or complete ms/cover letter; fax query OK. Pays $40-110 CAN, on acceptance for one-time rts. Articles 800-1,500 wds (15/yr); fiction 850-1,200 wds (4/yr). Responds in 5 wks. Seasonal 10 mos ahead. Accepts simultaneous submissions & reprints. Prefers disk. Guidelines.

> **Tips:** "Canadians/Lutherans receive priority, but not the only consideration. Want material that is clear, concise and fresh. Articles that talk about real life experiences of faith receive our best reader response."

*THE CANADIAN BAPTIST, 414-195 The West Mall, Etobicoke ON M3C 5K1 Canada. (416)622-8600. Fax (416)622-0780. E-mail: canbap@user.rose.com. Baptist Convention of Ontario and Quebec/Western Canada. Dr. Larry Matthews, ed. Covers issues relevant to and events/stories about people in the Baptist community. Monthly mag; 32 pgs; circ 11,000. Subscription $18 CAN. 90% freelance. Query; phone/fax query OK. Pays negotiable rates on publication for one-time rts. Not copyrighted. Articles. Responds in 6 wks. Seasonal 3 mos ahead. Accepts simultaneous submissions & reprints (occasionally). Kill fees negotiated. Prefers disk. Sidebars OK. Guidelines; copy for 9x13 SAE.

THE CANADIAN CATHOLIC REVIEW, St. Thomas More College, 1437 College Dr., Saskatoon SK S7N 0W6 Canada. (306)966-8959. Fax (306)966-8904. E-mail: callam@duke.usask.ca. Catholic. Rev. Daniel Callam, CSB, ed. For intelligent (but not scholarly) Catholics who take their faith seriously. Monthly (11X) mag; 40 pgs; circ 1,000. Subscription $25, US 30% freelance. Query; phone/fax/e-mail query OK. Pays $50-300 on publication for 1st NASR. Articles 500-6,000 wds (10/yr); book reviews 300-700 wds/$25. Responds in 9 wks. Seasonal 6 mos ahead. Prefers disk. No sidebars. Prefers RSV. Guidelines; copy $3/9x12 SAE/IRCs. (Ads)

> **Columns/Departments:** Buys 10/yr. Scripture; Liturgy; American Notes; The Church in Quebec; 500-1,200 wds; $50.
>
> **Tips:** "Most open to columns and general articles. Be lucid, articulate, faithful and brief."

*CATHEDRAL AGE, Mount St. Alban, Massachusetts & Wisconsin Aves NW, Washington DC 20016-5098. (202)537-6249. Fax (202)364-6600. Washington National Cathedral (Episcopal). Sherwood Harris, ed. About what's happening in and to cathedrals and their programs. Quarterly mag; 36 pgs; circ 32,000. Subscription $15. 20% freelance. Query/clips; phone/fax query OK. Pays to $500 on acceptance for all rts. Articles 1,000-1,500 wds (10/yr); book reviews 600 wds, $100. Responds in 4 wks. Seasonal 6 mos ahead. Requires disk. Kill fee 50%. Sidebars OK. Prefers RSV. Copy $5/9x12 SAE/5 stamps.

> **Special Needs:** Art, architecture, and music.
>
> **Tips:** "We assign all articles, so query/clips first. Always write from the viewpoint of an individual first, then move into a more general discussion of the topic. Human interest angle important."

*THE CATHOLIC ANSWER, 207 Adams St., Newark NJ 07105. (219)356-8400. Our Sunday Visitor/Catholic. Father Peter Stravinskas, mng. ed. Answers to questions of belief for orthodox Catholics. Bimonthly mag; 64 pgs; circ 60,000. 50% freelance. Query/clips. Pays $100 on publication for 1st rts. Articles 1,200-2,200 wds (80/yr). Seasonal 6 mos ahead. Guidelines; free copy (from 200 Noll Plaza, Huntington IN 46750).

CATHOLIC COURIER, 1150 Buffalo Rd., Rochester NY 14624. (716)328-4340. Fax (716)328-8640. Catholic. Karen M. Franz, ed. Newspaper for the Diocese of Rochester NY. Weekly newspaper; 20 pgs; circ 48,000. Subscription $20. Less than 1% freelance. Query/clips or complete ms/cover letter. Pays $30-100 on publication for one-time rts. Articles 1,200 wds. Responds in 4-9 wks. Accepts simultaneous submissions. Prefers disk. (Ads)

> **Columns/Departments:** News; Leisure; Opinion; Youth; 750 wds.
>
> **Tips:** "We publish very little freelance and virtually none from non-local writers."

CATHOLIC DIGEST, Box 64090, St. Paul MN 55164-0090. Phone/fax (612)962-6725. E-mail: cdigest@stthomas.edu. Catholic/University of St. Thomas. Richard Reece, ed.; Kathleen Stauffer, mng. ed. Primarily for Catholic families with teens or grown children; most reprinted from other publications. Monthly mag; 145 pgs; circ 500,000+. Subscription $16.97. 10% freelance. Complete ms (for original material)/cover letter, tear sheets for reprints; e-mail submissions OK. Pays $200-400 ($100 for reprints) on acceptance for one-time rts. On-line only articles receive $100, plus half of any traceable revenue. Articles 1,000-3,500 wds (60/yr). Responds in 4-6 wks. Seasonal 4 mos ahead. Accepts reprints (tell when/where appeared). Sidebars OK. Guidelines; copy for 6x9 SAE/5 stamps.

Fillers: Fillers Editor. Buys 200/yr. Anecdotes, games, jokes, quizzes, prayers, quotes, short humor; to 500 wds; $2/published line.

Columns/Departments: Buys 100/yr. Open Door (personal stories of conversion to Catholicism); 200-500 wds; $20-50. See guidelines for full list.

Tips: "We favor the anecdotal approach. Stories must be strongly focused on a definitive topic that is illustrated for the reader with a well-developed series of true-life, interconnected vignettes."

** This periodical was #29 on the 1996 Top 50 Christian Publishers list. (#30 in 1995, #25 in 1994)

CATHOLIC FORESTER, Box 3012, Naperville IL 60566-7012. (630)983-3380. Fax (630)983-3384. Catholic Order of Foresters. Dorothy Deer, ed. For mixed audience, primarily parents and grandparents between the ages of 30 and 80. Bimonthly mag; 36 pgs; circ 100,000. Free/membership. 10% freelance. Complete ms/cover letter; phone/fax query OK. Pays .20/wd & up, on acceptance for all, 1st, one-time or reprint. Articles 1,000-1,800 wds (10/yr); fiction for all ages 500-1,000 wds (10/yr). Responds in 8-10 wks. Seasonal 6 mos ahead. Accepts simultaneous submissions & reprints (tell when/where appeared). Accepts disk. Kill fee 20-25%. Sidebars OK. Prefers NAS. Guidelines; copy for 9x12 SAE/4 stamps.

Fillers: Buys 6-8/yr. Cartoons, games, quizzes, word puzzles. Pays $25-60.

Tips: "Looking for articles on retirement."

** This periodical was #50 on the 1995 Top 50 Christian Publishers list.

#CATHOLIC HERITAGE, 200 Noll Plaza, Huntington IN 46750. (219)356-8400. Fax (219)356-9117. E-mail: 76440.3571@compuserve.com. Catholic. Bill Dodds, ed. For those interested in Catholic history. Bimonthly mag; circ 25,000. 75% freelance. Query; e-mail query OK. Pays $200 on acceptance for 1st rts. Articles 1,000-2,000 wds (15/yr). Responds in 3-5 wks. Seasonal 6 mos ahead. Accepts reprints (payment negotiable). Kill fee 33% or $50-75. Prefers disk. Guidelines; free copy.

Tips: "Most open to general features."

*CATHOLIC NEW YORK, 1011 1st Ave, 17th Fl., New York NY 10126. (212)688-2399. Fax (212)688-2642. Catholic. Anne Buckley, ed-in-chief. To inform New York Catholics. Weekly newspaper; 44 pgs; circ 130,000. Subscription $20. 10% freelance. Query or complete ms/cover letter. Pays $15-100 on publication for one-time rts. Articles 500-800 wds. Responds in 5 wks. Copy $1.

Columns/Departments: Comment; Catholic New Yorkers (profiles of unique individuals); 325 wds.

Tips: "Most open to articles that show how to integrate Catholic faith into work, hobbies or special interests."

CATHOLIC PARENT, 200 Noll Plaza, Huntington IN 46750. (800)348-2440. Catholic. Woodeene Koenig-Bricker, ed. Practical advice for Catholic parents, with a specifically Catholic slant. Bimonthly mag; 52 pgs; circ 40,000. Subscription $18. Est. 1993. 90% freelance. Query/clips or complete ms/cover letter; fax query OK. Pays $100-200 on acceptance for 1st rts. Articles 250-1,000 wds

(30-40/yr). Responds in 6-8 wks. Seasonal 6 mos ahead. Kill fee. Accepts disk. Sidebars OK. Guidelines; copy $3/10x13 SAE/5 stamps.

Fillers: Mary Bazzett. Accepts 40/yr. Parenting tips, 100-200 wds, $25.

Columns/Departments: This Works! (short parenting tips).

Tips: "Be practical in your advice. Read the publication to see how we use a blend of how-to and some personal experience."

** This periodical was #51 on the 1996 Top 50 Christian Publishers list. (#25 in 1995, #26 in 1994)

CATHOLIC PEACE VOICE (Formerly **PAX CHRISTI USA**), 532 W. 8th, Erie PA 16502-1343. (814)453-4955. Fax (814)452-4784. E-mail: PAXCHRIST@igc.apc.org. Website: http://www.nonviolence.org/nvweb/pcusa. Dave Robinson, ed. For members of US Catholic Peace Movement. Quarterly newspaper; 16 pgs; circ 20,000. Distributed free. 5% freelance. Query; phone/fax/e-mail query OK. Pays on publication for one-time rts. Accepts simultaneous submissions & reprints. Prefers disk. Guidelines; copy for 9x12 SAE/2 stamps. Not in topical listings. (Ads)

Tips: "Emphasis is on non-violence. No sexist language."

CATHOLIC RURAL LIFE (Formerly **RURAL LANDSCAPES**), 4625 Beaver Ave., Des Moines IA 50310-2199. (515)270-2634. Fax (515)270-9447. E-mail: ncrlc@aol.com. Website: http://www.netins.net/showcase/ncrlcnet. Catholic. Sandra A. LaBlanc, commun. dir. Biannual mag; 40 pgs; circ 3,000. Membership $25. 50% freelance. Query/clips; phone/fax/e-mail query OK. Pays for 1st rts. Articles 1,000-1,500 wds. Responds in 6 wks. Seasonal 6 mos ahead. Prefers disk. Sidebars OK. Guidelines/theme list; copy for 9x12 SAE/3 stamps.

Columns/Departments: Building Community, 350 wds; Closer Look (think piece), 750-1,000 wds; no payment.

*****CATHOLIC SENTINEL**, PO Box 18030, Portland OR 97218-0030. (503)281-1191. Fax (503)282-3486. Catholic. Robert Pfohman, ed. For Catholics in the Archdiocese of western and eastern Oregon. Weekly tabloid; 16-24 pgs; circ 15,000. Subscription $22. 25% freelance. Query; phone/fax query OK (if timely). Pays $25-150 on publication for one-time rts. Not copyrighted. Articles 800-1,800 wds (15/yr). Responds in 6 wks. Seasonal 1 month ahead. Accepts reprints (on columns, not news or features; tell them). Prefers disk or modem. Kill fee 100%. Sidebars OK. Copy 50 cents/9x12 SAE/2 stamps.

Columns/Departments: Buys about 30/yr. Opinion Page, 600 wds, $10. Send complete ms.

Tips: "Find active Catholics living their faith in specific, interesting, upbeat, positive ways."

*****CATHOLIC TELEGRAPH**, 100 E. 8th St., Cincinnati OH 45202. (513)421-3131. Fax (513)381-2242. Catholic. Tricia Hempel, gen. mng. Diocese newspaper for Cincinnati area. Weekly newspaper; 20 pgs; circ 27,000. 10% freelance. Send resume and writing samples for assignment. Pays varying rates on publication for all rts. Articles. Responds in 2-3 wks. Kill fee. Guidelines sent/acceptance; free copy.

Fillers: Newsbreaks (local).

#CATHOLIC TWIN CIRCLE, 33 Rossotto Dr., Hamden CT 06514. (203)288-5600. Fax (203)288-5157. Catholic/Circle Media. Loretta G. Seyer, ed., submit to Eileen Callahan. Features writing for Catholics and/or Christian families of all ages. Weekly newspaper; 20 pgs; circ 30,000. 45% freelance. Complete ms/cover letter. Pays .10/wd on publication for all rts. Articles 1,000-2,000 wds. Responds in 13 wks. Seasonal 2 mos ahead. Serials 3 parts. Kill fee. No sidebars. Prefers Catholic Bible. Guidelines/theme list; copy for 9x12 SAE/2 stamps or $2.

   Columns/Departments: Point of View (opinion on various Catholic issues), 600-800 wds, $50.

+CBA FRONTLINE, PO Box 200, Colorado Springs CO 80901. (719)576-7880. Fax (719)576-0795. Christian Booksellers Assn. Steve Parolini, ed. To give product knowledge and inspiration to the frontline staff in Christian retail bookstores. Monthly trade journal; 38 pgs; circ 11,000. Est. January 1997. 10-20% freelance. Query/clips; phone/fax/e-mail query OK. Pays .16-.25/wd. on acceptance for all rts. Articles. Responds in 4 wks. Seasonal 4-5 mos ahead. Accepts simultaneous submissions. Accepts disk. Kill fee. Sidebars OK. Prefers NIV. Guidelines/theme list.

   Fillers: Buys many/yr. Anecdotes, cartoons, facts, ideas, newsbreaks, short humor; 25-100 wds. Pays $20.

   Columns/Departments: Buys many/yr. Quick "did-you-know" product pieces in these columns: Music, Video, Software, Apparel, Books, Bibles, 25-100 wds. Inspiration (short devotionals), 250 wds; Humor (true retail-oriented anecdotes & cartoons), 25-100 wds. Pays $20.

   Tips: "We rarely accept unsolicited mss, but assign 2-5 articles per month to freelancers based on our agenda. Send cover letter, including experience and areas of interest, plus clips. Also looking for retail and product anecdotes."

CBA MARKETPLACE (formerly **BOOKSTORE JOURNAL**), PO Box 200, Colorado Springs CO 80901. (719)576-7880. Fax (719)576-0795. E-mail: 74521,43@compuserve.com. Christian Booksellers Assn. Sue Grise, ed. To provide Christian bookstore owners with professional retail skills, product information, and industry news. Monthly trade journal; 110 pgs; circ 8,000. Subscription $47. 10-20% freelance. Query/clips; phone/fax query OK. Pays .16-.25/wd on acceptance for all rts. Articles 1,500-2,500 wds (30/yr assigned); book reviews 150-200 wds, $30; music/video reviews 100-200 wds, $25. Responds in 4 wks. Seasonal 4-5 mos ahead. Accepts simultaneous submissions. Accepts disk. Kill fee 90%. Sidebars OK. Prefers NIV. Guidelines; copy $5/9x12 SAE/6 stamps. (Ads)

   Fillers: Buys 12/yr. Anecdotes, cartoons ($100), facts, ideas, newsbreaks, short humor; $20.

   Columns/Departments: Buys 10-20/yr. Industry Watch; Music News; Gift News; Video & software News; Book News; all 100-800 wds. Pays $25 or .25/wd. Query.

   Tips: "All our articles focus on producing and selling Christian products. We rarely accept unsolicited mss, but assign 2-5 articles per month to freelancers. Send cover letter, including experience and areas of interest, plus clips. We also assign 25-30 book reviews, 8-12 music reviews, and 2-5 video reviews per month."

*CELEBRATE LIFE, Box 1350, Stafford VA 22555. (540)659-4171. Fax (540)659-2586. E-mail: ALL.ORG@aol.com. American Life League. Steve Dunham, mng ed. A pro-life, pro-family magazine for Christian audience. Bimonthly mag; 48

pgs; circ 145,000. Subscription $12.95. 60% freelance. Query; phone/fax/e-mail query OK. Pays $25-150 on publication for one-time rts. Articles 500-2,000 wds (70/yr); book reviews 250 wds, $25. Responds in 2-8 wks. Seasonal 6 mos ahead. Accepts reprints. Prefers disk. Kill fee. Sidebars OK. Guidelines/theme list; copy for 9x12 SAE/5 stamps.

Fillers: Buys 6/yr. Newsbreaks (local or special pro-life news); 50-100 wds; $10.

Columns/Departments: Buys 3/yr. Prayer and Fasting (personal spirituality), 500 wds, $25-50. Query.

Special Needs: Abortion, adoption, euthanasia, post-abortion healing, natural family planning and teen chastity. Looking for articles by high school or college students.

Tips: "We need good color photos to accompany human-interest stories. Most open to human-interest stories to fit themes."

** #66 on the 1994 Top 50.

*CHANGES, 3201 SW 15th St., Deerfield FL 33442. (800)851-9100. U.S. Journal, Inc. Jeffrey Laign, mng ed. Recovery magazine for adults (from alcohol and other issues). Bimonthly mag; 100 pgs; circ 100,000. 25% freelance. Query or complete ms/cover letter; fax query OK. Pays .15/wd on publication for one-time rts. Articles & fiction to 2,000 wds. Responds in 9-18 wks. Accepts simultaneous submissions. Prefers disk or modem. Kill fee $15. Guidelines; free copy.

Poetry: Accepts poetry.

Tips: "We want self-help pieces, not personal experiences."

CHARISMA & CHRISTIAN LIFE, 600 Rinehart Rd., Lake Mary FL 32746. (407)333-0600. Fax (407)333-7133. E-mail: charisma@strang.com. Strang Communications. Lee Grady, exec. ed.; Marcia Ford, assoc. ed. (e-mail: mford@strng.com); Jimmy Stewart, book & music review ed. Primarily for the Pentecostal and Charismatic Christian community. Monthly mag; 100+ pgs; circ 220,000. Subscription $21.97. 75% freelance. Query; no phone/fax/e-mail query. Pays $100-800 on publication for 1st rts. Articles 2,000 wds (120/yr); book/music reviews, 200 wds, $20. Responds in 8-12 wks. Seasonal 4 mos ahead. Kill fee $50. Prefers disk. Sidebars OK. Guidelines; copy $3. (Ads)

Tips: "Most open to news section, reviews or features. Query (published clips help a lot)."

+CHESAPEAKE CITIZEN, 408 Cranes Roost, Annapolis MD 21401. (410)757-7599. Fax (410)757-6245. E-mail: CurtisEdit@aol.com. Maryland Family Forum. Carolyn Curtis, ed. To inform constituents of news events and public policy trends impacting pro-family Marylanders. Monthly newsletter; circ 4,500. Subscription $20. Open to freelance.

CHRISTIAN ADVOCATE, PO Box 30, Beech Grove IN 46107. (317)787-3291. Fax (317)787-3325. Reporter-Times, Inc. Joe Skuarenina, ed. Indianapolis-area regional paper for the evangelical Christian community. Monthly newspaper; circ. 14,000. Subscription $18. 99% freelance. Query; phone query OK. **NO PAYMENT.** Articles 650 wds (up to 100/yr); Fiction 500 wds; book/music reviews, 500 wds. Responds in 1-4 wks. Seasonal 2 mos ahead. Accepts simultaneous submissions & reprints. Kill fee 30%. Prefers disk. Sidebars OK. Prefers RSV. Copy $1.

Fillers: Anecdotes, cartoons, facts.

Columns/Departments: Accepts up to 40/yr. Query.

#CHRISTIAN AMERICAN NEWSPAPER, 1801-L Sara Dr., Chesapeake VA 23320. (804)424-2630. Fax (804)424-4326. E-mail: camerica@infi.net. Christian Coalition, Inc. Michael Ebert, ed. To provide a Christian perspective on the news, enabling them to be more effective citizens by being better informed. Bimonthly newspaper; circ 400,000. Subscription $14.95. Open to freelance. Query. (Ads)

+THE CHRISTIAN ARTS REVIEW, 783 Hwy. 90E., Chipley FL 32428. (908)638-0643. E-mail: BRIGHT@aol.com. Brightwater Communications Group. William Curtis Bridenback, ed. For evangelical Christians, 25-55, who enjoy Christian books and music. Quarterly newsletter; online edition updated monthly, and 2 special editions/yr; 6-8 pgs; circ 1,500. Subscription $12. 50% freelance. Query/clips; e-mail query OK. Pays $5-25 on publication for 1st & electronic rts. Articles 175-350 wds (10-15/yr); book/music/video reviews 75-150 wds, $5/product. Responds in 2 wks. Seasonal 4-5 mos ahead. Prefers disk. Kill fee. Sidebars OK. Guidelines/theme list; copy for #10 SAE/1 stamp. (Ads)

> **Fillers:** Buys 50/yr. Anecdotes, facts, newsbreaks, quotes; 75-150 wds; $5-25.
>
> **Columns/Departments:** Buys 10-15/yr. Feature Artist (celebrity interview/profile), 350 wds; Spotlight (new product), 275 wds; Etcetera (news & information soundbites), 75-150 wds. Pays $5-25.
>
> **Special Needs:** Bible reviews, essays on Christian media. Always looking for good reviewers who have the time and enjoy the work.
>
> **Contest:** At end of year, gives $25 certificates to best writers in each area.
>
> **Tips:** "Short items are a good way to go. We'd like to do more issues-oriented stories and op/ed pieces on Christian media. Our summer special issue is also a good place to start; write for topic information."

*CHRISTIAN CHRONICLE, PO Box 11000, Oklahoma City OK 73136. (405)425-5070. Church of Christ. Glover Shipp, mng ed. Denominational; international; focus on evangelism. Monthly newspaper; 32 pgs; circ 100,000. 5% freelance. Complete ms/cover letter. Pays varying rates on acceptance for one-time rts. Articles to 1,000 wds. Responds in 2-3 wks. Guidelines; free copy.

> **Tips:** "We prefer to get submissions from members of the Church of Christ."

*THE CHRISTIAN CHRONICLE, PO Box 12623, Reading PA 19612-2623. (610)378-1245. Fax (610)378-1378. E-mail: TCCjustice@aol.com. Non-denominational. Alice Swoyer-Smolkowicz, pub. For non-Charismatic Christians. Bimonthly newsletter; 8 pgs; circ. 2,000. Subscription $12. Est. 1994. 90% freelance. Complete ms/cover letter; phone/fax/e-mail query OK. **NO PAYMENT** for one-time rts. Articles 100-500 wds (18/yr); fiction (2/yr). Seasonal 3 mos ahead. Accepts reprints. Prefers disk. Prefers NIV. Copy for #10 SAE/1 stamp.

> **Fillers:** Accepts 24/yr. Anecdotes, cartoons, facts, ideas, quotes, short humor; 50-200 wds.

*THE CHRISTIAN CIVIC LEAGUE OF MAINE RECORD, Box 5459, Augusta ME 04332. (207)622-7634. Jasper S. Wyman, ed. Focuses on church, public service and political action. Monthly newsletter; 12 pgs; circ 4,600. 10% freelance. Query. **NO PAYMENT** for one-time rts. Articles (10-12/yr). Responds in

4-8 wks. Seasonal 2 mos ahead. Accepts simultaneous query & reprints. Free copy. Not in topical listings.

*CHRISTIAN COMPUTING MAGAZINE, PO Box 198, 309 S. Washington, Raymore MO 64083. (816)331-3881. Fax (816)331-5510. E-mail: BOBCC MAG@aol.com. Bob Dasal, mng. ed. For Christian/church computer users. Monthly (11X) mag; 2 pgs; circ. 90,000. Subscription $14.95. 40% freelance. Query/clips; fax/e-mail query OK. **NO PAYMENT** for all rts. Articles 1,000-1,800 wds (12/yr). Responds in 4 wks. Seasonal 2 mos ahead. Accepts reprints. Requires disk. Sidebars OK. Guidelines; copy for 9x12 SAE.

Fillers: Accepts 6 cartoons/yr.

Columns/Departments: Accepts 12/yr. Telecommunications (computer), 1,500-1,800 wds.

Special Needs: Articles on Internet, DTP, and computing.

*THE CHRISTIAN COURIER, 1933 W. Wisconsin Ave., Milwaukee WI 53233. (414)344-7300. Fax (414)344-7375. ProBuColls Assn. John M. Fisco, Jr., pub. To propagate the Gospel of Jesus Christ in the Midwest. Monthly newspaper; circ 10,000. 10% freelance. Query. **PAYS IN COPIES**, for one-time rts. Not copyrighted. Articles 300-1,500 wds (6/yr). Responds in 2-4 wks. Seasonal 2 mos ahead. Accepts reprints. Guidelines; free copy.

Fillers: Anecdotes, facts, newsbreaks; 10-100 wds.

CHRISTIAN COURIER, 4-261 Martindale Rd., St. Catherines ON L2W 1A1 Canada. (US address: Box 110, Lewiston NY 14092). (416)682-8311. Fax (416)682-8313. Independent (Protestant Reformed). Bert Witvoet, ed; Bob Vander Vennen, book review ed. To present Canadian and international news, both religious and secular, from a Reformed Christian perspective. Weekly (44X) newspaper; 20 pgs; circ 5,000. 25% freelance. Complete ms/cover letter; phone query OK. Pays .05-.10/wd on publication for one-time rts. Articles 700-1,000 wds (20/yr); fiction 1,000-2,000 wds (10/yr); book reviews 100-500 wds. Responds in 3 wks. Seasonal 1 yr ahead. Accepts reprints. Guidelines; copy for 9x12 SAE/IRC.

Poetry: Buys 20/yr. Avant-garde, free verse, traditional; 10-30 lines; $15-30. Submit max. 5 poems.

*CHRISTIAN CRUSADE NEWSPAPER, PO Box 279, Neosho MO 64850. (918)438-4234. Fax (417)451-4319. Interdenominational. Billy James Hargis, pub. A Christian, pro-American approach to current social and political issues. Monthly newspaper; 24 pgs; circ 25,000. 50% freelance. Query. Pays varying rates on publication for all rts. Articles (any length). Responds in 9 wks. Free copy.

CHRISTIAN DRAMA MAGAZINE, 1824 Celestia Blvd., Walla Walla WA 99362-3619. (509)522-5242. Suspending publication until March 1999.

THE CHRISTIAN EDGE, 6501 Bronson Ln., Bakersfield CA 93309. Phone/fax (805)837-1378. E-mail: THECHREDGE@aol.com. Chase Productions/evangelical. Don Chase, pub. Activity and resources guide; not an issues-driven publication. Monthly newspaper; 8-12 pgs; circ 15,000. Subscription $18. 10% freelance. Query/clips; e-mail query OK. **NO PAYMENT** for one-time rts. Articles 350-1,000 wds (10/yr); book/music/video reviews 150 wds. Responds in 3 wks. Seasonal 2 mos ahead. Accepts simultaneous submissions & reprints (tell when/where appeared). Prefers disk. Sidebars OK. Copy for 9x12 SAE/4 stamps. (Ads)

Fillers: Accepts 20-30/yr. Anecdotes, cartoons, facts, games, ideas, newsbreaks, quotes, short humor; 50-100 wds. Pays $10.

*THE CHRISTIAN FOCUS, PO Box 2891, 725 Kingsley Ave., Orange Park FL 32073. (904)269-7362. Fax (904)269-7362. Teresa D. Foster, ed. Committed to truth in Christian news around the world, nation and community. Monthly newspaper. Circulation 15,000. Subscription $19. Open to freelance.

CHRISTIAN HISTORY, 465 Gundersen Dr., Carol Stream IL 60188. (630)260-6200. Fax (630)260-0114. E-mail: CHedit@aol.com. Christianity Today, Inc. Submit to The Editor. To teach Christian history to educated readers in an engaging manner. Quarterly mag; 52 pgs; circ 70,000. Subscription $19.95. 75% freelance. Query; fax/e-mail query OK. Pays .10/wd on acceptance for 1st , electronic & some ancillary rts. Articles 1,000-3,000 wds (1/yr). Responds in 2 wks. Accepts reprints (tell when/where appeared). Requires disk. Kill fee 50%. Sidebars OK. Guidelines/theme list; copy $5.50. (Ads)

Tips: "Let us know your particular areas of specialization and any books or papers you have written in the area of Christian history."

** 1995 EPA Award of Merit—General.

CHRISTIAN HOME & SCHOOL, 3350 East Paris Ave. SE, Box 8709, Grand Rapids MI 49512. (616)957-1070x234. Fax (616)957-5022. E-mail: chsschlnt@aol.com. Christian Schools Intl. Dr. Gordon L. Bordewyk, ed; submit to Roger Schmurr, sr. ed. Focuses on parenting and Christian education; for parents who send their children to Christian schools. Bimonthly mag; 32 pgs; circ 58,000. Subscription $11.95. 30% freelance. Query or complete ms/cover letter. Pays $75-150 on publication for 1st rts. Articles 500-2,000 wds (40/yr); fiction 1,200-2,000 wds. Responds in 5 wks. Seasonal 4 mos ahead. Accepts simultaneous query. Guidelines/theme list; copy for 9x12 SAE/4 stamps.

Tips: Most open to features.

** 1995 EPA Award of Merit—Organizational.

CHRISTIAN INFORMATION ASSOCIATES NEWSLETTER (C.I.A.), PO Box 940335, Maitland FL 32794. (407)263-7776. J. Atwood, ed. For the Christian who wants specific information on Bible prophecy that is being fulfilled today; patriotic. Monthly newsletter; circ. 130. Free subscription (donation expected). Est. 1993. 50% freelance. Complete ms/cover letter. **PAYS IN SUBSCRIPTION**, for one-time rts. Not copyrighted. Accepts simultaneous submissions and reprints. Articles to 1,000 wds. Responds in 3 wks. Seasonal 1 mo ahead. Considers simultaneous submissions and reprints. Prefers disk. Sidebars OK. Copy for #10 SAE/2 stamps.

Fillers: Accepts 40-60/yr. Anecdotes, cartoons, facts, ideas, newsbreaks, prayers, Bible quotes; 60-100 wds.

#THE CHRISTIAN LEADER, PO Box V, Hillsboro KS 67063. (316)947-5543. Fax (316)947-3266. Mennonite Brethren. Don Ratzlaff, ed. Denominational. Monthly mag; circ. 9,800. Subscription $16. Query. Open to freelance. Not included in topical listings.

CHRISTIAN LIVING, 616 Walnut Ave. Scottdale PA 15683-1999. (412)887-8500. Fax (412)887-3111. E-mail: SKRISS%MPH@mcimail.com. Mennonite. Steve Kriss, ed. Denominational with focus on contemporary stories of faith in action in a variety of contexts. Monthly (8X) mag; 36 pgs; circ 5,000. Subscription $21.95.

20% freelance. Complete ms/cover letter; e-mail query OK. Pays .03-.05/wd on acceptance for 1st, one-time, reprint or simultaneous rts. Articles 500-1,800 wds (16/yr); fiction 500-1,500 wds (1-2/yr). Responds in 6 wks. Seasonal 8 mos ahead. Accepts simultaneous submissions & reprints (tell when/where appeared). Accepts disk. Sidebars OK. Prefers NRSV. Guidelines; copy for 9x12 SAE/3 stamps. (Ads)

Poetry: Buys 25/yr. Avant-garde, free verse, haiku, light verse; 3-35 lines; pays $1/line. Submit max. 5 poems.

Fillers: Buys 2-3/yr. Newsbreaks, prayers; 50-30 wds; $5-20.

Ethnic: Targets all ethnic groups involved in the Mennonite religion.

Tips: "We are always looking for good articles on prayer and multicultural issues. A good understanding of issues related to our emphasis and community, family and peace and justice will help the writer."

** This periodical was #51 on the 1995 Top 50 Christian Publishers list. (#56 in 1994)

CHRISTIAN MEDIA, Box 448, Jacksonville OR 97530. (541)899-8888. James Lloyd, ed/pub. For emerging Christian songwriters, artists, and other professionals involved in music, video, film, print, and broadcasting. Bimonthly tabloid; 16 pgs; circ 2,000-6,000. Query; prefers phone query. **NO PAYMENT** for negotiable rts. Articles; book & music reviews, 3 paragraphs. Accepts simultaneous submissions & reprints. Prefers disk. KJV only. Copy for 9x12 SAE/2 stamps.

Special Needs: Particularly interested in stories that expose dirty practices in the industry—royalty rip-offs, misleading ads, financial misconduct, etc. No flowery pieces on celebrities; we want well-documented articles on abuse in the media.

#THE CHRISTIAN OBSERVER, 9400 Fairview Ave., Ste. 200, Manassas VA 22110. (703)335-2844. Fax (703)368-4817. E-mail: Christiano@aol.com. Christian Observer Foundation; Presbyterian Reformed. Edwin P. Elliott, ed. To encourage and edify God's people and families. Newspaper published 2X/month; circ 2,000. Subscription $27. Query. Not in topical listings. (Ads)

CHRISTIAN PARENTING TODAY, 4050 Lee Vance View, Colorado Springs CO 80918-7100. (719)531-7776. Fax (719)535-0172. E-mail: CPTmag@aol.com. Cook Communications. Erin Healy, ed. Practical advice for parents (of kids birth-12), from a Christian perspective, that runs the whole gamut of needs: social, educational, spiritual, medical, etc. Bimonthly mag; 68-96 pgs; circ 200,000. Subscription $18.95. 95% freelance. Query or complete ms/cover letter; fax/e-mail query OK. Articles 800-2,000 wds (100/yr); product reviews (games, toys, etc), 150 wds, $25-35. Pays .20-.25/wd on acceptance for assigned (on publication for unsolicited) for 1st and reprint rts. Responds in 6-8 wks. Seasonal 1 yr ahead. Accepts simultaneous submissions & reprints (tell when/where appeared). Kill fee 25%. Accepts disk. Sidebars OK. Prefers NIV. Guidelines/guidelines addendum; copy for 9x12 SAE/$3 postage. (Ads—Debbie Mitchell, ext. 3324)

Columns/Departments: Buys 70-80/yr. Train Them Up, 300-400 wds, $50-75; Your Child Today, 300-400 wds, $50-75; Healthy & Safe, 300-400 wds, $50-75; Family Room, 600-700 wds, $125; The Lighter Side, 600-700 wds, $125; The Homefront Store, $25-35; Parent Exchange (parenting tips), 25-

100 wds, $40; Life in Our House (humorous anecdotes), 25-100 wds, $25. Complete ms.

Tips: "Write first for Your Child Today, Train Them Up or Healthy & Safe (departments). We often introduce new writers here and then draw upon those who have demonstrated skill and expertise to write features."

** This periodical was #20 on the 1996 Top 50 Christian Publishers list (#2 in 1995, #27 in 1994). 1996 EPA Award for Most Improved Publication.

+THE CHRISTIAN RANCHMAN, 7022-A Lake County Dr., Fort Worth TX 76179. (817)236-0023. Fax (817)236-0024. Interdenominational. Monthly tabloid; 12 pgs; circ 28,000. No subscription. Open to freelance. Complete ms/cover letter. **NO PAYMENT** for all rts. Articles; book/video reviews (length open). No sidebars.

Poetry: Accepts 40/yr. Free verse. Submit max. 3 poems.

Fillers: Accepts all types.

#CHRISTIAN READER, 465 Gundersen Dr., Carol Stream IL 60188. (630)260-6200. Fax (630)260-0114. E-mail: creditoria@aol.com. Christianity Today, Inc. Bonne Steffen, ed. A Christian "Readers Digest" that uses both reprints and original material. Bimonthly mag; 112 pgs; circ 225,000. Subscription $17.50. 60% freelance. Complete ms/cover letter; phone/fax/e-mail query OK. Pays $100-250 (.10/wd) on acceptance for 1st rts. Articles 500-1,500 wds (50/yr). Responds in 3 wks. Seasonal 9 mos ahead. Accepts reprints ($50-100, tell when/where appeared). Kill fee. No sidebars. Guidelines/theme list; copy for 6x9 SAE/4 stamps. (Ads)

Poetry: Buys 2/yr. Free verse, light verse, traditional; 5-35 lines; $10-50. Submit max. 3 poems.

Fillers: Buys 25-35/yr. Anecdotes, facts, short humor (see Lite Fare); 25-400 wds; pays $15-25.

Columns/Departments: Cynthia Thomas. Buys 150/yr. Lite Fare (adult church humor); Kids of the Kingdom (kids say and do funny things); Rolling Down the Aisle (true humor from weddings/rehearsals); all to 250 wds; $25-35.

Tips: "Keep articles short; we edit everything. First-person non-fiction stories are a top priority editorially for final selection."

Contest: Annual contest, March 1 deadline. Prizes $1,000, $500, $250. Send SASE for contest fact sheet.

** This periodical was #7 on the 1996 Top 50 Christian Publishers list. (#63 in 1995)

CHRISTIAN RENEWAL, Box 770, Lewiston NY 14092-0770. (905)562-5719. Fax (905)562-7828. E-mail: JVANDYK@aol.com. Reformed (Conservative). John Van Dyk, mng. ed. Church-related and world news for members of the Reformed community of churches in North America. Biweekly newspaper; 20 pgs; circ 4,300. Subscription $29. 5% freelance. Query/clips; e-mail query OK. Pays $25-100 for one-time rts. Articles 500-3,000 wds; fiction 2,000 wds (6/yr); book reviews 50-200 wds. Responds in 9 wks. Seasonal 3 mos ahead. Accepts simultaneous submissions & reprints. Prefers disk. Copy $1. (Ads)

#CHRISTIAN RESEARCH JOURNAL, Box 500, San Juan Capistrano CA 92693-0500. (714)855-4428. Fax (714)855-9927. E-mail: CRITALK@aol.com. Christian Research Institute. Elliot Miller, ed-in-chief. For those who have been affected by cults and the occult. Quarterly mag; 56 pgs; circ 40,000. Subscription $20. 80% freelance. Complete ms. Pays .15/wd on publication for 1st rts. Articles to 5,000 wds (1/yr); book reviews 1,000-2,500 wds. Responds in 16-20 wks. Kill fee up to 50%. Requires disk. Rarely uses sidebars. Guidelines; copy $6.

Columns/Departments: Witnessing Tips (evangelism), 1,000 wds; Viewpoint (opinion on cults, ethics, etc.), 875 wds.

Tips: "Be patient; we sometimes review mss only twice a year, but we will get back to you. Most open to features (on cults), book reviews, opinion pieces and witnessing tips."

** 1996 EPA Award of Merit—Organizational.

CHRISTIAN RETAILING, 600 Rinehart Rd., Lake Mary FL 32746. (407)333-0600. Fax (407)333-7133. E-mail: retailing@strang.com or stertzer@strang.com. Strang Communications Co. Carol Chapman Stertzer, mng ed. Business/trade publication directed toward Christian retail/bookstore owners, managers and clerks. Tabloid published 22X/yr; 56 pgs; circ 9,000. Subscription $45. 60% freelance. Query/clips; no phone/fax/e-mail query. Pays .10-.12/wd (to $325) on publication for all rts. Articles 1,500-2,000 wds (36/yr); book/music/video reviews, 250 wds, $15; industry news, to 800 wds. Responds in 8 wks. Seasonal 6 mos ahead. Accepts some reprints. Prefers disk. Kill fee $50. Accepts reprints. Sidebars OK. Free guidelines/copy. (Ads)

Special Needs: Music & video reviews, gift features and business.

Tips: "Most open to features. Pitch good idea that will benefit Christian retailers."

CHRISTIAN SINGLE, 127 9th Ave. N, Nashville TN 37234-0140. (615)251-5721. Fax (615)251-5008. Southern Baptist. Submit to The Editor. To encourage singles, primarily in their 20s and 30s, to integrate the biblical principles of their faith into their everyday lifestyle. Monthly mag; 52 pgs; circ 67,000. Subscription $19.95. 10% freelance. Query/clips; fax query OK. Query for electronic submissions. Pays $25 & up (negotiable) on acceptance for all, 1st, one-time, reprint, and electronic rts. Articles 600-2,500 wds (50/yr) & fiction 1,200-1,500 wds (10/yr); book/music reviews 300 wds, $25 (music), $50 (book). Responds in 8 wks. Seasonal 6 mos ahead. Accepts reprints (tell when/where appeared). Prefers disk. Likes sidebars. Prefers NIV. Guidelines; copy for 9x12 SAE/4 stamps.

Poetry: Buys 6/yr. Free verse, light verse, traditional; 5-25 lines; pay negotiable. Submit max. 3 poems.

Fillers: Buys 12/yr. Facts, newsbreaks, quotes, 200-500 wds. Pay negotiable.

Columns/Departments: Single Parenting (self-help), 1,200 wds; Body Shop (physical, mental, emotional, spiritual fitness), 1,200 wds; Closing Moment (devotional), 150 wds; Micro Info (filler bits), 800 wds; Profiles (singles putting faith to work), 2,000 wds. Query.

Tips: "Most open to Single Parenting & Body Shop Departments, or to general features. Send outline and opening paragraph with query."

** This periodical was #30 on the 1996 Top 50 Christian Publishers list. (#47 in 1995 & 1994)

CHRISTIAN SOCIAL ACTION, 100 Maryland Ave. NE, Washington DC 20002. (202)488-5621. Fax (202)488-1617. E-mail: LRANCK@igc.org. United Methodist. Lee Ranck, ed. Information and analysis of critical social issues from the perspective of Christian faith. Monthly (11X) mag; 48 pgs; circ 2,000. Subscription $15. 20% freelance. Query/clips or complete ms/cover letter. Pays $75-150 on publication for all rts (negotiable). Articles 2,000 wds (12/yr); book reviews 500 wds, $25. Responds in 4 wks. Consider simultaneous submissions & reprints (tell when/where appeared). Prefers disk. Sidebars OK. Prefers RSV. Guidelines; copy for 9x12 SAE/2 stamps. (Ads)

> **Columns/Departments:** Buys 10/yr. Talking (reader's write), 1,000 wds; Media Watch (reviews), 500 wds. Pays $25-50.
>
> **Special Needs:** Urban issues, children's issues, and environment.
>
> **Tips:** "Most open to regular articles on issues."

#CHRISTIAN STANDARD, 8121 Hamilton Ave., Cincinnati OH 45231. (513)931-4050. Fax (513)931-0904. Standard Publishing/Christian Churches/Churches of Christ. Sam E. Stone, ed. Devoted to the restoration of New Testament Christianity, its doctrines, its ordinances, and its fruits. Weekly mag; 24 pgs; circ 59,000. Subscription $19. 50% freelance. Complete ms/cover letter. Pays $10-80 on publication for 1st or one-time rts. Articles 400-1,600 wds (200/yr). Responds in 9 wks. Seasonal 8-12 mos ahead. Accepts reprints. Guidelines; copy for 9x12 SAE/3 stamps or $1.

CHRISTIANITY AND THE ARTS, P0 Box 118088, Chicago IL 60611. (312)642-8606. Fax (312)266-7719. E-mail: chrnarts@aol.com. Nondenominational. Marci Whitney-Schenck, ed/pub. Fiction editor: Terrence Brown, PO Box 381528, Germantown TN 38183. Celebrates the revelation of God through the arts and encourages Christian artistic expression. Quarterly mag; 56 pgs; circ 5,000. Subscription $21. Est. 1994. 40% freelance. Query or complete ms/cover letter; phone/fax/e-mail query OK. **NO PAYMENT** for one-time rts. Articles to 3,000 wds (20/yr); fiction to 4,000 wds (uses little). Responds in 4 wks. Seasonal 6 mos ahead. Accepts simultaneous submissions. Accepts disk. Sidebars OK. Theme list; copy $6.

> **Poetry:** Robert Engler, c/o Richard J. Daley College, 7500 S. Pulaski, Chicago IL 60652. Buys 12/yr. Avant-garde, free verse, haiku, traditional.
>
> **Special Needs:** Visual arts, dance, music, literature, drama.
>
> **Tips:** "Interested in features and interviews that focus on ethnic celebration of Christian arts, social problems and the arts, and Jewish-Christian links. I need three contributors to write on drama, dance, and film (four articles a year—no payment). Be knowledgeable, but readable to mass market."

#CHRISTIANITY TODAY, 465 Gundersen Dr., Carol Stream IL 60188-2498. (630)260-6200. Fax (630)260-0114. E-mail: CTedit@aol.com. Michael G. Maudlin, mng. ed. For evangelical Christian thought leaders who seek to integrate their faith commitment with responsible action. Magazine published 14X/yr; 90 pgs; circ 180,000. Subscription $24.95. 80% (little unassigned) freelance. Query/clips. Pays $200-500 (.10/wd) on acceptance for 1st rts. Articles 1,500-3,000 wds (60/yr); book reviews 500-750 wds, pays $75. Responds in 13 wks. Seasonal 8 mos ahead. Accepts reprints (payment 25% of regular rate). Kill fee. Guidelines; copy for 9x12 SAE/3 stamps.

> **Columns/Departments:** Buys 7/yr. Church in Action (profile of unusual person/ministry), 900-1,000 wds (query); Speaking Out (op/ed), 800 wds (complete ms); $75-150.

Tips: "Most of our freelance material is assigned."
** 1996 EPA Award of Merit—General.

*CHRISTMAS, An Annual Treasury, Box 1209, Minneapolis MN 55440. (612)330-3442. Augsburg Fortress. Bob Klausmeier, ed. Birth of Christ central to celebration of Christmas. Annual book; 64 pgs; circ 40,000. 75% freelance. Complete ms/cover letter. Pays $150-300 on acceptance for one-time rts. Articles 1,500-2,500 wds (2-3/yr); fiction 1,500-2,000 wds (3-4/yr). Responds in 12 wks. Works 14-18 mos ahead. Accepts reprints. Guidelines/themes; copy $12.95 + postage (call 800-328-4648).

> **Poetry:** Buys 3-4/yr. Free verse, light verse, traditional; to 30 lines; $75-125. Submit max. 3 poems. Nothing on Santa Claus.
>
> **Tips:** "Short stories related to Christmas only. Nonfiction related to yearly theme, check first."

+CHRYSALIS READER, Rte. 1 Box 184, Dillwyn VA 23936. (804)983-3021. Fax (804)983-1074. E-mail: lawson@aba.org. Swedenborg Foundation. Carol S. Lawson, ed.; Phoebe Loughrey, fiction ed. Focuses on spiritual life and literature. A semiannual collection of stories, articles and poetry in book form; 130-190 pgs; circ. 3,000. 60% freelance. Query. Pays $50-100 on publication for one-time rts. Articles (30/yr) and short stories (10/yr) 2,000-3,500 wds. Responds in 4-8 wks. Seasonal 8-9 mos ahead. Sidebars OK. Requires disk. Guidelines/theme list; copy $10/9x12 SAE/5 stamps.

> **Poetry:** Rob Lawson. Buys 15/yr. Avant-garde, Haiku; $25-35. Submit max. 3 poems.

#CHURCH & STATE, 1816 Jefferson Pl. NW, Washington DC 20036. (202)466-3234. Fax (202)466-2587. Americans United for Separation of Church and State. Joseph L. Conn, mng. ed. Emphasizes religious liberty and church/state relations matters. Monthly mag; 24-32 pgs; circ 33,000. 10% freelance. Query. Pays negotiable fee on acceptance for all rts. Articles 600-2,600 wds (11/yr), prefers 800-1,600. Responds in 9 wks. Accepts simultaneous query & reprints. Guidelines; copy for 9x12 SAE/3 stamps.

> **Tips:** "We are not a religious magazine. You need to see our magazine before you try to write for it."

#THE CHURCH ADVOCATE, Box 926, 700 E. Melrose Ave., Findlay OH 45839. (419)424-1961. Fax (419)424-3433. E-mail: CGGCWB@aol.com. Churches of God General Conference. Linda M. Draper, ed. Denominational. Quarterly mag; circ 13,000. Subscription $10. Little freelance. Query. Pays $10/printed pg. on publication for one-time rts. Articles 750 wds & up (6/yr). Seasonal 3 mos ahead. Accepts simultaneous submissions & reprints. Sidebars OK. Guidelines; copy for 9x12 SAE.

> **Tips:** Most open to personal experience.

CHURCH HERALD AND HOLINESS BANNER, 7415 Metcalf, Box 4060, Overland Park KS 66204. (913)432-0331. Fax (913)722-0351. Website: http://www.sunflower.org/kccbslib. Church of God (Holiness)/Herald and Banner Press. Ray Crooks, ed. Denominational; conservative/evangelical people. Biweekly mag; 20 pgs; circ 2,500. Subscription $12.50. 50% freelance. Complete ms/cover letter; phone/fax query OK. **NO PAYMENT,** for one-time rts. Not copyrighted. Articles 200-800 wds (25+/yr); fiction 500-1,000 wds. Responds in 9 wks. Seasonal 6 mos ahead. Accepts simultaneous submissions & reprints. Guidelines.

Poetry: Buys few. Traditional; 8-24 lines.

Fillers: Anecdotes, facts, prose, quotes; 150-400 wds.

Tips: "Most open to devotional articles. Must be concise, well-written, and get one main point across; 200-400 wds."

CHURCH OF GOD EVANGEL, PO Box 2350, Cleveland TN 37320-2250. (423)476-4512. Fax (423)478-7521. Church of God (Cleveland, TN). Homer G. Rhea, ed-in-chief. Denominational. Monthly journal; 36 pgs; circ 50,000. Subscription $12. 25% freelance. Query or complete ms/cover letter. Pays $10-40 on acceptance for 1st rts. Articles 500-1,500 wds (60/yr). Responds in 2 wks. Seasonal 6 mos ahead. Accepts few reprints (tell when/where appeared). Prefers disk. Some sidebars. Guidelines (2 stamps); copy for 9x12 SAE/4 stamps.

Fillers: Anecdotes & ideas.

Tips: "Need human interest articles. Always willing to buy thoughtful, well-written pieces that speak to people where they live. Always need humor with a point."

#COLUMBIA, PO Box 1670, New Haven CT 06510. (203)772-2130. Fax (203)777-0114. Knights of Columbus (Catholic). Richard McMunn, ed. Geared to a general Catholic family audience. Monthly mag; 92 pgs; circ 1.5 million. Subscription $6; foreign add $2. 50-60% freelance. Query. Pays to $250-500 on acceptance for 1st rts. Articles 1,000-1,500 wds (30/yr). Responds in 2-3 wks. Seasonal 4 mos ahead. Kill fee $125. Free guidelines/copy.

Tips: "Keep eye out for K of C activity in local area and send a query letter about it. Articles must be accompanied by photos or transparencies."

** This periodical was #25 on the 1996 Top 50 Christian Publishers list. (#32 in 1995, #19 in 1994)

+COMMAND, 3784 S. Inca, Englewood CO 80110. (303)761-1984. Fax (303)761-6226. E-mail: 75512.3123@compuserve.com. Officers Christian Fellowship. Don Martin, Jr., ed. To uplift Christ and evangelize the military forces. Monthly mag; circ 8,000. Subscription $15. Open to freelance. Query.

*COMMENTS FROM THE FRIENDS, Box 819, Assonet MA 02702. David A. Reed, ed. For ex-Jehovah's Witnesses, their relatives, Christians reaching out to them, and dissident Witnesses. Quarterly newsletter; 16 pgs; circ 1,200. Subscription $11. 5% freelance. Complete ms/cover letter. Pays $20 (sometimes copies or subscription) on publication for all rts. Articles 100-1,000 wds (4/yr); book reviews 50-1,000 wds. Responds in 4-8 wks. Seasonal 3 mos ahead. Accepts simultaneous submissions & reprints. Macintosh disks only. No sidebars. Any version. Guidelines; copy $1/8x10 SAE/2 stamps.

Columns/Departments: Witnessing Tips, 500-1,000 wds.

Tips: "Acquaint us with why you are qualified to write about J.W.'s. Write well-documented, concise articles relevant to J.W.'s today. We automatically reject all material not specifically about Jehovah's Witnesses."

COMMON BOUNDARY, 5272 River Rd., Ste. 650 Bethesda MD 20816-1405. (301)652-9495. E-mail: SIMPKINS@tmn.com. Ecumenical. Mark Judge, ed. asst. Explores relationship between psychotherapy and spirituality. Bimonthly mag; 64 pgs; circ 26,000. 50% freelance. Query. Pays varying rates on publication for 1st rts. Articles 3,000-4,000 wds. Responds in 13-26 wks. Accepts simultaneous submissions. Kill fee 1/3. Guidelines; copy $5.

Fillers: Newsbreaks, 200-600 wds.

Contest: Annual $1,000 Dissertation/Thesis award for best psycho-spiritual topic.

#COMMONWEAL, 15 Dutch St., New York NY 10038. (212)732-0800. Catholic. Patrick Jordan, mng ed. A review of public affairs, religion, literature and the arts. Biweekly mag; 32 pgs; circ 19,000. Subscription $39. 30% freelance. Query; phone query OK. Pays $75-100 (.03/wd) on acceptance for all rts. Articles 1,200-3,000 wds (20/yr). Responds 9 wks. Seasonal 2 mos ahead. Kill fee 2%. Occasional sidebars. Guidelines; free copy.

Poetry: Rosemary Deen. Buys 25-30/yr. Free verse, traditional; to 75 lines; .75/line. Submit max. 5 poems. Submit October-May.

Columns/Departments: Upfronts (brief, newsy facts and info behind the headlines), 750-1,000 wds; The Last Word (commentary based on insight from personal experience or reflection), 700 wds.

Tips: "Most open to meaningful articles on social, political, religious and cultural topics; or columns."

*COMPANION MAGAZINE, Box 535, Station F., Toronto ON M4Y 2L8 Canada. (800)461-1619. Fax (416)690-3320. E-mail: FranCentre@aol.com. Website: http://www.cmpa.ca. Catholic/Franciscan. Fr. R. Riccioli, ed; submit to Betty McCrimmon, man. ed. An adult, Catholic, inspirational, devotional family magazine. Monthly (11X) mag; 32 pgs; circ 5,000. 50% freelance. Complete ms, with cover letter. Phone/fax/e-mail query OK. Pays .06/wd CAN, on publication for 1st rts. Articles 500-1,000 wds (35/yr); fiction 500-1,000 wds (7/yr). Responds in 6 wks. Seasonal 5 mos ahead. Accepts disk (Mac). Guidelines; copy for 7x10 SAE with IRCs. (Ads)

Poetry: Free verse, light verse, traditional. Pays .60/line CAN.

Fillers: Anecdotes, cartoons, prayers, quotes, short humor, word puzzles.

Special Needs: Articles on St. Francis, Franciscan spirituality, and social justice.

Tips: Most open to human interest.

COMPANIONS, Rt. 4 Box 3926, Seymour MO 65746. (417)935-4639. Mennonite/Christian Light Publications. Roger L. Berry, ed. Consistent with conservative Mennonite doctrine: believer baptism, nonresistance, and nonconformity. Weekly take-home paper; 4 pgs; circ 7,000. Subscription $9.70. 80% freelance. Complete ms; no phone query. Pays .02-.05/wd on acceptance for all, 1st, one-time or reprint rts. Articles 100-800 wds (140/yr). Responds in 4 wks. Seasonal 5 mos ahead. Accepts simultaneous submissions & reprints (tell when/where appeared). No disk. No sidebars. KJV only. Guidelines; copy for 9x12 SAE/2 stamps.

Poetry: Buys 40/yr. Traditional, 4-32 lines; .30-.70/line. Submit max. 4 poems.

Fillers: Buys 15/yr. Anecdotes, facts, prose, quizzes; 50-150 wds.

Columns/Departments: Buys 24/yr. Science and Scripture (creationist/Biblicist), 400-600; Archaeology (archaeology that supports biblical truths); 400-600 wds; Truth for Youth, 200-800 wds.

Tips: "Looking for Anabaptist history/theology/ethics. Don't submit to us without studying the do's & don'ts in our guidelines. 70-75% of our material

comes from our readers, who understand our teachings and unique lifestyle."
** This periodical was #45 on the 1996 Top 50 Christian Publishers list. (#14 in 1995, #28 in 1994)

COMPASS: A Jesuit Journal, Box 400, Sta. F, 50 St. Charles St. E., Toronto ON M4Y 2L8 Canada. (416)921-0653. Fax (416)921-1864. E-mail: 74263.247@compuserve.com. Website: http://www.io.org/gvanv/. Catholic. Robert Chodos, ed. Ethical and ecumenical discussion of social and religious topics; for educated, but non-specialized readership. Bimonthly mag; 52 pgs; circ 3,700. Subscription $19. 10% freelance. Query/clips. Pays $100-500 CAN, on publication for 1st rts. Articles 1,500-2,500 wds (60/yr); fiction 1,000-2,500 wds/pays $100-250); book reviews 2,000 wds/$300. Responds in 8 wks. No seasonal. Accepts simultaneous submissions. Prefers disk. Kill fee 50%. Guidelines/theme list; copy $2/9x12 SAE/$1.35 postage CAN.

Fillers: Accepts 60/yr. Short, pithy quotes from other writers; 10-150 wds. Pays 1-yr subscription.

Columns/Departments: Buys 24/yr. Testament (contemporary application of scripture); Colloquy (theology & daily life); Saint (fresh perspective on a Saint); all 750 wds; $100-150. Query.

Special Needs: Every January/February issue examines the state of peace on earth.

Tips: "We are interested primarily in analytical and reflective articles. Write for themes."

*CONNECTING POINT, Box 685, Cocoa FL 32923. (407)632-0130. Linda G. Howard, ed. For and by the mentally challenged (retarded) community; primarily deals with spiritual and self-advocacy issues. Monthly mag; circ 1,000. 75% freelance. Complete ms. **NO PAYMENT** for 1st rts. Articles (24/yr) & fiction (12/yr), 250-750 wds; book reviews 150 wds. Responds in 3-6 wks. Seasonal 3 mos ahead. Accepts simultaneous submissions & reprints. Guidelines; copy for 9x12 SAE/6 stamps.

Poetry: Accepts 4/yr. Any type; 4-66 lines. Submit max. 10 poems.

Fillers: Accepts 12/yr. Cartoons, games, word puzzles; 50-250 wds.

Columns/Departments: Accepts 24/yr. Devotion Page, 1,000 wds; Bible Study, 500 wds. Query.

Special Needs: Record reviews, self-advocacy, integration/normalization, justice system.

Tips: "All ms need to be in primary vocabulary."

CONQUEST, 1300 N Meacham Rd., Schaumburg IL 60173-4888. (847)843-1600. Fax (847)843-3757. Regular Baptist. Joan E. Alexander, ed. For adults associated with fundamental Baptist Churches. Weekly take-home paper; 4 pgs; circ 55,000. 60% freelance. Complete ms/cover letter (first time); no phone/fax query. Pays .03-.07/wd on acceptance for all, 1st or reprint rts. Articles 400-1,000 wds (50/yr); fiction 500-1,200 wds (50/yr). Responds in 4-8 wks. Seasonal 1 yr ahead. Accepts disk. Sidebars OK. Prefers KJV. Guidelines; copy for #10 SAE/2 stamps or full quarter for $1.45.

Fillers: Buys 20-30/yr. Anecdotes, ideas, prose, word puzzles; must teach bible content in an enjoyable way; 100-400 wds; $10.

Tips: "Not everything that is Christian is suitable for readers in fundamental

Baptist churches. Address the spiritual dimension that is integral to the interests, concerns and daily living of the adult years without sentimentality, moralizing or preachiness."

+CONTACT, PO Box 5002, Antioch TN 37011-5002. (615)731-6812. Fax (615)731-0771. National Assn. of Free Will Baptists. Jack Williams, ed. Denominational. Monthly mag; circ 5,200. Subscription $12. Open to freelance. Complete ms. Not in topical listings. (Ads)

#CORNERSTONE, 939 W. Wilson, Chicago IL 60640-5718. (312)561-2450x2080. Fax (312)989-2076. Cornerstone Communications, Inc. Misty Files, sub. ed. For young adults, 18-35; covers contemporary issues in light of evangelical Christianity. Quarterly mag; 64 pgs; circ 30,000. Subscription $15. 10% freelance. Complete ms/cover letter; fax query OK. Pays .08-.10/wd after publication for 1st rts. Articles 250-4,000 wds (20/yr); fiction 250-2,500 wds (1-4/yr); book/music/film reviews 500-1,000 wds. Responds in 8-12 wks to accepted mss only (discards others, don't send SASE). Seasonal 6 mos ahead. Encourages simultaneous submissions; accepts reprints. Prefers disk. Sidebars OK. Guidelines; copy for 9x12 SAE/5 stamps.

> **Poetry:** Tammy Boyd. Buys 20-30/yr. Any type; $10-25. Submit max. 5 poems.

> **Fillers:** Buys 1-4/yr. Facts, quotes; 500-1,000 wds.

> **Columns/Departments:** Buys 3-4/yr. News items, 500-1,000 wds; Music Interviews (Christian & secular artists) to 2,700 wds; Music & Book Reviews (Christian & secular).

> **Tips:** "Most open to high-quality fiction, poetry, and book or music reviews."

THE COVENANT COMPANION, 5101 N. Francisco Ave., Chicago IL 60625. (773)784-3000x328. Fax (312)784-4366. E-mail: 73430.3316@compuserve.com. Website: http://www.npcts.edu/cov/. Evangelical Covenant Church. Jane Swanson-Nystrom, mng ed. Denominational. Monthly mag; 40 pgs; circ 22,000. Subscription $26. 10% freelance. Complete ms/cover letter; fax/e-mail query OK. Pays $25-50 on publication for one-time or simultaneous rts. Articles 750-1,200 wds (15/yr), fiction 750-1,200 (3/yr). Responds in 4 wks. Seasonal 3-4 mos ahead. Accepts simultaneous submissions & reprints (tell when/where appeared). Some kill fees. Sidebars OK. Prefers NRSV. Guidelines/theme list; copy for 9x12 SAE/4 stamps; or $2.25 (w/o SASE). (Ads)

> **Poetry:** Buys 5/yr. Avant-garde, free verse, traditional; $15-35. Submit max. 5 poems.

> **Fillers:** Cartoons, short humor, word puzzles.

> **Tips:** "Send articles well organized and with depth—our readers tend to have a long history of spiritual life."

+CREATION ILLUSTRATED, PO Box 7955, Auburn CA 95604. (800)360-2732. 68 pgs. New. Not included in topical listings.

*THE CRESSET, A Review of Arts, Literature & Public Affairs, Huegli Hall #29, Valpariaso IN 46383. (219)464-5274. Fax (219)464-5496. E-mail: geifrig@exodus. valpo.edu. Valpariaso University/Lutheran. Gail McGrew Eifrig, ed. For college educated, professors, pastors, lay people; serious review essays on religious-cultural affairs. Bimonthly (7X) mag; 36 pgs; circ 4,700. Subscription $8.50.

50% freelance. Complete ms/cover letter. Pays $25 on publication for 1st rts. Articles 2,500-5,000 wds (20-30/yr). Responds in 12 wks. Seasonal 3 mos ahead. Prefers disk. No sidebars. Copy for 9x12 SAE/5 stamps.

> **Poetry:** John Ruff. Buys 15-20/yr. Avant-garde, free verse, traditional; to 40 lines; $10. Submit max. 5 poems.

*CROSSWAY/NEWSLINE, 103 Ambleside Rd., Lightwater, Surrey GU185UJ England. Tel. 02764 72724. Airline Aviation & Aerospace Christian Fellowship. J. Brown, gen. sec. For non-Christians working in aviation. Crossway is an annual magazine; Newsline a quarterly newsletter; 16 pgs. Free subscription. 100% freelance. Complete ms/cover letter. **NO PAYMENT.** Sometimes copyrighted. Articles on aviation to 2,000 wds. Accepts simultaneous submissions & reprints. Guidelines.

THE DALLAS/FORT WORTH HERITAGE, PO Box 1424, Ennis TX 75120. (972)846-2900. Fax (972)445-5029. E-mail: DFWHERITAGE@FNI.com. John J. Dwyer, ed. To help preserve and sustain America's Christian heritage and pass it on to the nation's children. Monthly newspaper; 40-44 pgs; circ 50,000. Subscription $25. Open to freelance. Query.

DECISION, PO Box 779, Minneapolis MN 55440-0779. (612)338-0500. Fax (612)335-1299. E-mail: 103115.2747@compuserve.com. Billy Graham Evangelistic Assn. Roger C. Palms, ed. Evangelism/Christian nurture. Monthly mag; 44 pgs; circ 1,700,000. Subscription $9. 25% freelance. Complete ms/cover letter; no phone/fax/e-mail query. Pays $55-200 on publication for all or 1st rts. Articles 1,000-1,500 wds (40/yr). Responds 10-12 wks. Seasonal 10-12 mos ahead. Kill fee. Accepts disk. Some sidebars. Guidelines/theme list; copy for 10x13 SAE/3 stamps.

> **Poetry:** Buys 6/yr. Free verse, light verse, traditional; 4-16 lines; .50/wd. Submit max. 7 poems.
>
> **Fillers:** Buys 50/yr. Anecdotes, prose; 300-600 wds; $10-75.
>
> **Columns/Departments:** Buys 24/yr. Where Are They Now? (people who have become Christian through Billy Graham ministries); 600-900 wds; $75. My Greatest Struggle (overcoming in areas like vices, illness, loss, etc.), 1,100-1,400 wds.
>
> **Tips:** "Looking for articles for new series, My Greatest Struggle; for people to be vulnerable and honest in writing about how they have gained a measure of victory over sin, tragedy or crisis. We want personal experience stories/salvation testimonies in first person. Testimonies should include anecdotes from before and after your conversion, in addition to description of conversion itself. Let the reader learn through your experiences."
>
> **** #59 on the 1994 Top 50.**

DISCIPLESHIP JOURNAL, Box 35004, Colorado Springs CO 80935. (719)531-3529. Fax (719)598-7128. E-mail: smaycini@navigato.mhs.compuserve.com. The Navigators. Jon Graf, sr ed. For motivated, maturing Christians desiring to grow spiritually and to help others grow; biblical and practical. Bimonthly mag; 96+ pgs; circ 100,000. Subscription $21.97. 95% freelance. Query; fax query OK. Query for electronic submissions. Pays .20/wd on acceptance for 1st & electronic rts. Articles 1,500-2,500 wds (60/yr); fiction 1,500-2,500 wds (1-2/yr). Responds in 4-6 wks. Seasonal 4-6 mos ahead. Accepts simultaneous submissions. Prefers disk. Kill fee. Sidebars OK. Prefers NIV. Guidelines/theme list; copy for 9x12 SAE/9 stamps. (Ads)

Columns/Departments: Buys 15+/yr. On the Home Front (Q & A regarding family issues); 1,000 wds; Bible Study Methods (how-to), to 1,000 wds; DJ Plus (ministry how-to on missions, evangelism, serving, discipling, teaching & small groups), to 500 wds. Pays .20/wd.

Tips: "Most open to non-theme articles, DJ Plus and sidebars."

** This periodical was #2 on the 1996 Top 50 Christian Publishers list. (#15 in 1995, #8 in 1994). Also 1996 EPA Award of Merit—General.

+DISCIPLE'S JOURNAL, 200 Jefferson St., PO Box 100, Wilmington MA 01887. (508)657-7373. Fax (508)657-5411. Kenneth A. Dorothy, ed. To strengthen, edify, inform and unite the body of Christ. Monthly newspaper; circ 10,000. Subscription $9.95. 50% freelance. Query/clips. Pays $25-50. Articles to 400 wds; book/music/video reviews 200 wds. Responds in 2 wks. Seasonal 1 mo ahead. Accepts simultaneous submissions & reprints (tell when/where appeared). Prefers disk. Free guidelines/theme list/copy. (Ads)

Fillers: Buys 9/yr. Most types; to 400 wds. Pays $25-50.

Columns/Departments: Financial; Singles; Men; Women. 400 wds. Pays $25-50.

DISCOVERY, 400 W. Lake Brantley Rd., Altamonte Springs FL 32714-2715. (407)682-9494. Fax (407)682-7005. E-mail: JOYFUL953@aol.com. Radio Station WTLN FM/AM. Chris Shenk, features ed. For Christian community in Central Florida. Monthly newspaper; circ 25,000. Subscription free/$9 for home delivery. 20% freelance. Complete ms; phone/fax query OK. **NO PAYMENT**. Not copyrighted. News driven & informative articles under 500 wds. Seasonal 1+ mos ahead. Accepts reprints. Sidebars OK. No disk. Theme list. (Ads)

Columns/Departments: Christians in Business, Words for Women, Children's, Seniors, and (future) Singles.

Tips: "We may submit articles to our other publications in Knoxville and Philadelphia."

THE DOOR, 118 N. 30th St., Waco TX 76710. (817)752-1468. Fax (817)752-4915. E-mail: 103361.23@compuserve.com. Trinity Foundation. Bob Darden, ed. Satire of evangelical church plus issue-oriented interviews. Bimonthly mag; 44 pgs; circ 16,000. Subscription $24. 90% freelance. Complete ms. Pays $40-200 after publication for 1st rts. Not copyrighted. Articles 750-1,500 wds (25/yr). Responds in 6 wks. Accepts simultaneous submissions & reprints (if from non-competing markets). Kill fee $40-50. Sidebars OK. Guidelines; copy $4.50.

Tips: "We look for biting satire/humor—National Lampoon not Reader's Digest. You must understand our satirical slant. Read more than one issue to understand our 'wavelength.' We desperately need genuinely funny articles with a smart, satiric bent."

DOVETAIL: A Journal By and For Jewish/Christian Families, PO Box 19945, Kalamazoo MI 49019. (616)342-2900. Fax (616)342-1012. E-mail: dovetail@mich.com. Joan C. Hawxhurst, ed. Offers balanced, non-judgmental articles for interfaith families and the professionals who serve them. Bimonthly journal; 16-20 pgs; circ 1,000. Subscription $24.99. Complete ms/cover letter; fax/e-mail query OK. Pays $10-20 on publication for 1st or reprint rts. Articles 800-1,000 wds (10/yr); book reviews 400 wds, $10. Responds in 6-8 wks. Seasonal 6 mos ahead. Accepts simultaneous submissions & reprints (tell when/where appeared). Prefers disk. Some sidebars. Guidelines/theme list; copy for 9x12 SAE/3 stamps. (Ads)

Fillers: Buys 5/yr. Anecdotes, cartoons, ideas, short humor; 25-50 wds.

Tips: "Looking for articles profiling other interfaith families (other than Christian/Jewish); and humor. We only deal with interfaith issues. Best if you are in or close to an interfaith family."

DREAMS & VISIONS, 35 Peter St. S., Orillia ON L3V 5A8 Canada. Fax (705)329-1770. E-mail: skysong@bconnex.net. Skysong Press. Steve Stanton, ed. Quality fiction for Christian readers. Irregular journal; 56 pgs; circ 200. Subscription $12. 100% freelance. Complete ms/cover letter; fax/e-mail query OK. Pays .005/wd on publication for 1st rts & one non-exclusive reprint. Fiction 2,000-6,000 wds (10/yr). Responds in 4-6 wks. Seasonal 6 mos ahead. Accepts simultaneous submissions & reprints (tell when/where appeared). Accepts disk. Guidelines; copy $4.95 (4 back issues to writers $10).

DUSK & DAWN, PO Box 916, Berea OH 44017. E-mail: RiverGP@aol.com.Website: http://members.aol.com/RiverGP/Home.HtmL. River Gate Press. Michelle L. Levigne, ed/pub. Fiction in all genres for Christian teens and adults. Bimonthly mag; 44-48 pgs; circ 100 + Website. Subscription $26. Est. 1995. 100% freelance. Complete ms; e-mail query OK. Not copyrighted. Pays .005 -.01/wd on acceptance for one-time rts. Fiction 500-5,000 wds (20-30/yr). Responds in 6 wks. Seasonal 6-8 mos ahead. Accepts simultaneous submissions & reprints (tell when/where appeared). Guidelines; copy $5. (Ads)

Poetry: Buys 12-18/yr. Avant-garde, free verse, light verse, traditional; any length; $5-10. Submit max. 4 poems.

Fillers: Buys 5-10 cartoons/yr.

Tips: "Write stories that catch the imagination, and ask questions and offer answers. Have fun!"

#EMPHASIS ON FAITH AND LIVING, Box 9127, Fort Wayne IN 46899-9127. (219)747-2027. Fax (219)747-5331. E-mail: missionary.church@internetmci. com. Missionary Church. Robert Ransom, mng ed. Denominational; for adults 40 and older. Bimonthly mag; 16 pgs; circ 13,000. Subscription free. 10% freelance. Complete ms/cover letter. Pays .03-.04/wd on publication for 1st, one-time, reprint or simultaneous rts. Not copyrighted. Articles 200-800 wds (3/yr); fiction 200-1,600 wds (1-2/yr). Responds in 4-8 wks. Seasonal 4 mos ahead. Accepts simultaneous submissions & reprints. Guidelines; copy for 9x12 SAE/2 stamps.

Tips: "Our publication provides church news, missions information, and spiritual reading for members and friends of the Missionary Church denomination. We seek material that is compatible with our Wesleyan-Armenian church doctrine."

*ENCOURAGER PROVIDER, 4102 NW Dondee, Topeka KS 66618. (913)286-0388. Interdenominational. Charles White, sr ed. Serves home day-care providers for 2-5 year olds. Biweekly newsletter; 6 pgs; circ 1,600. Est. 1994. 5% freelance. Complete ms. Pays $5-30 on acceptance for one-time rts. Articles 50-300 wds (5/yr). Seasonal 1 yr ahead. Accepts simultaneous submissions & reprints. Sidebars OK.

Columns/Departments: Buys 5/yr. Pays $5.

*EPISCOPAL LIFE, 815 2nd Ave., New York NY 10017. (212)922-5398. Episcopal Church. Jerrold F. Hames, ed; Edward P. Stannard, mng. ed. Denominational. Monthly newspaper; 32 pgs; circ 180,000. 35% freelance. Query/clips or complete ms/cover letter; phone query on breaking news only. Pays $50-300 on publication for 1st, one-time or simultaneous rts. Articles 250-1,200 wds (12/yr); assigned book reviews 400 wds ($35). Responds in 5 wks. Seasonal 4 mos ahead. Accepts simultaneous submissions & reprints. Kill fee 50%. Free copy.

   Columns/Departments: Nan Cobbey. Buys 36/yr. Commentary on political/religious topics; 300-600 wds; $35-75. Query.

   Tips: "All articles must have Episcopal Church slant or specifics. We need topical/issues, not devotional stuff. Most open to feature stories about Episcopalians—clergy, lay, churches, involvement in local efforts, movements, ministries."

EVANGEL, Box 535002, Indianapolis IN 46253-5002. (317)244-3660. Free Methodist/Light and Life Communications. Julie Innes, ed. For young to middle-aged adults; encourages spiritual growth. Weekly take-home paper; 8 pgs; circ 22,000. Subscription $7.40. 100% freelance. Complete ms/cover letter. Pays .04/wd (.03/wd for reprints) on publication for 1st, one-time or reprint rts. Articles to 1,200 wds (100/yr); fiction to 1,200 wds (100/yr). Responds in 6-8 wks. Seasonal 9-12 mos ahead. Accepts simultaneous submissions & reprints (tell when/where appeared). Some sidebars. Prefers NIV. Guidelines; copy for #10 SAE/1 stamp.

   Poetry: Buys 30/yr. Free verse, light verse, traditional; 3-16 lines; $10. Submit max. 5 poems. Rhyming not usually taken too seriously.

   Fillers: Buys 30/yr. Cartoons, short humor, word puzzles; to 100 wds; puzzles $10, cartoons $20.

   Tips: "Write about a topic that is new and fresh. Avoid redundancy and focus on thesis for clarity of submission."

+THE EVANGEL, PO Box 348, Marlow OK 73055. (405)658-5631. Fax (405)658-2867. E-mail: Michael.Reynolds@sbbs.com. Home Mission Board, Southern Baptist Church. Michael H. Reynolds, ed. To expose Mormonism and explain its views of doctrine, history and current events. Bimonthly; circ 20,000. Subscription free. Open to freelance. Complete ms. Not in topical listings. (Ads)

+THE EVANGELICAL ADVOCATE, 1426 Lancaster Pike, Circleville OH 43113. (614)474-8856. Fax (614)477-7766. Churches of Christ in Christian Union. Wes Humble, ed. Denominational; emphasizing fundamental evangelical holiness. Monthly mag; circ 5,000. Subscription $10. Open to freelance. Query. Not in topical listings.

THE EVANGELICAL BAPTIST, 679 Southgate Dr., Guelph ON N1G 4S2 Canada. (519)821-4830. Fax (519)821-9829. E-mail: 103523.361@compuserve.com. The Fellowship of Evangelical Baptist Churches in Canada. Lois Peck, mng ed. Denominational; conservative evangelical. Monthly (11X) mag; 36 pgs; circ 4,000. Subscription $14.95 CAN, $16.95 US. 20-30% freelance. Query or complete ms/cover letter; phone/fax query OK. Pays $25-50 on publication for one-time rts. Articles 750-1,500 wds; fiction 750-1,500 wds; book reviews 200-375 wds. Responds in 5 wks. Seasonal 2 mos ahead. Accepts simultaneous submissions &

reprints. Accepts disk. Rarely uses sidebars. Guidelines; copy for 9x12 SAE/Canadian postage. (Ads)

   Tips: "If you expect payment for your submission, you must say so when submitting."

#THE EVANGELICAL BEACON, 901 E. 78th St., Minneapolis MN 55420-1360. (612)854-1300. Fax (612)853-8488. Evangelical Free Church of America. Carol Madison, ed; submit to Joyce K. Ellis, asst. ed. Denominational; informational, inspirational, and evangelistic. Monthly (7x) mag; 32 pgs; circ 30,000. Subscription $12. Very little freelance. Complete ms. Feature articles assigned. Looking for short news items, 150-200 words about exciting ministries, prayer movements, or evangelistic efforts of Evangelical Free Churches. B&W or color prints that illustrate the story a plus. Responds in 6 wks. Accepts simultaneous submissions & reprints. Guidelines; copy $1/ 9x12 SAE/4 stamps. (Ads)

*EVANGELICAL FRIEND, 110 S. Elliott Rd., Newberg OR 97132-2120. (503)538-7345. Evangelical Friends Intl. Paul Anderson, ed. Denominational organ. Bimonthly mag; 27 pgs; circ 10,500. 5% freelance. Query. **NO PAYMENT.** Not copyrighted. Articles 500-1,800 wds (6/yr). Responds in 4 wks. Seasonal 4 mos ahead. Accepts simultaneous submissions. Guidelines; copy for 9x12 SASE.

#EVANGELICAL VISITOR, PO Box 166, Nappanee IN 46550-0166. (219)773-3164. Fax (219)773-5934. Brethren in Christ. Glen Pierce, ed. Denominational. Monthly mag; circ 4,500. Subscription $12. 10% freelance. Complete ms. Pays $15-39 on publication for reprint rts. Articles 750-1,200 wds (3-5 pgs); fiction or true stories 900 wds. Responds in 10 wks. Seasonal 3-4 mos ahead. Accepts simultaneous submissions. Guidelines; copy $1.

EXPLORER MAGAZINE, PO Box 210, Notre Dame IN 46556. (219)277-3465. Flory Literary Foundation. Raymond Flory, ed/pub. Givers writers & poets a platform to reach others with Christian literature. Semiannual booklet; 32 pgs; circ 300+. Subscription $6. 99% freelance. Complete ms/cover letter. **PAYS COPY OR CASH PRIZE TO $25** (winners determined by readers), for one-time rts. Not copyrighted. Articles 200-300 wds (7/yr); fiction to 300-600 wds (7/yr). Responds in 2 wks. Seasonal 1 yr ahead. Accepts simultaneous submissions. No disk. No sidebars. Prefers NIV. Guidelines; copy $3. (Ads)

   Poetry: Accepts 100+/yr. Free verse, haiku, traditional; 2-20 lines. Submit max. 4 poems.

   Fillers: Accepts 6/yr. Anecdotes, prose, prayers; 200-300 wds.

   Contest: Each issue has a contest.

   Tips: "Send one poem per page and camera-ready, if possible. Poems should have an inspirational slant, nature, or love theme."

EXPRESSION CHRISTIAN NEWSPAPER, PO Box 44148, Pittsburgh PA 15205. (412)921-1300. Fax (412)921-1537. E-mail: express@nauticom.net. Website: http://www.nauticom.net/www/express. The Sonshine Foundation. Barbara Wilson, dir. of operations; Cathy Hickling, ed. Geared toward bringing unity among the churches in the Pittsburgh and west PA area. Monthly newspaper; 32 pgs; circ 15,000. Subscription by donation. 40-50% freelance. Query or complete ms/cover letter; phone/fax/e-mail query OK. **NO PAYMENT** for all rts. Articles 300-500 or 750-1,000 wds. Responds in 13 wks. Seasonal 1 mo ahead. Accepts simultaneous submissions. Accepts disk. Guidelines; copy for 9x12 SAE/3 stamps. (Ads)

Columns/Departments: Editorial and news summary.

Tips: "Send local/state stories, for example: Interview with local guy, Mel Blount (ex-Steeler), who has a half-way house for boys. Most open to editorials; PA stories of interest."

FAITH TODAY, M.I.P. Box 3745, Markham ON L3R 0Y4 Canada. (905)479-5885. Fax (905)479-4742. E-mail: ft@efc-canada.com. Evangelical Fellowship of Canada. Marianne Meed Ward, mng ed. Canadian news and current issues from an evangelical perspective. Bimonthly mag; 62-80 pgs; circ 18,000. Subscription $17.65 CAN. 80% freelance. Query/clips; fax/e-mail query OK. Query for electronic submissions. Pays $50-800 on acceptance for 1st rts. Articles (90/yr) 400-3,000 wds; news stories 400 wds; profiles 900 wds; book reviews 100 wds ($75). Responds in 4-6 wks. Prefers disk. Kill fee 30-50%. Sidebars OK. Guidelines/theme list; copy for 9x12 SAE/$1.35 Canadian postage. (Ads)

   Fillers: Buys 6/yr. Cartoons. Pays $25.

   Columns/Departments: Buys 6/yr. Guest Column (current social/political/religious issues of concern to Canadian church); 900 wds; $75.

   Special Needs: "All topics to be approached in a journalistic—not personal viewpoint—style."

   Contest: The God Uses Ink Awards Contest, held in conjunction with annual writer's conference. See listing under Canadian conferences. Open to Canadian Christian writers. Categories: Nonfiction book or article and fiction book or short story.

   Tips: "Most open to Guest column. Suggest a short news piece; if I'm happy with the idea and delivery, I'll assign a larger feature article."

   ** This periodical was #65 on the 1996 Top 50 Christian Publishers List. (#43 in 1994)

THE FAMILY DIGEST, PO Box 40137, Fort Wayne IN 46804. Our Sunday Visitor/Catholic. Corine Erlandson, ed. Geared to young Catholic families. Bimonthly journal; 48 pgs; circ 150,000. Distributed through parishes. 95% freelance. Complete ms/cover letter. Pays .05/wd, 4-6 wks after acceptance for 1st rts. Articles 750-1,200 wds (60/yr). Responds in 4-8 wks. Seasonal 7 mos ahead. Accepts reprints. No disk. No sidebars. Prefers NAB. Guidelines; copy for 6x9 SAE/2 stamps. (Ads- Call 612-929-6765)

   Fillers: Buys 15-20/yr. Anecdotes, 25-125 wds, $10.

   Tips: "Reading and getting to know the publication (and guidelines) is the best way to break in."

   ** This periodical was #52 on the 1995 Top 50 Christian Publishers list. (#57 in 1994)

THE FAMILY JOURNAL, PO Box 506, Bath NY 14810-0506. (607)776-4151. Fax (607)776-6929. E-mail: famlife@aol.com Interdenominational. Jack Hager, ed. A ministry center and 8 radio stations in northern PA and southern NY. Bimonthly newspaper; circ 22,000. Free to donors. 10% freelance. Complete ms/cover letter; phone/fax query OK. **NO PAYMENT.** Not copyrighted. Articles 250-500 wds (6/yr). Responds in 1 wk. Seasonal 3 mos ahead. Accepts simultaneous submissions & reprints. Requires disk. No sidebars. Copy for 10x13 SAE/2 stamps. (Ads)

   Poetry: Accepts 4/yr. Free verse, light verse, traditional; 32-40 lines. Submit max. 3 poems.

Tips: "We lean, but not exclusively, on stories/writers from NY and PA."

THE FAMILY NETWORK, RR1 Box 354, Claude TX 79019. Phone/fax (806)944-5414. Stacy Lewis, ed. To encourage Christian living, purity, modesty, home education, trusting God in family planning, homebirth, and prayer. Bimonthly newsletter; 12 pgs; circ.150. Subscription $15. 100% freelance. Complete ms; phone query OK. **NO PAYMENT.** Not copyrighted. Articles 50-800 wds (50/yr); fiction to 800 wds (15/yr). Responds in 3 wks. Seasonal 4 mos ahead. Accepts simultaneous submissions & reprints. Accepts disk. Sidebars OK. Guidelines; copy $3. (Ads)

Poetry: Accepts 12-20/yr. Any type; any length. Submit max.5 poems.

Fillers: Accepts 30/yr. All types.

Columns/Departments: Accepts 6/yr. Herbs (how to grow, dry, prepare own medicinals) 50-200; Child Training 50-1,000 wds; Marriage 50-1,000 wds.

Special Needs: Organizational helps and large family concerns.

Tips: "Any family/marriage/serving-God type articles. We love testimonies, articles that glorify God and encourage the believer."

+FATTED CALF FORUM, Fatted Calf Enterprises, Box 4031, San Marcos CA 92069. Department Editor. Regional Christian newspaper. Quarterly mag; 32+ pgs; circ 100. Subscription $20. 100% freelance. Complete ms. **PAYS IN COPIES/SUBSCRIPTION** for one-time rts. Articles to 2,000 wds (6/yr); fiction up to 2,000 wds (20/yr); music/video reviews, 250 wds. Responds in 6 wks. Seasonal 3 mos ahead. Accepts simultaneous submissions & reprints (tell when/where appeared). Prefers disk. Some sidebars. Guidelines; copy $2/9x12 SAE/4 stamps. (Ads)

Poetry: Accepts 20/yr. All types; any reasonable length. Submit max. 3 poems.

Columns/Departments: Accepts 4/yr. Pastor's Corner (church issues), 500 wds.

Contest: Sponsors a contest.

Tips: "We specialize in the unusual. Make me think. No self-help or counseling. Fiction! Poetry! Commentary, satire; preferably with an attitude. If everyone else is afraid of it, send it along."

+FEELINGS QUARTERLY, PO Box 85, Easton PA 18044-0085. (610)559-9287. E-mail: FEELINGS@itw.com. Website: http:\\www.SILO.com\FEELINGS. Anderie Poetry Press. Carole J. Heffley, exec. ed; submit to Michael Steffen, acq. ed. For the publication of fine poetry. Quarterly journal; 56-60 pgs; circ. 3,000. Subscription $24. Est.12/96. 90% freelance. Complete ms/cover letter; phone/e-mail query OK. Query for electronic submissions. **NO PAYMENT** for one-time rts. Responds in 4-6 wks. Seasonal 6 mos ahead. Reprints if it's been more than a year (tell when/where appeared). Guidelines; copies $6.50. (Ads)

Poetry: Accepts 1,000+/yr; to 38 lines. Submit max. 3 poems.

Fillers: Quotes: must pertain to poetry, poets or writing. Pays one copy.

Columns/Departments: Buys 20/yr. Pays $25. "Would accept a column on writing inspirational poetry; markets for inspirational poetry."

Contest: Sponsors several contests. Send for guidelines. Also collects poetry for an annual edition of praise poetry; 100 poems/edition.

+FELLOWSHIP IN PRAYER, 291 Witherspoon St., Princeton NJ 08542. (609)924-

6863. Fax (609)924-6910. Fellowship In Prayer, Inc. Rebecca Laird, ed. An interfaith spirituality journal. Bimonthly journal; 48 pgs; circ 6,000. 100% freelance. Query/clips; phone/fax query OK. **NO PAYMENT** for one-time rts. Articles to 1,500 wds (50/yr); book reviews 300 wds. Responds in 8 wks. Seasonal 6 mos ahead. Accepts reprints (tell when/where appeared). Accepts disk. Some sidebars. Guidelines; copy for SAE/3 stamps.

Poetry: Accepts 10/yr. Avant-garde, free-verse, light verse; to 35 lines. Submit max. 3 poems.

Columns/Departments: Buys 15/yr. A Transforming Experience (personal experience of spiritual significance); Pilgrimage (journey taken for spiritual growth of service); Spirituality and the Family; Spirituality and Aging; to 750 wds.

+**THE FELLOWSHIP LINK**, 679 Southgate Dr., Guelph ON N1G 4S2 Canada. (519)821-4830. Fax (519)821-9829. Fellowship of Evangelical Baptist Churches in Canada. Dr. T. Starr, ed. To edify and strengthen people 55+ through the various stages of aging. Quarterly mag; 24 pgs; circ. 2,000. Subscription $12. 90% freelance. Query w/wo clips. **NO PAYMENT** for all rts. Not copyrighted. Articles 300-350 wds (12/yr); fiction 300-350 wds (12/yr); book reviews 100 wds. Responds in 2 weeks. Seasonal 3 mos ahead. Accepts simultaneous submissions & reprints (tell when/where appeared). Guidelines; copy for 9x12 SAE/.90 postage or IRCs. (Ads)

Poetry: Accepts 3/yr. Traditional; short. Submit max. 2 poems.

Fillers: Accepts 6/yr. Anecdotes, cartoons, games, ideas, jokes, quizzes, short humor; to 250 wds.

Tips: "Most open to devotional articles or short stories, true or fictional."

*****FELLOWSHIP TODAY**, Box 237, Barrie ON L4M 4T2, Canada. (705)737-0114. United Church Renewal Fellowship. Gail Reid, mng. ed. Not included in topical listings.

#**FELLOWSHIP TODAY**, Fellowship Press, 4909 E. Buckeye Rd., Madison WI 53716. (608)221-1528. Fax (608)221-4934. E-mail: LAKECITY@MSN. FULLFEED.COM. Fellowship of Christian Assemblies. Kim Cortez, ed. Inspirational and teaching, informational. Monthly mag; circ 3,900. Subscription $10.60. 15% freelance. Query. Pays $7-20 on publication for 1st or reprint rts. Articles 500-1,800 wds (12/yr). Responds in 8 wks. Seasonal 3-4 mos ahead. Accepts simultaneous submissions. Guidelines; copy for 9x12 SAE/3 stamps. (Ads)

*****FIDELITY MAGAZINE**, 206 Marquette Ave., South Bend IN 46617. (219)289-9786. Fax (219)289-1461. E-mail: 71554.445@compuserve.com. Ultramontagne Associates, Inc. Dr. E. Michael Jones, ed. Issues relating to Catholic families and issues affecting America that impact all people. Monthly (11X) mag; 35 pgs; circ. 3,500. Subscription $25. 20% freelance. Complete ms/cover letter; fax/e-mail query OK. Pays $100 & up on publication for all rts. Articles (25/yr); book reviews $50. Responds in 12-24 wks. Query about reprints. Prefers disk. Some sidebars. Developing guidelines; copy for 9x12 SAE/5 stamps.

Poetry: Buys 15/yr. Free verse, light verse, traditional; 10-50 lines; $25. Submit max. 2 poems.

Fillers: Buys 15/yr. Cartoons, quotes; 25 wds & up; variable payment.

Columns/Departments: Buys 25/yr. Commentary, 2,500 wds; Feature, 5,000 wds; $100-250.

Tips: "All fairly open except cartoons. Single-spaced preferred; avoid dot matrix; photocopies must be clear."

FIRST THINGS: A Monthly Journal of Religion and Public Life, 156 Fifth Ave., Ste. 400, New York NY 10010. (212)627-1985. Fax (212)627-2184. Institute on Religion & Public Life. James Nuechterlein, ed. Shows relation of religion and religious insights to contemporary issues of public life. Monthly (10X) mag; 64-88 pgs; circ 26,000. Subscription $29. 80-85% freelance. Complete ms/cover letter. Pays $125-450 on publication for all rts. Articles 4,000-6,000 wds, opinion 1,000-2,000 wds; (50-75/yr); book reviews, 1,000-2,000 wds, $125. Responds in 1-3 wks. Seasonal 4-5 mos ahead. Prefers disk. Kill fee. No sidebars. Guidelines; copy for 9x12 SAE/9 stamps. (Ads)

> **Poetry:** Poetry Editor. Buys 10-20/yr. Free verse, traditional; to 45 lines; $50.
>
> **Columns/Departments:** Opinion, 800-1,600 wds.
>
> **Tips:** "Most open to opinion and articles."

FOCUS ON THE FAMILY MAGAZINE, 8605 Explorer Dr., Colorado Springs CO 80920. (719)531-3400. Fax (719)531-3499. Focus on the Family. Mike Yorkey, ed. To help families utilize Christian principles in the problems and situations of everyday living. Monthly mag; 16 pgs; circ 2,100,000. Free to donors. 15% freelance. Complete ms/cover letter; no phone/fax query. Pays $150-750 on acceptance for one-time rts. Articles 300-2,000 wds (15/yr). Responds in 2 wks. Seasonal 6 mos ahead. Accepts simultaneous submissions & reprints (tell when/where appeared). Accepts disk. Kill fee 1/3. Sidebars OK. Prefers NIV. Guidelines; copy for 9x12 SAE/3stamps.

> **Tips:** "Unfortunately it's getting harder and harder each year to break into this magazine since so much work is staff-written or excerpted from books."
> ** #54 on the 1994 Top 50.

FOURSQUARE WORLD ADVANCE, 1910 W. Sunset Blvd., Ste. 200, Los Angeles CA 90026-3282. (213)484-2400. Fax (213)413-3824. E-mail: comm@foursquare. org. International Church of the Foursquare Gospel. Dr. Ronald Williams, ed. Denominational. Bimonthly magazine; 23 pgs; circ 100,000. Free subscription. 5% freelance. Complete ms/cover letter. Pays $75 on publication for 1st, one-time, simultaneous, or reprint rts. Not copyrighted. Articles 800-1,200 wds (2-3/yr). Responds in 2 wks. Accepts simultaneous submissions & reprints. Sidebars OK. Free guidelines/theme list/copy.

> **Poetry:** Buys 1-2/yr. Pays $50.
>
> **Fillers:** Buys 1-2/yr. Anecdotes, cartoons; 250-300 wds; $50.

FRIENDS JOURNAL, 1501 Cherry St., Philadelphia PA 19102-1497. (215)241-7277. Fax (215)568-1377. E-mail: FriendsJnl@aol.com. Friends Publishing Corp. (Quaker). Vinton Deming, ed.; Kenneth Sutton, articles ed. Denominational. Monthly mag; 32-48 pgs; circ 9,000. Subscription $25. 95% freelance. Complete ms/cover letter; no phone/fax/e-mail query. **PAYS 4 COPIES**, for 1st rts. Articles to 2,500 wds (80/yr); fiction to 2,500 wds (1/yr); book reviews 500 wds. Responds in 2-15 wks. Seasonal 3 mos ahead. Accepts simultaneous submissions & reprints (rarely). Sidebars OK. Prefers NRSV. Guidelines; free copy. (Ads)

> **Poetry:** Judith Brown. Accepts many/yr. Any type, to 25 lines. Submit max.

3 poems. Only on Quaker themes: meditation, peace concerns.

Fillers: accepts 5/yr. Quaker-related humor and crossword puzzles.

Columns/Departments: Timothy Drake. Accepts 30/yr. Quaker writers only.

Tips: "Most open to poetry. Feature articles need to show an awareness of moderate-to-liberal thought in the Religious Society of Friends."

#THE GEM, 700 E. Melrose Ave., Box 926, Findlay OH 45839-0926. (419)424-1961. Fax (419)424-3433. E-mail: CGGCWB@aol.com. Churches of God, General Conference. Evelyn Sloat, ed. Weekly take-home paper for youth and adults; 8 pgs; circ 7,100. Subscription $9. 90% freelance. Complete ms/cover letter. Pays $7.50-15 on publication for one-time rts. Not copyrighted. Articles 1,000-2,000 wds (125/yr); fiction 500 wds. Responds in 18-26 wks. Seasonal 6 mos ahead. Accepts simultaneous submissions & reprints. Guidelines/copy for #10 SAE/1 stamp.

Tips: "We are accepting more material that is 400 wds or less as fillers (pays $5-10). Holiday material always welcome, although often we don't use it the first year we have it."

*GOD'S REVIVALIST, 1810 Young St., Cincinnati OH 45210. (513)721-7944x296. Ronald E. Shew, ed. Salvation theme; Wesleyan persuasion. Monthly mag; 24 pgs; circ 20,000. Subscription $8. 75% freelance. Complete ms/cover letter. **NO PAYMENT** for one-time rts. Articles 600-1,400 wds (3/yr). Responds in 9 wks. Seasonal 2 mos ahead. Accepts simultaneous submissions. Guidelines; copy $1/9x12 SAE.

Poetry: Accepts 5/yr. Free verse, light verse, traditional; 8-20 lines. Submit max. 10 poems.

Fillers: Accepts 5/yr. Facts, ideas, prose, short humor; 50-90 wds.

Tips: "We need some information about the author."

#GOOD NEWS, Box 150, Wilmore KY 40390. (606)858-4661. Fax (606)858-4972. E-mail: gnmag@aol.com. United Methodist/Forum for Scriptural Christianity. James V. Heidinger II, ed. Focus is church renewal—a return to Scriptural Christianity. Bimonthly mag; circ 65,000. Subscription $15 or contribution. 20% freelance. Query only. Pays .05-.07/wd on acceptance for 1st, simultaneous or reprint rts. Articles 1,500-1,800 wds (25/yr). Responds in 13 wks. Seasonal 6 mos ahead. Kill fee. Guidelines; copy $2.75. (Ads)

GOOD NEWS, ETC., PO Box 2660, Vista CA 92085. (619)724-3075. Fax (619)724-8311. E-mail: RICKMONR@aol.com. Good News Publishers, Inc. Rick Monroe, ed. Feature stories and local news of interest to Christians in San Diego County. Monthly tabloid; 24-28 pgs; circ 40,000. Subscription $15. 5% freelance. Query; query for electronic submissions, phone/fax query OK. Pays $20-25 on publication for 1st, one-time or reprint rts. Articles 500-700 wds (10/yr). Responds in 2 wks. Seasonal 2 mos ahead. Accepts simultaneous submissions & reprints. Prefers disk. Sidebars OK. Guidelines/theme list; copy for 9x12 SAE/4 stamps. (Ads)

Tips: "Most open to local, personality-type articles."

** 1994 EPA Award of Merit—Newspaper.

#GOOD NEWS JOURNAL, Box 1882, 10900 E Hwy WW, Columbia MO 65205. (573)875-8755. Fax (573)874-4964. Good News Publishers. Teresa Shields Parker, ed. Christian newspaper for mid-Missouri area. Bimonthly or monthly tabloid; 16 pgs; circ 50,000. Subscription $20. 25% freelance. Query/clips;

phone/fax query OK. **NO PAYMENT**, for one-time rts. Not copyrighted. Articles 250-1,000 wds (12-24/yr); kid's fiction 500-1,000 wds (6-12/yr); book/music reviews, 50-100 wds. Responds in 9 wks. Seasonal 2 mos ahead. Accepts simultaneous submissions & reprints. Prefers disk. Sidebars OK. Copy $1/ 9x12 SAE. (Ads)

Fillers: Accepts 12/yr. Cartoons, games, quizzes, quotes, word puzzles.

Columns/Departments: Accepts 12/yr. Good News Kids (fiction for kids up to 12 yrs), 500-750 wds; Golden Digest (testimonies or devotionals for those over 55), 1,000 wds.

Special Needs: Testimonies of healing with verification of physician.

Tips: "Interested in testimonies and personal experience stories that illustrate Christian growth or Christian principles."

GOOD NEWS REPORTER, PO Box 23664, Little Rock AR 72221-3664. (501)224-7508. Fax (501)224-3464. E-mail: gnrjames@aol.com. Kerusso Intl. James Strand, ed. News and information; dedicated to promoting revival in the church and community. Monthly tabloid; 24 pgs; circ 10,000. Subscription $20. 90% freelance. Query/clips; e-mail query OK. **NO PAYMENT** for one-time rts. Not copyrighted. Articles 250 wds (20/yr); book/music/video reviews, 150 wds. Responds in 6 wks. Seasonal 2 mos ahead. Accepts simultaneous submissions & reprints (tell when/where appeared). Accepts disk. Sidebars OK. Prefers KJV or NIV. Copy for 4 stamps. (Ads)

Fillers: Accepts 100/yr. All types; 25 wds.

Columns/Departments: Accepts 10/yr. Current Events; Politics; Opinion; all 100-500 wds. Complete ms.

Special Needs: Stories of people sharing their faith with others.

#GOSPEL TIDINGS, 5800 S. 14th St., Omaha NE 68107-3584. (402)731-4780. Fax (402)731-1173. E-mail: FEBComa@aol.com. Fellowship of Evangelical Bible Churches. Robert L. Frey, ed. To inform, educate and edify members of affiliate churches. Bimonthly mag; 16-20 pgs; circ 2,100. Subscription $8. 5% freelance. Complete ms; fax/e-mail query OK. Pays to $15-35 on publication for all rts. Articles (2-3/yr) & fiction (2-3/yr); 800-2,000 wds. Responds in 4-8 wks. Seasonal 4 mos ahead. Accepts simultaneous submissions & reprints. Prefers disk. Sidebars OK. Guidelines; copy for 9x12 SAE/3 stamps.

Poetry: Light verse, traditional.

GOSPEL TODAY MAGAZINE, 2201 Murfreesboro Rd. #C-203, Nashville TN 37217. (615)360-9444. Fax (615)361-1274. E-mail: gospel@usit.net. Horizon Concepts. Teresa Hairston, pub.; submit to Editorial Dept. Ministry and Christian/gospel music; Christian lifestyles directed toward African Americans. Bimonthly (8X) mag; 64 pgs; circ 50,000. Subscription $20. 50% freelance. Query; fax/e-mail query OK. Pays $75-250 on publication for 1st rts. Articles 1,500-3,000 wds. Responds in 4-9 wks. Seasonal 3 mos ahead. Prefers disk. Kill fee 10%. Sidebars OK. Prefers KJV. Guidelines/theme list; copy for 10x13 SAE/8 stamps. (Ads)

Poetry: Accepts.

Columns/Departments: Precious Memories (historic overview of renowned personality), 500 wds; From the Pulpit (issue-oriented observation from clergy), 1,000-1,500 wds; Life & Style (travel, health, beauty, fashion tip, etc.), 1,000-1,500 wds. No payment.

Tips: "Looking for more human-interest pieces—ordinary people doing extraordinary things."

+GREAT PLAINS MAGAZINE, PO Box 266, Downs KS 67437. (913)454-3973. Fax (913)454-3866. Lara Miller, ed. For readers 35+ in Kansas, Nebraska and Oklahoma. Bimonthly mag; 40 pgs; circ 12,500. Subscription $18. 60% freelance. Complete ms/cover letter; phone/fax query OK. Pays $30-100 on publication for 1st rts. Articles (18/yr). Responds in 4 wks. Seasonal 2 mos ahead. Accepts reprints (tell when/where appeared). Accepts disk. Guidelines/copy. Not in topical listings.

Columns/Departments: Buys 6/yr. Religion opinion, 800 wds.

+GREEN CROSS MAGAZINE, 1907 E. Main St., Richmond IN 47374. Phone/fax (317)939-2841. E-mail: mcrook@igc.apc.org. Website: http://www.northcoast.com/savetz/pd/pd.html. Evangelicals for Social Action. Michael Crook, ed. A biblically Christian magazine advocating care for God's creation. Quarterly mag; 32 pgs; circ 5,000. Subscription $25. 75% freelance. Query/clips; phone/fax/e-mail query OK. Pays to $150 on publication for one-time rts. Articles 600-1,800 wds (6-12/yr). Responds in 4-6 wks. Seasonal 4 mos ahead. Accepts simultaneous submissions & reprints (tell when/where appeared). Requires disk. Kill fee. Sidebars OK. Prefers NRSV or NIV. Copy for 9x12 SAE/ 2 stamps. (Ads)

Poetry: All types; 5-30 lines. No payment. Submit max. 3 poems.

Fillers: Cartoons, newsbreaks, prayers; $25.

Tips: "Looking for well-written personal testimony on writer's discovery of Christian/biblical basis for conservation. Other than that, we don't need articles that say "What a surprise! The Bible says to care for God's creation."

#GUIDEPOSTS, 16 E 34th St., New York NY 10016. (212)251-8100. Website: http://www.guideposts.org. Interfaith. Fulton Oursler, Jr., ed-in-chief; submit to The Editors. Personal faith stories showing how faith in God helps each person cope with life in some particular way. Monthly mag; 48 pgs; circ 3.9 million. Subscription $11.94. 30% freelance. Complete ms/cover letter. Pays $100-400 on acceptance for all & reprint rts. Articles 750-1,500 wds (40-60/yr). Responds in 4-8 wks. Seasonal 6 mos ahead. Accepts simultaneous submissions. Kill fee 25%. Some sidebars. Free guidelines/copy.

Poetry: Colleen Hughes. Buys 2-3/yr. Free verse, light verse, traditional; 2-20 lines; $10-25.

Fillers: Colleen Hughes. Buys 10-12/yr. Anecdotes; quotes, short humor; 10-200 wds; $25-100. "This is new for us."

Columns/Departments: Celeste McCauley. Buys 24/yr. His Mysterious Ways (divine intervention), 250 wds; This Thing Called Prayer, 250 wds; The Quiet People, 300 wds ("This is our most open area. Write in 3rd person."); $100.

Tips: "Be able to tell a good story, with drama, suspense, description and dialogue. The point of the story should be some practical spiritual help the reader receives from what the author learned through his experience." First person only.

** This periodical was #47 on the 1996 Top 50 Christian Publishers list. (#54 in 1995, #44 in 1994)

HALLELUJAH! (CAN), PO Box 223, Postal Stn. A, Vancouver BC V6C 2M3 Canada. (604)498-3895. Cable: Hallelujah. Bible Holiness Movement. Wesley H. Wakefield, ed. For evangelism and promotion of holiness revivals; readership mostly ethnic, non-white minorities. Bimonthly mag; 32-40 pgs; circ 5,000. Subscription $5. 3-5% freelance. Query or complete ms; no phone query. Pays $10-50 on acceptance for one-time or simultaneous rts. Articles 300-2,500 wds (4/yr). Responds in 5 wks. Accepts simultaneous submissions & reprints (tell when/where appeared). No disk. No sidebars. Prefers KJV. Guidelines; copy for 6x9 SAE/$1 postage.

> **Poetry:** Buys 4/yr. Traditional, hymn length (5 stanzas). Pays $5 or royalties. Submit max. 5 poems. Prefers poetry of hymn or song quality with identifiable meter.
>
> **Fillers:** Buys few. Prefers striking quotes from early Methodism or salvationers; 10-50 wds; $5.
>
> **Special Needs:** Spiritual warfare; religious conditions in southern Sudan; child labor/slavery; and Christian revival movements.
>
> **Ethnic:** Distributes to Nigeria, Canada and US
>
> **Tips:** "Avoid Americanisms. No Calvinistic articles or premillenialism. Be very familiar with evangelistic emphasis, doctrines, life standards, social stands of holiness churches."

+HALLELUJAH! (FL), 2701 Hodges Blvd., Jacksonville FL 32224. (904)223-6000. Fax (904)223-8400. E-mail: brichards@nlcf.org. New Life Christian Fellowship. Billy Richards, ed. Denominational; to spread the Gospel, educate Christians on issues, and advance the work of the Kingdom of God. Bimonthly mag; circ 7,000. Subscription free. Open to freelance. Complete ms. Not in topical listings.

+HARVEST TIMES, PO Box 868, Cleveland TX 77328. (713)592-4224. George Brohawn, ed. To spread the gospel, unite the church body, strengthen families and the community, encourage the body, and bring good community news. Biweekly newspaper; circ 3,000. Subscription $20. Open to freelance. Not in topical listings. (Ads)

*HEAD TO HEAD, PO Box 711, St. Johnsbury VT 05819-0711. Phone/fax (802)748-8000. Nondenominational. Paul A. Webb, ed-in-chief. Shows Christ as the greatest hope for brain-injury survivors and caretakers. Bimonthly mag; 24+ pgs; circ 1,000. Subscription $24. Est. 1994. 50% freelance. Complete ms/cover letter; fax query OK. **PAYS IN COPIES**, for 1st rts. Articles 250-1,200 wds (to 36/yr); fiction for all ages 500-1,000 wds; book/music/video reviews, 500 wds. Responds in 5 wks. Seasonal 3-6 mos ahead. Accepts reprints. Prefers disk. Guidelines/theme list; copy for 6x9 SAE/2 stamps.

> **Poetry:** Accepts 12/yr. All types, 4-60 lines. Submit max. 5 poems.
>
> **Fillers:** Most types; 50-250 wds.
>
> **Columns/Departments:** Tips & Hints; Caregiver Concerns & Family Matters, 250 wds.
>
> **Special Needs:** All topics should relate to brain injury, traumatic or congenital brain injury, cerebral palsy, encephalitis, multiple sclerosis, strokes, or alcohol/drug induced brain injury.
>
> **Tips:** "Need how-tos on survival, coping skills, cognitive strategies, social skills, job skills, and communication."

THE HEALING INN, 1813 Northwood Center NE, Tacoma WA 98422. Phone/fax (206)952-1188. Christian Airline Personnel Missionary Outreach. June Shafhid, ed. Offers healing for Christians wounded by a church or religious cult. Semiannual mag; 20 pgs; circ. 5,000. No subscriptions. 100% freelance. Complete ms; phone/fax query OK. **PAYS IN COPIES** for 1st or reprint rts. Articles 500-2,500 wds; fiction 500-3,000 wds. Responds in 3-4 wks. Seasonal 6 mos ahead. Accepts simultaneous submissions & reprints (tell when/where appeared). No disk. Some sidebars. Prefers KJV, NIV or NAS. Theme list; free copy. (Ads)

> **Poetry:** All types; 5-20 lines. Accepts 10-20/yr. Submit max. 10 poems.
> **Fillers:** Accepts 20/yr. Anecdotes, facts, games, ideas, jokes, newsbreaks, prose, quizzes, prayers, quotes, short humor, word puzzles.
> **Tips:** "All areas open. Looking for stories that will woo the lost back to Christ."

*HEARING HEARTS, 4 Silo Mill Ct., Sterling VA 20164. Phone/Fax (703)430-7387. American Ministries to the Deaf. Beverly Cox, ed. For deaf adults and those with whom they live, work and worship. Quarterly mag; 24 pgs; circ 500. Subscription $12. 75% freelance. Query/clips; phone/fax query OK. **PAYS IN COPIES**. Articles 100-600 wds (50-100/yr). Responds in 2 wks. Seasonal 3 mos ahead. Sidebars OK. Theme list; copy for 9x12 SAE/4 stamps.

> **Poetry:** Accepts 100/yr. Free verse, haiku, light verse, traditional; 5-30 lines. Submit max. 5 poems.
> **Fillers:** Cartoons, games, ideas, party ideas, quizzes, word puzzles.
> **Special Needs:** Wants interviews with interesting deaf Christians.
> **Tips:** "Needs Bible-application articles—lively & brief. Best if it can have a deaf twist—not using standard verses that refer to deaf. Show creativity to touch people within the 'don't fix me; I ain't broke' deaf culture."

#HERALD OF HOLINESS, 6401 The Paseo, Kansas City MO 64131. (816)333-7000 x2302. Fax (816)333-1748. Church of the Nazarene. Dr. Wesley D. Tracy, ed. For adult members of the denomination. Monthly mag; 64 pgs; circ 76,000. Subscription $12. 20% freelance. Complete ms/cover letter or query. Pays .05/wd (.04/wd for reprints) within 30 days of acceptance for 1st or one-time rts. Not copyrighted. Articles 800-2,000 wds. Responds in 6-8 wks. Seasonal 6 mos ahead. Accepts reprints. Kill fee 50%. Guidelines/theme list.

> **Poetry:** Buys 30/yr. Free verse & traditional/religious theme; short. Pays .75/line. Submit max. 3 poems.
> **Fillers:** Buys 30 cartoons/yr. Pays $10-50.
> **Tips:** "Need personality pieces about Nazarenes who are making a difference in their world (need not be celebrities); plus personal experiences of God at work in a person's life."
> ****** This periodical was #16 on the Top 50 Christian Publishers list.

HIGHWAY NEWS AND GOOD NEWS, PO. Box 303, Denver PA 17517-0303. (717)721-9800. Fax (717)721-9351. E-mail: GoTFC@AOL.COM. Craig Hartranft, ed. For truck drivers and their families; evangelistic, with articles for Christian growth. Monthly mag; 16 pgs; circ 35,000. Subscription $25. 75% freelance. Complete ms/cover letter; phone, fax, e-mail query OK. **PAYS IN COPIES** for rights offered. Articles (12/yr) & fiction (2/yr), 400-1,000 wds. Responds in 2 wks. Seasonal 6 mos ahead. Accepts simultaneous submissions &

reprints. Prefers disk. Sidebars OK. Prefers NIV. Guidelines/theme list; free copy.

Fillers: Accepts 6-12 cartoons/yr.

Tips: "All articles/stories must relate to truckers; need pieces on marriage, parenting, and fatherhood. Most open to features."

HOME LIFE, 127 9th Ave. N., Nashville TN 37234-0140. (615)251-5721. Fax (615)251-5008. E-mail: 70423,3242@compuserve.com. Southern Baptist. Jon Walker, ed-in-chief. Concentrates primarily on marriage issues, with parent and family issues secondary. Monthly mag; 66 pgs; circ 560,000. Subscription $19.95. 40% freelance. Query (complete ms for fiction); no phone/fax/e-mail query. Pays $75-275 on acceptance for all, 1st, one-time or reprint rts. Articles 600-1,800 wds (50/yr); fiction to 1,800 wds (10-12/yr). Responds in 8 wks. Seasonal 7 mos ahead. Accepts reprints (tell when/where appeared). Prefers disk. Sidebars OK. Prefers NIV. Guidelines; copy for 9x12 SAE/4 stamps.

Poetry: Buys 7-10/yr. Traditional; 4-24 lines; $10-75. Submit max. 5 poems.

Fillers: Cartoons & short humor.

Special Needs: Fiction on family relationships.

Tips: "Know who we are and who our audience is. This year we are moving to using more assigned material. A writer is more likely to get an assignment if we have worked with him/her on a query."

** This periodical was #16 on the 1996 Top 50 Christian Publishers list. (#26 in 1995, #24 in 1994)

#HOMESCHOOLING TODAY, PO Box 1425, Melrose FL 32666. Phone/fax (352)475-3088. E-mail: 74672.2004@compuserve.com. S. Squared Productions. Debbie Ward, ed. To equip homeschooling families. Bimonthly; circ 21,000. Subscription $17.95. Open to freelance. Query. (Ads)

HOME TIMES, Box 16096, West Palm Beach FL 33416. (561)439-3509. Neighbor News, Inc. Dennis Lombard, ed/pub. Conservative, pro-Christian community newspaper. Weekly tabloid; 20-32 pgs; circ 4,500. Subscription $12. 80% freelance. Complete ms/cover letter; no phone query. Pays $5-25 on publication for one-time rts. Articles 800 wds (25/yr); fiction 900 wds (5/yr); book reviews 500 wds; video reviews 400 wds; $5-15. Responds in 2-4 wks. Seasonal 6 wks ahead. Accepts simultaneous submissions & reprints (tell when/where appeared). Accepts disk Sidebars OK. Guidelines; 1 copy for $1/3 for $3. (Ads)

Poetry: Buys 5-6/yr. Free verse, light verse, traditional; 2-32 lines; $5. Submit max. 3 poems.

Fillers: Accepts many/yr. Anecdotes, cartoons, jokes, newsbreaks, quotes, short humor; to 100 wds; pays 6 issues.

Columns/Departments: Buys 15/yr. See guidelines for columns, to 600 wds; $5-15.

Special Needs: Op-eds and current affairs.

Tips: "Very open to new writers, but study guidelines (several new categories) and sample first; we are different. We need timely movie reviews, not too moralistic. Published by Christians, but not religious."

*HOMEWORK, The Home Business Newsletter with a Christian Perspective, 20 Whitcomb Dr., PO Box 394, Simsbury CT 06070. (203)651-5503. Christian. Posy Lough, ed. For people who work at home, or plan to. Bimonthly newsletter; 8 pgs. Subscription $20. Open to freelance. Complete ms. Short articles relating to home business. No additional information. Not included in topical listings.

IDEALS MAGAZINE, Ideals Publishing, Inc., PO Box 305300, Nashville TN 37230-5300. (615)333-0478. Lisa Ragan, ed. Seasonal, inspirational, nostalgic magazine for mature men and women of traditional values. Mag published 6 times/yr; 88 pgs; circ 180,000. Subscription $19.95. 90% freelance. Complete ms/cover letter; no phone query. Pays .10/wd on publication for one-time rts. Articles 1,000 wds (30/yr). Responds in 6-8 wks. Seasonal 6 mos ahead. Accepts simultaneous submissions & reprints (tell when/where appeared). No disk. No sidebars. Prefers KJV. Guidelines; copy $4.

> **Poetry:** Buys 100+/yr. Free verse, light verse, traditional; 8-40 lines; $10. Submit max. 5 poems.
>
> **Tips:** "Most open to optimistic poetry oriented around a season or theme."

*IMMACULATE HEART MESSENGER, 240 - 5th St. W., Alexandria SD 57311-0158. Catholic/Fatima Family Apostate. Fr. Robert J. Fox, ed. Bimonthly mag; circ. 10,000. Subscription $13. 50% freelance. **NO PAYMENT** for one-time rts. Articles 5 double-spaced pgs. Seasonal 6 mos ahead. Not in topical listings.

*IMPACT MAGAZINE, 12 B East Coast Rd., 1542 Singapore. 65-345-0444. Fax 65-345-3045. Evangelical Fellowship of Singapore. Andrew Goh, ed. To help young working adults apply Christian principles to contemporary issues. Bimonthly mag; circ 6,000. Subscription $22. 10-15% freelance. Complete ms/cover letter; phone query OK. **NO PAYMENT** up to $20/pg, for all rts. Articles (12/yr) & fiction (6/yr); 1,000-2,000 wds. Seasonal 2 mos ahead. Accepts reprints. Copy for $3 & $1.70 postage (surface mail).

> **Poetry:** Accepts 2-3 poems/yr. Free verse, 20-40 lines. Submit max. 3 poems.
>
> **Fillers:** Accepts 6/yr. Anecdotes, cartoons, jokes, quizzes, short humor, and word puzzles.
>
> **Columns/Departments:** Closing Thoughts (current social issues), 600-800 wds; Testimony (personal experience), 1,500-2,000 wds; Parenting (Asian context), 1,000-1,500 wds.
>
> **Tips:** "We're most open to fillers."

INDIAN LIFE, PO Box 3765, RPO Redwood Center, Winnipeg MB R2W 3R6 Canada. US address: Box 32, Pembina ND 58271. (204)661-9333. Fax (204)661-3982. E-mail: 103100.2735@compuserve.com. Website: http://www.indianlife. org. Intertribal Christian Communications. Jim Uttley, ed; Viola Fehr, asst. ed. An evangelistic publication for English-speaking aboriginal people in North America. Bimonthly newspaper; 16 pgs; circ 28,000. Subscription $7. 20% freelance. Query; fax/e-mail query OK. **NO PAYMENT** for 1st rts. Articles 250-1,500 wds (6/yr). Responds in 4 wks. Seasonal 6 mos ahead. Accepts reprints. Sidebars OK. Accepts disk. Guidelines; copy $1. (Ads)

> **Columns/Departments:** Jim Uttley. Accepts 12/yr. Family Life (native families); Native Business (natives in business); Crossword Puzzles; native pastor's column; all 500 wds.
>
> **Tips:** "Most open to historical pieces, news items and personal experience. Native authors preferred, but some others are published. Aim at an 8th grade reading level; short paragraphs; avoid multi-syllable words and long sentences."

#INLAND NORTHWEST CHRISTIAN NEWS, 222 W. Mission #107, Spokane WA 99201. (509)328-0820. Fax (509)326-4921. Zeda Leonard, ed. To inform, motivate and encourage evangelical Christians in Spokane and the inland Northwest. Newspaper published 18X/yr; 12 pgs; circ 2,500. Subscription $17.95. 30% freelance. Query; phone query OK. Pays $1/column inch on publication for 1st rts. Articles 500 wds. Responds in 9 wks. Copy $1.50. (Ads)

INSIDE JOURNAL, PO Box 17429, Washington DC 20041-0429. (703)478-0100x560. Fax (703)318-0235. E-mail: 74171.511@compuserve.com. Prison Fellowship Ministries. Terry White, ed. To proclaim the gospel to non-Christian prisoners within the context of a prison newspaper. Bimonthly (8X) tabloid; circ 371,000. Free subscription. 60% freelance. Query; phone/fax/e-mail query OK. Modest payment, depending on situation, on acceptance for one-time rts. Articles to 1,200 wds (25/yr). Responds in 4 wks. Seasonal 4 mos ahead. Accepts disk. Sidebars OK. Guidelines; free copy.

> **Columns/Departments:** Buys 15-20/yr. Shortimer (those preparing for release within 6 wks), 500 wds; Especially for Women (issues for incarcerated women), 600-800 wds. Variable payment.
>
> **Tips:** "Always need seasonal material for Christmas, Easter and Thanksgiving. Also celebrity stories that demonstrate triumph over adversity."
>
> ** 1995 EPA Award of Merit—Newspaper.

+INSPIRATIONAL NEWS NETWORK, 450 N. Claude A. Lord Blvd., Pottsville PA 17901. (717)628-2166. Fax (717)628-2167. Shirley C. Cicioni, pres/ed. A syndication that distributes articles dealing with news from an inspirational point of view. Not included in topical listings.

*THE INSPIRER, 737 Kimsey Ln. #620, Henderson KY 42420-4917. (502)826-5720. Billy Edwards, ed. To encourage believers in their Christian life. (Especially open to writers who are physically disabled.) Quarterly newsletter; 8 pgs; circ 2,500. Subscription for donation. 50% freelance. Query. Articles 250-700 wds (15/yr); fiction 250-500 wds (5/yr);book reviews, 500 wds. **PAYS IN COPIES/SUBSCRIPTION.** Not copyrighted. Responds in 2 wks. Seasonal 2 mos ahead. Accepts simultaneous submissions & reprints. No sidebars. Prefers KJV. Guidelines; copy for #10 SASE/2 stamps.

> **Poetry:** Accepts 5-10/yr. Traditional, 10-50 lines. Submit max. 3 poems.
>
> **Fillers:** Accepts 10-15/yr. Anecdotes, cartoons, facts, games, ideas, jokes, newsbreaks, prose, quizzes, prayers, quotes, short humor, word puzzles; 50-250 wds.
>
> **Columns/Departments:** Accepts 10/yr. Let the Redeemed Say So (testimonies), 250-500 wds; The Lighter Side (humor), to 300 wds.
>
> **Special Needs:** Issues of interest to (and from) the physically disabled; biblically-based and Christ-centered.

*INTERCHANGE, 412 Sycamore St., Cincinnati OH 45202. (513)421-0311. Fax (513)421-0315. Episcopal. Michael R. Barwell, ed. Regional paper for the Episcopal and Anglican Church in southern Ohio. Bimonthly tabloid; 28 pgs; circ 12,600. Free. 5% freelance. Query or complete ms/cover letter. Pays $35-50 on publication for all rts. Articles 500-2,000 wds (1-2/yr). Responds in 9 wks. Accepts simultaneous submissions. Prefers disk (Mac compatible). Sidebars OK. Copy for 9x12 SASE.

Tips: "Most open to features, especially with a local angle."

*THE INTERIM, 53 Dundas St. E. #306, Toronto ON M5B 1C6 Canada. (416)368-0250. Fax (416)368-8575. Catholic. Peter Muggeridge, ed. Abortion, euthanasia, pornography, feminism and religion from a pro-life perspective. Monthly newspaper; circ 25,000. 50% freelance. Query; phone query OK. Pays $100-150 CAN, on publication. Articles 700-1,000 wds. Responds in 2 wks. Seasonal 2 mos ahead. Accepts simultaneous submissions & reprints.

*INTERVARSITY, Box 7895, Madison WI 53707-7895. (608)274-9001. Fax (608)274-7882. E-mail: nKunde@ivcfnsc.fulfeed.com. InterVarsity Christian Fellowship. Neal Kunde, ed. To inform donors and other interested readers of InterVarsity's work on campus. Quarterly mag; circ 55,000. Subscription for donation. 5% freelance. Query. Pays $250 on publication for 1st rts. Articles 750 wds (21/yr). Seasonal 6 mos ahead. Guidelines; free copy.

Columns/Departments: Buys 4/yr. Campus Datelines (news about life on college campuses); 100 wds; $50.

Tips: "Most open to nonfiction features. Call the editor and ask specific questions."

ISLAND CHRISTIAN INFO, PO Box 5062, Sta. B, Victoria BC V8R 6N3 Canada. (250)744-3690. Fax (250)727-2667. E-mail: bbrian@islandnet.com. Vancouver Island Christian Communication Society. Lloyd Mackey, ed. Easy-to-read local news and inspiration for churches and businesses on Vancouver Island. Monthly tabloid; 24 pgs; circ. 14,000. Subscription $20, $25 US 98% freelance. Query; phone/fax/e-mail query OK. Not copyrighted. **NO PAYMENT**. Articles 300-750 wds; little fiction; a few book/music reviews, 400 wds. Seasonal 2 mos ahead. Accepts simultaneous submissions and reprints. Copy for 9x12 SAE/IRCs or $1. (Ads)

Poetry: Accepts 24-36/yr.

Fillers: Anecdotes; accepts few.

*IT'S YOUR CHOICE MAGAZINE, PO Box 7135, Richmond VA 23221-0135. (804)662-9596. Voice mail: (804)254-9940. FutureWend Publications. Dr. James Rogers, ed. For people seeking fresh and effective approaches to domestic and international crime and violence; emphasis on ethics. Monthly newsletter; 8-24 pgs; circ. 2,000. Subscription $9.84. Est. 1993. Complete ms. Pays $0-$1/wd ($1,000 max.), for all (contest winner), 1st, reprint or simultaneous rts. Articles (12/yr) & fiction (12/yr), to 1,000 wds; book reviews, to 1,000 wds. Responds in 4 wks (longer if interested). Seasonal 6 mos ahead. No sidebars. Accepts simultaneous submissions & reprints. Guidelines; copy for $2/#10 SAE/2 stamps.

Fillers: Buys 24-50/yr. Facts, ideas, quotes; to 50 wds. Pays $5.

Columns/Departments: Op-Ed (ethical issues), to 1,000 wds; Personal Experience (ethical issues), 1,000 wds; Bottom Line (fillers—ethical principles); 50 wds max; $5.

Special Needs: Ethical reviews/critiques of articles in other publications; educational system failure; criminal justice system failure. Accepts juvenile fiction only by juveniles.

Tips: "All fiction related to ethical issues in some way. 'Bottom Line' fillers best place to break in."

Contest: Two divisions, one for public, one for school children. March 31,

1997 deadline. First prize: $1,000. Runners up (4): $250. Send SASE & $2 fee for guidelines and a submission form (one for each entry).

JEWEL AMONG JEWELS ADOPTION NEWS, 9302 Seascape Dr., Indianapolis IN 46256. Phone/fax (317)849-5651. Independent Christian. Sherrie Eldridge, ed. Targets the interests and needs of adoptees and those touched by adoption. Quarterly newsletter; circ. 1,500. Free subscription in US. Est. 1994. Complete ms/cover letter; fax/e-mail query OK. **NO PAYMENT**. Articles 250-500 wds. Responds in 2 wks. Seasonal 3 mos ahead. Accepts simultaneous submissions & reprints. Prefers disk. Prefers NIV. Guidelines/theme list; copy for 1 stamp.

Poetry: Free verse, traditional. Submit any number.

Fillers: Accepts 10/yr. Anecdotes, cartoons, facts, ideas, newsbreaks, prose, quizzes, prayers, quotes, short humor, word puzzles; 25-300 wds.

Columns/Departments: Common Threads, Passages of Adoption, The Great Awakening, Trigger Points, Reframing the Loss, The Blessings of Adoption; all 250 wds. See guidelines for descriptions.

Special Needs: Adoptive parenting, adoption, grief & loss, identity in Christ, bonding & attachment perspectives, 12-step writing about adoption, how to find therapist who understands adoption issues.

Tips: "Most open to columns and transparent testimonials from adoptees willing to share their story."

JOHN MILTON MAGAZINE, 475 Riverside Dr., Rm. 455, New York NY 10115. (212)870-3335. Fax (212)870-3229. John Milton Society for the Blind/nonsectarian. Darcy Quigley, mng dir.; Ingrid Peck, fiction ed. Reprints material from over 60 religious periodicals in a large-type digest for the visually impaired. Quarterly tabloid; 24 pgs; circ 5,355. 1% freelance. Complete ms/cover letter; fax query OK. **NO PAYMENT**, for reprint rts. Not copyrighted. Articles 250-1,000 (1/yr); fiction 250-1,000 (1/yr); book reviews 200-500 wds. Responds in 6 wks. Seasonal 9-12 mos ahead. Accepts simultaneous submissions & reprints (tell when/where appeared). Some sidebars. Guidelines; copy for 9x12 SAE/3 stamps.

Poetry: Accepts 1/yr. Any type; to 40 lines. Submit max. 3 poems. Seasonal/holiday.

Fillers: Accepts 5/yr. Anecdotes, prayers, short humor; 25-500 wds.

Tips: "Most open to poetry/prayers pertaining to Christian holidays/seasonal themes and visual impairments. If writing about blindness, don't be patronizing. Look at the magazines we typically reprint from (see guidelines)."

JOURNAL OF CHRISTIAN NURSING, PO Box 1650, Downers Grove IL 60515-0780. (630)887-2500. Fax (630)887-2520. E-mail: jcn@ivpress.com. Nurses Christian Fellowship of InterVarsity Christian Fellowship. Melodee Yohe, mng. ed. Personal, professional, practical articles that help nurses integrate Christian faith with nursing profession. Quarterly mag.; 48 pgs; circ 9,000. Subscription $19.95. 35% freelance. Complete ms/cover letter; phone/fax query OK. Pays $25-80 on publication for all (rarely), one-time or reprint (occ.) rts. Not copyrighted. Articles 6-12 pgs (20/yr). Responds in 4-6 wks. Seasonal 1 yr ahead. Accepts some reprints (tell when/where appeared). Accepts disk. Kill fee 50%. Sidebars OK. Prefers NRSV. Guidelines/theme list; copy $4.50/9x12 SAE/6 stamps. (Ads)

Columns/Departments: Pulse Beats (this and that).

Special Needs: Congregational health, nursing history, environmental issues, professional issues, conflict management, and dealing with disabilities.

Contests: Sponsors an occasional contest. None planned for now.

Tips: "All topics must relate to nursing, or contain illustrations using nurses. freelancers can interview and write about Christian nurses involved in creative ministry (include pictures). Interview/profile a Christian nurse involved in a creative ministry."

** 1996 EPA Award of Merit—Christian Ministry.

JOURNAL OF CHURCH AND STATE, Baylor University, PO Box 97308, Waco TX 76798-7308. (817)755-1510. Fax (817)755-1571. E-mail: Derek_Davis@Baylor.edu. Baylor University/Interdenominational. Dr. Derek H. Davis, dir. Provides a forum for the critical examination of the interaction of religion and government worldwide. Quarterly jour; 225 pgs; circ 1,700. Subscription $20. 50% freelance. Complete ms (3 copies)/cover letter. **NO PAYMENT** for all rights. Articles 25-30 pgs/footnotes (24/yr). Responds in 6-8 wks. Prefers disk. No sidebars. Guidelines; copy $8 + $1.50 postage. (Ads)

Special Needs: Church-state issues.

*JOYFUL NOISE**, 4259 Elkcam Blvd. SE, St. Petersburg FL 33705-4216. Nondenominational. William W. Maxwell, ed. Deals with African-American life and religious culture. Bimonthly mag. Est. 1993. Complete ms/cover letter or query/clips. Pays $50-250 on acceptance for 1st rts. Articles 700-3,000 wds. Guidelines.

+JOYFUL NOISE: A Journal of Christian Poetry**, PO Box 401, Bowling Green KY 42102. Jim Erskine, ed. Christian-oriented poetry. Est. 1996. **PAYS IN COPIES**. Guidelines.

Poetry: Traditional; to 30 lines.

Tips: "We prefer personal, small subjects, over large themes such as love, brotherhood, etc. No political, new age, or social issues."

+THE KANSAS CHRISTIAN**, PO Box 47003, Topeka KS 66647. (913)273-4424. Fax (913)272-5595. E-mail: ChrstnNews@aol.com. Eagle Christians, Inc. Everett R. Daves, ed. To promote the gospel of Jesus Christ. Weekly; circ 3,800. Subscription $18 donation. Open to freelance. Complete ms. Not in topical listings. (Ads)

*KANSAS CITY CHRISTIAN NEWSPAPER**, PO Box 1114, Lee's Summit MO 64063. (816)524-4522. Non-denominational. Dwight Widaman, pub; Alecia Chai, ed. To promote Christian business, ministries and organizations; provide thought-provoking commentary for edification of the body of Christ. Monthly newspaper; circ 35,000. Subscription $14. 50% freelance. Complete ms/cover letter; short phone query OK. **PAYS IN COPIES** or limited amount for well-researched pieces, for one-time or reprint rts. Not copyrighted. Articles to 1,200 wds (100/yr). Responds in 6 wks. Seasonal 6 mos ahead. Accepts reprints. Guidelines; copy for 9x12 SAE/$1 postage.

Fillers: Accepts 12/yr. Anecdotes, cartoons, ideas, newsbreaks, quotes, short humor; to 500 wds.

Tips: "We look for up-to-date information. Willing to work with new writers who want to learn."

+KENTUCKY CHRISTIAN NEWS,**, 3191 Nicholasville Rd., Ste. 600, Lexington

KY 40503. Beverly Byrd, ed. Christian Newspaper. Not in topical listings.

LIBERTY, Religious Liberty Dept., 12501 Old Columbia Pike, Silver Springs MD 20904. (301)680-6448. Fax (301)680-6695. E-mail: 74617.263@compuserve. com. Seventh-day Adventist. Clifford R. Goldstein, ed. Deals with religious liberty issues for government officials, civic leaders, and laymen. Bimonthly mag; 32 pgs; circ 250,000. 90% freelance. Query; phone/fax/e-mail query OK. Pays $500-750 on acceptance for 1st rts. Articles & essays to 2,500 wds. Responds in 4 wks. Requires disk. Guidelines.

*LIFE GATE, 2026 Boulder Run Dr., Richmond VA 23233. (804)750-1504. Fax (804)750-1504. E-mail: lifegate@richmond,hofi.net. By His Design, Inc. Randy Moore, ed. Positive news for Protestant Christians. Monthly tabloid; circ. 23,000. 40% freelance. Query; fax/e-mail query OK. **NO PAYMENT.** Articles 250-500 wds (12/yr); book/music reviews 350 wds. Seasonal 4 mos ahead. Accepts simultaneous submissions & reprints. Prefers disk. Prefers NIV. Copy $1.50.

> **Poetry:** Accepts 8-10/yr. Avant-garde, free verse, light verse, traditional; 100-500 wds. Submit max. 5 poems.
>
> **Fillers:** Anecdotes, facts.

*LIFEGLOW, Box 6097, Lincoln NE 68506. (402)489-5922. Christian Record Services. Richard J. Kaiser, ed-in-chief. For sight-impaired adults over 25; interdenominational Christian audience. Quarterly mag; 65-70 pgs (lg. print); circ 30,000. Free to sight-impaired. 95% freelance. Query; phone query OK. Pays .04-.05/wd on acceptance for one-time rts. Articles & true stories 750-1,400 wds. Responds in 1-4 wks. Seasonal 18 mos ahead. Accepts simultaneous query & reprints. Guidelines; copy for 9x12 SAE/5 stamps.

> **Special Needs:** Nostalgia. Overstocked on historical.
>
> **Tips:** "Remember the readers are sight impaired or physically handicapped. Would the topics be relevant to them?"

#LIGHT AND LIFE, Box 535002, Indianapolis IN 46253. (317)244-3660. Fax (317)244-1247. Free Methodist Church of North America. Doug Newton, ed. Christian growth, ministry to saved and unsaved, denominational news. Monthly mag; 32 pgs; circ 23,000. Subscription $15. 40% freelance. Query; phone query OK. Pays .04-.05/wd on publication for 1st, one-time, or simultaneous rts. Articles 500-600 or 1,000-1,200 wds (60/yr). Responds in 4-6 wks. Seasonal 8 mos ahead. Accepts simultaneous submissions. Prefers disk (WordPerfect); pays $2 extra. Kill fee 50%. Sidebars OK. Guidelines; copy $1.50. (Ads)

> **Poetry:** Buys 6-10/yr. Free verse, traditional; 4-16 lines; $10. Send max. 5 poems. Uses as sidebars to articles.
>
> **Columns/Departments:** Buys 6-10/yr. Personal Opinion; Young Voice (ages 16-22); 500-600 wds.
>
> **Tips:** "Most open to feature articles. Write to the readers' interest. Our age groupings are approximately: 25% baby boomers, 25% over 65, 30% between boomers and retired; 20% younger than boomers."
>
> ** 1994 EPA Award of Excellence—Denominational.

*LIGHTHOUSE FICTION COLLECTION, PO Box 1377, Auburn WA 98071-1377. Tim Clinton, ed/pub. Timeless fiction for the whole family. Quarterly mag; 56 pgs; circ 300. Subscription $7.95 for 6/$14.95 for 12. 100% freelance. Complete ms/cover letter. Pays to $5-50 on publication for 1st or one-time rts. Fiction for all ages 250-5,000 wds (40-50/yr). Responds in 6-18 wks. Seasonal any time. Guidelines; copy $3.

Poetry: Buys 12-20/yr. Free-verse, light verse, traditional; 6-80 lines; $1-5. Submit max. 5 poems.

Tips: "Read and follow guidelines. Basic need is for good stories and poems—well-written, interesting, new plot."

LIGUORIAN, One Liguori Dr., Liguori MO 63057-9999. (314)464-2500. Fax (800)325-9526. E-mail: 104626.1547@compuserve.com. Website: http://www. liguori.org. Catholic. Allan Weinert, CSSR, ed-in-chief. To help readers lead a fuller Christian life through the sharing of experiences, scriptural knowledge, and a better understanding of the church. Monthly mag; 72 pgs; circ 340,000. Subscription $18. 30% freelance. Query or complete ms/cover letter; phone/fax/e-mail query OK. Pays .10/wd (to $200) on acceptance for all rts. Articles 750-2,000 wds (2-5/yr); fiction 2,000 wds (12/yr). Responds in 6-8 wks. Seasonal 6 mos ahead. Prefers disk. Some sidebars. Guidelines; copy for 6x9 SAE/3 stamps.

Fillers: Anecdotes, jokes, prose, prayers, short humor; .10/wd.

Columns/Departments: Buys 12/yr. Five-Minute Meditation (reflective essay), 750 wds. Complete ms.

Tips: "Polish your own ms. Need marriage and parenting articles, articles that touch a reader's life in a personal way. If writing a personal experience piece, beware of limited subjectivity. Most open to Five-Minute Meditation, fiction and fillers."

LIVE, 1445 Boonville Ave., Springfield MO 65802-1894. (417)862-2781x4356. Fax (417)862-6059. Assemblies of God. Paul W. Smith, adult ed. Inspiration and encouragement for adults. Weekly take-home paper; 8 pgs; circ 130,000. Subscription $8. 100% freelance. Complete ms; no phone/fax query. Pays .05/wd (.03/wd for reprints) on acceptance for 1st, one-time or reprint rts. Articles 800-1,600 wds (50/yr); fiction 800-1,600 wds (50/yr). Responds in 6 wks. Seasonal 18 mos ahead. Accepts simultaneous submissions & reprints. No disk. No sidebars. Prefers NIV. Guidelines/copy for #10 SAE/1 stamp.

Poetry: Buys 25-30/yr. Free verse, traditional; 12-20 lines; $10-15. Submit max. 3 poems.

Fillers: Buys 50/yr. Anecdotes, facts, prose, short humor; 200-500 wds; .02-.03/wd. short humor, word puzzles; to 200-700 wds; $10-25.

Tips: "Encourage our readers to live more productive Christian lives. We want them to be uplifted, not preached at or merely informed. Our purpose is mainly Christian inspiration and encouragement. Send no more than two articles in the same envelope and send SASE. "

** This periodical was #26 on the 1996 Top 50 Christian Publishers list. (#16 in 1995, #20 in 1994)

LIVING, Rt. 2 Box 656, Grottoes VA 24441. Phone/fax (540)249-3177. E-mail: Tgether@aol.com. Shalom Foundation, Inc. Melodie Davis, ed. A positive, practical and uplifting publication for the whole family; mass distribution. Quarterly magazine & tabloid; 36 pgs; circ 90,000 tabloid, 160,000 mag. Free subscription. 60% freelance. Complete ms. Pays $50 on publication for one-time or reprint rts. Articles 750-1,250 wds (30/yr); fiction (5/yr). Responds in 6 wks. Seasonal 6 mos ahead. Accepts simultaneous submissions & reprints (tell when/where appeared). No disk. Sidebars OK. Prefers NIV. Guidelines; copy for 9x12 SAE/4 stamps. (Ads)

Fillers: Buys 15/yr. Various; 50-100 wds; $10-25.

Tips: "Most open to first-person stories on family relationships—spouse and parent-child. Strong on anecdotes, short on moralism. Touch family needs in a practical way with a Christian slant, without being overly religious."

THE LIVING CHURCH, PO Box 92936, Milwaukee WI 53202-0936. (414)276-5420. Fax (414)276-7483. E-mail: livngchrch@aol.com. Episcopal/The Living Church Foundation, Inc. John Schuessler, mng ed. Independent news coverage of the Episcopal Church for clergy and lay leaders. Weekly mag; 16+ pgs; circ 9,000. Subscription $39.50. 70% freelance. Complete ms/cover letter; phone/fax/e-mail query OK. **PAYS IN COPIES** for one-time rts. Articles 800-1,000 wds (50/yr); fiction (1/yr). Responds in 4 wks. Seasonal 2 mos ahead. Accepts disk. Sidebars OK. Copy for 9x12 SAE/3 stamps. (Ads)

Poetry: Accepts 5-10/yr. Free verse, traditional; 4-15 lines. Submit max. 3 poems.

Columns/Departments: Accepts 10/yr. Benediction (devotional/inspirational), 200 wds.

Tips: "Most open to features, as long as they have something to do with the Episcopal Church."

+LIVING LIGHT NEWS, #200, 5304-89 St., Edmonton AB T6E 5P9 Canada. (403)468-6397. Fax (403)468-6872. Living Light Ministries. Jeff Caporale, ed. To motivate and encourage Christians; witnessing tool to the lost. Bimonthly (7X) mag; 28 pgs; circ 10,000. Subscription $12.95. Est. 1995. 80% freelance. Query/clips; phone/fax query OK. Pays $25-150 on publication for 1st, one-time, simultaneous or reprint rts. Not copyrighted. Articles 600-800 wds (20/yr); fiction to 1,500 wds (10/yr); book reviews 200 wds, music/video reviews 150 wds, $20. Responds in 4 wks. Seasonal 3 mos ahead. Accepts reprints (tell when/where appeared). Prefers disk. Kill fee 20%. Sidebars OK. Prefers NIV. Guidelines/theme list; copy for 9x12 SAE/ 9 stamps. (Ads)

Special Needs: Celebrity interviews/testimonials; interesting fiction and nonfiction stories related to Christmas; unique ministries.

LIVING WITH TEENAGERS, 127 Ninth Ave. N, Nashville TN 37234-0140. (615)251-2226. (615)251-5008. LifeWay Press. Michelle Hicks, mng. ed. Christian parenting for parents of teenagers. Monthly mag; 34 pgs; circ. 45,000. Subscription $18.95. 50% freelance. Query or complete ms/cover letter; fax query OK. Pays $100-300 on acceptance for all, 1st, one-time rts. Articles 400-1,000 wds (15/yr); fiction (1-2/yr); book/music reviews, 200 wds. Responds in 6 wks. Seasonal 6 mos ahead. Rarely accepts reprints (tell when/where appeared). Sidebars OK. Prefers NIV. Guidelines/theme list; copy for 9x12 SAE/4 stamps.

Fillers: Anecdotes, cartoons, party ideas, short humor; 25-200 wds; $20-100.

Tips: "Looking for holiday topics."

THE LOOKOUT, 8121 Hamilton Ave., Cincinnati OH 45231-9981. (513)931-4050. Fax (513)931-0950. E-mail: dahlmasj@ucenglish.mcm.uc.edu. Standard Publishing. David Faust, ed. For adults in Sunday school who are interested in learning more about applying the gospel to their lives. Weekly take-home paper; 16 pgs;

circ 105,000. Subscription $23.50. 25% freelance. Query; no phone/fax/e-mail query. Pays up to.09/wd (for unsolicited) on acceptance for 1st, one-time, or reprint rts. Articles 500-1,800 wds (50/yr); fiction 1,000-1,800 wds (15/yr). Responds in 10 wks. Seasonal 6 mos ahead. Accepts simultaneous submissions & reprints (tell when/where appeared). Accepts disk. Kill fee 33%. Sidebars OK. Prefers NIV. Guidelines/theme list; copy for 9x12 SAE/3 stamps.

Fillers: Cartoons, $50.

Columns/Departments: Buys 24/yr. Outlook (personal opinion), 500-900 wds; Salt & Light (innovative ways to reach out into the community), 500-900 wds. Pays .05-.07/wd.

Tips: "Show evidence of solid research. In feature articles on hot issues, present accurate information and measured judgments and let the reader decide. Most open to columns. Cover topics that are important to our readers, are backed up by some research (quotes, statistics, etc.), and be willing to express a strong opinion without being harsh or unfair to opposing opinions." ** This periodical was #1 on the 1996 Top 50 Christian Publishers list. (#3 in 1993 & 1995) Also EPA 1996 Award of Excellence—Sunday School Take-Home.

#THE LUTHERAN, 8765 W. Higgins Rd., Chicago IL 60631-4183. (773)380-2540. Fax (773)380-2751. E-mail: lutheranmagazine.partl@ecunet.org. Evangelical Lutheran Church in America. Edgar R. Trexler, ed.; Roger R. Kahle, mng ed.; submit to David L. Miller, sr. ed. Addresses broad constituency of the church. Monthly mag; 68 pgs; circ 800,000. 30% freelance. Query only; fax/e-mail query OK. Pays $400-1,000 (assigned), $100-500 (unsolicited) on acceptance for 1st rts. Articles 1,000-1,500 wds (40/yr). Responds in 3 wks. Seasonal 4 mos ahead. Accepts reprints. Disk/modem OK Kill fee 50%. Guidelines/theme list; free copy.

Fillers: Roger Kahle. Buys 50/yr. Cartoons, jokes, short humor. Uses only true anecdotes from ELCA congregations.

Columns/Departments: Roger Kahle. Lite Side (church and religious humor), In Focus, Living the Faith, Values & Society, In Our Churches, Our Church at Work; 25-100 wds; $10.

Tips: "Most open to feature articles."
** This periodical was #31 on the 1996 Top 50 Christian Publishers list. (#7 in 1995, #9 in 1994)

+THE LUTHERAN AMBASSADOR, 86286 Pine Grove Rd., Eugene OR 97402. (541)687-8643. Fax (541)683-8496. E-mail: CraigJN@aol.com. Assn. of Free Lutheran Congregations. Craig Johnson, ed. Denominational. Magazine published 16X/yr; circ 4,800. Subscription $16. Open to freelance. Complete ms. Not in topical listings.

THE LUTHERAN DIGEST, Box 4250, Hopkins MN 55343. (612)933-2820. Fax (612)933-5708. Lutheran. David L. Tank, ed. Blend of secular and light theological material used to win non-believers to the Lutheran faith. Quarterly mag; 72 pgs; circ 155,000. Subscription $20/2 yrs. 100% freelance. Query/clips or complete ms/cover letter. Pays $25 on acceptance for one-time rts. Articles to 1,000 wds (25-30/yr). Responds in 4-9 wks. Seasonal 6-9 mos ahead. Accepts reprints (70% is reprints). No disk. Some sidebars. Guidelines; copy $2/6x9 SAE/3 stamps.

Poetry: Accepts 45-50/yr. Light verse, traditional; any length; no payment. Submit max. 3 poems.

Fillers: Anecdotes, cartoons, facts, jokes, short humor; to 100 wds; no payment.

Tips: "We would like more short articles, 1 page or less. We also look for good-quality nature articles."

** #50 on the 1994 Top 50.

THE LUTHERAN JOURNAL, 7317 Cahill Rd., Ste. 201, Minneapolis MN 55439-2081. (612)941-6830. Fax (612)941-3010. Independent. Michael Beard, pub. Family magazine for church members, middle age and older. Quarterly mag; 32 pgs; circ 120,000. Subscription $6. 60% freelance. Query; fax query OK. Pays $10-50 on publication for one-time or reprint rts. Articles 300-1,500 wds (40/yr); book reviews, 150 wds, $5. Responds in 9 wks. Seasonal 4-6 mos ahead. Accepts simultaneous submissions & reprints. Sidebars OK. Prefers NIV, ASV or KJV. Guidelines; copy for 9x12 SAE/3 stamps. (Ads)

Fillers: Buys 5-10/yr. Anecdotes, cartoons, facts, jokes, quotes, short humor; to 100 wds; $5-10.

Columns/Departments: Buys 40/yr. Apron Strings (short recipes); About Books (reviews), 50-150 wds. Pays $5-25.

*****THE LUTHERAN LAYMAN,** 2185 Hampton Ave., St. Louis MO 63139-2983. (314)647-4900x18 or (800)944-3450. Lutheran Laymen's League/Lutheran Church-Missouri Synod. Gerald Perschbacher, ed. Lutheran news for lay adults. Monthly tabloid; 16 pgs; circ 80,000. 10% freelance. Query. Pays negotiable fees (about $110/tabloid pg) on publication for all rts. Not copyrighted. Articles 600-1,500 wds (10+/yr). Responds in 2 wks. Seasonal 3 mos ahead. Guidelines; free copy.

Columns/Departments: Buys 5/yr. Celebrities or Personalities (L.L.L. related, when possible—members, supporters); 600-1,500 wds.

Tips: "No opinion pieces or heavy doctrine. Be in Lutheran Church-Missouri Synod and know about Intl. L.L.L."

#LUTHERAN WITNESS, 1333 S. Kirkwood Rd., St. Louis MO 63122-7295. (314)965-9000. Lutheran Church-Missouri Synod. Rev. David Mahsman, ed; submit to David L. Strand, mng ed. Denominational. Monthly mag; 26 pgs; circ 325,000. 50% freelance. Complete ms/cover letter. Pays $100-300 on acceptance for 1st rts. Articles 250-1,600 wds (40-50/yr); fiction 500-1,500 wds. Responds in 9 wks. Seasonal 6 mos ahead. Considers simultaneous submissions & reprints. Kill fee 50%. Free guidelines/copy.

Fillers: Accepts 60+/yr. Cartoons ($50), short humor; no payment.

Columns/Departments: Buys 60/yr. Bible Studies, Humor, Opinion; $50-100.

*****MANNA,** 7041 Angelsea Dr., West Jordan UT 84084-2602. Christian. Roger A. Ball, ed. Features short, unrhymed poetry by beginning and intermediate writers. Biannual mag; 40 pgs; circ 250. 100% freelance. Complete ms. **NO PAYMENT** but gives cash prizes of $3-7 for best poems in each issue; for 1st rts. Responds in 5 wks. Guidelines; copy $3.50.

Poetry: Free verse. Submit max. 5 poems.

*****MARIAN HELPERS BULLETIN,** PO Box 951, Stockbridge MA 01263.

(413)298-3691. Catholic. Vincent Flynn, ed. Quarterly mag; circ 500,000. 20% freelance. Query/clips or complete ms/cover letter. Pays .10/wd on acceptance for all, 1st, or reprint rts. Articles 500-900 wds; book reviews. Responds in 3 wks. Seasonal 6 mos ahead. Accepts reprints. Kill fee 30%. Free guidelines/copy.

Tips: "Also needs articles on mercy in action or devotion to Blessed Virgin Mary."

MARRIAGE PARTNERSHIP, 465 Gundersen Dr., Carol Stream IL 60188. (630)260-6200. Fax (630)260-0114. E-mail: MPedit@aol.com. Christianity Today, Inc. Louise Ferrebee, assoc. ed. To promote and strengthen Christian marriages. Quarterly mag; 80 pgs; circ 59,000. Subscription $19.95. 5% freelance. Query; fax/e-mail query OK. Pays .15/wd on publication for 1st rts. Articles 500-2,000 wds. Responds in 8-10 wks. Seasonal 6 mos ahead. Some sidebars. Guidelines; copy $5.

Fillers: Cartoons; pays $75 .

Columns/Departments: For Women Only (women's issues) & For Men Only (men's issues), 400-500 wds; Work it Out (working out a marriage problem).

#MATURE LIVING, 127 9th Ave. N., Nashville TN 37234. (615)251-2274. Southern Baptist. Al Shackleford, ed. Christian leisure-reading for senior adults (50+) characterized by human interest and Christian warmth. Monthly mag; circ 350,000. 70% freelance. Complete ms. Pays .055/wd ($75 min.) on acceptance for one-time rts. Articles 400-1,200 (100/yr); fiction 900-1,200 wds (12/yr). Responds in 13 wks. Seasonal 1 yr ahead. Serials. Guidelines; copy for 9x12 SAE/4 stamps.

Poetry: Buys 30/yr. Light verse, traditional; senior adult themes; any length; $13-20. Submit max. 5 poems.

Fillers: Buys 120/yr. Anecdotes, facts, games short humor; to 50 wds; $10.

Columns/Departments: Cracker Barrel (brief humor), $10; Grandparent's Brag Board, $10.

Tips: "Most open to human-interest stories. All articles and fiction must relate to senior adults."

MATURE YEARS, Box 801, Nashville TN 37202. (615)749-6292. Fax (615)749-6512. United Methodist. Marvin W. Cropsey, ed. Inspiration, information, and leisure reading for persons of retirement age. Quarterly mag; 112 pgs; circ 70,000. Subscription $12. 50% freelance. Complete ms/cover letter. Pays .05/wd on acceptance for one-time rts. Articles 900-2,000 wds (60/yr); fiction 1,200-2,000 wds (4/yr). Responds in 3-8 wks. Seasonal 14 mos ahead. Accepts reprints. Sidebars OK. Guidelines; copy $3.75.

Poetry: Buys 24/yr. Free verse, haiku, light verse, traditional; 4-16 lines; pays .50-$1/line. Submit max. 6 poems.

Fillers: Buys 20/yr. Cartoons, jokes, prayers, word puzzles (religious only); to 30 wds; $5-25.

Columns/Departments: Buys 20/yr. Health Hints, 900-1,200 wds; Modern Revelations (inspirational), 900-1,100 wds; Fragments of Life (true life inspirational), 250-600 wds; Going Places (travel), 1,000-1,500 wds; Money Matters, 1,200-1,800 wds.

Special Needs: Articles on crafts and pets. Fiction on older adult situation.

** This periodical was #56 on the 1996 Top 50 Christian Publishers list. (#65 in 1995, #51 in 1994)

THE MENNONITE, Box 347, Newton KS 67114. (316)283-5100. Fax (316)283-0454. E-mail: TheMennonite@gcmc.org. General conference Mennonite Church. Gordon Houser, ed. Practical articles on aspects of Christian living. Semimonthly mag; 24 pgs; circ 8,000. Subscription $28. 10% freelance. Complete ms/cover letter; fax/e-mail query OK. Pays .05/wd on publication for one-time rts. Articles 700-1,200 wds (10/yr); book/music/video reviews, 300 wds, $10. Responds in 1-2 wks. Seasonal 6 mos ahead. Accepts simultaneous submissions & reprints (tell when/where appeared). Accepts disk. Kill fee 50%. Sidebars OK. Prefers NRSV. Guidelines/theme list; copy for 9x12 SAE/6 stamps.

> **Poetry:** Buys 5-10/yr. Avant-garde, free verse; $20-50. Submit max. 3 poems.
>
> **Fillers:** buys 3-5/yr. Anecdotes, cartoons, facts; 25-100 wds; $10-30.
>
> **Columns/Departments:** Buys 5/yr. Speaking Out (opinion); Bible (Bible study with application); Profile (example of discipleship); all 700 wds. Pays .05/wd.
>
> **Tips:** "Most open to feature articles (1,000-1,500 wds): should be anecdotal, with practical ideas for living the Christian life; stories of people who have changed for the better are especially considered; needs to fit Mennonite theology."

MENNONITE BRETHREN HERALD, 3-169 Riverton Ave., Winnipeg MB R2L 2E5 Canada. (204)669-6575. Fax (204)654-1865. E-mail: mbherald@ cdnmbconf.ca. Canadian Conference of Mennonite Brethren Churches. Susan Brandt, mng. ed. Denominational; for information, communication and spiritual enrichment. Biweekly mag; 32 pgs; circ 15,000. Subscription $30. 40% freelance. Complete ms/cover letter. Pays .07/wd on publication for 1st rts. Articles 1,200 wds (40/yr); fiction 1,000-2,000 wds (10/yr). Responds in 20 wks. Seasonal 5 mos ahead. Accepts reprints (tell when/where appeared). Prefers disk. Sidebars OK. Prefers NIV. Guidelines/theme list; copy for 9x12 SAE/$1 Canadian postage. (Ads)

> **Poetry:** Buys 15/yr. Avant-garde, free verse, traditional; any length; pays to $10.

MENNONITE HISTORIAN, 600 Shaftesbury Blvd., Winnipeg MB R3P 0M4 Canada. (204)888-6781. Fax (204)831-5675. Conference of Mennonites in Canada. Lawrence Klippenstein, ed. Gathers and shares historical material related to Mennonites; focus on North America, but also beyond. Quarterly newsletter; 8 pgs; circ. 2,600. Subscription $9. 60% freelance. Complete ms/cover letter; phone/fax query OK. **NO PAYMENT EXCEPT BY SPECIAL ARRANGEMENT** for 1st rts. Articles 250-1,000 wds (6/yr). Responds in 3 wks. Seasonal 3 mos ahead. Accepts simultaneous submissions & reprints (depending on where published). Copy $1/9x12 SAE.

> **Tips:** "Most open to lead articles. Write with your ideas. Also genealogical articles."

*MENNONITE REPORTER, 3-312 Marsland Dr., Waterloo ON N2J 3Z1 Canada. (519)884-3810. Fax (519)884-3331. Mennonite. Ron Rempel, ed. Denominational. Biweekly newspaper; 20 pgs; circ 11,000. 20% freelance. Query; fax query

OK. Pays .10/wd on publication for 1st rts. Articles 750-1,250 wds; news 500-750 wds. Responds in 4 wks. Accepts simultaneous submissions. Guidelines; free copy.

Tips: "Most of our readers are Canadians; give us a Canadian perspective."

*MENNONITE WEEKLY REVIEW, Box 568, Newton KS 67114-0568. (316)283-3670. Mennonite. Robert Schrag, ed. Features religious and Mennonite news. Weekly newspaper; 12-16 pgs; circ 11,000. 5% freelance. Complete ms/cover letter. Pays .05/wd on publication for one-time rts. Articles 400-500 wds. Responds in 5 wks. Accepts simultaneous submissions. Copy $1/SAE/2 stamps.

MESSAGE, Review and Herald Pub. Assn., 55 W. Oak Ridge Dr., Hagerstown MD 21740. (301)791-7000x2565. Fax (301)714-1753. E-mail: 74617.3047@compuserve.com. Seventh-day Adventist. Stephen P. Ruff, ed. Blacks and other minorities who have an interest in current issues and are seeking a better lifestyle. Bimonthly mag; 32 pgs; circ 80-90,000. Subscription $11.95. 60% freelance. Complete ms/cover letter; fax query OK. Pays $50-300 on acceptance for 1st rts. Articles to 700 wds (50/yr); parables; fiction for children (elementary age, 8-10/yr), 400-800 wds. Responds in 3-10 wks. Seasonal 5+ mos ahead. Prefers disk. Sidebars OK. Prefers NIV. Guidelines; free copy for 9x12 SAE.

Fillers: Facts, quizzes; $25.

Columns/Departments: Healthspan (health issues), 400-800 wds; Voices in the wind (facts/community-related info).

Contests: Sometimes has a black history contest and/or Bible-related contest.

Tips: "Submissions should be reader-friendly—written for a 6th-8th grade reading level. The use of humor, anecdotes and personal experiences is encouraged."

** This periodical was #28 on the 1995 Top 50 Christian Publishers list. Also 1996 EPA Award of Merit—Missionary.

#MESSAGE OF THE OPEN BIBLE, 2020 Bell Ave., Des Moines IA 50315. (515)288-6761. Fax (515)288-2510. Open Bible Standard Churches. Delores Winegar, ed. To inspire, inform and educate the Open Bible family. Bimonthly mag; 16 pgs; circ 4,100. Subscription $9.75. 5% freelance. Complete ms/cover letter; phone/fax query OK. **NO PAYMENT.** Not copyrighted. Articles 700-800 or 1,400-1,600 wds (10-15/yr). Responds in 2-4 wks. Seasonal 3-4 mos ahead. Some sidebars. Prefers NIV. Guidelines/theme list; copy $2 or 9x12 SAE/4 stamps.

Tips: "We have a brand new format and are unsure of future needs. Mostly looking for writers in our denomination but will consider an exceptionally written testimony article."

** 1996 EPA Award of Merit—Denominational.

*MESSENGER, Box 18068, Covington KY 41018-0068. (606)283-6270. Catholic. Jean Bach, news ed. Diocese paper of Covington KY. Weekly (45X) newspaper; 24 pgs; circ 16,000. Subscription $18. 40% freelance. Query/clips. Pays $1.25/column inch on publication for 1st rts. Articles 500-800 wds. Responds in 1 wk. Seasonal 1 mo ahead. Accepts simultaneous submissions. Guidelines; free copy.

#MESSENGER OF THE SACRED HEART, 661 Greenwood Ave., Toronto ON

M4J 4B3 Canada. (416)466-1195. Catholic/Apostleship of Prayer. Rev. F.J. Power, S.J., ed. Help for daily living on a spiritual level. Monthly (11x) mag; 32 pgs; circ 16,000. 20% freelance. Complete ms/cover letter. Pays from .04/wd on acceptance for 1st rts. Articles 700-1,500 wds (30/yr); fiction 750-1,500 wds (11/yr). Responds in 5 wks. Seasonal 5 mos ahead. No sidebars. Guidelines; copy $1/9x12 SAE.

> **Tips:** "Most open to inspirational stories and articles."

THE MESSENGER OF ST. ANTHONY, Via Orto Botanico, 11, 34123 Patua, Italy (no longer has a US editor or address). Catholic. Submissions Editor. For middle-age and older Catholics in English-speaking world; articles that address current issues. Monthly mag; 36 pgs; circ 300,000. Subscription $20. 25% freelance. Query or complete ms/cover letter. Pays $50-150 on publication for one-time & electronic rts. Articles 600-1,800 wds (95/yr); fiction 700-2,000 wds (6/yr). Responds in 5 wks. Seasonal 9 mos ahead. No sidebars. Guidelines; free copy.

> **Poetry:** To 300 wds.

> **Tips:** "We prefer articles with accompanying photos."

METHODIST HISTORY, 36 Madison Ave., Madison NJ 07940. (201)408-3189. Fax (201)408-3909. United Methodist. Charles Yrigoyen Jr., ed. History of the United Methodism and Methodist/Wesleyan churches. Quarterly journal; 64 pgs; circ 1,000. 100% freelance. Query; phone query OK. **PAYS IN COPIES** for all rts. Historical articles to 5,000 wds (15/yr); book reviews 500 wds. Responds in 8 wks. Requires disk. No sidebars. Guidelines; copy $5. (Ads)

*MINISTRY TODAY, Box 9127, Fort Wayne IN 46899. (219)747-2027. Fax (219)747-5331. Missionary Church. Robert Ransom, mng ed. Denominational; for young adults, 20-45 years old. Bimonthly tabloid; 4 pgs; circ 5,000. 15% freelance. Complete ms/cover letter. Pays .03-.04/wd on publication for 1st, one-time, reprint or simultaneous rts. Not copyrighted. Articles 200-800 wds (3-4/yr); fiction 200-1,600 wds (1-2/yr). Responds in 4-8 wks. Seasonal 4 mos ahead. Accepts simultaneous submissions & reprints. Guidelines; copy for 9x12 SAE/2 stamps.

> **Tips:** "Limited due to being only 4 tabloid pages with six issues/yr. Family and parenting material is most selected category."

#MINNESOTA CHRISTIAN CHRONICLE, 7317 Cahill Rd., Minneapolis MN 55439. (612)941-1605. Fax (612)941-3010. E-mail: trouten@compuserve.com. Beard Communications. Doug Trouten, ed. Local news and features of interest to the Christian community. Biweekly newspaper; 36 pgs; circ 6,000. Subscription $19.95. 10% freelance. Query; phone query OK. Pays .05/wd after publication for one-time rts. Articles 500-1,000 wds (50/yr); book reviews 500 wds. Responds in 13 wks. Seasonal 2 mos ahead. Accepts simultaneous query & reprints. Guidelines; copy $2. (Ads)

> **Tips:** "Not interested in anything without a Minnesota 'hook.' Inspiration section has room for two general personality features each issue; tell us about people and ministries we're not aware of."

> ****** 1996 EPA Award of Excellence—Newspaper.

THE MIRACULOUS MEDAL, 475 E. Chelten Ave., Philadelphia PA 19144-5785. (215)848-1010. Catholic. Rev. William J. O'Brien, ed. Fiction & poetry for Catholic adults, mostly women. Quarterly mag; 30 pgs; circ 340,000. 40% freelance. Complete ms/cover letter; phone query OK. Pays .02/wd & up on acceptance for 1st rts. Religious fiction 1,600-2,400 wds (6/yr). Responds in 26-40 wks. Seasonal 1 yr ahead. Accepts simultaneous submissions. Guidelines; copy for 9x12 SAE/3 stamps.

Poetry: Buys 6/yr. Free verse, traditional; to 20 lines; .50 & up/line. Send any number. "Must have religious theme, preferably about the Blessed Virgin Mary."

THE MONTANA CATHOLIC, PO Box 1729, Helena MT 59624-1729. (406)442-5820. Fax (406)442-5191. Catholic. Gerald M. Korson, ed. News and features for the Catholic community of western Montana. Tabloid published 16X/yr; 16-28 pgs; circ 9,200. Subscription $13.50 MT, $18 US. 5% freelance. Complete ms/cover letter. Pays .05/wd on acceptance for one-time rts. Articles 500-1,000 wds (5/yr); book reviews, 200-600 wds. Responds in 4 wks. Seasonal 2-3 mos ahead. Accepts simultaneous submissions & reprints (tell when/where appeared). Accepts disk. Kill fee 35%. Sidebars OK. Prefers NAS or RSV. Guidelines/theme list; copy for 9x12 SAE/4 stamps.

Tips: "Submit to annual special supplements on colleges, religious vocations, respect for life, senior citizens, bereavement, Christmas, Easter and Lent. Articles pertaining to the Catholic Church in western Montana are always welcome."

MOODY MAGAZINE, 820 N. LaSalle Blvd., Chicago IL 60610. (312)329-2164. Fax (312)329-2149. E-mail: MoodyLtrs@moody.edu. Website: http://www. moody.edu. Moody Bible Institute. Andrew Scheer, mng. ed. To encourage and equip evangelical Christians to think and live biblically. Bimonthly mag; 84-104 pgs; circ 100,000. Subscription $18.95. 60% freelance. Query only; no phone/fax/e-mail query. Query for electronic submissions. Pays $210-500 ($210-375 for fiction), or .15/wd (.20/wd for assigned) on acceptance for 1st & non-exclusive electronic rts. Articles 1,400-2,500 wds (60/yr); fiction 1,400-2,500 wds (1-3/yr). Responds in 6-8 wks. Seasonal 9 mos ahead. Accepts reprints (tell when/where appeared). Kill fee 50%. Requires disk. Sidebars OK. Prefers NIV. Guidelines; copy for 9x12 SASE/8 stamps. (Ads)

Columns/Departments: Buys 12/yr. Just For Parents (application of scriptural principle to parenting), 1,500 wds; First Person (salvation testimonies— may be as-told-to), 800-1,000 wds; $150-225.

Special Needs: "Looking for articles reflecting the ethnic/racial diversity in the body of Christ; articles sensitive to singles in the church."

Tips: "We want feature articles from freelancers for the second (non-cover) section of each issue. In generating article ideas, consider these questions: What has God been working on in my life the last few years? How am I applying a new realization of what the Bible is directing me to do? What difference has this obedience made? Answers should lead you to appropriate content for a Moody article."

** This periodical was #9 on the 1996 Top 50 Christian Publishers list. (#4 in 1995 & 1994)

+MOVIEGUIDE, PO Box 64, Camarillo CA 93010. (805)383-2000. Fax (805)383-4089. E-mail: 74512.2260@compuserve.com. Christian Film & TV Commission. Dr. Theodore Baehr, ed. Family guide to media entertainment from a biblical perspective. Biweekly; 30+ pgs.; circ 7,000. Subscription $40. 20% freelance. Query/clips. Pays $20 for all rts. Articles 1,500 wds (20/yr); book/music/video/movie reviews, 1,500 wds. Responds in 26 wks. Requires disk. Guidelines. (Ads)

*NATIONAL CATHOLIC REPORTER, 115 E. Armour Blvd., Kansas City MO 64141. (816)531-0538. Catholic. Thomas Fox, ed. Independent. Weekly (44X) newspaper; 44-48 pgs; circ 48,000. Query/clips. Pays varying rates on publication. Articles any length. Responds in 9 wks. Accepts simultaneous submissions.

    Columns/Departments: Query with ideas for columns.

*NATIONAL REVIEW, 150 E. 35th St., New York NY 10016. (212)679-7330. Fax (212)696-0309. National Review, Inc. Drew Oliver, ed. Conservative journal of news and commentary covering politics, international affairs, the economy, and cultural trends. Biweekly mag; 72 pgs; circ. 225,000. Subscription $57. 80% freelance. Query; phone/fax query OK. Pays negotiable rates on publication for all rts. Articles 1,200-8,000 wds. Kill fee. Prefers disk. Sidebars OK.

    Fillers: Cartoons.

*NETWORK, Box 320627, Birmingham AL 35232-0637. (205)328-7112. Interdenominational. Dolores Milazzo Hicks, ed/pub. To encourage and nurture dialog, understanding and unity in Jewish and Christian communities. Monthly tabloid; 12-16 pgs; circ 15,000. 50% freelance. Negotiable payment. Not copyrighted. Accepts simultaneous submissions. Articles and news.

NEW COVENANT, 200 Noll Plaza, Huntington IN 46750. (219)356-8400. Fax (219)356-8472. E-mail: NewCov@aol.com.Catholic/Our Sunday Visitor. Mike Aquilina, ed. Serves readers interested in orthodox Catholic spirituality. Monthly mag; 36 pgs; circ 20,000. Subscription $18. 85% freelance. Query/clips or complete ms/cover letter; fax/e-mail query OK. Pays $100-200 on acceptance for 1st or one-time rts. Articles 1,000-1,200 wds (40/yr). Responds in 5 wks. Seasonal 5 mos ahead. Prefers disk. Guidelines; copy for 9x12 SAE/5 stamps. (Ads)

    Tips: "Most open to practical, useful approaches to deepening one's spiritual life and relationship with Christ. Be familiar with New Covenant's style so you can speak to our audience."

    ** This periodical was #33 on the 1996 Top 50 Christian Publishers list. (#48 in 1995, #46 in 1994)

A NEW HEART, Box 4004, San Clemente CA 92674-4004. (714)496-7655. Fax (714)496-8465. Aubrey Beauchamp, ed. For Christian healthcare-givers; info regarding medical/Christian issues. Quarterly mag; 16 pgs; circ 5,000. Subscription $20. 20% freelance. Complete ms/cover letter; phone/fax query OK. **PAYS 2 COPIES** for one-time rts. Not copyrighted. Articles 600-1,800 wds (20-25/yr). Responds in 2-3 wks. Accepts simultaneous submissions & reprints. No sidebars. Guidelines; copy for 9x12 SAE/ 3 stamps.

    Poetry: Accepts 1-2/yr. Submit max. 1-3 poems.

    Fillers: Accepts 3-4/yr. Anecdotes, cartoons, facts, jokes, short humor; 100-120 wds.

    Columns/Departments: Accepts 20-25/yr. Chaplain's Corner, 200-250 wds; Physician's Corner, 200-250 wds.

    Tips: "Most open to true stories, short, medically related, including caregivers."

+NEW HORIZONS, 607 N. Easton Rd., Bldg. E, PO Box P, Willow Grove PA 19090-0920. (215)830-0900. Fax (215)830-0350. E-mail: tomtyson@aol.com. Committee on Christian Education, Orthodox Presbyterian Church. Thomas E. Tyson, ed. Denominational. Monthly (11X) newsletter; circ 12,000. Subscription $15. Open to freelance. Complete ms. Not in topical listings.

NEW MAN, 600 Rinehart Rd., Lake Mary FL 32746. (407)333-0600. Fax (407)333-7133. E-mail: newman@strang.com. Strang Communications Co. Brian Peterson, ed. dir. To inform and equip men with Christ-centered perspectives in every aspect of their lives to be a godly influence in their worlds. Bimonthly (8X) mag; 100 pgs; circ. 300,000. Subscription $15. Est. 1994. 60% freelance. Query/clips; no phone/fax/e-mail query. Pays $75-800 on publication for all rts. Articles 100-1,800 wds (50/yr). Responds in 10 wks. Seasonal 8 mos ahead. Accepts simultaneous submissions & reprints (tell when/where appeared). Prefers disk. Kill fee. Sidebars OK. Prefers NIV. Guidelines; copy $3. (Ads)

> **Tips:** "We're looking for articles on everyday men who are doing something extraordinary in their area, from all parts of the world. Also action-packed stories, outdoor family adventures (true)."
>
> **Fillers:** Buys 24/yr.Facts, ideas, prose, quizzes, quotes; to 250 wds. Pays .10/wd.
>
> **Columns/Departments:** Buys 15/yr, Women (written to men, about women, by women); Health (men's health concerns); Finances; Career; all to 1,000 wds; $100-300.
>
> ** This periodical was #67 on the 1996 Top 50 Christian Publishers List. Also 1996 EPA Award of Excellence—Organizational.

*NEW OXFORD REVIEW, 1069 Kains Ave., Berkeley CA 94706. (510)526-5374. Catholic. Dale Vree, ed. Orthodox Catholic, but open to compatible evangelical views; highly educated audience. Monthly (10X) mag; circ 14,000. Subscription $19. 50% freelance. Query or complete ms; phone query OK. **PAYS IN COPIES**, for all rts. Articles 750-3,750 wds (15/yr). Responds in 3-6 wks. Seasonal 4 mos ahead. Copy for $3.50.

> **Tips:** "Manuscripts must have intellectual depth."

NEW THOUGHT JOURNAL, 2520 Evelyn Dr., Dayton OH 45409. (513)293-9717. Fax (513)866-9603. E-mail: ntjmag@aol.com. Jeff Ohl, ed. Present-day philosophers, prophets, poets, authors, artists and musicians share their thoughts with refreshing openness as they travel their intuitive paths. Quarterly mag; 44 pgs; circ 5,000. Subscription $14. 100% freelance. Query; fax/e-mail query OK. Pays negotiable rates (indicate your expectation with submission) on publication for one-time rts. Articles & fiction 500-1,500 wds (16 of ea./yr); book/music/video reviews, 250 wds. Does not respond to all submissions. Seasonal 3 mos ahead. Accepts simultaneous submissions & reprints (tell when/where appeared). Prefers disk. Sidebars OK. Guidelines/theme list; copy $5. (Ads)

> **Poetry:** Buys 50/yr. Avant-garde, free verse, light verse; any length. Submit max. 6 poems.
>
> **Fillers:** Ideas, prose, quotes. No payment.
>
> **Tips:** "Always looking for writings inspired by transformative experiences and personal growth, creativity and spirituality, the arts and humanities, health and positive living."

THE NEW TRUMPET, TH130 590 Lower Landing Rd., Blackwood NJ 08012. (609)228-4243. Mae Hart Lovett, ed. To help Christians in their walk and to prepare them for the return of Christ. Irregular newsletter; 16 pgs; circ 1,200. Est. 1993. 100% freelance. Complete ms/cover letter; phone query OK. **PAYS IN COPIES** for one-time rts. Articles 350-800 wds (33/yr); fiction 1,500-2,000 wds (3/yr); book/video reviews, 300 wds. Responds in 4 wks. Accepts simultaneous submissions & reprints (tell when/where appeared). Prefers disk. Sidebars OK. Prefers NIV or NAS. Guidelines; copy for 2 stamps.

> **Poetry:** Accepts 3-5/yr. Free verse, light verse, traditional; 4-24 lines. Submit max. 3-6 poems.
>
> **Fillers:** Accepts 3-4/yr. Anecdotes, cartoons, facts, ideas, jokes, prayers, prose, quizzes, quotes, short humor; 15-30 wds.
>
> **Tips:** "Call to discuss your idea. Looking for men writers. Your idea should excite you and the reader, be biblically based, and comfort or build the reader's faith. I like story, fact or fiction."

NEW WRITING MAGAZINE, Box 1812, Amherst NY 14226-7812. (716)834-1067. E-mail: newwriting@aol.com. Website: http://members.aol.com/Box1812/. New Writing Agency. Sam Meade, co-ed. The best of new writing by beginning and established writers. Semiannual electronicmag. Free on the Internet. 95% freelance. Complete ms/cover letter; e-mail query ok. **NO PAYMENT** for one-time rts. Not copyrighted. Articles (3/yr); fiction (10/yr). Responds in 4-8 wks. Seasonal 6 mos ahead. Accepts simultaneous submissions & reprints (tell when/where appeared). Guidelines. (Ads)

> **Poetry:** Buys 10/yr. Avant-garde, free verse, traditional; any length. Submit max. 5 poems.
>
> **Contest:** "We run a writing contest and agency. Send SASE for details."

NO-DEBT LIVING, PO Box 282, Veradale WA 99037-0282. Phone/fax (509)927-1322 (call for fax). E-mail: nodebtnews@aol.com or nodebt@NS.poweramp.com. Robert E. Frank, ed. Financial and home-management information from a Christian perspective. Monthly newsletter; 8-12 pgs; circ. 1,000. Subscription $25.95. Est. 1993. 50% freelance. Query/clips; fax/e-mail query OK. Pays $20-50 on publication for 1st rts. Articles 200-1,000 wds (30/yr); 400-600 wds (vignettes). Responds in 3 wks. Seasonal 3 mos ahead. Accepts simultaneous submissions & reprints (tell when/where appeared). Prefers disk or E-mail in ASCII format. Sidebars OK. Prefers NIV or NAS. Guidelines/theme list; copy for 6x9 SAE/3 stamps.

> **Tips:** "Follow AP style. Use original quotes from two well-known professionals (preferably Christians). Link story to a current news trend or issue."

*THE NORTH AMERICAN VOICE OF FATIMA, 1023 Swan Rd., Youngstown NY 14174. (716)754-7489. Catholic. Rev. Stephen McGee, C.R.S.P., ed. To foster Christian ideals with emphasis on Mary, Mother of God, and Mother of the Church. Bimonthly mag; 20 pgs; circ 3,000. 40% freelance. Query or complete ms. Pays .02/wd on publication for 1st rts. Not copyrighted. Articles & fiction 700 wds. Responds in 6 wks. Seasonal 6 mos ahead. Accepts simultaneous submissions. Free copy.

+NORTHSTATE CHRISTIAN TIMES,, PO Box 493954, Redding CA 96049. (916)221-0326. Rick Flynn, ed. Christian Newspaper. Not in topical listings.

NORTHWEST CHRISTIAN JOURNAL, Box 59014, Renton WA 98058. (206)255-3552. Fax (206)228-8749. Tami Tedrow, ed. News with an evangelical perspective for NW Christians; local features & news stories. Monthly tabloid; 16-32 pgs; circ 27,000. Subscription $15. Little freelance. Query/clips. Pays $35 on publication for one-time or simultaneous rts. Articles 500-750 wds. Responds in 6-8+ wks. Accepts simultaneous submissions & reprints. Accepts disk. Some sidebars. Prefers NIV. Guidelines; copy $1.50. (Ads)

> **Tips:** "This is a news publication, which means we look for stories that are timely and reflect what's happening in the Northwest. No devotional material; we have a news focus/news style. Local writers wanted. Most open to news/interviews assigned by the editor."

NORTHWESTERN LUTHERAN, 2929 N Mayfair Rd., Milwaukee WI 53222-4398. (414)256-3888. Fax (414)256-3899. E-mail: nl@sab.wels.net. Wisconsin Evangelical Lutheran Synod. Gary P. Baumler, ed. Denominational. Monthly mag; 36 pgs; circ 55,000. Subscription $9. 25% freelance. Complete ms/cover letter; no phone/fax/e-mail query. Pays $50/pg on publication for one-time rts. Articles 500-1,000 wds (50/yr). Responds in 4-6 wks. Seasonal 4 mos ahead. Accepts reprints (tell when/where appeared). Accepts disk. Sidebars OK. Prefers NIV. Guidelines; copy for 9x12 SAE/2 stamps.

> **Tips:** "Most of our writers belong to the denomination and write about our members, organizations or institutions. Most open to strong personal witness; strong inspirational example of Christian living."

OBLATES, 9480 N. De Mazenod Dr., Belleville IL 62223-1160. (618)398-4848. Fax (618)398-8788. Catholic/Missionary Assn. of Missionary Oblates of Mary Immaculate. Mary Mohrman, mss ed. To inspire, comfort, uplift, and motivate an older Catholic/Christian audience. Bimonthly mag; 20 pgs; circ 500,000. Free to members. 33% freelance. Complete ms/cover letter; no phone/fax query. Pays $80 on acceptance for 1st rts. Articles 500-600 wds (40/yr). Responds in 6-8 wks. Seasonal 6 mos ahead. Considers simultaneous submissions. No disk. No sidebars. Prefers NAB. Guidelines; copy for 6x9 SAE/2 stamps.

> **Poetry:** Buys 20-25/yr. Free verse, traditional; 12-20 lines; $30. Submit max. 3 poems.
>
> **Tips:** "Need personal, inspirational articles with a strong spiritual theme firmly grounded to a particular incident and poetry."

OUR FAMILY, Box 249, Battleford SK S0M 0E0 Canada. (306)937-7771. Fax (306)937-7644. Catholic/Missionary Oblates of St. Mary's Province. Fr. Nestor Gregoire, ed. All aspects of family life in the light of Christian faith. Monthly (11X) mag; 40 pgs; circ 10,000. Subscription $15.98. 50% freelance. Query or complete ms. Pays .07-.10/wd on acceptance for 1st rts. Articles 500-2,500 wds (75/yr). Responds in 4-6 wks. Seasonal 4 mos ahead. Accepts simultaneous submissions & reprints. Sidebars OK. Guidelines/theme list; copy $2.50/9x12 SAE./Canadian postage or IRCs. (Ads)

> **Poetry:** Buys 44/yr. Free verse, haiku, light verse, traditional; 2-25 lines; $.75-$1/line.
>
> **Fillers:** Buys 40/yr. Anecdotes, cartoons, jokes, short humor; to 150 wds.
>
> **Tips:** "Your SASE must have Canadian postage. We aim at the average reader. Looking for articles which deal with specific Catholic issues; articles

that are rooted in social justice, service to others, and the Sunday liturgy. Articles need an experiential point of view with practical guidelines."

** This periodical was #39 on the 1996 Top 50 Christian Publishers list. (#39 in 1995, #29 in 1994)

*OUR SUNDAY VISITOR, 200 Noll Plaza, Huntington IN 46750. (219)356-8400. Fax (219)356-8472. Catholic. David Scott, ed. Vital news, spirituality for today's Catholic. Weekly newspaper; 24 pgs; circ 120,000. Subscription $36. 5% freelance. Query. Pays $150-250 on acceptance for 1st rts. Articles to 1,000 wds (25/yr). Responds in 5 wks. Seasonal 2 mos ahead. Kill fee. Guidelines; Copy for #10 SASE.

Columns/Departments: Buys 50/yr. Viewpoint (editorial/op-ed), 750 wds, $100.

Tips: "Need familiarity with Catholic Church issues and with Catholic Press—newspapers and magazines."

** #1 on the 1994 Top 50.

PARENTLIFE, 127 Ninth Ave. N., Nashville TN 37234-0140. (615)251-2226. Fax (615)251-5008. Southern Baptist/LifeWay Press. Michelle Hicks, mng. ed. For parents of children—birth to 12 years. Monthly mag; 50 pgs; circ 115,000. Subscription $19.95. Est. 1994. 50% freelance. Query or complete ms/cover letter; phone/fax query OK. Pays $75-300 on acceptance for all, first, or one-time rts. Articles 500-1,000 wds (15-20/yr); fiction (1-2/yr). Responds in 6 wks. Seasonal 6 mos ahead. Considers simultaneous submissions. No disk. Sidebars OK. Prefers NIV. Guidelines/theme list; copy for 9x12 SAE/4 stamps.

Fillers: Buys 50+/yr. Anecdotes, cartoons, ideas, party ideas; 25-200 wds; $20-75.

Columns/Departments: Kid's Kitchen (cooking), 100-400 wds; Make It (crafts), 100-400 wds; Growth Spurt (age-appropriate advice), 400-500 wds. Pays $25-100. Complete ms.

Tips: "Looking for holiday topics. Query for fiction."

** This periodical was #27 on the 1996 Top 50 Christian Publishers list. (#40 in 1995)

+THE PARENT PAPER, PO Box 1313, Manchester TN 37355. (615)728-8309. Fax (615)723-1902. E-mail: rhurst@edge.net. Rebekah Hurst, pub. A Christian perspective on topics that benefit the family. Monthly newspaper; circ. 5,000; free subscription. Complete ms. **PAYS 3 COPIES FOR NOW** for 1st or reprint rts. Articles; fiction from youth writers (400-600 words). Seasonal 6 mos ahead. Accepts simultaneous submissions & reprints. Guidelines; copy for 9x12 SAE/4 stamps.

Poetry: Accepts 6/yr

THE PEGASUS REVIEW, PO Box 88, Henderson MD 21640-0088. (410)482-6736. Art Bounds, ed. Theme oriented poetry, short fiction & essays; not necessarily religious. Bimonthly mag; 6-8 pgs; circ 125. Subscription $10. 100% freelance. Query or complete ms/cover letter; no phone query. **PAYS 2 COPIES** for one-time rts. Fiction 2 pgs, single-spaced (10-12/yr); also one-page essays. Responds in 4 wks. Accepts simultaneous submissions & reprints (tell when/where appeared). No sidebars. Guidelines/theme list; copy $2.50/#10 SAE/1 stamp.

Poetry: Accepts 60-80/yr. Any type; to 24 lines (shorter the better). Theme oriented. Submit max. 5 poems.

Fillers: Accepts 6 cartoons /yr.

Special Needs: 1997 themes are: laughter, earth, home, patriotism, books, and holidays.

Tips: "We are open to beginners as well as professional writers, with the emphasis on beginner writers."

PENTECOSTAL EVANGEL, 1445 Boonville, Springfield MO 65802-1894. (417)862-2781. Fax (417)862-0416. E-mail: pevangel@ag.org. Assemblies of God. Hal Donaldson, ed.; submit to Ann Floyd, tech. & research ed. Denominational; Pentecostal. Weekly mag; 32 pgs; circ 245,000. Subscription $23.95. 10% freelance. Complete ms/cover letter. Pays .06/wd (.03/wd for reprints) on acceptance for 1st rts. Articles 1,000-1,200 wds (100/yr); book reviews 150-200 wds, $20. Responds in 8-10 wks. Seasonal 3 mos ahead. Kill fee 100%. Accepts disk. Sidebars OK. Prefers NIV or KJV. Guidelines; copy $1. (Ads)

Tips: "General inspirational articles with a strong focus; salvation-type articles for the unsaved; feature articles targeted to the unsaved (we will have 12 evangelism issues a year."

** This periodical was #28 on the 1996 Top 50 Christian Publishers list. (#11 in 1995, #23 in 1994)

PENTECOSTAL HOMELIFE, 8855 Dunn Rd., Hazelwood MO 63042-2299. (314)837-7300. Fax (314)837-4503. E-mail: Gyouth8855@aol.com. United Pentecostal Church. Scott Graham, ed. Addresses relevant topics for the Christian family. Bimonthly mag; 16 pgs; circ 1,500. 40% freelance. Complete ms/cover letter; phone/fax/e-mail query OK. Pays $30 on publication for one-time or simultaneous rts. Articles 500-1,500 wds (12/yr); fiction 500-1,500 wds (12/yr). Responds in 3-4 wks. Seasonal 6 mos ahead. Accepts simultaneous submissions & reprints(tell when/where appeared). No disk. Some sidebars. Prefers KJV. Guidelines; copy for 10x13 SAE.

Poetry: Buys 3-4/yr. Light verse, traditional; 4-50 lines. Pays $15-30. Submit max. 2 poems.

Fillers: Buys 2/yr. Cartoons, games, quizzes, word puzzles. Pays $15-30.

Tips: "Most open to fiction and relationships."

#THE PENTECOSTAL TESTIMONY, 6745 Century Ave., Mississauga ON L5N 6P7 Canada. (905)542-7400. Fax (905)542-7313. E-mail: testimony@paoc.org. The Pentecostal Assemblies of Canada. Rick Hiebert, ed. Focus is inspirational and Christian living; Pentecostal holiness slant. Monthly mag; 28 pgs; circ 23,500. Subscription $24 US/$17 CAN. 10-15% freelance. Query; phone/fax query OK. Pays $20-60 ($50-75 for fiction) on publication for all or 1st rts. Articles 600-1,300 wds (20/yr); fiction 1,400-1,600 wds (6/yr). Responds in 12-24 wks. Seasonal 6 mos ahead. Accepts reprints. Prefers disk. Sidebars OK. Prefers NIV. Guidelines; copy $2. (Ads)

Poetry: Buys 4-6/yr. Avant-garde, free verse; 8-20 lines; $20. Submit max. 3 poems.

Fillers: Buys 10-12/yr. Anecdotes, cartoons, short humor; 300-500 wds; $20-30.

Tips: "Sell your idea with a concise, yet detailed, query with some humor.

Don't make references to US locations or events."

#PERSPECTIVES, A Journal of Reformed Thought, PO Box 470, Ada MI 49301-0470. (616)285-8074. E-mail: 70134.222@compuserve.com. Reformed Church Press. Craig W. Stapert, mng ed. To express the Reformed faith theologically; to engage issues that Reformed Christians meet in personal, ecclesiastical, and societal life. Monthly (10X) mag; 24 pgs; circ. 3,000. Subscription $19.95. Query; phone/e-mail query OK. **NO PAYMENT.** Articles, and fiction (2/yr) 1,750-3,500 wds. Responds in 4-6 wks. Seasonal 4+ mos ahead. Prefers disk (IBM). Rarely uses sidebars. Prefers NRSV. Copy for 9x12 SAE/$1.50 postage. (Ads)

> **Poetry:** Francis Fike. Accepts 5-10/yr. Submit max. 6 poems.

+PHYSICIAN, 8605 Explorer Dr., Colorado Springs CO 80920. (719)548-4575. Fax (719)531-3499. Focus on the Family. Melissa Cox, ed. To encourage physicians and their families. Bimonthly mag; 24 pgs; circ 55,000. Free to medical profession. 15% freelance. Query; fax query OK. Pays .10/wd on publication for 1st rts. Articles 800-2,400 wds. Responds in 8 wks. No seasonal. Requires disk. Kill fee. Sidebars OK. Copy available.

> **Fillers:** Cartoons; $75.

> **Tips:** "Call ahead. Be a physician. Understand the medical industry."

+A PLACE TO ENTER, 1328 Broadway, Ste. 1054, New York NY 10001. Brian Iton, ed-in-chief. Literary magazine that publishes some religious fiction. Complete ms/one-page bio. Pays $100 after publication. Fiction to 5,000 wds. Guidelines.

+THE PLAIN TRUTH, 300 W. Green St., Pasadena CA 91129. (818)304-6077. Fax (818)795-0107. E-mail: Susan_Stewart@ptm.org. Plain Truth Ministries. Susan Stewart, assoc. ed. Proclaims the Gospel of Jesus Christ, emphasizing the central teachings of Christianity and making those teachings plain and truthful. Bimonthly mag; 48 pgs; circ 102,000. Subscription $12.95. 75% freelance. Query/clips; fax/e-mail query OK. Pays .25/wd on publication for one-time and world (all languages) rts. Articles 550-2,500 wds (30/yr); book/music/video reviews 100 wds, $25. Responds in 4-6 wks. Seasonal 4-6 mos ahead. Accepts simultaneous submissions & reprints (tell when/where appeared). Requires disk. Kill fee 10%. Sidebars OK. Prefers NIV. Guidelines; copy for 10x13 SAE/4 stamps. (Ads)

> **Columns/Departments:** Buys 18/yr. Family (family issues), 1,500 wds; Commentary (hot topic editorials), 550-650 wds; Christian People (testimonial/interviews), 1,500 wds. Query or complete ms.

> **Tips:** "Best to send tear sheets of previously published articles and submit detailed query for standard articles."

*PLENTY GOOD ROOM, 1800 N. Hermitage Ave., Chicago IL 60622-1101. (773)486-8970. Catholic. J. Glen Murray, ed. Focuses on African-American worship within the church. Bimonthly mag; 12 pgs. Est. 1993. Query. Pays $25/pg, for all rts. Articles. Responds in 13 wks. Guidelines; free copy.

+PLOUGH, Spring Valley, RD 2 Box 446, Farmington PA 15437. (412)329-1100. Fax (412)329-0914. E-mail: brud@esslink.com. Bruderhof Communities. Christoph Arnold, ed. Dedicated to all who work for a personal transformation in Christ and for a radical turn away from the materialism, militarism, racism, and impurity of this world towards the coming of God's kingdom. Mag pub. 4-6X/yr;

circ 7,500. No subscription. Some freelance. Query. Not in topical listings.

THE PLOWMAN, Box 414, Whitby ON L1N 5S4 Canada. (905)668-7801. The Plowman Ministries/Christian. Tony Scavetta, pub. Poetry and prose of social commentary; any topics. Irregular newspaper; 20 pgs; circ 10,000. Subscription $10/$12 outside Canada. 90% freelance. Query; phone query OK. **NO PAYMENT**. Articles (10/yr) & fiction (50/yr), 20-25 lines; book reviews 6-8 lines. Responds in 1 wk. Accepts simultaneous submissions & reprints. No disk. No sidebars. Free guidelines/copy. (Ads)

> **Poetry:** Accepts 100/yr. Free verse, haiku, traditional; to 38 lines (55 characters across max.). Submit max. 5 poems.
>
> **Fillers:** Accepts 25/yr. Anecdotes, prose, prayers; 25-30 wds.
>
> **Special Needs:** Also publishes chapbooks; 20% royalties. Open to all topics.
>
> **Contest:** Sponsors a poetry contest; $2/poem.

*PLUS, 66 E. Main St., Pawling NY 12564. (914)855-5000. Fax (914)855-1462. Peale Center for Christian Living. Pat Planeta, sr. ed. Spiritually oriented, based on positive thinking and faith. Monthly (10X) mag; 36 pgs; circ 600,000. Subscription $10. 30% freelance. Complete ms/cover letter; phone/fax query OK. Pays $25/pg on publication for 1st or one-time rts. Articles 500-2,500 wds (8/yr). Responds in 3-4 wks. Seasonal 6 mos ahead. Accepts reprints. Some sidebars. Guidelines; copy for #10 SAE/1 stamp.

> **Tips:** "Have a deep, living knowledge of evangelical Christianity. Our audience is 65-70% female, average age is 55."
>
> ****** This periodical was #31 on the 1995 Top 50 Christian Publishers list.

POETRY FORUM SHORT STORIES, 5713 Larchmont Dr., Erie PA 16509. Phone/fax (814)866-2543. E-mail: 75562.670@compuserve.com. Interdenominational. Gunvor Skogsholm, ed. Poetry and prose that takes an honest look at the human condition. Bimonthly mag; 20-24 pgs; circ 500+. Subscription $18. 90% freelance. Complete ms/cover letter; fax/e-mail query OK. **NO PAYMENT** for one-time rts (buys only from subscribers). Articles 100-800 wds; fiction 800-3,000 wds. Responds in 4-13 wks. Accepts simultaneous submissions. Guidelines; copy $3. (Ads)

> **Poetry:** Inspirational; any type.
>
> **Contest:** Send SASE for information.

POET'S PARK, 2745 Monterey Hwy #76, San Jose CA 95111-3129. E-mail: soos@soos.com. Website: http://www.soos.com/poetpark. Redwood Family Chapel. Submit to: poetry@soos.com. Known as "the resting spot on the information super highway;" on-line to provide spiritual refreshing for those who are browsing the Web. Quarterly mag. Free. 100% freelance. Query on-line only/one poem. **NO PAYMENT** for one-time rts. Articles 350-2,500 wds (12/yr). Responds in 4 wks. Accepts simultaneous submissions & reprints. Requires disk or e-mail. Sidebars OK. Guidelines; view online only at above Website. (Ads)

> **Poetry:** Accepts 600-800/yr. Any type; 1-60 lines; submit via e-mail; one only.

*POSITIVE LIVING, 66 E. Main St., Pawling NY 12564. (914)855-5000. Fax (914)855-1462. Peale Center for Christian Living. Ric Cox, exec. ed.; submit to Pat Planeta, sr. ed. A spiritual, motivational, self-improvement magazine for the 40 year old. Monthly (10X) mag; 40 pgs. Est. 1995. Query or complete ms/cover letter. Pays $125- $500 ($125/pg) on acceptance. Articles 1,500-2,500 wds. Responds in 4 wks. Seasonal 4 mos ahead. Accepts reprints ($50/pg). Guidelines.

POURASTAN, 615 Stuart Ave., Outremont QB H2V 3H2 Canada. (514)279-3066. Fax (514)276-9960. Canadian Diocese of the Armenian Holy Apostolic Church. Mr. N. Ouzounian, ed. Denominational; religious, social and community oriented. Bimonthly mag; 24-28 pgs; circ 1,000. Free for donations. 100% freelance. Complete ms/cover letter; phone/fax query OK. **NO PAYMENT.** Not copyrighted. Articles 250-1,500 wds(10/yr); book reviews, 300 wds. Seasonal 1 mo ahead. Accepts simultaneous submissions & reprints. No sidebars. Accepts disk. Copy for 9x12 SAE/90 cents.

Poetry: Accepts 10/yr. Traditional, 4-40 lines. Submit max. 2 poems.

Fillers: Anecdotes, ideas, prayers, quotes, short humor, 10-50 wds.

Note: This publication is published in Armenian with occasional English and French.

POWER FOR LIVING, Box 36640, Colorado Springs CO 80936. (719)536-0100x3989. Fax (719)536-3243. Cook Communications/Scripture Press. Don Alban Jr., ed. To help adults relate the Power of God and His Word to their everyday lives. Weekly take-home paper; 8 pgs; circ 250,000. Subscription $11. 35% freelance. Complete ms; no phone/fax/e-mail query. Pays up to 15/wd (reprints up to .10/wd) on acceptance for 1st, one-time, or reprint rts. Articles to 1,500 wds (25/yr). Responds in 13-18 wks. Seasonal 1 yr ahead. Accepts reprints (tell when/where appeared). Accepts disk. Few sidebars. Guidelines/copy for #10 SAE/1 stamp.

Fillers: Buys 10-15/yr. Cartoons, word puzzles; $25-50.

Tips: "Most open to vignettes, 450-1,000 wds, of prominent Christians with solid testimonies or profiles from church history. Focus on the unusual. Signed releases required. We prefer paraphrases of Bible verses, not direct quotes."

** This periodical was #11 on the 1996 Top 50 Christian Publishers list. (#9 in 1995, #21 in 1994)

#PRAIRIE MESSENGER, PO Box 190, Muenster SK S0K 2Y0 Canada. (306)682-1772. Fax (306)682-5285. E-mail: ccnpm@explorer.sasknet.sk.ca. Catholic. Marion Noll, OSU, assoc. ed. For Catholics in Saskatchewan & Manitoba, and Christians in other faith communities. Weekly journal; circ 7,800. Subscription $22.50 CAN. 10% freelance. Complete ms/cover letter; phone/fax/e-mail query OK. Pays to $40-60 ($2/column inch for news items) on publication for 1st, one-time, simultaneous & reprint rts. Not copyrighted. Articles to 250-600 wds (15/yr). Responds in 9 wks. Seasonal 3 mos ahead. Accepts simultaneous submissions & reprints. Sidebars OK. Guidelines; copy for 9x12 SAE/$1 CAN/$1.24 US.

Poetry: Accepts 48/yr. Free verse; 6-25 lines.

Special Needs: Ecumenism; social justice; native concerns.

Tips: "Comment/feature section is most open. Send topic of concern or interest to Prairie readership. It's difficult to break into our publication."

** This periodical was selected #1 for general excellence by the Canadian Church Press.

PRAYERWORKS, PO Box 301363, Portland OR 97294. (503)761-2072. Fax

(503)760-1184. E-mail: 7653.3202@compuserve.com. V. Ann Mandeville, ed. For prayer warriors in retirement centers; focuses on prayer. Weekly newspaper; 4 pgs; circ 600. Free subscription. 100% freelance. Complete ms; phone/fax query OK. **PAYS IN COPIES**, for one-time rts. Not copyrighted. Articles (30-40/yr) & fiction (30/yr); 300-500 wds. Responds in 3 wks. Seasonal 2 mos ahead. Accepts simultaneous submissions & reprints. No sidebars. Guidelines; copy for #10 SAE/1 stamp.

> **Poetry:** Accepts 20-30/yr. Free verse, haiku, light verse, traditional. Submit max. 10 poems.
>
> **Fillers:** Accepts up to 50/yr. Facts, jokes, prayers, quotes, short humor; to 50 wds.
>
> **Tips:** "Write tight. Half our audience is over 70, but 30% is young families. Subject matter isn't important as long as it is scriptural and designed to help people pray."

#THE PRESBYTERIAN LAYMAN, 520 Mulberry St. SW, Lenoir NC 28645. (704)758-8716. Fax (704)758-0920. Presbyterian Lay Committee. Parker T. Williamson, exec. ed. For the conservative/evangelical members of the Presbyterian Church (USA). Bimonthly newspaper; 24 pgs; circ. 520,000. No subscriptions. 10% freelance. Query. Pays negotiable rates on publication for 1st rts. Articles 800-1,200 wds (12/yr). Responds in 2 wks. Seasonal 2 mos ahead. Prefers disk. Sidebars OK. Copy for 9x12 SAE/3 stamps.

> **Poetry:** Traditional; pay negotiable. Submit max. 1 poem.

THE PRESBYTERIAN OUTLOOK, Box 85623, Richmond VA 23285-5623. (804)359-8442. Fax (804)353-6369. E-mail: outlook.parti@pcusa.org. Presbyterian Church (USA)/Independent. Robert H. Bullock Jr., ed. For ministers, members and staff of the denomination. Weekly (43X) mag; 16-40 pgs; circ 11,700. Subscription $27.25. 5% freelance. Query; phone/fax /e-mail query OK. **NO PAYMENT** for all rts. Not copyrighted. Articles to 1,000 wds; book reviews 1 1/2 pgs. Responds in 1-2 wks. Seasonal 2 mos ahead. Requires disk. Occasional sidebar. Prefers NRSV. Guidelines; copy for #10 SAE/2 stamps.

> **Tips:** "Correspond with editor regarding current needs. Most material is commissioned; anything submitted should be of interest to Presbyterians."

#PRESBYTERIAN RECORD, 50 Wynford Dr., North York ON M3C 1J7 Canada. (416)444-1111. Fax (416)441-2825. E-mail: perecord@web.ape.org. Website: http://www.presbycan.ca/. Presbyterian Church in Canada. Rev. John Congram, ed. Denominational. Monthly (11X) mag; 52 pgs; circ 60,000. 50% freelance. Query (preferred) or complete ms/cover letter; fax query OK. Pays $50 (CAN) on publication for 1st, one-time, reprint or simultaneous rts. Articles 1,000-1,500 wds (15-20/yr); book/music reviews, to 400 wds/no pay. Responds in 9-13 wks. Seasonal 3 mos ahead. Accepts simultaneous submissions & reprints. Sidebars OK. Guidelines; copy for 9x12 SAE/$1 Canadian postage or IRCs from US writers.

> **Poetry:** Thomas Dickey. Buys 8-15/yr. Free verse, haiku, light verse traditional; 10-30 lines preferred; $35-50. Send any number.
>
> **Fillers:** Buys 6/yr. Anecdotes, cartoons, facts, ideas, prose, prayers, short humor; to 200 wds; $15-25.
>
> **Columns/Departments:** Buys 12/yr. Full Count (controversial issues), 750 wds; $35-50.

Tips: "It helps if submissions have some connection to Canada and/or the Presbyterian Church."

#PRESBYTERIANS TODAY, 100 Witherspoon St., Louisville KY 40202-1396. (502)569-5637. Fax (502)569-8632. E-mail: today@pcusa.org. Presbyterian Church (USA). Catherine Cottingham, mng. ed. Denominational; not as conservative or evangelical as some. Monthly (10X) mag; 44 pgs; circ 90,000. Subscription $12.95. 65% freelance. Complete ms/cover letter; fax/e-maile query OK. Pays $200 before publication for 1st rts. Articles 1,200-1,500 wds (20/yr). Responds in 4-5 wks. Seasonal 4 mos ahead. Some reprints. Kill fee. Guidelines; free copy. (Ads)

Fillers: Cartoons, $25, short humor to 100 wds, no payment.

Tips: "Most open to feature articles or news articles about Presbyterian people and programs (600-800 wds, $75). Do not often use inspirational or testimony-type articles."

** This periodical was #64 on the 1996 Top 50 Christian Publishers list. (#41 in 1995)

PRISM, 10 Lancaster Ave., Wynnewood PA 19096-3495. (610)645-9391. Fax (610)649-8090. E-mail: prism@esa.mhs.compuserve.com. Evangelicals for Social Action. Dwight Ozard, ed. For Christians who are interested in the social and political dimensions of the gospel. Bimonthly mag; 44 pgs; circ 10,000. Est. 1993. Subscription $25. 15% freelance. Query/clip; fax/e-mail query OK. Pays $200 ($100 for fiction) 6 wks after publication for 1st or reprint rts. Articles 500-2,800 wds (5/yr); fiction, 700-1,600 wds (1/yr); book/video reviews, 500 wds, $0-100. Responds in 8-12 wks. Seasonal 6 mos ahead. Accepts reprints (tell when/where appeared). Prefers disk. Sidebars OK. Prefers NRSV. Guidelines; copy $3. (Ads)

Tips: "Looking for analysis on religious right; social justice fiction. Understand progressive evangelicals and E.S.A. Read Tony Campolo, Ron Sider and Richard Foster. Most open to features."

PROGRESS, Box 9609, Kansas City MO 64134. (816)763-7800. Fax (816)765-2522. Stonecroft Ministries. Susan Collard, mng. ed. For women and their families who are involved in some aspect of Stonecroft Ministries. Bimonthly mag; 64 pgs; circ 30,000. Subscription $8.50. 30% freelance. Complete ms/cover letter; phone/fax query OK. **PAYS IN COPIES,** for 1st rts. Not copyrighted. Articles 300-2,000 wds (25/yr). Responds in 2-3 wks. Seasonal 5-6 mos ahead. Accepts reprints. Guidelines; copy for 6x9 SAE/3 stamps.

Columns/Departments: Buys 12-15/yr. Coping Series (how God helped through crisis or stress—prefers other than illness); Family Builders (help for families); 1,000-1,500 wds.

Tips: "We do not include controversial or doctrinal issues about which Christians disagree. Material should be Christ-centered and biblically based. Most open to columns."

PROVIDENCE, PO Box 879, Westerville OH 43081. (614)882-1990. Fax (614)882-9197. E-mail: Prov@netset.com. Bonna, Ltd. Bonnie Peebles, pub. An issues-oriented paper with a Christian "spin." Monthly newspaper; 24 pgs; circ. 25,000. Subscription $20. Est. 1995. 30% freelance. Query/clips; phone/fax/e-mail query OK. Pays $15-40 on publication for 1st rts. Articles 400-500 wds. Responds in 4 wks. Accepts reprints (tell when/where appeared). Requires disk. Sidebars OK. Prefers NAS or NIV. Copy available. (Ads)

Fillers: Cartoons.

Columns/Departments: Commentary (current issues), 1,000 wds.

Tips: "Most areas of the paper open. Follow guidelines and meet deadlines."

#PURPOSE, 616 Walnut Ave., Scottdale PA 15683. (412)887-8500. Fax (412)887-3111. E-mail: purpose%mph@mcimail.com. Mennonite Church. James E. Horsch, ed. Denominational, for older youth and adults. Weekly take-home paper; 8 pgs; circ 15,000. Subscription $14.45. 95% freelance. Complete ms (only)/cover letter; phone query OK. Pays .05/wd on acceptance for one-time rts. Articles & fiction, to 750 wds (130/yr). Responds in 9 wks. Seasonal 6 mos ahead. Accepts simultaneous submissions & reprints (tell when/where appeared). Sidebars OK. Guidelines; copy for 6x9 SAE/2 stamps.

Poetry: Buys 130/yr. Free verse, light verse, traditional; 3-12 lines; $2/line. Submit max. 10 poems.

Fillers: Buys 15/yr. Anecdotes, cartoons, short humor; 200-500 wds; .04/wd.

Tips: "Articles must carry a strong story line. First person is preferred. Don't exceed maximum word length."

** This periodical was #48 on the 1996 Top 50 Christian Publishers list. (#20 in 1995, #22 in 1994)

#PURSUIT, 901 E. 78th St., Minneapolis MN 55420. (800)995-5360. (612)854-1300. Fax (612)853-8488. Evangelical Free Church. Carol Madison, ed; submit to Joyce Ellis, asst. ed. An evangelistic magazine written for the unchurched. Quarterly mag; 32 pgs; circ 50,000. Subscription $8. 100% freelance. Query. Pays .10/wd on publication for one-time rts. Articles 800-2,000 wds (20/yr). Responds in 4-6 wks. Seasonal 6 months ahead. Accepts simultaneous submissions & reprints if advised. Kill fee 25%. Guidelines; copy $1/9x12 SAE/4 stamps. (Ads)

Tips: "Study the magazine. Write about what the unchurched are interested in, touching especially on felt needs. Along with complete article, please submit suggested theme for issue and two or three companion article ideas."

#QUEEN OF ALL HEARTS, 26 S. Saxon Ave., Bay Shore NY 11706-8993. (516)665-0726. Fax (516)665-4349. Catholic/Montfort Missionaries. Rev. Roger M. Charest, SMM, mng. ed. Focus is Mary, the Mother of Jesus. Bimonthly mag; 48 pgs; circ 4,000. Subscription $17. 50% freelance. Complete ms/cover letter. Pays $40-60 on acceptance for one-time rts. Not copyrighted. Articles (25/yr) and fiction (6/yr)1,000-2,000 wds. Responds in 9 wks. Seasonal 6 mos ahead. No sidebars. Guidelines; copy for 9x12 SAE/$2.50.

Poetry: Joseph Tusiani. Buys 10/yr. Free verse; to 25 lines. Pays 2 year subscription and 6 copies. Submit max. 2 poems. Pays copies.

*THE QUIET REVOLUTION, 1655 St. Charles St., Jackson MS 39209. (601)353-1635. Voice of Calvary Ministries. Cornelius J. Jones, ed. Interracial ministry to the poor; conservative/evangelical. Quarterly mag; 7 pgs; circ 3,000. 10% freelance. Query or complete ms/cover letter. **NO PAYMENT** for one-time rts. Articles 3-4 pgs. Responds in 5 wks. Accepts reprints. Free copy.

Tips: "Most open to articles about ministering to the poor."

*RATIO: Essays in Christian Thought, 350 Canner St. #405, New Haven CT 06511-2254. Jeff Bearce, ed. For an academic/intellectual audience anchored in the humanities; deals with theology, biblical studies, psychology, science, etc. Semiannual journal; circ 100. 15-20% freelance. Query. **NO PAYMENT.** Not copyrighted. Articles, fiction & book reviews.

#RELEASE INK, 404 BNA Dr., Bldg. 200, Ste. 508, Nashville TN 37217. (615)872-8080. Fax (615)889-0437. Thomas Nelson, Inc. Chris Well, ed. Covers Christian books and their authors. Bimonthly mag; circ 100,000. Subscription $12. Open to freelance. (Ads)

RELIGIOUS BROADCASTING, National Religious Broadcasters, 7839 Ashton Ave., Manassas VA 22109. (703)330-7000. Fax (703)330-6996. E-mail: ssmith@ nrb.com. Christine L. Pryor, assoc. ed. Topics relate to Christian radio, television and satellite; promoting access excellence in religious broadcasting. Monthly (10X) mag; 84 pgs; circ 8,500. Subscription $24. 30% freelance. Complete ms/cover letter; fax/e-mail query OK. **PAYS 6 COPIES** for 1st or reprint rts. Articles 2,00-2,500 wds (25/yr). Responds in 3 wks. Seasonal 4 mos ahead. Accepts reprints (tell when/where appeared). Prefers disk. Sidebars OK. Prefers NIV & KVJ. Guidelines/theme list; copy for 9x12 SAE/6 stamps. (Ads)

> **Columns/Departments:** Sarah E. Smith. Accepts 100/yr. Trade Talk or Media Focus (news items/events in religious broadcasting), 300 wds; Socially Speaking (social issues), 1,000 wds.
>
> **Special Needs:** Electronic media; education. All articles must relate in some way to broadcasting; radio, TV, programs on radio/TV.
>
> **Tips:** "Most open to feature articles relevant to religious broadcasters. Become acquainted with religious broadcasters in your area and note their struggles, concerns, and victories. Find out what they would like to know, research the topic, then write about it."

*RELIGIOUS EDUCATION, 15600 Mulholland Dr., Los Angeles CA 90077. (310)476-9777x326. Fax (310)471-1278. Religious Education Assn. Hanan A. Alexander, ed-in-chief. A forum for interreligious dialogue for people concerned with issues surrounding religious education. Quarterly journal; circ 3,000. Subscription/membership $40. 95% freelance. Complete ms/cover letter. **PAYS 3 COPIES**, for all rts. Articles to 6,500 wds; book reviews, 250 wds. Responds in 2-3 wks. Guidelines; copy $2.

> **Columns/Departments:** Insights from Scholarship; Insights from Practice; Forum (diverse points of view on topics of interest); and Critique (reviews of books, media and curricula).
>
> **Special Needs:** Religious, theological, values, moral education, spiritual formation or development, character development.

+REMEMBRANCE, Box 394, Society Hill SC 29593. E-mail: EBOONE@aol.com. RSVP Press. Gene Boone, ed. A tribute to loved ones who have passed away. Biannual mag (semi-book form); 60 pgs; circ 250. Subscription $8.95. Est. 1996. 100% freelance. Complete ms/cover letter; e-mail query OK. **PAYS IN COPIES** for one-time rts. Articles to 200-3,000 wds (50/yr). Responds in 2-3 wks. Accepts reprints (tell when/where appeared). Accepts disk. No sidebars. Guidelines/theme list; copy $4.95.

> **Poetry:** Accepts 100-200/yr. Free verse, traditional; 3-50 lines.

*THE REVELATION POST, 187 Cooper St., Cambridge ON N3C 2N9 Canada. (519)651-2896. Fax (519)651-2521. Shining Light Ministries. Brent Hackett, ed.

Gospel outreach newspaper sent to all homes in area; focus is evangelical. Irregular (as funds provide) newspaper; 8-12 pgs; circ. 15,000-45,000. Freewill gifts. Query; phone/fax query OK. **NO PAYMENT** for one-time rts. Articles 300-1,000 wds (flexible). Responds in 2 wks. Accepts simultaneous submissions & reprints. Prefers disk. Prefers KJV. Guidelines/theme list; copy for 6x9 SAE.

Poetry: Accepts 1-2/yr. Traditional. Submit max. 2 poems.

Fillers: Accepts 4-5/yr. Facts, quotes.

Special Needs: Current events in relation to Bible prophecy.

*ROLE MODEL MAGAZINE, PO Box 1336, Lake Arrowhead CA 92352-1336. (909)337-0759. Fax (909)337-0794. Christine Cot, ed. Views entertainment, fashion, and media from a Christian perspective. Quarterly mag; 40-50 pgs; circ. 20,000. Subscription $14. 30% freelance. Query/clips or complete ms/cover letter; fax query OK. Pays on publication for 1st rts. Articles 500-1,500 wds; book reviews 50-500 wds. Responds in 5 wks. Seasonal 3 mos ahead. Copy $3.75.

Poetry: Traditional; short.

RUTHERFORD MAGAZINE, PO Box 7482, Charlottesville VA 22906-7482. (804)978-3888. Fax (804)978-1789. E-mail: rutherford@fni.com. The Rutherford Institute. Tanya Stanciu, ed. Examines current cultural trends, particularly issues affecting religious liberty. Monthly mag; 28 pgs; circ. 30,000. Subscription $21. 50% freelance. Query/clips; phone/fax/e-mail query OK. Pays $75-500 on acceptance for all rts. Articles 600-3,500 wds (15/yr). Responds in 4-6 wks. Accepts simultaneous submissions. Prefers disk. Kill fee. Sidebars OK. Free copy. (Ads)

Fillers: Cartoons. Also needs illustrations.

Columns/Departments: Bobby Maddex. Buys 8/yr. Culture (current book/film/art/theater reviews), 600 wds; $75-150. Query.

Tips: "Looking for probing articles on aspects of popular culture. Send query with clips; we prefer to assign articles to freelancers. Best be familiar with cultural or religious liberty issues."

ST. ANTHONY MESSENGER, 1615 Republic St., Cincinnati OH 45210-1298. (513)241-5615. Fax (513)241-0399. Catholic. Norman Perry, O.F.M., ed. Catholic. Monthly mag; 56 pgs; circ 340,100. Subscription $19. 50% freelance. Query; no phone/fax query. Pays .15/wd on acceptance for 1st, reprint (right to reprint), & electronic rts. Articles to 2,500-3,000 wds (40-50/yr); fiction 2,500-3,000 wds (12/yr); book reviews 500 wds/$25. Responds in 8-10 wks. Seasonal 6 mos ahead. Kill fee. Some sidebars. Prefers NAB. Guidelines; copy for 9x12 SAE. (Ads)

Poetry: Susan Hines-Brigger. Buys 40-50/yr. Free verse, haiku, light verse, traditional; 3-25 lines; $2/line ($10 min.) Submit max. 5 poems.

Special Needs: Catholic celebration of the Millennium.

Tips: "Most open to articles, profiles, interviews of Catholic personalities. Writing must be professional, use Catholic terminology and vocabulary. Writing must be faithful to Catholic belief and teaching, life and experience."
** #40 on the 1994 Top 50.

#ST. JOSEPH'S MESSENGER AND ADVOCATE OF THE BLIND, PO Box 288, Jersey City NJ 07303-0288. (201)798-4141. Catholic/Sisters of St. Joseph of Peace. Sister Ursula Maphet, CSJP, ed. For older Catholics interested in supporting ministry to the aged, young, blind, and needy. Semiannual mag; 16 pgs; circ

20,000. Subscription $5. 30% freelance. Complete ms. Pays variable rates on publication for 1st rts. Articles 500-1,000 wds (24/yr); fiction 1,000-1,500 wds (30/yr). Responds in 5 wks. Seasonal 3 mos ahead. Accepts simultaneous submissions & reprints. No sidebars. Guidelines; copy for 9x12 SAE/2 stamps.

Poetry: Buys 25/yr. Light verse, traditional; 4-40 lines; $5-20 on publication. Submit max. 10 poems.

Fillers: Buys 20/yr. Ideas, 50-100 wds; $5-10.

Tips: "Most open to contemporary fiction."

*ST. WILLIBRORD JOURNAL, Box 271751, Houston TX 77277-1751. Christ Catholic Church. Charles E. Harrison, ed. Strictly Catholic; concentrating on the unchurched. Quarterly journal; 40 pgs; circ 500. 5% freelance. Complete ms/cover letter. **NO PAYMENT** for one-time rts. Not copyrighted. Articles to 1,000 wds. Responds in 9 wks. Seasonal 6 mos ahead. Copy $2.

Columns/Departments: Question Box; Q & A column on doctrinal and biblical questions.

Tips: "We will read anything if it is sincere and orthodox. Most open to what's happening in the Christian church: doctrinal changes, attitude adjustments, moral attitudes."

SALT OF THE EARTH, 205 W. Monroe St., Chicago IL 60202. (312)236-7782. Fax (312)236-8207. E-mail: sote@claret.org. Claretian Publications. Dob Beaulieu, asst. ed. Focus is on social justice and prayer. Bimonthly mag; 40 pgs; circ 9,000. Subscription $18. 90% freelance. Query/clips; fax/e-mail query OK. Pays $300-600 on acceptance for 1st rts. Articles 3,000 wds (50/yr). Responds in 9 wks. Seasonal 6 mos ahead. Accepts simultaneous submissions & reprints (tell when/where appeared). Prefers disk. Kill fee. Sidebars OK. Prefers NAB. Guidelines; free copy. (Ads)

Columns/Departments: Buys 18/yr. Parish File (profile of parish involved in social justice work), 600 wds; Roundtable (responses to survey questions), 1,000 wds; Sourcebook (social service agency profile), 600 wds. Pays $150.

Tips: "All features and departments open. Read guidelines and sample, send in a good query, any background information on the topic, and clips of articles that show proficiency in this type of article."

*THE SALT & THE LIGHT, 27013 Pacific Hwy. S. #157, Kent WA 98032. (206)927-4738. E-mail: JohnOdz@aol.com. J. Jireh Desktop Publishing. Geoff M. Pope, ed. Charismatic; for people who seek unique uses of language that entertain, exhort, confront, and magnify Jesus. Quarterly jour; 26 pgs; circ. 300. Subscription $16. Est. 1995. 75% freelance. Complete ms. **PAYS 3 COPIES** for 1st rts. Seasonal 3 mos ahead. Accepts simultaneous submissions & reprints. Articles 500-2,500 wds (6/yr); fiction 500-2,500 wds (4/yr); book reviews to 2,500 wds. No sidebars.

Tips: "Looking for essays and testimonies."

#SCP JOURNAL/SCP NEWSLETTER, (Spiritual Counterfeits Project), PO Box 4308, Berkeley CA 94704-4308. (510)540-0300. Fax (510)540-1107. Tal Brooke, ed. Christian apologetics for the college educated. Quarterly; 55 pgs; circ 18,000. Subscription $25. 5-10% freelance. Query/clips; phone query encouraged. Pays $20-35/typeset pg on publication for negotiable rts. Articles 2,500-3,500 wds

(5/yr); book reviews 1,500 wds. Responds in 13 wks. Accepts simultaneous query & reprints. Guidelines; copy $8.75

Tips: "Talk to us first."

#SEEK, 8121 Hamilton Ave., Cincinnati OH 45231. (513)931-4050x365. Standard Publishing. Eileen H. Wilmoth, ed. For young and middle-age adults. Weekly take-home paper; 8 pgs; circ 45,000. 98% freelance. Complete ms/cover letter. Pays .05-.07/wd on acceptance for 1st rts, .025/wd for reprint rts. Articles 400-1,200 wds (150-200/yr); fiction 400-1,200 wds. Responds in 13 wks. Seasonal 1 yr ahead. Accepts reprints. Guidelines; copy for 6x9 SAE/2 stamps.

Fillers: Buys 50/yr. Ideas, jokes, short humor; $15.

** This periodical was #49 on the 1996 Top 50 Christian Publishers list. (#57 in 1995, #36 in 1994)

THE SHANTYMAN, 2476 Argentia Rd., Ste. 213, Mississauga ON L5N 6M1 Canada. (905)821-6310. Fax (905)821-6311. Shantymen's Christian Assn. Margaret Sharpe, mng ed. Distributed by their missionaries in remote areas of Canada and northern US as an evangelism tool. Bimonthly mini tabloid; 16 pgs; circ 17,000. Subscription $6. 90% freelance. Complete ms/cover letter; no phone/fax query. Pays $20-50 CAN, on publication for one-time or reprint rts. Articles 800-1,600 wds (30/yr). Responds in 4-6 wks. Seasonal 6 mos ahead. Accepts reprints (tell when/where appeared). No disk. Some sidebars. Prefers NASB. Guidelines; copy for #10 SAE/2 stamps or IRC's.

Columns/Departments: Accepts 6/yr. Way of Salvation (fresh look at Gospel message), 300-400 wds.

Tips: "We always have a need for salvation testimonies, first person (preferred) on as-told-to. We always have too many inspirational stories. No reprints, please, until 1998."

*SHARING, A Journal of Christian Healing, Box 1974, Snoqualmie WA 98065-1974. Phone/fax (206)888-9255. E-mail: rustyra@halcyon.com. Order of St. Luke the Physician. Rusty Rae, ed. For Christians interested in spiritual and physical healing. Monthly (10X) journal; 32 pgs; circ 10,000+. Subscription $20. 100% freelance. Query or complete ms; e-mail query OK. **NO PAYMENT.** Not copyrighted. Articles to 5 typed pages (100-150/yr). Responds in 6 wks. Seasonal 3 mos ahead. Accepts simultaneous submissions & reprints. Prefers disk. Guidelines; copy for 6x9 SAE/2 stamps.

Poetry: Accepts 20-30/yr. Any type or length.

Tips: "Most open to stories of personal healing. We do not return mss or poems, nor do we reply to inquiries regarding mss status."

#SIGNS OF THE TIMES, Box 5353, Nampa ID 83653-5353. (208)465-2500. Fax (208)465-2531.Seventh-day Adventist. Marvin Moore, ed. Biblical principles relevant to all of life; for general public. Monthly mag; 32 pgs; circ 245,000. 40% freelance. Query/clips or complete ms. Pays $100-400 (.20/wd) on acceptance for 1st rts. Articles 500-2,000 wds (75/yr). Responds in 4-9 wks. Seasonal 8 mos ahead. Accepts reprints (tell when/where appeared). Kill fee 50%. Guidelines; copy for 9x12 SAE/3 stamps.

** This periodical was #34 on the 1996 Top 50 Christian Publishers list. (#42 in 1995, #33 in 1994)

*SILVER WINGS, PO Box 1000, Pearblossom CA 93553. (805)264-3726. Jackson

Wilcox, ed. Christian understanding and uplift through poetry. Quarterly mag; 32 pgs; circ 450. Subscription $7. 100% freelance. Complete ms. **PAYS A SUB-SCRIPTION**, for 1st rts. Not copyrighted. Responds in 3 wks. Seasonal anytime. Accepts simultaneous submissions & some reprints. Guidelines; copy $2.

> **Poetry:** Accepts 250/yr. Free verse, haiku, light verse, traditional; 2-20 lines. Submit max. 5 poems.

#SINGLE-PARENT FAMILY, 8605 Explorer Dr., Colorado Springs CO 80920. (719)548-4588. Fax (719)531-3499. Focus on the Family. Dr. Lynda Hunter, ed. To encourage and equip single parents to do the best job they can at creating stable, godly homes for themselves and their children. Monthly mag; 32 pgs; circ. 72,000. Subscription $15. Open to freelance. Query or complete ms. (Ads)

*SMART DADS NEWSLETTER, Box 270616, San Diego CA 92198-2616. (619)487-7099. Fax (619)487-7356. Paul Lewis, ed. Christian fathering/parenting, with strong crossover to secular dads. Bimonthly newsletter; 8 pgs; circ 10,000. Subscription $24 (includes 2 tapes). Little freelance. Complete ms; fax query OK. Pays negotiable rates on publication for 1st rts. Articles 350-900 wds (5/yr). Responds in 2-4 wks. Seasonal 4 mos ahead. Accepts simultaneous submissions. Prefers disk. Some sidebars. Copy for 6x9 SAE/3 stamps.

> **Fillers:** Buys 10/yr. Games, ideas, quotes.
>
> **Columns/Departments:** Buys 5/yr. Making Your Marriage Better; The Single Parent; To Better Love Her; Good Advice; 325-600+ wds.
>
> **Tips:** "We are not a magazine and have tight length requirements. Because of crossover audience, we do not regularly print Scripture references or use traditional God-word language."

+SMILE, PO Box 1534, New Milford CT 06776. Joyce M. Johnson, ed. Poetry journal devoted to cheering up people. Journal. Subscription $7. Complete ms. **PAYS ONE COPY** for 1st or reprint rts. Articles 200 wds (essay or first-person reminiscences). Guidelines; copy $2.

> **Poetry:** To 28 lines.
>
> **Fillers:** Quotes (state source) and short humor.
>
> **Contest:** You must be a subscriber to be eligible for poetry prizes awarded four times per year.
>
> **Tips:** "One-third is devoted to nostalgia, one-third to light humor, and one-third to spiritual/religious thought."

#SOCIAL JUSTICE REVIEW, 3835 Westminster Pl., St. Louis MO 63108-3472. (314)371-1653. Catholic Central Verein of America. Rev. John H. Miller, C.S.C., ed. For those interested in the social teaching of the Catholic Church. Bimonthly journal; 32 pgs; circ 4,600. Subscription $15. 25% freelance. Query. Pays .02/wd on publication for 1st rts. Not copyrighted. Articles 2,000-3,000 wds (80/yr); book reviews 750 wds (no pay). Responds in 2 wks. Seasonal 3 mos ahead. Accepts reprints (tell when/where appeared). No sidebars. Guidelines; copy for 9x12 SAE/3 stamps.

> **Columns/Departments:** Virtue; Economic Justice; variable length. Query.
>
> **Tips:** "Fidelity to papal teaching and clarity and simplicity of style; thoughtful and thought-provoking writing. All areas open."

#SOJOURNERS, 2401 - 15th St. NW, Washington DC 20009. (202)328-8842. Fax (202)328-8757. E-mail: sojourners@ari.net. Karen Lattea, mng ed. For those who seek to turn their lives toward the biblical vision of justice and peace. Bimonthly mag; 68 pgs; circ. 24,000. Subscription $30. 30% freelance. Query. Pays $75-200 on publication for variable rts (no reprints). Articles 600-3,600 wds (10/yr); fiction 600-3,600 wds; book/music reviews, 650-1,300 wds, $50-100. Responds in 6 wks. Seasonal 6 mos ahead. Kill fee. Prefers NRSV. Sidebars OK. Guidelines; copy for 9x12 SAE. (Ads)

Poetry: Rose Marie Berger. Accepts 6-10/yr. Free verse, haiku; $50.

Fillers: Accepts 6 cartoons/yr.

Columns/Departments: Buys 15/yr. Culture Watch (reviews), 650-1,300 wds; Commentary (editorials), 650 wds; New Wineskins (faith issues), 650 wds; and Close to Home (parenting, family, singles), 650 wds; $50-75.

Tips: "Most open to features, Culture Watch, New Wineskins, or Close to Home."

+THE SOMETHING BETTER NEWS,, 2900 Wilson SW, Ste. 107, Grandville MI 49418. (616)530-3957. Fax (616)530-0728. E-mail: SOMEBETNEWS.COM. Jerry Fennell, ed. Christian Newspaper. Monthly tabloid; 20-24 pgs; circ 75,000. Subscription $20. 10% freelance. Query/clips; phone/fax query OK. Negotiable payment on publication for 1st or one-time rts. Articles 750-1,000 wds (8-10/yr); book reviews 500 wds, music/video reviews 750-1,000 wds, $10. Responds in 4 wks. Seasonal 2 mos ahead. Accepts reprints (tell when/where appeared). Requires disk. Some sidebars. Prefers KJV. Guidelines; copy for SAE/ 4 stamps. (Ads)

Columns/Departments: Buys 36/yr. God & Money; Revival; Advice; all 1,000 wds. Pays $10. Query or complete ms.

Special Needs: Wants to expand their Christian entertainment section. Always looking for sports/recreation pieces.

Tips: "Most open to concert reviews and news stories."

+SPIRIT OF REVIVAL, 2000 Morris Dr., Niles MI 49102. (616)684-5905. Fax (616)684-0923. Life Action Ministries. Nancy Leigh DeMoss, ed. Proclaiming and preserving the message of revival. Biannual mag; circ 74,000. Subscription free. Open to freelance. Query. Not in topical listings.

#SPIRITUAL LIFE, 2131 Lincoln Rd. NE, Washington DC 20002-1199. (202)832-8489. Fax (202)832-8967. E-mail: edodonnell@aol.com. Website: http://www. ocd.or.at/. Catholic. Edward O'Donnell, O.C.D., ed. For college-educated Christians interested in spirituality. Quarterly mag; 64 pgs; circ 12,000. 90% freelance. Subscription $15. 80% freelance. Complete ms/cover letter; phone/fax query OK. Pays $50-250 ($10/ms pg) on acceptance for 1st rts. Articles/essays 3,000-5,000 wds (20/yr); book reviews 1,500 wds, $15. Responds in 9 wks. Seasonal 9 mos ahead. Accepts simultaneous submissions. Requires disk. No sidebars. Prefers NAB. Guidelines; copy for 7x10 SAE/5 stamps.

Tips: "No stories of personal healing, conversion, miracles, etc."

SPORTS SPECTRUM, Box 3566, Grand Rapids MI 49501-3566. (616)954-1276. Fax (616)957-5741. E-mail: ssmag@sport.org. Discovery House Publishers. Dave Branon, mng. ed. An evangelistic tool that sports fans can use to witness to non-Christian friends. Monthly mag; 32 pgs; circ 50,000. Subscription $18.97. 60% freelance. Query/clips; fax/e-mail query OK. Pays .15/wd on publication for 1st rts. Articles 725-2,000 wds (60/yr). Responds in 4 wks. Kill fee. Sidebars OK.

Prefers NIV. Guidelines; copy for 9x12 SAE/4 stamps.

Columns/Departments: Buys 18/yr. Leaderboard (Christian athletes serving others), 725 wds; Front Row (on the scene sports scenarios), 800 wds. Pays .15/wd.

Tips: "Show an ability to interview professional athletes and create a well-written article from that interview. Don't interview an athlete on our behalf without our approval. We do welcome ideas/leads from freelancers."

** #69 on the 1994 Top 50. 1996 EPA Award of Merit—General.

#STANDARD, 6401 The Paseo, Kansas City MO 64131. (816)333-7000. Fax (816)333-4439. Nazarene. Rev. Everett Leadingham, ed. Examples of Christianity in everyday life for adults college-age through retirement. Weekly take-home paper; 8 pgs; circ 160,000. Subscription $8.95. 100% freelance. Complete ms/cover letter. Pays .035/wd (.02/wd for reprints) on acceptance for 1st or reprint rts. Articles or fiction 300-1,700 wds (200/yr). Responds in 10 wks. Seasonal 6 mos ahead. Accepts simultaneous submissions & reprints. Few sidebars. Prefers NIV. Guidelines/copy for #10 SAE/2 stamps.

Poetry: Buys 50/yr. Free verse, haiku, light verse, traditional; to 20 lines; $5 (.25/line). Submit max. 5 poems.

Fillers: Buys 25/yr. Cartoons, word puzzles; $5.

Tips: "Fiction or true-experience stories must demonstrate Christianity in action. Show us, don't tell us. Action in stories must conform to Wesleyan-Armenian theology and practices."

** This periodical was #41 on the 1996 Top 50 Christian Publishers list. (#12 in 1995, #2 in 1994)

#THE STANDARD, 2002 S. Arlington Hts. Rd., Arlington Hts. IL 60005. (847)228-0200. Fax (847)228-5376. E-mail: gmbgcstd@aol.com. Baptist General Conference. Jodi Hanning, mng. ed. Denominational. Monthly (10X) mag; 32 pgs; circ. 11,000. Subscription $15.75. 90% freelance. Query; fax/e-mail query OK. Pays $20-200 on publication for 1st rts. Articles 250-2,000 wds (60/yr). Responds in 4-6 wks. Seasonal 3 mos ahead. Accepts reprints. Kill fee 50%. Prefers disk. Sidebars OK. Prefers NIV. Guidelines/theme list; copy for 10x13 SAE/4 stamps. (Ads)

Fillers: Cartoons, facts, ideas, jokes, newsbreaks, party ideas, prose, short humor; $10-20.

Columns/Departments: Buys 10/yr. Page 31 (op/ed), 350-400 wds, $30-40.

Tips: "When we use a general article, it has to be tailor-made to fit our themes."

** 1996 EPA Award of Excellence—Denominational.

+STAND FIRM, God's Challenge for Today's Man, 127 Ninth Ave. N., Nashville TN 37234-0140. (615)251-5955. Fax (615)251-5008. E-mail: vhancoc@bssb.com. Lifeway Press/Baptist Sunday School board. Valerie Hancock, copy ed. Addresses the unique and distinctive needs of men of the 90s. Monthly digest-size mag; 36 pgs; circ 40,000. Subscription $18.95. 25-30% freelance. Complete ms/cover letter; fax/e-mail query OK. Pays negotiable rates on acceptance for all (preferred), 1st, or electronic rts. Articles 50-400 wds; book/music/video reviews, 20-50 wds. Responds in 4-6 wks. Seasonal 6-8 mos ahead. Accepts simultaneous submissions & reprints (tell when/where appeared). Prefers disk. Sidebars OK.

Prefers NIV. Guidelines/theme list; copy for 6x9 SAE/3 stamps.

Tips: "Looking for feature articles for week-ends; interviews with recognized Christian leaders, reviews of men's products/books/events, news/ideas/projects/activities for men, ministry news, and insights into sports, finances, and other topics of interest to men."

*THE STAR OF ZION, 401 E. 2nd St., Charlotte NC 28231. (704)377-4329. Fax (704)333-1769. African Methodist Episcopal Zion Church. Dr. Morgan W. Tann, ed. Ethnic publication; moderate; conservative. Weekly tabloid; 12-20 pgs; circ 8,000+. Subscription $22. 90% freelance. Query; phone query OK. **PAYS 5 COPIES**. Not copyrighted. Articles & fiction to 600 wds. Responds in 9 wks. Seasonal 2 mos ahead. Accepts simultaneous submissions. No sidebars. Guidelines; copy $1/10x14 SAE/2 stamps.

Poetry: African-American themes.

Fillers: Short humor.

*STEWARDSHIP, 32401 Industrial Dr., Madison Heights MI 48071. (810)585-7800. Fax (810)585-2193. Parish Publications, Inc. Richard Meurer, ed. To help church members understand stewardship. Monthly newsletter; 4 pgs. 50% freelance. Query or complete ms/cover letter; fax query OK. Pays $25-100 on publication for all rts. Articles 200-300 wds. Free copy.

SUNDAY DIGEST, 4050 Lee Vance View, Colorado Springs CO 80918-7100. (719)536-0100. Fax (719)536-3296. Cook Communications. Vicki Huffman, ed. To encourage Christian adults (mostly women 30-55) of various denominations in their faith. Weekly take-home paper; 8 pgs; circ 100,000. Subscription $9.95. 70% freelance. Complete ms; fax query OK. Pays .10-.15/wd on acceptance for one-time rts. Articles 400, 800, 1,200 or 1,600 wds (100/yr) & fiction 1,200-1,700 wds (10/yr). Responds in 6-8 wks if accepted. (New policy: Do not send SASE or expect response unless accepted.) Seasonal 8 mos ahead. Encourages simultaneous submissions & reprints. Kill fee 5%. Sidebars OK. Prefers disk. Likes sidebars. Prefers NIV. Accepts disk. Guidelines; copy for #10 SAE/1 stamp.

Poetry: Buys 10-15/yr. Free verse, light verse, traditional; 4-20 lines; $25-50. Submit max. 10 poems.

Fillers: Buys 20/yr. Anecdotes, prose; 50-200 wds; $10-40.

Columns/Departments: Buys 20-30/yr. Well Versed (poetry), to 20 lines; God At Work (special ways God works in a life), 400-500 wds. Pays $50-75.

Tips: "Submit stories that impart spiritual truth in down-to-earth ways. Make sure the reader has something to relate to and take away. We receive so many submissions, our policy of not returning mss is the only way we can continue to accept unsolicited material."

** This periodical was #4 on the 1996 Top 50 Christian Publishers list (#1 in 1995, #18 in 1994). Also 1996 EPA Award of Merit—Sunday School Take-Home.

TABLE TALK, 6401 The Paseo, Kansas City MO 64131. (816)333-7000x2359. Fax (816)333-4439. E-mail: childmin@nazarene.org. Nazarene. Submit to Kathleen Johnson, asst. ed. A family magazine for parents of elementary age children; offers helps, hints, ideas and encouragement. Quarterly mag; 80 pgs; circ 12,000. Subscription $6.75. 40% freelance. Complete ms/cover letter; phone/fax/e-mail query OK. Pays $25 or .05/wd (.03 for reprints) on publication for multi-use rts.

Articles 1,200 wds (20/yr). Responds in 16 wks. Seasonal 15 mos ahead. Accepts simultaneous submissions and reprints (tell when/where appeared). Accepts disk. Some sidebars. Prefers NIV. Guidelines; copy for 6x9 SAE/4 stamps.

Poetry: Free verse, light verse, traditional; $10 or .05/wd.

Fillers: Buys 12/yr. Anecdotes, cartoons, games, ideas, short humor; 75-1500 wds; $10 or .05/wd.

Tips: "Offer encouragement and advice on how to deal with family and parenting issues." Margins should be 1.5" all around.

TEAK ROUNDUP, #5 - 9060 Tronson Rd., Vernon BC V1T 6L7 Canada. (6250)545-4186. Fax (250)545-4194. West Coast Paradise Publishing. Robert or Yvonne Anstey, owners. General, family-oriented poetry and prose. Quarterly mag; 52 pgs; circ. 120. Subscription $17 CAN. 100% freelance. Query; phone/fax query OK. **NO PAYMENT** for one-time rts. Articles (100/yr) & fiction to 1,000 wds; book reviews 250 wds. Responds in 1 wk. Seasonal 2 mos ahead. Accepts reprints. Accepts disks. Sidebars OK. Prefers KJV. Guidelines; copy $5/6x9 SAE/.90 CAN postage or $1.17 US.

Poetry: Accepts 100/yr. Avant-garde, free verse, haiku, light verse, traditional; 10-40 lines. Submit max. 3 poems.

Fillers: Anecdotes, cartoons, ideas, newsbreaks, party idea, prose, short humor. Also accepts line art drawings.

Contest: For subscribers only.

Tips: Subscribers only are eligible for publication.

*THE TEXAS MESSENGER NEWSPAPER, PO Box 309, Del Valle TX 78617. (512)385-0090. Fax (512)385-0091. Faith Communication Ministries, Inc. Charles W. Sanders, ed/pub. Bimonthly tabloid; circ. 18,100. Subscription $15. 10% freelance. Query. Pays .05-.07/wd on publication for one-time rts. Articles 500-1,100 wds (10/yr); fiction (5/yr). Responds in 3 wks. Seasonal 2 mos ahead. Accepts reprints. Sidebars OK. Prefers KJV. Copy for 8x10 SAE/4 stamps. Not in topical listings.

*THIS ROCK, 7290 Engineer Rd. Ste. H, PO Box 17490, San Diego CA 92111. (619)541-1131. Fax (619)541-1154. Catholic. Karl Keating, ed. Deals with doctrine, evangelization and apologetics. Monthly (11X) mag; 48 pgs; circ 10,000. Subscription $24. 70% freelance. Query. Pays $300 on publication for 1st rts. Articles 1,500-4,000 wds. Responds in 5-13 wks. Guidelines; copy $4.

+TIME FOR RHYME, Battleford SK S0M 0E0 Canada. (306)445-5172. Richard W. Unger, ed. Not strictly Christian (but editor is). Quarterly mag; 32 pgs. Subscription $12, US or CAN. Est. 1995. Guidelines; copy $3.25 US or CAN.

Poetry: Buys poetry only. Rhyming only.

TIME OF SINGING, A Magazine of Christian Poetry, PO Box 149, Conneaut Lake PA 16316. (814)382-5911. High Street Community Church. Charles A. Waugaman, ed. We try to appeal to all poets and lovers of poetry. Quarterly mag; 44 pgs; circ 300. Subscription $15. 95% freelance. Complete ms/cover letter; phone query OK. Pays $1-4/poem or .25/line on publication for 1st or reprint rts. Poetry only. Responds in 4-6 wks. Seasonal 4-6 mos ahead. Accepts some reprints. Guidelines/theme list; copy $4/6x9 SAE.

Poetry: Buys 150-200/yr. Free verse, haiku, light verse (rarely), traditional; any length (prefers short). Submit max. 5 poems.

Contest: Sponsors an annual poetry contest (send SASE for rules).

Tips: "We only review books by our poets. Send SASE and put name and address on every poem."

+TODAY'S CHRISTIAN DOCTOR, PO Box 5, Bristol TN 37621-0005. (423)844-1000. Fax (423)844-1005. E-mail: 75364.331@compuserve.com. Christian Medical & Dental Society. David B. Biebel, ed. To change the face of health care by changing the hearts of doctors. Bimonthly mag; circ 12,000. Subscription $25. Open to freelance. Query. Not in topical listings. (Ads)

+TODAY'S CHRISTIAN SENIOR, 40 Berkshire Ct., Wyomissing PA 19610-1224. (610)372-1111. Fax (610)372-1122. E-mail: ScepterCom@aol.com. Scepter Publication. Bryan Bice, ed. Geared to senior citizens in the areas of health, finances, ministry and travel. Quarterly mag; 24 pgs; circ 50,000. Free subscription. Est. 1996. Accepts freelance. Complete ms/cover letter; fax query OK. Pays $150 on publication for 1st, one-time or simultaneous rts. Not copyrighted. Articles 800-1,000 wds. Responds in 4-6 wks. Seasonal 1 yr ahead. Accepts simultaneous submissions & reprints (tell when/where appeared). Prefers disk. Sidebars OK. Prefers KJV. Theme list; copy for 9x12 SAE/3stamps. (Ads)

TODAY'S FAMILY MATTERS, 9005 Macsvega Ct., Lorton VA 22079. Phone/fax (703)339-6467. C~ ~ Services, Inc. Donna G. Spann, ed. Ministers to the family on b~ ~~, household management and home-based business, with h~ ~~e evangelical, home-schooling families. Bimonthly newslet-t~ ~~; circ. 250. Subscription $15. Est. 1994. 25% freelance. Query; ph~ ~uery OK. **PAYS 5 COPIES** for one-time rts. Not copyrighted. Articles 250-2,000 wds (24/yr); book reviews 350 wds. Responds in 3-4 wks. Seasonal 4 mos ahead. Accepts simultaneous submissions & reprints (tell when/where appeared). Prefers disk (Mac). Sidebars OK. Guidelines; copy for 9x12 SAE/4 stamps. (Ads)

Fillers: Anecdotes, cartoons, short humor; to 100 wds; no payment.

Columns/Departments: Thrifty Thoughts (money-saving tips), 100-500 wds; Organization Corner (organize household), 100-500 wds; Good Works (Successful home businesses), 500-1,000; Home Remedies, 100-250 wds; Smile-For-Awhile (humor from real life), Home Works, any length; $15. Query or complete ms.

Special Needs: Alternative/natural health issues, including home remedies and organic gardening; how to organize in the home. Looking for humor.

Tips: "Impart important, helpful info in a friendly, humorous style. Most open to columns; be realistic. Get guidelines and copy before submitting."

*TODAY'S SINGLE, 1933 W. Wisconsin Ave., Milwaukee WI 53233. (414)344-7300. National Association of Christian Singles. John M. Fisco, Jr., pub.; submit to Rita Bertolas, ed. For Christian single adults: never married, divorced, widowed, or separated. Quarterly newspaper; circ 10,000. 85% freelance. Complete ms. **PAYS IN COPIES**, for one-time or reprint rts. Not copyrighted. Articles 300-2,000 wds (12-15/yr). Responds in 2-4 wks. Seasonal 4-5 mos ahead. Guidelines; free copy.

Poetry: Buys 15-20/yr. Free verse, haiku; 4-30 lines. Submit max. 5 poems.

Tips: Deadlines: January 1, April 1, July 1, and October 1.

*TOTAL HEALTH, 165 N. 100 E. Ste 2, St. George UT 84770-2505. Submit to Arpi

Coliglow, asst. ed. A family health magazine. Bimonthly mag; 70 pgs; circ 90,000. Subscription $16. 75% freelance. Query or complete ms. Pays $50-75 on publication for all and reprint rts. Articles 1,400-1,800 wds (48/yr). Responds in 4 wks. Seasonal 4 mos ahead. Accepts simultaneous submissions. Query or complete ms/cover letter. Sidebars OK. Requires disk (Mac). Guidelines; copy $1/9x12 SAE/5 stamps.

Columns/Departments: Contemporary Herbal, 1,000 wds, $50.

Tips: "Most open to self-help and prevention articles."

*TOUCHSTONE, A Journal of Ecumenical Orthodoxy, 3300 W. Cullom Ave., Chicago IL 60618. (773)267-1440. Fellowship of St. James. James Kushiner, ed. News and opinion devoted to a thoughtful appreciation of orthodox Christian faith. Quarterly jour; 44 pgs; circ 2,500. 25% freelance. Query/clips or complete ms/cover letter. **PAYS IN COPIES** for one-time rts. Articles 2,400 wds; little fiction 3,000 wds. Responds in 13 wks. Accepts simultaneous submissions. Prefers disk. Guidelines; copy for 10x13 SAE/7 stamps.

Poetry: Accepts.

Fillers: Cartoons.

THE UNITED CHURCH OBSERVER, 478 Huron St., Toronto ON M5R 2R3 Canada. (416)960-8500. Fax (416)960-8477. E-mail: observer@inforamp.net. United Church of Canada. Muriel Duncan, ed. Denominational news. Monthly mag; 52-60 pgs; circ 130,000. Subscription $20. 20% freelance. Query or complete ms/cover letter; fax/e-mail query OK. Pays negotiable rates on publication for 1st rts. Articles 1,500-2,500 wds (8/yr); juvenile fiction (6-12 yrs), query; book reviews (all assigned), $50. Responds in 12 wks. Seasonal 3-4 mos ahead. Kill fee. Some sidebars. Guidelines; copy $2. (Ads)

Fillers: Buys 24 cartoons/yr; $20.

Columns/Departments: Buys 40-50/yr. Faith; Living; world; Ministry; Front Page (church-related opinion pc.), 800 wds. Pays $200.

#UNITED VOICE, 8032 Cottonwood, Lenexa KS 66215-4120. (913)438-2607. Fax (913)438-2608. E-mail: DLLeBLANC@aol.com. Episcopalians United for Revelation Renewal and Reformation. Douglas LeBlanc, ed. To provide reporting and commentary on the Episcopal church for supporters and friends. Bimonthly newspaper; circ 25,000. Free subscription. Open to freelance. Complete ms. (Ads)

UPSOUTH, 3627 Hammett Hill Rd., Bowling Green KY 42101. (502)843-8018. Catholic. Galen Smith, ed/pub. By freelance poets and writers interested in spiritual and Southern life and issues. Quarterly newsletter; 12-16 pgs; circ 75. Subscription $5. 98% freelance. Query. **PAYS FREE COPY** for one-time rts. Articles & fiction to 500 wds; book/music/video reviews to 500 wds. Responds in 2 wks. Accepts simultaneous submissions & reprints. No sidebars. Guidelines; copy $1/#10 SAE/1 stamp.

Poetry: Buys large number. Any type, to 21 lines. Submit max. 3 poems.

Tips: "Prefer short, concise pieces that are crisp, interesting and uplifting. Writing about the South should be culture-centered. Most open to good poetry—spiritual, inspirational and uplifting poems that can move a reader."

U.S. CATHOLIC, 205 W. Monroe St., Chicago IL 60606. (312)236-7782. Fax (312)236-7230. E-mail: uscath@aol.com. Website: http://www.claret.org~uscath. Catholic/Claretian. Tom McGrath, exec. ed.; Patrice Tuohy, mng ed. Devoted to starting and continuing a dialogue with Catholics of diverse lifestyles and opinions about the way they live their faith. Monthly mag; 52 pgs; circ 35,000. Subscription $18. 95% freelance. Complete ms/cover letter; phone/fax/e-mail query OK. Pays $250-600 (fiction $300-400) on acceptance for all rts. Articles 2,500-4,000 wds; fiction 2,500-3,500 wds. Responds in 2 wks. Seasonal 2 mos ahead. Accepts disk. Sidebars OK. Guidelines; free copy. (Ads)

Columns/Departments: (See guidelines first.) Sounding Board, 1,100-1,300 wds, $250; Gray Matter and A Modest Proposal, 1,100-1,800 wds, $250; Practicing Catholic, 750 wds, $150.

Tips: "All articles should have an explicit religious dimension that enables readers to see the interaction between their faith and the issue at hand. Fiction should be well-written, creative, with solid character development."

#VIBRANT LIFE, 55 W. Oak Ridge Dr., Hagerstown MD 21740-7390. (301)791-7000. Fax (301)790-9734. Seventh-day Adventist. Larry Becker, ed. Total health publication (physical, mental and spiritual); plus articles on family and marriage improvement; ages 25-45. Bimonthly mag; 32 pgs; circ 50,000. Subscription $12.97. 80% freelance. Complete ms; fax query OK. Pays $75-250 on acceptance for 1st rts. Articles 500-1,500 wds (20-25/yr). Responds in 9 wks. Seasonal 9 mos ahead. Accepts simultaneous submissions & reprints (tell when/where appeared). Sidebars OK. Guidelines; copy $1/9x12 SAE.

Columns/Departments: Buys 6-10/yr. Woman to Woman (health, family, emotional issues); At Your Best (self-help); Challenges & Triumphs (overcoming difficulty); all 600 wds; $75-150.

Tips: "Remember the Christian tie-in. How-to sidebars help a lot. Make the stories focus on people, not problems. Health information should be scientifically sound. The whole magazine is wide open."

** This periodical was #22 on the 1996 Top 50 Christian Publishers List.

*VISION, 20 Corporate Park #3fl 18101, Irvine CA 92714-5116. (714)754-1400. Full Gospel Business Men's Fellowship. Dr. Jerry Jensen, ed.; submit to Kay Mangio. For members only (men). Quarterly mag; 32-40 pgs; circ 70,000. Query. Pays .10/wd on acceptance for various rts. Articles. Responds in 6 wks. Seasonal 6 mos ahead. Kill fee. Accepts reprints. Free guidelines/copy.

Columns/Departments: 1st Person Male Testimonies (spirit-filled); 2,200 wds.

Tips: "We accept material on an assignment basis, which we delegate."

*THE VISION, 8855 Dunn Rd., Hazelwood MO 63042-2299. (314)837-7300. Fax (314)837-4503. United Pentecostal Church. Richard M. Davis, ed. Denominational. Weekly take-home paper; 4 pgs; circ 10,000. Subscription $4.40. 95% freelance. Complete ms/cover letter. Pays $18-25 on publication for 1st rts. Articles 1,200-1,600 wds (to 120/yr); fiction 1,200-1,600 wds (to 120/yr). Seasonal 9 months ahead. Accepts simultaneous submissions & reprints. Guidelines; free copy.

Poetry: Buys 30/yr. Pays $3-12.

Tips: "Most open to good stories and articles for a traditional, fundamental, conservative church." Accepts material primarily from members of the denomination.

#VOICE, PO Box 19714, Irvine CA 92713-9714. (714)754-1400. Fax (714)557-

9916. Full Gospel Business Men's Fellowship Intl. Jerry Jensen, ed. An evangelistic outreach to the business men in the marketplace. Monthly mag; 40 pgs; circ 200,000. Subscription $7.95. 20% freelance. Query; fax query OK. **NO PAYMENT.** First Person Male Testimonies (spirit-filled) 600-2,500 wds (200/yr). Responds in 2 wks. Seasonal 2 mos ahead. Accepts simultaneous submissions & reprints. Guidelines; copy for 6x9 SAE/2 stamps. (Ads)

*THE VOICE, 7537 Holly Park Dr. S. #665, Seattle WA 98118. (206)721-1983. A & A Enterprises/Pentecostal. Rev. Daniel Ashcraft, ed. Christ-honoring poetry and devotionals for street people and everyday folks. Monthly newsletter; 1 pg; circ 500. Subscription $10. 100% freelance. Complete ms. **PAYS IN COPIES** for all rts. Articles 25-75 wds. Responds in 4 wks. Seasonal 6 mos ahead. Accepts simultaneous submissions & reprints. No sidebars. Guidelines/theme list; copy for $2/#10 SAE/1 stamp.

Poetry: Accepts 50/yr. Free verse, light verse, traditional; 5-20 lines. Submit max. 5 poems.

Tips: "Most open to poetry. Avoid preaching. Keep it simple, to the point and neat."

WAR CRY, 615 Slaters Ln., Alexandria VA 22313. (703)684-5500. Fax (703)684-5539. E-mail: USWarCry@aol.com. The Salvation Army. Lt. Col. Marlene Chase, ed. Pluralistic readership reaching all socioeconomic strata and including distribution in institutions. Biweekly mag; 24 pgs; circ 300,000. Subscription $7.50. 5% freelance. Complete ms/brief cover letter; no phone/fax/e-mail query. Pays .15-.20/wd on acceptance for 1st, one-time or reprint rts. Articles 700-1,500 wds (60/yr). Responds in 4 wks. Seasonal 6 mos ahead. Accepts simultaneous submissions & reprints. Accepts disk. Sidebars OK. Prefers NIV. Guidelines/theme list; free copy.

Poetry: Buys 30/yr. Any type; to 16 lines. Pays by the word.

Tips: "Much of what we receive consists of personal experience pieces, which don't fit our format. We prefer essays about 800 wds."

** This periodical was #6 on the 1996 Top 50 Christian Publishers List. (#70 in 1994)

+THE WATCHMAN, PO Box 614, Madison FL 32341. (904)973-6101. Nondenominational. Lu Castillo, ed. End-time Bible prophecy subjects; general Christian growth; articles of interest to home churches. Quarterly newsletter; 8 pgs. 20% freelance. Complete ms/cover letter. **NO PAYMENT.** Not copyrighted. Articles.

+THE WAY OF ST. FRANCIS, 1500 - 34TH Ave., Oakland CA 94601. Phone/fax (707)763-9189. Franciscan Friars of California. Camille Franicevich, mng. ed. For those interested in the message of St. Francis of Assisi as lived out by contemporary people. Bimonthly mag; 40+ pgs; circ 3,500. Subscription $9. 10% freelance. Complete ms/cover letter; no phone/fax query. **NO PAYMENT** for one-time or reprint rts. Articles 250-1,500 wds (5-6/yr); fiction 250-1,500 wds. Responds in 6-8 wks. Seasonal 4 mos ahead. Accepts simultaneous submissions & reprints. Prefers disk. Sidebars OK. Guidelines/theme list; copy for 6x9 SAE/6 stamps.

Tips: "Make direct connection to Francis or the Franciscan way of life."

WEAVINGS, 1908 Grand Ave., PO Box 189, Nashville TN 37202-0189. (615)340-

7254. Fax (615)340-7006. E-mail: 102615.3133@compuserve.com. The Upper Room. John S. Mogabgab, ed.; submit to Kathleen Stephens, assoc. ed. A thoughtful, thematic focus on the Christian spiritual life. Bimonthly journal; 48 pgs; circ. 40,000. Subscription $24. 75% freelance. Complete ms/cover letter. Pays .10 & up/wd on publication for 1st or one-time rts. Articles 2,000 wds (35/yr); fiction (6/yr) 2,000 wds (vignettes 500 wds); book reviews 750 wds. Responds in 8 wks. Seasonal 8 mos ahead. Accepts reprints (tell when/where appeared). Accept disk. Kill fee. No sidebars. Prefers NRSV. Guidelines/theme list; copy for 7x10 SAE/5stamps.

Poetry: Buys 4-5/yr. Free verse, haiku, light verse. Must have a spiritual focus; $50 & up.

#WESLEYAN ADVOCATE, Box 50434, Indianapolis IN 46250-0434. (317)595-4204. Fax (317)842-1649. E-mail: weslynDOC@aol.com. The Wesleyan Church. Jerry Brecheisen, mng ed. A full salvation family mag; denominational. Monthly mag; 36 pgs; circ 15,000. Subscription $15. 50% freelance. Complete ms/cover letter; phone query OK. Pays $10-40 for assigned, $5-25 for unsolicited, .01-.02/wd for reprints on publication for 1st or simultaneous rts. Not copyrighted. Articles 250-650 wds (50/yr). Responds in 2 wks. Seasonal 6 mos ahead. Accepts simultaneous submissions & reprints. Guidelines; copy $2. (Ads)

Poetry: Buys 30/yr. Free verse or traditional; $5-10. Send max. 6 poems.

Fillers: Prose, 100-300 wds. Pays $2-6.

Columns/Departments: Personal Experiences, 700 wds; Ministry Tips, 600 wds; $10.

+THE WICHITA CHRONICLE, PO Box 781079, Wichita KS 67278. Karen McBride, ed.

#THE WITNESS, 1249 Washington Blvd., Detroit MI 48226-1868. (313)962-2650. Fax (313)962-1012. E-mail: thewitness@edunet.org. Episcopal Church Publishing Co. Jeanie Wylie-Kellermann, ed. Seeks to examine society in light of faith and conscience, with clear advocacy for the poor, women, people of color, and other minority groups, from a left perspective. Monthly mag; 28 pgs; circ 4,000. Subscription $20. 20% freelance. Query or complete ms/cover letter (on first submission). Pays $50-250 (assigned) or $50-100 (unsolicited) on publication for 1st rts. Articles 250-1,800 wds (10/yr). Responds in 6 wks on accepted mss, no response to unaccepted. Seasonal 3 mos ahead. Accepts simultaneous submissions. Kill fee 50%. Free guidelines/copy.

Poetry: Buys 10/yr. Pays to $30. Submit max. 5 poems.

Tips: "We like brevity, wit and humor. Anything long-winded gets dismissed quickly—so it's worth editing your material ruthlessly before you send it."

+YESTERDAY'S FAMILY, PO Box 450, Milligan College TN 37682-0450. E-mail: CJH@MCNET.MILLIGAN.MILLIGAN-COLLEGE.TN.US. Sonja Haskins, ed. To help readers deal with and overcome issues like alcoholism, the various facets of physical, emotional, and sexual abuse, co-dependency, violence and depression. Bimonthly newsletter. Subscription $10. **PAYS IN COPIES.** Guidelines; copy $2.

CHILDREN'S MARKETS

+BIBLE-IN-LIFE PIX, 4050 Lee Vance View, Colorado Springs CO 80918-7100.

(719)536-0100. David C. Cook Church Ministries. Judy Gillespie, ed. For elementary-aged children. Weekly take-home paper; circ 200,000. Query. Not in topical listings.

BREAD FOR GOD'S CHILDREN, Box 1017, Arcadia FL 34265. (941)494-6214. Fax (941)993-0154. Bread Ministries, Inc. Judith M. Gibbs, ed. A family magazine for serious Christians who are concerned about their children or grandchildren (ages 6-18). Monthly mag; 32 pgs; circ 10,000. Free subscription. 25% freelance. Complete ms. Pays $10-25 ($30-40 for fiction) on publication for 1st or one-time rts. Not copyrighted. Articles 500-900 wds (10/yr); fiction & true stories 800-900 wds for 4-10 yrs, 900-1,500 wds for teens (20/yr). Responds in 8-12 wks (may hold longer). Accepts simultaneous submissions & reprints (tell when/where appeared). Some sidebars. Guidelines; 3 copies for 9x12 SAE/7 stamps; 1 copy 3 stamps.

> **Tips:** "Most open to fiction for children and youth. Stories must be centered on Christian growth and teach positive spiritual values without being preachy or sugary sweet. Articles for children and teens must have the same teaching value. The Bible is our guideline for morality, not current social values. Creative approaches to scriptural truth are the best way to get our acceptance for publication."

+CLUB CONNECTION, 1445 Boonville Ave., Springfield MO 65802-1894. (417)862-2781. Fax (417)862-0503. E-mail: mettes@ag.org. Kerry Clarensau, ed. For girls ages 3 through high school (with leader edition for Missionettes leaders). Est. 1997. Quarterly mag; 32 pgs. Subscription $6.50 (leader's $7.50). 10% freelance. Complete ms/cover letter. Pays $10-50 on publication for 1st or one-time rts. Articles 500 wds (4-6/yr). Responds in 10 wks. Seasonal 10-12 mos ahead. Accepts simultaneous submissions & reprints (tell when/where appeared). Accepts disk. Kill fee. Sidebars OK. Prefers NIV. Guidelines/theme list; copy for 9x12SAE/3 stamps.

> **Poetry:** Buys 1-2 /yr. Light verse; 4-20 lines; $5-10. Submit max. 2 poems.
> **Fillers:** Buys 6-8/yr. Anecdotes, cartoons, facts, games, ideas, jokes, newsbreaks, party ideas, quizzes, short humor, word puzzles; 20-100 wds; $5-20.
> **Columns/Departments:** Buys 4-6/yr. Pays $10-50.
> **Tips:** "Articles with a Christian slant of interest to girls."

*CLUBHOUSE, c/o Your Story Hour, Box 15, Berrien Springs MI 49103. (616)471-3701. Fax (616)471-4661. Non-denominational. Krista Phillips, ed. To help young people (9-14) feel good about themselves. Monthly newsletter; 4 pgs; circ 8,000. Subscription $5. 75% freelance. Complete ms. Pays $12-35 on acceptance for one-time rts. Articles 25-1,200 wds (150/yr); fiction 100-1,200 wds (30/yr). Responds in 4-5 wks. Seasonal 6 mos ahead. Accepts simultaneous submissions & reprints. No disk. Guidelines; copy for 5x7 SAE/2 stamps.

> **Poetry:** Buys 60/yr. Free verse, light verse, traditional; to 12 lines; $12. Submit max. 3 poems.
> **Fillers:** Buys 60/yr. Anecdotes, cartoons, games, jokes, word puzzles; 50-100 wds; $12.
> **Tips:** "Send all material once a year in March."
> ** This periodical was #50 on the 1996 Top 50 Christian Publishers List.

#COUNSELOR, 4050 Lee Vance View, Colorado Springs CO 80918. (719)536-

0100. Cook Communications/Scripture Press. Janice K. Burton, ed. Presents the way spiritual truths in the weekly lesson can be worked out in everyday life—a correlated teaching tool for 8-11 yr olds. Weekly take-home paper; 4 pgs. Subscription $11.50. 60% freelance. Complete ms/cover letter. Pays .07-.10/wd on acceptance for all, 1st, one-time, or reprint rts. Articles 300-500 wds (10-20/yr); fiction/true stories 900-1,100 wds (10-15/yr). Responds in 9 wks. Seasonal 1 yr ahead. Accepts simultaneous submissions & reprints (pays .05-.07/wd). No sidebars. Guidelines/theme list; copy for #10 SAE/1 stamp.

> **Fillers:** Buys 8-12/yr. Games, puzzles, fun activities; to 150 wds.
>
> **Columns/Departments:** Kids in Action (unusual activities to benefit others); World Series (missions story from child's perspective); 300-500 wds.
>
> **Tips:** "Should have a feel for the age level. Know your readers and what is appropriate in terms of concepts and vocabulary. Submit only best quality manuscripts." Uses ethnic short stories. Include Social Security number.
>
> ** This periodical was #61 on the 1996 Top 50 Christian Publishers List. (#67 in 1994). 1996 EPA Award of Merit—Sunday School Take-Home.

+COURAGE, 1300 N. Meacham Rd., Schaumburg IL 60173-4888. (847)843-1600. Fax (847)843-3757. Regular Baptist Press. Joan Alexander, ed. For children, 9-12, in Sunday school. Weekly take-home paper; 4 pgs; circ 40,000. Subscription $5.80. 50% freelance. Complete ms/cover letter the first time only; no phone/fax query. Pays .03-.07/wd on acceptance for all rts (negotiable). Articles 200-600 wds (30/yr); fiction 600-1,200 wds (30/yr). Responds in 4-8 wks. Seasonal 1 yr ahead. Rarely accepts reprints. Accepts disk. Sidebars OK. Prefers KJV. Guidelines; copy for #10 SAE/2 stamps; or order a full quarter for $1.45.

> **Fillers:** Buys 35-40/yr. Games, prose, word puzzles, crafts, other puzzles; 150-250 wds. Pays $10.
>
> **Tips:** "Address the spiritual dimension that is present in the interests, concerns, and daily lives of children 9-12 without sentimentality, moralizing or preachiness."

#CRUSADER, Box 7259, Grand Rapids MI 49510. (616)241-5616. Fax (616)241-5558. E-mail: cadets@aol.com. Calvinist Cadet Corp. G. Richard Broene, ed. To show cadets and their friends, boys 9-14, how God is at work in their lives and in the world around them. Mag published 7X/yr; 24 pgs; circ 14,000. Subscription $8.05. 40% freelance. Complete ms/cover letter. Pays .04-.06/wd on acceptance for 1st, one-time, or simultaneous rts. Articles 400-1,000 wds (20-25/yr); fiction 900-1,500 wds (12/yr). Responds in 9 wks. Seasonal 5 mos ahead. Accepts simultaneous submissions & reprints. Prefers NIV. Guidelines/theme list; copy for 9x12 SAE/3 stamps. (Ads)

> **Fillers:** Robert DeJonge. Buys 7-10/yr. Cartoons, games, short humor, word puzzles; 20-200 wds; $5-20.
>
> **Tips:** "Fiction tied to themes; request new theme list after January of each year."
>
> ** 1995 EPA Award of Merit—Youth.

*CRUSADER, 1548 Poplar Ave., Memphis TN 38104. (901)272-2461. Fax (901)726-5540. Southern Baptist. James Warren, ed. For children, primarily boys, grades 4-6; missions education. Monthly mag; 20 pgs; circ. 60,000. Subscription $12.36. Complete ms/cover letter; fax query OK. Pays variable rate on acceptance for all rts. Responds in 4 wks. Seasonal 1 yr ahead. Prefers NAS. Guidelines/theme list; copy $1.25/9x12 SAE/4 stamps.

Tips: "Be Southern Baptist—involved in Royal Ambassadors or children's missions education group."

DISCOVERIES, 6401 The Paseo, Kansas City MO 64131. (816)333-7000. Fax (816)333-4439. Nazarene/Wesleyan Churches. Kathleen Johnson, asst. ed. For 8-9 yr olds, emphasizing Christian values and holy living. Weekly take-home paper; 4 pgs; circ 30,000. 100% freelance. Complete ms/cover letter; fax query OK. Pays .05/wd one year before publication for 1st, one-time, reprint and multiuse rts. Articles (10/yr) & fiction (10/yr), 500-700 wds. Responds in 6-8 wks. Seasonal 1 yr ahead. Accepts reprints (tell when/where appeared). No disk. Sidebars OK. Prefers NIV. Guidelines/theme list/copy for #10 SAE/1 stamp.

Fillers: Buys 15/yr. Cartoons, games, quizzes, word puzzles/yr; $15.

Tips: "Follow guidelines and theme list. Most open to nonfiction and fiction."

+DISCOVERY, 475 Riverside Dr., Rm. 455, New York NY 10115. (212)870-3335. Fax (212)870-3229. The John Milton Society for the Blind. Darcy Quigley, mng. dir. For blind children ages 8-18, in Braille; reprints articles from Christian and other magazines for youth. Quarterly mag; 44 pgs; circ 2,000. Free subscription. 5% freelance. Complete ms/cover letter. **NO PAYMENT** for reprint rts. Not copyrighted. Articles 1,500 wds (1/yr); fiction 1,500 wds (1/yr). Responds in 6 wks. Seasonal 9-12 mos ahead. Accepts simultaneous submissions & reprints (tell when/where appeared). No sidebars. Guidelines; free copy.

Poetry: Accepts 1/yr. Any type; to 500 lines.

Fillers: Anecdotes, games, ideas, jokes, quizzes, prayers, short humor.

Tips: "Look at magazines we typically reprint from (see guidelines). Send complete manuscript with little or no editing required. We are most in need of poetry/prayers pertaining to Christian themes/holidays."

FOCUS ON THE FAMILY CLUBHOUSE, 8605 Explorer Dr., Colorado Springs CO 80920. (719)531-3400. Fax (719)531-3499. Focus on the Family. Lisa Brock, ed. For children 8-12 yrs in Christian homes. Monthly mag; 24 pgs; circ 100,000. Subscription $15. 50% freelance. Complete ms/cover letter; no phone/fax/e-mail query. Pays $25-350 for articles, $25-500 for fiction on acceptance for all rts. Articles 1,200 wds (15/yr); fiction 1,200 wds (30/yr). Responds in 6-8 wks. Seasonal 4 mos ahead. Accepts simultaneous submissions & reprints. Accepts disk. Some kill fees. Sidebars OK. Prefers NIV or NCV. Guidelines; copy for 9x12 SAE/6 stamps. (Ads)

Fillers: Buys 10/yr. Facts, games, ideas, party ideas, quizzes, short humor, word puzzles; 150-500 wds; $25-200.

Columns/Departments: Buys 2-5/yr. Usually staff-written. Complete ms. Pays $20-250.

Contest: Contest only for children 8-12 years.

Tips: "Biggest need is for fiction. Send mss with list of credentials. Read past issues."

** This periodical was #62 on the 1996 Top 50 Christian Publishers list. (#38 in 1995, #15 in 1994) Also 1995 EPA Award of Merit—Youth.

#FOCUS ON THE FAMILY CLUBHOUSE JR., 8605 Explorer Dr., Colorado

Springs CO 80920. (719)548-4595. Fax (719)531-3499. Focus on the Family. Lisa Brock, ed. For ages 4-8 yrs. Monthly mag; 16 pgs; circ 80,000. Subscription $12. 25% freelance. Complete ms/cover letter; fax query OK. Pays $100 ($100-200 for fiction) on acceptance for 1st rts. Articles 300-750 wds (1-2/yr); fiction 300-1,000 wds (10/yr). Responds in 4 wks. Seasonal 5-6 mos ahead. Kill fee. No sidebars. Guidelines; copy for 9x12 SAE/2 stamps.

Poetry: Buys 3/yr. Free verse, light verse, traditional; 10-25 lines; $25-100.

Fillers: Buys 1-2/yr. Cartoons, games, word puzzles; $15-30.

Special Needs: Bible stories.

Tips: "Most open to short, non-preachy fiction, beginning reader stories, and read-to-me."

** This periodical was #53 on the 1996 Top 50 Christian Publishers list. (#53 in 1995, #15 in 1994) 1996 EPA Award of Excellence—Youth.

#GOD'S WORLD TODAY/IT'S GOD'S WORLD, PO Box 2330, Asheville NC 28803. Phone/fax (704)253-1556. God's World Publications. Norman W. Bomer, ed. Current events, published in 5 editions, for kindergarten through jr. high students, mostly in Christian and home schools. Weekly newsletter (during school yr); 8 pgs; circ 301,000. Subscription $19.95. 16% freelance. Complete ms/cover letter. Pays $75 on acceptance for one-time rts. Articles 700-900 wds. Responds in 9 wks. Guidelines; free copy.

Tips: "Keep vocabulary simple. Must present a distinctly Christian world view without being moralistic."

***GOOD NEWS FOR CHILDREN**, 330 Progress Rd., Dayton OH 45449. (513)847-5900. Fax (513)847-5910. Catholic. Joan Mitchell CSJ, ed. For 2nd & 3rd graders. Weekly take-home paper. Not in topical listings.

#GUIDE, 55 W. Oak Ridge Dr., Hagerstown MD 21740. (301)791-7000. Fax (301)790-9734. E-mail: 74617.3100@compuserve.com. Seventh-day Adventist. Carolyn Rathbun, ed.; Randy Fishell, assoc. ed. A Christian journal for 10-14 yr olds, presenting true stories relevant to their needs. Weekly take-home paper; 32 pgs; circ 34,000. Subscription $36.97/yr. 50% freelance. Complete ms/cover letter. Pays $25-125 (.03-.07/wd) on publication for 1st, one-time or simultaneous rts. Articles (75-100/yr) or true stories (35-50/yr) or fiction; 500-1,200 wds. Responds in 3 wks. Seasonal 6 mos ahead. Accepts simultaneous submissions & reprints (tell when/where appeared—pays 1/2). Sidebars usually assigned. Guidelines; copy for #10 SAE/2 stamps. (Ads)

Fillers: Buys 40/yr. Games & word puzzles on a spiritual theme; 20-50 wds; $15-30.

Special Needs: "Most open to true action/adventure and Christian humor. Kids want that—put it together with dialogue and a spiritual slant, and you're on the 'write' track for our readers. School life."

** This periodical was #22 on the 1995 Top 50 Christian Publishers list. (#38 in 1994)

GUIDEPOSTS FOR KIDS, PO Box 538, Chesterton IN 46304. (219)929-4429. E-mail: WALLYT5232@aol.com. Website: http://www.guideposts.org. Guideposts Inc. Mary Lou Carney, ed; Sailor Metts, articles editor; Lurlene McDaniel, fiction editor. For kids 7-12 yrs (emphasis at upper level). Bimonthly mag; 32 pgs; circ 200,000+. Subscription $15.95. 75% freelance. Query/clips (complete ms for fiction); prefers not to get electronic submissions. Pays $150-450 ($250-400 for fiction) on acceptance for all & electronic rts. Articles 300-1,200 wds (30/yr); fiction 500-1,200 wds (10/yr). Responds in 6 wks. Seasonal 6 mos ahead. Kill fee. Likes sidebars. Prefers NIV or NKJV. Guidelines; copy $3.25/10x13 SAE.

Poetry: Mary Lou Carney. Buys 4-6/yr. Free verse, haiku, light verse, traditional; 3-20 lines; $15-50. Submit max. 5 poems.

Fillers: Buys 15-20/yr. Facts, games, jokes, quizzes, short humor, word puzzles; to 300 wds; $20-75.

Columns/Departments: Buys 20/yr. Featuring Kids (true, interesting kid profiles), 300-600 wds; Tips From the Top (Christian celebrities/sport figures), 500-700 wds; $150-350.

Tips: "Looking for historical fiction; mini-series/brain teasers; true action stories suitable comic book format."

** This periodical was #54 on the 1996 Top 50 Christian Publishers list. (#55 in 1995)

HIGH ADVENTURE, 1445 Boonville Ave., Springfield MO 65802-1894. (417)862-2781 x4178. Fax (417)831-8230. Assemblies of God. Marshall Bruner, ed-in-chief. For the Royal Rangers (boys), 5-17 yrs; slanted toward teens. Quarterly mag; 16 pgs; circ 86,000. 90% freelance. Complete ms/cover letter. Pays .03-.04/wd on acceptance for 1st, one-time, simultaneous or reprint rts. Articles 500-900 wds (30/yr); fiction 500-900 wds (15/yr). Responds in 4-5 wks. Seasonal 7 mos ahead. Accepts simultaneous submissions & reprints (tell when/where appeared). Sidebars OK. Prefers NIV. Guidelines/theme list; copy for 9x12 SAE/3 stamps.

Fillers: Buys 30/yr. Cartoons, jokes, short humor; 50 wds; $2-20.

JUNIOR TRAILS, 1445 Boonville Ave., Springfield MO 65802-1894. (417)862-2781. E-mail: UElemCurr@ag.org. Assemblies of God. Sinda S. Zinn, ed. Teaching of Christian principles through fiction stories about children (10-12 yrs). Weekly take-home paper; 8 pgs; circ 50,000. Subscription $6.20. 98% freelance. Complete ms. Pays .03-.05/wd on acceptance for one-time rts. Articles 300-500 wds (50/yr); fiction 1,000-1,200 wds (50/yr). Responds in 2-4 wks. Seasonal 15-18 mos ahead. Accepts simultaneous submissions & reprints. No disk. No sidebars. Prefers NIV. Guidelines/theme list; copy for #10 SAE/1 stamp.

Poetry: Buys 6-8/yr. Free verse, haiku, light verse, traditional; $5 & up. Submit max. 3 poems.

Fillers: Buys 8-10/yr. Facts, short humor; 300-500 wds; .03-.05/wd.

Tips: "Most open to fiction based on relevant problems for today's kids. Submit well-written, believable stories in which character overcomes real problem based on biblical principles. Use third person; move story through action and dialogue, rather than narration."

** This periodical was #17 on the 1996 Top 50 Christian Publishers list. (#23 in 1995)

*KEYS FOR KIDS, Box 1, Grand Rapids MI 49501. (616)451-2009. Hazel Marett, ed. A daily devotional booklet for children (8-14) or for family devotions. Bimonthly booklet; 96 pgs; circ 40,000. No subscriptions. 100% freelance. Complete ms. Pays $12-16 on acceptance for 1st or simultaneous rts. Not copyrighted.

Devotionals (includes short fiction story) 375-425 wds (60-70/yr). Responds in 2-4 wks. Seasonal 4-5 mos ahead. Accepts simultaneous submissions & reprints. Prefers KJV or NIV. Guidelines; copy for 6x9 SAE/$1.24 postage.

Tips: "If you are rejected, go back to the sample and study it some more."

*LAD, 1548 Poplar Ave., Memphis TN 38104. (901)272-2461. Fax (901)726-5540. Southern Baptist. Charlotte Teas, ed. For boys, grades 1-3; missions education. Monthly mag; 20 pgs; circ. 60,000. Subscription $12.36. Complete ms/cover letter; fax query OK. Pays variable rate on acceptance for all rts. Responds in 4 wks. Seasonal 1 yr ahead. Prefers NAS. Guidelines/theme list; copy $1.25/9x12 SAE/4 stamps.

Tips: "Be Southern Baptist—involved in Royal Ambassadors or children's missions education group."

LISTEN, 6401 The Paseo, Kansas City MO 64131. (816)333-7000 x2244. Fax (816)333-4439. E-mail: gpryor@nazarene.org. Nazarene/Wesleyan. George Pryor, ed. Weekly activity/story paper for 5-6 yr olds; 4 pgs; circ 18,000. Subscription $8.40. 75% freelance. Complete ms/cover letter. Pays .05/wd on publication for all rts. Articles 100-200 wds (5/yr); contemporary fiction & true stories 300-400 wds (52/yr). Responds in 6-8 wks. Seasonal 12 mos ahead. Accepts simultaneous submissions. Accepts disk. Kill fee 5%. No sidebars. Prefers NIV. Guidelines/theme list/copy for #10 SAE/1 stamp.

Poetry: Buys 20/yr. Free verse; 4-12 lines; $2 or .25/line.

Fillers: Buys 30/yr. Games, ideas/activities (age-appropriate); $5-15.

Special Needs: Exciting, age-appropriate activities for back page; adventure stories and children's life situation stories.

MY FRIEND, The Catholic Magazine for Kids. 50 St. Paul's Ave., Boston MA 02130. (617)522-8911. Fax (617)541-9805. E-mail: chaire@interramp.com. Website: http://www.pauline.org. Pauline Books & Media. Sr. Kathryn James, mng. ed. Christian values and basic Catholic doctrines for children, ages 6-12. Monthly mag; 32 pgs; circ 12,000. Subscription $18. 20-40% freelance. Complete ms/cover letter; fax/e-mail query OK. Pays $75-150 on acceptance for all or 1st rts. Articles 500-900 wds (20/yr) & fiction 500-900 wds (8/yr). Responds in 4 wks. Seasonal 6 mos ahead. No disk. Kill fee. Sidebars OK. Guidelines; copy $2/9x12 SAE/5 stamps.

Fillers: New area. Cartoons, jokes.

Tips: "In fiction, include physically challenged, and universality or ethnic inclusion."

** This periodical was #32 on the 1996 Top 50 Christian Publishers list. (#34 in 1995, #39 in 1994)

*NATURE FRIEND MAGAZINE, 22777 State Rd. 119, Goshen IN 46526. (219)534-2245. Pilgrim Publishers/Fundamental Creationist. Stanley K. Brubaker, ed. For children (ages 4-14); about God's wonderful world of nature and wildlife. Monthly mag; 36 pgs; circ 10,000. 40% freelance. Complete ms/cover letter. Pays .05/wd on publication for one-time rts. Articles 300-1,500 wds; true stories 300-1200 wds. Responds in 13-26 wks. Seasonal 3 mos ahead. Accepts simultaneous submissions & reprints. Guidelines & 2 copies for $5/6x9 SAE.2

Poetry: Buys 10-20/yr. Traditional; $8-20. Submit max. 5 poems.

Tips: "Don't bother submitting to us unless you have seen our guidelines and a sample copy. We are very conservative in our approach."

#ON THE LINE, 616 Walnut Ave., Scottdale PA 15683-1999. (412)887-8500. Fax (412)887-3111. E-mail: MARY%5904477@mcimail.com. Mennonite. Mary Clemens Meyer, ed. Reinforces Christian values in 10-14 yr olds. Weekly take-home paper; 8 pgs; circ 6,500. Subscription $17.10. 90% freelance. Complete ms only/cover letter. Pays .03-.05/wd ($10-30) on acceptance for one-time rts. Articles 350-500 wds (95/yr); fiction 1,000-1,800 wds (52/yr). Responds in 5 wks. Seasonal 6 mos ahead. Accepts simultaneous submissions & reprints. Sidebars OK. Prefers NIV or NRSV. Guidelines; copy for 9x12 SAE/2 stamps.

    Poetry: Buys 10-15/yr. Free verse, haiku, light verse, traditional; 3-12 lines; $5-15.

    Fillers: Buys 100+/yr. Cartoons, facts, games, jokes, party ideas, quizzes, prayers, word puzzles; $10-25.

    Ethnic: Targets all ethnic groups involved in the Mennonite religion.

    Tips: "Watch kids 10-14. Listen to them talk. Write stories that sound natural—not moralizing, preachy, with adults quoting Scripture. Our readers like puzzles, especially theme crosswords."

    ** This periodical was #38 on the 1996 Top 50 Christian Publishers list. (#44 in 1995, #52 in 1994)

OUR LITTLE FRIEND, Box 5353, Nampa ID 83653-5353. (208)465-2500. Fax (208)465-2531. E-mail: ailsox@pacificpress.com. Website: http://www.pacificpress.com. Seventh-day Adventist. Aileen Andres Sox, ed. For theme and comments, see **Primary Treasure**. Weekly take-home paper for 1-6 yr olds (through 1st grade); 8 pgs; circ 45,000-50,000. 80% freelance (assigned), 20% unsolicited. Complete ms; fax/e-mail query OK (not preferred). Pays $25-50 on acceptance for one-time or reprint rts. True stories to 650 wds. Responds in 13 wks. Seasonal 7 mos ahead. Accepts simultaneous submissions & reprints. No disk. Guidelines (also on webpage)/theme list; copy for 9x12 SAE/2 stamps.

    Poetry: 12 lines; $1/line.

    Tips: "Stories need to be crafted for this age reader in plot and vocabulary."

PARTNERS, Christian Light Publications, Inc., Box 1212, Harrisonburg VA 22801-1212. (540)434-0768. Fax (540)433-8896. Mennonite. Crystal Shank, ed. For 9-14 yr olds. Weekly take-home paper; 4 pgs; circ 5,900. Subscription $9.20. Almost 100% freelance. Complete ms. Pays up to .05/wd on acceptance for all, 1st, one-time or reprint rts. Articles 200-1,000 wds (50/yr); fiction & true stories 1,000-1,600 wds (50/yr). Responds in 6 wks. Seasonal 6 mos ahead. Accepts simultaneous submissions (treated as reprints) & reprints; serials 2-13 parts (2-4 parts preferred). Requires KJV. Guidelines/theme list/copy for 9x12 SAE/3 stamps.

    Poetry: Buys 25/yr. Traditional, story poems; 4-24 lines; .50/line. Submit max. 6 poems.

    Fillers: Buys 50-75/yr. Quizzes, word puzzles (Bible related). Payment varies, about $5.

    Columns/Departments: Character Corner; Cultures & Customs; Historical Highlights; Maker's Masterpiece; Missionary Mail; Torches of Truth; or Nature Nooks; all 200-800 wds.

Tips: "Personal familiarity with conservative Mennonite applications of biblical truth is very helpful. Follow themes. We do not require that you be Mennonite, but we do send a questionnaire for you to fill out."

** This periodical was #63 on the 1996 Top 50 Christian Publishers list. (#66 in 1995)

POCKETS, PO Box 189, Nashville TN 37202-0189. (615)340-7333. Fax (615)340-7006. E-mail: 102615.3127@compuserve.com. United Methodist. Janet Knight, ed; submit to Lynn W. Gilliam, assoc. ed. Devotional magazine for children (6-11 yrs). Monthly (11X) mag; 48 pgs; circ 100,000. Subscription $16.95. 75% freelance. Complete ms. Pays.12/wd on acceptance for 1st rts. (Will start buying software application rts if commissioned.) Articles 400-800 wds (20/yr) & fiction 500-1,600 wds (45-50/yr). Responds in 6 wks. Seasonal 1 yr ahead. Accepts reprints (tell when/where appeared). Kill fee 33%. Some sidebars. Prefers NRSV. Guidelines/theme list (new each Dec.); copy for 7x9 SAE/4 stamps.

Poetry: Buys 25/yr. Free verse, haiku, light verse, traditional; 4-20 lines; $25-50 or $2/line. Submit max. 7 poems.

Fillers: Buys 44 games/puzzles/yr. Games, ideas, jokes, prayers, riddles, word puzzles; $25.

Columns/Departments: Buys 40/yr. Kids Cook; Pocketsful of Love (ways to show love), 200-300 wds; Peacemakers at Work, 500-800 wds; Pocketsful of Prayer, 400-600 wds.

Special Needs: "New feature is a 2-pg story for ages 5-8, 650 words max. Need role model stories and retold Bible stories. Stories about someone you'd like to know. Interesting articles about children doing unusual things, 250-600 wds."

Contest: Fiction-writing contest; submit between 4/1 & 8/15 every yr. Prize $1,000. Length 1,000-1,600 wds. Must be unpublished and not historical fiction. Previous winners not eligible. Send to Pockets Fiction Contest at above address.

Tips: "Get our theme list first. Nonfiction probably easiest to sell and Peacemakers at Work."

** This periodical was #10 on the 1996 Top 50 Christian Publishers list. (#8 in 1995, #18 in 1994)

POWER AND LIGHT, 6401 The Paseo, Kansas City MO 64131. (816)333-7000x2243. Fax (816)333-4439. E-mail: mhammer@nazarene.org. Nazarene/WordAction Publishing Co. Beula Postelwait, ed; Melissa Hammer, assoc. ed. For pre-teens, 11-12 year olds. Weekly take-home paper; 8 pgs; circ 40,000. Subscription $10. Est. 1993. 35% freelance. Query or complete ms/cover letter; fax/e-mail query OK. Pays .05/wd on publication for multiple use rts (writer retains right to reuse). Articles 400-800 wds (10/yr); fiction 400-800 wds (50/yr); book/music reviews, 200-300 wds. Responds in 6-12 wks. Seasonal 6 mos ahead. Accepts reprints (.035/wd—tell when/where appeared). Kill fee $15. Accepts disk. Some sidebars. NIV only. Guidelines/theme list (avail. May 1997); copy for #10 SAE/2 stamps.

Fillers: Buys 104/yr. Cartoons, games, jokes, short humor, word puzzles; $15.

Columns/Departments: Buys 52/yr. Spotlight the Past (biblical background/archeological information), 400-500 wds. Query.

Tips: "Most open to fiction, puzzles and cartoons. Request a theme list. Write about preteens from a preteen perspective."

#PRIMARY DAYS, PO Box 36640; Colorado Springs CO 80936. (719)536-0100. Fax (719)536-3243. Cook Communications/ Scripture Press. Janice K. Burton, ed. To show children, 6-8, how Bible truths can work out in everyday life. Weekly take-home paper; 4 pgs. Subscription $11. 100% freelance. Complete ms/cover letter. Pays .07-.10/wd on acceptance for all, 1st, one-time, or simultaneous rts. Articles 300-350 wds (10-20/yr); fiction 300-350 wds (10-15/yr). Responds in 9 wks. Seasonal 1 yr ahead. Accepts simultaneous submissions & reprints. No sidebars. Guidelines/theme list/copy for #10 SAE/1 stamp.

Fillers: Buys 8-12/yr. Games, puzzles, fun activities.

** This periodical was #69 on the 1996 Top 50 Christian Publishers list. (#56 in 1995)

PRIMARY PAL, 1300 N. Meacham Rd., Schaumburg IL 60173-4888. (847)843-1600. Fax (847)843-3757. Regular Baptist Press. Joan Alexander, ed. For ages 6-8; fundamental, conservative. Weekly take-home paper; 4 pgs; circ. 50,000. Subscription $5.80. complete ms; no phone/fax query. Pays .03-.07/wd on acceptance for all rts (negotiable). Articles 150 wds (20/yr); fiction 500-600 wds (30/yr). Responds in 4-8 wks. Seasonal 1 yr ahead. Accepts disk. No sidebars. Prefers KJV. Guidelines; copy for #10 SAE/2 stamps.

Fillers: Accepts 35-40/yr. Games, prayers, word puzzles; craft projects (with step-by-step photos); visual puzzles, mazes, What's wrong with this picture? What's missing? Etc. Pays $10.

Tips: "Primary Pal is fiction with a supporting nonfiction article or activity. Know the children/families/pastors in the denomination. Know the spiritual dimension that is present in the interests, concerns and daily lives of children 6-8."

PRIMARY TREASURE, Box 5353, Nampa ID 83653-5353. (208)465-2500. Fax (208)465-2531. E-mail: ailsox@pacificpress.com. Website: http://www.pacificpress.com. Seventh-day Adventist. Aileen Andres Sox, ed. To teach children Christian belief, values, and practice. God's loving us and our loving Him makes a difference in every facet of life, from how we think and act to how we feel. Weekly take-home paper for 7-9 yr olds (2nd-4th grades); 16 pgs; circ 35,000. 50% freelance (assigned), 50% reprints or unsolicited. Complete ms; fax/e-mail query OK (not preferred). Pays $25-50 on acceptance for one-time or reprint rts. True stories 900-1,000 wds; articles used rarely (query). Responds in 13 wks. Seasonal 7 mos ahead. Accepts simultaneous submissions; serials to 10 parts (query). No disk. Guidelines (also on Website); copy for 9x12 SAE/2 stamps.

Poetry: 12 lines; $1/line.

Tips: "We need positive, lively stories about children facing modern problems and making good choices. We always need strong stories about boys. We need a spiritual element that frequently is missing from submissions. We're changing; refer to guidelines."

*PROMISE, 330 Progress Rd., Dayton OH 45449. (513)847-5900. Fax (513)847-5910. Catholic. Joan Mitchell CSJ, ed. For preschoolers. Weekly (32X) take-home paper. Not in topical listings.

R-A-D-A-R, 8121 Hamilton Ave., Cincinnati OH 45231. (513)931-4050. Fax (513)931-0904. Standard Publishing. Elaina Meyers, ed. For 8-11 yr olds; correlates with Sunday-school lesson themes. Weekly take-home paper; 12 pgs; circ 112,000. Subscription $12. 80-90% freelance. Complete ms; no phone/fax query. Pays .03-.07/wd on acceptance for 1st, one-time, simultaneous or reprint rts. Articles 300-500 wds (50/yr) & fiction 700-1,000 wds (50/yr). Responds in 2-4 wks. Seasonal 1 yr ahead. Accepts simultaneous submissions & reprints (tell when/where appeared). Few sidebars. Prefers NIV. Guidelines/theme list/copy for #10 SAE/1 stamp.

Poetry: Buys 25/yr. Traditional, any length; .50/line. Submit any number.

Fillers: Buys 25/yr. Cartoons, facts, games, jokes, quizzes, prayers, word puzzles; .03-.07/wd.

Tips: "We mail theme list automatically if you request to be put on list. Keep abreast with the times and where kids are. I rely on freelancers to supply all my needs. Follow theme list."

** This periodical was #24 on the 1996 Top 50 Christian Publishers list. (#24 in 1995, #13 in 1994)

SKIPPING STONES, A Multicultural Children's Quarterly, PO Box 3939, Eugene OR 97403. (541)342-4956. Not specifically Christian. Arun N. Toke, ed. Multi-cultural and multi-ethnic writings for children 8-14. Bimonthly mag; 36 pgs; circ 3,000. Subscription $20. 80% freelance. Complete ms/cover letter; no phone query. **PAYS IN COPIES** for 1st or reprint rts. Articles (15-25/yr) 750 wds; fiction (15-25/yr—usually by children), 750-1,000 wds; book reviews 100 wds. Responds in 10-12 wks. Seasonal 4 months ahead. Accepts simultaneous submissions. Accepts disk. Sidebars OK. Guidelines; copy $5/9x12 SAE/5 stamps.

Poetry: Only from kids under 19. Accepts 50/yr. Any type; 3-30 lines. Submit max. 3 poems.

Fillers: Accepts 10-20/yr. Anecdotes, cartoons, facts, games, ideas, jokes, newsbreaks, quizzes, quotes, word puzzles; to 200 wds.

Columns/Departments: Accepts 10/yr. Noteworthy News (multicultural/nature/intl./social, appropriate for youth), 200 wds.

Special Needs: Multicultural, international experiences, ecological awareness, and social issues. Accepts fiction from adults only if it illustrates multicultural or social issues.

Contest: 1997 Youth Honor Awards. Theme: How I'm Making a Difference. June 20, 1997 deadline for students 16 and under, May 1, 1997 deadline for adult authors. Send SASE for guidelines.

Tips: "We're seeking submissions by minority, multicultural, international, and/or youth writers. Do not be judgmental or preachy; be open or receptive to diverse opinions."

#STORY FRIENDS, 616 Walnut St., Scottdale PA 15683. (412)887-8500. Fax (412)887-3111. E-mail: MPH%590-4477@mcimail.com. Mennonite. Rose Mary Stutzman, ed. For children 4-9 yrs; reinforces Christian values in a non-moralistic manner. Weekly take-home paper; 4 pgs; circ 7,000. Subscription $10. 50-80% freelance. Complete ms/cover letter. Pays .03-.05/wd on acceptance for one-time rts. Not copyrighted. Articles (5-10/yr) & fiction (10-20/yr), 300-800 wds. Responds in 5 wks. Seasonal 6 mos ahead. Accepts simultaneous submissions & reprints (tell when/where appeared). Prefers NIV or NRSV. Guidelines; copy for 9x12 SAE/2 stamps.

Poetry: Buys 20-25/yr. Free verse, haiku, light verse; to 8 lines (unless story poem); $10. Submit max. 4 poems.

Fillers: Buys 2-3/yr. Facts, games, party ideas, word puzzles.

Ethnic: Targets all ethnic groups involved in the Mennonite religion.

Tips: "Send stories that show rather than tell. Nothing that portrays children being unnaturally religious or pious. Cover letter should give your experience with children."

*STORY MATES, Christian Light Publications, Inc., Box 1212, Harrisonburg VA 22801-1212. (703)434-0768. Mennonite. Miriam Shank, ed. For 4-8 yr olds. Weekly take-home paper; 4 pgs; circ 5,200. 95% freelance. Complete ms/cover letter. Pays .02-.05/wd on acceptance for all, 1st, & reprint rts. Realistic or true stories to 800 wds; picture stories 120-150 wds. Responds in 9 wks. Seasonal 7 mos ahead. Guidelines/theme list; copy for 6x9 SAE/2 stamps. Will send questionnaire to fill out.

Poetry: Traditional, any length. Likes story poems.

Fillers: Quizzes, word puzzles, craft ideas. "Need fillers that correlate with theme list."

Tips: "No fantasy, child evangelism, Valentine's Day, Halloween, secular Christmas or Easter material." Very conservative.

TOGETHER TIME, 6401 The Paseo, Kansas City MO 64131. (816)333-7000x2347. Fax (816)333-4439. E-mail: lboardman@naz.org.WordAction Publishing Co./Church of the Nazarene. Lynda Boardman, ed. For 3-4 yr olds and parents. Weekly take-home paper; 4 pgs; circ 19,000. Subscription $9.95. 75% freelance. Query; fax/e-mail query OK. Pays .05/wd on publication for all rts. Articles 150-200 wds, fiction 150-200 wds (30/yr). Responds in 12 wks. Seasonal 12 mos ahead. Accepts simultaneous submissions. Kill fee 5%. Prefers disk. Prefers NIV. Guidelines/theme list; copy for #10 SAE/1 stamp.

Poetry: Buys 52/yr. Free verse, traditional; 4-8 lines; .25/line. Submit max. 5 poems.

Fillers: Games, ideas, activities; 150-200 wds.

Tips: "Know the age level of 3-4 year olds. Integrate Christian education throughout; don't tack it on the end."

TOUCH, Box 7259, Grand Rapids MI 49510. (616)241-5616. Fax (616)241-5558. GEMS Girls Clubs/(Christian Reformed, Reformed, and Presbyterian). Carol Smith, mng ed. To show girls, ages 9-14, that God is at work in their lives and the world around them. Monthly (10X) mag; 24 pgs; circ 14,000. Subscription $12.50. 75% freelance. Complete ms/cover letter; fax query OK. Pays $10-70 or .025/wd on publication for 1st or simultaneous rts. Articles 200-500 wds (10/yr); fiction 500-1,000 wds (30/yr); book/music/video reviews, 200 wds, $25. Responds in 4 wks. Seasonal 1 yr ahead. Accepts simultaneous submissions & reprints. No disk yet. Sidebars OK. Prefers NIV. Guidelines/theme list; copy $1/9x12 SAE/3 stamps.

Poetry: Buys 3/yr. Haiku, light verse, traditional; 4-16 lines; $10-20. Poetry fits themes.

Fillers: Buys 8/yr. Cartoons, games, ideas, party ideas, quizzes, short humor, word puzzles; 50-200 wds; $15-25.

Columns/Departments: Buys 3/yr. Crafts (things of interest to girls), 200-300 wds; $20-30.

Special Needs: Annual theme is "Come, Celebrate the King!" so all articles and stories should be of a celebrative nature. See Update for ideas.

Tips: "Fiction most open to freelancers. Know what girls face today and how they cope in their daily lives. We need angles from home life and friendships, peer pressure and the normal growing-up challenges girls deal with."

** This periodical was #42 on the 1996 Top 50 Christian Publishers list. (#45 in 1995)

*VENTURE, 1884 Randolph Ave., St. Paul MN 55105. (612)690-7010. Editorial Development Associates. Sr. Joan Mitchell, ed. Connects young people's real life experiences—successes and conflicts in family, neighborhood, classroom, playground—with the Sunday gospels; for intermediate-age children. Weekly take-home paper; 8 pgs; circ 140,000. 40% freelance. Query. Pays $75-125 on publication for all rts. Articles (6-8/yr) & fiction (8-10/yr), 800-900 wds. Responds in 2-8 wks. Seasonal 4-6 mos ahead. Accepts simultaneous query. Guidelines; copy $1.85.

Tips: "We want realistic fiction and nonfiction that raises current ethical religious questions and conflicts in multi-racial settings, believable and detailed, to which intermediate-age children can relate."

WONDER TIME, 6401 The Paseo, Kansas City MO 64131. (816)333-7000. Fax (816)333-4439. E-mail: lperrigo@nazarene.org. Church of the Nazarene. Lois Perrigo, ed.; submit to Shirley Smith, asst. ed. For 6-8 yr olds (1st & 2nd graders); emphasis on principles, character-building, and brotherhood. Weekly take-home paper; 4 pgs; circ 40,000. 50% freelance. Query; no phone/fax/e-mail query. Pays $25 on publication for multi-use rts. Fiction 250-350 wds (52/yr). Responds in 5 wks. Seasonal 6 mos ahead. Kill fee. Guidelines/theme list; copy for 9x12 SAE/2 stamps.

Tips: "We accept freelance stories to relate to our lesson Bible truth. Stories should be contemporary, life-related, and at a 1st-2nd grade readability. Avoid trite situations."

CHRISTIAN EDUCATION/LIBRARY MARKETS

#BAPTIST LEADER, Box 851, Valley Forge PA 19482-0851. (610)768-2143. Fax (610)768-2056. American Baptist. Donald Ng, ed. Practical "how-to" or thought-provoking articles for local church Christian education lay leaders and teachers. Quarterly mag; 32 pgs; circ 5,000. Subscription $8. 5% freelance. Complete ms/cover letter; fax query OK. Pays $10-50 on acceptance for 1st rts. Articles 1,200-2,000 wds (4/yr). Responds in 2-12 wks. Seasonal 1 yr ahead. Accepts simultaneous submissions & reprints. Prefers disk. Sidebars OK. Prefers NRSV. Guidelines; copy $1.50.

Poetry: Accepts 2-3/yr. Haiku, light verse, traditional; $10-20.

Fillers: Buys 4-8/yr. Cartoons, jokes, prayers; 25-100 wds; $10-20.

Special Needs: Plays & skits related to holidays that churches celebrate: Christmas, Easter, Mother's Day, Children's Day, Reformation Sunday,

Black History Month, etc; 1,300-2,000 wds; pays $25-50.

Tips: "Most open to feature articles, new program ideas for holidays, and holiday-related dramas or plays."

BRIGADE LEADER, Box 150, Wheaton IL 60189. (630)665-0630. Fax (630)665-0372. E-mail: BrigadeCSB@aol.com. Christian Service Brigade. Deborah Christensen, mng. ed. For men leading boy's clubs; emphasis on fathering issues. Quarterly mag; 16 pgs; circ 8,000. Subscription $6. 25% freelance. Query (most articles assigned). Pays .05-.10/wd on publication for 1st or reprint rts. Articles 1,000-1,500 wds (8/yr). Responds in 2 wks. Seasonal 4 mos ahead. Accepts reprints. Prefers disk. Kill fee $35. Sidebars OK. Prefers NIV. Guidelines; copy $1.50/9x12 SAE/4 stamps.

Tips: "We're especially looking for men who are familiar with Christian Service Brigade and how to disciple boys."

+CARAVAN: A Resource for Adult Religious Educators, 90 Parent Ave., Ottawa ON K1N 7B1 Canada. (613)241-9461. Fax 613)241-8117. Canadian conference of Catholic Bishops. Joanne Chafe, ed. A resources for adult educators who work in church settings. Quarterly mag; 16 pgs; circ 1,500. Subscription $17.12. 100% freelance. Complete ms/cover letter. Pays variable rate on acceptance or publication. Copyrighted; rights released on request. Articles (30-40/yr). Responds in 4-6 wks. Seasonal 3 mos ahead. Accepts simultaneous submissions. Sidebars OK. Guidelines/copy.

Columns/Departments: Adult religious education: New Initiatives, New Releases, Creative program ideas.

Special Needs: Workshop models.

#CATECHIST, 330 Progress Rd., Dayton OH 45449. (513)847-5900. Fax (513)847-5910. Catholic. Patricia Fischer, ed. For Catholic school teachers. Mag. published 8x/yr; 52 pgs; circ 45,700. Query (preferred) or complete ms. Pays $25-100 on publication for all rts. Articles 1,200-1,500 wds. Responds in 9-18 wks. Guidelines; copy $2.50. Not in topical listings.

***CE CONNECTION**, Box 12609, Oklahoma City OK 73157. (405)787-7110. General Christian Education Dept./IPHC. Talmage Gardner, asst to dir. Targets pastors and local Christian education workers/leaders for training/how-to. Quarterly mag/newsletter; circ 6,600. 100% freelance. Complete ms/cover letter. **NO PAYMENT.** Not copyrighted. Articles. Seasonal 4 mos ahead. Accepts reprints. Free copy.

+CE CONNECTION COMMUNIQUE, PO Box 12624, Roanoke VA 24027. Phone/fax (540)342-7511. E-mail: cccbbr@worldnet.att.net. Betty Robertson, ed. Virginia Christian Education Assn. Bimonthly newsletter; 8 pgs; circ 1,350. Subscription $19.95. 25% freelance. Query; no phone/fax/e-mail query. Pays $5-10 on acceptance for 1st, one-time, simultaneous rts. Not copyrighted. Articles 100-600 wds. Responds in 6 wks. Seasonal 6 mos ahead. Accepts simultaneous submissions & reprints. Guidelines; copy $3.

CHILDREN'S MINISTRY, PO Box 481, Loveland CO 80539. (970)669-3836. Fax (970)669-3269. E-mail: CMM Editor@aol.com. Website: http://www.grouppublishing. com. Group Publishing. Barbara Beach, dept. ed. For Christians who work with kids from birth to 6th grade. Monthly mag; 70 pgs; circ 50,000. Subscription $24.95. 75% freelance. Query/clips; fax/e-mail query OK. Pays

$10-175 on acceptance for all rts. Articles 50-1,500 wds (40/yr). Responds in 4 wks. Seasonal 5 mos ahead. Accepts disk. Sidebars OK. Prefers New Century. Guidelines; copy $2/9x12 SASE. (Ads)

Columns/Departments: Buys up to 50/yr. Teacher Telegram (practical teacher tips); For Parents Only (practical parenting tips); Preschool Page (hints, songs, bible activities); Group Games; Seasonal Specials (parties, service projects, worship celebrations—4-5 mos ahead); 5-Minute Messages; 50-125 wds; $25. Complete mss.

Special Needs: Working with volunteers, discipling children, morals, issues for the professional children's minister, and Sunday school programming that works; children's issues; seasonal.

Tips: "Most open to departments. Need 'ah-ha' ideas—practical. Read CM to familiarize yourself with our magazine. Understand our unique and innovative approach to Christian education."

#CHRISTIAN EDUCATION COUNSELOR, 1445 Boonville Ave., Springfield MO 65802-1894. (417)862-2781. Fax (417)862-0503. E-mail: Sylbil@aol.com. Assemblies of God. Sylvia Lee, ed. Presents teaching and administrative helps to lay leaders in local churches. Monthly mag; 16/24 pgs; circ 22,500. Subscription $10/leader $14. 40% freelance. Complete ms/cover letter. Pays .05-.10/wd on acceptance for 1st, one-time, simultaneous & reprint rts. Articles 600-800 wds (50/yr); book reviews, 400-500 wds, $35. Responds in 4 wks. Seasonal 6 mos ahead. Accepts simultaneous submissions & reprints. Prefers disk (Microsoft Word 5.1). Sidebars OK. Guidelines/theme list; copy for 9x12 SAE/2 stamps.

Fillers: Buys cartoons, games, ideas, quizzes; $35-85.

Tips: "Writers should have first-hand experience in Christian education in the local church. Articles strong on how-to. Offer practical material for classroom teachers who are short on time and resources."

** This periodical was #52 on the 1996 Top 50 Christian Publishers list. (#62 in 1995, #64 in 1994)

CHRISTIAN EDUCATION LEADERSHIP, 1080 Montgomery Ave., Cleveland TN 37311. (423)476-4512. E-mail: lancewc@aol.com. Pentecostal Church of God/Pathway Press. Lance Colkmire, ed. For Christian education teachers and leaders. Quarterly mag; 32 pgs; circ 10,000. Subscription $7. 40% freelance. Complete ms/cover letter. Pays $25-55 on acceptance for one-time, simultaneous or reprint rts. Articles 400-1,200 wds (12/yr). Responds in 4 wks. Seasonal 4 mos ahead. Accepts simultaneous submissions & reprints (tell when/where appeared). Accepts disk. Sidebars OK. Guidelines; copy for 9x12 SAE/4 stamps.

Columns/Departments: Sunday School; Singles Ministry; Outreach; Music Ministry; The Pastor and C.E.; Kid's Church; 400-800 wds; $25-50.

Special Needs: Articles on children's ministry and Sunday school.

#CHRISTIAN EDUCATORS JOURNAL, 1828 Mayfair NE, Grand Rapids MI 49503. (712)722-6252. Fax (712)722-1198. E-mail: lgilst@dordt.edu. Lorna Van Gilst, mng. ed. For educators in Christian day schools at the elementary, secondary, and college levels. Quarterly journal; 36 pgs; circ 4,200. Subscription $7.50. 50% freelance. Query; phone query OK. Pays $30 on publication for one-time rts. Articles 600-1,200 wds (20/yr); fiction 600-1,200 wds. Responds in 5 wks. Seasonal 4 mos ahead. Accepts simultaneous submissions & reprints. Guidelines/theme list; copy $1 or 9x12 SAE/4 stamps. (Ads)

Poetry: Buys 6/yr. On teaching day school; 4-30 lines; $10. Submit max. 5 poems.

Tips: "No articles on Sunday school, only Christian day school. Most open to theme topics and features."

THE CHRISTIAN LIBRARIAN, Box 4000, Three Hills AB T0M 2N0 Canada. US address: Box 4, Cedarville OH 45314. (403)443-5511 x3343. Fax (403)443-5540. E-mail: ron.jordahl@pbi.ab.ca. Assn. of Christian Librarians. Ron Jordahl, ed. Christian librarianship. Quarterly (3X) jour; 40 pgs; circ 500. Subscription $20. 25% freelance. Query; phone/fax query OK. **NO PAYMENT**, for one-time rts. Not copyrighted. Articles 1,000-3,500 words; research articles to 5,000 wds (6/yr); reviews 150-300 wds. Responds in 5 wks. Accepts simultaneous query & reprints. Prefers disk. Sidebars OK. Guidelines; copy $5.

Fillers: Anecdotes, cartoons, newsbreaks, short humor; 25-300 wds.

Special Needs: Articles on libraries, books, and reading.

CHRISTIAN LIBRARY JOURNAL, 1101 SW Rogue River Ave., Grants Pass OR 97526. (541)479-5277. Fax (541)479-5178. E-mail: NANCYHCLJ@aol.com. Christian Library Services. Nancy Hesch, ed/pub. Primarily published for the Christian school (K-12) library and teachers of reading and English; also of interest to librarians, teachers, and home-schooling parents. Bimonthly (5X) mag; 88 pgs; circ. 1,000. Subscription $45. Est. 1995. 10% freelance. Query or complete ms/cover letter; fax/e-mail query OK; query for electronic submissions. Pays $50-100 on publication for 1st or reprint rts. Articles (15/yr) 500-1,200 wds; book reviews, 200-400 wds (ask to be a reviewer), no payment. Responds in 8-12 wks. Seasonal 4 mos ahead. Accepts reprints (tell when/where appeared). Prefers disk. Sidebars OK. Free guidelines/copy. (Ads)

Fillers: Quotes; 10-100 wds. No payment.

Columns/Departments: Accepts 4-6/yr. Book Nook (using books with students), 500-800 wds; no payment. Complete ms.

Tips: "Looking for discussions of various genres of Christian literature, especially as related to K-12 and staff."

*CHRISTIAN SCHOOL, 1308 Santa Rosa, Wheaton IL 60187. (708)653-4588. Phil Landrum, pub. A publication for Christian-school educators and parents. Quarterly mag; 48 pgs; circ 3,000 schools. 2% freelance. Query; phone query OK. **NO PAYMENT.** Articles 500-1,500 wds (1/yr); fiction 1,000-1,500 (1/yr). Responds in 2-4 wks. Free guidelines/copy.

Poetry: Accepts 1/yr. Traditional. Submit max. 5 poems.

Fillers: Accepts 1/yr. Anecdotes.

Special Needs: Education how-to; youth trends; training techniques; children's books.

CHURCH & SYNAGOGUE LIBRARIES, PO Box 19357, Portland OR 97280-0357. (503)244-6919; (800)LIB-CSLA. Fax (503)977-3734. E-mail: CSLA@worldaccess.com. Church and Synagogue Library Assn. Judith Janzen, exec. dir. To help librarians run congregational libraries. Bimonthly; 20 pgs.; circ. 2,500. Subscription $25, $35 CAN, $45 foreign. Query. **NO PAYMENT.** Requires disk. Articles. Book & video reviews 1-2 paragraphs. (Ads)

Fillers: Ideas.

CHURCH EDUCATOR, 165 Plaza Dr., Prescott AZ 86303. (520)771-8601. Fax (520)771-8621. E-mail: edmin2@aol.com. Linda Davidson, ed. For mainline Protestant Christian educators. Monthly journal; 36 pgs; circ 5,000. Subscription $28. 90% freelance. Complete ms/cover letter; phone/fax/e-mail query OK. Pays .03/wd after publication for 1st rts. Articles (100/yr) & fiction (20/yr), 500-2,000 wds. Responds in 3-6 wks. Seasonal 5 mos ahead. Accepts some reprints (tell when/where appeared). Sidebars OK. Guidelines/theme list; copy for 9x12 SAE/4 stamps.

> **Fillers:** Bible games and Bible puzzles.
>
> **Columns/Departments:** Buys 20/yr. Noah's Ark (crafts for children); Youth Notebook (tips for working with teens); 200-500 wds.
>
> **Special Needs:** Developing children's spirituality.
>
> **Tips:** "Talk to the educator at your church. What would they find useful? Most open to seasonal articles dealing with the liturgical year. Write up church programs with specific how-tos of putting the program together."

CHURCH LIBRARIES (formerly **LIBRARIAN'S WORLD**), 9731 Fox Glen Dr. #6F, Niles IL 60714-5861. (847)296-3964. Fax (847)296-0803. E-mail: 102661.3622 @compuserve.com. Evangelical Church Library Assn. Lin Johnson, ed. To assist church librarians in setting up, maintaining, and promoting church libraries and media centers. Quarterly mag; 36-44 pgs; circ 550. Subscription $20. 99% freelance. Complete ms; fax/e-mail query OK. Pays .04/wd on acceptance for 1st, reprint or simultaneous rts. Not copyrighted. Articles 500-1,000 wds (20/yr); book/video/cassette reviews by assignment (send SASE for application form), 75-150 wds, free product. Responds in 4-6 wks. Seasonal 6 mos ahead. Accepts simultaneous submissions & reprints (tell when/where appeared). Requires disk. Sidebars OK. Prefers NIV. Guidelines; copy for 9x12 SAE/5 stamps. (Ads)

> **Columns/Departments:** Buys 12/yr. Idea Cards (3x5 card ideas on any aspect of running a library), 100 wds; pays a free book.
>
> **Tips:** "Talk to church librarians or get involved in library or reading programs. Most open to articles, card ideas, and promotional ideas; profiles of church libraries. Not currently looking for reviewers."

*CHURCH MEDIA LIBRARY MAGAZINE, 127 9th Ave. N., Nashville TN 37234. (615)251-2752. Southern Baptist. Floyd B. Simpson, ed. Supports the establishment and development of church media libraries; provides how-to articles and articles of inspiration and encouragement to media library workers. Quarterly mag; 52 pgs; circ 30,000. Query. Pays .055/wd on publication for all, 1st, or reprint rts. Articles 600-1,500 wds (40-60/yr). Responds in 5 wks. Seasonal 14 mos ahead. Free guidelines/copy.

CHURCH WORSHIP, 165 Plaza Dr., Prescott AZ 86303. (602)771-8601. Fax (602)771-8621. E-mail: edmin2@aol.com. Robert Davidson, ed. Supplementary resources for church worship leaders. Monthly journal; 24 pgs; circ 1,200. Subscription $24. 75% freelance. Complete ms/cover letter; phone/fax/e-mail query OK. Pays .03/wd on publication for 1st rts. Articles to 100-1,500 wds; fiction 100-1,500 wds. Responds in 2-6 wks. Seasonal 4 mos ahead. Guidelines/theme list; copy for 9x12 SAE/3 stamps.

> **Poetry:** Submit max. 5 poems.
>
> **Special Needs:** Complete worship services.

Tips: "Most open to creative worship services using music, drama or art."

EVANGELIZING TODAY'S CHILD, Box 348, Warrenton MO 63383-0348. (314)456-4321. Fax (314)456-2078. E-mail: ETCLIP@aol.com. Child Evangelism Fellowship. Elsie C. Lippy, ed. To equip Christians to win the world's children (4-11) to Christ and disciple them. Bimonthly mag; 64 pgs; circ 20,000. Subscription $20. 50% freelance. Complete ms; no phone/fax/e-mail query. Pays .10-.12/wd (.07/wd for fiction) within 60 days for all, 1st, one-time or reprint rts. Articles 1,200-1,500 wds (24/yr); fiction 700-900 (12/yr). Responds in 4-6 wks. Seasonal 1 yr ahead. Accepts reprints (tell when/where appeared). Accepts disk. Kill fee 30%. Sidebars OK. Guidelines; copy $2/9x12 SAE/6 stamps. (Ads)

    Resource Center: Buys 40-60/yr. Complete ms, 200-250 wds. Pays $15-25 for teaching hints, bulletin board ideas, object lessons, missions incentives, etc.

    Special Needs: Salvation testimonies of adults saved before age 12, 700-900 wds; 6/yr. Creative ideas for involving children in ministry.

    Tips: "Most open to Resource Center. Study the publication. Know children and/or children's workers."

    ** This periodical was #64 on the 1995 Top 50 Christian Publishers list. (#49 in 1994)

#GROUP MAGAZINE, Box 481, Loveland CO 80538. (303)669-3836. Fax (303)669-3269. E-mail: rick_lawrence@ministrynet.usa.net. Rick Lawrence, ed. Aimed at leaders of high-school-age, Christian youth groups. Bimonthly mag; 56 pgs; circ 57,000. Subscription $25.95. 60% freelance. Query. Pays $35-200 on acceptance for all rts. Articles 500-1,700 wds (50-60/yr). Responds in 9 wks. Seasonal 7 mos ahead. Kill fee $20. Guidelines; copy $2/9x12 SAE.

    Columns/Departments: Barbara Beach. Buys 160/yr. Try This One (youth group activities), 125 wds; Strange But True (strange youth-ministry stories), 600 wds; Hands-on Help (tips for leaders), 125 wds; $35. Complete ms.

    Tips: "All areas open; new slant; not preachy. Looking for short how-to pieces, up to 250 words."

INSIGHT INTO CHRISTIAN EDUCATION, Box 23152, Charlotte NC 28227-0272. (704)545-6161. Fax (704)573-0712. Advent Christian. Millie Griswold, ed. For local church Christian education volunteers. Quarterly mag; 8 pgs; circ 2,200. Subscription $6. 20% freelance. Query or complete ms. Pays $25 on publication. Articles 600-1,000 wds. Accepts reprints. Seasonal 6 mos ahead. Free copy.

#THE JOURNAL OF ADVENTIST EDUCATION, 12501 Old Columbia Pike, Silver Springs MD 20904-6600. (301)680-5075. Fax (301)622-9627. E-mail: 74617.1231@compuserve.com. Seventh-day Adventist. Beverly J. Rumble, ed. For Seventh-day teachers teaching in the church's school system, K-University. Bimonthly journal; 48 pgs; circ 7,500. Subscription $16.25. 10% freelance. Query; phone/fax/e-mail query OK. Pays $25-100 on publication for 1st & translation rts. Articles to 1,000-1,500 wds (2-20/yr); book reviews to $25. Responds in 6-18 wks. Seasonal 5-6 mos ahead. Kill fee rarely. Accepts reprints. Few sidebars. Guidelines; copy for 9x12 SAE/5 stamps or $1.25.

    Fillers: Cartoons only, no pay.

    Special Needs: "All articles in the context of denominational schools (*not* Sunday school tips); professional enrichment and teaching tips for Christian teachers. Need feature articles."

KIDS' STUFF, 55 W. Oak Ridge Dr., Hagerstown MD 21740. (301)791-7000. Fax (301)790-9734. Seventh-day Adventist. Suzanne Perdew, mng ed. For adults leading children (birth-eighth grade) to Christ. Quarterly mag; 32-40 pgs; circ. 7,500. Subscription $16.95. 10% freelance. Query; fax/e-mail query OK. Pays $25-125 on acceptance for one-time or reprint rts. Articles 500-1,300 wds (10/yr). Responds in 6-8 wks. Seasonal 9 mos ahead. Accepts simultaneous submissions & reprints (tell when/where appeared). Sidebars OK. Prefers NIV. Guidelines; copy for 9x12 SAE/4 stamps.

> **Columns/Departments:** Try This (short ideas that have worked in teaching kids), 2-3 paragraphs. Pays free book.
>
> **Tips:** "Looking for program ideas, outreach ideas, something that has worked to draw kids closer to Jesus. This is a how-to oriented magazine. I'd be interested in active teaching ideas on general themes, such as faith, trust, prayer and grace."

LEADER IN THE CHURCH SCHOOL TODAY, 201 Eighth Ave. N, Nashville TN 37202. (615)749-6538. Fax (615)749-6061. E-mail: 102521.1513@compuserve. com. United Methodist. Jill S. Reddig, ed. For pastors and Christian education leaders in the church. Quarterly mag; 64 pgs; circ 10,000. Subscription $14. 50% freelance. Complete ms/cover letter; phone/fax/e-mail query OK. Pays .05/wd on acceptance for all or 1st rts. Articles to 400-2,500 wds (98/yr). Responds in 2-8 wks. Seasonal 14 mos ahead. Accepts reprints. Sidebars OK. Prefers NRSV (never Living). Prefers disk. Guidelines/search list; copy $3.50.

> **Fillers:** Buys 4 cartoons/yr. Christian ed themes only; $15-30.
>
> **Columns/Departments:** Buys 30/yr. Idea Exchange (what worked for us), 50-150 wds; Teacher/leader Development (teacher training), 700-2,500 wds; Days & Seasons (seasonal Christian ed.), 700-2,500 wds.
>
> ** This periodical was #66 on the 1996 Top 50 Christian Publishers List.

*LEVEL C TEACHER—EARLY CHILDHOOD, 6401 The Paseo, Kansas City MO 64131. (816)333-7000. Nazarene. Lynda T. Boardman, ed. Lessons and guidelines for Sunday school teachers of 3-4 yr. olds. Quarterly; 64 pgs; circ 1,800. 5% freelance. Complete ms/cover letter; phone query OK. Pays .035/wd on publication for all rts. Accepts simultaneous submissions & reprints. Kill fee. Copy for 6x9 SAE/2 stamps.

> **Poetry:** Traditional; 4-8 lines; .25/line ($2 min.). Submit max. 5 poems.
>
> **Tips:** "Mostly assigned. If interested in writing for us, give editor a call. We do accept poems periodically."

*LOLLIPOPS, The Magazine for Early Childhood Educators, Good Apple, Inc., Box 2649, Columbus OH 43216-2649. Donna Borst, ed. Easy-to-use, hands-on, practical teaching ideas and suggestions for early childhood educators. Mag published 5 times/yr; circ 20,000. 20% freelance. Query or complete ms. Pays $10-100 on publication for all rts. Articles 200-1,000 wds; fiction (for young children) 500-1,200 wds. Seasonal 6 mos ahead. Guidelines (2 stamps); copy for 9x12 SAE/3 stamps.

> **Poetry:** Light verse.
>
> **Tips:** "Looking for something new and different for teachers of young children; seasonal material."

#MEMOS, 1445 Boonville Ave., Springfield MO 65802-1894. (417)862-2781. Fax (417)862-0503. Assemblies of God. Kerry Clarensau, ed. Leadership magazine for girl's program (ages 3-teens), called Missionettes. Quarterly mag; 24 pgs; circ 14,100. Subscription $6.50. 30% freelance. Query or complete ms/cover letter; phone query OK. Pays $10-50 on acceptance for 1st rts. Articles to 1,200 wds; book reviews 50-75 wds. Responds in 4 wks. Seasonal 1 yr ahead. Accepts reprints. Free guidelines/copy.

Special Needs: Children and divorce; children and self image.

Tips: "Most writers are involved as a coordinator/sponsor in Missionettes. Most open to articles on how to work with children; age-level crafts and projects."

*PARISH TEACHER, 426 S. 5th St., Box 1209, Minneapolis MN 55440-1209. (612)330-3423. Fax (612)330-3455. ELCA/Augsburg Fortress Publishers. Carol A. Burk, ed. Articles and ideas for Lutheran church school teachers. Monthly (10X) newsletter; 16 pgs; circ 50,000. Subscription $7.75. 12.5% freelance. Complete ms/cover letter. Pays $50 on publication for 1st rts. Not copyrighted. Articles 650-750 wds (15/yr); plays 400-800 wds (3-4/yr). Responds in 12-16 wks. Seasonal 4-6 mos ahead. Accepts simultaneous submissions & reprints. Prefers disk. No sidebars. Prefers NRSV. Guidelines; copy for 9x12 SAE/4 stamps.

Fillers: Buys 100 ideas/yr.; 100-200 wds; $15.

Tips: "Most open to ideas or feature articles that are practical and useful in the classroom."

PERSPECTIVE, Box 788, Wheaton IL 60189-0788. (630)293-1600x340/342. Fax (630)293-3053. Pioneer Clubs. Rebecca Powell Parat, ed. To help and encourage Pioneer Club leaders (for children ages 2-18). Triannual mag; 32 pgs; circ 27,000. Subscription $6. 15% freelance. Query/clips or complete ms; fax query OK. Pays .05-.10/wd ($50-90) on acceptance for all, 1st, one-time or reprint rts. Articles 500-1,500 wds (0-3/yr). Responds in 6 wks. Seasonal 9 mos ahead. Accepts simultaneous query & reprints (tell when/where appeared). Prefers disk. Sidebars OK. Prefers NIV. Guidelines; copy $1.75/9x12 SAE/4 stamps.

Fillers: Buys 1-2/yr. Games, party ideas.

Columns/Departments: Buys 0-3/yr. Storehouse (ideas for crafts, games, service projects, tips for leaders, etc.); 100-200 wds; $7-15. Complete ms.

Tips: "Most articles done on assignment. We'd like to hear from freelancers who have experience with, or access to, a Pioneer Clubs program or Camp Cherith. They should send samples of their work along with a letter introducing themselves."

+REACHING CHILDREN AT RISK, PO Box 633, Oxford OX1 4YP, England UK. Phone/fax +44-1865-203-567. E-mail: 100423.2255@compuserve.com. The Viva Network. B. Ripley Robinson, ed. To meet the needs of project leaders and workers ministering to children at high risk (street children of the world). Journal. Est. 1996. Query; phone/e-mail query OK. **PAYS IN COPIES.** Articles 1,500-3,000 wds. Guidelines. Not in topical listings.

Tips: "We are forming a pool of writers who would contribute material on an ongoing basis. A contributing writer may be asked to write one or two articles a year. Topics will be suggested by the writers."

RELIGION TEACHER'S JOURNAL, Box 180, Mystic CT 06355. (860)536-2611. Fax (860)572-0788. E-mail: ttpubsedit@aol.com. Twenty-Third Publications/Catholic. Gwen Costello, ed. dir. For volunteer religion teachers who need practical, hands-on information as well as theological background for teaching religion to K through high school. 7X yearly mag; 40 pgs; circ 40,000. Subscription $18.95. 40% freelance. Query; fax/e-mail query OK. Pays to $100 on acceptance for 1st rts. Not copyrighted. Articles to 6 pgs (50/yr). Responds in 2-4 wks. Seasonal 2 mos ahead. Prefers disk. Sidebars OK. Guidelines/theme list; copy for 9x12 SAE/4 stamps. (Ads)

Fillers: Jennifer Johnson. Buys 20-30/yr. Anecdotes (about teaching), games, ideas, prayers, successful class activities; to 1 pg; $5-25.

Tips: "Know our audience and address their needs. Most open to feature articles about teaching skills, spirituality, successful class activities or projects."

RESOURCE, 6401 The Paseo, Kansas City MO 64131. (816)333-7000x2224. Fax (816)363-7092. E-mail: dfelter@nazarene.org. Church of the Nazarene. David Felter, ed. To provide information, training, and inspiration to those who are involved in ministering within the Christian Life and Sunday school departments of the local church. Quarterly journal; 34 pgs; circ 6,000. Subscription $6.25. 50-65% freelance. Complete ms/cover letter; fax/e-mail query OK. Query for electronic submissions. Pays .04/wd on acceptance for all, 1st, one-time, or reprint rts. Articles 1,000-4,000 wds (150/yr); book reviews 300 wds. Responds in 2 wks. Seasonal 6 mos ahead. Accepts reprints. Accepts disk. Sidebars OK. Prefers NIV or NRSV. Guidelines/theme list; copy for 9x12 SAE/2 stamps.

Poetry: Buys 4/yr. Seasonal or on outreach/Sunday school; to 30 lines; .25/line, $5 minimum. Submit max. 1 poem.

Fillers: Buys 4 cartoons/yr; $10-25.

Tips: "Looking for succinct pieces that instruct, train, motivate, etc."

** This periodical was #18 on the 1996 Top 50 Christian Publishers list. (#10 in 1995)

*SHINING STAR MAGAZINE, Box 399, Carthage IL 62321. (217)357-6093. Silver Burdett & Ginn. Mary Tucker, ed. Reproducible Bible activities, games, etc. for K-7th grades. Quarterly mag; 80 pgs; circ 20,000. Subscription $16.95. 99% freelance. Query; phone/fax query OK. Pays $10-50 on publication for all rts. Articles 100-500 wds (20/yr); fiction 100-500 wds (10/yr). Responds in 5-9 wks. Seasonal 9 mos ahead. Accepts simultaneous submissions; serials 4 parts. No sidebars. Guidelines/theme list; copy $3/9x12 SAE/3 stamps.

Poetry: Buys 10/yr. Traditional; 8-36 lines; $10-30. Submit max. 4 poems.

Fillers: Buys 25/yr. Anecdotes, facts, games, ideas, quotes, word puzzles; 100-300 wds; $10-40.

Special Needs: Puzzles, games, crafts for kids.

Tips: "Try out material on children before you consider it ready to submit."

TEACHERS IN FOCUS, 8605 Explorer Dr., Colorado Springs CO 80920. (719)548-4578. Fax (719)531-3499. Focus on the Family. Charles W. Johnson, ed. To encourage, inform and support Christian teachers in public and private education (K-12). Monthly (9X) mag; 32 pgs; circ 35,000. Subscription $20. 80% freelance. Query; fax query OK. Pays $200 & up on acceptance for 1st rts. Articles 1,500 wds (4/yr); book reviews (educational resources), $25-50. Responds in 4 wks. Accepts reprints (tell when/where appeared). Accepts disk. Kill fee 50%. Sidebars OK. Prefers NIV. Guidelines/theme list; copy for 9x12 SAE/4 stamps.

Fillers: Buys 50/yr. Humorous classroom anecdotes; 50-150 wds; $25.

Columns/Departments: Accepts 9/yr. Laughs From the Lounge (student humor), 100-150 wds; Teammates (profiles on support staff), 500 wds. Pays $75.

Tips: "Uses articles of interest to teachers trying to cope in the classroom situation. Education issues. Avoid educational and religious jargon."

** This periodical was #12 on the 1996 Top 50 Christian Publishers list (#29 in 1995, #55 in 1994). 1995 EPA Award of Excellence—Christian Ministry.

#TEACHERS INTERACTION, 3558 S. Jefferson Ave., St. Louis MO 63118-3968. (314)268-1000. Fax (314)268-1329. Concordia Publishing House/Lutheran Church-Missouri Synod. Jane Haas, ed. A magazine church-school workers grow by. Quarterly mag (newsletter 7X/yr); 32 pgs; circ. 20,400. Subscription $10.25. 20% freelance. Complete ms/cover letter. Pays $20-100 on publication for all rts. How-tos to 100 wds, articles 750-1,500 wds (6/yr); fiction 750-1,200 wds. Responds in 13 wks. Seasonal 1 yr ahead. No sidebars. Guidelines/theme list; copy $2.75/9x12 SAE/2 stamps.

Poetry: Christian; 5-20 lines; $30-50. Also Christian songs.

Fillers: Buys 48/yr. Prayers; teacher tips/ideas, 200 wds; $20.

Special Needs: Practical, how-to articles that will help the volunteer church worker.

*****TEAM**, Box 7259, Grand Rapids MI 49510. (616)241-5616. Young Calvinist Federation. Dale Dieleman, ed. Geared to leaders of youth programs, not Sunday school. Quarterly mag; circ 2,000. 10% freelance. Complete ms. Pays $30 on publication for 1st, simultaneous or reprint rts. Articles 700-2,000 wds (6/yr). Responds in 5 wks. Seasonal 6 mos ahead. Kill fee 50%. Accepts simultaneous submissions & reprints. Guidelines; copy $1/9x12 SAE/2 stamps.

Fillers: Cartoons, ideas, party ideas, short humor.

Columns/Departments: Street Beat (issues in urban youth ministry).

TODAY'S CATHOLIC TEACHER, 330 Progress Rd., Dayton OH 45449. (937)847-5900. Fax (937)847-5910. Catholic/Peter Li Education Group. Mary C. Noschang, ed. Directed to personal and professional concerns of teachers and administrators in K-12 Catholic schools. Monthly mag (6X during school yr); 60 pgs; circ 50,000. Subscription $14.95. 75% freelance. Query or complete ms/cover letter; phone/fax query OK. Pays $100-250 on publication for all rts. Articles 1,500 wds (20/yr). Responds in 8 wks. Seasonal 6 mos ahead. Accepts simultaneous submissions & reprints (tell when/where appeared). Kill fee. Prefers disk. Sidebars OK. Guidelines/theme list; copy $3. (Ads)

Special Needs: Activity pages teachers can copy and pass out to students to work on. Try to provide classroom-ready material teachers can use to supplement curriculum.

Tips: "Looking for material teachers in grades 3-9 can use to supplement curriculum material. Most open to articles or lesson plans."

#VISION MAGAZINE, Box 41300, Pasadena CA 91114. (818)798-1124. Fax (818)798-2346. E-mail: educa@aol.com. Christian Educators Assn., Intl. Judy Turpen, ed. To encourage and equip Christian educators and parents in public education; inserted in Teachers in Focus. Monthly (9X) insert; 8 pgs; circ 6,000. Subscription $35 (free to members). 50% freelance. Query; fax query OK. Pays

$30-40 on publication for 1st & reprint rts. Articles 50-1,200 wds (2/yr); book reviews, 40-50 wds, pays copies. Responds in 4-6 wks. Seasonal 4 mos ahead. Accepts simultaneous submissions & reprints. Sidebars OK. Guidelines/theme list; copy for 9x12 SAE/6 stamps. (Ads)

Poetry: Accepts 3-4/yr. Free verse, haiku, light verse, traditional; 4-16 lines; no payment. Submit max. 3 poems.

Fillers: Accepts 2-6/yr. Anecdotes, cartoons, facts, ideas, newsbreaks, prose, prayers, quotes; 100 wds; no payment. Educational only.

Special Needs: Legal and other issues in public education.

Tips: "Know public education, write from a positive perspective as our readers are involved in public ed. by calling and choice. Most open to tips for teachers for living out their faith in the classroom in legally appropriate ways."

DAILY DEVOTIONAL MARKETS

Due to the nature of the daily devotional market, the following market listings may include only the name, address, phone number (if available) and editor's name. Because most of these markets assign all material, they do not wish to be listed in the usual way, if at all.

If you are interested in writing daily devotionals, send to the following markets for guidelines and sample copies, write up sample devotionals to fit each one's particular format, and send to the editor with a request for an assignment. **DO NOT** submit any other type of material to these markets unless indicated.

*CHRIST IN OUR HOME, 426 S. 5th St., Box 1209, Minneapolis MN 55440-1209. (612)330-3423. Fax (612)330-3455. Carol A. Burk, ed. Pays $15/devotion.

*COME YE APART, Box 419527, Kansas City MO 64131. Paul Martin, ed.

DAILY DEVOTIONS FOR THE DEAF, 21199 Greenview Rd., Council Bluffs IA 51503-9500. (712)322-5493. Fax (712)322-7792. Duane King, ed. Prefers to see completed devotionals; 225 wds. **NO PAYMENT.**

DEVOTIONS, 8121 Hamilton Ave., Cincinnati OH 45231. (513)931-4050. Eileen Wilmoth, ed. No devotions or poetry. Buys photos only.

FORWARD DAY BY DAY, 412 Sycamore St., Cincinnati OH 45202-4195. (513)721-6659. Fax (513)421-0315. E-mail: forward.movement@ecunet.org. E.S. Gleason, ed. Send a couple of sample devotions to fit our format and request an assignment. Devotionals each 1305 characters. Pays about $200 for a month's devotions. Uses almost no freelance.

*THE HOME ALTAR, Meditations for Families with Young Children, 426 S. 5th St., Box 1209, Minneapolis MN 55440-1209. (612)330-3423. Fax (612)330-3455. Carol A. Burk, ed. 64 pgs. Pays $15/devotion.

*LIGHT FROM THE WORD, Box 50434, Indianapolis IN 46250-0434. (317)595-4144. Carl W. Pierce, sr. ed.

+PATHWAYS TO GOD, PO Box 2499, Anderson IN 46018-2499. (800)347-7721. (317)644-7721. Fax (317)622-9511. Kathleen Buehler, ed. Send an SASE for information on becoming a Pathways writer.

#THE QUIET HOUR, 4050 Lee Vance View, Colorado Springs CO 80919. Cook Communications Ministries. Gary Wilde, ed. Pays $15 on acceptance. Send resume and list of credits, rather than a sample.

REJOICE!, 1218 Franklin St. NW, Salem OR 97304-3902. (503)585-4458. Mennonite. Philip Wiebe, ed. Quarterly. Pays $110 for 7-day assigned meditations, 300 wds. Doesn't send samples or guidelines to unsolicited writers. Prefers that you send couple of sample devotions and inquire about assignment procedures. Don't apply for assignment unless you are familiar with the publication and Anabaptist theology.

THE SECRET PLACE, Box 851, Valley Forge PA 19482-0851. (610)768-2240. Kathleen Hayes, mng. ed. Prefers to see completed devotionals, 125-200 wds (use unfamiliar Scripture passages). Uses poetry and photos. 64 pgs. Pays $15 for all rts. Guidelines.

THE UPPER ROOM, PO Box 189, Nashville TN 37202-0189. (615)340-7252 (no "cold" calls; get guidelines first). Fax (615)340-7006. Website: http://www. upperroom.org. Mary Lou Redding, mng. ed. 95% freelance. Pays $20 per 250-word devotional. 72 pgs. Note: This publication does accept freelance submissions and does not make assignments. Phone/fax/e-mail query OK. Send devotionals up to 250 wds. Buys one-time use of art work (transparencies/slides requested). No disk. Guidelines; copy for 5x7 SAE/2 stamps.

> **Tips:** "We do not return submissions. Accepted submissions will be notified in 6-9 wks. Follow guidelines."

THE WORD IN SEASON, PO Box 1209, Minneapolis MN 55440-1209. (800)426-0115x216. Fax (612)330-3455. Andrea Lee Schieber, ed. 96 pgs. Devotions 250 wds. Pays $15/devotion. Guidelines for #10 SAE/2 stamps.

> **Tips:** "We prefer that you write for guidelines. We will send instructions for preparing sample devotions. We accept new writers based on the sample devotions we request and make assignments after acceptance."

MISSIONS MARKETS

#AMERICAN HORIZON, 1445 Boonville Ave., Springfield MO 65802-1894. (417)862-2781x3264. Fax (417)863-7276. Assemblies of God. Traci L. Countryman, ed. Denominational magazine of home missions/mostly on assignment. Bimonthly mag; 20 pgs; circ 36,000. Free to contributors. 75% freelance. Query or complete ms/cover letter; phone query OK. Pay .03/wd on publication for 1st rts. Articles 750-1,200 wds (17/yr). Responds in 6 wks. Seasonal 5 mos ahead. Accepts simultaneous submissions & reprints. Free guidelines/copy.

AREOPAGUS MAGAZINE, PO Box 33, Shatin, New Territories, Hong Kong. (852)2691-1904. Fax (852)2695-9885. E-mail: areos@asiaonline.net. Website: http://www.areopagus.org.hk.Tao Fong Shan Christian Centre. John G. LeMond, ed. Provides a forum for dialogue between the good news of Jesus Christ and people of faith both in major world religions and new religious movements. Quarterly mag; 50 pgs; circ 1,000. Subscription $24. 75% freelance. Query; e-mail OK. Pays $100-300 on publication for one-time rts. Articles 1,000-5,000 wds (20/yr); book reviews, 500-750 wds, $100. Responds in 6-12 wks. Seasonal 3 mos ahead. Accepts simultaneous submissions & reprints. Prefers disk. Kill fee 50%. Guidelines; free copy.

> **Columns/Departments:** Query.
> **Special Needs:** Interfaith dialogue.

Tips: "We look for compassionate, direct, and unselfconscious prose that reflects a writer who is firmly rooted in his/her own tradition but is unafraid to encounter other religions."

#CATHOLIC NEAR EAST, 1011 First Ave., New York NY 10022-4195. (212)826-1480. Fax (212)826-8979. Catholic. Michael La Civita, ed. Interest in cultural, religious, human rights development in Middle East, NE Africa, India and Eastern Europe. Bimonthly mag; 32 pgs; circ 110,000. Subscription $10. 50% freelance. Query/clips; phone query OK. Pays .20/wd on acceptance for all rts. Articles 1,500-2,000 wds (15/yr). Responds in 9 wks. Seasonal 4 mos ahead. Kill fee. Sidebars OK. Guidelines; copy for 7x10 SAE/2 stamps.

Tips: "We strive to educate our readers about the culture, faith, history, issues and people who form the Eastern Christian churches. Material should not be academic."

#CHILDLIFE, PO Box 9716, Federal Way WA 98063-9716. (206)815-1000. Fax (206)815-3445. E-mail: worvismag@aol.com. World Vision, Inc. Bruce Brander, mng. ed. Child/family life in poverty areas, disaster areas of the Third World; success stories of sponsored children. Quarterly mag; 16 pgs; circ 275,000. Free to sponsors. Some freelance. Query only. Pays $100-350 for assigned (otherwise **PAYS IN COPIES**) on acceptance for 1st rts. Articles 800-2,800 wds (50/yr). Seasonal 6-7 mos ahead. Kill fee. Guidelines; copy for 9x12 SAE/2 stamps.

Tips: "Send a letter with resume of past work experience. Most open to personality profiles, testimonies of children, families whose lives have been enriched through World Vision child sponsorship. Third World 'issue' pieces dealing with children and families, i.e., hunger, poverty, child exploitation, etc."

#COMPASSION MAGAZINE, 3955 Cragwood Dr., Colorado Springs CO 80933. (719)594-9900. Fax (719)536-9618. Compassion Intl. Jennifer L. Ball, pub. mng. Covering Compassion's worldwide Christian child development activities. Quarterly mag; 24 pgs; circ 160,000. Free to donors. 0% freelance, but open. Query; phone query OK. Pay negotiable on publication for 1st rts. Articles 700-1,200 wds. Responds in 2-4 wks. Seasonal 3 mos ahead. Prefers disk. Sidebars OK. Theme list; copy for 9x12 SAE/3 stamps. Not in topical listings.

Tips: "Articles for consideration would need to incorporate our work around the world. Interested writers should call for specific details."

#EAST-WEST CHURCH AND MINISTRY REPORT, Dept. IEWCS, Wheaton College, Wheaton IL 60187-5593. (630)752-5917. Fax (630)752-5555. E-mail: iewcs@david.wheaton.edu. Institute for East-West Christian Studies. Dr. Mark Elliot, ed. Encourages Western Christian ministry in East Central Europe and the former Soviet Union that is effective, culturally sensitive and cooperative. Quarterly newsletter; 16 pgs; circ. 430. Subscription $42.75. Est. 1993. 70% freelance. Query or complete ms; fax/e-mail query OK. **NO PAYMENT** for 1st rts. Articles 100-2,500 wds (40/yr); book reviews, 100-300 wds. Responds in 4-12 wks. Accepts reprints. Sidebars OK. Guidelines/theme list; free 4-pg sample.

Columns/Departments: Accepts 8-12/yr. News Notes, 50-200 wds; Resources (missionary resources), 100-300 wds; Practically Speaking (practical tips on living & ministering in our field), 100-500 wds. Query.

Tips: "All submissions must relate to East-Central Europe, the former Soviet Union or evangelical missions. "

THE GREAT COMMISSION HANDBOOK, 701 Main St., Evanston IL 60202. (847)869-1573. Fax (847)869-4825. E-mail: 73041.2471@compuserve.com. Berry Publishing Services, Inc. Dala Bruemmer, mng ed. For people of all ages who want to get involved with missions; motivates and informs evangelical Christians about needs and opportunities. Annual mag; 96 pgs; circ. 170,000. 25-30% freelance (rest from missionaries/experts). Query; phone/e-mail query OK. Pays .10/wd on publication for one-time and electronic. Articles 1,200-1,500 wds. Responds in 4-6 wks. Accepts simultaneous submissions & reprints (tell when/where appeared). Requires disk. Sidebars OK. Guidelines; copy for 9x12 SAE. (Ads)

>**Special Needs:** "Training for missions."

>**Tips:** "Our readers are a combination of missions-minded adults, Christian college students, mission agency inquirers, prospects and short-term alumni, and attendees at various North American mission conferences."

#HEARTBEAT, 5233 Mt. View Rd., Antioch TN 37013. (615)731-6812. Fax (615)731-5345. E-mail: MHS:don@fwbfm.compuserve.com. Free Will Baptist. Don Robirds, ed. To inform and challenge church members with mission needs. Bimonthly mag; 16 pgs; circ 20,000. Subscription free. 3% freelance. Query; fax/e-mail query OK. Pays .03/wd on publication for one-time rts. Articles 600-1,000 wds (2/yr). Responds in 6 wks. Seasonal 4 mos ahead. Accepts reprints. No sidebars. Guidelines; copy for 9x12 SAE.

INTERNATIONAL JOURNAL OF FRONTIER MISSIONS, 321 W. Rio Grande, El Paso TX 79902. (915)533-4975. Fax (915)532-0990. E-mail: 103121,2610 @compuserve.com. Hans Weerstra, ed. Dedicated to frontier missions in people groups that have no viable Christian church. Quarterly journal; circ 600. Subscription $15. 100% freelance. Complete ms/cover letter; phone/fax/e-mail query OK. **NO PAYMENT**, for one-time rts. Articles 6-7 pgs. Seasonal 3 mos ahead. Accepts simultaneous submissions & reprints. Guidelines/theme list; copy $1/9x12 SAE/$1.05 postage. (Ads)

>**Special Needs:** Contextualization, church in missions, comparative religions, training for missions, trends for missions, biblical basis for missions.

>**Tips:** "Although the circulation is small, the print run is 3,000 and used for motivational purposes."

#LATIN AMERICA EVANGELIST, Box 52-7900, Miami FL 33152-7900. (305)884-8400. Fax (305)885-8649. E-mail: 74114.1052@compuserve.com. Latin America Mission. John D. Maust, ed. To present God's work through the churches and missionaries in Latin America. Quarterly mag; 22 pgs; circ 17,000. Subscription $10. 10% freelance. Query only. Pays variable rates on publication for 1st rts. Articles 1,000 wds. Reporting time varies. Accepts simultaneous submissions. Not in topical listings. Free copy.

>**Tips:** "Looking for news and analysis of the religious climate and social conditions in Latin America."

+LEADERS FOR TODAY, Box 13, Atlanta GA 30370. (770)449-8869. Fax (770)449-8457. E-mail: 104437.610@compuserve.com. Haggai Institute. Scott Schreffler, mng. ed. Primarily for donors to ministry; focus is alumni success stories. Quarterly mag; 24 pgs; circ 6,500. 75% freelance. Query; fax query OK. Pays .10-.25/wd on acceptance for all rts. Articles 1,000-2,000 wds. Responds in

2-3 wks. Requires disk. Kill fee 100%. Sidebars OK. Prefers NIV. Guidelines/theme list; copy for 9x12 SAE/4 stamps.

Tips: "All articles are pre-assigned. Query first."

*THE MAP INTERNATIONAL REPORT, MAP International, Box 50, Brunswick GA 31521-5000. (912)265-6010. Phil Craven, ed. Deals with health care in developing countries. Bimonthly newsletter; 8-12 pgs; circ 13,500. 5% freelance. Prefers query. **NO MENTION OF PAYMENT.** Articles 500 wds. Seasonal 4 mos ahead. Not in topical listings. Free guidelines/theme list/copy.

#MESSAGE OF THE CROSS, 6820 Auto Club Rd., Minneapolis MN 55438. (612)829-2492. Fax (612)829-2753. Bethany Fellowship, Inc. George Foster, ed. Deeper life and Christian missions for a general Christian public. Quarterly mag; 32 pgs; circ 10,000. Subscription free. 20% freelance. Complete ms/cover letter; fax query OK. Pays $20-35 on publication for 1st or reprint rts. Articles (8/yr). Responds in 4 wks. Seasonal 6 mos ahead. Accepts reprints. No sidebars. Copy for 6x9 SAE.

MISSION TODAY, 701 Main St., Evanston IL 60202. (847)869-1573. Fax (847)869-4825. E-mail: 73041.2471@compuserve.com. Berry Publishing Services, Inc. Dala Bruemmer, ed. Gives a comprehensive overview of evangelical missionary activity worldwide, focusing on current opportunities and developments. Annual mag; 184 pgs; circ. 60,000. Est. 1994. 25-30% freelance (rest from missionaries/experts). Query; phone/e-mail query OK. Query for electronic submissions. Pays .10/wd on publication for one-time and electronic rts. Articles 1,200-1,500 wds. Responds in 4-6 wks. Accepts simultaneous submissions & reprints (tell when/where appeared). Requires disk. Sidebars OK. Guidelines/theme list; copy for 9x12 SAE. (Ads)

Special Needs: Training for missions.

Tips: "We seek articles by people personally involved in missions. Material should reflect fresh thinking and analysis on current missions issues. Get guidelines & theme list; contact editor to discuss your ideas."

MISSIOLOGY, Asbury Theological Seminary, Wilmore KY 40390. (606)858-2215/2216. Fax (606)858-2375. American Society of Missiology. Darrell L. Whiteman, ed. A professional organization for mission studies. Quarterly journal; 128 pgs; circ 2,000. Subscription $18. 75% freelance. Complete ms (3 copies)/cover letter; phone/fax query OK. **PAYS 20 COPIES**, for one-time & reprint rts. Articles to 20 typed pgs (20/yr); book reviews, 200 wds. Responds in 8-10 wks. Requires disk. Guidelines; copy for 7x10 SAE. (Ads)

Tips: "Whole journal is open to freelancers as long as they write from a missiological perspective and have adequate documentation."

#NEW WORLD OUTLOOK, 475 Riverside Dr., Room 1333, New York NY 10115-0122. (212)870-3765. Fax (212)870-3940. United Methodist. Alma Graham, ed.; submit to Christie R. House. Denominational missions. Bimonthly mag; 48 pgs; circ 30,000. Subscription $12. 20% freelance. Query; phone/fax query OK. Pays $50-300 on publication for all rts. Articles 500-2,000 wds (5-7/yr); book reviews 200-500 wds (assigned). No guaranteed response time. Seasonal 4 mos ahead. Kill fee 50%. Prefers disk (WordPerfect preferred). Sidebars OK. Prefers NRSV. Guidelines; copy $2.50.

Tips: "Ask for a list of United Methodist mission workers and projects in your area. Investigate them, propose a story, and consult with the editors before writing. Most open to articles and/or color photos of US or foreign mission sites visited as a stringer, after consultation with the editor."

*THE OBLATE WORLD AND VOICE OF HOPE, Box 680, 486 Chandler St., Tewksbury MA 01876. (508)851-7258. Missionary Society of the Oblate Fathers of Texas. Rev. Thomas J. Reddy, OMI, ed. Missions publication for Catholic clergy and laity. Bimonthly newspaper; circ 25,000. Pays .01-.02/wd on acceptance. Missions stories 1,000-1,600 wds. Responds in 3 wks. Not in topical listings. Copy.

#PARTNERS, PO Box 9716., Federal Way WA 98063-9716. (206)815-1000. Fax (206)815-3445. E-mail: worvismag@aol.com. World Vision. Submit to Jane Sutton, asst. ed. To educate and affirm donors to World Vision. Quarterly mag; 16 pgs; circ 198,000. Free to donors. 0-1% freelance. Query; phone/fax query OK. Pays $100-500 or .20/wd on acceptance for 1st rts. Articles 600-1,400 wds (3/yr). Responds in 6-8 wks. Seasonal 10 mos ahead. Prefers disk. Kill fee 70%. Sidebars OK. Guidelines; copy for 9x12 SAE/$1 postage.

> **Tips:** Call or query editors.

+PFI WORLD REPORT, Box 17434, Washington DC 20041. (703)481-0000. Fax (703)481-0003. E-mail: chris@pfi.org. Prison Fellowship, Intl. Christopher P. Nicholson, mng. ed. Targets issues and needs of prisoners, ex-prisoners, justice officials, victims, families and PFI staff, and volunteers in 75 countries. Bimonthly newsletter; 4-8 pgs; circ 7,000. Free subscription. 15% freelance. Query; phone/fax/e-mail query OK. Pays to $250 on acceptance. Articles 500-700 wds (3/yr). Responds in 3 wks. Seasonal 4 mos ahead. Accepts simultaneous submissions & reprints (tell when/where appeared). Accepts disk. Kill fee. Sidebars OK. Copy for #10 SAE/ 1 stamp.

> **Special Needs:** Prison issues, justice issues, anything that relates to international prison ministry.

> **Tips:** "Looking for personal profiles of people active in prison ministry (preferably PFI officials); Ex-prisoner success stories; how-to articles about various aspects of prison ministry. Avoid American slant."

#P.I.M.E. WORLD, 17330 Quincy St., Detroit MI 48221-2765. (313)342-4066. Fax (313)342-6816. Pontifical Inst. for Foreign Missions/Catholic. Paul W. Witte, mng. ed. For those interested in and supportive of foreign missions. Monthly (10X) mag; 16 pgs; circ 30,000. Subscription $5. 10% freelance. Complete ms/cover letter. Pays .06/wd on publication for all rts. Photos $5-10. Not copyrighted. Articles 600-1,200 wds (10/yr). Responds in 9 wks. Seasonal 4 mos ahead. Accepts simultaneous submissions. Prefers disk. No sidebars. Prefers NAB. Guidelines; copy for 9x12 SAE/3 stamps.

> **Tips:** "Issues like hunger, human rights, women's rights, peace and justice as they are dealt with in developing countries by missionaries and locals alike; stories of missionary service."

THE QUIET HOUR ECHOES, 630 Brookside Ave., Box 3000, Redlands CA 92373. (909)793-2588. Fax (909)793-4754. Website: http://www.tagnet.org/quiethour. The Quiet Hour (radio broadcast). Sharon Bird, gen. mgr. Provides radio listeners with challenges from the mission field and heart-to-heart messages from God. Monthly mag; 32 pgs; circ. 80,000. Subscription $5. 50%

freelance. Query only. **NO PAYMENT.** Not copyrighted. Few sidebars. Prefers KJV.

Poetry: Accepts 12-36/yr. Traditional.

Tips: Most open to articles on health, and poetry.

*THE RAILROAD EVANGELIST, PO Box 3846, Vancouver WA 98662. (360)699-7208. Joe Spooner, ed. For railroad and transportation employees and their families. Quarterly mag; circ 2,500. Subscription $6. 100% freelance. Complete ms; phone query OK. **NO PAYMENT.** Articles 100-700 wds (10-15/yr). Seasonal 4 months ahead. Accepts simultaneous submissions & reprints. Guidelines; copy for 9x12 SAE/2 stamps.

Poetry: Accepts 4-8/yr. Traditional, any length. Send any number.

Fillers: Accepts many. Anecdotes, cartoons, quotes; to 100 wds.

Tips: "We need 400-700 word salvation testimonies."

SAVE OUR WORLD (S.O.W.), 2490 Keith St. NW, PO Box 8016, Cleveland TN 37320-8016. (423)478-7190. Fax (423)478-7155. E-mail: tlr@cogwm.org. Church of God (Cleveland TN). Robert D. McCall, ed. Denominational publication for missions awareness. Quarterly tabloid; 16 pgs; circ. 97,000. Free.10% freelance. Query/clips; phone/fax/e-mail query OK. **NO PAYMENT** (pays $50 for some) for one-time rts. Articles 400-650 wds. Responds in 4 wks. Accepts reprints. Prefers disk. Sidebars OK. Prefers KJV. Copy $3/9x12 SAE.

Fillers: Accepts 4/yr. Facts, newsbreaks; 50-100 wds.

Tips: "Most open to missions trips made to foreign fields, missions experiences, material promoting missions giving and its rewards, missions-related stories, etc."

*URBAN MISSION, Box 27009, Philadelphia PA 19118. (215)887-5511. Fax (215)887-5404. Westminster Theological Seminary. H.M. Conn, ed. Dedicated to advancement of Christ in cities throughout the world. Quarterly journal; circ 1,300. Subscription $16. 100% freelance. Complete ms/cover letter. **PAYS 3 COPIES.** Articles 2,100-6,000 wds (40/yr). Responds in 1-2 wks. Accepts reprints.

#WHEREVER, Box 969, Wheaton IL 60189-0969. (630)653-5300. Fax (630)653-1826. E-mail: 76060.713@compuserve.com. The Evangelical Alliance Mission/interdenominational. Dana Felmly, ed. coord. For yg. adults interested in overseas missions, short or long term. Triannual mag; 16 pgs; circ 7,700. Free subscription. 70% freelance. Query. Pays $75-125 on publication for all or one-time rts. Articles 500-1,000 wds (13/yr); fiction 500-1,000 wds (1/yr). Responds in 5 wks. Sidebars OK. Guidelines/theme list; copy for 9x12 SAE/3 stamps.

Poetry: Buys 3/yr. Any type. Pays $75. Submit max.1 poem.

Tips: "Write and ask to be put on mailing list for themes, then query. No first-mission-trip stories unless it has dramatic conflict. You need some kind of experience with overseas missions."

*WORLD CHRISTIAN, Box 25, Colfax WA 99111. Independent. Submit to Gordon Aeschliman, ed.; June Mears, mng. ed. Missions slant. Monthly mag; circ 40,000. Query. **NO PAYMENT FOR NOW.** Responds in 6-8 wks. Accepts reprints. Articles 1,500-4,500 wds. Accepts simultaneous query. Guidelines/theme list; copy for SASE.

WORLD MISSION PEOPLE, PO Box 535002, Indianapolis IN 46253. (317)244-

3660. Fax (317)244-1247. Free Methodist World Missions. Daniel V. Runyon, ed. People features and worldwide news for supporters of Free Methodist missions. Bimonthly mag; 32 pgs; circ. 7,000. Subscription $10. 100% freelance. Complete ms/cover letter; phone/fax query OK. **NO PAYMENT** for one-time rts. Articles 600-1,200 wds (40-50/yr). Responds in 4 wks. Seasonal 6 mos ahead. Considers simultaneous submissions & reprints (tell when/where appeared). Prefers disk. Sidebars OK. Prefers NIV. Copy for 9x12 SAE/4 stamps.

> **Tips:** "Visit a Free Methodist overseas ministry and tell us about your experience."

WORLD VISION MAGAZINE, PO Box 9716, Federal Way WA 98063-9716. (206)815-2371. Fax (206)815-3445. E-mail: LWilson@MARY.WVUS.org. World Vision Inc. Larry Wilson, sr ed.; Bruce Brander, mng ed. Relevant issues pertaining to the US and the Third World, as well as poverty. Bimonthly mag; 24 pgs; circ 84,000. Subscription free. 50% freelance. Query/clips; fax query OK. Pays $200-1,000 or .20-.25/wd on acceptance for 1st & electronic rts. Articles 750-2,500 wds (6/yr). Responds in 6 wks. Seasonal 8 mos ahead. Accepts simultaneous submissions & reprints (tell when/where appeared). Accepts disk. Kill fee. Sidebars OK. Prefers NRSV. Guidelines; copy for 9x12 SAE/2 stamps.

> **Columns/Departments:** Buys 6/yr. Turning Points (personal experience relating to poor), 450-700 wds; .20/wd.
>
> **Tips:** "Send us copies of anything written previously. Have experience in nonfiction writing for publications. Be fairly knowledgeable about the Third World. To break in, call an editor—Terry Madison, Bruce Brander or Larry Wilson."
>
> ** This periodical was #59 on the 1996 Top 50 Christian Publishers list (#36 in 1995, #61 in 1994). Also 1996 EPA Award of Merit—Missionary.

#WORLDWIDE CHALLENGE, 100 Sunport Ln., Dept. 1600, Orlando FL 32809. (407)826-2390. Fax (407)826-2374. E-mail: WChallenge@aol.com. Campus Crusade for Christ. Diane McDougall, ed. For financial supporters of Campus Crusade. Bimonthly mag; 52 pgs; circ 90,000. Subscription $12.95. 10% freelance. Query only/clips. Pays .10/wd + a flat fee of $100, $150 or $200 (depending on research) on acceptance for 1st rts (all rts for assigned articles). Articles 300-1,000 wds. Responds in 2-4 wks. Seasonal 4-5 mos ahead. Accepts reprints. Kill fee. Guidelines; copy $2/9x12 SAE/5 stamps.

> **Columns/Departments:** Buys 2-5/yr. Upfront (personal experience/commentary); 300-1,000 wds. Most open area. People (with unique ministry of evangelism or discipleship), 1,900 wds; History's Hero, 1,350 wds.
>
> **Tips:** "Give the human face behind a topic or story. Show how the topic relates to evangelism and/or discipleship."
>
> ** This periodical was #43 on the 1996 Top 50 Christian Publishers List. (#35 in 1994) Also 1996 EPA Award of Merit—Organizational.

MUSIC MARKETS

#CCM MAGAZINE, 107 Kenner Ave., Nashville TN 37205. (615)386-3011. Fax (615)385-4112. E-mail: Contemporary Christian Music/CCM Communications. April Hefner, mng ed. Encourages spiritual growth through contemporary music; provides news and information about the Christian music market. Monthly mag;

circ. 85,000. Subscription $21.95. 75% freelance. Query/clips; phone/fax query OK. Pays .20/wd for short pieces, or $100/published page for features, on publication for all rts. Articles 500-2,500 wds; music reviews 250-350 wds. Responds slowly. Seasonal 3 mos ahead. Kill fee 50%. Prefers disk or e-mail. Sidebars OK. Guidelines; copy for 9x12 SAE/$4. (Ads)

** 1996 EPA Award of Merit—Youth.

CHRISTIAN COMPOSER, Box 448, Jacksonville OR 97530. (541)899-8888. James Lloyd, ed/pub. The only songwriter and artists Top Sheet in the business; includes a relevant essay on music-related subjects. Bimonthly newsletter, supplement to Christian Media; circ 2,000-6,000. Query; prefers phone query. **PAYS IN COPIES OR PRODUCT** for all rts. Articles; book & music reviews, 3 paragraphs. Responds in 3 wks. Accepts simultaneous submissions & reprints. Prefers disk. KJV only. Copy for 9x12 SAE/2 stamps. Not in topical listings.

> **Special Needs:** Material should focus on the craft of song writing, musical performance, or marketing of the same.
>
> **Tips:** "We like 'street-smarts' when it comes to articles. Tell it like it is in the music industry; we want our readers forewarned about the various pitfalls in Christian music. "

CHRISTIAN COUNTRY RESEARCH BULLETIN (CCRB), 7057 Bluffwood Ct., Brownsburg IN 46112. (317)892-5031. Fax (317)892-5034. E-mail: ccrb@ ai2a.net. Website: http://www.achiever.com/freehmpg/christiancountry. Joyful Sounds. Les Roberts, ed. Trade journal for Christian country radio industry. Biweekly trade journal; 8-12 pgs; circ. 300-1,200. Subscription $36. 75% freelance. Query or complete ms/cover letter; phone/fax/e-mail query OK. Negotiable payment & rights. Articles 600-2,000 wds; music reviews, 100-300 wds. Responds in 2 wks. Seasonal 2 mos ahead. Accepts reprints. Requires disk (DOS-ASCII). Copy for 9x12 SAE/2 stamps. (Ads)

> **Fillers:** Cartoons, short humor.
>
> **Columns/Departments:** Insider (artist interview); Programming 101 (radio technique); retail, inspirational, especially for musicians and radio people; 600-2,000 wds.
>
> **Tips:** "Most open to artist interviews. Must be familiar with Christian country music."

#THE CHURCH MUSICIAN, 127 9th Ave. N., Nashville TN 37234. (615)251-2961. Fax (615)251-2614 or 5951. Southern Baptist. Jere Adams, ed. For church music leaders. Quarterly; 16 pages (music), 98 pgs total; circ 16,000. 20% freelance. Complete ms. Pays to .055/wd (.06 on disk) on acceptance for all rts. Articles & fiction (related to church music), to 1,300 wds. Responds in 9 wks. Accepts reprints (pays 50%- tell when/where appeared). Copy for 9x12 SAE/3 stamps.

> **Poetry:** Church music slant/inspirational, 8-24 lines; $5-15.
>
> **Fillers:** Short humor (with a musical slant); $5-15.

*THE CHURCH MUSIC REPORT/CHURCH MUSIC WORLD, Box 1179, Grapevine TX 76099. (817)488-0141. Bill Rayborn, ed. For church music leaders. Monthly newsletter; 8-12 pgs. Ideas, tips, how-tos, and the like. Articles; interviews.

*CHURCH PIANIST/SAB CHOIR/THE CHOIR HERALD, Box 268, Alcoa TN

37701. (615)982-5669. Now a division of The Lorenz Corp. Hugh S. Livingston Jr., ed. Each of these music magazines has one page devoted to articles that deal with problems/solutions of choirs and accompanists. Bimonthly mag; 36-52 pgs; circ 25,000. 45% freelance. Complete ms/cover letter. Pay $15-150 on publication for all rts. Articles 250-1,250 wds (10-20/yr). Seasonal 1 yr ahead. Responds in 3-6 wks. Guidelines; copy for 9x12 SAE/3 stamps.

> **Poetry:** Accepts 25/yr. Free verse, light verse, traditional, or poetry suitable for song lyrics; $10. Submit max. 5 poems.
>
> **Fillers:** Accepts 5-10/yr. Anecdotes, cartoons.
>
> **Special Needs:** Choir experiences; pianist/organist articles.
>
> **Tips:** "Best approach is from direct experience in music with the small church."

CREATOR MAGAZINE, PO Box 64775, Tucson AZ 85748. (520)885-8281. Fax (520)885-8996. E-mail: CreatorMag@aol.com. Marshall Sanders, pub. For interdenominational music ministry; promoting quality, diverse music programs in the church. Bimonthly mag; 48-56 pgs; circ 5,500. 40% freelance. Complete ms/cover letter; fax/e-mail query OK. Pays $35-60 on publication for 1st or one-time rts. Articles 1,000-6,000 wds (12/yr); book reviews $20. Responds in 4-12 wks. Seasonal 6 mos ahead. Accepts reprints (tell when/where appeared). Prefers disk. Sidebars OK. Prefers NRSV. Guidelines/theme list; copy for 9x12 SAE/6 stamps. (Ads)

> **Fillers:** Buys 20/yr. Anecdotes, cartoons, ideas, jokes, party ideas, short humor; 10-75 wds; $5-25.
>
> **Special Needs:** Articles on worship; staff relationships.

#GLORY SONGS, 127 9th Ave. N. Nashville TN 37234. (615)251-2913. Southern Baptist. Jere V. Adams, ed. Easy choral music for church choirs; practical how-to articles for small church music programs. Quarterly mag; 26 pgs; circ 85,000. 100% freelance. Complete ms. Pays .055/wd on acceptance for 1st rts. Articles 550-1,000 wds (6-7/yr). Responds in 2-4 wks. Seasonal 1 yr ahead. Accepts simultaneous submissions & reprints. Guidelines; free copy.

> **Poetry:** Buys 2-3/yr. Free verse, traditional.
>
> **Fillers:** Cartoons, ideas, party ideas, musical quizzes, short humor.
>
> **Special Needs:** Vocal techniques, choir etiquette, mission/outreach ideas, music training, etc.

+GOSPEL INDUSTRY TODAY, 2201 Murfreesboro Rd. #C-203, Nashville TN 37217. (615)360-9444. Fax (615)361-1274. E-mail: gospel@usit.net. Horizon Concepts. Teresa Hairston, pub.; submit to Editorial Dept. About the Christian and Gospel music industry. Monthly (10X) mag; 16 pgs; circ 3,500. Subscription $24. 50% freelance. Query; fax/e-mail query OK. Pays $75-250 on publication for 1st rts. Articles 1,500-3,000 wds. Responds in 5-9 wks. Seasonal 3 mos ahead. Prefers disk. Kill fee 10%. Sidebars OK. Prefers KJV. Guidelines/theme list; copy for 10x13 SAE/8 stamps. (Ads)

*GOSPEL MUSIC EXCLUSIVE, 420 N McKinley St. #111-406, Corona CA 91719-6504. (909)875-7404. Fax (909)272-4338. E-mail: DDALEY1956@aol.com. Rhonda Daley, ed-in-chief. Bimonthly mag; circ. 40,000. Subscription $24.99. Est. 1994. 50% freelance. Query; fax/e-mail query OK. Pays: .10-.25/wd on publication for 1st rts. Articles 500-1,000 wds (20/yr). Responds in 2-4 wks.

Seasonal 6 mos ahead. Prefers disk. Sidebars OK. Prefers NIV. Guidelines; copy for 9x12 SAE/8 stamps.

Poetry: Buys 5/yr. Light verse; $25-50. Submit max. 5 poems.

Fillers: Buys 20/yr. Anecdotes, cartoons; $25-50.

Columns/Departments: Nite Life (profiles of Christian clubs/coffeehouses), 500+ wds; Artist profiles, 500-1,000 wds; Music Reviews, 250 wds; Concerts/Events (with photos), 500 wds; pays $100-250. Complete ms.

Tips: "Looking for new ideas or new slant on an old idea. Most open to artist profiles, concerts and events."

+GUITAR MASTER MAGAZINE, 4909 Stockdale Hwy. #201, Bakersfield CA 93309. (805)664-0281. David Serfozo, ed. Technical magazine geared toward guitar players; not exclusively Christian. Monthly mag. Est. 1995.

Tips: "Features articles in which Christian guitarists discuss their technique, musical influences, and Christian testimonies. Also includes transcriptions of songs, solos and riffs; reviews of guitar-oriented recordings; news and notes about upcoming projects and tours; information on guitars and equipment; and a guitar-player employment listing."

THE HYMN, School of Theology, Boston University, 745 Commonwealth Ave., Boston MA 02215-1401. (800)THEHYMN. Hymn Society in the US & Canada. Carl P. Daw, Jr., exec. dir. For church musicians, hymnologists, scholars; articles related to the congregational song. Quarterly journal; 60 pgs; circ 3,000. Subscription $45. 100% freelance. Query. **NO PAYMENT** for all rts. Articles any length (12/yr); book & music reviews any length. Responds in 4 wks. Seasonal 4 mos ahead. Prefers disk. Sidebars OK. Guidelines; free copy.

Poetry: Hymn poetry.

Special Needs: Hymns and articles on history of hymns.

#THE MUSIC LEADER, 127 9th Ave. N., Nashville TN 37234. (615)251-2513. Southern Baptist. Anne Trudel, coordinating ed. How-to material for leaders of preschool and children's choirs. Quarterly mag; 92 pgs; circ 35,000. 5% freelance. Complete ms/cover letter. Pays .055-.065/wd on acceptance for all or one-time rts. Articles 75-80 lines (to 800 wds), or 150-170 lines typed 40 characters/line; 250 lines max. Seasonal dramas, 7-8 pgs. Responds in 5 wks. Guidelines; copy $3.

Poetry: For choir leaders.

*MUSIC MAKERS, 127 9th Ave. N., Nashville TN 37234. (615)251-2961. Southern Baptist. Darrell Billingsley, ed. For children ages 6-11. Quarterly mag; circ 105,000. Pays .06/wd on acceptance for all rts. Articles & fiction 250-500 wds. Responds in 4 wks. Not in topical listings. Guidelines/copy.

*MUSIC TIME, 127 9th Ave. N., Nashville TN 37234. (615)251-2000. Southern Baptist. Derrell Billingsley, literary design ed. For 4 & 5 yr olds; directly related to unit material found in **The Music Leader.** Quarterly mag; circ 60,000. Complete ms. Pays .05/wd for stories. Pays $9-12 on acceptance for all rts. Stories for 4 & 5 yr olds. Responds in 2-5 wks. Not in topical listings. Guidelines; free copy.

Poetry: 1-7 lines; $5-9.

*QUEST, PO Box 14804, Columbus OH 43214. Rick Welke, ed. Geared to 16-30 year olds and radio personnel. Monthly newsletter. Est. 1995. Query; fax query OK. **PAYS A SUBSCRIPTION.** Articles 100-500 wds (4/yr); fiction, 150-750 wds (4/yr); book/music reviews, 30-75 wds. Seasonal 3 mos ahead. Accepts simultaneous submissions & reprints. Theme list; copy for #10 SAE/2 stamps.

Poetry: Accepts 12/yr. Any type, 4-24 lines. Submit max. 4 poems.

Fillers: Accepts 36/yr. Cartoons, facts, jokes, quizzes, quotes, short humor, word puzzles.

Columns/Departments: Artist Action (any specific artist information).

Special Needs: Organizational pieces; new music releases/photos; artist's concert schedules; radio station playlists.

Tips: "Submit between the 10th and 20th of each month for best review."

+RELEASE, 404 BNA Dr., Bldg 200, Ste. 508, Nashville TN 37217. (615)872-8080. Fax (615)889-0437. E-mail: 76711.3500@compuserve.com. Thomas Nelson, Inc. Roberta Croteau, ed. Covers contemporary Christian music. Bimonthly mag; circ 200,000. Subscription $12. Open to freelance. Complete ms. Not in topical listings. (Ads)

*RENAISSANCE,The Resource Publication for the Christian Musician, Box 2134, Lynnwood WA 98036. Renaissance Artists Group/Christian Artists International. Nathan L. Csakany, ed. Issues of interest to Christian musicians. Not in topical listings. Copy.

*RING! PO Box 1179, Grapevine TX 76099-1179. (817)488-0141. Fax (817)481-4191. TCMR Communications Inc. Lynann Rayborn, ed. For handbell choir members. Monthly (10X) newsletter.

#THE SENIOR MUSICIAN, 127 9th Ave. N, Nashville TN 37234. (615)251-2913. Southern Baptist. Jere V. Adams, ed. For music directors and choir members of senior adult choirs. Quarterly mag; 26 pgs; circ 32,000. 100% freelance. Complete ms. Pays .055/wd on acceptance for 1st rts. Articles 500-900 wds (6-7/yr). Responds in 2-4 wks. Seasonal 1 yr ahead. Some simultaneous submissions; reprints. Guidelines; free copy.

Poetry: Buys 2-3/yr. Traditional.

Fillers: Buys 3-4/yr. Cartoons, ideas, party ideas, musical quizzes, short humor.

Special Needs: Senior adults' testimonials, inspirational stories, personal growth and development, music training, and choir projects.

Tips: "All topics must relate to senior adult musicians and senior choirs—anything else will be returned."

+(SEVEN) 7 BALL, 404 BNA Dr., Bldg. 200, Ste. 508, Nashville TN 37217. (615)872-8080. Fax (615)889-0437. E-mail: 76710.251@compuserve.com. Thomas Nelson, Inc. Chris Well, ed. covers modern and alternative Christian rock. Bimonthly mag; circ 50,000. Open to freelance. Not in topical listings. (Ads)

*SHOUT! 86 Elm St., Peterborough NH 03458-1052. Connell Communications, Inc. Angela Casteel, ed. Designed to appeal to both a Christian and mainstream music market. Bimonthly mag. Est. 1995. 50% freelance. Query/clips. Pays on publication for all rts. Articles 300-6,000 wds; music reviews 200 wds, $20. Responds in 4 wks. Seasonal 3 mos ahead. Kill fee. Sidebars OK. Guidelines; copy for 9x12 SAE.

Columns/Departments: Shout Bits (news bits about artists); Friends (features on established artists); Finds (features on new artists).

Tips: "Send a resume and samples. Follow up with a phone call. Most open to music reviews."

*SING! PO Box 1179, Grapevine TX 76099-1179. (817)488-0141. Fax (817)481-4191. TCMR Communications Inc. Lynann Rayborn, ed. For adult choir members. Monthly newsletter.

*SING! JR., PO Box 1179, Grapevine TX 76099-1179. (817)488-0141. Fax (817)481-4191. TCMR Communications Inc. Lynann Rayborn, ed. For children's choir members & their parents. Monthly (9X) newsletter.

*TRADITION, Box 438, Walnut IA 51577. (712)366-1136. Prairie Press Ltd. Robert Everhart, ed. Devoted to acoustic traditional music with an over-35 audience. Bimonthly mag; circ 2,500. 20% freelance. Query. Pays $10-15 on publication for one-time rts. Not copyrighted. Articles 800-1,200 wds (2/yr). Responds in 5 wks. Seasonal 6 mos ahead. Accepts simultaneous query & reprints. Copy $1.

Poetry: Buys 4/yr. Free verse, traditional; 5-20 lines; $2-5. Submit max. 2 poems.

Fillers: Buys 5/yr. Anecdotes, clippings, jokes; 15-50 wds; $5-10.

Special Needs: Articles on gospel music.

*YOUNG MUSICIANS, 127 9th Ave. N., Nashville TN 37234. (615)251-2944. Southern Baptist. Clinton Flowers, ed. For children 9-11 yrs. Quarterly mag.; 52 pgs; circ 85,000. Query. Pays .05/wd on acceptance for 1st rts. Music and music-related articles, stories 400-800 wds. Responds in 5 wks. Free guidelines/copy.

Fillers: Prose, word puzzles (music-related).

PASTOR/LEADERSHIP MARKETS

ART+PLUS, Reproducible Resources, Box 4710, Sarasota FL 34230-4710. (941)955-2950. Fax (941)955-5723. E-mail: MMediaInc@aol.com. Mission Media Inc. Wayne Hepburn, pub. Reproducible illustrations and verse for church bulletins and newsletters. Quarterly glossy book; 26 pgs; circ 3,000. Subscription $49. 100% freelance. Send copy; phone/fax/e-mail query OK. Pays $5-50 on acceptance for all rts only. Responds in 6-8 wks. Seasonal anytime. Accepts simultaneous submissions. Prefers disk. Guidelines/theme list; copy $2/9x12 SAE.

Poetry: Buys 15-20/yr. Traditional only; to 16 lines; $15-25. Submit max. 10 poems.

Fillers: Buys 150+/yr. Anecdotes, cartoons, jokes, quizzes, prayers, short humor (church-related anecdotes); to 25 wds; $8.

Tips: "We are seasonally oriented; more open to art/images than writing. We need 3-5 poems per quarter and 3-10 anecdotes or fillers."

CATECHUMENATE: A JOURNAL OF CHRISTIAN INITIATION, 1800 N. Hermitage Ave., Chicago IL 60622-1101. (773)486-8970. Fax (800)933-7094. E-mail: editors@ltp.org. Catholic. Victoria M. Tufano, ed. For clergy and laity who work with those who are planning to become Catholic. Bimonthly jour; 48 pgs; circ 5,600. Subscription $20. Complete ms/cover letter; phone/fax/e-mail query OK. Pays $100-250 on publication for all rts (poetry, one-time rts). Articles 1,500-3,000 wds (10/yr). Responds in 2-6 wks. Accepts simultaneous submissions. Prefers disk. Kill fee. No sidebars. Guidelines; copy for 6x9 SAE/4 stamps.

Poetry: Buys 6/yr. Free verse, traditional; 5-20 lines; $75. Submit max. 5 poems.

Columns/Departments: Buys 12/yr. Sunday Word (Scripture reflection on Sunday readings, aimed at catechumers); 450 wds; $200-250. Query for assignment.

Special Needs: Christian initiation; reconciliation.

Tips: "It helps if the writer has experience working with Christian initiation. Approach is that this is something we are all learning together through experience and scholarship."

#CELEBRATION (SDA), 55 W Oak Ridge Dr., Hagerstown MD 21740. (301)791-7000x2547. Fax (301)790-9734. E-mail: 74617.1455@compuserve.com. Review & Herald. Faith Crumbly, mng. ed. For adult leaders in SDA churches. Monthly mag; 32 pgs; circ 10,000. Subscription $23.97. 60% freelance. Query; fax query OK. Pays .10/wd (varies) on acceptance for 1st rts. Articles any length. Responds in 2-8 wks. Seasonal 6 mos ahead. Accepts reprints (tell where & when published). Prefers disk when assigned. Sidebars OK. Prefers NKJV. Guidelines; copy .50/9x12 SAE/2 stamps. (Ads)

Fillers: Cartoons and short humor relevant to monthly themes.

Special Needs: Program helps for Mother's Day, Father's Day, Christmas, Thanksgiving. Submit 6 mos in advance. Write for specific guidelines.

+CELEBRATION(Catholic), 207 Hillsboro Dr., Silver Spring MD 20902-3125. William J. Freburger, ed. National Catholic Reporter Publishing House. Monthly mag; 48 pgs; circ 9,000. Subscription $64.95. 15% freelance. Complete ms/cover letter. Pays $100-200 on acceptance for one-time rts. Articles 1,000-2,500 wds (15-20/yr). Responds in 2 wks. Seasonal 7 mos ahead. Prefers disk. No sidebars. Copy for 10x13 SAE/4 stamps. (Ads)

Contest: Monthly contest on different themes, usually worship ideas for specific occasions (New Year, Easter, etc.).

Tips: "I am always looking for descriptions of worship services (texts), ideas for worship occasions (seasonal., special), unsentimental and non-obvious stories as teaching/preaching aids, etc."

+CELL CHURCH MAGAZINE, 14925 Memorial Dr., Ste. 101, Houston TX 77079. (281)497-7901. Fax (281)497-0904. E-mail: farah@domi.net. Touch Outreach Ministries. Farah A. Antangan, mng. ed. For Cell Church pastors, leaders and consultants working to impact the world for Christ, through the church. Quarterly mag; 24 pgs; circ 11,000. Subscription $14. 70-80% freelance. Query/clips; fax/e-mail query OK. **PAYS 10 COPIES.** Articles 1,000-1,500 wds (20-30/yr). Responds in 2 wks. Seasonal 3 mos ahead. Accepts simultaneous submissions & reprints (tell when/where appeared). Prefers disk. Some sidebars. Prefers NIV .Guidelines/theme list; copy $3.50/9x12 SAE/3 stamps.

Columns/Departments: Accepts 20-25/yr. Youth, Children's Ministry, Transitioning (to Cell Church), Global Input, Lone Service (lone pastor/supervisor), Pastor's Pilgrimage (pastor's testimonial about Cell Church), and Heart to Heart (heartfelt testimony about cell life); all 1,000-1,500 wds.

Special Needs: Global issues; practical tips and ideas relevant to Cell Church concept. Needs youth Cell Church writer.

CELL LIFE FORUM, 131 Tilman Cir., Markham ON L3P 6A4 Canada. (905)471-

5015. Fax (905)471-6912. E-mail: 75273,3241@compuserve.com. World Team Canada. Nancy J. Lindquist, ed. A resource to connect cell-based churches across Canada. Quarterly mag; 16 pgs; circ. 300+. Subscription $12 CAN. Est. 1994. 75% freelance. Query; phone/e-mail query OK. Pays .05/wd on publication for 1st or one-time rts. Not copyrighted. Articles 500-2,000 wds (8-12/yr); book/music reviews, 100-500 wds, $5-25. Responds in 3-4 wks. Accepts simultaneous submissions & reprints. Accepts disk (prefers e-mail). Sidebars OK. Prefers NIV. Guidelines/theme list; copy for 9x12 SAE. (Ads)

Poetry: Buys 4/yr. Any type as long as on theme; 5-30 lines; $5-10. Submit max. 4 poems.

Fillers: Buys 8+/yr. Anecdotes, cartoons, tips; to 100 wds; $5-10.

Tips: "All material must relate to Canadian cell churches or Canadians involved in cell churches. Most open to profiles, My Story, or fillers."

*CHICAGO STUDIES, Box 665, Mundelein IL 60060. (708)566-1462. Catholic. Rev. George J. Dyer, ed. For the continuing theological development of priests and other religious educators. Triannual journal; circ 6,100. Subscription $17.50. 50% freelance. Complete ms. Pays $35-100 on acceptance for all rts. Articles 3,000-4,000 wds (30/yr). Responds in 9 wks. Seasonal 6 mos ahead. Guidelines; copy $5.

Tips: "Include cover letter with information about yourself."

CHRISTIAN CENTURY, 407 S. Dearborn St., Chicago IL 60605. (312)427-5380. Fax (312)427-1302. Christian Century Foundation. Submit to Manuscripts. For ministers, educators and church leaders interested in events and theological issues of concern to the ecumenical church. Magazine published 38X/yr; 32-48 pgs; circ 33,000. Subscription $38. 90% freelance. Query/clips (complete ms for fiction); phone/fax query OK. Query for electronic submissions. Pays $75-150 on publication for all rts. Articles to 3,000 wds (150/yr); fiction to 3,000 wds (4/yr); book reviews, 800-1,000 wds. Responds in 4 wks. Seasonal 6 mos ahead. No disk. Kill fee. Sidebars OK. Prefers NRSV. Guidelines/theme list; free copy.

Poetry: Buys 50/yr. Any type (religious but not sentimental); 3-25 lines; $25. Submit max. 10 poems.

Fillers: Buys 20 cartoons/yr.

Tips: "Looking for more fiction. Keep in mind our audience of sophisticated readers, eager for analysis and critical perspective that goes beyond the obvious."

#CHRISTIAN COUNSELING TODAY, 1821 Walden Office Sq., Ste. 111, Schaumburg IL 60173-4267. E-mail: 102124.2061@compuserve.com. Dr. Gary Collins, ed. Provides practical, relevant, up-to-date biblically and psychologically accurate information about Christian counseling for professional, pastoral, and lay counselors. Quarterly mag; circ. 20,000. Subscription $35. Open to freelance. Query. (Ads)

#CHRISTIAN MANAGEMENT REPORT, PO Box 4638, Diamond Bar CA 91765-0638. (909)861-8861. Fax (909)860-8247. E-mail: 74407.233@compuserve.com. Church Management Association. Sandy Scruggs, dir. For Christian managers of nonprofit organizations and people from ministries in general. Bimonthly journal; 40 pgs; circ 2,600. Subscription $29.95. 75% freelance. Query or complete ms/cover letter; fax query ok. **NO PAYMENT** for all rts. Articles 800 wds

(20/yr); book reviews 200-500 wds. Responds in 5-13 wks. Seasonal 6 mos ahead. Accepts simultaneous submissions & reprints. Guidelines; free copy. (Ads)

Fillers: Anecdotes, cartoons, facts, newsbreaks, prose, prayers, quotes, short humor; 50-100 wds.

Columns/Departments: Management Q & A; Hiring Insights; both 500-700 wds. Query.

Special Needs: Non-profit management; fund-raising; marketing; and hiring issues.

CHRISTIAN MINISTRY, 407 S. Dearborn St., Ste. 1405, Chicago IL 60605-1150. (312)427-5380. Fax (312)427-1302. The Christian Century Foundation. Victoria Rebeck, mng. ed. For clergy seeking thoughtful, practical advice for parish ministry challenges. Bimonthly mag; 48 pgs; circ 6,000. Subscription $14. 90% freelance. Complete ms/cover letter; fax query OK. Pays $60-100 on publication for all rts. Articles 1,800-2,500 wds (50/yr); book reviews, 400 wds (keep book). Responds in 6 wks. Seasonal 6-9 mos ahead. Kill fee 50%. Sidebars OK. Prefers disk. Sidebars OK. Prefers NRSV. Guidelines/theme list; copy for 9x12 SAE/45stamps. (Ads)

Fillers: Buys 6/yr. Anecdotes, cartoons, facts; 100 wds. Pays $25.

Contest: Sponsors a sermon contest. Write for qualifications and requirements.

Tips: "Looking for articles on faith in the workplace. The following areas are open to freelancers: From the Pulpit: sermons in manuscript format. Reflection on Ministry: personal perspectives on being a minister, 2,000 wds. Minister's Workshop: practical advice on common ministry problems, 2,000 wds. Tricks of the Trade: Brief practical tips, 250 wds. Read our magazine first."

*CHRISTIAN RECREATION (formerly **CHURCH RECREATION**), 127 Ninth Ave. N, Nashville TN 37234. (615)251-3841. Southern Baptist. Laura Stallins, asst ed. Focus is on using recreation in all church programs. Quarterly mag; 60 pgs; circ 17,000. 70% freelance. Query or complete ms/cover letter; fax query OK. Pays .055/wd on acceptance for all or one-time rts. Articles 800 wds; fiction (scripts, skits, puppet plays and monologues) 800-1,200 wds. Responds in 5 wks. Accepts simultaneous submissions. Prefers disk. Guidelines; copy for 9x12 SASE.

THE CHRISTIAN SENTINEL, Box 11322, Philadelphia PA 19137. (215)289-7885. Fax (215)289-8808. Calvary Chapel. Jackie Alnor, ed. Leaders-oriented publication exploring Christian apologetics issues; cults; issues affecting the church. Quarterly mag; 36 pgs; circ 10,000. 10% freelance. Query/clips. **NO PAYMENT** for 1st rts. Articles 100-700 wds; book reviews 500 wds. Responds in 2 wks. Sidebars OK. Copy for 9x12 SAE/2 stamps.

Fillers: Accepts 10/yr. Cartoons.

Special Needs: Heresy in the church; defense of the faith; signs of the times; eye-witness accounts of the introduction of lying signs and wonders in the church.

Tips: "Be called to a discernment ministry; be provoked by evil and false teachings. Most open to news. Be big on fact, short on opinion."

*CHURCH ADMINISTRATION, MSN 157, 127 9th Ave. N., Nashville TN 37234.

(615)251-2062. Fax (615)251-3866. Southern Baptist. George Clark, ed. Practical pastoral ministry/church administration ideas for pastors and staff. Monthly mag; 50 pgs; circ 12,000. 15% freelance. Query. Pays .055-.065/wd on acceptance for all rts. Articles 1,500-1,800 wds (60/yr). Responds in 8 wks. Guidelines/copy for #10 SAE/2 stamps.

> **Columns/Departments:** Buys 60/yr. Weekday Dialogue; Minister's Mate; Secretary's File; all 2,000 wds.

CHURCH BYTES, 304C Crossfield Dr., Versailles KY 40383. (606)873-0550. Fax (606)879-0121. E-mail: deerhavn@lex.infi.net. Deerhaven Press. Neil B. Houk, ed. Everything about church computing. Bimonthly mag; 56 pgs; circ 40,000. Subscription $18. 33% freelance. Query; phone/fax/e-mail query OK. Pays $35 on publication for 1st rts. Articles 800-1,500 wds (30-50/yr). Responds in 1-2 wks. Accepts simultaneous submissions. Prefers disk. Sidebars OK. Guidelines; copy for 9x12 SAE/3 stamps. Not in topical listings. (Ads)

> **Tips:** "Most open to personalized stories of how computer technology is used and what difference it makes. Pictures are a plus—color or black & white. No software reviews needed."

*CHURCH GROWTH NETWORK, 3630 Camellia Dr., San Bernardino CA 92404. Phone/fax: (909)882-5386. Dr. Gary L. McIntosh, ed. For pastors and church leaders interested in church growth. Monthly newsletter; 2 pgs; circ 5,000. Subscription $12. 20% freelance. Query; fax query OK. **PAYS FREE SUBSCRIPTION** for 1st rts. Articles 1,200-1,250 wds (2/yr). Responds in 4 wks. Accepts reprints. Prefers disk. No sidebars. Copy for #10 SAE/1 stamp.

> **Tips:** "All articles must have a church growth slant. Should be very practical, how-to material; very tightly written with bullets, etc."

+CIRCUIT RIDER, 201 - 8th Ave S., Nashville TN 37203. (615)749-6488. Fax (615)749-1079. United Methodist. Jill Reddig, mng. ed. Denominational clergy. Monthly mag; 24 pgs; circ 42,000. 1% freelance. Complete ms. Buys 1st rts. Articles 650-1,200 wds. Responds in 3 wks. Prefers disk. Sidebars OK. Prefers NRSV. Guidelines; copy for 9x12 SAE. Not in topical listings.

*THE CLERGY JOURNAL, PO Box 240, S. St. Paul MN 55075-0240. (612)451-9945. Fax (612)457-4617. Logos Productions, Inc. Sharilyn Figueroa, mng. ed. "How-to" articles on church administration, ministry/personal issues for Protestant ministers, Christian educators and church personnel. Monthly (10X) mag; 48-52 pgs; circ 10,000. Subscription $27. 20% freelance. Complete ms/cover letter; phone/fax query OK. Pays $25-100 on publication for 1st rts. Articles 250-500, up to 2,000 wds (20/yr); book reviews 250 wds/no pay. Responds in 2-3 wks. Seasonal 6 mos ahead. Accepts reprints. Kill fee 50%. Prefers disk. Sidebars OK. Prefers NRSV. Free guidelines/copy.

> **Fillers:** Buys 50-60 cartoons/yr; $10.

> **Tips:** Send a completed article for evaluation. If editor likes style/content, contact will be made for future assignment.

CROSS CURRENTS, College of New Rochelle, New Rochelle NY 10805-2339. (914)654-5425. Fax (914)654-5925. Association for Religion and Intellectual Life. Shelley Schiff, mng ed. For thoughtful activists for social justice and church reform. Quarterly jour; 144 pgs; circ 4,500. Subscription $30. 99% freelance. Mostly written by academics. Complete ms/cover letter; phone/fax query OK.

NO PAYMENT for all rts. Articles 3,000-5,000 wds; book reviews 1,000 wds (James Giles). Responds in 2-8 wks. Seasonal 6 mos ahead. Accepts simultaneous submissions & reprints. Prefers disk. No sidebars. Guidelines; copy for 9x12 SAE/4 stamps. (Ads)

> **Poetry:** Tom O'Brien. Accepts 8/yr. Any type or length; no payment. Submit max. 5 poems.
>
> **Tips:** "Send 3 double-spaced copies; SASE; use Chicago Manual of Style; non-sexist language."

*DIACONALOGUE, 1304 LaPorte Ave., Valparaiso IN 46383. (219)464-0909. Lutheran Deaconess Assn. Dot Nuechterlein, ed. Focus on ministries of Christian service in everyday life. Semiannual (2-3X) newsletter; 4-6 pgs; circ 1,000. 50% freelance. Complete ms/cover letter. Pays $25 on publication for one-time rts. Not copyrighted. Articles 1,000 wds (3/yr). Responds in 2-4 wks. Seasonal 6 mos ahead. Accepts reprints. Guidelines/copy for #10 SAE/1 stamp.

> **Poetry:** Free verse.
>
> **Tips:** "Most open to articles or poems that advocate or illustrate service and caregiving."

DIOCESAN DIALOGUE, 16565 S. State St., South Holland IL 60473. (708)331-5485. Fax (708)331-5484. Catholic. Fr. Michael Gilligan, editorial dir. Targets Latin-Rite dioceses in the US that sponsor a mass broadcast on TV or radio. Semiannual tabloid; circ. 750. Free. 20% freelance. Complete ms/cover letter; no phone/fax query. Pays on publication for all rts. Responds in 10 wks. Accepts simultaneous submissions & reprints. Prefers New American Bible (Confraternity). Copy $3/9x12 SAE/2 stamps.

> **Fillers:** Cartoons, 2/yr.

*DISCIPLESHIP TRAINING, 127 9th Ave. N., Nashville TN 37234. (615)251-2831. Southern Baptist. Richard Ryan, sr. ed. Training Christians for discipleship. Quarterly mag; 64 pgs; circ 30,000. 10% freelance. Query. Pays .05/wd 30 days after acceptance for all or 1st rts. Articles 500-1,500 wds (15/yr). Responds in 6 wks. Seasonal 1 yr ahead. Free guidelines/copy.

> **Tips:** "Most open to testimonies regarding discipleship in the lives of growing Christians."

*ECUMENICAL TRENDS, Box 16136, Ludlow KY 41016. (606)581-6216. Catholic. William D. Carpe, ed. For ecumenical officers, pastors, academics; ecumenical news and articles on ecumenical topics. Monthly jour; circ 9,000. Subscription $10. 100% freelance. Complete ms. Pays $50 & up on publication. Not copyrighted. Articles 3,000-6,000 wds (40/yr); book reviews, $50. Accepts simultaneous submissions & reprints. No sidebars.

> **Poetry:** 2-3 pgs maximum; $35.
>
> **Tips:** Also uses meditations, 1,000-1,250 wds. Pays $50.

EMMANUEL, 5384 Wilson Mills Rd., Cleveland OH 44143-3092. (216)442-4752. Fax (216)449-3862. Catholic. Rev. Anthony Schueller, ed. Eucharistic spirituality for priests and others in church ministry. Monthly (10X) mag; 62 pgs; circ 4,500. Subscription $19.95. 50% freelance. Query or complete ms/cover letter; phone/fax query OK. Pays $100 for articles, $50 for meditations, on publication for all rts. Articles 2,000-2,500 wds; meditations 1,000-1,250 wds. Accepts disk. (Ads)

Poetry: Buys 10/yr. Maximum 2-3 pgs; $35.

ENRICHMENT: A Journal for Pentecostal Ministry, 1445 Boonville Ave., Springfield MO 65802. (417)862-2781. Fax (417)862-0416. E-mail: enrichment@ ag.org. Assemblies of God. Rick Knoth, mng ed. Directed to denominational ministers and church leaders. Quarterly jour; 128 pgs; circ 32,000. Subscription $18. 30% freelance. Complete ms/cover letter. Pays up to .10/wd on acceptance (sometimes publication) for 1st or reprint rts. Articles 2,000 wds; book reviews, 200-300 wds, $25. Responds in 6-8 wks. Seasonal 8-12 mos ahead. Accepts simultaneous submissions & reprints (tell when/where appeared). Accepts disk. Kill fee. Sidebars OK. Prefers NIV. Free guidelines/theme list/copy. (ads)

Fillers: Cartoons.

Columns/Departments: Buys 150/yr. Sermon Seed (sermon outlines), 100-300 wds; Ministry Ideas (for churches and pastors), 200-300 wds; and Illustrate It (sermon illustrations; original or give credit), 200-350 wds.

Special Needs: Articles on burnout and small groups.

Tips: "Most open to sermon outlines, sermon illustrations, ministry ideas that work, book reviews, and Managing Your Ministry section."

*ENVIRONMENT & ART LETTER, 1800 N. Hermitage Ave., Chicago IL 60622-1101. (773)486-8970 x64. Fax (773)486-7094. Catholic. David Philippart, ed. For artists, architects, building professionals, pastors, parish committees interested in church architecture, art and decoration. Monthly newsletter; 12 pgs; circ 2,500. Subscription $20. 80% freelance. Query/clips; phone/fax query OK. Pays $25/ms page on publication for all rts. Responds in 18 wks. Seasonal 2 mos ahead. Accepts simultaneous submissions. Theme list; copy for 9x12 SAE/3 stamps.

Tips: "Need a thorough knowledge of the liturgical documents pertaining to architecture and art, especially environment and art for Catholic worship."

*EUCHARISTIC MINISTER, 115 E. Armour Blvd., Box 419493, Kansas City MO 64141. (816)531-0538. Catholic. Rich Heffern, ed. For eucharistic ministers. Monthly newsletter; 4-8 pgs; circ 50,000. 90% freelance. Complete ms. Pays $20-200 on acceptance for one-time rts. Articles 200-2,000 wds (30+/yr). Responds in 1-2 wks. Seasonal 4-6 mos ahead. Accepts simultaneous submissions & reprints. Guidelines; free copy.

Fillers: Buys 10-12/yr. Anecdotes, cartoons, short humor.

Tips: "We want articles to be practical, inspirational, or motivational. They need to be simple and direct enough for the average person to read easily—no heavy theology, pious inspiration, or excess verbiage."

#EVANGELISM, 12800 N. Lake Shore Dr., Mequon WI 53097-2402. (414)243-4207. Fax (414)243-4409. E-mail: HeckYes@aol.com. Dr. Joel Heck, ed. For pastors and lay people concerned about personal evangelism. Quarterly journal; 40 pgs; circ 800. Subscription $15. 50% freelance. Query. Sometimes pays for one-time rts. Articles 1,000-3,000 wds (8/yr). Responds in 5 wks. Seasonal 3 mos ahead. Accepts simultaneous submissions & reprints. Guidelines/theme list; copy $3. (Ads)

Columns/Departments: Accepts 10/yr. Idea Bank (evangelism ideas), 50-500 wds; News Bank (evangelism news), 50-500 wds; Conference Bank (evangelism conferences), 50-500 wds; Introducing... (info on outreach organizations), 1,000-5,000 wds.

346 PASTOR/LEADERSHIP MARKETS/Periodical Publishers

Special Needs: Assimilation and church growth.

Tips: "We need articles on evangelism programs, witnessing, and profiles of outreach organizations."

+EVANGELISM USA, PO Box 12609, Oklahoma City OK 73157. (405)787-7110. Fax (405)789-3957. International Pentecostal Holiness Church. Talmadge Gardner, ed. For pastors/leaders interested in church growth/revitalization, church planting, and intercultural ministries. Monthly (10X) mag; 8 pgs. 100% freelance. Complete ms/cover letter. **NO PAYMENT** for all rts. Not copyrighted. Articles; book reviews 1 column long. Responds in 1 wk. Accepts disk. Sidebars OK. Free guidelines/copy.

THE FIVE STONES, 135 Pine St., Norton MA 02766-2812. Phone/fax (508)285-7145. E-mail: TONY_PAPPAS@ecunet.com. Ecumenical-American Baptist. Anthony G. Pappas, ed. Primarily to small church pastors and laity, denominational staff, and seminaries; to equip for service. Quarterly newsletter/journal; 24 pgs; circ 1,000+. Subscription $12.50. 60% freelance. Query/clips or complete ms/cover letter; phone/fax query OK. Pays $5, copies or subscription, on publication for one-time rights. Not copyrighted. Articles (20/yr) & fiction, 1,000-5,000 wds; book reviews 1,000 wds, $5. Responds in 4 wks. Seasonal 1 yr ahead. Accepts simultaneous submissions & reprints (tell when/where appeared). Guidelines; copy for 9x12 SAE/4 stamps.

Fillers: Buys 12/yr. Anecdotes, cartoons, ideas, jokes, short humor; 20-200 wds; $5.

Tips: "Always looking for everything related to small church life; fresh programming. Good place for unpublished to break in. Best to call and talk."

*GROUP'S JR. HIGH MINISTRY, Box 481, Loveland CO 80539. (970)669-3836. Fax (970)669-3269. E-mail: JHEditor@aol.com. Group Publications, Inc. Rick Lawrence (articles); Barbara Beach (columns). For youth ministers who work with the junior-high age group. Mag published 5 times/yr; 31 pgs; circ 20,000. Subscription $19.95. 75% freelance. Query; fax query OK. Pays $25-100 on acceptance for all rts. Articles 125-1,200 wds (60/yr). Responds in 4-8 wks. Seasonal 5 mos ahead. Kill fee .05%. Sidebars OK. Guidelines; copy $2/9x12 SAE.

Columns/Departments: Buys 30/yr. Parents Page (tips for parents of jr. highers); 125-200 wds; $25.

Tips: "Potential authors should be familiar with our magazine and its style. Most successful authors have experience working with jr. highers in church. We like new ideas with 'ah-has'."

*HOMILETIC AND PASTORAL REVIEW, 86 Riverside Dr., New York NY 10024. (212)799-2600. Catholic. Kenneth Baker S.J., ed. Promotion of Catholic faith, primarily for priests. Monthly journal; 80 pgs; circ 15,000. 90% freelance. Complete ms/cover letter. Pays $100 after publication for all rts. Articles to 6,000 wds. Responds in 5 wks. Free copy.

THE IVY JUNGLE REPORT, 2639 Iron St., Bellingham WA 98225. (360)733-6212. Fax (360)738-8057. E-mail: ivyjungle@aol.com. Woodruff Resources. Mike Woodruff, pub. For people who minister to collegians. Quarterly mag; circ 800. Subscription $20. 75% freelance. Query; fax/e-mail query OK. **NO PAYMENT** for one-time rts. Not copyrighted. Articles 500-1,500 wds (16/yr);

book/music reviews, 500 wds. Responds in 2 wks. Accepts simultaneous submissions & reprints. Prefers disk. Sidebars OK. Copy for 2 stamps. (Ads)

Fillers: Accepts 10+/yr. Anecdotes, cartoons, facts, jokes, newsbreaks, quizzes, quotes, short humor; 15-100 wds.

Columns/Departments: Out of the Classroom (student missions), 750-1,000 wds (4/yr). Query.

Tips: "We are looking for writers who understand the unique demands and challenges of college ministry, both church and parachurch."

*JOURNAL OF BIBLICAL ETHICS IN MEDICINE, PO Box 13231, Florence SC 29504. (803)665-6853. Dr. Hilton Terrell, ed. Ethical issues in medicine for physicians, pastors, health professionals, and concerned citizens. Quarterly jour; circ 1,200. Subscription $18. 90% freelance. Complete ms/cover letter. Pays variable rates on publication for all rts. Articles to 5,000 wds; book reviews, no pmt. Responds in 2-4 wks. Accepts simultaneous submissions & reprints. Guidelines; copy for 9x12 SAE/4 stamps.

#JOURNAL OF CHRISTIAN CAMPING, PO Box 62189, Colorado Springs CO 80962-2189. (719)260-9400. Fax (719)260-6398. E-mail: CCIUSA@aol.com. Christian Camping Intl. Dean Ridings, ed. For those involved in organized camps and conference centers. Bimonthly mag; 32-40 pgs; circ 7,000. Subscription $24.95. 75% freelance. Query; fax/e-mail query OK. Pays .06/wd on publication for all rts. Articles 250-1,000 wds (5-8/yr). Responds in 2-6 wks. Seasonal 4 mos ahead. Accepts simultaneous submissions. Prefers disk. Sidebars OK. Prefers NIV. Guidelines/theme list; copy $2.25/9x12 SAE/5 stamps. (Ads)

Fillers: Buys 3-5 cartoons/yr; $25-50.

Special Needs: Outdoor setting; purpose and objectives; administration and organization; personnel development; camper/guest needs; programming; health and safety; food service; site/facilities maintenance; business/operations; marketing and PR; and fund raising. Also prominent Christian making a difference because of Christian camping experience and/or in Christian camping.

Tips: "Most open to feature articles. Writer must be rooted in the camping industry. Before sending, ask yourself if this is a MUST READ for Christian camping professionals."

*JOURNAL OF CHRISTIAN HEALING, 3661 S. Kinnickinnie Ave., St. Francis WI 53235. (414)481-3696. Assoc. of Christian Therapists. Father Louis Lussier, OSCAS, ed. Focuses on the healing power and presence of Jesus Christ, for health and mental health professionals and healing ministries. Quarterly journal; 40 pgs; circ 1,200. 100% freelance. Complete ms/cover letter; phone query OK. **PAYS IN COPIES,** for all rts. Articles 10-20 pgs (12/yr); fiction 2-5 pgs; book reviews, 2-5 pgs. Accepts reprints. Responds in 8 wks. Guidelines; copy $8.

Poetry: Charles Zeiders. Accepts 12/yr. Free verse, haiku, light verse or traditional; to 40 lines. Submit max. 10 poems.

Fillers: Accepts 10/yr. Various; to 250 wds.

Columns/Departments: Accepts 12/yr. Resources, Medical practices, Nursing, Pastoral Ministry, Psychiatry, Prayer Ministry, Sexuality, Dreams; 2-5 pgs.

Tips: "All articles or short stories must relate to healing."

*THE JOURNAL OF PASTORAL CARE, 1068 Harbor Dr. SW, Calabask NC 28467. Phone/fax (910)579-5084. E-mail: Orlo@aol.com. Orlo Strunk, Jr., mng ed. For chaplains/pastors/professionals involved with pastoral care and counseling in other than a church setting. Quarterly jour; 112 pgs; circ. 12,000. Subscription $22.95. 90% freelance. Complete ms; phone/fax/e-mail query OK. **PAYS IN COPIES** for 1st rts. Articles 5,000 wds (20/yr); fiction 1,000-3,000 wds (1/yr). Responds in 2-8 wks. Seasonal 1 yr ahead. Prefers disk. No sidebars. Guidelines; copy $5.50/6x9 SAE/2 stamps.

> **Poetry:** Accepts 12/yr. Free verse, haiku, traditional; 3-24 lines. Submit max. 3 poems.

> **Tips:** "Readers are highly trained clinically, as well as holding professional degrees in religion/theology. Writers need to be professionals on topics covered."

+JOURNAL OF THE AMERICAN SOCIETY FOR CHURCH GROWTH, Talbot School of Theology, 13800 Biola Ave., La Mirada CA 90639. (310)903-6000. Fax (909)882-5386. E-mail: gary-mcintosh@peter.biola.edu. American Society for Church Growth. Dr. Gary L. McIntosh, ed. Targets professors, pastors, denominational executives and seminary students interested in church growth and evangelism. Quarterly journal (3X-fall, winter, spring); 125 pgs; circ. 200. Subscription $24. 100% freelance. Complete ms/cover letter; phone/fax/e-mail query OK. **PAYS IN COPIES** for 1st rts. Not copyrighted. Articles 15 pgs (12/yr). Responds in 8 wks. Accepts reprints (tell when/where appeared). Prefers disk. No sidebars. Guidelines/theme list; copy $10/ 6x9 SAE. (Ads)

> **Tips:** "All articles must have a church growth slant."

LEADERSHIP JOURNAL, 465 Gundersen Dr., Carol Stream IL 60188. (630)260-6200. Fax (630)260-0114. E-mail: LeaderJ@aol.com. Christianity Today, Inc. Kevin A. Miller, ed. Practical help for pastors/church leaders. Quarterly journal; 130 pgs; circ 69,000. Subscription $22. 75% freelance. Query; fax/e-mail query OK. Pays $50-400 (.10/wd) on publication for 1st rts, rt. to reprint & & electronic rts. Articles 500-3,000 wds (80/yr). Responds in 2-3 wks. Seasonal 5 mos ahead. Accepts disk. Kill fee 50%. Sidebars OK. Guidelines/theme list; copy $3/9x12 SAE/7 stamps. (Ads)

> **Fillers:** Buys 80/yr. Anecdotes, cartoons, ideas, short humor; to 150 wds. Pays $25-50.

> **Columns/Departments:** Buys 80/yr. Ideas That Work, 150 wds; To Illustrate (sermon illustrations), 150 wds; To Quip (humorous sermon illustrations); Back Page (opinion), 1,200 wds. Complete ms. Pays $25-50.

> **Special Needs:** Material on pastoral care, church health, contemporary preaching, and the pastor's soul.

> **Tips:** "Writers should be involved in the ministry/leadership of the church. "
> ** This periodical was #14 on the 1996 Top 50 Christian Publishers list. (#27 in 1995, #16 in 1994)

LITURGY, 8750 Georgia Ave., Ste. 123, Silver Spring MD 20910. (301)495-0885. Fax (301)495-5945. E-mail: litconf@aol.com. The Liturgical Conference. Blair Gilmer Meeks, ed. For clergy, liturgy planners, musicians, and religious educators. Bimonthly jour; 80 pgs; circ 2,500. Subscription $45. 5% freelance. Query; phone/fax/e-mail query OK. Pays $50 on publication for all rts. Articles 1,500-

2,200 wds (3/yr). Responds in 3-6 wks. Seasonal 10 mos ahead. Accepts simultaneous submissions & reprints. Prefers disk. No sidebars. Guidelines/theme list; copy $10.95.

Tips: "An ecumenical perspective is required. No poetry."

LUTHERAN FORUM, PO Box 327, Delhi NY 13753-0327. (607)746-7511. Fax (607)829-2158. American Lutheran Publicity Bureau. Ronald Bagnall, ed. For church leadership, clerical and laity. Quarterly journal; 64 pgs; circ 3,200. 100% freelance. Complete ms/cover letter. **NO PAYMENT.** Articles 1,000-3,000 wds. Responds in 26-32 wks. Accepts simultaneous submissions & reprints. Requires disk. Guidelines; copy for 9x12 SAE/6 stamps. (Ads)

LUTHERAN PARTNERS, 8765 W. Higgins Rd., Chicago IL 60631-4195. (800)638-3522x2875 or 2884. (773)380-2884 or 2875. Fax (773)380-2829. E-mail: 1partmag@elca.org or LUTHERAN_PARTNERS.parti@ecunet.org. Evangelical Lutheran Church in America. Carl E. Linder, ed.; William A. Decker, mng ed. To encourage and challenge rostered leaders in the ELCA, including pastors and lay leaders. Bimonthly mag; 40-48 pgs; circ 20,000. Subscription $10 (free to leaders). 5-10% freelance. Query or complete ms/cover letter; phone/fax/e-mail query OK. Query for electronic submissions. Pays $25-150 on publication for 1st rts. Articles 500-2,000 wds (12/yr); book/video reviews 700 wds (contact book review ed.). Responds in 12-16 wks. Seasonal 6-8 mos ahead. Accepts simultaneous submissions & reprints (tell when/where appeared). Kill fee. Prefers disk. Sidebars OK. Prefers NRSV. Guidelines; copy for 9x12 SAE/5 stamps. (Ads)

Poetry: Buys 6/yr. Free verse, traditional: $50. Submit max. 4 poems.

Fillers: Buys 4-6/yr. Ideas for parish ministry (called Jottings); to 500 wds; $25.

Special Needs: Book & video reviews. Query Thelma Megill-Cobbler, Trinity Lutheran Seminary, 2199 E. Main St., Columbus OH 43209, (614)235-4136. Uses books predominately from mainline denominational publishers. Payment is copy of book.

Tips: "Query us with solid idea. Understand Lutheran Christian theology and congregational life. Be able to see life from a pastor/lay leader's point of view. With limited freelance, most sections hard to get into, but you might try the Jottings section first (see Fillers)."

MINISTRIES TODAY, 600 Rinehart Rd., Lake Mary FL 32746. (407)333-0600. Fax (407)333-7133. E-mail: ministries@strang.com. Strang Communications. Lee Grady, exec. ed; Marcia Ford, assoc. ed (e-mail: mford@strng.com); Jimmy Stewart, book & music review ed. Helps for pastors and church leaders in charismatic churches. Bimonthly mag; 90 pgs; circ 30,000. Subscription $24.95. 60-80% freelance. Query; fax/e-mail query OK. Pays $50 or $500-800 on publication for all rts. Articles 2,000-2,500 wds (25/yr); book/music/video reviews, 300 wds, $25. Responds in 4 wks. Prefers disk. Kill fee. Sidebars OK. Prefers NIV. Guidelines; copy $4/9x12 SAE. (Ads)

Columns/Departments: Michele Buckingham. Buys 36/yr. Soap Box (opinion pcs); The Next Generation (youth/children's ministry); 800 or 1,050 wds; $100-150.

Tips: "Most open to columns. Write for guidelines and study the magazine."

MINISTRY MAGAZINE, 12501 Old Columbia Pike, Silver Spring MD 20904.

(301)680-6510. Fax (301)680-6502. Seventh-day Adventist. Submit to The Editor. For Pastors. Monthly mag; 32 pgs.; circ.16,000. Subscription $25. 90% freelance. Query; fax query OK. Pays $50-150 on acceptance for all rts. Articles 750-1,500 wds; book reviews 2 paragraphs ($25). Responds in 2 wks. Requires disk. Some sidebars. Guidelines; copy for 9x12 SAE/5 stamps. (Ads)

+MODERN LITURGY, 160 E. Virginia St. #290, San Jose CA 95112. (408)286-8505. Fax (408)287-8748. E-mail: mdrnlitrgy@aol.com. Resource Publications, Inc. Nick Wagner, ed. dir. To help liturgists and ministers make the imaginative connection between liturgy and life. Monthly (10X) mag; 50 pgs; circ 20,000. Subscription $45. Query; fax/e-mail query OK. Query for electronic submissions. **PAYS A SUBSCRIPTION** on publication for 1st rts. Articles 1,000 wds (30/yr). Responds in 4 wks. Seasonal 6 mos ahead. Accepts reprints (tell when/where appeared). Requires disk. Sidebars OK. Guidelines/theme list; copy $4/11x14 SAE/2stamps. (Ads)

    Contest: Visual Arts Awards.

*NATIONAL DRAMA SERVICE, 127 Ninth Ave. N, MSN 158, Nashville TN 37234. (615)251-3837. Fax (615)251-2066. Southern Baptist. Matt Tullos, creative dir. Conservative, evangelical dramas for stage, street and sanctuary. Quarterly drama script collections; 3,000 members. Subscription $35. Est. 1993. 100% freelance. Complete ms/cover letter. Pays $25 or .055/wd on acceptance for all or 1st rts. Scripts 5-7 minutes in length. Responds in 10 wks. Seasonal 6-12 mos ahead. Accepts simultaneous submissions. Prefers NIV. Guidelines; copy for 9x12 SAE.

*NETWORKS, Box 685, Cocoa FL 32923. (407)632-0130. Fax (407)631-8207. Christian Council on Persons with Disabilities. Linda G. Howard, ed. For those with specialized ministry to the mentally retarded. Bimonthly newsletter; 8 pgs; circ 1,700. 80% freelance. Query or complete ms. **NO PAYMENT** for 1st rts. Articles 250-450 wds (12/yr); book reviews 350 wds. Responds in 6 wks. Seasonal 4 mos ahead. Accepts simultaneous submissions & reprints. Guidelines; copy for 9x12 SAE/6 stamps.

    Poetry: Accepts 4/yr. Any type; to 66 lines. Submit max. 10 poems.

    Columns/Departments: Accepts 8/yr. Program Highlights, 1,000 wds; Teachers' Tips, 750 wds.

    Special Needs: Advocacy, normalization/integration, church/state issues. June 15 deadline for annual issue on the Christian Council on Persons with Disabilities.

+THE NEWSLETTER NEWSLETTER, 4150 Belden Village St. 4th Floor, Canton OH 44718. (330)493-7880. Fax (330)493-7897. E-mail: newsletter@comresources. com. Communication Resources. Stan Purdum, exec. ed. To help church secretaries and church newsletter editors prepare their newsletter. Monthly newsletter; 12 pgs. Subscription $39.95. 30% freelance. Complete ms. Pays $150 on acceptance for all rts. Articles 800-1,000 wds (8/yr). Responds in 4 wks. Seasonal 8 mos ahead. Accepts simultaneous submissions. Requires disk. Kill fee. Sidebars OK. Copy for 9x12 SAE/3 stamps.

+PARISH LITURGY, 16565 S. State St., South Holland IL 60473. (708)331-5485. Catholic. Father Gilligan, ed. dir. A planning tool for Sunday and Holyday liturgy. Quarterly mag; 32 pgs; circ 22,000. Subscription $18/2 yrs. 10% freelance.

Query; no phone query. All rts. Articles 400 wds. Responds in 4 wks. Seasonal 4 mos ahead. Accepts simultaneous submissions & reprints (tell when/where appeared). Some sidebars. Prefers NAB.

+**PASTORAL LIFE**, Box 595, Canfield OH 44406-0595. (330)533-5503. Fax (330)533-1076. Catholic. Rev. Anthony Chenevey, ed. Focuses on the current problems, needs, issues and all important activities related to all phases of pastoral work and life. Monthly mag. Query. Pays .04/wd & up. Articles to 3,000 wds. Responds in 2 wks. Guidelines; free copy.

   Tips: "We feature pastoral homilies for Sundays and Holydays. Articles should be eminently pastoral in approach and content."

+**PASTOR'S FAMILY**, 8605 Explorer Dr., Colorado Springs CO 80920. (719)531-3400. Fax (719)531-3499. Focus on the Family. Simon J. Dahlman, ed. To support and strengthen ministers and other church workers, their spouses, and children in area of family life. Bimonthly mag; 32 pgs; circ 14,000. Subscription $18. Est. 1996. Query; phone/fax query OK. Pays .15-.20/wd on acceptance for 1st rts. Articles 400-1,600 wds (40/yr). Responds in 6 wks. Accepts disk. Kill fee 50%. Sidebars OK. Prefers NIV. Guidelines/theme list; copy for 9x12 SAE/ 2 stamps.

   Fillers: Buys 40/yr. Anecdotes, cartoons, quotes; 25-100 wds. Pays $15.

   Columns/Departments: After Church (roundtable on specific topic), 1,300-1,500 wds, query; Better Homes and Parsons (humorous anecdotes related to ministry lifestyle), 50-100 wds; Stuff (brief info and reviews), 50-100 wds. Complete ms. Pays $15-300.

   Tips: "You must have a history in ministry or be able to understand, empathize, and communicate within that experience. We're looking for subjects and treatments that are unique to the ministry life. This is a family-life magazine, not a professional development journal."

*__PASTOR'S TAX & MONEY__, PO Box 50188, Indianapolis IN 46250. (800)877-3158. Fax (317)594-8311. Daniel D. Busby, ed. Guidance for pastors in management of church and personal finances. Quarterly newsletter; 8 pgs; circ 6,000. Subscription $59.95. 50% freelance. Complete ms/cover letter. Pays $50 on publication for 1st rts. Articles 600-800 wds (8/yr). Responds in 13 wks. No sidebars. Copy $1/6x9 SAE/2 stamps.

   Special Needs: Minister's taxes; computers; personal finances and church finances.

THE PREACHER, PO Box 757800, Memphis TN 38175-7800. (901)757-7977. Fax (901)757-1372. E-mail: olford@memphisonline. Encounter Ministries, Inc. Mark N. Boorman, dir. of commun. Triennial mag; 16-24 pgs; circ. 4,000. Subscription $10 (voluntary). 10% freelance. Query; phone query OK. **NO PAYMENT** for one-time rts. Articles (3-6/yr) 250-500 wds; fiction; book reviews 100-200 wds. Responds in 2 wks. Seasonal 3-4 mos ahead. Accepts simultaneous submissions. Prefers disk. Sidebars OK. Prefers NKJ. Copy for 6x9 SAE/2 stamps.

   Poetry: Accepts 1-2 /yr. Traditional; 4-20 lines. Submit max. 2 poems.

   Fillers: Accepts 4-6/yr. Prayers, 100-200 wds.

   Tips: "Be a pastor or actively involved in Christian ministry."

*__PREACHER'S ILLUSTRATION SERVICE__, Box 3102, Margate NJ 08402. (609)822-9401. Fax (609)822-1638. James Colaianni, pub. Sermon illustration resource for professional clergy. Bimonthly loose-leaf booklet, 16 pgs. 15% freelance. Complete ms. Pays .15/wd on publication for any rts. Illustrations/anecdotes 50-250 wds. Responds in 6 wks. Seasonal 4 mos ahead. Accepts reprints. Prefers disk. Guidelines/topical index; copy for 9x12 SAE.

Poetry: Light verse, traditional; 50-250 lines; .15/wd. Submit max. 3 poems.

Fillers: Various; sermon illustrations; 50-250 wds; .15/wd.

THE PREACHER'S MAGAZINE, 10814 E. Broadway, Spokane WA 99206. (509)226-3464. Fax (509)926-8740. Nazarene. Rev. Randal E. Denny, ed. A professional journal for holiness pastors and other preachers. Quarterly mag; 80 pgs; circ 18,000. Subscription $7.50. 30% freelance. Complete ms/cover letter; phone query OK. Pays .035/wd on publication for one-time rts. Articles 700-2,500 wds (40/yr); book reviews 300-400 wds. Responds in 4-6 wks. Seasonal 6 mos ahead. Accepts simultaneous submissions & reprints (tell when/where appeared). No disk. Some sidebars. Prefers NIV. Guidelines.

Fillers: Buys 10/yr. Anecdotes, cartoons, ideas; 300-700 wds.

Tips: "Material must be relevant to pastor's ministry or personal life."

PREACHING, PO Box 369, Jackson TN 38302-0369. (901)668-9948. E-mail: 74114.275@compuserve.com. Preaching Resources, Inc. Dr. Michael Duduit, ed; submit to Mark Johnson, mng ed. Professional magazine for evangelical preachers; focus is on preaching and worship leadership. Bimonthly mag; 64-80 pgs; circ 10,000. Subscription $24.95. 80% freelance. Query; fax/e-mail query OK. Query for electronic submissions. Pays $35-50 on publication for 1st rts & reprint rts. Articles 1,200-1,500 wds (30-40/yr). Responds in 8-10 wks. Seasonal 1 yr ahead. Prefers disk. Prefers NIV. Some sidebars. Guidelines/theme list; copy $2.50. (Ads)

Fillers: Buys 10-15/yr. Cartoons only; $25.

Tips: "Need how-to articles about specific areas of preaching and worship leadership. We only accept articles from pastors or seminary/college faculty."

THE PRIEST, 200 Noll Plaza, Huntington IN 46750-4304. (219)356-8400. Fax (219)359-9117. Catholic/Our Sunday Visitor, Inc. Msgr. Owen F. Campion, ed. For Catholic priests, deacons and seminarians; to help in all aspects of ministry. Monthly mag; 48 pgs; circ 8,200. Subscription $35.97. 80% freelance. Complete ms/cover letter; phone query OK. Pays $175-250 on acceptance for 1st rts. Articles to 1,500-5,000 wds (96/yr); some 2-parts. Responds in 6-8 wks. Seasonal 6 mos ahead. Free guidelines/copy. (Ads)

Fillers: George Foster. Cartoons; $35.

Columns/Departments: Buys 36/yr. Viewpoint (about priests or the church), under 1,000 wds, $50. Complete ms.

Tips: "Write to the point, with interest, and when you have said your piece, quit. Most open to features. Keep the audience in mind. Include Social Security number."

** #62 on the 1994 Top 50.

*PROCLAIM, 127 Ninth Ave. N, Nashville TN 37234. (615)251-2874. Fax (615)251-3866. Southern Baptist. Bill Chitwood, ed. Sermons, illustrations and worship materials for pastors. Quarterly mag; 50 pgs; circ 15,000. Subscription $13.30. 75% freelance. Query; phone query OK. Pays .055/wd ($8 min) on acceptance for all or 1st rts. Articles 600-4,000 wds (50-60/yr). Responds in 2-16 wks. Seasonal 6 mos ahead. Accepts reprints. No sidebars. Guidelines; free copy for 9x12 SAE.

Columns/Departments: Features, 2,400 wds; Sermon Workshop (sermon helps), 50-700 wds; Worship Workshop, 2,400 wds; Pulpit Performance, 3,000 wds.

** #68 on the 1994 Top 50.

*PUBLISHERS WEEKLY RELIGION BOOKLINE**, 1813 Monroe St., Evanston IL 60202-1903. (847)328-4043. Fax (847)328-0048. E-mail: 72624.3562@ compuserve.com. Cahners Publishing. Lynn Garrett, ed. Covers religious books and publishing for pastors, leaders, religious bookstores, libraries, etc.; all religions from a nonsectarian point of view. Biweekly tabloid; 8 pgs; circ. 6,000. Subscription $79. Est. 1996. 50-60% freelance. Query/clips; phone/fax/e-mail query OK. Pays $75/column (@350 wds) on publication for 1st and electronic rts. Articles 350-1,500 wds; book/CD-Rom/audio book/video reviews, 150 wds, $35 + book. Seasonal material by arrangement only. Might accept reprints. Kill fee. Requires disk, modem or e-mail. Sidebars OK. Guidelines; copy for 9x12 SAE/2 stamps.

Tips: "Writing for us requires expertise in some area of religion and/or publishing as a business, as well as a world view that is not too constricted (remember we are nonsectarian). Most open to reviews and features. All pieces are book-focused."

PULPIT HELPS, 6815 Shallowford Rd., Chattanooga TN 37421. (800)251-7206. Fax (423)894-6863. E-mail: AMGpublish@aol.com. Ted Kyle, ed. To help preachers and serious students of the Bible. Monthly tabloid; 28 pgs; circ 105,000. Subscription $15. 10% freelance. Complete ms; no phone/fax/e-mail query. **NO PAYMENT.** Articles to 100-1,200 wds (30-40/yr). Responds in 2 wks. Seasonal 4-5 mos ahead. Accepts simultaneous submissions & reprints (tell when/where appeared). MacIntosh disk. Few sidebars. Prefers KJV or NIV. Guidelines/theme list; copy for 9x12 SAE. (Ads)

Poetry: Accepts 20-30/yr. Traditional; short. Submit max 3 poems.

Fillers: Anecdotes, prose, quotes, short religious humor; to 150 wds.

Columns/Departments: Family Helps, to 1,000 wds; Illustrations (for sermons), 100-150 wds; Bulletin Inserts (religious 1-liners), 50 wds; Sermon Outlines (brief).

Tips: "Most open to short, pointed anecdotes/articles preachers can use as illustrations; also need one-sentence fillers for our Bulletin Inserts."

QUARTERLY REVIEW, A Journal of Theological Resources for Ministry, 1001 - 19th Ave. S., Nashville TN 37202-0871. (615)340-7334. Fax (615)340-7048. E-mail: shels@bhem.org. United Methodist. Dr. Sharon J. Hels, ed. A theological approach to subjects of interest to clergy—Scripture study, ethics, and practice of ministry in Wesleyan tradition. Quarterly journal; 112 pgs; circ 1,500. Subscription $24. 75% freelance. Complete ms/cover letter; phone/fax query OK. **PAYS IN COPIES** for 1st rts. Articles to 5,000 wds (20/yr); book reviews to 1,000 wds. Responds in 6-8 wks. Seasonal 8 mos ahead. Prefers disk. No sidebars. Prefers NRSV. Guidelines/theme list; copy for 9x12 SAE/$2 postage.

Tips: "We look for writers who have strong academic/theological training and whose work addresses concerns and interests of those in ministry. Awareness of current scholarly literature, a well-developed argument, and clear expository prose are essential."

REFORMED WORSHIP, 2850 Kalamazoo SE, Grand Rapids MI 49560. (616)246-0781. Fax (616)246-0834. Christian Reformed Church in North America. Dr. Emily R. Brink, ed. To provide liturgical and musical resources for pastors, church musicians, and other worship leaders. Quarterly journal; 48 pgs; circ 3,700. Subscription $23. 90% freelance (15% unsolicited). Complete ms/cover letter; phone/fax query OK. Pays .05/wd on publication for one-time rts; book reviews $25. Articles 250-1,500 wds (1-2/yr); book reviews 250 wds, $25. Responds in 4-6 wks. Seasonal 8 mos ahead. Rarely accepts reprints. Kill fee 50%. Prefers disk. Sidebars OK. Prefers NIV or NRSV. Guidelines; copy $5/9x12 SASE.

Fillers: Buys 4-5/yr. Cartoons, prayers; $20-50.

Columns/Departments: View From the Pew (humorous or reflective vignettes on worship experiences), 1,000-1,500 wds.

Tips: "You need to understand the Reformed tradition of worship. Most open to cartoons."

*RESOURCE: The National Leadership Magazine, 6745 Century Ave., Mississauga ON L5N 6P7 Canada. (905)542-7400. Fax (905)542-7313. Pentecostal Assemblies of Canada. Michael Horban, ed. For church leadership and practical how-tos on leadership issues. Bimonthly mag; 48 pgs; circ 10,000. Subscription $20. 20% freelance. Query. Pays $30-100 on publication for all rts. Articles 500-1,500 wds (8-10/yr); book reviews 250 wds, $20. Responds in 4-6 wks. Seasonal 3 mos ahead. Accepts reprints. Prefers disk. Sidebars OK. Guidelines/theme list; copy $2/9x12 SAE.

Fillers: Buys 4-8/yr. Anecdotes, cartoons, short humor; 200-300 wds; $20-30.

Columns/Departments: Kevin Johnson. Buys 6-12/yr. Resources for Youth Workers; Resources for CE Workers; 300 wds; $20-30.

Special Needs: Good missions promotional features.

Tips: "Say something positive to leaders that stretches and enriches them."

REVIEW FOR RELIGIOUS, 3601 Lindell Blvd., Rm. 428, St. Louis MO 63108-3393. (314)977-7363. Fax (314)977-7362. E-mail: FOPPEMA@sluca.slu.edu. Catholic/Jesuits of Missouri Province. Rev. David L. Fleming, S.J., ed. For Catholic Women and Men Religious, clergy and laity involved in church ministry; to reflect on the church's rich heritage of spirituality. Bimonthly journal; 112 pgs; circ 9,500. Subscription $20. 85% freelance. Complete ms/cover letter; no phone/fax/e-mail query. Pays $18-72 on publication for 1st rts. Articles 2,000-5,000 wds (50/yr). Responds in 8 wks. Seasonal 8 mos ahead. Accepts disk. No sidebars. Prefers RSV or NAB. Guidelines; copy for 10x13 SAE/5 stamps.

Poetry: Buys 10/yr. Light verse, traditional; 3-12 lines; $6.

Tips: "Be familiar with at least three past issues."

SERMON NOTES, 1420 Osborne St., Ste. 10, Humboldt TN 38343. (901)784-9239. Fax (901)784-8154. E-mail: stevemay@sermonnotes.com. Alderson Press. Stephen May, ed. Sermon helps for ministers. Bimonthly mag; 64 pgs; circ 3,000. Subscription $39. Est. 1994. 25% freelance. Complete ms/cover letter; fax/e-mail query OK. Pays $35-50 for articles & sermons ($5 for illustrations on publication for one-time rts. Sermons & articles (8/yr)1,500 wds; illustrations 80-100 wds); book reviews 500 wds ($20). Responds in 5 wks. Seasonal 4 mos ahead. Accepts reprints (tell when/where appeared). Prefers disk. Sidebars OK. Prefers NIV. Guidelines/theme list; copy $2/6x9 SAE. (Ads)

Fillers: Buys 12/yr. Cartoons, short humor on church newsletter ideas. Pays $15.

Columns/Departments: Buys 6/yr. Q & A (interview with Christian leader), 1,000-1,500 wds; Pastor's Library (book or product review), 500 wds. Pays $35-50.

Tips: "Looking for profiles of ministers and/or churches that are effectively reaching seekers. We also need articles that will help a minister communicate more effectively with congregation (not just articles on how to preach sermons). Would also like to see a positive, constructive analysis of a high profile pastor—what makes him effective, etc."

SINGLE ADULT MINISTRIES JOURNAL, Box 62056, Colorado Springs CO 80962. (800)487-4726. Fax (719)533-3041. E-mail: 70702.1001@compuserve. com. Cook Communications Ministries. Jerry D. Jones, ed. For pastors and lay leaders involved in ministry with single adults. Bimonthly journal; 16-24 pgs; circ 5,000. Subscription $24. 5% freelance. Query; fax/e-mail query OK. **USUALLY NO PAYMENT** for 1st rts. Articles 200-2,500 wds (0-4/yr); book reviews 50-300 wds/$15-75. Responds in 6-12 wks. Seasonal 4-6 mos ahead. Prefers disk. Theme list; copy for 9x12 SAE/4 stamps. (Ads)

Fillers: Buys 0-5/yr. Facts, newsbreaks, quotes; 25-200 wds; $10-50.

Tips: "Write to the pastor or leader, not to singles themselves. Interview singles or the leaders who work with them."

*THE SUNDAY SCHOOL LEADER: LARGER CHURCH EDITION, 127 Ninth Ave. N., Nashville TN 37234. (615)251-2074. (615)251-2074. Fax (615)251-5091. Southern Baptist. Judith S. Hayes, sr. ed. Focuses on the Sunday school programs of larger Baptist churches (over 150 people). Monthly mag; 66 pgs; circ 50,000. Subscription $19.80. 10% freelance. Query or complete ms/cover letter; fax query OK. Pays .055/wd on acceptance for all rts. Articles 650-1,250 wds. Responds in 5 wks. Accepts disk. Guidelines.

*SUNDAY SERMONS, PO Box 3102, Margate NJ 08402. (609)822-9401. Fax (609)822-1638. Ecumenical. J. Colaianni, ed-in-chief. Full-text sermon resource for clergy. Bimonthly bound workbook; 54-60 pgs. 5% freelance. Pays on publication for all rts. Responds in 6 wks. Seasonal 6 mos ahead. Accepts reprints. Prefers disk. Guidelines/theme list; copy for 9x12 SAE. Not in topical listings.

Tips: "Sermons must include several relevant illustrations."

TECHNOLOGIES FOR WORSHIP (Formerly, **RELIGION**), PO Box 35, Aurora ON L4G 3H1 Canada. (905)830-4300. Fax (905)853-5096. E-mail: amip@ inforamp.net. Website: http://www.TFWM.com. AMI Publishing. Lisa Anastasoff, ed. Bimonthly mag; 40 pgs; circ. 5,000. Subscription $29.95. 90% freelance. Query; phone/fax/e-mail query OK. Articles 750-2,500 wds. **NO PAYMENT** for one-time rts. Responds in 4-8 wks. Seasonal 2 mos ahead. Accepts simultaneous submissions & reprints. Prefers disk. Some sidebars. Guidelines/theme list; copy for 9x12 SAE/$1.85 postage. (Ads)

Special Needs: Technologies: audio, video, music, computers, broadcast, lighting, and drama; 750-2,500 wds.

Tips: Call the editor to discuss idea for article or column. Should know a lot about today's technologies.

#THEOLOGY TODAY, PO Box 29, Princeton NJ 08542. (609)497-7714. Nondenominational. The Editors. Explores key issues, current thoughts and trends in the fields of religion and theology. Quarterly jour; 72 pgs; circ 13,000. Subscription $21. Little unsolicited accepted. Complete ms/cover letter. Pays $75-200 on publication for all rts. Articles 1,500-3,500 wds. Sidebars OK. Guidelines; free copy. Incomplete topical listings.

Tips: "Articles should be scholarly without being pedantic and of general interest without being faddish. We expect exclusive language."

TODAY'S CHRISTIAN PREACHER, 40 Berkshire Ct., Wyomissing PA 19610-1224. (610)372-1111. Fax (610)372-1122. E-mail: ScepterCom@aol.com. Scepter Publication. Jerry Thacker, ed. To provide material on current topics to help preachers in their personal lives. Quarterly mag; 24 pgs; circ 25,000. Free subscription. Est. 1993. 20% freelance. Complete ms/cover letter; fax query OK. Pays $150 on publication for one-time or simultaneous rts. Not copyrighted. Articles 800-1,000 wds (10-15/yr). Responds in 3-4 wks. Seasonal 1 yr ahead. Accepts simultaneous submissions & reprints (tell when/where appeared). Prefers disk. Sidebars OK. Prefers KJV. Guidelines; copy for 9x12SAE/3stamps. (Ads)

*TODAY'S PARISH, Box 180, Mystic CT 06355. (860)536-2611. Fax (860)572-0788. Catholic. Daniel Connors, ed. Practical ideas and issues relating to parish life, management and ministry; human interest relevant to parish life. Mag published 7 times/yr; 40-42 pgs; circ 14,800. Subscription $22. 25% freelance. Query or complete ms. Pays $50-100 on publication for 1st rts. Articles 800-1,800 wds (45/yr). Responds 13 wks. Seasonal 6 mos ahead. Guidelines; copy for 9x12 SASE.

Poetry: Free verse; to 25 lines.

+VOICE OF THE VINEYARD, PO Box 17580, Anaheim CA 92817. (714)777-1433. Fax (714)777-8841. E-mail: 102100.2657@compuserve.com. Assn. of Vineyard Churches. Jon Bogart, ed. Quarterly mag; 24 pgs; circ. 12,000. 5% freelance. Query; fax/e-mail query OK. Pays negotiable rates on publication for 1st rts. Articles 750-1,200 wds; book reviews 300 wds. Responds in 2 wks. Accepts simultaneous submissions & reprints (tell when/where appeared). Requires disk. Kill fee, Prefers NIV. Sidebars OK. Copy for 9x12 SAE/2 stamps.

Fillers: Anecdotes, cartoons, facts, games, ideas, jokes, newsbreaks, quizzes, quotes, short humor, word puzzles; 50 wds.

WCA MONTHLY, PO Box 3188, Barrington IL 60011-5046. (847)765-0070. Fax (847)765-5046. E-mail: www.willowcreek.org. Willow Creek Assn. Paul Braoudakis, mng ed. For church leaders that are willing to take risks for the sake of the Gospel. Monthly newsletter; 16-20 pgs; circ. 10,000. Subscription $29. 10% freelance. Query/clips; phone/fax/e-mail query OK. Pays $25 on publication for all rts. Articles 500-1,000 wds; book/music reviews 500 wds, video reviews 300 wds. Responds in 2 wks. Seasonal 2 mos ahead. Accepts simultaneous submissions & reprints (tell when/where appeared). Requires disk. Some sidebars. Prefers NIV. Free copy.

Fillers: Accepts many. Cartoons, ideas, short humor; 50-75 wds. Pays $10.

Columns/Departments: On the Lighter Side (humor), 100 wds; News From the Frontlines (creative ministries within the church), 50-100 wds; Strategic Trends (trends from growing churches), 200-250 wds. Pays $10-25. Complete ms.

Tips: "Any articles that pertain to doing a seeker-sensitive type of ministry will be considered."

*WORD & WORLD: Theology for Christian Ministry, 2481 Como Ave., St. Paul MN 55108. (612)641-3482. Fax (612)641-3354. E.L.C.A./Luther Northwestern Theological Seminary. Frederick J. Gaiser, ed. Addresses ecclesiastical and secular issues from a theological perspective and addresses pastors and church leaders with the best fruits of theological research. Quarterly journal; 104 pgs; circ 3,100. Subscription $18. 10% freelance. Complete ms/cover letter; phone query OK. Pays $50 on publication for all rts. Articles 5,000-6,000 wds. Responds in 2-8 wks. Guidelines/theme list; copy $5.

Tips: "Most open to general articles. We look for serious theology addressed clearly and interestingly to people in the practice of ministry. Creativity and usefulness in ministry are highly valued."

#WORSHIP LEADER, 107 Kenner Ave., Nashville TN 37205-2207. (615)386-3011. Fax (615)385-4112. E-mail: mriddle@ccmcom.com. CCM Communications. Melissa L. Riddle, mng ed. Intellectual tone with practical advice on leading worship. Bimonthly mag; 40+ pgs; circ 43,000. Subscription $14.95. 20-40% freelance. Query/clips or complete ms. Pays .20/wd on publication for all rts. Articles 800-2,000 wds (15/yr). Responds in 6-8 wks. Seasonal 6-8 mos ahead. Kill fee 50%. Prefers disk. Sidebars OK. Prefers NIV. Guidelines. (Ads)

Fillers: Buys 6-12/yr. Anecdotes, quotes; 150-300 wds.

Columns/Departments: Buys 6-12/yr. Viewpoint (op/ed), 600-800 wds; Putting it All Together (experience with church), 1,200 wds. Several others, see guidelines.

Tips: "We need writers from all parts of the country to do profiles of churches, worship leaders/ministers of music in their home cities. Also, suggest articles on worship applications outside the church."

YOUR CHURCH, 465 Gundersen Dr., Carol Stream IL 60188. (630)260-6200. Fax (630)260-0114. E-mail: YCEditor@aol.com. Christianity Today Inc. Richard Doebler, mng. ed. Focuses on church business/administration, purchasing and facilities management. Bimonthly mag; 60-76 pgs; circ 150,000. Subscription free to qualified readers. 75% freelance. Query; phone/fax/e-mail query OK. Query for electronic submissions. Pays .12-.20/wd on acceptance for 1st rts. Articles 900-1,300 wds (60/yr). Responds in 2-4 wks. Seasonal 6 mos ahead. Accepts reprints (tell when/where appeared). Kill fee 1%. Sidebars OK. Guidelines/theme list; copy for $1 postage. (Ads)

Columns/Departments: Accepts 30/yr. In the Know (conference, video, book & software reviews); Product Notes (new product information); 120 wds; no payment.

Special Needs: Audio/visual equipment; books/curriculum resources; music equipment; church products; furnishings; office equipment; computers/software.

Tips: "Almost all articles are assigned to writers with expertise in a certain area. Write and ask for an assignment; tell your strengths, interests and background."

YOUTHWORKER, 1224 Greenfield Dr., El Cajon CA 92021. (619)440-2333. Fax (619)440-4939. E-mail: leslie@youthspecialties.com. Youth Specialties Inc. Dave Urbanski, ed. For youth workers/church and parachurch. Monthly journal; 72 pgs; circ 13,200. Subscription $39.95. 90% freelance. Query; phone query OK. Pays $100-150 on acceptance for 1st & reprint rts. Articles 2,000-3,500 wds (30/yr). Responds in 5 wks. Seasonal 10 mos ahead. Accepts reprints. Kill fee $50. Guidelines/theme list; copy $3/10x13 SAE.

Columns/Departments: Buys 10/yr. High School Minister; Middle School Minister; 2,000-3,000 wds; $100-150.

Special Needs: Upcoming themes include Music in Ministry, Growing Up: pitfalls, conflict, conflict, expectations.

Tips: "Read Youthworker; imbibe its tone (professional, though not academic; conversational, though not chatty). Query me with specific, focused ideas that conform to our needs. Writer needs to be a youth minister."

** This periodical was #46 on the 1995 Top 50 Christian Publishers list. (#53 in 1994) Also 1995 EPA Award of Merit—Christian Ministry.

TEEN/YOUNG ADULT MARKETS

+BEAUTIFUL CHRISTIAN TEEN, #7 Bergoo Rd., Webster Spring WV 26288. (304)847-7537. Kimberly Short Wolfe, ed. Conservative publication for Christian teen girls. Bimonthly mag. 75% freelance. **NO PAYMENT.** Guidelines; copy $3.

#BREAKAWAY, 8605 Explorer Dr., Colorado Springs CO 80920. (719)548-4576. Fax (719)531-3499. Focus on the Family. Michael Ross, ed. The 14-year-old, unchurched teen (boy) in the public school is our target; boys 11-18 yrs. Monthly mag; 24-32 pgs; circ 90,000. Subscription $15. 60-70% freelance. Complete ms/cover letter; phone query OK. Pays .12-.15/wd on acceptance for all, 1st, one-time & reprint rts. Articles 400-1,800 wds (40/yr); fiction 1,200-2,200 wds (15/yr); music reviews, 300 wds, $30-40. Responds in 5 wks. Seasonal 8 mos ahead. Accepts simultaneous submissions & reprints. Kill fee 33-50%. Guidelines/theme list; copy for 9x12 SAE/3 stamps. (Ads)

Fillers: Buys 50/yr. Cartoons ($75), facts, quizzes; 200-600 wds; .20-.25/wd.

Columns/Departments: Buys 12/yr. Plugged In (devotional); 700-900 wds.

Tips: "Need strong lead. Brevity and levity a must. Have a teen guy or two read it. Make sure the language is up-to-date, but not overly hip."

** This periodical was #3 on the 1996 Top 50 Christian Publishers list. (#6 in 1995, #5 in 1994)

#BRIO, 8605 Explorer Dr., Colorado Springs CO 80920. (719)548-4577. Fax (719)531-3499. Focus on the Family. Susie Shellenberger, ed. For teen girls, 12-16 yrs. Monthly mag; 32 pgs; circ 160,000. Subscription $15. 25-50% freelance. Complete ms/cover letter; phone query OK. Pays .08-.15/wd on acceptance for 1st rts. Articles 800-1,000 wds (50/yr); fiction 1,000-2,000 wds (40/yr). Responds in 6 wks. Seasonal 6 mos ahead. Sometimes pays kill fee. Guidelines; copy for 9x12 SAE/6 stamps.

Fillers: Buys 10/yr. Cartoons, facts, ideas, quizzes, short humor; 500 wds.

Special Needs: All topics of interest to female teens are welcome: boys, make-up, dating, weight, ordinary girls who have the extraordinary, female adjustments to puberty, etc. Also teen-related female fiction.

Tips: "Study at least 3 issues of *Brio* before submitting. We're looking for a certain, fresh, hip-hop conversational style. Most open to fiction, articles and quizzes."

** This periodical was #60 on the 1996 Top 50 Christian Publishers list. (#61 in 1995, #37 in 1994) Also 1995 EPA Award of Merit—Youth.

CALEB ISSUES & ANSWERS, The Caleb Campaign, 11973 S. County Line Rd., West Frankfort IL 62896-9661. (618)937-2348. Tim Hastings, ed. A newspaper written from a biblical/creationist viewpoint for young people, 12-20 yrs. Newspaper published 4X during school yr; 16 pgs; circ 10,000. 20-50% freelance. Query or complete ms; phone query OK. **NO PAYMENT** for all rts. Articles 1,000-2,000 wds (25/yr). Responds in 8 wks. Accepts disk. Guidelines/theme list; copy $1.

Tips: "We are eager for new writers. Need history (list available) and sports interviews. Make articles interesting and relevant."

#CAMPUS LIFE, 465 Gundersen Dr., Carol Stream IL 60188. (630)260-6200. Fax (630)260-0114. E-mail: CLedit@aol.col. Christianity Today, Inc. Christopher Lutes, mng. ed. Seeks to help high school students and early college students navigate adolescence with their faith intact; not overtly religious. Monthly (10X) mag; 62 pgs; circ 100,000. Subscription $19.95. 35% freelance. Query; fax query OK. Pays .15-.20/wd on acceptance for 1st or one-time rts. Articles 250-2,500 (1/yr); fiction 1,000-3,500 wds (1-5/yr). Responds in 5-9 wks. Seasonal 5 mos ahead. Accepts simultaneous submissions & reprints. Disk OK. Kill fee 50%. Sidebars OK. Guidelines; copy $2/9x12 SAE/3 stamps. (Ads)

Poetry: Buys 1-5/yr. Free verse; 5-20 lines; $25-50. Submit max. 2 poems.

Fillers: Buys 30 cartoons/yr; $50; anecdotes, facts, short humor, 25-250 wds, $10-50.

Columns/Departments: Buys 20/yr. Making the Grade (study tips), 100-250 wds, $25-50.

Tips: "Most open to as-told-to stories. Interview students and get their stories."

** This periodical was #49 on the 1995 Top 50 Christian Publishers list. (#63 in 1994)

CERTAINTY, 1300 N. Meacham Rd., Schaumburg IL 60173-4888. (847)843-1600. Fax (847)843-3757. Regular Baptist Press. Joan E. Alexander, ed. For senior high youth (15-18); conservative/fundamental. Weekly take-home paper; 4 pgs; circ 18,000. Subscription $5.80. 40% freelance. Complete ms/cover letter (first time); no phone/fax query. Pays .03-.07/wd on acceptance for all, 1st or reprint rts. Articles 400-800 wds (15-20/yr); fiction 500-1,200 wds (some multipart), (15-20/yr). Responds in 4-8 wks. Seasonal 1 yr ahead. Accepts disk. Sidebars OK. Prefers KJV. Guidelines; copy for #10 SAE/2 stamps or full quarter for $1.45.

Fillers: Buys 20-30/yr. Ideas, prose, word puzzles; 100-400 wds; $10. Must teach Bible content in an enjoyable way.

Tips: "Not everything that is Christian is suitable in a publication intended for readers in fundamental Baptist churches. Address the spiritual dimension that is integral to the interests, concerns, and daily lives of teenagers."

CHALLENGE (IL), 1300 N. Meacham Rd., Schaumburg IL 60173-4888. (847)843-1600. Fax (847)843-3757. Regular Baptist Press. Joan E. Alexander, ed. For junior high youth (12-14); conservative/fundamental. Weekly take-home paper; 4 pgs; circ. 16,000. Subscription $5.80. complete ms/cover letter (first time); no phone/fax query. Pays .03-.07/wd on acceptance for all (negotiable)& reprint rts. Articles 500-800 wds (30/yr); fiction 700-1,200 wds (30/yr). Responds in 4-8 wks. Seasonal 1 yr ahead. Accepts disk. Sidebars OK. Guidelines; copy for #10 SAE/2 stamps or full quarter for $1.45.

> **Fillers:** Games, ideas, word puzzles, individual or small-group ministry projects; 100-300 wds; $10.

> **Tips:** "Not everything that is Christian is suitable in a publication intended for readers in fundamental Baptist churches. Address the spiritual dimension that is integral to the interests, concerns, and daily lives of young teens."

CHALLENGE (TN), 1548 Poplar Ave., Memphis TN 38104-2432. (901)272-2461. Fax (901)726-5540. Southern Baptist. Joe Conway, ed. Missions interest articles for young men, ages 12-18. Monthly mag; leader edition + 16 pgs; circ 24,000. Subscription $3.09/3.75 quarterly. 20% freelance. Complete ms. Pays .05/wd on publication for 1st rts. Articles 600-900 wds (36/yr). Responds in 2 wks. Seasonal 8 mos ahead. Accepts simultaneous submissions and reprints (tell when/where appeared). No disk. Sidebars OK. Prefers NAS or NIV. Guidelines/theme list; copy for 9x12 SAE/3 stamps.

> **Fillers:** Buys 12/yr. Ideas, word puzzles; 25-50 wds; $10-25.

> **Tips:** "Looking for articles of male youth interest and articles with a Christian testimony, especially sports. Mission stories involving youth are also very good."

*CHRISTTEEN MAGAZINE, PO Box 1519, Inglewood CA 90308. (213)750-7573. Franklin Publications. Sharon Jones, mng. ed. For African-American teens and their parents. Quarterly mag. Subscription $15. Est. 1994. Complete ms/cover letter. **PAYS IN COPIES** (for now) for 1st rts. Articles 500-1,100 wds (18/yr); open to fiction; book, music, movie reviews, 200 wds. Responds in 6-8 wks. Seasonal 6 mos ahead. Accepts simultaneous submissions & reprints. Wants sidebars. Prefers KJV or NIV. Guidelines; copy $3/9x12 SAE/5 stamps.

> **Poetry:** From teens only. Free verse, traditional. Submit max. 2 poems.

> **Fillers:** Various; 25-150 wds.

> **Columns/Departments:** Teenview (by teens), 400-500 wds; Education (info on career planning, college, etc.), 500-850 wds.; The Way They Do It (youth programs), 400 wds; Parent Exchange (encouraging info/testimonies by parents), 500-850 wds; Let's Celebrate (holidays/special ways to celebrate), 400-500 wds.

> **Tips:** "All departments & feature articles open (you don't have to be African-American to write for us). Write in a down-to-earth style, with lots of anecdotes, and don't use a lot of slang."

#THE CONQUEROR, 8855 Dunn Rd., Hazelwood MO 63042. (314)837-7300. United Pentecostal Church, Intl. Nathan C. Reever, ed. For teenagers in the denomination. Bimonthly mag; 16 pgs; circ 6,000. Subscription $7.50. 90% freelance. Complete ms. Pays $20-30 on publication for various rts. Articles & fiction (many/yr) 600-800. Responds in 10 wks. Seasonal 4 mos ahead. Accepts simultaneous submissions & reprints. Prefers KJV. Guidelines; copy for 11x14 SAE/2 stamps.

Fillers: Various.

Tips: "Articles should be written with the idea of strict morals, standards and ethics in mind."

#CROSS WALK, 6401 The Paseo, Kansas City MO 64131. (816)333-7000x2211. Fax (816)333-4315. E-mail: RCPrivett@aol.com. Holiness denominations. Becki Privett, ed. Written by teens (and youth leaders) for teens. Weekly take-home paper; circ 35,000. Subscription $7.60. Est. 1995. By assignment only. Query only. Pays on acceptance for all rts. Responds in 2 wks. Kill fee 50%. No sidebars. Guidelines; copy for 9x12 SAE/2 stamps.

Tips: "Open only to a youth worker (professional or volunteer) and five teens from his/her youth group. The youth leader will write devotionals for Saturday and Sunday, and the five teens will write devotionals for Monday-Friday."

+DEVO'ZINE, 1908 Grand Ave., Nashville TN 37202-9890. (615)340-7247. Fax (615)340-7006. E-mail: 102615.3145@compuserve.com. The Upper Room. Robin Pippin, ed. Devotional; to help teens (12-18) maintain their maximum connection with God and other Christians. Bimonthly mag; 64 pgs; circ 58,000. Subscription $16.95. Est. 1996.100% freelance. Query; phone/fax/e-mail query OK. Pays $20 for meditations, $75 for feature articles (assigned) on acceptance for one-time, electronic rts (newspaper, software-driven format). Meditations 150-250 wds (350/yr), articles 350-500 wds; book/music/video reviews, 350-500 wds, $75. Responds in 16 wks. Seasonal 6-8 mos ahead. Accepts reprints (tell when/where appeared). Accepts disk. Kill fee. Sidebars OK. Prefers NRSV, NIV, CEV. Guidelines/theme list; copy $1/7x10 SAE.

Poetry: Buys 25-30/yr. Free verse, light verse, haiku, traditional.; to 150 wds. Pays 20. Submit max. 1 poem/theme, 9 themes/issue.

Tips: " Call with ideas for week-end features related to specific themes."

*ESSENTIAL CONNECTIONS, 127 Ninth Ave. N., Nashville TN 37234. (615)251-5679. Southern Baptist. Dwayne Ulmer, ed.

+I.D., 4050 Lee Vance View, Colorado Springs CO 80918. (719)536-0100. Fax (719)536-3296. Cook Communications Ministries. C. Celeste Palmer, ed. Articles/stories relating Christianity to a teen's daily life. Weekly take-home paper; circ 75,000. Open to freelance. Query. Not in topical listings.

INSIGHT, 55 W. Oak Ridge Dr., Hagerstown MD 21740-7301. (301)791-7000. Fax (301)790-9734. E-mail: 74617.3077@compuserve.com. Seventh-day Adventist. Lori Peckham, ed. For Adventist teenagers, 14-19 yrs. Weekly take-home paper; 16 pgs; circ 20,000. Subscription $37.97. 80% freelance. Complete ms/cover letter; phone/fax/e-mail query OK. Pays $40-125 on acceptance for 1st rts. Articles 500-1,200 wds (120/yr); fiction 500-1,200 wds (few/yr, $40-85). Responds in 8-10 wks. Seasonal 4-6 mos ahead. Accepts reprints. Prefers disk (Wordperfect 6.0). Kill fee. Sidebars OK. Prefers NIV. Guidelines; copy for 9x12 SAE/4 stamps.

Poetry: Buys to 36/yr. All types; to 1 pg; $15-30. By teens only.

Fillers: Buys to 100/yr. Cartoons, facts, quizzes, quotes, short humor, statistics; to 200 wds; $10-40.

Columns/Departments: Buys 52/yr. Well-Versed (personal story that demonstrates truth of a Bible verse), 1,000-1,500 wds; On the Edge (drama in real life), 800-1,500 wds, $75-125. It Happened To Me (personal experience in first-person), 600-900 wds, $50-100. So I Said (true shorts or opinion pcs.), 200-400 wds, $40-60. How I Became Friends with God, 600-900 wds, $50-100; Service with a Smile, 600-1,500 wds, $50-125.

Contest: Sponsors a fiction & poetry contest; includes a category for students under 21. Prizes to $250. June 1 deadline (may vary). Send SASE for rules.

Tips: "Read other youth publications. Put yourself in teens' place, looking at the adult world from the outside. Talk to teens informally. Most open to true, dramatic stories. Think through spiritual implications, but don't preach."

** This periodical was #8 on the 1996 Top 50 Christian Publishers list. (#18 in 1995, #6 in 1994)

LISTEN, 55 W. Oak Ridge Dr., Hagerstown MD 21740. (301)745-3888. Fax (301)790-9734. The Health Connection. Lincoln Steed, ed. To educate teens against alcohol/drugs in a uniquely positive way; emphasizes moral values in a secular tone. Monthly mag; 32 pgs; circ. 40,000. Subscription $24.95. 60% freelance. Query (query for fiction)or complete ms/cover letter; phone/fax query OK. Pays $50-200 on acceptance for 1st or reprint rts. Articles 1,200 wds (50/yr); fiction 1,200 wds (20/yr). Responds in 12 wks. Seasonal 6 mos ahead. Accepts simultaneous submissions & reprints (tell when/where appeared). Accepts disk. Sidebars OK. Guidelines; copy for 9x12 SAE/2 stamps. (Ads)

** This periodical was #15 on the 1996 Top 50 Christian Publishers List.

ON COURSE, 1445 Boonville Ave., Springfield MO 65803-1894. (417)862-2781. Fax (417)866-1146. E-mail: oncourse@ag.org(mbooze). Assemblies of God. Melinda Booze, ed. Contemporary issues/themes for teens. Quarterly mag; 32 pgs; circ. 160,000. Distributed free. 60% freelance. Query or complete ms; fax/e-mail query OK. Query for electronic submissions. Pays .08/wd, up to $85, on acceptance for 1st, one-time or reprint rts. Articles 800-1,000 wds (30/yr); fiction 800-1,200 wds (2/yr). Responds in 6 wks. Seasonal 6 mos ahead. Accepts reprints (tell when/where appeared). Prefers disk. Sidebars OK. Prefers NIV. Guidelines/theme list; copy for 10x13 SAE/2 stamps. (Ads)

Poetry: Buys 4/yr. Any type; any length; $25.

Fillers: Cartoons.

Tips: "Most open to features—include stories about, quotes from teens. Need more fiction. Let us know as much about yourself and writing as you can. Call and talk to us, send samples, send ideas based on themes. An assignment may result."

** This periodical was #68 on the 1996 Top 50 Christian Publishers List. Also1996 EPA Award of Merit—Youth.

PATHWAYS, 1316 Convention Plaza, St. Louis MO 63166. (314)231-8500. Fax (314)231-8524. E-mail: cbpxchg@aol.com. Christian Board of Publication. Deana L. Perdue, ed. For middle school/junior high students; grades 6-9; compliments leader guide for church school curriculum. Quarterly mag; 32 pgs; circ. 3,000. Est. 1994. 1% freelance. Query or complete ms/cover letter; phone/fax/e-mail (if short) query OK. Pays .03/wd on publication for one-time, simultaneous or reprint rts. Articles 600-1,000 wds (4/yr); fiction 1,000 wds (4/yr). Responds in 4 wks. Seasonal 8-10 mos ahead. Considers simultaneous submissions & reprints (tell when/where appeared). Sidebars OK. Prefers NRSV. Guidelines/theme list; copy $2/9x12 SAE/5 stamps.

> **Poetry:** Buys 8-12/yr. Any type, to 20 lines. Pays $3 for 10 lines; then .30/line.
>
> **Fillers:** Buys 20-25/yr. Anecdotes, cartoons, games, jokes, prayers, prose, short humor, word puzzles; $15-25.
>
> **Tips:** "We use freelance only to support topics in the curriculum. Material that addresses relevant concerns of youth, especially trying to live out their faith, is most likely to match a theme. Humor always needed; also age-appropriate puzzles."

THE ROCK, 4050 Lee Vance View, Colorado Springs CO 80918-7100. (719)536-0100. Fax (719)536-3296. Cook Communications Ministries. Vicki Otter, ed. For junior high youth, grades 6-8. Weekly take-home paper; 8 pgs; circ. 125,000. 80% freelance (assigned). Query. Pays on acceptance for all rts. Requires disk. Prefers NIV. Also produces an edition for African-American youth.

> **Tips:** "We are not currently accepting freelance material; perhaps in a year or two."

#SHARING THE VICTORY, 8701 Leeds Rd., Kansas City MO 64129-1680. (816)921-0909. Fax (816)921-8755. Fellowship of Christian Athletes (Protestant and Catholic). John Dodderidge, ed. Equipping and encouraging athletes and coaches to take their faith seriously, in and out of competition. Monthly (Sept-May) mag; 32 pgs; circ 55,000. Subscription $18. 65% freelance. Query only/clips. Pays $50-200 on publication for 1st rts. Articles 500-1,000 wds (18/yr). Responds in 3 wks. Seasonal 4 mos ahead. Kill fee. Sidebars OK. Guidelines; copy $1/9x12 SAE/3 stamps. (Ads)

> **Poetry:** Buys 9/yr. Free verse, traditional; 8-24 lines; $25-50. Submit max. 3 poems.
>
> **Special Needs:** Articles on FCA camp experiences (40th anniversary of camps). All articles must have an athletic angle.
>
> **Tips:** "FCA angle important; pro & college athletes and coaches giving solid Christian testimony; we run stories according to athletic season; need articles/poetry on female athletes."

#SPIRIT, Lectionary-based Weekly for Catholic Teens, 1884 Randolph Ave., St. Paul MN 55105-1700. (612)690-7005. Fax: (612)690-7039. Catholic. Therese Sherlock, CSJ, mng. ed. For the religious education of high schoolers (14-18 yrs). Weekly newsletter; 4 pgs; circ 26,000. 50% freelance. Query (complete ms/cover letter for fiction). Pays $75-150 on publication for all rts. Articles & fiction 1,100-1,200 wds (12 ea./yr). Responds in 2-6 wks. Seasonal 6 mos ahead. Accepts simultaneous submissions. Free guidelines/copy.

STRAIGHT, 8121 Hamilton Ave., Cincinnati OH 45231. (513)931-4050. Fax (513)931-0950. Standard Publishing. Heather Wallace, ed. For Christian teens (13-19 yrs). Weekly take-home paper; 12 pgs; circ 35,000. Subscription $11.49. 90% freelance. Complete ms/cover letter. Pays .05-.06/wd on acceptance for 1st, one-time, or reprint rts. Articles to 800-1,100 wds (25-30/yr); fiction 900-1,500 wds (100/yr). Responds in 4-8 wks. Seasonal 9-12 mos ahead. Accepts simultaneous submissions & reprints. No disk. Some sidebars. Prefers NIV. Guidelines/theme list; copy for #10 SAE/2 stamps.

Poetry: Buys 25-30/yr. Free verse, light verse, traditional; from teens only; $10. Submit max. 5 poems.

Fillers: Buys 10-15/yr. Prayers, short humor, 300-700 wds.

Columns/Departments: Buys 12/yr. Straight Spotlight (teens making a difference), 900 wds.

Tips: "Request to be put on our theme list. Be aware of the current trends with teens. Write about everyday issues (for teens) from a Christian perspective."

** This periodical was #13 on the 1996 Top 50 Christian Publishers list. (#5 in 1995, #17 in 1994)

#STUDENT LEADERSHIP JOURNAL, Box 7895, Madison WI 53707-7895. (608)274-9001x425. Fax (608)274-7882. InterVarsity Christian Fellowship. Jeff Yourison, ed. Undergraduate college student Christian leaders, single, ages 18-36. Quarterly journal; 32 pgs; circ 8,500. Subscription $16. 20-30% freelance. Query/clips. Pays $35-125 on acceptance for 1st or one-time rts. Articles to 2,000 wds (1/yr); fiction to 1,500 wds (0-1/yr), $25-100; book reviews 150-400 wds, $25-50. Responds in 16 wks. Seasonal 8 mos ahead. Accepts reprints. Guidelines/theme list; copy $3/9x12 SAE/4 stamps.

Poetry: Buys 4-6/yr. Avant-garde, free verse; to 15 lines; $25-50. Submit max. 5 poems.

Fillers: Buys 0-5/yr. Facts, games, party ideas, quizzes; to 200 wds; $10-50.

Columns/Departments: Buys 6-10/yr. Collegiate Trends, 20-100 wds; Student Leadership Network, 500-800 wds; Chapter Strategy (how-to planning strategy for campus groups), 500-800; $10-75. Query.

Special Needs: Campus issues/trends/ministry/spiritual growth/leadership; Kingdom values.

Tips: "Most open to main features targeted to college-age students. Be upbeat, interesting and fresh. Use both Scripture and life illustrations."

** 1996 EPA Award of Merit—Christian Ministry.

TAKE FIVE, 1445 Boonville Ave., Springfield MO 65802. (417)862-2781x4359. Fax (417)862-8558. E-mail: YouthCurr@ag.org. Assemblies of God. Tammy Bicket, youth ed. A daily devotional for teens, grades 7-12. Quarterly booklet; 112 pgs; circ 30,000. Subscription $8. 80% freelance. Write for assignment. Pays $15/devotion on acceptance for all rts (one-time rts for poetry). Responds in 13 wks. Seasonal 15 mos ahead. Accepts simultaneous submissions & reprints on poetry only. Prefers disk. Guidelines; copy for 6x9 SAE/3 stamps.

Poetry: Buys 36/yr. Any type; 8-20 lines; $15. Submit max. 5 poems. "Poetry is held on file unless writer requests its return."

Special Needs: Photos; photos of ethnic groups are a plus. Poetry from teens (SASE required for return).

Tips: "All devotional writing is done on assignment to Assemblies of God writers only. Sample devotional or similar writing can be submitted for editors evaluation and for future consideration when writing assignments are made."

*TEENAGE CHRISTIAN, 179 Wimbledon Ct., Gallatin TN 37033. (502)753-1881. Church of Christ/Christian Publishing Inc. Shana Curtis, ed. Spiritual answers to tough questions for Christian teens (13-19 yrs). Bimonthly mag; 32 pgs; circ 11,600. Subscription $2.50. 60% freelance. Complete ms. Pays $15-25 on publication for one-time rts. Articles 600-1,200 wds (60/yr); fiction 600-1,200 wds (20/yr); book/music reviews, 750 wds ($15-25). Responds in 6-8 wks. Seasonal 4 mos ahead. Accepts simultaneous submissions & reprints. Sidebars OK. Guidelines; copy for 9x12 SAE/4 stamps.

> **Poetry:** Buys 10/yr. Free verse, light verse, traditional; 10-25 lines; $15-25. Submit max. 5 poems.
>
> **Fillers:** Buys 5-10/yr. Cartoons, quizzes, prayers, word puzzles; 150-350 wds; $15-25.
>
> **Tips:** "Write general-interest articles for Christian teens, 'teen friendly,' not preachy. All areas open except columns."

TEEN LIFE (AG), 1445 Boonville Ave., Springfield MO 65802-1894. (417)862-2781x4359. Fax (417)862-6059. Assemblies of God. Nancy Williams, asst. ed. To emphasize Christian living through biblical principles for Spirit-filled young people ages 15-17. Quarterly take-home paper; 36 pgs; circ 55,000. Subscription $6.20. Est. 1994. 50% freelance. Complete ms/cover letter; no phone/fax query. Pays .05-.08/wd ($25-100) on publication (.03-.05/wd or $25-75 for fiction) for 1st, reprint or simultaneous rts. Articles 1,000-1,200 wds (200/yr); fiction 800-1,000 wds (200/yr). Responds in 6-8 wks. Seasonal 18 mos ahead. Accepts simultaneous submissions & reprints (tell when/where appeared). Prefers disk. Sidebars OK. Prefers NIV. Guidelines/theme list; copy for 9x12 SAE/2 stamps

> **Fillers:** Buys less than 100/yr. Cartoons, facts, short humor; 100-250 wds; no payment.
>
> **Special Needs:** Looking for discipleship, dating and family life.
>
> **Tips:** "The best opening is in the area of short story, true or fiction. Get a theme list and write to the themes."
>
> ** This periodical was #37 on the 1996 Top 50 Christian Publishers list. (#37 in 1995, #11 in 1994)

*TEEN LIFE (UPC), 8855 Dunn Rd., Hazelwood MO 63042. (314)837-7304. United Pentecostal Church. R. M. Davis, ed. For teens 13-15 yrs. Weekly take-home paper. 90% freelance. Complete ms. Pays $8-25 on publication for all rts. Articles 800-1,800 wds (up to 120/yr); fiction 1,200-1,800 wds (up to 120/yr). Seasonal 9 mos ahead. Accepts simultaneous submissions & reprints. Guidelines; free copy.

> **Poetry:** Accepts 30/yr; $3-12.
>
> **Tips:** "Most open to good stories and articles for a traditional, fundamental audience."

+TEEN MISSIONS LAUNCH PAD, 885 E. Hall Rd., Merritt Island FL 32953. (407)453-0350. Fax (407)452-7988. Website: http://www.teenmissions.goshen.net/. Teen Missions Intl., Inc. Paula Yost, ed. To present information about current news, needs, and developments of Teen Missions youth and adult ministries around the world. Biannual mag; circ 65,000. Subscription free. Open to freelance. Complete ms. Not in topical listings. (Ads)

#TEEN POWER, 4050 Lee Vance View, Colorado Springs CO 80918. (719)536-0100. Cook Communications/Scripture Press. Sarah M. Peterson, ed. To help young teens (11-15 yrs) explore ways Jesus relates to them in everyday life.

Weekly take-home paper; 8 pgs. Subscription $11.50. 100% freelance. Complete ms/cover letter. Pays $25-120 on acceptance for one-time or simultaneous rts. Articles 300-1,000 wds (75/yr); fiction & true stories 600-1,200 wds (75/yr— $45-120). Responds in 13 wks. Seasonal 6 mos ahead. Accepts simultaneous submissions & reprints (pays .05-.07/wd). Guidelines/theme list/copy for #10 SAE/1 stamp.

Poetry: From teens only. Free verse, light verse, traditional.

Fillers: Buys 10/yr. Cartoons, jokes, prose, quizzes, word puzzles; $15.

Tips: "Looking for fresh, creative true stories, true-to-life fiction and articles. Show how God and the Bible are relevant in the lives of today's teens. Use slice-of-life vignettes. All manuscripts must have a clear, spiritual message." Send Social Security number.

** This periodical was #21 on the 1996 Top 50 Christian Publishers list. (#21 in 1995, #41 in 1994)

#TEEN QUEST (TQ), 465 Gundersen Dr., Carol Stream IL 60188. (630)260-6200. Fax (630)260-0114. E-mail: TeenQuest@aol.com. Campus Life. Lisa Proctor, ed. asst. To show teens (13-19 yrs) why a relationship with Christ is important now and how to grow in this relationship. Monthly (10X) mag; 48 pgs; circ 25,000. Subscription $14.50. 50% freelance. Complete ms; phone query OK. Pays .10-.15/wd (reprints .03/wd) on publication for 1st rts. Accepting no articles; fiction (all types) 1,500-2,250 wds (20-25/yr). Responds in 8 wks. Seasonal 3 mos ahead. Accepts simultaneous submissions & reprints. Some kill fees. Guidelines; copy for 9x12 SAE/6 stamps. (Ads)

Tips: "Writer must be able to communicate with teens in a relevant and entertaining way. We accept fiction only."

*TEENS ON TARGET, 8855 Dunn Rd., Hazelwood MO 63042. (314)837-7300. Fax (314)837-4503. Word Aflame Publications. P. Daniel Buford, assoc. ed. For teens 12-14 years. Weekly take-home paper; circ. 7,000. Subscription $4.40. 75% freelance. Complete ms/cover letter. Pays .01-.02/wd on publication for 1st or simultaneous rts. Articles 1,200-1,400 wds; fiction 1,200-1,400 wds (40/yr). Seasonal 1 yr ahead. Accepts simultaneous submissions & reprints. Few sidebars. Prefers KJV. Guidelines; copy for 6x9 SAE/2 stamps.

Fillers: Buys 2-3/yr. Quizzes, word puzzles; $5-12.

Tips: "Articles should be human interest with practical application of Christian principles for 12-14 year olds."

TODAY'S CHRISTIAN TEEN, 40 Berkshire Ct., Wyomissing PA 19610-1224. (610)372-1111. Fax (610)372-1122. E-mail: ScepterCom@aol.com. Scepter Publication. Jerry Thacker, ed. To help today's Christian teens by presenting material which applies the Bible to contemporary issues. Quarterly mag; 24 pgs; circ 75,000. Free subscription. 25% freelance. Complete ms/cover letter; fax query OK. Pays $150 on publication. Not copyrighted. Articles 800-1,000 wds (10/yr). Responds in 3-4 wks. Seasonal 1 yr ahead. Accepts simultaneous submissions & reprints (tell when/where appeared). Prefers disk. Sidebars OK. Prefers KJV. Guidelines; copy for 9x12SAE/3stamps.

*TRANSCEND, 4 Daniels Farms Rd., Ste. 134, Trumbell CT 06611. (203)924-5646. Transcend Publishing. Quentin Plair, ed. For teens 14-17. Biannual mag; 40 pgs; circ 10,000. Subscription $5. Est. 1995. 60% freelance. Query/clips or complete ms/cover letter. Pays $25 on acceptance for one-time rts. Articles any length; fiction to 5,000 wds. Responds in 13 wks. Accepts simultaneous submissions. Guidelines; copy $3.

Poetry: Any length.

*VISIONS, Lectionary-based Weekly for Catholic Junior Highs, 330 Progress Rd., Dayton OH 45449. (513)847-5900. Fax (513)847-5910. Peter Li, Inc./Catholic. Joan Mitchell, CSJ, mng. ed. Connects young people's real life experiences—successes and conflicts in family, neighborhood, classroom—with the Sunday gospels; for grades 7-9. Weekly (28X during school yr) take-home paper; circ 140,000. 40% freelance. Query. Pays $75-125 on publication for all rts. Articles (6-8/yr) & fiction (8-10/yr), 900-1,000 wds. Responds in 2-8 wks. Seasonal 4-6 mos ahead. Accepts simultaneous query. Guidelines; copy $1.85.

WITH, The Magazine for Radical Christian Youth, Box 347, Newton KS 67114-0347. (316)283-5100. Fax (316)283-0454. Faith & Life Press/Mennonite, Brethren & Mennonite Brethren. Carol Duerksen (fillers & poetry) & Eddy Hall (articles & fiction), co-eds. For high-school teens (15-18 yrs), Christian and non-Christian. 8 time/yr mag; 32 pgs; circ 6,100. Subscription $18.95. 95% freelance. Query (on first-person and how-to articles); complete ms on others/cover letter; no phone/fax query. Pays .05/wd (.03/wd for reprints) on acceptance for 1st, one-time, simultaneous or reprint rts. Articles 1,000-1,700 wds (15/yr); fiction 1,000-2,000 wds (15/yr); music/video reviews, 400-500 wds, $40 (query for assignment). Responds in 4 wks. Seasonal 6-8 mos ahead. Accepts simultaneous submissions & reprints. No disk. Kill fee 33-50%. Sidebars OK. Prefers NRSV. Guidelines/theme list; copy for 9x12 SAE/5 stamps. Separate guidelines for 1st-person and how-to articles sent only when requested.

Poetry: Buys 1/yr. Any type; 4-50 lines; $10-25. Submit max. 3 poems.

Fillers: Buys 20 cartoons/yr; $35.

Contest: Sponsors contests for teen writers only.

Tips: "Most open to fiction; match upcoming theme."

** This periodical was #23 on the 1996 Top 50 Christian Publishers list. (#17 in 1995, #12 in 1994)

YOU! MAGAZINE, 31194 La Baya Dr., Suite 200, West Lake Village CA 91362-4022. (818)991-1813. Fax (818)991-2024. E-mail: Youmag@earthlink.net. Website: http://www/home.earthlink.net/youmag/. Catholic. Juliette Buerkle, asst. ed. An alternative teen magazine (13-18 yrs) aimed at bridging the gap between religion and pop culture. Monthly (10X) mag; 28 pgs; circ 35,000. (Youthbeat, a newspaper insert, also available.) Subscription $19.95. 40% freelance. Complete ms; phone/fax/e-mail query OK. Pays .05-.075/wd ($10-105) on publication for one-time & reprint rts. (Prefers volunteer submissions; will use those first.) Articles 900 wds (130/yr); fiction 900 wds (15/yr); book reviews, 500 wds, .07/wd. Responds in 4 wks. Seasonal 2 mos ahead. Accepts simultaneous query & reprints (but not priority). Accepts disk. Sidebars OK. Free guidelines/copy. (Ads)

Poetry: Accepts 24/yr. Any type. No pay.

Fillers: Any type; to 300 wds. No pay.

Columns/Departments: Buys 60/yr. Gimme a Break (strange stuff going on in world), 100 wds; Retro (historical events for this month), 75 wds; Soundbites (mainstream music artists doing something Christian), 100 wds.

Special Needs: Interviews with celebrities willing to share their faith.

Tips: "Write in the language of teens. Must be 'hip.' Most open to sports, school, friends & family, sexuality, and Your Stuff. Be brief, positive and powerful."

*YOUNG ADULT TODAY, 1350 W. 103rd St., Chicago IL 60643. (312)233-4499. Urban Ministries, Inc. Dr. Colleen Birchett, ed. Young adult curriculum for ages 18-24 (student and teacher manuals). Quarterly booklet; 72 pgs; circ 7,500. 60% freelance. Complete ms. Pays $35-50 on publication for all rts. Articles (24/yr) & fiction (12/yr); 2,900-3,500 characters. Responds in 1-2 wks. Seasonal 3 mos ahead. Free guidelines/theme list/copy.

Tips: "Send resume and writing sample. Writer must be able to relate the writing to the outline given and the biblical material."

*YOUNG AND ALIVE, Box 6097, Lincoln NE 68506. (402)488-0981. Christian Record Services. Richard Kaiser, ed. For sight-impaired young adults, 16-20 yrs; for interdenominational Christian audience. Quarterly mag; 65-70 pgs; circ 26,000. 90% freelance. Query or complete ms/cover letter; phone query OK. Pays .03-.05/wd on acceptance for one-time rts. Articles & true stories 800-1,400 wds (30/yr). Responds in 9-13 wks. Seasonal 1 yr ahead. Accepts simultaneous query & reprints. Guidelines; copy for 9-12 SAE/6 stamps.

Special Needs: Adventure and relationships for the handicapped.

Tips: "Although many blind and visually impaired young adults have the same interests as their sighted counterparts, the material should meet their needs specifically."

Note: This publication has cut back to fewer issues and is overstocked.

*YOUNG CHRISTIAN, PO Box 1264, Huntington WV 25714. Tellstar Productions. Shannon Bridget Murphy, ed. For young Christians—children, teens and young adults. Bimonthly mag; circ. 1,500. Subscription $18. 95-100% freelance. Complete ms/cover letter. Pays on publication for 1st or one-time rts. Articles 500+ wds; fiction 500+ wds (24/yr). Responds in 4-8 wks. Seasonal 2-6 mos ahead. Accepts simultaneous submissions & reprints. Sidebars OK. Guidelines; copy $3 ($5 for 2).

Columns/Departments: Open to suggestions for columns.

Special Needs: How to write and make sales; articles for or by teens/young adults; food/recipes; party ideas for children and young adults.

Contest: Sponsors contests throughout the year. Send SASE for details.

Tips: "Submissions always welcome from children, teens or young adults. Writers, artists, or photographers should send a resume or letter with info on experiences and background."

YOUNG SALVATIONIST, PO Box 269, Alexandria VA 22313. (703)684-5500. Fax (703)684-5539. E-mail: USWarCry@aol.com. The Salvation Army. Lesa Davis, prod. mngr. For teens & young adults in the Salvation Army. Monthly (10X) mag; 16 pgs; circ 48,000. Subscription $4. 90% freelance. Complete ms. Pays .15/wd (.10 for reprints) on acceptance for one-time & reprint rts. Articles (25/yr) & fiction (6/yr); 1,000-1,500 wds. Responds in 4 wks. Seasonal 3-6 mos ahead. Accepts reprints (tell when/where appeared). Accepts disk. Some sidebars. Prefers NIV. Guidelines/theme list; copy for 9x12 SAE/3 stamps.

Contest: Sponsors a contest for fiction, nonfiction, poetry, original art and photography. Send SASE for details.

Tips: "We are always looking for articles/interviews about Christian entertainers or athletes. Ask for theme list. Be contemporary—no stories about how it used to be."

** This periodical was #36 on the 1996 Top 50 Christian Publishers list. (#43 in 1995, 314 in 1994)

*YOUTH CHALLENGE, 8855 Dunn Rd., Hazelwood MO 63042. (314)837-7300. Fax (314)837-4503. Word Aflame Publications. P. Daniel Buford, assoc. ed. For teens in 10th-12th grades. Weekly take-home paper; circ. 5,500. Subscription $4.40. 75% freelance. Complete ms/cover letter. Pays .01-.02/wd on publication for 1st or simultaneous rts. Articles 1,200-1,400 wds; fiction 1,200-1,400 wds (40/yr). Seasonal 1 yr ahead. Accepts simultaneous submissions & reprints. Few sidebars. Prefers KJV. Guidelines; copy for 6x9 SAE/2 stamps.

Fillers: Buys 2-3/yr. Quizzes, word puzzles; $5-12.

Tips: "Articles should be human interest with practical application of Christian principles for 15-17 year olds."

*YOUTH FOCUS, Paywoods Communications, 4 Daniels Farm Rd., Ste. 134, Trumbull CT 06611. (203)924-5646. For African-American youth, ages 12-17. Quentin Plair, ed. Monthly newsletter; circ 10,000. 75% freelance. Complete ms. Pays $15-100 on publication for 1st or one-time rts. Articles 10-3,000 wds (2/yr). Responds in 9 wks. Seasonal 5 mos ahead. Accepts simultaneous submissions & reprints. Guidelines; copy $1.

Poetry: Buys 7/yr. Any type; 1-200 lines; $10-30.

YOUTH 97, PO Box 23462, Evansville IN 47724. Phone/fax (812)471-3769. E-mail: Youth97@aol.com. House of White Birches/interdenominational. Rick Shallenberger, ed. Real answers to real questions based on Christian values; targets 15-19-year-olds. Bimonthly mag; 36 pgs; circ. 40,000. Subscription $14.95. 70% freelance. Query/clips. Pays $50-450 ($50-300 for fiction) on acceptance for 1st rts. Articles (30yr) & fiction (10/yr); 600-1,800 wds; book/music/video reviews, 100-150 wds, $25-30. Responds in 4 wks. Seasonal 6 mos ahead. Accepts simultaneous submissions & few reprints. Kill fee 30-50%. Prefers disk. Sidebars OK. Prefers NIV. Guidelines; copy for 9x12 SAE/3 stamps. (Ads)

Poetry: By teens only. Accepts 20/yr. Avant-garde, free verse, light verse, traditional. Submit max. 3 poems. No payment.

Fillers: Buys 6-10/yr. Anecdotes, facts, quizzes; 25-250 wds; .25/wd.

Columns/Departments: Buys 12-20/yr. Ideas Plus (ideas for home life, education, relationships, etc.), 200 wds; $20-50.

Tips: "Write to an older teenager in a style that relates to teens. Avoid slang. Articles on relationships always needed."

#YOUTH UPDATE, 1615 Republic St., Cincinnati OH 45210-1298. (513)241-5615. St. Anthony Messenger Press/Catholic. Carol Ann Morrow, ed. For high-school teens, to support their growth in a life of faith. Monthly newsletter; 4 pgs; circ 26,000. 90% freelance. Query. Pays $350-400 (.14/wd) on acceptance for 1st rts. Articles 2,200-2,300 wds (12/yr). Responds in 13 wks. Seasonal 6 mos ahead. Prefers disk. Sidebars OK. Guidelines; copy for #10 SAE/1 stamp.

*YOUTH WORLD, 8855 Dunn Rd., Hazelwood MO 63042. (314)837-7304. United

Pentecostal Church. R. M. Davis, ed. For teens 13-15 yrs. Weekly take-home paper. 90% freelance. Complete ms. Pays $8-25 on publication for all rts. Articles 800-1,800 wds (up to 120/yr); fiction 1,200-1,800 wds (up to 120/yr). Seasonal 9 mos ahead. Accepts simultaneous submissions & reprints. Guidelines; free copy.

Poetry: Accepts 30/yr; $3-12.

Tips: "Most open to good stories and articles for a traditional, fundamental audience."

#ZELOS, 4050 Lee Vance View, Colorado Springs CO 80918. (719)536-0100. Cook Communications /Scripture Press. Sarah M. Peterson, ed. Spiral notebook to help high schoolers grow in daily relationship with God. Quarterly Sunday school student curriculum notebook. Est. 1995. Subscription $4.99. 50% freelance. Complete ms/cover letter. Pays .08-.12/wd ($30-120) on acceptance for one-time or simultaneous rts. Articles (40/yr) & fiction (20/yr) 400-1,000 wds. Responds in 9-13 wks. Seasonal 1 yr ahead. Accepts simultaneous submissions & reprints (tell when/where appeared). No sidebars. Guidelines/theme list; copy of sample article for #10 SAE/1 stamp; copy of booklet $5.50

Poetry: Buys 5/yr. Free verse, light verse, traditional; on relevant teen issues; 5-30 lines; $15-50. Submit Max. 3 poems.

Tips: "We use one freelance-written feature which correlates with the theme for each week. When possible, use true stories, personal experience, as-told-to, profiles and interviews. All material must have a clear, Christian perspective. Be realistic; no too-good-to-be-true characters or subjects." Include Social Security number on all submissions.

** This periodical was #44 on the 1996 Top 50 Christian Publishers List.

WOMEN'S MARKETS

ANNA'S JOURNAL, PO Box 341, Ellijay GA 30540. (706)276-2307. Catherine Ward-Long, ed. Spiritual support for childless couples who for the most part have decided to stay that way. Quarterly newsletter; 8 pgs; circ. 45. Subscription $14. Est. 1995. 90% freelance. Complete ms; phone query OK. **PAYS IN COPIES**, for 1st, simultaneous or reprint rts. Not copyrighted. Articles 500-1,500 wds (8-12/yr); fiction 1,000-2,000 wds (103/yr). Responds in 4-8 wks. Seasonal 3 months ahead. Accepts simultaneous submissions & reprints. No sidebars. Prefers KJV. Guidelines/theme list; copy $3/9x12 SAE/3 stamps.

Poetry: Accepts 4-10/yr. Any type. Submit max. 3 poems.

Fillers: Accepts 3-4/yr. Prose, prayers, letters; 50-250 wds.

Special Needs: Articles from married, childless men; articles discussing the meaning of: childless, childfree and childless by choice.

Tips: "Looking for innovative ways to improve the child-free lifestyle and self-esteem. No articles on adoption or infertility. It helps if writer is childless or knows someone who is."

*ASPIRE, 107 Kenner Ave., Nashville TN 37205. (615)386-3011. Fax (615)385-4112. CCM Communications. Charlotte Rose, ed. asst. Entertains, encourages, and inspires '90s women (25-45) to pursue a more balanced and fulfilling life experience. Monthly mag; 84 pgs; circ. 180,000. Subscription $17.95. Est. 1994. 80% freelance. Query/clips; fax/e-mail query OK. Pays .20-.50/wd on acceptance for 1st & electronic rts. Articles; book and music reviews, 100 wds, $30. Responds in 8 wks. Seasonal 5 mos. ahead. Kill fee 20%. Sidebars OK. Prefers NKJV. Guidelines; copy $2.95/9x12 SAE.

Columns/Departments: Family Matters, Food for Thought, BodyWise, Your Image, Smart Money, and On the Job; 800 wds; .20/wd.

Tips: Send previously published clips along with thoroughly outlined query. Most open to Food for Thought, BodyWise, Family Matters, or Smart Money.

** This periodical was #19 on the 1996 Top 50 Christian Publishers list. (#59 in 1995)

*THE CHURCH WOMAN, 475 Riverside Dr., Room 812, New York NY 10115. (212)870-2347. Fax (212)870-2338. Church Women United. Margaret Schiffert, ed. Highlights women's, peace and justice issues. Quarterly mag; 24 pgs; circ 10,000. Little freelance. Query. **PAYS IN COPIES.** Articles to 3 pgs. Guidelines; copy $1.

COLABORER, Box 5002, Antioch TN 37011-5002. (615)731-6812. Fax (615)731-0071. E-mail: colaborer@nafwb.com. Free Will Baptist/Women Nationally Active for Christ. Suzanne Franks, ed. To help Free Will Baptist women fulfill the great commission. Bimonthly mag; 32 pgs; circ 11,000. Subscription $6.75. 10% freelance. Query or complete ms/cover letter; no phone/fax/e-mail query. **PAYS IN COPIES.** Articles (2/yr) 1,500-2,000 wds; fiction (2/yr) 1,000-2,000. Responds in 8 wks. Seasonal 9 mos ahead. Accepts reprints. Accepts disk. Some sidebars. Guidelines; copy $1.25/ 9x12 SAE.

Fillers: Accepts 2-3/yr. Anecdotes, party ideas, prayers, short humor; to 500 wds.

Tips: "Looking for stewardship of life articles. Most open to articles on missions and prayer."

Contest: Creative Arts Contest open to women in the Free Will Baptist Church. March 1 deadline each year. $25 first prize, plus others. Categories include art, feature articles, plays, poetry, and programs. Send SASE for details.

#CONSCIENCE, A Newsjournal of Prochoice Catholic Opinion, 1436 U St. NW, Ste. 301, Washington DC 20009-3997. (202)986-6093. Catholic. Maggie Hume, ed. For laypeople, theologians, policymakers, and clergy. Quarterly newsjournal; 48 pgs; circ 12,000. Subscription $10. 80% freelance. Query/clips or complete ms/cover letter. Pays $25-150 on publication for 1st rts. Articles 1,000-5,000 wds (8-12/yr); book reviews 500-800 wds, $25-50. Responds in 18 wks. Seasonal 6 mos ahead. Accepts simultaneous submissions & reprints. Kill fee. Guidelines; copy for 9x12 SAE/4 stamps.

Poetry: Buys 16/yr. Any type, on subject, to 50 lines; $10 + copies. Submit max. 5 poems.

Fillers: Buys 6/yr. Newsbreaks; 100-300 wds; $25-35.

Tips: "Focus on issues of reproductive choice. Raise serious ethical questions within a generally prochoice framework. Most open to feature articles and book reviews."

+COTTAGE CONNECTIONS, 1113 Radisson Ct., Burnsville MN 55337. Mary Bevis, ed/pub. Encouragement for stay-at-home moms. Quarterly mag. Subscription $10. 100% freelance. Complete ms/cover letter. **NO PAYMENT** for one-time rts. Articles (16/yr) 1 pg; fiction (16/yr) 2-3 pgs (single-space all submissions). Responds in 3 wks. Seasonal 6 mos ahead. Accepts simultaneous submissions & reprints (tell when/where appeared). No sidebars. Guidelines; copy $3.

Poetry: Accepts 40/yr. Traditional, to 2 pgs. Submit max. 5 poems.

Fillers: Anecdotes, facts, prose, prayers, quotes, short humor; 100 wds.

Tips: "We need poetry, as well as essays (not necessarily inspirational). We will publish creative writing and journal entries, but also tackle issues and controversies our members feel strongly about. Be constructive, down to earth, humble and honest." Publishes subscribers.

+DOMESTIQUE, PO Box 509013, Indianapolis IN 46250-9013. (317)552-0285. Fax (317)552-3290. E-mail: PenWorks@netUSA1.net. PenWorks Publishing. Penny E. Stone, ed. For women who run a home. Monthly booklet; 20-24 pgs; circ growing. Subscription $18.95. Est. 1996. 50% freelance. Complete ms/cover letter; fax/e-mail query OK. Pays .01-.05/wd after publication for 1st, one-time, simultaneous or reprint rts. Not copyrighted. Articles 300-800 wds (100/yr). Responds in 2-4 wks. Seasonal 4 mos ahead. Accepts simultaneous submissions & reprints (tell when/where appeared). No disk. Prefers KJV or NKJV. Few sidebars. Guidelines; 2 copies for $3. (Classified ads)

Poetry: Buys 10-15/yr; 4-12 lines; $5.

Fillers: Anecdotes, facts, jokes, prose, short humor, household tips, spiritual questions. Pays 2 copies.

Columns/Departments: Behind the Scenes (pertinent news items), 400-800 wds; Rejuvenate! (morale-building, self-help, positive thinking), 300-600 wds; Domestic Engineering (household tips), 200-400 wds; Tea Time (short humor-pays in copies); Ways to Date Your Mate, 300-500 wds; Home Front (parenting), 300-500 wds; Quiet Moments (devotional with scripture from KJV), 300-500 wds; Mood Food (recipes—pays in copies); A Penny for Your Thoughts (opinion), to 500 wds.

Tips: "We need articles which fit within our column guidelines. We try to touch on most aspects of domestic engineers. Preferred writers are subscribers."

ESPRIT, Evangelical Lutheran Women, 1512 St. James St., Winnipeg MB R3H 0L2 Canada. (204)775-8591. Fax (204)775-8628. Evangelical Lutheran Church in Canada. Lorie Battershill, ed. For denominational women. Quarterly mag; 56 pgs; circ 6,580. Subscription $15.50 CAN, $25 US. 50% freelance. Complete ms/cover letter; phone/fax query OK. Pays $12.50-15/pg CAN on publication for one-time rts. Articles (34/yr) and fiction (4/yr) 325-1,400 wds; book reviews 150 wds ($6.25 CAN). Responds in 2 wks. Seasonal 3 mos ahead. Accepts simultaneous submissions & reprints (tell when/where appeared). Accepts disk (Macintosh). Some sidebars. Prefers NRSV. Guidelines/theme list; copy for 6x9 SAE/.90 CAN postage or $1 for non-Canadians.

Poetry: Buys 8-12/yr. Free verse, light verse, traditional; 8-100 lines; $10-20. Submit max. 2 poems.

Fillers: Buys 20/yr. Anecdotes, cartoons, prose, prayers, short humor, word puzzles; 50-350 wds; $3.25-12.50.

Columns/Departments: Buys 4/yr. Over the Fence (conversational), 325 wds. Pays $12.50-15/pg.

Tips: "Be a Lutheran woman living in Canada. Use inclusive language (no male pronoun references to God), focus on women and spiritual/faith issues. Check our theme calendar; almost all articles and poems are theme related."

#THE HELPING HAND, Box 12609, Oklahoma City OK 73157-2609. (405)787-7110. Fax (405)789-3957. Pentecostal Holiness Church/Women's Ministries. Doris L. Moore, ed. Denominational; for women. Bimonthly mag; 20 pgs; circ 4,000. Subscription $6.50. 70% freelance. Query. Pays $20 on publication for 1st, one-time, reprint & simultaneous rts. Articles 500-1,800 wds (12/yr); fiction 500-1,800 wds (20/yr). Responds in 2-4 wks. Seasonal 4 mos ahead. Accepts simultaneous submissions & reprints. Prefers NIV or KJV. Guidelines; copy for 9x12 SAE/2 stamps.

> **Poetry:** Buys 5/yr. Traditional; $10-20. Submit max. 4 poems.

HORIZONS, 100 Witherspoon St., Louisville KY 40202-1396. (502)569-5379. Fax (502)569-8085. Presbyterian Church (USA). Submit to Editorial Dept. Justice issues and spiritual life for Presbyterian women. Bimonthly mag & Annual Bible study; 40 pgs; circ 40,000. Subscription $14. 40% freelance. Complete ms/cover letter; fax query OK. Pays $50-250 on publication for all rts. Articles 1,000-1,200 wds (20/yr) & fiction 500-1,200 wds (2/yr); book/music/video reviews 100-150 wds ($25). Responds in 2 wks. Seasonal 5 mos ahead. Accepts simultaneous submissions and reprints (tell when/where appeared). Requires disk. Some kill fees. Sidebars OK. Prefers NRSV. Guidelines/theme list; copy $2/9x12 SAE.

> **Poetry:** Buys 5/yr. All types; $25-100.
>
> **Fillers:** Cartoons, jokes, prayers, short humor, word puzzles; 50-175 wds; $25.
>
> **Tips:** "Write articles focused at women 35-45. On work, lifestyle, family and church (especially Presbyterian Church). We want to reach younger women as well, so articles that integrate generations, speak to younger women and introduce forward thinking would be welcomed." Most open to personal experience/profiles.

*JOURNAL OF WOMEN'S MINISTRIES, 46 Olive St., Methuen MA 01844. (800)334-7626. Episcopal/Council for Women's Ministries. Marcy Darin, ed. Deals with issues of interest to women from a liberal perspective. Biannual mag; 36 pgs; circ 10,000. Query. Pays $50 on publication for 1st rts. Articles 1,200-1,500 wds. Responds in 5 wks. Seasonal 3 mos ahead. Guidelines; copy for 9x12 SAE/3 stamps.

> **Poetry:** Free verse, traditional. Submit max. 2 poems.

JOURNEY, 127 Ninth Ave. N., Nashville TN 37234. (615)251-5659. Fax (615)251-5008. Southern Baptist. Pamela Nixon, mng. ed. Devotional magazine for women of the 90s (30-45 years old). Monthly mag; 44 pgs; circ 100,000. 20% freelance. Subscription $18.50. Est. 1994. Query/clips or complete ms/cover letter. Pays $20-150 on acceptance for all, 1st or one-time rts. Articles 350-1,000 wds (25/yr). Responds in 6-8 wks. Seasonal 6-7 mos ahead. Accepts simultaneous submissions & reprints. Short sidebars OK. Prefers NIV. Accepts disk. Guidelines; copy for 6x9 SAE/2 stamps.

> **Poetry:** Buys 2-3/yr. Free verse, light verse, traditional; $20. Submit max. 5 poems.
>
> **Fillers:** Prayers, short humor; 200-350 wds.

Columns/Departments: Buys 12-15/yr. Prayer Diary (short, woman's prayer in first-person), 250-300 wds.

Special Needs: Profiles on well-known Christian women. "We would like to see personal stories of faith applied to challenging situations that would encourage, inspire or motivate. Also articles on career, health, and personal development with a faith angle."

Tips: "Would like to see brief, descriptive articles about relationships (marriage, parent-child, friends, etc.), personal stories of faith or spiritual growth, or time management for busy women—some serious, some light in tone."

** This periodical was #55 on the 1996 Top 50 Christian Publishers List.

#THE JOYFUL WOMAN, PO Box 90028, Chattanooga TN 37412-6028. (423)894-4500. Fax (423)894-0907. Joyful Christian Ministries. Joy Rice Martin, ed. For and about Bible-believing women who want God's best. Bimonthly (5X) mag; 24-36 pgs; circ 8,350. Subscription $16. 50% freelance. Query only; fax query OK. Pays $15-50 (.03-.04/wd) on publication for 1st rts. Articles & fiction 500-1,200 wds (15/yr); music reviews, 200-400 wds, $20. Responds in 2-6 wks. Seasonal 4 mos ahead. Accepts simultaneous submissions & reprints. Prefers disk. Sidebars OK. Guidelines/theme list; copy $3/9x12 SAE/4 stamps. (Ads)

Poetry: Buys 6/yr. Free verse, light verse, traditional; 15-40 lines; $15-40. Submit max. 2 poems.

Fillers: Buys 10/yr. Cartoons, jokes, newsbreaks, prayers, quotes, short humor; 25-300 wds; $15-25.

Tips: "Our biggest need is true-life stories. We prefer 1,000 word or less manuscripts, and would like color pictures of author and/or manuscript subject. Please allow 16 weeks before you call about your manuscript."

#JUST BETWEEN US, 777 S. Barker Rd., Brookfield WI 53045. (414)786-6478 or (800)260-3342. Fax (414)796-5752. Elmbrook Church, Inc. Shelly Esser, ed. Ideas, encouragement and resources for wives of evangelical ministers. Quarterly mag; 32 pgs; circ 2,700. Subscription $14.95. 90% freelance. Query; phone/fax query OK. **NO PAYMENT** for one-time rts. Articles 250-500 wds or 800-1,500 wds (50/yr). Responds in 6 wks. Accepts simultaneous submissions & reprints. Sidebars OK. Prefers NIV. Guidelines/theme list; copy $2/9x12 SAE. (Ads)

Fillers: Buys 15/yr. Anecdotes, cartoons, ideas, prayers, quotes, short humor; 50-250 wds.

Columns/Departments: Buys 12/yr. Money Savers; Keeping Your Kids Christian; Women's Ministry (program ideas); all 500-700 wds.

Tips: "Articles need to relate to unique ministry issues. Most open to columns or feature articles. Follow themes."

THE LINK & VISITOR, 30 Arlington Ave., Toronto ON M6G 3K8 Canada. (416)651-7192. Fax (416)651-0438. Baptist Women's Missionary Society of Ontario and Quebec. Esther Barnes, ed. A positive, practical magazine for Canadian Baptist women who want to make a difference in our world. Monthly mag; 16 pgs; circ 4,500. Subscription $14 CAN. 50% freelance. Complete ms/cover letter; phone query OK. Pays .05/wd CAN, on publication for one-time, reprint or simultaneous rts. Articles (25/yr) 700-2,000 wds. Responds in 52 wks. Seasonal 4 mos ahead. Accepts simultaneous submissions & reprints (tell when/where appeared). Some kill fees. Some sidebars. Prefers NRS. Guidelines/theme list; copy for 9x12 SAE/$1 Canadian postage.

Poetry: Buys 3/yr. Free verse; 12-32 lines; $10-30. Submit max. 4 poems.

Tips: "Canadian writers preferred. If US writers send US postage for returns, they will be rejected. Too many writers seem too focused on themselves and their own experiences. Canadian perspective, please."

*LUTHERAN WOMAN TODAY, 8765 W. Higgins Ave., Chicago IL 60631-4189. (312)380-2743. Evangelical Lutheran Church in America. Nancy J. Stelling, ed. For women in the denomination. Monthly (11X) mag: 48 pgs; circ 230,000. 25% freelance. Complete ms/cover letter or query. Pays $60-280 on publication for 1st rts. Articles (24/yr) & fiction (5/yr), to 1,050 wds. Responds in 16 wks. Seasonal 7 mos ahead. Guidelines/theme list; copy $1.

Poetry: Buys 5/yr. Free verse, haiku, light verse, traditional; to 60 lines; $15-60. Submit max. 3 poems. Poetry must have a spiritual and women's focus.

Columns/Departments: Buys 5/yr. Devotion, 350 wds; Season's Best (reflection on the church yr), 350-700 wds; About Women; Forum (essay); $50-250.

Tips: "Submit a short, well-written article using inclusive language and offering a women's and spiritual focus."

*LUTHERAN WOMAN'S QUARTERLY, 1860 Greenfield Dr., El Cajon CA 92021. Phone/fax (619)444-6089. Lutheran Women's Missionary League. Patricia Beach Schutte, ed-in-chief. For women of the Lutheran Church—Missouri Synod. Quarterly mag; 48 pgs; circ. 200,000. Subscription $2.50. 100% freelance. Complete ms/cover letter. **NO PAYMENT.** Not copyrighted. Articles 750-1,200 wds (4/yr); fiction 750-1,200 wds (4/yr). Responds in 2 wks. Seasonal 5 mos ahead. Sidebars OK. Prefers NIV. Guidelines/theme list.

Tips: "Most open to articles. Must reflect the Missouri synod teachings. Most of our writers are from the denomination."

*PROBE, 529 S. Wabash, Ste. 404, Chicago IL 60605. (312)663-1980. National Assembly of Religious Women/Catholic/Ecumenical. Ann Wetherilt, ed. Networking tool for members with a progressive, social justice and feminist thrust. Quarterly newspaper; 12 pgs; circ 3,000. 90% freelance. Query. **PAYS A SUBSCRIPTION** for one-time rts. Articles to 2,000 wds; fiction to 2,000 wds. Accepts simultaneous submissions. Copy $1.

Poetry: Must be theme-related.

THE PROVERBS 31 HOMEMAKER, PO Box 17155, Charlotte NC 28227. (704)849-2270. Fax (704)849-2270. E-mail: P31home@aol.com. Mary Ellen Bianco, ed. Encouragement and information for stay-at-home mothers. Monthly newsletter; 10 pgs; circ. 2,000. Subscription $15. 90% freelance. Query. **NO PAYMENT** for one-time rts. Articles 200-400 wds (24/yr); book reviews 200-250 wds. Responds in 4 wks. Seasonal 4 mos ahead. Accepts simultaneous submissions & reprints (tell when/where appeared). No disk. Sidebars OK. Prefers NIV. Guidelines/theme list; copy for 9x12 SAE/2 stamps.

Poetry: Accepts up to 12/yr.

Fillers: Accepts 12/yr. Anecdotes, cartoons, ideas, party ideas, prose, prayers, quotes, short humor; to 100 wds.

Tips: "Looking for articles on relationship with God; how homemakers organize time; marital relationships; how to keep kids busy."

SISTERS TODAY, The Liturgical Press, St. John's Abbey, PO Box 7500, Collegeville MN 56321-7500. (320)363-2213. Fax (800)445-5899. E-mail: mwagner @CSBSJU.edu. Catholic. Sr. Mary Anthony Wagner, O.S.B., ed. (St. Benedict's Convent, St. Joseph MN 56374, [320]363-7065). To explore the role of women and the Church in our time. Bimonthly journal; 80 pgs; circ 3,500. Subscription $20. 50% freelance. Complete ms/cover letter; phone/e-mail query OK. Pays $5/printed page on publication for 1st rts. Articles 10-12 pgs (50-70/yr). Responds in 4-6 wks. Seasonal several mos ahead. Accepts disk. No sidebars. Guidelines/theme list; copy $4. (Ads)

> **Poetry:** Sr. Mary Virginia Micke, C.S.J. (1884 Randolph Ave., St. Paul MN 55105) Buys 30-40/yr. Free verse, haiku, light verse, traditional; to 34 lines (prefers 16-20); $10. Submit max. 4 poems.
>
> **Tips:** "Most open to articles and poems."

+TEA AND SUNSHINE, S63 W 35530 Piper Rd., Eagle WI 53119. (414)392-9761. Fax (414)547-8871. E-mail: MLJBeen@aol.com. Margaret Been, pub. For women whose hearts are at home. Bimonthly newsletter; 12-16 pgs; circ. 500. Est. 1995. Subscription free (donations welcome). 40% freelance. Complete ms/cover letter. **PAYS IN COPIES.** for one-time rts. Articles 200-800 wds; fiction 600-1.200 wds; book reviews 300 wds. Responds promptly. Seasonal 6 mos ahead. No disk. Some sidebars. Prefers KJV, NIV or NAS. Copy for 9x12 SAE/ 3 stamps.

> **Poetry:** Accepts many/yr. Literary; around 8-30 lines.
>
> **Fillers:** Prose, short humor.
>
> **Special Needs:** Craft ideas, such as spinning, weaving, knitting, soap making, etc.
>
> **Tips:** "We like essays about quality of life and savoring the beauty around us, things about the creativity of homemaking, and stories of God's victory over and in all circumstances."

TODAY'S CHRISTIAN WOMAN, 465 Gundersen Dr., Carol Stream IL 60188-2498. (630)260-6200. Fax (630)260-0114. E-mail: TCWedit@aol.com. Submit to Camerin Courtney, asst. ed. To help Christian women grow in their relationship to God by providing practical, biblical perspectives on marriage, sex, parenting, work, health, friendship, and self. Bimonthly mag; 80-150 pgs; circ 309,000. Subscription $17.95. 25% freelance. Query; fax/e-mail query OK. Query for electronic submissions. Pays .15/wd on publication (on acceptance for assignments) for 1st or reprint rts. Articles 1,000-1,500 wds (6-12/yr); no fiction. Responds in 4-6 wks. Seasonal 6 mos ahead. Accepts simultaneous submissions and reprints (tell when/where appeared). Some sidebars. Prefers NIV. Guidelines; copy $5. (Ads)

> **Columns/Departments:** Buys 12/yr. One Woman's Story (dramatic story of overcoming a difficult situation), 1,000-1,500 wds, $150, query; Faith on Job (sharing faith at work), 100-200 wds, $25; Small Talk (humorous, inspirational anecdotes), 50-100 wds, $25. Send complete ms for last two/not acknowledged or returned.
>
> **Tips:** "Most open to One Woman's Story: Should tell how you, through a

personal experience, came to a spiritual turning point, solved a problem, or overcame a difficult situation."

** This periodical was #57 on the 1996 Top 50 Christian Publishers List. (#34 in 1994)

*UNIQUE, PO Box 2430, Cleveland TN 37320-2430. (423)478-7095. Fax (423)478-7891. Church of God (Cleveland TN)/Dept. of Ladies Ministries. Rebecca J. Jenkins, exec. dir. Denominational magazine for Pentecostal women. Bimonthly mag; 20 pgs; circ 7,500. Subscription $7.50. 100% freelance. Complete ms. **NO PAYMENT** for all rts. Articles 500-600 (preferred), up to 1,200 wds. Responds in 2-4 wks. Seasonal 4 mos ahead. Accepts reprints. Prefers disk. Some sidebars. Guidelines; copy for 9x12 SAE/3 stamps.

> **Poetry:** Accepts 8/yr. To one pg. Submit max. 3 poems.
>
> **Fillers:** Accepts 8/yr. Prayers & short humor.

VIRTUE, 4050 Lee Vance View, Colorado Springs CO 80918-7102. (719)531-7776. Fax (719)535-0172. E-mail: VirtueMag@aol.com. Good Family Magazines. Debbie Colclough, assoc. ed. For Christian women who seek spiritual perspectives and personal enrichment in every aspect of their lives. Bimonthly mag; 80-85 pgs; circ 115,000. Subscription $18.95. 40% freelance. Query; no phone/fax query. Pays .20-.25/wd on publication for 1st rts (sometimes exclusive rts). Articles 900-1,200 wds (60/yr) & fiction 1,200-1,500 wds (4-6/yr). Responds in 8-9 wks. Seasonal 6-7 mos ahead. Accepts reprints only from non-competing markets (tell when/where appeared). Prefers disk. Kill fee. Encourages sidebars. Guidelines; copy for 9x12 SAE/9 stamps or $3. (Ads)

> **Poetry:** Buys 6-12/yr. Avant-garde, light verse; any length; .15-.20/wd. ($25-50). Submit max. 3 poems.
>
> **Departments:** Buys 30/yr. One Woman's Journal, to 1,200 wds (send complete ms); Family Matters (News and information for families), to 300 wds; Virtue in Action (about virtue, values and character in our culture), to 200 wds.
>
> **Tips:** "Looking for examples of Christ-like character. We have a brand new format and new columns. Most open to 'One Woman's Journal' (story of how a woman works through a struggle—not necessarily solving it—and where God is in that)."
>
> ** #42 on the 1994 Top 50.

*WELCOME HOME, 8310A Old Courthouse Rd., Vienna VA 22182. (703)827-5903 or (800)783-4MOM. Fax(703)790-8587. Mothers at Home, Inc. Submit to Manuscript Coordinator. For women who have chosen to stay at home with their children. Monthly jour; circ. 15,000. Subscription $18. 100% freelance. Complete ms/cover letter. **NO (OR LIMITED) PAYMENT** for one-time rts. Articles to 2,400 wds, most 500-1,500 wds (20/yr). Responds in 6-12 wks. Seasonal 1 yr ahead. Some sidebars. Guidelines (request specific guidelines for departments interested in); copy $2/7x10 SAE.

> **Poetry:** Winnie Peterson Cross. Accepts 48/yr. Free verse, haiku, light verse, traditional.
>
> **Columns/Departments:** Accepts 36/yr. From a Mother (surprising/sudden insights); Resource Roundup (books/resources); New Dimensions (personal growth/development); Heartwarming (cooking/recipes); Health & Safety

(mother's/child's health, family safety); Time to Care (volunteer work; all 700-1,000 wds.

THE WESLEYAN WOMAN, PO Box 50434, Indianapolis IN 46250-0434. (317)570-5164. Fax (317)570-5280. E-mail: vanhornn@wesleyan.org. Wesleyan Church. Martha Blackburn, ed. Inspiration, education and sharing to meet the needs of Wesleyan women. Quarterly mag; circ 3,500. Subscription $10. Complete ms/cover letter; phone/fax query OK. Pays .04/wd (.02/wd for reprints) on publication for 1st & one-time rts. Articles to 700 wds. Seasonal 6 mos ahead. Accepts simultaneous submissions & reprints. Accepts disk. Guidelines/theme list; free copy.

    Poetry: Accepts 4-5/yr. Avant-garde, free verse, light verse, traditional.

    Fillers: Cartoons, facts, newsbreaks.

    Tips: "Most open to personal stories of 'guts' and grace to follow the Lord. Ways you see God at work in your life."

WOMAN'S TOUCH, 1445 Boonville Ave., Springfield MO 65802-1894. (417)862-2781. Fax (417)862-0503. E-mail: womanstouch@ag.org. Assemblies of God. Peggy Musgrove, ed. A general readership magazine committed to providing help and inspiration for Christian women, strengthening family life, and reaching out in witness to others; also leadership edition. Bimonthly mag; 36 pgs; circ 18,000+. Subscription $7/leader $8.50. 95% freelance. Complete ms/cover letter. Pays $10-40 (.03/wd) on publication for 1st, one-time, or reprint rts. Articles to 1,200 wds (50-60/yr). Responds in 10 wks. Seasonal 10-12 mos ahead. Accepts simultaneous submissions & reprints (tell when/where appeared). Accepts disk. Kill fee. Sidebars OK. Prefers KJV or NIV. Guidelines/theme list; copy for 9x12 SAE/3 stamps.

    Poetry: Buys 2-3/yr. Light verse, traditional; 10-50 lines; $5-20. Submit max. 3 poems.

    Fillers: Buys 10/yr. Anecdotes, ideas; 50-200 wds; $5-15.

    Columns/Departments: Buys 30/yr. A Better You (health/fitness), 500 wds; A Final Touch (human interest on home/family/career), 350 wds; A Lighter Touch (true humorous anecdotes); 100 wds; History's Women (great women of faith), 500 wds. Pays $10-40.

    ** This periodical was #35 on the 1996 Top 50 Christian Publishers List.

WOMEN ALIVE!, Box 4683, Overland Park KS 66212. (913)649-8583. Fax (913)649-8583. Aletha Hinthorn, ed. To encourage Holiness women to apply Scripture to their daily lives. Bimonthly mag; 20 pgs; circ 3,500. Subscription $13.95. 50% freelance. Complete ms/cover letter. Pays $15-40 on publication for 1st, simultaneous or reprint rts. Articles 400-1,500 wds (30/yr). Responds in 6-8 wks. Seasonal 4-6 mos ahead. Accepts simultaneous submissions & reprints. Some sidebars. Guidelines; copy for 9x12 SAE/4 stamps.

    Poetry: Buys 0-3/yr. Traditional, $10-40. Submit max. 3.

    Fillers: Buys 0-1/yr. Cartoons, jokes, short humor.

    Columns/Departments: Buys 6/yr. Senior Savvy (for older women); 900-1,200 wds; $15-40.

    Tips: "We look for articles that draw women into a deeper spiritual life—articles on surrender, prayer, Bible study—yet written with personal illustrations."

#WOMEN OF SPIRIT, 55 W. Oak Ridge Dr., Hagerstown MD 21740-7390. (301)790-9737. Fax (301)790-9734. E-mail: 74617.4104@compuserve.com. Seventh-day Adventist. Penny Wheeler, ed. To be a friend and mentor to women, stimulating spiritual vitality, nurturing emotional growth, fostering balanced, healthy living, and encouraging a dynamic witness in home and community. Quarterly mag,; circ. 17,000. Subscription $14.95. Query first. (Ads)

WRITER'S MARKETS

BYLINE, Box 130596, Edmond OK 73013-0001. (405)348-5591. E-mail: ByLineMP @aol.com. Secular. Kathryn Fanning, mng. ed. Offers practical tips, motivation and encouragement to freelance writers and poets. Monthly mag; 36 pgs; circ 3,000+. Subscription $20. 85% freelance. Query or complete ms; no phone/fax/e-mail query. Pays $50 ($100 for fiction) on acceptance for 1st rts. Articles 1,500-1,800 wds (100/yr); personal experiences 800 wds; fiction 2,000-4,000 wds (10/yr). Responds in 4-6 wks. Seasonal 6 mos ahead. Accepts simultaneous submissions. Prefers disk. Encourages sidebars. Guidelines; copy $4.
>   **Poetry:** Betty Shipley. Buys 110-120/yr. Any type; to 30 lines; $5-10. Writing themes. Submit max. 4 poems.
>   **Fillers:** Short Humor for humor page only, 200-400 wds, pays $15-20.
>   **Columns/Departments:** Buys 50-60/yr. End Piece (personal essay on writing theme), 750 wds; First Sale accounts, 200-400 wds; Only When I Laugh (writing humor), 100-500 wds; End Piece; $15-35. Complete ms.
>   **Contests:** Sponsors many year round; details included in magazine.
>   **Tips:** "Most open to First Sale account; be upbeat about writing. Need articles, essays and poetry on writing topics; general interest short stories (no religious)."

#CANADIAN WRITER'S JOURNAL, Box 6618, Stn LDC 1, Victoria BC V8P 5N7 Canada. (604)477-8807. Gordon M. Smart, ed. How-to articles for writers. Quarterly mag; circ 350. Subscription $15. 75% freelance. Query. Pays $5 CAN/published pg on publication for 1st, one-time or reprint rts. Not copyrighted. Articles 500-1,200 wds (50-55/yr); book reviews 250-500 wds/$5. Responds in 9 wks. Seasonal 3 mos ahead. Accepts reprints (tell when/where appeared). Kill fee. Guidelines; copy $4.
>   **Poetry:** Elizabeth St. Jacques (406 Elizabeth St., Saulte St. Marie ON P6B 3H4 Canada). Traditional, haiku: on writing; to 15 lines. Pays $1. Send 5 poems max.
>   **Fillers:** Anecdotes, cartoons, ideas, short humor; 100-250 wds.
>   **Contest:** Sponsors annual poetry contest (June 30 deadline). Also a fiction contest.

*CHIPS OFF THE WRITER'S BLOCK, Box 83371, Los Angeles CA 90083. Secular. Wanda Windham, ed. For beginning writers. Bimonthly newsletter; circ 500+. 100% freelance. Complete ms/cover letter. **PAYS IN COPIES**, for one-time rts. Articles to 1,500 wds (100/yr); fiction to 1,200 wds (50+/yr). Responds in 6 wks. Seasonal 6 mos ahead. Accepts simultaneous submissions & reprints. Guidelines; copy $3.
>   **Poetry:** All forms (on writing only); 1-40 lines. Submit max. 5 poems.
>   **Fillers:** Anything on writing; to 300 wds.

Tips: "Need more one-page, well-researched, how-to articles. Open to new columns and ideas."

THE CHRISTIAN COMMUNICATOR, 3133 Puente St., Fullerton CA 92835-1952. (714)990-1532. Fax (714)990-0310. E-mail: Susanosb@aol.com. American Christian Writers/Reg Forder, Box 110390, Nashville TN 37222, (800)21-WRITE (for advertising or subscriptions). Susan Titus Osborn, ed. For Christian writers/speakers who want to polish writing skills, develop public-speaking techniques, and sell their mss. Monthly mag; 24 pgs; circ 4,000. Subscription $25. 50% freelance. Complete ms/cover letter; phone/fax query OK. Pays $5-10 on publication for 1st, one-time or reprint rts. Articles 600-1,200 wds (62/yr). Responds in 6-8 wks. Seasonal 6 mos ahead. Accepts reprints. Free guidelines/copy.

Poetry: Accepts 12/yr. Poems on writing; $5. Submit max. 4 poems.

Fillers: Accepts 12/yr.

Columns/Departments: Buys 12/yr. Communicator Interview (published author), 800-1,200 wds; Publisher's Profile, 800-1,200 wds; Speaker's Corner (techniques for speakers), 600-1,000 wds; Book Reviews (writing/speaking books), 300-400 wds; $5-10.

Tips: "Most in need of publisher profiles."

*THE CHRISTIAN RESPONSE, PO Box 125, Staples MN 56479-0125. (218)894-1165. Christian Writers of America. Hap Corbett, ed. Exposes anti-Christian bias in America & encourages readers to write letters in defense of such bias. Bi-monthly newsletter; 6 pgs; circ 400. Subscription $15. Est. 1993. 10% freelance. Complete ms/cover letter; phone query OK. Pays $2.50-20 on acceptance for 1st or simultaneous rts. Articles 50-300 wds (6/yr). Responds in 2 wks. Seasonal 6 mos ahead. Accepts simultaneous submissions & reprints. No sidebars. Guidelines; copy for $1 or 3 stamps.

Fillers: Anecdotes, facts, quotes; 25-100 wds; $2.50-10.

Special Needs: Articles on anti-Christian bias; tips on writing effective letters to the editor; pieces on outstanding accomplishments of Christians in the secular media.

Tips: "We are looking for news/articles about anti-Christian bias in the media, and how you, as a writer, responded to such incidents."

CROSS & QUILL, Rt. 3 Box 1635, Jefferson Davis Rd., Clinton SC 29325. Phone/fax (864)697-6035. E-mail: CWFI@aol.com. Christian Writers Fellowship Intl. Sandy Brooks, ed/pub. For Christian writers, editors, agents, conference directors. Bimonthly newsletter; 12 pgs; circ 1,000+. Subscription $20; CWFI membership $40. 75% freelance. Complete ms; e-mail query OK. Pays small honorarium for articles on publication for 1st rts. Articles 800-1,000 wds (12/yr); book reviews 100 wds (pays copies). Responds in 2 wks. Seasonal 4 mos ahead. Accepts reprints (tell when/where appeared). Sidebars OK. Accepts disk. Guidelines; copy $2/9x12 SAE/2 stamps. (Ads)

Poetry: Accepts 12/yr. Any type; to 12 lines. Submit max. 3 poems. Must pertain to writing/publishing. Currently overstocked.

Fillers: Accepts 12/yr. Anecdotes, cartoons, facts, prayers; to 100 wds. Pays in copies.

Columns/Departments: Accepts 36/yr. Writing Rainbows! (devotional),

600 wds; Writer to Writer (how-to), 900 wds; Editor's Roundtable (interview with editor), 200-800 wds; Tots, Teens & In-Betweens (juvenile market), 200-800 wds; BusinessWise (business side of writing), 200-800 wds; Connecting Points (how-to on critique group), 200-800 wds.

Tips: "Most open to feature articles, devotions for writers or book reviews on writing books."

EXCHANGE, #104-15 Torrance Rd., Scarborough ON M1J 3K2 Canada. (416)439-4320. (416)439-5089. E-mail: 104611.1454@compuserve.com. Audrey Dorsch, ed. A forum for Christian writers to share information and ideas. Quarterly newsletter; 8 pgs; circ 200. Subscription $11.50 US/$16 Canada. 60% freelance. Complete ms/cover letter; fax/e-mail query OK. Pays .08/wd (CAN) on publication for one-time rts. Not copyrighted. Articles 400-600 wds (20/yr). Responds in 4-6 wks. Accepts reprints (.06/wd—tell when/where appeared). Kill fee 30-50%. No sidebars. Accepts disk. Guidelines/copy for #10 SAE/2 Canadian stamps (.52).

Fillers: Ideas, quotes; 25-100 wds; no payment.

Columns/Departments: Buys 4/yr. Did You Know Your Computer Can Do This? (software features), 300 wds. Query.

Special Needs: Material for advanced writers; well-researched pieces on Christian literary agents.

Tips: "Ask yourself what article you wish would appear somewhere for your own writing development. Then research it and write it yourself."

*FELICITY, HCR-13, Box 21AA, Artemas PA 17211. (814)458-3102. Ann Weems, ed. Thematic issues from writers for adults of all ages. Quarterly newsletter; 30-40 pgs; circ 200+. Subscription $15. 100% freelance. Complete ms/cover letter. **PAYS IN COPIES,** small payment to contest winners, for one-time, reprint & simultaneous rts. Articles 100-250 wds (12/yr); fiction to 2,500 wds (see Contests). Responds in 6-24 wks. Seasonal 3 mos ahead. Accepts simultaneous submissions & reprints. No sidebars. Guidelines/theme list; copy for #10 SAE/2 stamps.

Poetry: Any type, to 36 lines.

Fillers: Anecdotes, cartoons, writing ideas, jokes, quizzes, word puzzles. Pays one copy.

Contests: Sponsors two contests/issue. Send for information.

#GOTTA WRITE NETWORK LITMAG, 612 Cobblestone Cr., Glenview IL 60025. Phone/fax (847)296-7631. E-mail: netera@aol.com. Secular/Maren Publications. Denise Fleischer, ed. A support system for writers, beginner to well established. Semiannual mag; circ 200. Subscription $12.75. 80% freelance. Query or complete ms/cover letter; e-mail query OK. Pays $5 ($10 for fiction) after publication for 1st rts. Articles 3-5 pgs (25/yr); fiction to 5-10 pgs (10+/yr) on writing techniques; book reviews 2.5 pgs. Responds in 18 wks. Seasonal 6 mos ahead. Guidelines; copy $5.

Poetry: Accepts 75+/yr. Avant-garde, free verse, haiku, experimental; 4 lines to 1 pg. Submit max. 5 poems.

Fillers: Accepts 100/yr. Anecdotes, facts, newsbreaks, tips; 100-250 wds; pays in copies.

Tips: "Most open to articles on writing techniques. Give me something different and in-depth. No I-love-writing, how-I-did-it."

*HEAVEN, HCR-13 Box 21AA, Artemas PA 17211. (814)458-3102. Kay Weems, ed. Published for Easter. New publication. $5/copy. Annual booklet. Est. 1995. 100% freelance. **NO PAYMENT.** Responds in 4-12 wks. Accepts simultaneous submissions and reprints.

　　Poetry: All types of poetry on heaven, to 36 lines. Submit max. 10 poems.

*HOUSEWIFE-WRITER, Box 780, Lyman WY 82937-0780. (307)782-7003. Secular. Emma Bluemel, ed; Edward Wahl, fiction ed. For new and unpublished writers who are home-based. Bimonthly magazine; 48 pgs; circ 2,000. Subscription $18. 80-90% freelance. Complete ms; phone query OK. Pays .01/wd on acceptance for 1st rts. Articles (60-100/yr) and fiction (6-12/yr) to 2,000 wds. Responds in 4-12 wks. Seasonal 6 mos ahead. Accepts simultaneous submissions & reprints. Sidebars OK. Guidelines; copy $4/#10 SAE.

　　Poetry: Maria Reed. Buys 36/yr. Any type; to 45 lines; $1-5. Submit max. 5 poems.

　　Fillers: Buys 24-30/yr. Anecdotes, cartoons, ideas, jokes, short humor; hints (on writing/running a home); 25-200 wds; $1-4.

　　Columns/Departments: Buys 30-40/yr. Confessions of a Housewife-Writer, 250-750 wds; or various writing tips, 150-250 wds; $3. Complete ms.

　　Contests: Sponsors annual contests with a June 1 deadline. Prizes are $30, $20 & $10, plus publication. Send SASE for rules.

　　Tips: "Need how-tos on juggling home, children and writing. We rank verse and emotion ahead of linguistic gymnastics."

INKLINGS, Threads of Truth From Art and Story, 1650 Washington St., Denver CO 80203-1407. (303)861-8191. Fax (303)861-8194. E-mail: inkhick@aol.com. Paradox Publishing. Brad Hicks, pub.; Nancy Hicks, fiction ed. For thinking Christians and seekers interested in the arts and literature. Quarterly mag.; circ 10,000. Subscription $15. Est. 1993. 50-75% freelance. Query or complete ms/cover letter; phone/fax/e-mail query OK. Pays $100 for lead article only, on publication for 1st rts. Articles 250-3,000 wds (4/yr); fiction 250-3,000 wds (8/yr); book/music reviews, 350 wds (pays in copies). Responds in 4 wks. Seasonal 3-6 mos ahead. Prefers disk. Kill fee 50%. Sidebars OK. Prefers NIV. Guidelines/theme list; copy $4. (Ads)

　　Poetry: Joy Sawyer & Nancy Hightower. Accepts 20-30/yr. All types, 2-100 lines. Submit max. 10 poems.

　　Columns/Departments: Buys 112-20/yr. Stories (fiction & short stories, all genres), 250-3,000 wds; Theme Pages (articles/features on theme), 250-3,000 wds. Pays $50-100.

　　Special Needs: Fiction, poetry, articles, essays and features on 1997 themes: Responsibility of the Artist, Home, and Humor and the Fool.

　　Contest: Called Flash Fiction, up to 1,000 wds; $5/submission entry fee. $100 cash prize, $50 gift certificate, and publication in Inklings.

　　Tips: "Be able to write stories well. See Tips in writer's guidelines."

+INSPIRATIONAL MARKET NEWS, 1132 - 21st St. SE, Cedar Rapids IA 52403. Helen Hunt, ed.

*MERLYN'S PEN, The National Magazine of Student Writing, Box 1058, East Greenwich RI 02818. Secular. R. James Stahl, ed. Written by students in grades 7-12 only. Mag. printed in 2 editions: Intermediate, 6th-9th grades; Senior, 9th-

12th grades. Fiction to 2,500 wds; reviews and travel pieces to 1,000 wds. **PAYS IN COPIES**. Not in topical listings. Students send for guidelines.

Poetry: To 200 lines.

*MY LEGACY, HCR-13 Box 21AA, Artemas PA 17211. (814)458-3102. Ann Weems, ed. For young adults and up. Quarterly booklet; 70-80 pgs; circ 200+. 100% freelance. **NO PAYMENT**. No articles; fiction to 2,500 wds (100/yr). Responds in 14-16 wks. Accepts simultaneous submissions & reprints. Guidelines; copy for 6x9 SAE/4 stamps & $3.50.

Poetry: Accepts 200+/yr. Any types; to 36 lines.

NORTHWEST CHRISTIAN AUTHOR, 10663 NE 133rd Pl., Kirkland WA 98034-2030. (206)821-6647. Fax (206)823-8590. E-mail: lkfnewton@aol.com. Northwest Christian Writers' Assn. Lorinda Newton, ed. To encourage Christian authors to share the gospel through the written word and to promote excellence in writing. Bimonthly newsletter; 8 pgs; circ. 80. Subscription $10. 70% freelance. Complete ms/cover letter; e-mail query OK. Query for electronic submissions. **PAYS 3 COPIES** for one-time, reprint or simultaneous rts. Not copyrighted. Articles 500-1,000 wds (20/yr). Responds in 4 wks. Accepts simultaneous submissions & reprints (tell when/where appeared). Prefers disk. Sidebars OK. Guidelines; copy for 6x9 SAE/2 stamps.

Fillers: Accepts 1-2 cartoons/yr.

Tips: "Looking for how-to articles on fiction and nonfiction."

*OMNIFIC, HCR-13 Box 21AA, Artemas PA 17211. (814)458-3102. Kay Weems, ed. Family-type publication for writers/adults. Quarterly booklet; 100+ pgs; circ 300+. Subscription $16. 100% freelance. **SMALL AWARDS GIVEN**. Accepts simultaneous submissions & reprints. No articles; poetry only. Guidelines; copy for 6x9 SAE/4 stamps & $4.

Poetry: Any type; to 36 lines. Submit max. 4-8 poems.

ONCE UPON A TIME, 553 Winston Ct., St. Paul MN 55118. (612)457-6223. Fax (612)457-9565. E-mail: AUDREYOUAT@aol.com. Audrey B. Baird, ed/pub. A support publication for children's writers and illustrators. Quarterly mag; 32 pgs; circ 1,000. Subscription $20. 50% freelance. Complete ms/cover letter; phone/fax query OK. **PAYS IN COPIES** for one-time rts. Articles 100-800 wds. Responds in 4 wks. Seasonal 4 mos ahead. Accepts simultaneous submissions & reprints (if non-overlapping; wait 2 yrs if competing). Accepts disk. Some sidebars. Guidelines; copy $4.50. (Ads)

Poetry: Buys 10/yr. Free verse, haiku, light verse, traditional; any length. Writing related. Submit max. 5 poems.

Tips: "Emphasis is on children's writing, but we take general writing pieces too. I don't get enough humor. Half our magazine is open to freelancers. I like how-to pieces. Overstocked on rejection pieces. Looking for articles on viewpoint, collaboration, figures of speech, or avoiding clichés."

THE POETRY CONNECTION, 13455 SW 16th Ct. #F-405, Pembroke Pines FL 33027. (954)431-3016. Sylvia Shichman, ed/pub. Information for poets, writers and song writers; also greeting card markets. Monthly newsletter; circ. 200. Subscription $20. Phone query OK. Not copyrighted. Guidelines; copy $7/10x13 SAE/$2 postage.

Poetry: Free verse.

Contests: Lists contests in newsletter.

Note: Also offers membership in the Magic Circle, a reading network service for poetry and lyrics. Membership $20. Poems and lyrics will be read over a Florida radio station, WLRN. In addition, rents a mailing list that includes poets, writers, song writers, professional artists, sound recorders, and demo-tape organizations.

SOUTHWESTERN WRITERS NEWSLETTER, PO Box 331509, Ft. Worth TX 76163-1509. (817)346-6188. Fax (817)292-9525. Protestant. Tillie Read, pub. Quarterly newsletter; 8-12 pgs; circ. 45. Subscription $10. 100% freelance. Not copyrighted. Query; fax query OK. **PAYS IN COPIES** for one-time rts. Articles (5/yr). Responds in 4 wks. Accepts reprints. Sidebars OK. Guidelines; copy $2.50.

    Poetry: Accepts 10/yr. Free verse, haiku, light verse, traditional. Submit max. 3 poems.

    Fillers: Accepts 5/yr. Anecdotes, facts, ideas, newsbreaks, prose, quizzes, prayers, quotes, short humor, word puzzles.

*TEACHERS & WRITERS, 5 Union Square W, New York NY 10003. (212)691-6590. Ron Padgett, ed. On teaching creative and imaginative writing. Mag published 5 times/yr; circ 1,500-2,000. Query. **PAYS IN COPIES.** Articles 3,000-6,000 wds. Not in topical listings. Copy $2.50.

TICKLED BY THUNDER, 7385 - 129 St., Surrey BC V3W 7B8 Canada. Phone/fax (604)591-6095. E-mail: larry-lindner@mindlink.bc.ca. Larry Lindner, ed. For intermediate writers; fiction and poetry need not be about writing. Quarterly mag; 20 pgs; circ 500. Subscription $12 (or $10 US). 100% freelance. Complete ms/cover letter; e-mail query OK. Pays $2-5 (in Canadian or US stamps) on publication for 1st or one-time rts. Articles to 2,000 wds (4/yr); fiction to 2,000 wds (8-12/yr); book reviews 300 wds. Responds in 16 wks. Seasonal 4 mos ahead. Accepts simultaneous submissions & reprints (tell when/where appeared). Prefers disk. Sidebars OK. Guidelines; copy $1/9x12 SAE/2 US stamps or .90 CAN (unattached).

    Poetry: Accepts 12-24/yr. Free verse, haiku, light verse, traditional; to 40 lines. Submit max. 7 poems.

    Fillers: Anecdotes, ideas, short humor; to 100 wds.

    Contest: For fiction, articles and poetry. For subscribers only. Send SASE for guidelines.

    Tips: "Participate in contests. If writing a religious story, it must do more than push religious buttons. It must stand on its own and not be dragged down by the 'moral' at the end. Looking for articles about writing and writer's groups."

+TODAY'S $85,000 freelance WRITER (formerly **THE PROLIFIC freelanceR**), PO Box 554, Oradell NJ 07649. Phone/fax (201)262-3277. E-mail: BSKCom@ internexus.net. BSK Communications & Assoc. Brian Konradt, ed. Focuses on the business and marketing side of freelance writing. Bimonthly mag; 40 pgs; circ 3,000. Subscription $23.70. 90% freelance. Query/clips; phone/fax query OK. Pays .05-.10/wd on acceptance or publication for 1st rts. Articles 2,000 wds. Responds in 5 wks. Requires disk. Kill fee. Requires sidebars. Guidelines; copy $4.95.

Poetry: To 24 lines.

Filler: Prose, 50-150 wds; newsbreaks, 50-300 wds.

VIRGINIA CHRISTIAN WRITER, PO Box 12624, Roanoke VA 24027. Phone/fax (540)342-7511. E-mail: ccmbbr@worldnet.att.com. A division of Creative Christian Ministries. Betty Robertson, ed. To inform, encourage and unite writers in Virginia. Quarterly newsletter; 4 pgs; circ. 556. Subscription $4. Est. 1994. 25% freelance. Query; fax query OK. Pays $3-5 on acceptance for one-time or simultaneous rts. Not copyrighted. Articles & book reviews to 500 wds. Responds in 6 wks. Seasonal 6 mos ahead. Accepts simultaneous submissions & reprints. Prefers disk. No sidebars. Guidelines; copy $1/#10 SAE/2 stamps.

Fillers: Ideas.

Tips: "Short how-to articles needed. Use a creative approach."

*THE WRITE TOUCH, PO Box 695, Selah WA 98942. (509)966-3524. Tim Anderson, ed. For writers trying to get published. Monthly newsletter; 12 pgs; circ 40. Subscription $15/yr. Est. 1994. 100% freelance. Complete ms/cover letter. **PAYS 3 COPIES**, for one-time rts. Essays on various subjects (120/yr) & fiction for all ages (120/yr), 100-500 wds. Responds in 2-4 wks. Seasonal 2 mos ahead. Discourages simultaneous submissions & reprints. Disk OK. Guidelines; copy $1.

Poetry: Any type; 4-30 lines. Submit maximum 3 poems.

Fillers: Anecdotes, facts, ideas, prose, short humor; 15-50 wds.

THE WRITER, 120 Boylston St., Boston MA 02116-4615. Secular. Sylvia Burack, ed/pub. How-to for writers; lists religious markets in December. Monthly mag; 52 pgs; circ 50,000. 70% freelance. Complete ms/cover letter. Pays $100 on acceptance for 1st rts. Articles to 2,000 wds (60/yr). Responds in 2-3 wks. No disks. No sidebars. Copy $3. (Ads)

Poetry: Accepts poetry for critiques in "Poet to Poet" column; to 30 lines; no payment. No religious poetry. Submit max. 3 poems.

Columns/Departments: Buys 24+/yr. Rostrum (shorter pcs. on the craft of writing), 1,000 wds; Off the Cuff (somewhat more personal tone), 1,000-1,200 wds; $75.

Special Needs: How-to on the craft of writing only.

#WRITERS CONNECTION, PO Box 24770, San Jose CA 95154-4770. (408)554-2090. Fax (408)554-2099. Jan Stiles, ed. Nuts and bolts information on writing and publishing in all fields (except poetry). Monthly newsletter; circ 1,500. Subscription/membership $45. Also distributed electronically. 60% freelance. Complete ms; query/clips for profiles. Pays $25-75 on publication for 1st or reprint rts. Articles 800-2,200 wds (25-32/yr); book reviews, 200-300 wds (pays 2 copies). Responds in 9 wks. Seasonal 4 mos ahead. Accepts reprints. Guidelines; copy $3.

Fillers: Accepts 4-10/yr. Facts, newsbreaks, tips, resources; 50-350 wds.

Columns/Departments: Profiles (useful info/insights from professional editors/agents), 725-800 wds; Business & Technical Writing (hard info on how to write), 750-825 wds; $25-50.

Special Needs: In-depth articles on how to write or market your writing (technique). No religious slant or tone.

Tips: "Most open to short features or columns; shorter articles that offer specific, in-depth help for writers."

WRITER'S DIGEST, 1507 Dana Ave., Cincinnati OH 45207. (513)531-2222. Fax (513)531-1843. E-mail: WritersDig@juno.com. Secular/F & W Publications. Amanda Boyd, asst. ed. To inform, instruct or inspire the freelancer. Monthly mag; 76 pgs; circ 250,000. Subscription $27. 90% freelance. Query/clips; e-mail query OK. Pays .15-.30/wd on acceptance for 1st and reprint rts. Articles 750-3,000 wds (100/yr). Responds in 6-8 wks. Seasonal 6 mos ahead. Kill fee 20%. Prefers disk. Sidebars OK. Guidelines; copy $3.50 ($3.70 in OH). (Ads—Call Joan Wright, 800-234-0963)

> **Poetry:** Buys 10-15/yr. Light verse on writing; 2-20 lines; $10-50. Submit max. 8 poems.
>
> **Fillers:** Buys to 50/yr. Anecdotes & short humor on writing; 50-250 wds; .10-.15/wd.
>
> **Columns/Departments:** Buys 100-150/yr. The Writing Life (anecdotes about writing life & short profiles), 50-800 wds; Tip Sheet (short solutions to writer/business-related problems), 50-600 wds; Chronicle (1st-person narrative about writing life), 1,200-1,500 wds. Pays .10-.15/wd.
>
> **Contests:** Sponsors annual contest for articles, short stories, poetry and scripts. Also The National Self-Publishing Book Awards. Send SASE for rules.
>
> **Tips:** "Always in the market for technique pieces. Writing Life and Tip sheet items are great ways to break in."

WRITER'S EXCHANGE, Box 394, Society Hill SC 29593. E-mail: Eboone@ aol.com. Eugene Boone, ed. Features writings and small press markets for writers and poets. Quarterly mag; 32 pgs; circ 350. Subscription $12. 100% freelance. Complete ms/cover letter; e-mail query OK. **PAYS IN COPIES** for one-time rts. Articles 200-3,000 wds (30/yr). Responds in 2-3 wks. Seasonal 6-8 mos ahead. Accepts reprints (tell when/where appeared). Accepts disk. Sidebars OK. Guidelines/theme list; copy $3. (Ads)

> **Poetry:** Accepts 50-100/yr. Any type; 3-30 lines. Submit max. 8 poems.
>
> **Fillers:** Accepts 300/yr. Various; 10-750 wds.
>
> **Contest:** Poetry contest; send SASE for rules.

WRITER'S FORUM, Writer's Digest School, 1507 Dana Ave., Cincinnati OH 45209. (513)531-2222. Fax (513)531-1843. E-mail: writersdig@juno.com. F&W Publications. Amanda Boyd, ed. Writing techniques, marketing and inspiration for Writer's Digest correspondence school students. Quarterly newsletter; 16 pgs; circ 13,000. Subscription $10. 100% freelance. Complete ms/cover letter; e-mail query OK. Pays $10-25 on acceptance for reprint rts. Articles 750-1,500 wds (20/yr). Responds in 4-8 wks. Seasonal 4 mos ahead. Accepts reprints (tell when/where appeared). Accepts disk. Free guidelines/copy for #10 SAE/3 stamps.

> **Tips:** "A great market for reprints. How-to pieces geared toward beginning writers always stand a good chance. Articles must have a how-to slant; focus on writing technique."

WRITERS INFORMATION NETWORK (WIN), Box 11337, Bainbridge Island WA 98110. Phone/fax (206)842-9103. Professional Assn. of Christian Writers. Elaine Wright Colvin, ed. Bimonthly mag; 24 pgs; circ 1,000+. Subscription $29.95. 30% freelance. Complete ms/cover letter. Pays $10-50 (copies or subscription) on acceptance for 1st rts. Articles 50-300 wds; book reviews, 300 wds. Responds in 4-6 wks. Kill fee. Guidelines; copy $5/9x12 SAE/4 stamps.

Poetry: Any type.

Fillers: Anecdotes, facts, ideas, newsbreaks, quizzes, quotes, prayers, short humor; 50-300 wds; $10-50.

Columns/Departments: Buys 48/yr. Industry News, Market News, Word from the Warrior Bard, Bulletin Board, Computer Corner, Speakers Corner, Resources for Writers, and Our Readers Write; $10-25.

Tips: "Attend writer's conferences, C.B.A., and EPA, and report on what's happening in the industry. Most columns open."

*WRITER'S INK, PO Box 93156, Henderson NV 89009-3156. (800)974-8465. Panabaker Publications. Darla R. Panabaker, ed. Supplies writers with information on writing and selling. Monthly newsletter; 12 pgs; circ. 100. Subscription $24. Est. 1995. 90-95% freelance. Query or complete ms. **PAYS IN COPIES** for 1st, one-time or simultaneous rts. Articles 50-1,000 wds (200/yr); book reviews, 500 wds. Responds within 4 wks. Seasonal 3-6 mos ahead. Accepts simultaneous submissions & reprints. Sidebars OK. Guidelines; copy for 9x12 SAE/2 stamps.

Poetry: All types; on writing topics; to 50 lines. Send any number.

Fillers: Ideas, newsbreaks, quizzes, quotes; to 50 wds.

Columns/Departments: Looking for freelancers to write columns. Topics and subject matter open. Please inquire.

Contest: 1996 Poetry Competition. $100 grand prize. Deadline November 15. Send SASE for rules.

Tips: "Send article with letter describing your previous experience. All areas open. We use a different writer for each cover article. "

#WRITER'S JOURNAL, PO Box 25376, St. Paul MN 55125-0376. (612)730-4280. Fax (612)730-4356. Secular. Valerie Hockert, ed. Bimonthly journal; circ 52,000. 40% freelance. Complete ms. Pays to $50, 60 days after publication, for 1st rts. Articles 700-1,000 wds (30-40/yr). Responds in 4-6 wks. Seasonal 6 mos ahead. Accepts simultaneous query. Not in topical listings. Guidelines; copy $4.

Poetry: Esther M. Leiper. Buys 20-30/yr. All types; to 25 lines; .25/line. Submit max. 5 poems.

Contest: Runs 2 poetry contests each year, spring and fall.

*WRITER'S LIFELINE, Box 1641, Cornwall ON K6H 5V6 Canada. (613)932-2135. Stephen Gill, mng. ed. For professional freelancers and beginning writers. Bimonthly mag; 16-35 pgs; circ 1,500. Needs articles of interest to writers, news items of national and international interest, letters to the editor, poetry, interviews. Needs book reviewers; **PAYS IN BOOK REVIEWED & COPIES**. Not in topical listings.

+WRITER'S NEWS, 2130 Sunset Dr. #47, Vista CA 92083. Phone/fax (619)941-9293. Elizabeth Klungness, ed. Monthly newsletter; 10 pgs. Subscription $15. 20% freelance. Query; phone/fax query OK. **PAYS IN COPIES** for 1st rts. Not copyrighted. Articles to 600 wds (24/yr). Responds in 2 wks. Seasonal 2 mos ahead. Accepts simultaneous submissions & reprints (tell when/where appeared). No disk. No sidebars. Guidelines; copy for #10 SAE/2 stamps.

Fillers: Writing-related jokes and fillers.

Tips: "We encourage writers to tell us their experiences with editors, agents, and publishers, and to offer craft suggestions."

*THE WRITER'S NOOK NEWS, 38114 3rd St. #181, Willoughby OH 44094-6140. (216)953-9292. Fax (216)354-6403. Secular. Eugene Ortiz, ed./pub. Dedicated to giving freelance writers specific information for their immediate practical use in getting published and staying published. Quarterly newsletter; circ 2,000. Subscription $18. 100% freelance. Complete ms. Pays .06/wd on acceptance for 1st rts. Not copyrighted. Articles 100-400 wds (80/yr); book reviews 50-100 wds (.06/wd). Responds in 26 wks. Guidelines; copy $5.

Fillers: Buys 20/yr. Facts, newsbreaks; 20-100 wds.

Tips: "Most open to tips and suggestions about the process of writing and publishing."

*WRITER'S RESOURCE NETWORK, Box 940335, Maitland FL 32794. (407)260-5150. Jeffrey Atwood, ed. News and resources for writers and editors. Bimonthly newsletter; circ 1,500. 30% freelance. Complete ms/cover letter. Pays .03/wd on publication for all rts. Articles 350 wds (4/yr). Responds in 2-4 wks. Seasonal 6 mos ahead. Accepts simultaneous submissions & reprints. Guidelines/theme list; free copy.

Poetry: Buys 2/yr. Haiku, light verse, traditional; 4-20 lines; .03/wd. Submit max. 5 poems.

Fillers: Accepts 10-15/yr. Anecdotes, cartoons ($1), facts, newsbreaks; 10-100 wds.

Tips: "Most open to short techniques/how-tos on how you overcame a specific problem to get published; first-person articles."

WRITER'S WORLD, 204 E. 19th St., Big Stone Gap VA 24219. (540)523-0830. Fax (540)523-5757. Mar-Jon Publications. Gainelle Murray, ed. Secular magazine for writers with an underlying religious slant. Bimonthly mag; 24 pgs; circ 3,600. Subscription $15. 100% freelance. Complete ms/cover letter. **PAYS 2 COPIES** for one-time rts. Articles (90-100/yr) 900-1,500 wds; fiction (6/yr)1,000-1,900 wds. Responds in 5 wks. Seasonal 6 mos ahead. Accepts simultaneous submissions & reprints (tell when/where appeared). No disk. Sidebars OK. Prefers KJV. Guidelines; copy $4.50/9x12 SAE/4 stamps.

Poetry: Submit to Diane L. Krueger, 17 Oswego Ave., Rockaway NJ 07866. Accepts 150-200/yr. Free verse, light verse, traditional, humorous (on writing); 4-16 lines. Submit max. 5 poems. Cash payment for cover poetry.

Fillers: Accepts 20-25/yr. Anecdotes, cartoons, prose, quotes, short humor (on writing life), writing tips; 100-400 wds.

Columns/Departments: Accepts 6/yr. Yesterday's Scrapbook (nostalgia), 900-1,000 wds; Fiction Feature, 1,500-2,000 wds; Poets & Poetry, 4-16 lines; Interview/Profile (established writers), 900-1,000 wds.

Tips: "Most open to writing-related articles and poetry that makes the reader laugh or cry. Would like to see articles on every aspect of the business of writing."

+WRITING & SURFING, The Writer's & Journalist's Guide to Making the Most Out of Online Services, 223 Wall St., Huntington NY 11743-2060. (516)421-1682. E-mail: SurfWrite@aol.com. Write Way Communications. Debra A. Velsmid, ed. Monthly newsletter; 8 pgs. Subscription $18. Est. 1996. Query or complete ms. **PAYS 2 COPIES.** Articles 500 wds. Guidelines; copy $1.50, free 4-pg intro issue.

*WRITING RIGHT NEWSLETTER, Box 35132, Elmwood Park IL 60635. (708)453-5023. John Biardo, ed. Helping writers and poets with their writing career. Monthly newsletter; circ 500. 50% freelance. Complete ms (query for fiction). **PAYS IN COPIES,** for one-time rts. Articles 600-1,000 wds (50/yr); fiction 500-700 wds (10/yr); book reviews 600 wds. Responds in 2-4 wks. Accepts reprints. Guidelines; copy $4.

Fillers: Accepts 10/yr. Ideas, newsbreaks; 200-300 wds.

Tips: "Most open to writer's tips that have worked for you."

MARKET ANALYSIS

PERIODICALS IN ORDER BY LARGEST CIRCULATION

ADULT/GENERAL
Guideposts 3,900,000
Focus on the Family
2,100,000
Decision 1,700,000
Columbia 1,500,000
The Lutheran 800,000
Plus 600,000
Home Life 560,000
Presbyterian Layman 520,000
Catholic Digest 500,000+
Marion Helpers 500,000
Oblates 500,000
Mature Living 350,000
St. Anthony Messenger
340,100
Liguorian 340,000
Miraculous Medal 340,000
Lutheran Witness 325,000
Messenger of St. Anthony
300,000
New Man 300,000
War Cry 300,000
American Bible Society
Record 275,000
Anglican Journal 272,000
Liberty 250,000
Power for Living 250,000
Pentecostal Evangel 245,000
Signs of the Times 245,000
Christian Reader 225,000
National Review 225,000
Charisma & Christian Life
220,000
Christian Parenting Today
200,000
Voice (CA) 200,000
Aspire 180,000
Christianity Today 180,000
Episcopal Life 180,000
Ideals 180,000
Living (magazine) 160,000
Standard 160,000
Lutheran Digest 155,000
The Family Digest 150,000
Celebrate Life 145,000
Live 130,000

Unit Church Observer 130,000
Lutheran Journal 120,000
Our Sunday Visitor 120,000
ParentLife 115,000
The Lookout 105,000
Presbyterian Survey 105,000
The Plain Truth 102,000
Catholic Forester 100,000
Changes 100,000
Discipleship Journal 100,000
Foursquare World Advance
100,000
Kaleidoscope 100,000
Moody 100,000
Release Ink 100,000
Sunday Digest 100,000
Christian Computing 90,000
Living (tabloid) 90,000
Total Health 90,000
Message 80-90,000
Lutheran Layman 80,000
Herald of Holiness 76,000
Something Better News
75,000
Spirit of Revival 74,000
Single Parent Family 72,000
Christian History 70,000
Mature Years 70,000
Vision (CA) 70,000
Christian Single 67,000
alive now! 65,000
Good News 65,000
Indian Life 62,000
Catholic Answer 60,000
Christian Standard 59,000
Marriage Partnership 59,000
Presbyterian Record 59,000
Christian Home & School
58,000
Conquest 55,000
InterVarsity 55,000
Northwestern Lutheran 55,000
Physician 55,000
Church of God Evangel
50,000
Dallas/Ft Worth Heritage
50,000

Good News Journal 50,000
Gospel Today 50,000
Pursuit 50,000
Sports Spectrum 50,000
Today's Christian Senior
50,000
Vibrant Life 50,000
Annals of St. Anne 45,000
Living with Teenagers 45,000
Seek 45,000
Catholic Parent 40,000
Christian Research Journal
40,000
Christmas 40,000
A Positive Approach 40,000
Stand Firm 40,000
Weavings 40,000
America 36,000
Highway News 35,000
U.S. Catholic 35,000
Church & State 33,000
Cathedral Age 32,000
The Banner 30,000
Catholic Twin Circle 30,000
Cornerstone 30,000
Evangelical Beacon 30,000
Lifeglow 30,000
Progress 30,000
Rutherford 30,000
At Ease 28,000
Christian Ranchman 28,000
Indian Life 28,000
Common Boundary 26,000
First Things 26,000
African-American Heritage
25,000
Catholic Heritage 25,000
Interim 25,000
Providence 25,000
United Voice 25,000
Sojourners 24,000
Pentecostal Testimony 23,500
Light and Life 23,000
Canada Lutheran 23,000
Life Gate 23,000
Covenant Companion 22,000
The Family Journal 22,000

Evangel 22,000
Homeschooling Today 21,000
B.C. Catholic 20,000
Catholic Peace Voice 20,000
The Evangel 20,000
God's Revivalist 20,000
New Covenant 20,000
Role Model 20,000
St. Joseph's Messenger 20,000
Commonweal 19,000
Texas Messenger 18,100
Faith Today 18,000
Experiencing God 17,000
The Shantyman 17,000
The Door 16,000
Messenger/Sacred Heart 16,000
AXIOS 15,670
Christian Edge 15,000
Mennonite Brethren Herald 15,000
Network 15,000
Poet's Park 15,000
SCP Journal 15,000
Wesleyan Advocate 15,000
Island Christian Herald 14,000
New Oxford Review 14,000
Purpose 13,800
Bible Advocate 13,500
Church Advocate 13,000
Emphasis on Faith & Living 13,000
Great Plains 12,500
New Horizons 12,000
Table Talk 12,000
Today's Christian Doctor 12,000
Presbyterian Outlook 11,700
Canadian Baptist 11,000
CBA Frontline 11,000
Spiritual Life 11,000
The Standard 11,000
Evangelical Friend 10,500
Review for Religious 10,200
Sharing 10,000+
Awareness Tennessee 10,000
Baptist Informer 10,000
Celebration (SDA) 10,000
Disciple's Journal 10,000
Good News Reporter 10,000
Immaculate Heart Messenger 10,000
Living Light News 10,000
The Plowman 10,000
Prism 10,000
Smart Dads 10,000
This Rock 10,000
Today's Single 10,000

The Vision 10,000
The Christian Leader 9,800
Montana Catholic 9,200
Celebration (Catholic) 9,000
Christian Retailing 9,000
Friends Journal 9,000
Journal of Christian Nursing 9,000
Living Church 9,000
Salt of the Earth 9,000
Prairie Messenger 8,600
Our Family 8,500
Religious Broadcasting 8,500
Star of Zion 8,000+
CBA Marketplace 8,000
Command 8,000
The Family 8,000
The Mennonite 8,000
Atlantic Baptist 7,500
Plough 7,500
Brethren Evangelist 7,325
The Gem 7,100
Companions 7,000
Hallelujah! (FL) 7,000
The Bible Today 7,000
Master's Community 7,000
MN Christian Chronicle 7,000
MovieGuide 7,000
Alive! 6,000
Christian Courier (CAN) 6,000
Fellowship in Prayer 6,000
Impact 6,000
John Milton 5,355
Bread of Life 5,200
Contact 5,200
AGAIN 5,000
Christianity & the Arts 5,000
Christian Living 5,000
Companion 5,000
The Evangelical Advocate 5,000
Green Cross 5,000
Hallelujah! 5,000
Healing Inn 5,000
Ministry Today 5,000
A New Heart 5,000
New Thought Journal 5,000
Parent Paper, The 5,000
Queen of All Hearts 5,000
The Lutheran Ambassador 4,800
Cresset 4,700
Christian Civic League/ME 4,600
Social Justice Review 4,600
Chesapeake Citizen 4,500
Evangelical Visitor 4,500

Home Times 4,500
Christian Renewal 4,300
Message/Open Bible 4,100
ADVOCATE 4,000
Evangelical Baptist 4,000
The Witness 4,000
Fellowship Today 3,900
The Kansas Christian 3,800
Compass 3,700
Cross Currents 3,500
Fidelity 3,500
Servant Life 3,500
Way of St. Francis 3,500
Perspectives on Science 3,300
Advent Christian Witness 3,200
Catholilc Insight 3,100
Chrysalis Reader 3,000
Feelings Quarterly 3,000
Harvest Times 3,000
North American Voice 3,000
Perspectives 3,000
Quiet Revolution 3,000
Religious Education 3,000
Rural Landscapes 3,000
The Witness 3,000
Mennonite Historian 2,600
Church Herald/Holiness Banner 2,500
The Inspirer 2,500
The Messenger (NC) 2,500
Railroad Evangelist 2,500
Touchstone 2,500
Gospel Tidings 2,100
Christian Media 2-6,000
Apocalypse Chronicles 2-3,000
Answers in Action 2,000
Baptist History & Heritage 2,000
Christian Chronicle 2,000
Christian Observer 2,000
Christian Social Action 2,000
Fellowship Link 2,000
It's Your Choice 2,000
Journal/Church & State 1,700
Encourager Provider 1,600
Christian Arts Review 1,500
Jewel Among Jewels 1,500
Pentecostal Homelife 1,500
Comments From the Friends 1,200
The New Trumpet 1,200
Bible Reflections 1,100
Canadian Catholic Review 1,000
Connecting Point 1,000
Dovetail 1,000

Head to Head 1,000
Methodist History 1,000
No-Debt Living 1,000
Pourastan 1,000
Evangelism 900
Prayerworks 600
Poetry Forum Short Stories
   500+
Broken Streets 500
Hearing Hearts 500
St. Willibrord Journal 500
The Voice 500
Silver Wings 450
Burning Light 400
Explorer 300+
Baptist Beacon 300
Lighthouse Fiction 300
The Salt & The Light 300
Time of Singing 300
Manna 250
Remembrance 250
Today's Family Matters 250
Dreams & Visions 200
Family Network 150
Christian Information Assoc.
   130
Pegasus Review 125
TEAK Roundup 120
Dusk & Dawn 100
Fatted Calf Forum 100
Ratio 100
Upsouth 75

CHILDREN

God's World Today 301,000
Guideposts for Kids 200,000+
Bible-in-Life Pix 200,000
Venture 140,000
R-A-D-A-R 112,000
FOF Clubhouse 100,000
Pockets 100,000
High Adventure 86,000
FOF Clubhouse Jr. 80,000
Crusader (TN) 60,000
Junior Trails 50,000
Our Little Friend 45-50,000
Courage 40,000
Power & Light 40,000
Wonder Time 40,000
Primary Treasure 35,000
GUIDE 33,000
Together Time 19,000
Venture 18,000
Touch 14,000
My Friend 12,000
Crusader (MI) 12,300
BREAD for God's Children
   10,000

Nature Friend 10,000
CLUBHOUSE 8,000
Story Friends 7,000
On the Line 6,500
Partners 5,900
Story Mates 5,200
Skipping Stones 3,000
Discovery 2,000
Listen 18,000

CHRISTIAN EDUCATION/LIBRARY

GROUP 57,000
Children's Ministry 50,000
Parish Teacher 50,000
Today's Catholic Teacher
   50,000
Catechist 45,700
Religion Teacher's Journal
   40,000
Teachers in Focus 35,000
Church Media Library 30,000
Perspective 27,000
CE Counselor 22,500
Evangelizing Today's Child
   20,000
Group's Jr. High Ministry
   20,000
Lollipops 20,000
Shining Star 20,000
Memos 14,100
Teachers Interaction 14,000
CE Leadership 10,000
Leader/Church School Today
   10,000
Journal/Adventist Ed 7,500
Kids' Stuff 7,500
CE Connection 6,600
Resource 6,000
Vision (CA) 6,000
Church Educator 5,000
Christian Educator's Journal
   4,200
Leader 3,500
The Youth Leader 2,800
Church & Synagogue Librar-
   ies 2,500
Insight into CE 2,200
Team 2,000
Changing Lives 1,800
Caravan 1,500
CE Connection Communique
   1,350
Christian Library Journal
   1,000
Librarian's World 550
Christian Librarian 500

MISSIONS

Childlife 275,000
Partners 198,000
Great Commission Handbook
   170,000
Compassion 160,000
Catholic Near East 100,000
Save Our World 97,000
Worldwide Challenge 90,000
World Vision 84,000
Quiet Hour Echoes 80,000
Mission Today 60,000
World Christian 40,000
American Horizon 36,000
P.I.M.E. World 31,000
New World Outlook 30,000
Oblate World 25,000
Heartbeat 20,000
Latin America Evangelist
   17,000
Message of the Cross 10,000
PFI World Report 7,000
World Mission People 7,000
Leaders for Today 6,500
Wherever 6,000
Missiology 2,000
Urban Mission 1,300
Areopagus 1,000
Intl. Journal/Frontier 600
East-West Church 430

MUSIC

Release 200,000
Music Makers 105,000
CCM Magazine 85,000
Glory Songs 85,000
Young Musicians 85,000
Music Time 60,000
7 Ball 50,000
Gospel Music Exclusive
   40,000
Church Pianist 35,000
Music Leader 35,000
Senior Musician 32,000
Church Musician 16,000
Creator 5,500
Gospel Industry Today 3,500
The Hymn 3,000
Tradition 2,500
Christian Composer 2,000-
   6,000
Christian Country 300-1,200

NEWSPAPERS

United Methodist Reporter
   450,000
Christian American 400,000
Inside Journal 371,000

Anglican Journal 272,000
Episcopal Life 170,000
Catholic New York 130,000
Our Sunday Visitor 125,000
The Alabama Baptist 117,000
Pulpit Helps 105,000
Christian Chronicle 100,000
Arlington Catholic Herald
  53,000
Good News Journal 50,000
Catholic Courier 48,000
National Catholic Reporter
  48,000
Good News Etc. 40,000
Beacon Christian News
  35,000
Kansas City Christian 35,000
Catholic Twin Circle 30,000
Catholic Telegraph 27,000
NW Christian Journal 27,000
Christian Crusade 25,000
Discovery 25,000
The Interim 25,000
The Revelation Post 15,000-
  45,000
Catholic Sentinel 15,000
Christian Focus 15,000
Expression Christian Newspa-
  per 15,000
Issues & Answers (teen)
  15,000
Messenger (KY) 15,000
Christian Advocate 14,000
Interchange 12,600
Mennonite Reporter 11,000
Mennonite Weekly Review
  11,000
Christian Courier (WI) 10,000
Disciple's Journal 10,000
Today's Single 10,000
Montana Catholic 8,300
Arkansas Catholic 7,000
Minnesota Chr. Chronicle
  6,000
Christian Courier (Canada)
  5,000
Maranatha 5,000
Christian Renewal 4,500
Lead 3,600
Inland NW Christian 2,500
Probe 1,800
Christian Edge 1,500

PASTORS/LEADERS
Your Church 150,000
Pulpit Helps 105,000
Leadership Journal 69,000
Eucharistic Minister 50,000

Sunday School Leader 50,000
Worship Leader 43,000
Circuit Rider 42,000
Church Bytes 40,000
Christian Century 33,000
Enrichment 32,000
Today's Christian Preacher
  25,000
Parish Liturgy 22,000
Christian Counseling Today
  20,000
Lutheran Partners 20,000
Modern Liturgy 20,000
Preacher's Magazine 18,000
Christian Recreation 17,000
Ministry 16,000
Homiletic/Pastoral Review
  15,000
Proclaim 15,000
Today's Parish 14,800
Pastor's Family 14,000
Youthworker 13,200
Theology Today 13,000
Church Administration 12,000
Jour/Pastoral Care 12,000
Voice of the Vineyard 12,000
Cell Church 11,000
Christian Sentinel 10,000
Clergy Journal 10,000
Preaching 10,000
Resource 10,000
WCA Monthly 10,000
Review for Religious 9,500
Celebration 9,000
Ecumenical Trends 9,000
The Priest 8,200
Brigade Leader 8,000
Faith & Renewal 8,000
Student Leadership Journal
  8,000
Journal/Christian Camping
  7,000
Chicago Studies 6,100
Christian Ministry 6,000
Journal/Christian Camping
  6,000
Pastor's Tax & Money 6,000
PW Religion BookLine 6,000
Catechumenate 5,600
Baptist Leader 5,000
Church Growth Network
  5,000
Single Adult Min Jour 5,000
Technologies/Worship 5,000
Cross Currents 4,500
Emmanuel 4,500
The Preacher 4,000
Reformed Worship 3,700

Lutheran Forum 3,200
Word & World 3,100
National Drama Service 3,000
ArtPlus 3,000
Sermon Notes 3,000
Christian Management Report
  2,600
Environment & Art 2,500
Liturgy 2,500
Networks 1,700
Quarterly Review 1,500
Church Worship 1,200
Jour/Biblical Ethics 1,200
Jour/Christian Healing 1,200
Five Stones 1,000+
Diaconalogue 1,000
Evangelism 800
Ivy Jungle Report 800
Diocesan Dialogue 750
Cell Life 300+
Jour/Amer Soc/Chur Growth
  200

TEEN/YOUNG ADULT
Brio 160,000
On Course 160,000
Visions 140,000
The Rock 125,000
Campus Life 100,000
Breakaway 90,000
I.D. 75,000
Today's Christian Teen 75,000
Teen Missions Launch Pad
  65,000
Devo'Zine 58,000
Sharing the Victory 55,000
Teen Life 55,000
Young Salvationist 48,000
Listen 40,000
Youth 97 40,000
Cross Walk 35,000
Straight 35,000
You! 35,000
Spirit 30,000
Take Five 30,000
Youth Update 30,000
Young & Alive 26,000
Teen Quest 25,000
Challenge (TN) 24,000
Insight 20,000
Certainty 18,000
Challenge 16,000
Teenage Christian 11,600
Caleb Issues & Answers
  10,000
Transcend 10,000
Youth Focus 10,000
Student Leadership 8,500

Young Adult Today 7,500
Teens on Target 7,000
With 6,100
The Conqueror 6,000
Youth Challenge 5,500
Pathways 3,000
Young Christian 1,500

WOMEN
Today's Christian Woman
   309,000
Lutheran Woman Today
   230,000
Lutheran Woman's Quarterly
   200,000
Virtue 115,000
Journey 100,000
Horizons 40,000
Woman's Touch 18,000+
Women of Spirit 17,000
Welcome Home 15,000
CoLaborer 11,000
Church Woman 10,000
Conscience 10,000
Journal/Women's Ministries
   10,000
Joyful Woman 8,350
Unique 7,500

Esprit 6,580
Link & Visitor 4,500
Helping Hand 4,000
Sisters Today 3,500
Wesleyan Woman 3,500
Women Alive 3,500
Probe 3,000
Just Between Us 2,700
Proverbs 31 Homemaker 2,000
Tea and Sunshine 500
Salt & Light 300
Anna's Journal 45

WRITERS
Writer's Digest 250,000
Writer's Journal 52,000
The Writer 50,000
Writer's Forum (OH) 13,000
Inklings 10,000
Christian Communicator
   4,000
Writer's World 3,600
Byline 3,000+
Today's $85,000 Freelance
   Writer 3,000
Housewife-Writers Forum
   2,000
Writer's Nook News 2,000

Teachers & Writers 1,500-
   2,000
Writers Connection 1,500
Writer's Lifeline 1,500
Writer's Resource Network
   1,500
Cross & Quill 1,000+
Writers Information Network
   1,000+
New Writing 1,000
Once Upon a Time 1,000
Virginia Christian Writer 565
Chips off Writer's Block 500+
Tickled By Thunder 500
Writing Right Newsletter 500
Christian Response 400
Canadian Writer's Journal 350
Writer's Exchange 350
Omnific 300+
Felicity 200+
My Legacy 200+
Exchange 200
Gotta Write Network 200
The Poetry Connection 200
Writer's Ink 100
Northwest Christian Author 80
Southwestern Writers 45
The Write Touch 40

PERIODICAL TOPICS IN ORDER OF POPULARITY

NOTE: Following is a list of topics in order by popularity. To find the list of publishers interested in each of these topics, go to the Topical Listings for periodicals and find the topic you are interested in. The numbers indicate how many periodical editors said they were interested in seeing something of that type or topic. There are 310 photography markets this year. (*—new topics this year)

1. Christian Living 264
2. Family Life 263
3. Personal Experience 261
4. Poetry 260
5. Current/Social Issues 259
6. Inspirational 246
7. Prayer 243
8. Interviews/Profiles 238
9. Holiday/Seasonal 231
10. Evangelism/Witnessing 226
11. Spirituality 211
12. Humor 201
13. Marriage 186
14. True Stories 186
15. Book Reviews 180
16. How-To 175
17. Worship 173
18. Discipleship 167
19. Relationships 166
20. Church Outreach 163

21. Devotions/Meditations 162
22. Parenting 160
23. Controversial Issues 157
24. Fillers: Cartoons 157
25. Theological 147
26. Missions 146
27. Bible Studies 145
28. Christian Education 145
29. World Issues 142
30. Women's Issues 138
31. Ethics 137
32. Leadership 136
33. Historical 132
34. Short Story: Adult/Religious 127
35. Health 126
36. Think Pieces 125
37. Essays 117
38. Youth Issues 117
39. Fillers: Anecdotes 116

40. Environmental 115
41. Fillers: Short Humor 115
42. Men's Issues 115
43. Opinion Pieces 115
44. Religious Freedom 114
45. Ethnic/Cultural 113
46. Money Management 112
47. Celebrity Pieces 110
48. Salvation Testimonies 107
49. Senior Adult Issues 105
50. Book Excerpts 104
51. Divorce 101
52. Doctrinal 100
53. Short Story: Humorous 100
54. Singles Issues 98
55. Healing 94
56. Short Story: Contemporary 93
57. Stewardship 90
58. Short Story: Biblical 88

59. Fillers: Facts 87
60. Fillers: Ideas 87
61. Sports/Recreation 86
62. Cults/Occult 84
63. Social Justice 84
64. Short Story: Parables 81
65. Liturgical 79
66. Political 79
67. Economics 78
68. Home Schooling 78
69. Miracles 77
70. Music Reviews 76
71. Short Story: Adventure 74
72. Church Growth 73
73. Christian Business 73
74. Fillers: Word Puzzles 71
75. Church Management 69
76. Travel 64
77. *Church Life 63
78. Fillers: Newsbreaks 62
79. Spiritual Warfare 62

80. Fillers: Quizzes 60
81. Fillers: Quotes 60
82. Nature 58
83. How-To Activities 57
84. Short Story: Allegory 57
85. Short Story: Historical 57
86. Psychology 56
87. Short Story: Teen/Yg Adult 56
88. Fillers: Prose 55
89. Fillers: Games 54
90. Fillers: Prayers 54
91. Fillers: Jokes 53
92. *Death/Dying 52
93. Food/Recipes 52
94. Short Story: Juvenile 51
95. Prophecy 48
96. Sociology 48
97. Short Story: Mystery 44
98. Science 42
99. Sermons 42

100. Creation Science 39
101. *Self-Help 36
102. Short Story: Fantasy 36
103. Short Story: Literary 36
104. Short Story: Frontier 35
105. Short Story: Plays 28
106. Short Story: Romance 28
107. *Video Review 28
108. Fillers: Party Ideas 25
109. *Writing How-to 24
110. Short Story: Science Fiction 23
111. Short Story: Skits 21
112. Puppet Plays 17
113. *Short Story: Ethnic 15
114. Short Story: Mystery/ Romance 15
115. Short Story: Historical/ Romance 14
116. Short Story: Frontier/ Romance 13

Comments:

If you are a short story writer, the biggest market is for adult fiction (127 markets—down 4 from last year), then teen, holding second place (56 markets—2 more than last year), then juvenile (51 markets—2 more than last year). The most popular genres (in order) are Humorous, Contemporary, Biblical, Parables, Adventure, Allegory, and Historical. Compared to last year, Parables moved ahead of Adventure and Allegory moved ahead of Historical. The least popular are still the genre romances.

Although the market for poetry seems to be leveling off (the number of markets dropped by one this year, and it went from third most popular to fourth), you poets still have 260 markets and the potential for even more sales than in past years. The total number of poems expected to be bought or accepted by those markets is about 7,450—1,750 more than last year. Although there are again more book markets for poetry this year than ever before, the serious poet should pursue the periodical markets and can certainly sell regularly if care is taken to target poetry to fit the needs of the specific markets.

This year the same topics are in the top 11, except for Humor which dropped out of it, and Evangelism/Witnessing that moved into it. There was some shifting around, however, with Christian Living moving from 5th to 1st, Personal Experience and Prayer each moved up one place, and Current/Social Issues dropped three places and Poetry two places. In fiction, Contemporary, Biblical, Parables, Plays & Skits went up some; Mystery, Humorous, Adventure, Allegory and Historical went down; and the others stayed about the same. The biggest drop was in Historical which dropped 8 places in the ratings; the biggest gain in Biblical which moved up 5 places.

Following is a list of topics that either increased or decreased in demand since last year. The number following the topic indicates how many positions that particular topic moved up or down in the ratings. An asterisk (*) before a topic indicates that this is at least the second year in a row that it has increased or decreased.

DECREASED IN INTEREST:

Youth Issues—down 19
Christian Education— down 12
Home Schooling—down 11
Women's Issues—down 9

Theological—down 8
*Singles Issues—down 8
*Short Story: Historical— down 8
*Psychology—down 8
Miracles—down 7

Short Story: Mystery— down 7
Short Story: Humorous— down 6
Political—down 6
Fillers: Quotes—down 6

*Fillers: Prose—down 6
Senior Adult Issues—down 5
*Sociology—down 5

INCREASED IN INTEREST:
Church Growth—up 21
*Ethnic/Cultural—up 21
Spiritual Warfare—up 19

Essays—up 16
Church Management—up 15
Evangelism/Witnessing—
    up 13
Men's Issues—up 12
Fillers: Short Humor—up 11
How-To Activities—up 11
Sports/Recreation—up 10

Travel—up 10
*Discipleship—up 9
Creation Science—up 9
*Music Reviews—up 8
Liturgical—up 7
*Stewardship—up 7

SUMMARY OF INFORMATION ON CHRISTIAN PERIODICAL PUBLISHERS FOUND IN THE ALPHABETICAL LISTINGS

NOTE: *The following numbers are based on the maximum total estimate for each periodical. For example, if they gave a range of 4-6, the average was based on the higher number, 6. These figures were all calculated from those periodicals that reported information in each category.*

WANTS QUERY OR COMPLETE MANUSCRIPT:
Of those periodicals that indicated a preference, 45% will accept a complete manuscript (down 11% from last year), and 34% require or will accept a query (down 10% from last year). Thirteen percent of the combined group will accept either (up 1% from last year).

ACCEPTS PHONE QUERY:
This year, 168 periodical publishers are accepting phone queries—down from 170 last year. It is suggested that you reserve phone queries for timely material that won't wait for the regular mailed query. If you phone in a query, be sure you have your idea well thought out and can present it succinctly and articulately.

ACCEPTS FAX QUERY:
More and more publishers have fax numbers and a good many are willing (and even prefer) to accept fax queries. Last year, over 27% of all the periodical publishers accepted fax queries. This year, 214 publishers (42%) will accept them. Since a fax query will not have an SASE, it is suggested that you make fax queries only if you have your own fax machine to accept their response.

ACCEPTS E-MAIL QUERY:
This is only the second year we have asked about E-mail queries, and as predicted last year, the number of publishers with e-mail addresses has jumped dramatically. Last year only 52 publishers (8%) were open to receiving messages or submissions by e-mail. This year 270 publications have e-mail, and 135 publishers (50% of those) are open to e-mail queries.

SUBMISSIONS ON DISK:
Of the 298 periodicals that responded to the question about whether or not they accepted, preferred, or required submissions on disk, 83 (28%) said they accepted disks, 142 (47%) preferred disks, only 38 (13%) required disk, and 37 (12%) do not want disks.

PAYS ON ACCEPTANCE OR PUBLICATION:
Forty-three and one-half percent of the publishers pay on acceptance (down $\frac{1}{2}$% from last year), while 56% pay on publication.

PERCENTAGE OF FREELANCE:
Most of the publishers responded to the question about how much freelance material they use. The average indicates that 54% of material used is from freelancers (up 1% from last year). As to the question of whether the amount of freelance used is going up or down, of those who responded this year, 43 % are using the same amount of freelance material, 30% are using less, and 26 % are using more than last year (down 11%).

CIRCULATION:
In dividing the list of periodicals into three groups, according to size of circulation, the list comes out as follows: Publications with a circulation of 100,000 or more (up to 3,900,000), 14% (13.6% last year); publications with circulations between 50,000 and 100,000, only 10% (9.6% last year); the remaining 76% have circulations of 50,000 or less. If we break that last group into three more groups by circulation, we come out with 9% of those from 33,000-50,000 (same as last year); 16% from 17,000-32,000 (14% last year); and the remaining 75% with less than 17,000. That means that over 57% of all the periodicals that reported their circulation are at a circulation of 17,000 or less.

Looking at just those periodicals that completed questionnaires this year and indicated their circulation, for 27% their circulation went up (down 10%), for 42% their circulation went down (an increase of 9%), and the remaining 31% stayed the same.

RESPONSE TIME:
Although according to the 554 publishers who indicated response time, the average response has dropped below $7\frac{1}{4}$ weeks, those who are writing and submitting regularly generally believe that most publishers are taking longer than they used to to respond to submissions.

REPRINTS:
Just under 55% of the periodicals reporting accept reprints, that's over 1% less than last year. Although in the past it has not been necessary to tell a publisher where a piece has been published previously, that seems to be changing. Most Christian publishers are now wanting a tear sheet of the original publication and a cover letter telling when and where it appeared originally. This year the listings indicate if a publisher wants to know when and where a piece has appeared previously. They are also paying less for reprints than for original material.

PREFERRED BIBLE VERSION:
Again this year, the most preferred Bible version is the NIV, the preference of 47% of the publishers (down 5% from last year). Other preferred versions are the KJV with 21%, the New Revised Standard Version at 16%, the New American Standard with 5%, NAB with 5% and the NKJV and RSV with 2 % each. The NIV seems a good choice for those that didn't indicate a preference, although the more conservative groups seem to favor the KJV.

PERIODICALS THAT HAVE CHANGED NAMES OR CEASED PUBLICATION

Acts 29 (CO/bad address)
Advance—See Enrichment
All About Issues—See Cele-
   brate Life
Attention Please! (WA)
The Beacon (FL)—bad
   address
Beacon Christian News (NY)
The Bethany Choice (MI)
Better Tomorrow, A
Caregiver's Connection (VA)
Caring Connection (CO)
Choralation (IN)
Christian Author (IL)
Christianity & Crisis (NY)
Christian Singles
Christian Vision (Canada)
Church Business (Canada)
Church Recreation—See
   Christian Recreation
Church Teachers—See
   Church Educator

CLASS (NY - bad address)
The Communicator (OR)
Congregational Journal (CA)
Connection (CA/UT)
Contempo (AL)
Creation Social Science (KS)
Critic, The (IL)
Crystal Rainbow (FL)
Dads Only—See Smart Dads
Daughters of Sarah (IL)
End Times Bulletin (FL—bad
   address)
Enlace Informativo (FL—
   Bad address)
Equipping the Saints (CA)
ESA Advocate—See Prism
Event (TN)
Faith 'N' Stuff—See Guide-
   posts for Kids
For Parents (NY)
God's Special People (WA)
Growing Churches (TN)

Hayden Herald (ID)
HiCall—See Teen Life
His Garden (IL)
Home Office Opportunities
   (WY)
Inner Horizons (MA)
It's God's World—See God's
   World Today
Junebugs Knocking (IL)
Kiln, The (WA)
Light for Today (MN)
Kootenai Courier (ID)
Miracles (FL)
Moments With God (IL)
Newsletter (FL)
Opus One/Opus Two (TN)
Our Town (VA)
Paraclete (MO)
People & Places (NY)
Pioneer—See Challenge
Phoenix Rising (VA)
The Prayer Line (WA)

Primary Teacher—See Won-
    der Time
Professional Parents (CO)
Quest (NY)
Royal Service (AL)
Salt Shaker (CAN)
Score—See Gospel Today
Scoreboard Publications (UT)
Search (TN)

Starlight Magazine (NC)
Teens Today—See Cross Walk
Thirteen Poetry Magazine
    (NY)
Today's Better Life (TX)
The Trumpet Sounds (TX)
Urban Family (MS)
Voice of Sarah (KS)
Voices in the Wilderness (MA)

Worship Today (FL)
Writer's Anchor (PA)
Writer's Guidelines (MO)
Young Crusader (IL)
Youth & CE Leadership—See
    Christian Education Lead-
    ership

PERIODICALS NOT INTERESTED IN FREELANCE SUBMISSIONS, OR WHO ASKED NOT TO BE LISTED

Absolute Sound (NY)
Action Tracks
Acorn, The
Action Information (DC)
Adolescence (CA)
Adult Focus (TN)
Adult Teacher (MO)
AFA Journal (MS)
Alliance Life (CO)
The A.M.E. Church Review
    (GA)
Anglican Theological Review
    (IL)
Answers in Action (CA)
Assoc. Reformed Presby (SC)
Australian Evangel
Baptist Bulletin (IL)
Baptist Herald (IL)
Baptist World (VA)
Berean Statesman (MN)
Bible-in-Life Friends (CO)
Bible-in-Life Stories (CO)
Bible-Science News (MN)
Bible Time 4s and 5s
Bible World (NJ)
Biblical Illustrator (TN)
Bodywise (AR)
Books & Religion (NC)
Bookviews (WI)
Brethren Missionary Herald
    (IN)
Builder (PA)
Catholic Accent (PA)
Catholic Exponent (OH)
Catholic Health World (MO)
Catholic Insight (CAN)
Catholic Library World (PA)
CBMC Contact (TN)
Children's Church Exchange
    (MO)
The Chosen People (NC)
Christ for the Nations (TX)
Christian Conquest (AL)
Christian Education Journal

(IL)
Christian Example
Christianity & Crisis (IL)
Christian Info (Canada)
Christian Life (OH)
Christian Living (TN)
Christian Medical Society
    Journal (TX)
ChristianWeek (Canada)
Christian Woman (AZ/TN)
Christ in Our Home (MN)
Christopher News Notes (NY)
Church Herald (MI)
Church of God MISSIONS
    (IN)
Church Programs/ Mid-
    dlers/Jrs (MO)
Church Programs/ Pre-
    schoolers (MO)
Church Programs/Primaries
    (MO)
Columban Mission (NE)
Command (CO)
Compassion Today (Canada)
The Congregationalist (WY)
Contact Quarterly (TN)
Contempo (AL)
Contemporary Christian
    Music (TN)
Cornerstone Connections
    (MD)
COSMET Newsletter (CA)
Covenanter Witness (PA)
Daily Blessing (OK)
Daily Meditation (TX)
Dialog (MN)
Directions in Faith (TN)
The Disciple (MO)
Door of Hope (CA)
Doorways (CO)
Elmbrook (WI)
El Orador
Epiphany Journal (CA)
Eurovision Advance (CA)

Evangelical Missions Quar-
    terly (IL)
Exodus Standard (CA)
Faith & Renewal (MI)
Faith at Work, Inc. (Canada)
FaithQuest (IL)
Family Forum (MO)
Family Therapy (CA)
Family Voice (DC)
Family Walk (GA)
Fellowship (NY)
Festivals (CA)
Firm Foundation (TX)
Focus Magazine (TN)
The Forerunner (FL)—no
    response
Forward Day by Day (OH)
Four and Five (OH)
The Free Methodist Pastor
    (IN)
Fulness Magazine (TX)
God's Word for Today (MO)
Gospel Herald (PA)
Gospel Message (MO)
Greater Europe Report (IL)
Growing Together (IL)
The Herald (KY)
Heritage Herald (NC)
High School Teaching Guide
    (IL)
The Home Altar (MN)
Image (KS)
Image (PA)
IMAGE (VA)
IMPACT (IL)
Insight (NC)
Insights (CA)
Interest (IL)
Interlit (IL)
Invitation (TN)
It's Our World (DC)
Jubilee (DC)
KEY to CE (OH)
Kindred Spirit (TX)

Last Day Messenger (OR)
Level D Teacher (MO)
Light for Today (MN)
Listen Magazine (DC)
Living Faith (MO)
Living Light (DC)
Living Values (IL)
Look and Listen (TN)
The Lookout (NY)
Luke Society News (MS)
Lutheran Education (IL)
Lutheran Libraries (MN)
Maranatha Manna (MD)
Marketplace, The (Canada)
Marriage & Family (IN)
Maryknoll (NY)
Media Update (CA)
Men's Ministries (MO)
Messenger (IL)
Messenger, The (Canada)
Ministry (MD)
Miracle Living (AZ)
Mission (MD)
Missionary Monthly (MI)
Mission Frontiers (CA)
Missions Today (TN)
Momentum (DC)
Money Matters (GA)
Musicline (CA)
My Daily Visitor
My Delight (OH)
My Devotions (MO)
My Jewels (OH)
My Pleasure (OH)
Nat Christian Reporter (TX)
Nat/Intl. Religion Report (VA)
New Catholic World (NJ)
New Jerusalem Music (NJ)

Nor'Easter (NY)
OC International (CA)
Open Doors News Briefs
   (CA)
Opening the Word (KS)
Open Windows (TN)
The Other Side (PA)
Pathway I.D. (TN)
PCA Messenger (GA)
Pentecostal Messenger (MO)
People of Destiny (MD)
Poet & Writers (NY)
Portals of Prayer (MO)
Praying (MN)
Preschool Playhouse
   (assigned)
Preteen Teacher (MO)
Primary St. (assigned)
Quaker Life (IN)
Reflections (MD)
Reformed Journal (MI)
Response (NY)
Royal Service (AL)
Sally Ann (Canada)
Servant (Canada)
Single Adult Ministry Infor-
   mation (MO)
Southwestern News 50,000
Sower, The (IL)
Spiritual Women's Times
   (WA)
Student, The (TN)
Student Venture Newsletter
   (CA)
Sunday School Illustrator
   (TN)
The Sunday School Times &
   Gospel Herald (OH)

Tabletalk (FL)
Teacheraid (PA)
Teaching Home, The (OR)
Teen Triumph (TN)
Thema (LA)
These Days (GA)
The Trim Tab (GA)
The United Brethren (IN)
United Evangelical ACTION
   (IL)
United Methodist Reporter
   (TX)
Veritas (CA)—no response
Vista (IN)
Weekly Bible Reader (OH)
Wee Lambs (PA)
Wesleyan World (IN)
Wheaton Alumni (IL)
Wine Castles (MN)
The Winner (DC)
The Witness (PA)
Word & Way (MO)
Word in Season (MN)
Word of Faith (OK)
Words of Hope (MI)
World (NC)
World Encounter (IL)
Worldorama (OK)
World Pulse (IL)
Worldwide THRUST (PA)
Young Life (CO)
Young Missionary (IN)
Youth Alive (MO)
YouthGuide (KS)
Youth Illustrated (IL)
Youth Walk (GA)

GREETING CARD/GIFT/SPECIALTY MARKETS

PLEASE NOTE: This listing contains both Christian/religious card publishers and secular publishers who have religious lines or produce some religious or inspirational cards. Keep in mind that the secular companies may produce other lines of cards that are not consistent with your beliefs, and that for a secular company, inspirational cards usually do not include religious imagery.

(*) Indicates that publisher did not return questionnaire.
(#) Indicates that listing was updated from guidelines or other sources.
(+) Indicates new listing.

NOTE: See the end of this listing for specialty product lists.

*ALLPORT GREETING CARD CO., 532 NW 12th, Portland OR 97209. Michael & Victoria Allport, eds. General card publisher that does inspirational cards. 10% freelance. Pays on publication. Responds in 3 mos. Seasonal/holiday 6 mos ahead. Submit at least 8 ideas. Guidelines.

#RUSS BERRIE & CO., INC., 111 Bauer Dr., Oakland NJ 07436. (201)337-9000. Angelica Berrie, ed. A general card publisher/inspirational and religious lines. 50% freelance; buys 40 ideas/yr. Outright submission. Pays $25-100 on acceptance for all rts. Royalty 2%. Responds in 2-4 mos. Uses rhymed, unrhymed, traditional, light verse; various lengths. Produces conventional, humorous, inspirational, juvenile, religious, sensitivity, soft line. Needs card verse for anniversary, birthday, friendship, get well, keep in touch, love, miss you, new baby, please write, sympathy, thank you, wedding. Needs verses for other products for Christmas, Easter, graduation, Halloween, relatives, mother, St. Patrick's Day, Thanksgiving, Valentine's Day. Holiday/seasonal 24 mos ahead. Open to new card lines. Prefers 10-25 ideas/submission. Open to ideas for perpetual and undated calendars, gift books, greeting books, plaques, postcards, novelty products/copy, bookmarks, mugs, magnets, picture frames, gift bags, diaries, address books, stationery and gift items. Guidelines/market list for #10 SAE/2 stamps.

+BLUE MOUNTAIN ARTS, PO Box 1007, Boulder CO 80306. (303)449-0536. E-mail: bma@rmii.com. Publishes quality books, cards, calendars and prints. Lisa M. Truesdale, asst. ed. Pays $200 for all rts, or $25 for one-time use in a book. Uses sensitive poetry and prose on love, friendship, family, philosophies; Christmas, Valentine's Day, Easter, Mother's Day, and Father's Day. Holiday/seasonal 4 mos. ahead.

> **Tips:** "We are interested in reviewing poetry and writings for greeting cards, and expand our field of freelance poetry writers."

*THE BRANCHES, INC., PO Box 848, Chanhassen MN 55317-0848. (612)474-0924. Ronald Olson, marketing mngr. General card publisher/religious line. 5% freelance; 9 ideas/yr. Pays $240/camera-ready design, on publication. Royalties 2-5%. Responds in 6 mos. Prefers unrhymed. Produces traditional, inspirational, juvenile and sensitivity. Holiday/seasonal 1 yr ahead. Open to ideas for greeting books, plaques, postcards, mugs, coaster magnets, bookmarks. Catalog.

*CARING CARD COMPANY, Box 90278, Long Beach CA 90809. Shirley Hassell, ed. A specialty card publisher/inspirational and religious cards. 45% freelance. Outright submissions. Pays $10-25 on publication for all rts. Responds in 8-16 wks. Uses rhymed, unrhymed and traditional; length open. Produces inspirational, religious, sensitivity and soft line. Needs Christmas, friendship, get well, keep in touch, love, miss you, please write, Valentines, significant loss/sympathy (bereavement, hospice environment, life/death transitions). Holiday/seasonal 6-12 months ahead. Prefers 1-12 ideas/submission. Also open to ideas for calendars, posters, plaques, postcards, and T-shirts. Guidelines.

+CATHEDRAL ART METAL CO., 250 Esten Ave., Pawtucket RI 02860. (401)726-2100. Fax (401)726-1790. Fritzi Frey, art. dir. A Christian card publisher/specialty products. 50% freelance; buys 25 ideas/yr. Query. Pays on acceptance. Royalties 5%. Responds in 4 wks. Produces inspirational, novelty, religious. Produces cards with jewelry and other gift items. Open to new card lines. Also open to ideas for gift books, gift/novelty items and plaques. No guidelines; catalog available.

CEDAR HILL STUDIO, PO Box 328, Waynesville NC 28786. (704)456-6344. Fax (704)456-6303. E-mail: 103663.2047@compuserve.com. Mark B. Clasby, CEO. Christian/religious card publisher. Open to freelance. Prefers outright submission. Pays $10-25 on acceptance for all rts. No royalties. Responds in 6-8 wks. Buys short humor. Produces humorous, inspirational, and sensitivity. Needs anniversary, birthday, Christmas, congratulations, friendship, get well, graduation, keep in touch, love, miss you, new baby, please write, relative, sympathy, thank you, Valentines, and wedding. Seasonal 1 yr ahead. Open to new card lines. Also open to ideas for calendars, gift/novelty items, magnets, mugs, plaques, postcards, posters and T-shirts. Guidelines; no catalog.

Tips: "Messages must be uplifting and encouraging."

CELEBRATION GREETINGS (A div. of Leanin' Tree), Box 9500, Boulder CO 80301. (303)530-1442. Fax (303)530-7283. Barb Brackemyer, art/verse ed. Christian/religious card publisher & specialty products. 25% freelance. Buys 30 ideas/yr. Query. Pays $100 on publication for all rts. No royalties. Responds in 12 wks. Any type of verse, including humorous; 1-4 lines. Produces conventional, humorous, inspirational, religious. Needs anniversary, birthday, Christmas, friendship, get well, keep in touch, love, miss you, new baby, sympathy, thank you, wedding, and encouragement. Christmas ideas 12 mos ahead. Not open to new card lines. Prefers 12-20 ideas. Not open to ideas for specialty items. Guidelines; no catalog.

Tips: "We need birthday card ideas especially."

*CREATIVE CHRISTIAN MINISTRIES, PO Box 12624, Roanoke VA 24027. Phone/fax (540)342-7511. Barbara Shaffer; mkg. dir. Christian/religious card publisher. 50% freelance. Outright submissions. Pays $5-10 on acceptance for reproduction rts. No royalties. Responds in 6 wks. Rhymed, unrhymed & traditional. Produces inspirational, religious and sensitivity. Needs birthday, Christmas, friendship, get well, new baby, sympathy, thank you, wedding, and thinking of you. Seasonal 6 mos ahead. Open to ideas for new card lines. Submit any number. Also open to ideas for magnets, plaques, and post cards. Guidelines; catalog available in mid 1996.

Special Needs: Cards for older adults, caregivers, adult children of aging parents facing role reversal.

*CREATIVE GRAPHICS, 785 Grant, Eugene OR 97402. (503)484-2726. Submit to Terry Dusseault, corp. sec. General card publisher/religious lines. Open only to photographs/artwork. Query. Pays $50/card.

DAYSPRING GREETING CARDS, Box 1010, Hwy. 16 E., Siloam Springs AR 72761. (501)549-9303. Fax (501)524-8959. E-mail: ANNW@OUTREACH. MHS.compuserve.com. Ann Woodruff, ed. Christian/religious card publisher. 20% freelance; buys up to 1,000 ideas/yr. Query or outright submission. Pays from $35-50/idea on acceptance for all rts. No royalty. Responds in 4-8 wks. Uses unrhymed (preferred), light verse, conversational, contemporary; various lengths. Produces announcements, humorous, informal, inspirational, invitations, juvenile, novelty, religious. Needs anniversary, birthday, Christmas, congratulations, Easter, friendship, get well, graduation, keep in touch, love, miss you, new baby, please write, relatives, sympathy, Thanksgiving, thank you, Valentines, wedding, and all major sending seasons and everyday occasions. Also needs pastor and Christian service appreciation and encouragement. Seasonal 1 yr ahead. Open to new card lines and calendar ideas. Send 20 ideas or less. Guidelines; no catalog.

Special Needs: Boss's Day, Secretaries' Day, Pastor and Christian Service appreciation and encouragement.

Tips: "We need fresh, new ideas."

*DIVINE INSPIRATION, PO Box 90981, Washington DC 20090-0981. (202)291-0424. Fax (202)291-0420. Lori George, pres. Christian/religious card publisher. No freeláncе. Does inspirational and religious cards. All need to contain scriptures. Open to ideas for new card lines. Open to ideas for calendars, post cards, posters, bookmarks, wallet cards, note cards and spiral-bound booklets. No guidelines or catalog.

*FREEDOM GREETING CARDS, Box 715, Bristol PA 19007. (215)945-3300. J. Levitt, pres. General card publisher/religious and inspirational lines. Currently has all the freelancers they need. Let them know the kind of work you can do and they will put your name in their file.

*GALLANT GREETINGS, 4300 United Parkway, Schiller Park IL 60176. (708)671-6500. Fax (708)671-7500. General card publisher/a few inspirational/religious cards. Chris Allen, VP-Sales & Marketing. 90% freelance. Query. Responds in 1 month. Pays 60-90 days after acceptance for world greeting card rts. Pays royalties. Uses rhymed, unrhymed, traditional and light verse; 4-6 lines. Produces announcements, conventional, humorous, informal, inspirational, invitations, juvenile, religious. Needs all types of greetings. Holiday/seasonal 6 months ahead. Open to new card lines. Prefers 6-10 ideas/submission. Guidelines/needs list; no catalog.

*GENESIS MARKETING GROUP, 16 Wellington Ave., Greenville SC 29609. (803)233-2651. Fax (803)232-0059. Peter Sullivan, pres. Christian/religious card publisher. 100% freelance. Buys 10 ideas/yr. Outright submission. Royalty 5%. Traditional & light verse. Produces inspirational, religious, sensitivity. Needs anniversary, birthday, Christmas, congratulations, Easter, friendship, get well, graduation, keep in touch, love, miss you, new baby, please write, relatives, sympathy, thank you, valentines, wedding. Also produces calendars, gift books, magnets, mugs, plaques, posters, T-shirts.

HEART IMPRESSIONS, PO Box 12624, Roanoke VA 24027. Phone/fax (703)342-7511. E-mail: ccmbbr@worldnet.att.com. Creative Christian Ministries. Betty Robertson, ed. Christian card publisher. 25% freelance. Pays $5-10/idea on acceptance for all rts. Prefers outright submissions. Responds in 6 wks. Prefers rhymed, unrhymed, or traditional; variable length. Produces inspirational and religious. Does friendship, new baby, sympathy, thank you, and wedding. Seasonal 9 mos ahead. Open to ideas for new card lines. Submit any number. Also open to ideas for audio tapes, magnets, plaques and post cards. Guidelines; no catalog.

+HEART STEPS, INC., PO Box 307, King WI 54946. (715)258-8141. Fax (715)256-9170. General card publisher with a religious line. Open to freelance art; beginning to review copy. Bought 1 idea in 1996. Query. Pays variable rates on acceptance. No royalties. Responds in 4 wks. Unrhymed verse, 3-5 lines. Produces conventional, inspirational, juvenile, religious and sensitivity. Needs Christmas, sympathy and Valentines. Seasonal 1 yr ahead. Send any number. Also open to ideas for gift/novelty items, magnets, and T-shirts. No guidelines; catalog for 10x13 SAE/3 stamps.

*IMAGE CRAFT, INC., 1245 Franklin Blvd., Box 814, Cambridge ON N1R 5W6 Canada. (519)622-4310. Fax (519)622-6774. Jeanette Gilmour, ed. General card publisher with a religious line. Open to freelance. Prefers outright submission. Pays on acceptance. No royalties. Produces announcements, conventional, humorous, informal, inspirational, invitations, juvenile, religious and studio cards. Needs anniversary, birthday, Christmas, congratulations, Easter, friendship, get well, graduation, keep in touch, love, miss you, Mother's Day/Father's Day, new baby, relatives/all occasion, sympathy, Thanksgiving, thank you, Valentines, wedding, confirmation, and First Communion. Seasonal 7 mos ahead. Open to new card lines. Also open to ideas for gift books and plaques.

J-MAR, PO Box 23149, Waco TX 76702-3149. (817)751-0100. Fax (817)751-0054. C. M. Nevill, sales dir. Christian/Religious card publisher. 10% freelance; buys 10-15 ideas/yr. Query. Pays $25-50 on acceptance for all rts; no royalties. Responds in 2 wks. Prefers rhymed, unrhymed, traditional or light verse; 6-12 lines. Produces inspirational, juvenile, novelty, religious. Needs anniversary, birthday, Christmas, congratulations, Easter, friendship, get well, graduation, keep in touch, love, miss you, new baby, relative, sympathy, thank you, Valentines, wedding. Seasonal 12 mos ahead. Open to new card lines. Send 3-4 ideas. Open to ideas for plaques & magnets. No guidelines; catalog for 9x12 SAE.

*LIFE GREETINGS, Box 468, Little Compton RI 02837. (401)635-8535. Kathy Brennan, ed. Christian/religious card publisher. Open to freelance. Outright purchases. Pays $10 on acceptance for all rts. No royalties. Responds in 6 wks. Uses rhymed, unrhymed, traditional; 6-8 lines. Produces announcements, conventional, humorous, inspirational, and religious. Needs congratulations, friendship, get well, new baby, sympathy, thank you and wedding. Also clergy reassignment, ordination, anniversary of ordination, and pro-life Christmas. Seasonal 6 mos ahead. Open to new card lines. Prefers 6 ideas/submission. Guidelines; no catalog.

+MADISON PARK GREETINGS, 1407 11th Ave., Seattle WA 98105. (206)324-5711. Renee Capps, copywriting coor. General card publisher that does inspirational cards. 50% freelance. Holiday/seasonal 10 mos. ahead. Responds in 2 mos.

Pays on publication. Produces announcements, informal, studio, conventional, inspirational, sensitivity, humorous, invitations, and soft line.

*MANHATTAN GREETING CARD CO., 150 E 52 St. c/o Platzer/Fineberg, New York NY 10022. (718)894-7600. Paula Haley, ed. General card publisher/inspirational line. 100% freelance. Pays $5-250. Responds in 3 wks. Produces announcements, conventional, humorous, informal, inspirational, invitations, juvenile, sensitivity, soft line, studio, Christmas (85% of the line). Holiday/seasonal 18 months ahead. Also open to ideas for bumper stickers, calendars, gift books, greeting books, post cards, and promotions. Free guidelines.

NOVO CARD PUBLISHERS, INC., 4513 N Lincoln Ave., Chicago IL 60625. (312)769-6000. Fax (312)769-6769. Thomas Benjamin/Sheri Cline, art dirs. General card publisher that does a few inspirational and religious cards. 60-95% freelance; buys 200-500 ideas/yr. Prefers query for writers and outright submissions for art samples. Pays $2/line on publication for greeting card rts. No royalties. Responds in 3 wks. Uses any type verse, variable lengths. Produces all types of cards. Needs birthday, congratulations, friendship, graduation, keep in touch, relatives (all occasions), sympathy, thank you. Seasonal 8 mos ahead. Open to ideas for new card lines. Submit enough ideas to show style. Guidelines/needs list; samples for 9x12 SAE/5 stamps.

Tips: "Sympathy cards need to be a bit more inspirational than just 'my deepest sympathy'."

*PACIFIC PAPER GREETINGS, INC., Box 2249, Sidney BC V8L 3S8 Canada. (604)656-0504. Louise Rytter, ed. Inspirational cards. 50% freelance; buys 20 ideas/yr. Pays on acceptance for all rts. Responds in 3 wks. Produces conventional, inspirational, romantic, sensitivity, soft line. Holiday/seasonal 12 months ahead. Guidelines for SAE/1 IRC.

PAINTED HEARTS & FRIENDS, 1222 N. Fair Oaks Ave., Pasadena CA 91103-3614. (818)798-3633, Fax (818)798-7385. E-mail: teri@paintedhearts.com. Teri Willis, ed. General card publisher that does a few inspirational and religious cards. Accepts freelance. Query or outright submission (copies only, no original artwork). Pays $25/message on acceptance. 5% royalty on artwork only. Responds in 1-2 wks. Uses unrhymed, traditional, light verse; 2-3 liners. Produces announcements, inspirational, invitations. Needs most types of greetings (no Please Write), plus graduation and Jewish holidays. See guidelines for submission schedule. Open to ideas for new card lines. Submit 12 art designs max, or 24 messages. Open to ideas for banners, gift books, and stationery. Guidelines; no catalog.

RED FARM STUDIO, 1135 Roosevelt Ave., Pawtucket RI 02862. (401)728-9300. Fax (401)728-0350. Rebecca Burns, art dir. General card publisher with a religious line. 50% freelance; buys 10-20 ideas/yr. Outright submission. Pays variable rates on acceptance for exclusive rts. No royalties. Responds in 2 mos. Use traditional and light verse; 1-4 lines. Produces announcements, invitations, religious. Needs anniversary, birthday, Christmas, friendship, get well, new baby, sympathy, wedding. Holiday 6 months ahead. Not open to ideas for new card lines. Submit any number of ideas. Guidelines/needs list for SASE.

+BOB SIEMON DESIGNS INC., 11609 Martens River Cir., Fountain Valley CA 92708. (714)549-0678. Fax (714)979-2627. Eileen McMullen, ed. Christian card publisher. 20-25% freelance. Buys 5-10 ideas/yr. Query. Pays variable royalty and advance, on acceptance, based on artist and product. Responds in 4-6 wks. Prefers traditional or light verse; 1-2 verses. Produces humorous, inspirational, religious, sensitivity and soft line. Needs anniversary, birthday, Christmas, congratulations, Easter, friendship. Get well, graduation, keep in touch, love, miss you, new baby, please write, sympathy, thank you, Valentines, wedding. Seasonal 6 mos ahead. Open to ideas for new card lines. Send any number. Also open to ideas for gift/novelty items, magnets, mugs, plaques. No guidelines; catalog available.

SUNRISE PUBLICATIONS, INC., 1145 Sunrise Greeting Ct., Box 4699, Bloomington IN 47402-4699. (812)336-9900. Fax (812)336-8712. Submit to Text Editor. General card publisher that does inspirational cards. 1% freelance; buys 10 ideas/yr. Outright submission. Pays $50 on acceptance for worldwide exclusive rts. No royalties. Responds in 2-3 mos. Prefers unrhymed, traditional; 2 stanzas max. Produces conventional, humorous, inspirational. Needs anniversary, birthday, belated birthday, Christmas, congratulations, Easter, friendship, get well, graduation, Halloween, keep in touch, love, miss you, new baby, please write, relatives, St. Patrick's Day, sympathy, Thanksgiving, thank you, Valentines, wedding; also baptism, confirmation, bar and bat mitzvah. Holiday/seasonal 6 mos ahead. Open to ideas for new card lines. Up to 15 ideas/submission. Also open to ideas for gift/novelty items, greeting books, magnets and posters. Guidelines; no catalog.

> **Tips:** "We use very little religious imagery or verse. However, it is sometimes used in sympathy, Easter and Christmas captions."

#WARNER PRESS INC., 1200 E 5th St, PO Box 2499, Anderson IN 46018. (317)644-7721. Fax (317)649-3664. Robin Fogle, product ed. Christian/religious card publisher. 50% freelance; buys 100+ ideas/yr. Query. Pays $20-35 on acceptance for all rts. No royalties. Responds in 9 wks. Uses rhymed, unrhymed, traditional, light verse; 4-8 lines. Produces inspirational, religious. Needs anniversary, birthday, Christmas (needs a good amount for boxed cards), Easter, friendship, get well, graduation, new baby, sympathy, thank you, Valentines, wedding, secret pal, and from the pastor. Holiday/seasonal 6 months ahead. Accepts Christmas material in September for next year. Open to new card lines. Accepts 10 ideas/submission. Also open to ideas for calendars, coloring & activity books, gift books, postcards, posters and Sunday bulletins (devotional material). Guidelines (must send for before submitting); no catalog.

> **Special Needs:** "We purchase for boxed greeting cards. Verses should be warm and personal, but general enough to be sent by a group."
>
> **Tips:** "We prefer submissions be typed on 3x5 cards with name, address, telephone #, and freelance identification # on the back."

ADDITIONAL CARD PUBLISHERS

The following greeting card publishers do not use freelance material, or did not complete a questionnaire, but are included for reference or to contact on your own. Do not submit to them before you send for guidelines or ascertain their needs.

ABBEY PRESS, St. Meinrad IN 47577. No freelance.

ABUNDANT TREASURES, PO Box 605, Calimesa CA 92320-0605.

ACT NOW, INC., PO Box 294, Mogadore OH 44260. No freelance.

APPALACHIAN BIBLE CO. INC., 506 Princeton Rd, Johnson City TN 37601.

ART BEATS, 33 River Rd., Cos Cob CT 06807-2717.

BARTON-COTTON INC., 1405 Parker Rd., Baltimore MD 21227. No freelance.

CAROLYN BEAN PUBLISHING, 1700 Corporate Cir., Petaluma CA 94954-6924.

BERG CHRISTIAN ENTERPRISES, 4525 SE 63rd Ave., Portland OR 97206.

BETH HA DAVAR, 10 Brick Row, Athens NY 12015. No freelance.

+BLACK FAMILY GREETING CARDS, 20 Cortlandt Ave., New Rochelle NY 10801. Bill Harte, pres.

BRETT-FORER GREETINGS, Masterpiece Studio, Bedford Park IL 60499-2002. No freelance.

CARDS 4 YOU, 23011 Moulton Pkwy., #E-10, Dept. 113, Laguna Hills CA 92653. No freelance.

CAROLE JOY CREATIONS, INC., 107 Mill Plain Rd., Danbury CT 06811. (203)798-2060. African-American greetings cards.

+CD GREETING CARDS, PO Box 5084, Brentwood TN 37024-5084.

CURRENT, INC., PO Box 2559, Colorado Springs CO 80901. No freelance.

+T.S. DENISON GREETING CARDS, PO Box 1650, Grand Rapids MI 49501.

EARTH CARE PAPER, INC., PO Box 8507, Ukiah CA 95482.

EISNER ADVERTISING STUDIO (OH)—No freelance.

KRISTEN ELLIOTT, INC., 6 Opportunity Way, Newburyport MA 01950.

FAMILY LINE ALLISON GREETINGS, 79 - 5th Ave. 4th Fl, New York NY 10003-3034.

FAYE'S SPECIALTY CARDS (NY)—No freelance.

FLAVIA—No freelance.

+FREDERICK SINGER AND SONS, INC., 2-15 Borden Ave., Long Island City NT 11101.

+FRIENDLY SALES, PO Box 755, Quakertown PA 18951.

+FRIENDS OF ISREAL GOSPEL MINISTRIES, PO Box 908, Bellmawr NJ 08099-9900.

THE C.R. GIBSON CO. (bought out by Thomas Nelson)—No freelance.

GIFTED LINE, 999 Canal Blvd., Point Richmond CA 94804—No freelance.

GOSPEL GIGGLES, PO Box 11781, Portland OR 97211-0781. No freelance.

GREENLEAF, INC., 200 Wending Way, Spartanburg SC 29306.

GUERNICA EDITIONS (Canada)—No freelance.

THE HERMITAGE ART COMPANY INC., 5151 N. Ravenswood Ave., Chicago IL 60640.

HIGHER HORIZONS, Box 78399, Los Angeles CA 90016.

IDESIGN, 12020 W. Ripley, Milwaukee WI 53226. (414)475-7176.

IT TAKES TWO, INC., 100 Minnesota Ave., Le Sueur MN 56058. No freelance.

JONATHAN & DAVID INC, Box 1194, Grand Rapids MI 49501.

KIMBERLY ENTERPRISES INC., 15029 S. Figueroa St., Gardena CA 90248—Inspirational cards.

KINKA, 1 Orchard Park, Madison CT 06443. No freelance.

+LAWSON FALLE LTD., Eden Hall, 3330 Griswold Rd., Port Huron MI 48060.

THE LORENZ COMPANY, 1208 Cimmaron Dr., Waco TX 76712-8174.

MALENA PRODUCTIONS INC., Box 14483, Ft. Lauderdale FL 33302— Out of business.

MANUSCRIPTURES (WI)—No freelance.

MARIAN HEATH GREETING CARDS, 9 Kendrick Rd., Wareham MA 02571— No freelance.

MASTERPIECE STUDIOS, PO Box 2002, Bedford Park IL 60499-2002—No freelance.

+MCBETH CORP., PO Box 400, Chambersburg PA 17201.

MERI MERI, 11 Vista Ave., San Mateo CA 94403-4612.

+A MIRACLE PUBLISHING, INC. PO Box 310210, Atlanta GA 31131. (404)505-8321.—Open to freelance. Jennipher Thomas, ed.

+MORE THAN A CARD, 5010 Baltimore Ave., Bethesda MD 20816.

NORTHWESTERN PRODUCTS INC. (MN)—No freelance.

NU ART, 6247 W 74th St., Bedford Park IL 60499. No freelance.

OAKSPRINGS IMPRESSIONS, Box 572, Woodacre CA 94973.

OATMEAL STUDIOS, PO Box 138, Rochester VT 05767. Helene Lehrer, creative dir.

PARAMOUNT CARDS INC. (RI)—No freelance.

PALOMA CHRISTIANA, PO Box 1711, La Quinta CA 92253-1711. Bad address.

GROUP, INC., PO Box 977, Scranton PA 18501-0977. No freelance.

C.M. PAULA COMPANY, 6049 Hi-Tek Ct., Mason OH 45040. No freelance.

PRINTERY HOUSE (MO)—No freelance.

+PS GREETINGS/FANTUS PAPER PRODUCTS, 5060 N. Kimberly Ave., Chicago IL 60630-1744.

QUADRIGA ART (NY)—No freelance.

RAINFALL, INC. (MI)—No freelance.

RANDALL WILCOX PUBLISHING, 826 Orange Ave. #544, Coronado CA 92118. (619)437-1321.

RENAISSANCE GREETING CARDS (ME)—No freelance.

SANGAMON INC. (IL)—No freelance.

JOSEPH E. SCHULTZ ART STUDIO (IN)—No freelance.

MARCEL SCHURMAN CO., INC., 2500 N. Watney Way, Fairfield CA 94533-6724. Not open.

SECOND NATURE LTD. (England)—No freelance.

SEEDS EVANGELICAL GREETING CARDS (NC)—No freelance

SENDJOY GREETING CARDS, Laurel Park, Wappingers Falls NY 12590.

THESE THREE, INC., 2103 - 18th St. N. #1035, Arlington VA 22201-3537. Jean Bridgers, ed.

+THINGS GRAPHIC & FINE ARTS, 1522 - 14th St. NW, Washington DC 20005.

TLC GREETINGS, 615 McCall Rd., Manhattan KS 66502-8512. Out of business.

WEST GRAPHICS, 385 Oyster Point Blvd. #7, S. San Francisco CA 94080-1934. Carol West, ed.

WILDEST DREAMS, Fairview Dr. Rd 10, Carmel NY 10512.

WIZWORKS, Box 240, Masonville CO 80541.

NOTE: Most of the markets listed below for games, gift items and videos have not indicated their interest in receiving freelance submissions. Contact these markets on your own for information on submission procedures before sending them anything.

GAME MARKETS

BIBLE GAMES CO., 14389 Cassell Rd., Fredericktown OH 43019. Kelly Vozar, asst. Produces Bible games. 10% freelance. Buys 1-2 ideas/yr. Query. Pays on publication for all rts (negotiable). Royalties 8%. Responds in 6-8 wks. Open to new ideas. One game per submission. Guidelines; catalog for 9x12 SAE/6 stamps.

> **Tips:** "Send developed and tested game play; target market and audience. Must be totally non-sectarian and fully biblical—no fictionalized scenarios." Board games, CD-roms, computer games and video games.

BIBLE WALK GOSPEL EDUCATION GAMES. (800)829-1883. Board games.

CACTUS GAME DESIGN, INC. 8845 Stevens Chase Ct., Las Vegas NV 89129. Games.

GOOD STEWARD GAME CO., 6412 Sunnyfield Way., Sacramento CA 95823-5781. (916)393-4263. William Parker, ed. Board games.

*LATE FOR THE SKY PRODUCTION COMPANY, 561 Reading Rd., Cincinnati OH 45202. Fax (513)721-5757. Board games.

MARTIN LEVY INC., 1405 Brewester Dr., El Cerrito CA 94530. (510)234-8888. Board games.

M.J.N. ENTERPRISES, 1624 McMillan, Memphis TN 38106. (901)946-8185. Board games.

+TALICOR, 190 Gentry St., Pomona CA 91767-2100. (909)593-5877. Fax (909)596-6586. Lew Herndon, pres. Produces board games. 100% freelance. Prefers outright submissions. Pays royalties on publication of 5-7%. Responds in 2-3 wks. Looks for personal experience and insight. Seasonal 4 mos ahead. Open to new ideas. Submit 1-4 ideas. Catalog for 9x12 SAE/3 stamps.

> **Tips:** "We need family stories—fiction or nonfiction—where our products were used successfully. Stories on communication, or lack of it, where our products will fit."

WISDOM TREE, 2700 E. Imperial Hwy, Ste.A, Brea CA 92821-6711. (800)772-4253. King James Bible and action games for play on Game Boy.

GIFT/SPECIALTY ITEM MARKETS

#ARGUS COMMUNICATIONS, 200 E. Bethany, Allen TX 75002-3804. (214)390-6300. Fax (214)390-6555. Beth Davis, ed. Primarily interested in Christian posters. 90% freelance. Query. Outright purchase. Pays $75 on acceptance for all rts. Royalty 5-8%. Responds in 9 wks. Uses unrhymed, traditional, light verse; 1-2 lines. Produces humorous and inspirational (one line of sweet, light bear cards). Needs birthday, congratulations, friendship, get well, keep in touch, love, miss you, sympathy, thank you, and wedding. Submit maximum 20 ideas. Also open to calendars & postcards appropriate for Christian schools and Sunday school classrooms. Guidelines; catalog for 9x12 SAE/3 stamps.

> **Special Needs:** "We need Christian posters for teens and adults that are positive, inspirational and motivational."

#THE CALLIGRAPHY COLLECTION, 2604 NW 74th Pl., Gainesville FL 32653. (904)375-8530. Fax (904)374-9957. Katy Fischer, ed. General publisher/inspirational line of framed prints. 40% freelance; 20 ideas/yr. Outright submission. Pays $75-150 for framed print idea on publication for all rts; no royalties. Responds in 6 months. Uses rhymed, unrhymed (preferred), traditional, light verse; under 50 words. Produces inspirational (not too specific or overly religious), framed prints for friends, family, teachers, etc. Holiday/seasonal 6 months ahead. Send 3 ideas/batch. Also open to ideas for gift books, plaques, and musical framed pieces. Guidelines; no catalog.

*CONTENOVA GIFTS, 1820 E 46th St., Los Angeles CA 90058-1948. Vicki Boynton, dir. of marketing. Specializes in personalized gifts & novelties. Accepts outside submissions for mug sayings and artwork, but currently has no religious designs; mainly humorous birthday. Guidelines; no catalog.

DICKSONS, INC., 709 B Ave. E., PO Box 368, Seymour IN 47274. (812)522-1308. Fax (812)522-1319. Vice President of Product Development. Produces specialty products; no greeting cards. 1% freelance; open. Submit cover letter/sample. Outright purchases. Responds ASAP. Uses religious/inspirational verses for bookmarks, Quik Notes, plaques, etc. Seasonal 1 yr ahead. Open to ideas for specialty items. Send any number. Produces banners, board games, calendars, coloring books, computer software, gift/novelty items, magnets, mugs, plaques, puzzles and T-shirts. No guidelines or catalog.

INSPIRATIONS, Thomas Nelson Gifts, 506 Nelson Pl., Nashville TN 37214. (800)251-4000. Fax (800)448-8403. Stationery, journals, monthly planners, note pads, and gift collection.

MARYCANA, 23 Great Oaks Blvd., Ste. S, San Jose CA 95119. (800)869-3733. Gift items, including: gift dolls, notepaper, bookmarks, etc.

NEW VENTURES, 137 Barre St., Montpelier VT 05602. (802)229-1020. Fax (802)229-1020. Action figures.

PEELE ENTERPRISES SHIRT PRINTS, LTD., 3401 Hwy 25N, Hodges SC 29653. (803)374-7339. Christian T-shirts and sweatshirts.

QUALITY ARTWORKS, INC., 2262 N. Penn Rd., Hatfield PA 19440-0369. (215)822-0125. Fax (215)822-2619. A bookmark and scroll publisher with inspirational/religious lines. Linda Tomezsko Morris, creative dir. 5% freelance; buys 0-10 ideas/yr. Query. Pays $50-300 on publication for all rts; no royalties. Responds in 4-6 wks. Uses rhymed, unrhymed, traditional, light verse; medium length. Produces bookmarks, decorative scrolls, blank journals, stationery, blank note card sets and notepads. Anniversary, congratulations, friendship, love, new baby, relative and thank you. Not open to ideas for new products. Guidelines; no catalog.

*RAYS OF SONSHINE, 910 Ave. E/Box 736, Wisner NE 68791. (402)529-6531. Marlene Colligan, owner. Christian/religious card publisher. New company. Open to freelance. Needs anniversary, birthday, get well, new baby, sympathy. Open to ideas for new card lines. Current line mostly designed for seniors.

#SCANDECOR, 430 Pike Rd., Southampton PA 18966. (215)355-2410. Fax (215)364-8737. Lauren Harris Karp, product mngr. A general poster publisher that does a few inspirational posters for children, teens and adults. 40% freelance; buys 50 ideas/yr. Makes outright purchase, for world-wide, exclusive rts. Pays $100 on publication, depends on size of poster. No royalties. Responds in 9 wks. Uses rhymed, unrhymed and light verse; one line up to 20 lines. Produces humorous, inspirational, juvenile, novelty and soft line. No holiday posters. Submit several ideas. Open to ideas for calendars, posters and novelty products/copy. Guidelines; no catalog.

+SWANSON CHRISTIAN SUPPLIES, 1200 Park Ave., Murfreesboro TN 37133-1257. (615)896-4114. Fax (615)898-1313. Carmel S. Tritschler, adver. dir. Produces specialty products. Just opening up to freelancers. Query. Pays on publication. No royalties. Responds in 4-8 wks. Uses rhymed, unrhymed, traditional and light verse; short. Inspirational/Christian. Open to new ideas. Send any number. Open to ideas for coloring books, gift/novelty items, magnets, mugs, plaques, post cards. No guidelines or catalog.

YOUTH LIFE CREATIONS, 2004 Carrolton, Muncie IN 47304. (800)784-0078. Action cards.

SOFTWARE DEVELOPERS
BAKER BOOK HOUSE, see book section.
BIBLESOFT, 22014 17TH Ave. S., Seattle WA 98198. (206)824-0647.
EPIPHANY SOFTWARE, 15897 Alta Bista Way, San Jose CA 95127. (408)251-9788.
EXEGESES (exeGeses), PO Box 1776, Orange CA 92668. (714)835-1705. (714)835-1705.
KIRKBRIDE TECHNOLOGIES, PO Box 606, Indianapolis IN 46206. (317)633-1900.
LOGOS RESEARCH SYSTEMS, 2117 200th Ave. W., Oak Harbor WA 98277. (360)679-6575. (360)679-6575.
LOIZEAUX BROTHERS, see book listing.
NAVPRESS SOFTWARE, 16002 Pool Canyon Rd., Austin TX 78734. (512)266-1700.
PARSONS TECHNOLOGY, 1 Parsons Dr., Hiawatha IA 52233. (319)378-7006.
SAGE SOFTWARE, PO Box 1926, Albany OR 97321-0509. (541)967-8337.
ZONDERVAN CORP., see book listing.

VIDEO/CD MARKETS
CHRISTIAN DUPLICATIONS INTL., INC., 1710 Lee Reed Rd., Orlando FL 32810. (800)327-9332. Videos.
CITY ALIVE, PO Box 4952, Chicago IL 60680-4952. (312)433-3838. Fax (312)433-3839. Music and teaching videos.
DALLAS CHRISTIAN VIDEO, 1878 Firman, Richardson TX 75081. (800)231-0095.
+RUSS DOUGHTEN FILMS, INC., 5907 Meredith Dr., Des Moines IA 50322. (515)278-4737. Fax (515)278-4738. E-mail: rdfilms_msi@adsmnet.com. Gene McKelvey, marketing & art dir. Produces videos. Open to ideas. Guidelines; catalog.
EDDE ENTERTAINMENT, 19749 Dearborn Ave., Chatsworth CA 91311. (800)727-2229. Videos.
+HEARTSONG, PO Box 2455, Glenview IL 60025. (800)648-0755. Videos.
+HI-TEK HI-TOUCH, 3945 N. 900 W. #2, Pleasant View UT 84414-1055. (801)782-7605. CD-Roms.

+**MARK IV PICTURES VIDEO**, 5907 Meredith Dr., Des Moines IA 50322. (800)247-3456. Videos.

+**PROPHECY PARTNERS**, PO Box 2204, Niagara Falls NY 14302. (905)684-5561. Videos.

PROPHECY PUBLICATIONS, PO Box 7000, Oklahoma City OK 73153. (800)475-1111. Religious education videos.

RANDOLF PRODUCTIONS, 23181 Verdugo Dr., Laguna Hills CA 92653. (800)266-7741. Videos.

SOLDIERS OF LIGHT PRODUCTIONS, PO Box 16354, Encino CA 91416-6354. (813)345-3866. Fax (818)345-1162. Videos.

THIS WEEK IN BIBLE PROPHECY, PO Box 1440, Niagara Falls NY 14302. (905)684-7700. Videos.

+**VISUAL PROGRESSIONS**, PO Box 1327, Melbourne FL 32902. (800)922-1985. Videos.

PUBLISHERS PRODUCING SPECIALTY PRODUCTS

NOTE: Most of the following publishers are greeting card publishers, but some will be found in the book publisher listings.

ACTIVITY/COLORING BOOKS
Dicksons
Rainbow Books
Chariot (Rainfall)
Regina Press
Shining Star
Standard
Swanson
Warner Press

AUDIO TAPES
Eldridge Publishing
Heart Impressions
Liguori Publications
Success Publishers
Tyndale House
Word
World Publishing
Zondervan

BANNERS
Dicksons
Painted Hearts & Friends

BOARD GAMES
Bethel Publishing
Bible Games Co.
Chariot (Rainfall Inc.)
Dicksons
Good Steward Game Co.
Late for the Sky
Master Books
Joshua Morris Publishing

M.J.N.Enterprises
Shining Star
Standard Publishing
Talicor
Tyndale House
Warner Press (maybe)

CALENDARS/DAILY JOURNALS
Abingdon
American Tract Society
Argus Communications
Barbour & Co.
Russ Berrie
Caring Card Co.
Cedar Hill Studio
DaySpring/Outreach
Dicksons
Divine Inspiration
Garborg's
Genesis
Group Publishing
Manhattan Greeting Card
Neibauer Press
Pilgrim Press
Read 'N Run Books
Scandecor
Tyndale House
Warner Press

CD-ROMS
Bible Games Co.
Chariot
GROUP Publishing

Image Books/Doubleday
Lydia Press
NavPress
Our Sunday Visitor
World Publishing

CHARTS
Rose Publishing

COMIC BOOKS
Dicksons
Kaleidoscope Press
Thomas Nelson

COMPUTER GAMES
Bible Games Co.
Brown-ROA
Master Books
NavPress Software
Wood Lake Books

COMPUTER SOFTWARE
Baker (BakerBytes)
Biblesoft
Concordia
Dicksons
Epiphany Software
exeGeses
Gospel Light
Kirkbride Technology
Logos Research Systems
Loizeaux Brothers
NavPress Software
Parsons Technology

Resource Publications
Sage Software
Zondervan

GIFT BOOKS
(See listing under Book Topics)
Russ Berrie
Cathedral Art
Genesis
Image Craft
Painted Hearts & Friends
Review and Herald
Warner Press

GIFT/NOVELTY ITEMS
Abingdon
Russ Berrie
Cathedral Art
Cedar Hill Studio
Contenova Gifts
Dicksons
Heartsteps
Manhattan Greeting Card
New Boundary Designs
Scandecor
Bob Siemon Designs
Swanson
Sunrise Publications
Zondervan

GREETING BOOKS
Russ Berrie
Calligraphy Collection
Joshua Morris (novelty books)
Manhattan Greeting Card
New Boundary Designs
Sunrise Publications

MAGNETS
Russ Berrie
Cedar Hill Studio
Creative Christian
Dicksons
Genesis
Heart Impressions
Heartsteps
J-Mar
New Boundary Designs
Bob Siemon Designs
Sunrise Publications
Swanson

MUGS
Cedar Hill Studio

Contenova Gifts
Dicksons
Russ Berrie
Genesis
New Boundary Designs
Bob Siemon Designs
Swanson

PLAQUES
Dicksons
Russ Berrie
Calligraphy Collection
Caring Card Company
Cathedral Art
Cedar Hill Studio
Creative Christian
Dicksons
Genesis
Heart Impressions
Image Craft
J-Mar
New Boundary Designs
Bob Siemon Designs
Swanson

POST CARDS
Abingdon
Argus Communications
Russ Berrie
Caring Card Co.
Cedar Hill Studio
Creative Christian
Divine Inspiration
Heart Impressions
Manhattan Greeting Card
New Boundary Designs
Read 'N Run Books
Swanson
Warner Press
Zondervan

POSTERS
Argus Communications
Caring Card Co.
Cedar Hill Studio
Divine Inspiration
Eldridge Publishing
Genesis
Read 'N Run Books
Scandecor
Standard Publishing
Sunrise Publications
Warner Press

PUZZLES
Dicksons

STATIONERY
Dicksons
Painted Hearts & Friends

SUNDAY BULLETINS
Warner Press

T-SHIRTS
Caring Card Co.
Cedar Hill Studio
Dicksons
Eldridge Publishing
Genesis
Heartsteps
Peele Enterprises

VIDEOS/VIDEO GAMES
Abingdon
Augsburg
Bible Games Co.
Brentwood Music
Broadman & Holman
Brown-ROA
Chariot (Rainfall)
Church Street Press
City Alive
Destiny Image
Diamante
Russ Doughten Films
Editorial Unilit
Focus on the Family
Gospel Light/Regal
Group Publishing
Howard Publishing
Integrity Music
InterVarsity
Liguori Publications
Moody Press
Paraclete Press
Pauline Video
Prophecy Publications
Star Song
Tyndale Family Video
Vermont Story Works
Victor Books
Vision Video
Wisdom Tree
Word
Zondervan

CHRISTIAN WRITERS' CONFERENCES AND WORKSHOPS

(*) Asterisk before a listing means the information was not verified or updated by the group leader.
(+) A plus sign before a listing indicates a new listing.

ALABAMA
SOUTHERN CHRISTIAN WRITERS CONFERENCE. Birmingham/Samford University, June 13-14, 1997 Contact: Joanne Sloan, SCWC, PO Box 1106, Northport AL 35476. (205)333-8603. Fax (205)339-4528. Attendance: 150-200.

ARIZONA
AMERICAN CHRISTIAN WRITERS PHOENIX CONFERENCE. October 23-25, 1997. IMPACT Days, March 8, 1997. Contact: Reg A. Forder, Box 110390, Nashville TN 37222. 1-800-21-WRITE. Attendance: 50-150.
MINI WRITING WORKSHOPS. Held in various U.S. locations, throughout the year. Contact and speaker: Donna Goodrich, 648 S. Pima St., Mesa AZ 85210. (602)962-6694. One to three-day-long workshops on various topics. Attendance: 20-30.
+NORTH TUCSON CHRISTIAN WRITERS' SEMINAR. January 27, 1997. Speaker: Mona Hodgson. Contact: Marianne Matthews, 7887 N. LaCholla Blvd. #3191, Tucson AZ 85741-3460. Phone/fax: (520)797-2298. E-mail: MMATTHEWS @wow.com.
*PRESCOTT CHRISTIAN WRITERS SEMINAR. Prescott, September 1997 (usually 4th Saturday). Contact: Barbara Spangler, 2967 N Meadowlark Dr., Prescott Valley AZ 86314-2556. (602)772-6263 or Pauline Dunn, 1840 Iron Springs Rd. #A2F, Prescott AZ 86301. (601)778-7342.
*SOUTH-EASTERN ARIZONA CHRISTIAN WRITERS SEMINAR. Tucson; September 1997. Contact: Kristina Lorentzen, PO Box 64956, Tucson AZ 85728-4956.
*TUCSON CHRISTIAN WRITERS RETREAT. Tucson, May 1997. Contact: Annie Dearborn, 2581 W Sunset Rd., Tucson AZ 85741-5233. (520)888-6915.

ARKANSAS
AMERICAN CHRISTIAN WRITERS SILOAM SPRINGS IMPACT DAY May 24, 1997. Contact: Reg Forder, Box 110390, Nashville TN 37222. 1-800-21-WRITE. Attendance: 50-150.
+ARKANSAS WRITERS' CONFERENCE. Little Rock; June 1997. Contact: Peggy Vining, 6817 Gingerbread Ln., Little Rock AR 72204. (501)565-8889. Attendance: 200.

CALIFORNIA

*ADOPT A PRISONER INC. WRITER'S SEMINARS Long Beach; July 1, September 1, and December 1, 1997. Contact & speaker: Achim Rodgers, 6341 Johnson Ave., Long Beach CA 90805. (310)428-7349.

AMERICAN CHRISTIAN WRITERS ANAHEIM IMPACT DAY. March 22, 1997. Contact: Reg Forder, Box 110390, Nashville TN 37222. 1-800-21-WRITE. Attendance: 50-150.

AMERICAN CHRISTIAN WRITERS FULLERTON CONFERENCE. October 16-18, 1997. Contact: Reg Forder, Box 110390, Nashville TN 37222. 1-800-21-WRITE. Attendance: 50-150.

AMERICAN CHRISTIAN WRITERS SAN DIEGO CONFERENCE. March 14-15, 1997. Contact: Reg Forder, Box 110390, Nashville TN 37222. 1-800-21-WRITE. Attendance: 50-150.

CASTRO VALLEY CHRISTIAN WRITERS SEMINAR. Castro Valley, February 28-March 1, 1997. Speaker: Norman Rohrer. Contact: Pastor Jon Drury, 19300 Redwood Rd., Castro Valley CA 94546-3465. (510)886-6300 or (510)881-5888. Fax (510)581-5022. Attendance: 60.

+CEHUC SPANISH CHRISTIAN WRITERS SEMINAR . Los Angeles, San Diego or Tijuana; April 1997. Contact: Magdalena Latorre, 9802 Quail Canyon Rd., El Cajon CA 92021-6000. Phone/fax (619)390-3747. New.

CHRISTIAN LEADERS AND SPEAKERS SEMINARS (C.L.A.S.S.). Various dates & locations across the country. Speakers: Florence Littauer and Marita Littauer. Contact: Marita Littauer, 1645 S. Rancho Santa Fe #102, San Marcos CA 92069. (619)471-0233. Attendance: 100.

CHRISTIAN WRITERS FELLOWSHIP OF ORANGE COUNTY WRITER'S DAYS. Santa Ana, April and October 1997. Contact: Carol Hutchins, PO Box 538, Lake Forest CA 92630. (310)379-5646. Attendance: 100.

INLAND EMPIRE CHRISTIAN WRITERS SEMINARS. Riverside, February & September 1997. Contact: Bill Page or Carole Gift Page, 10653 Ridgefield Terr., Moreno Valley CA 92557-3806. (909)924-0610. Attendance: 80.

*LODI ALL-DAY WRITERS SEMINAR. Stockton, no date set for 1997. General writing conference; not just Christian writers. Contact: Walt Meryman, Box 1863, Lodi CA 95241. (209)368-9849. Write and ask to be put on mailing list.

MOUNT HERMON CHRISTIAN WRITERS CONFERENCE. Mount Hermon (near Santa Cruz), March 21-25, 1997. Keynote speaker: Bill Butterworth, author/humorist. Advanced track with Sally Stuart. Contact: David R. Talbott, Box 413, Mount Hermon CA 95041-0413. (408)335-4466. Attendance: 125-200.

*NARRAMORE CHRISTIAN WRITERS CONFERENCE. Narramore Christian Foundation/Rosemead, April 1997. Contact: Dr. Clyde M. Narramore, 1409 N Walnut Grove Ave., Rosemead CA 91770. (818)288-7000. Attendance: 30.

SAN DIEGO CHRISTIAN WRITERS GUILD ONE-DAY SEMINAR. San Diego, September 1997. Contact: Robert Gillespie, 17041 Palacio Pl., San Diego CA 92027. (619)487-7929. E-mail: bgill@adnc.com. Web Page: www.globalwebs. com/writers. Attendance: 150.

SAN DIEGO STATE UNIVERSITY WRITERS CONFERENCE. SDSU Aztec Center, January 18-19, 1997. To advanced writers offers a read and critique by editors and agents. Contact: Jan Wahl, Gateway Center, College of Extended

Studies, 5250 Campanile Dr., San Diego CA 92182. (619)594-2514. Attendance: 350.

WRITE TO BE READ WORKSHOP. Hume Lake; call for date. Speakers: Norm Rohrer and others. Contact: Norman B. Rohrer, 260 Fern Ln., Hume CA 93628-9999. (209)335-2333. Fax (209)335-2770. E-mail: NVRohrer@aol.com. Free workshop. Attendance: 40.

COLORADO

+AD LIB CHRISTIAN WRITERS RETREAT. Woodland Park/Colorado Rockies, October 2-5, 1997. Contact: Judith Deem Dupree, PO Box 365, Pine Valley CA 91962. Phone/fax (619)473-8683. E-mail: rdupree/MCI ID: 755-5321. Not a conference, but a retreat/workshop with three facilitators in fiction, non-fiction and poetry. Attendance: 25.

*CHRISTIAN ARTISTS' SEMINAR IN THE ROCKIES. Estes Park, July/August 1997. For anyone interested in Christian music industry and ministry. Has classes in song writing and sketch writing. Contact: Cam Floria, 7100 Broadway, Ste. 3-K, Denver CO 80221-2920. (303)452-1313. Attendance: 1,000-1,300.

*COLORADO CHRISTIAN COMMUNICATORS RETREAT. Colorado Springs, September 1997. Contact: Scoti Domeij, 5209 Del Paz Dr., Colorado Springs CO 80918-2001. Attendance: 100.

COLORADO CHRISTIAN WRITERS CONFERENCE. Estes Park, YMCA of the Rockies; March 6-8, 1997. Interim Director: Marlene Bagnull, 316 Blanchard Rd., Drexel Hill PA 19026-3507. Phone/fax (610)626-6833. E-mail: mbagnull@ aol.com. (Debbie Barker on a sabbatical). Attendance: 225.

*GLEN EYRIE WRITERS' WORKSHOPS. Glen Eyrie Conference Center, Colorado Springs; February, April, June, October 1997 advanced, August 1997.Contact: Grace Saint, Box 6000, Colorado Springs CO 80934. (719)594-2535. Attendance: 20 maximum in each.

+SPAN '97: MASTERFUL BOOK PROMOTION & SELLING. San Francisco; September 6-8, 1997. Sponsored by the Small Publishers Assn. of North America. Speakers: Tom & Marilyn Ross. For authors, self-publishers and small presses. Contact: Marilyn Ross, PO Box 1306, Buena Vista CO 81211-1306. (719)395-4790. Fax (719)395-8374. E-mail: SPAN@span-assn.org. Attendance: 200.

WRITE TO BE READ WORKSHOP. Denver; call for date. Speakers: Norm Rohrer and others. Contact: Norman B. Rohrer, 260 Fern Ln., Hume CA 93628-9999. (209)335-2333. Fax (209)335-2770. E-mail: NVRohrer@aol.com. Free workshop. Attendance: 40.

CONNECTICUT

*WESLEYAN WRITERS CONFERENCE. Middletown, June 1997 Contact: Anne Green, c/o Wesleyan University, Middletown CT 06459. (203)347-9411, ext. 2448. Attendance: 100.

FLORIDA

AMERICAN CHRISTIAN WRITERS MIAMI CONFERENCE. November 14-15, 1997. Contact: Reg A. Forder, Box 110390, Nashville TN 37222. 1-800-21-WRITE. Attendance: 50-150.

FLORIDA CHRISTIAN WRITERS CONFERENCE. Park Avenue Retreat Center/Titusville; January 23-27, 1997; January 29-February 2, 1998. Speaker 1997: Clint Kelly. Offers advanced track by application only. Contact: Billie Wilson, 2600 Park Avenue, Titusville FL 32780. (407)269-6702x202. Attendance: 200.

WRITING STRATEGIES FOR THE CHRISTIAN MARKET. Classes for beginning, intermediate & advanced writers March 1, May 3, October 4 & November 1, 1997. Also material available for an independent studies program by mail. Contact: Rosemary J. Upton, 2712 S. Peninsula Dr., Daytona Beach FL 32118. (904)322-1111. Write to be put on mailing list. Attendance: 10-20.

GEORGIA

AMERICAN CHRISTIAN WRITERS ATLANTA CONFERENCE. September 26-27, 1997. IMPACT Days, April 26, 1997. Contact: Reg Forder, Box 110390, Nashville TN 37222. 1-800-21-WRITE. Attendance: 50-150.

CHRISTIAN BOOKSELLERS ASSN. CONVENTION. Atlanta, Georgia (held in a different location each year), July 12-17, 1997. Contact: CBA, Box 200, Colorado Springs CO 80901. (719)576-7880. Entrance badges available through book publishers.

NORTHEAST GEORGIA WRITERS CONFERENCE. Gainesville, October 1998 (biennial/even-numbered years). Contact: Elouise Whitten, 660 Crestview Terrace, Gainesville GA 30501-3110. (770)532-3007. Attendance: 50-60.

SOUTHEASTERN WRITERS CONFERENCE, St. Simons Island; June 15-21,1997. Contact: Pay Laye, Rt. 1 Box 102, Cuthbert GA 31740. (912)679-5445. Attendance: 100 (limited).

HAWAII

*YWAM WRITERS SEMINAR. Kona, July 1997. Speakers: Janice Rogers & Beverly Caruso. Contact: Beverly Caruso, 1621 Baldwin Ave., Orange CA 92665. (714)637-1733. Fax (714)282-0496. Attendance: 30-40.

IDAHO

INTERNATIONAL NETWORK OF COMMUNICATORS & THE ARTS CONFERENCE. Coeur d'Alene; September 30-October 3, 1997. Contact: Sheri Stone, Box 1754, Post Falls ID 83854-1754. Phone/fax (208)667-9730. Attendance: 300.

ILLINOIS

AMERICAN CHRISTIAN WRITERS/CHRISTIAN WRITERS INSTITUTE CHICAGO CONFERENCE. August 15-16, 1997. Contact: Reg Forder, Box 110390, Nashville TN 37222. 1-800-21-WRITE. Attendance: 50-150

+ASSOCIATED CHURCH PRESS 1997 ANNUAL CONVENTION. Chicago, April 20-23, 1997. Contact: John Stapert, The Associated Church Press, PO Box 30215, Phoenix AZ 85046-0215. E-mail: John_Stapert@Ecunet.org. Workshops, individual critique, meet editors, discuss potential assignments, etc.

+ILLINOIS PRAIRIE WRITER'S CONFERENCE. Wyanet; June 1997. Contact: Illinois Prairie Writer's Assn., PO Box 372, Wyanet IL 61379.

INTERNATIONAL BLACK WRITERS CONFERENCE. Chicago, June 27-29, 1997. Contact: Mable Terrell, PO Box 1030, Chicago IL 60690-1030. (312)409-2292.

MISSISSIPPI VALLEY WRITERS CONFERENCE. (24th) Augustana College/Rock Island, June 8-13, 1997. Contact: David R. Collins, 3403 45th St., Moline IL 61265. (309)762-8985. Offers advanced novel track. Attendance: 80.

THE SALVATION ARMY CHRISTIAN WRITERS' CONFERENCE. Des Plaines IL, April 1998 (held every other year). Contact: Elizabeth Kinzie, 10 W. Algonquin Rd., Des Plaines IL 60016-6006. (847)294-2050. Attendance: 60. For S.A. officers, laymen, and employee staff.

WRITE-TO-PUBLISH CONFERENCE. Wheaton College (Chicago area); June 2-6, 1997. Keynoter: Neva Coyle. Contact: Lin Johnson, 9731 Fox Glen Dr., #6F, Niles IL 60714-5828. (847)296-3964. Fax (847)296-0754. E-mail: 102661. 3622@compuserve.com. Attendance: 150.

INDIANA

*BETHEL COLLEGE CHRISTIAN WRITERS' WORKSHOP. Mishawaka; July 1997. Contact: Carol Gravelyn, 1001 W. McKinley Ave., Mishawaka IN 46545-5509. (219)257-3352. Attendance: 120.

+IMAGE FESTIVAL OF LITERATURE AND THE ARTS. New Harmony; November 1997. Contact: Image, PO Box 674, Kennett Square PA 19348, or call Richard Wilkinson at (610)444-8065 or e-mail: gwolfe@isi.org.

MIDWEST WRITERS WORKSHOP. Muncie, July 30-August 2, 1997. Contact: Dr. Earl Conn, Dept. of Journalism, Ball State University, Muncie IN 47306-0675. (317)285-6000. Fax 317-285-6002. E-mail: %%ELCONN@BSU.edu. Attendance: 120.

OPEN DOOR CHRISTIAN WRITERS SEMINAR. Westport; May1998. Contact: Janet Teitsort, PO Box 78, Westport IN 47283-0078. Phone/fax (812)591-2210.

KANSAS

*BCCC CREATIVE WRITING WORKSHOP. Butler County Community College, El Dorado; Fall 1997. Contact: Vivien Minshull-Ford, 901 S. Haverhill Rd., El Dorado KS 67042. (316)321-5083, ext. 233. Attendance: 200.

BOONDOCKS RETREAT. Dodge City; possibly June, date not set. Contact: Linda Fergerson, 2500 Memory Ln., Dodge City KS 67801. (316)225-1126. Attendance: 25-40. Offers a spiritual retreat for writers, rather than a nuts & bolts conference.

+KANSAS CITY CHRISTIAN WRITERS' NETWORK FALL CONFERENCE. Kansas City area; October 11, 1997, October 10, 1998. Contact: Teresa Vining, 1438 N Lucy Montgomery Way, Olathe KS 66061-6706. Phone/fax: (913)764-4610. E-mail: KCCWN@aol.com. Offers advanced track and classes for teens. Attendance: 100. Also offers a spring writing retreat (May 10, 1997).

PITTSBURG CHRISTIAN WRITERS' SEMINAR. Pittsburg; April 1997 & 1998. Contact: LeAnn Campbell, 267 SW 1st Ln., Lamar MO 64759. (417)682-2713.

KENTUCKY

AMERICAN CHRISTIAN WRITERS LOUISVILLE CONFERENCE. February

1, 1997. Contact: Reg A. Forder, Box 110390, Nashville TN 37222. 1-800-21-WRITE. Attendance: 50-150.

LOUISIANA
*LOUISIANA CHRISTIAN WRITERS GUILD WORKSHOP. Shreveport; July 1997. Contact: Mark Sutton, 8900 Kingston Rd., Shreveport LA 71118. (318)686-2898. Attendance: 50+.

MAINE
*FOURTH ANNUAL CHRISTIAN WRITERS' CONFERENCE. China Lake Conference Center, August 1997. Contact: Dr. Ken Parker, Minister of Conferencing & Camping, China Lake Conference Center, PO Box 149, China ME 04926. (207)968-2101, Fax (207)968-2434. Attendance: 35-50.
STATE OF MAINE WRITERS' CONFERENCE. Ocean Park; August 19-22,1997. Contact: Richard F. Burns, PO Box 7146, Ocean Park ME 04063-7146. (207)934-9806 (summer) or (413)596-6734 (winter). E-mail: rburnsO@kraken. mvnet.wnec.edu. Attendance: 25-40. Contest announcement available March 1; brochure available June 1. Half-price tuition for teens.

MARYLAND
SANDY COVE CHRISTIAN WRITERS CONFERENCE. Sandy Cove/North East, October 5-9, 1997. Offers Advanced Track. Contact: Gayle Roper, 251 Water Works Rd., Coatesville PA 19320. (610)384-8125. E-mail: GGRoper@ aol.com. Attendance: 150.
*REVIEW AND HERALD WRITERS' WEEK. Review & Herald Publishing Assn., Hagerstown; July 1997. Contact: Penny E. Wheeler, 55 W. Oak Ridge Dr., Hagerstown MD 21740. (301)790-9731. Attendance: 50.

MASSACHUSETTS
AMERICAN CHRISTIAN WRITERS BOSTON CONFERENCE. June 20-21, 1997. Contact: Reg Forder, Box 110390, Nashville TN 37222. 1-800-21-WRITE. Attendance: 50-150.
*CAPE COD WRITERS' CONFERENCE. Craigville Conference Center, August 1997. Contact: Joseph Ryan, c/o Cape Cod Conservatory, Rt. 132, West Barnstable MA 02668. (508)375-0516. Attendance: 125. Also offers CAPE LITERARY ARTS WORKSHOPS: 6 simultaneous week-long workshops (poetry, romance novels, juvenile writing, children's book illustrating, and play writing), August 1997. Limited to 10 in each workshop.

MICHIGAN
*ANDREWS UNIVERSITY CHRISTIAN WRITER'S AND COMMUNICATOR'S CONFERENCE. Berrien Springs, June 1997. Contact: Dr. Kermit Netteburg, Communications Dept., Andrews University, Berrien Springs MI 49104. (616)471-3618. Attendance: 85.
EVANGELICAL PRESS ASSOCIATION CONVENTION. Grand Rapids; May 4-7,1997 (held in different location each year). Chicago IL, May 1998. 1997 speakers: John Perkins and Ken Medema. Contact: Ron Wilson, dir., 485 Pano-

rama Rd, Earlysville VA 22936. (804)973-5941. Fax (804)973-2710. E-mail: 74473.272@compuserve.com. Attendance: 300-400. Annual convention; freelance communicators welcome.

MARANATHA CHRISTIAN WRITERS SEMINAR. Maranatha Bible & Missionary Conference/Muskegon, August 18-22,1997 (20th anniversary). Contact: Leona Hertel, 4759 Lake Harbor Rd., Muskegon MI 49441-5299. (616)798-2161. Attendance: 50.

*MICHIGAN NORTHWOODS WRITERS CONFERENCE. Glen Arbor, July 1997. Contact: Robert Karner, 1 Old Homestead Rd., Glen Arbor MI 49636. (616)334-3072.

"SPEAK UP WITH CONFIDENCE" SEMINARS. Hillsdale, July 24-27, 1997. Contact: Carol Kent, 1614 Edison Shores Pl., Port Huron MI 48060. (810)982-0898. Fax (810)987-4163. Speaker: Carol Kent. Speaking seminar. Offers advanced training. Attendance: 100.

MINNESOTA

AMERICAN CHRISTIAN WRITERS MINNEAPOLIS CONFERENCE. August 8-9, 1997. Contact: Reg Forder, Box 110390, Nashville TN 37222. 1-800-21-WRITE. Attendance: 50-150.

MINNESOTA CHRISTIAN WRITERS GUILD SPRING SEMINAR. Minneapolis/St. Paul, April 19-20, 1997. Contact: Charette Barta, 5344 Ewing Ave. S., Minneapolis MN 55410. (612)922-4609. Attendance: 80-100.

MISSOURI

AMERICAN CHRISTIAN WRITERS ST. LOUIS CONFERENCE. September 12-13, 1997. Contact: Reg Forder, Box 110390, Nashville TN 37222. 1-800-21-WRITE. Attendance: 50-150.

*GREATER ST. LOUIS INSPIRATIONAL WRITERS WORKSHOP. St. Louis metro area. Contact: Lila Wold Shelburne, 707 Gran Lin Dr., St. Charles MO 63303-6025. (314)946-8533.

MARK TWAIN WRITERS CONFERENCE. Hannibal, Heartland Lodge, four separate weeks in June, July, August & September, 1997. Contact: Cyndi Allison, 921 Center St., Hannibal MO 63401. (800)747-0738. (573)221-2462. Fax (573)221-6409. Attendance: 25 per conference. Note: This is a general conference under the direction of evangelical Christians.

*NAZARENE WRITERS CONFERENCE. No date or location set for next conference. Contact: Shona Fisher, 6401 The Paseo, Kansas City MO 64131. (816)333-7000x2387. Attendance: 200.

WRITE TO BE READ WORKSHOP. St. Louis; call for date. Speakers: Norm Rohrer and others. Contact: Norman B. Rohrer, 260 Fern Ln., Hume CA 93628-9999. (209)335-2333. Fax (209)335-2770. E-mail: NVRohrer@aol.com. Free workshop. Attendance: 40.

NEW JERSEY

DAYSTAR COMMUNICATIONS WRITING WORKSHOPS. Half-day (3 hour) and full-day (6 hour) Workshops on a wide variety of writing topics. Send for brochure. Contact: Dr. Mary Ann Diorio, PO Box 405, Millville NJ 08332-0405.

(609)327-1231. Fax (609)327-0291. E-mail: 72602,1027@compuserve.com; or madiorio@aol.com.

NEW MEXICO

+GHOST RANCH WRITING WORKSHOPS. Abiquiu; October 1997. Contact: Ghost Ranch, HC 77 Box 11, Abiquiu NM 87510-9601.

GLORIETTA CHRISTIAN WRITERS' CONFERENCE. November 5-9, 1997. Contact: Mona Hodgson, PO Box 999, Cottonwood AZ 86326. (520)634-0384. New conference.

SOUTHWEST CHRISTIAN WRITERS ASSN. SEMINAR. Farmington, September 20, 1997 (18th Annual). Speaker: Susan Titus Osborn. Contact: Tom Walmsley, PO Box 1008, Flora Vista NM 87415. (505)334-0617. Attendance: 30.

SOUTHWEST WRITERS WORKSHOP. Albuquerque, August 1997. Contact: Paula Paul, 1338 Wyoming Blvd. NE, Ste. B, Albuquerque NM 87112-5067. (505)293-0303. Fax (505)237-2665. Attendance: 400.

WRITERS' CONFERENCE AT SANTA FE. Santa Fe, February 21-23, 1997. Contact: Michele Lis, Program Coordinator, Dept. of Continuing Education, Santa Fe Community College, Box 4187, Santa Fe NM 87502-4187. (505)438-1251. Attendance: 100-120.

NEW YORK

*GREATER SYRACUSE CHRISTIAN WRITER'S CONFERENCE. Liverpool, May 1997. Contact: Pat Spencer, 108 Woodpath Rd., Liverpool NY 13090. (315)652-3178. Attendance: 60-75.

OHIO

*ANTIOCH WRITERS WORKSHOP. Secular. Antioch College/Yellow Springs; July 1997. Contact: Judy DuPolito, PO Box 494, Yellow Springs OH 45387. (513)866-9060. Attendance: 70.

CINCINNATI BIBLE COLLEGE CHRISTIAN WRITERS WORKSHOP. Cincinnati, September 6,1997. Contact: Dr. Ward Patterson, 2852 McKinley Ave., Cincinnati OH 45211. (513)244-8445. Attendance: 80-100.

COLUMBUS CHRISTIAN WRITERS CONFERENCE. Columbus, May 1997. Contact: Brenda Custodio, 3069 Bocastle Ct., Reynoldsburg OH 43068. (614)861-1011. E-mail: custodiob2@aol.com. Attendance: 60.

+HEIGHTS WRITERS CONFERENCE. Beechwood, May 3, 1997 (always 1st Saturday of May). Contact: Lavern Hall, Writer's World Press, PO Box 24684, Cleveland OH 44124-0684. (216)481-1974.

NORTHWEST OHIO CHRISTIAN WRITERS SEMINAR. Toledo; September 27,1997. Contact: Linda Tippett, 4221 Woodmont Rd., Toledo OH 43613. (419)475-9169. Attendance: 75-100.

SET FORTH CHRISTIAN WRITERS GUILD SEMINAR. North Central OH/Mansfield area; July 1997. Contact: Donna Caudill, 836 Delph Ave., Mansfield OH 44906. (419)747-1755.

+STATELINE CHRISTIAN WRITER'S CLUB PEOPLE IN PRINT SEMINAR. Celina, October 18, 1997. Contact: Shirley Knox, 54106 Club Island Rd., Celina OH 45822. (419)268-2040.

+WEST-DAYTON CHRISTIAN WRITERS SEMINAR. Dayton; August 1997. Contact: Tina V. Toles, 518 Lambert Ln., Englewood OH 45323. (937)836-6600.

OKLAHOMA
AMERICAN CHRISTIAN WRITERS TULSA CONFERENCE. July 31-August 2, 1997. Contact: Reg Forder, Box 110390, Nashville TN 37222. 1-800-21-WRITE. Attendance: 50-150.
*WRITING WORKSHOPS. Various locations and dates. Contact: Kathryn Fanning, PO Box 18472, Oklahoma City OK 73154-0472.

OREGON
OREGON CHRISTIAN WRITERS COACHING CONFERENCE. Salem, July 21-24,1997. Speaker: Lonnie Hull Dupont. Contact: Sandy Cathcart, 341 Flounce Rock Rd., Prospect OR 97536-9726. (541)560-2367. E-mail: 75222.3643@compuserve.com. Attendance: 125-150.
WRITE TO BE READ WORKSHOP. Eugene; call for date. Speakers: Norm Rohrer and others. Contact: Norman B. Rohrer, 260 Fern Ln., Hume CA 93628-9999. (209)335-2333. Fax (209)335-2770. E-mail: NVRohrer@aol.com. Free workshop. Attendance: 40.

PENNSYLVANIA
*CATHOLIC PRESS ASSOCIATION ANNUAL CONVENTION. May 1997. Contact: Owen McGovern, exec. dir., 3555 Veterans Memorial Hwy Ste. O, Ronkonkoma NY 11779-7636. (516)471-4730. For media professionals. Attendance: 350.
GREATER PHILADELPHIA CHRISTIAN WRITERS' CONFERENCE. Dresher (N. of Philadelphia), May 29-31, 1997. Especially encourages African-American writers. Contact: Marlene Bagnull, 316 Blanchard Rd., Drexel Hill PA 19026-3507. Phone/fax (610)626-6833. E-mail: mbagnull@aol.com. Attendance: 300.
MONTROSE CHRISTIAN WRITERS CONFERENCE. Montrose, July 7-11, 1997. Contact: Jill Renich Meyers, 5 Locust St., Montrose PA 18801-1112. (717)278-1001. Fax (717)278-3061. Includes advanced track. Attendance: 85.
ST. DAVIDS 40TH CHRISTIAN WRITERS' CONFERENCE. Geneva College/Beaver Falls, near Pittsburgh, June 15-20, 1997. Offers advanced track. Marji Stewart, director. Contact: Audrey Stallsmith, registrar, 87 Pines Rd. E., Hadley PA 16130. (412)253-2738. Attendance: 60-100.
WEST BRANCH CHRISTIAN WRITERS SEMINAR. Williamsport, October 1997. Contact: Eileen Berger, RR 2 Box 378, Hughesville PA 17737. (717)584-2280.
*WRITING FOR PUBLICATION. Pittsburgh Theological Seminary, April 1997. Speaker: Dr. Roland Tapp. Contact: The Rev. Mary Lee Talbot, 616 N. Highland Ave., Pittsburgh PA 15206. (412)362-5610x296. Attendance: 25.

SOUTH CAROLINA
SOUTH CAROLINA CHRISTIAN WRITERS CONFERENCE. Conestee; September 27, 1997, September 26, 1998. Speaker for 1997: Muriel Larson. Contact: Betty Robertson, PO Box 12624, Roanoke VA 24027. Phone/fax (540)342-7511. E-mail: ccmbbr@worldnet.att.com. Attendance: 50.

TENNESSEE

AMERICAN CHRISTIAN WRITERS MEMPHIS CONFERENCE. May 31, 1997. Contact: Reg Forder, Box 110390, Nashville TN 37222. 1-800-21-WRITE. Attendance: 50-150.

AMERICAN CHRISTIAN WRITERS NATIONAL RETREAT. August 29-September 1, 1997. Speakers: Steve Laube, Susan Osborn, Dennis Hensley, and Lin Johnson. Contact: Reg Forder, Box 110390, Nashville TN 37222. 1-800-21-WRITE. Attendance: 50-150.

+PRESBYTERIAN WRITER'S GUILD WORKSHOP. Nashville; April 7-12. Perry Biddle, director. Contact: Jane Hines, registrar, PWGW, PO Box 1207, Brentwood TN 37024-1207. (615)370-4008.

*RELIGIOUS COMMUNICATIONS CONGRESS. Nashville, April 1997. Contact: RCC, Mail Stop 192, 127 Ninth Ave. N., Nashville TN 37234.

*SOUTHERN BAPTIST WRITERS WORKSHOP. Nashville, July 1997. Contact: Director, 127 Ninth Ave. N., Nashville TN 37234. (615)251-2939. Attendance: 50.

TEXAS

AMERICAN CHRISTIAN WRITERS AUSTIN CONFERENCE. February 21-22, 1997. Contact: Reg Forder, Box 110390, Nashville TN 37222. 1-800-21-WRITE. Attendance: 60-150.

AMERICAN CHRISTIAN WRITERS DALLAS CONFERENCE. May 16-17, 1997. Contact: Reg Forder, Box 110390, Nashville TN 37222. 1-800-21-WRITE. Attendance: 50-150.

AMERICAN CHRISTIAN WRITERS HOUSTON CONFERENCE. February 14-15, 1997. Contact: Reg Forder, Box 110390, Nashville TN 37222. 1-800-21-WRITE. Attendance: 50-150.

*THE ART OF WRITING, THE ACT OF WRITING. Longview, March 1997. Contact: Ernestine Finigan, Box 8513, Marshall TX 75670. (214)935-3047 or 938-0756 (days). Attendance: 50+.

+AUSTIN CHRISTIAN WRITERS' CONFERENCE. Austin, February 21-22, 1997. Contact: Bob Rose, 309 Summit Ridge North, Leander TX 78645-8645. (512)267-3630. Fax (512)219-5444 (voice activated). New conference.

*FRONTIERS IN WRITING. Amarillo College, August 1997. Sponsored by Panhandle Professional Writers. Contact: Doris R. Meredith, Box 19303, Amarillo TX 79114. (806)352-3889. Attendance: 100. Write for contest information.

INSPIRATIONAL WRITERS ALIVE!/AMARILLO SEMINAR. April 5, 1997. Speaker: Sally E. Stuart. Contact: Helen Luecke, 2921 S. Dallas, Amarillo TX 79103-6713. (806)376-9671.

*SOUTHWESTERN CHRISTIAN WRITERS GUILD CONFERENCE. Dallas, fall 1997. Contact: Jan Winebrenner, 2709 Winding Hollow, Plano TX 75093. (214)867-1119.

TEXAS CHRISTIAN WRITERS FORUM. Houston; August 1988 (first Saturday in August in even numbered years). Contact: Maxine E. Holder, Rt. 4 Box 81-H, Rusk TX 75785-9410.(903)795-3986. Attendance: 65.

+YWAM HANDS-ON WRITERS TRAINING WORKSHOPS. Lindale; various dates. Contact: Pamela Warren, PO Box 1380, Lindale TX 75771-1380. (903)882-5591x288. Send SASE for list of workshops.

VIRGINIA
AMERICAN CHRISTIAN WRITERS VIRGINIA BEACH CONFERENCE. June 27-28, 1997. Contact: Reg Forder, Box 110390, Nashville TN 37222. 1-800-21-WRITE. Attendance: 50-150.

NORTHERN VIRGINIA CHRISTIAN WRITERS ANNUAL CONFERENCE. Fairfax; March 15, 1997. Contact: Jennifer Ferranti, dir., PO Box 629, Dunn Loring VA 22027-0629. Phone/fax (703)698-7707. E-mail: 75327.3147@compuserve.com. Advanced track. Attendance: 100.

VIRGINIA CHRISTIAN WRITERS CONFERENCE. Roanoke; April 12, 1997. Speakers: Lt. Col. Marlene Chase and Yvonne Lehman. Contact: Betty B. Robertson, PO Box 12624, Roanoke VA 24027-2624. (540)342-7511. Fax (540)342-7511. E-mail: ccmbbr@worldnet.att.net. Attendance: 50.

***WRITING FOR CHRISTIAN PUBLISHERS.** Regent University/Virginia Beach; August 1997. Contact: Dr. Doug Tarpley, chairman, School of Journalism, Regent University, Virginia Beach VA 23464. (804)532-7091/436-2926. New—projected attendance: 100-200.

WRITING FOR THE LOCAL CHURCH . . . AND SOMETIMES BEYOND. Held in various locations by invitation. Contact: Betty B. Robertson, PO Box 12624, Roanoke VA 24027-2624. Phone/fax:(540)342-7511. E-mail: ccmbbr@ worldnet.att.com.

WASHINGTON
AMERICAN CHRISTIAN WRITERS SEATTLE CONFERENCE. April 4-5, 1997. Contact: Reg Forder, Box 110390, Nashville TN 37222. 1-800-21-WRITE. Attendance: 50-150.

+DOMINION COLLEGE WRITERS' CONFERENCE. Seattle area; November 1997. Contact: Geoff Pope, 20833 Highway 99S, Seattle Washington 98198. (206)870-3492. Fax (206)870-3553. E-mail: Geoffish@aol.com. Attendance:75-160.

***NORTHWEST CHRISTIAN WRITERS ASSN. SEMINARS.** Seattle area, date to be announced. Contact: Beth Harris, 14313 - 130th Ave. NE, Kirkland WA 98034.

***PACIFIC NORTHWEST WRITERS CONFERENCE.** Tukwilla (Seattle); no date given. Contact: Don Clark, 2033 - 6th Ave. #804, Seattle WA 98121. (206)443-3807. This is a secular conference that includes classes in Christian writing. Also sponsors a contest and conference for high school students. Attendance: 700.

SDA CAMP MEETING WRITING CLASS. Auburn, June 22-27, 1997. Open to non-Adventists. Contact: Marian Forschler, 18115 - 116th Ave. SE, Renton WA 98058-6562. (206)235-1435. Attendance: 50.

***SEATTLE PACIFIC CHRISTIAN WRITERS CONFERENCE.** Seattle. Contact for new schedule. Offers Mentoring Program, Process Sessions, Issues Forums, & Marketing Update Sessions. Contact: Linda Wagner, Humanities Dept., Seattle Pacific University, Seattle WA 98119. (206)281-2109.

***WASHINGTON CHRISTIAN WRITERS.** Seattle, February, June & September 1997. Contact: Elaine Colvin, PO Box 11337, Bainbridge Island WA 98110. (206)842-9103. Attendance: 75-100.

***WENATCHEE CHRISTIAN WRITERS MINI-SEMINAR.** Wenatchee, September 1997. Contact: Shirley Pease, 1818 Skyline Dr. #31, Wenatchee WA 98801-2302. (509)662-8392. Attendance: 50.

WRITERS HELPING WRITERS. Spokane; March 6-8, 1997. This is not a conference, but a booth offering manuscript evaluation and help to writers during the annual Christian Workers Conference. Contact: Pat Pfeiffer, PO Box 104, Otis Orchards WA 97027-0140. (509)927-7671 or 226-3532 (evenings).

WRITERS INFORMATION NETWORK (W.I.N.) SEMINARS. Seattle/February; Alaska/March; Texas/May; Seattle/June & September. Contact: Elaine Colvin, Box 11337, Bainbridge Island WA 98110. (206)842-9103. Attendance: 75-150.

WRITER'S WEEKEND AT THE BEACH. Ocean Park, February 1997. Contact: Pat Rushford, 3600 Edgewood Dr., Vancouver WA 98661. (206)695-2263 or Birdie Etchison, PO Box 877, Ocean Park WA 98640. (206)665-6576. Attendance: Limited to 45-50.

WISCONSIN

GREEN LAKE CHRISTIAN WRITER'S CONFERENCE. Green Lake, July 5-12,1997. Contact: Jan DeWitt, Program Dept., American Baptist Assembly, W2511 State Hwy 23,Green Lake WI 54941-9300. (800)558-8898. Fax (414)294-3878. Attendance: 80. Also provides Christian Writer's Weeks when you can stay at the conference center for writing time. Contact for dates.

TIMBER-LEE CHRISTIAN WRITER'S CONFERENCE. Timber-Lee Christian Center/East Troy, February or April 1997. Contact: Mary Kay Meeker, N8705 Scout Rd., East Troy WI 53120. (414)642-7345. Attendance: 30-40.

*WORD & PEN CHRISTIAN WRITERS CONFERENCE. Oshkosh, September 1997 (tentative). Contact: Beth A. Ziarnik, 1963 Indian Point Rd., Oshkosh WI 54901. (414)235-0664. Attendance: 75.

CANADA

ALBERTA CHRISTIAN WRITERS' SEMINARS. Last week-end of April (Rocky Mountain College, Calgary AB) & September 27, 1997 (King's University College in Edmonton AB). September Speakers: Sally Stuart, 1997; Luci Shaw, 1998. Contact: Elsie Montgomery, pres., 34 - 1130 Falconer Rd., Edmonton AB T6R 2J6, Canada. (403)988-5622. Fax (403)430-0139. E-mail: elsie_montgomery@enabel.ccinet.ab.ca

*GOD USES INK WRITERS AT BRIERCREST SCHOOLS. Caronport, SK, Briercrest Bible College; June 1997. Contact: Shirley Klassen, 510 College Dr., Caronport SK S0H 0S0 Canada. (306)756-3358. Attendance: 70.

GOD USES INK WRITERS CONFERENCE/ON. Guelph, Ontario; June 12-14,1997. Speaker: Ellen Santilli Vaughn. Contact: Marianne Meed Ward, M.I.P. Box 3745, Markham ON L3R 0Y4 Canada. (905)479-5885. Fax (905)479-4742. E-mail: ft@efccanada.com. Attendance: 110-120. Offers a Professional Track for advanced writers.

*SWAN VALLEY WRITERS GUILD CONFERENCE. Swan River, Manitoba; date unconfirmed. Contact: Julie Bell, Box 262, Bowsman MB R0L 0H0 Canada. (204)734-7890.

WORDPOWER. Clearbrook, none scheduled for 1997. Contact: MB Herald, 3-169

Riverton Ave., Winnipeg MB R2L 2E5 Canada. (204)669-6575. Offers workshops for advanced and young writers. Attendance: 100-150.

FOREIGN COUNTRIES

AMERICAN CHRISTIAN WRITERS CARIBBEAN CRUISE. November 16-23, 1997. Speakers: Dr. Dennis Hensley, Carole Gift Page, and Sally E. Stuart. Contact: Reg A. Forder, Box 110390, Nashville TN 37222. 1-800-21-WRITE. Attendance: 40-50.

WRITERS' SUMMER SCHOOL. Swanwick, Derbyshire, England; August 16-27, 1997. Contact: Brenda Courtie, The New Vicarage, Parsons St., Woodford Halse, Daventry, Northants, NN11 3RE, England, United Kingdom. Phone/fax: 01327-261477. E-mail: courties@dial.pipex.com. A secular conference attended by many Christians. Attendance: 300.

*YWAM WRITING SEMINARS. Seminars pending in Egypt, Israel, Great Britain, Chile, Guatemala during 1997. Open to invitations. Contact: Beverly Caruso, 1621 Baldwin Ave., Orange CA 92665. (714)282-0496. Attendance 15-50.

CONFERENCES THAT CHANGE LOCATIONS

CHRISTIAN BOOKSELLERS ASSN. CONVENTION. Atlanta, Georgia (held in a different location each year), July 12-17, 1997. Contact: CBA, Box 200, Colorado Springs Co 80901. (719)576-7880. Entrance badges available through book publishers.

EVANGELICAL PRESS ASSOCIATION CONVENTION. Grand Rapids; May 4-7,1997 (held in different location each year). Chicago IL, May 1998. 1997 speakers: John Perkins and Ken Medema. Contact: Ron Wilson, dir., 485 Panorama Rd, Earlysville VA 22936. (804)973-5941. Fax (804)973-2710. E-mail: 74473.272@compuserve.com. Attendance: 300-400. Annual convention; freelance communicators welcome.

"WRITE HIS ANSWER" SEMINARS. Various locations around U.S.; dates throughout the year; choice of article writing or books (includes self-publishing). Contact: Marlene Bagnull, 316 Blanchard Rd., Drexel Hill PA 19026-3507. Phone/fax (610)626-6833. E-mail: mbagnull@aol.com. Attendance: 30-100. Day or day-and-a-half seminars by the author of *Write His Answer—Encouragement for Christian Writers.*

THE WRITING ACADEMY SEMINAR Changes location every year. Contact: Nora Buys, 11534 Hillpark Ln., Los Altos CA 94024.

*YWAM CHRISTIAN WRITERS SEMINARS. Various states, Africa, Middle East, and South America; various dates. Contact: Registrar, YWAM Writer's Seminars, Box 3464, Orange CA 92665. (714)637-1733. Fax (714)282-0496.

AREA CHRISTIAN WRITERS' CLUBS, FELLOWSHIP GROUPS, AND CRITIQUE GROUPS

(*) An asterisk before a listing means the information was not verified or updated by the group leader.
(+) A plus sign before a listing indicates a new listing.

ALABAMA
CHRISTIAN freelanceRS, Tuscaloosa. Contact: Joanne Sloan, 3230 Mystic Lake Way, Northport AL 35476. (205)333-8603. Fax (205)339-4528. Membership (30+) open.

ARIZONA
*BETHANY CHRISTIAN WRITERS' CLUB. Phoenix. Contact: Rod Hugen, 2140 W. Nicolet, Phoenix AZ 85021. (602)995-1857. Membership (25+) open.
FOUNTAIN HILLS CHRISTIAN WRITERS. Contact: Rosemarie D. Malroy, 10413 N. Demaret Dr., Fountain Hills AZ 85268-5742. (602)837-8494. Membership (24) open. Occasionally sponsors a seminar.
*GRACE CHAPEL WRITERS CLUB. Scottsdale. Contact: Frances Klinkert, 4523 N. 34th St., Phoenix AZ 85018. Membership (11) open.
MESA CHRISTIAN WRITERS CLUB. Contact: Donna Goodrich, 648 S. Pima St., Mesa AZ 85210. (602)962-6694. Membership (15-20) open.
+NORTH TUCSON CHRISTIAN WRITERS' FELLOWSHIP. Contact: Marianne Matthews, 7887 N. LaCholla Blvd. #3191, Tucson AZ 85741-3460. Phone/fax: (520)797-2298. E-mail: MMATTHEWS@wow.com. Membership (20) open. Sponsors a January seminar.
PHOENIX CHRISTIAN WRITERS' FELLOWSHIP. Contact: Victor J. Kelly Sr., 2135 W. Cactus Wren Dr., Phoenix AZ 85021. (602)864-1390. E-mail: Vkelly@getnet.com. Membership (20) open.
*PRESCOTT CHRISTIAN WRITERS FELLOWSHIP. Contact: Barbara Spangler, 2967 N Meadowlark Dr., Prescott Valley AZ 86314-2556. (602)772-6263/778-7342. Membership (10-15) open. Sponsors one-day seminar (usually 4th Saturday in September).
*SOUTH-EASTERN ARIZONA CHRISTIAN WRITERS GROUP. Benson. Contact: Kristina Lorentzen, PO Box 64956, Tucson AZ 85728-4956. Membership (18) open. Sponsoring a September 1997 seminar.
TEMPE CHRISTIAN WRITERS GROUP. Contact: Andrea Huelsenbeck, 6510 S. Alder Dr., Tempe AZ 85283-3907. (602)730-0052. Membership (60) open.
*TUCSON CHRISTIAN WRITERS FELLOWSHIP. Contact: Annie Dearborn, 2581 W Sunset Rd., Tucson AZ 85741-5233. (520)888-6915. Membership (30) open. Sponsoring a May retreat.
*WORD OF GRACE WRITERS CLUB. Mesa. Contact: George & Valerie Martinez, 315 N. Hobson, Mesa AZ 85203. (602)969-3358. Membership (15+) open.

CALIFORNIA

CASTRO VALLEY CHRISTIAN WRITERS GROUP. Contact: Pastor Jon Drury, 19300 Redwood Rd., Castro Valley CA 94546. (510)886-6300. Fax (510)581-5022. Membership (10) open. Sponsoring a Christian Writers Seminar, February 28-May 1, 1997.

+CEHUC SPANISH CHRISTIAN WRITERS GROUP. El Cajon. Contact: Magdalena Latorre, 9802 Quail Canyon Rd., El Cajon CA 92021-6000. Phone/fax (619)390-3747. Membership (34) open. Sponsors a contest open to non-members. Planning a Spanish conference for April 1997 in Los Angeles, San Diego or Tijuana.

+CHILDREN'S WRITERS GROUP. Lake Forest. Contact: Eileen Reinoehl, 24902 Winterwood Dr., Lake Forest CA 92630. (714)859-6294. For serious children's writers

CHRISTIAN WRITERS FELLOWSHIP OF ORANGE COUNTY. Santa Ana. Contact: Louis Merryman or Carolyn Hutchins, PO Box 538, Lake Forest CA 92630. (310)379-5646. Membership (100) open. Monthly newsletter. Sponsors critique groups throughout southern California (contact critique group coordinator, Jessica Shaver, 186 E. Cameron Pl., Long Beach CA 90807-3851, (310)595-4162). Sponsors two annual Writers' Days: April and October 1997.

DIABLO VALLEY CHRISTIAN WRITERS GROUP. Danville. Contact: Marcy Weydemuller, 3623 Corte Segundo, Concord CA 94519. (510)676-6555. Fax (510)681-1771. Membership (10) open.

*GLENDALE CHRISTIAN SCRIBES. Contact: Stephanie Smedley, 7929 Beckett St., Sunland CA 91040-3303. (818)352-7017. Membership (8) open.

HAYWARD AREA CHRISTIAN WRITERS GROUP. Contact: Launa Herrmann, 21555 Eden Canyon Rd., Castro Valley CA 94552. Phone/fax (510)889-7564. Membership (12) open.

*HIGH DESERT CHRISTIAN WRITERS GUILD. Lancaster. Contact: Ellen Berg, 3600 Brabham Ave., Rosamond CA 93560-6891. Membership open.

INLAND EMPIRE CHRISTIAN WRITERS GUILD. Moreno Valley. Contact: Bill and Carole Gift Page, 10653 Ridgefield Terr., Moreno Valley CA 92557. (909)924-0610. Membership (46) open. Sponsors twice-yearly seminars in February & September.

*ADOPT A PRISONER INC. WRITER'S GROUP. Contact: Achim Rodgers, 6341 Johnson Ave., Long Beach CA 90805. (310)428-7349. Membership (35) open. Sponsoring seminars on July 1, September 1, and December 1, 1997.

*LODI WRITERS ASSOCIATION. Contact: Dee Porter, Box 1863, Lodi CA 95241. (209)334-0603. Membership (65) open. Sponsors one-day workshop.

NATIONAL WRITER'S ASSN./SOUTHERN CALIFORNIA CHAPTER. Fountain Valley. Liaison: Shirl Thomas, 9379 Tanager Ave., Fountain Valley CA 92708-6557. (714)968-5726. Membership (142) open. Secular group/many Christians.

*OAKLAND CHRISTIAN WRITERS CLUB. Contact: Sharon Haynes, 1068 - 85th Ave., Oakland CA 94621. (510)562-4743. Membership (20) open.

SACRAMENTO CHRISTIAN WRITER'S CLUB. Contact: Jan Roach, 8304 Bellsbrae Dr., Antelope CA 95843-5145. Phone/fax (916)729-3858. Membership (35) open.

SAN DIEGO COUNTY CHRISTIAN WRITERS' GUILD. Contact: Robert Gillespie, 17041 Palacio Pl., San Diego CA 92027. (619)487-7929. Fax (619)673-3921. E-mail: bgill@adnc.com. Membership (250+) open. Sponsors fall seminar and March awards banquet. Contest for members.

+SIERRA VALLEY AREA CHRISTIAN WRITERS' GROUP. Loyalton. Contact: Janet McHenry, PO Box 750, Loyalton CA 96118. Phone/fax (916)993-4019. Membership (10) open. May sponsor a fall seminar.

*THE WRITE BUNCH. Stockton. Contact: Shirley Cook, pres., 3123 Sheridan, Stockton CA 95219. (209)477-8375. Audrey Seitelman, secretary, (209)952-4977. Membership (7) open (to one more).

COLORADO

*COLORADO CHRISTIAN COMMUNICATORS. Colorado Springs. Contact: Madalene Harris, 810 Crystal Park Rd. 23, Manitou Springs CO, 80829. (719)685-9432. Membership (30+) open. Sponsors fall seminar.

COLORADO CHRISTIAN WRITERS. Longmont/Lyons. Contact: Debbie Barker, 67 Seminole Ct., Lyons CO 80540. (303)823-5718. Fax (303)823-6408. Membership (10+) open. Sponsors a March seminar.

CHRISTIAN WRITERS IN TOUCH. Denver. Contact: Christine Adams, 1257 Logan St., Apt. 204, Denver CO 80203-2442. (303)595-5857. Membership open.

DELAWARE

DELMARVA CHRISTIAN WRITERS' FELLOWSHIP. Georgetown. Contact: Candy Abbott, PO Box 777, Georgetown DE 19947-0777. Phone/fax (302)856-6649. E-mail: cabbott@outland.dtcc.edu. Membership (12) open.

FLORIDA

ADVENTURES IN CHRISTIAN WRITING. Orlando. Contact: Mary Shaw, 350 E. Jackson St. #811, Orlando FL 32801. (407)841-4866. Membership (15-20) open.

SUNCOAST CHRISTIAN WRITERS GROUP. Largo. Contact: Elaine Creasman, 13014 - 106th Ave. N., Largo FL 34644-5602. (813)595-8963. Membership (20) open.

TITUSVILLE CHRISTIAN WRITERS' FELLOWSHIP. Contact: Nancy Otto Boffo, 2625 Riviera Dr., Titusville FL 32780-5144. (407)267-7604. Membership (10) open.

WRITING STRATEGIES CRITIQUESHOP. Daytona Beach. Meets monthly (10X). Sponsors half-day seminars quarterly in January, February, May and October. Speakers: Rosemary Upton & Kistler London. Send SASE for brochure. Contact: Rosemary J. Upton, 2712 S. Peninsula Dr., Daytona Beach FL 32118. Phone/fax (904)322-1111. Membership (12+) open.

WRITING STRATEGIES FOR THE CHRISTIAN MARKET. Daytona Beach. Seminars held quarterly. Contact: Rosemary J. Upton, 2712 S. Peninsula Dr., Daytona Beach FL 32118. (904)322-1111. Membership (97) open.

GEORGIA

*NORTHEAST GEORGIA WRITERS. Gainesville. Contact: Elouise Whitten, 660

Crestview Terr., Gainesville GA 30501-3110. (770)532-3007. Membership (26) open. Sponsors day and night groups, contests, critique groups, two all-day workshops and a biennial writers' conference.

HAWAII
*HAWAII CHRISTIAN WRITERS. Contact: Steven Kirk, 85-794 Farrington Hwy., Waianae HI 96742. New group. Membership open.

IDAHO
INTERNATIONAL NETWORK OF COMMUNICATORS & THE ARTS. Couer d Alene. Contact: Sheri Stone, Box 1754, Post Falls ID 83854-1754. Phone/fax (208)667-9730. Membership (25) open. Sponsors a contest and an annual fall seminar.

ILLINOIS
INTERNATIONAL BLACK WRITERS. Chicago & New York. Contact: Mable Terrell, PO Box 1030, Chicago IL 60690-1030. (312)409-2292. Membership (2,000) open. Sponsors a contest open to nonmembers. Conference in Chicago, June 27-29, 1997.
*JUVENILE FORUM. Moline. Contact: David R. Collins, 3403 45th St., Moline IL 61265. (309)762-8985. Membership (6-12) open to those writing for children or youth.
*TRUE VINE CHRISTIAN FELLOWSHIP. Springfield. Contact: Faith Logan, 813 S. 13th St., Springfield IL 62702. Membership (8) open.

INDIANA
BLOOMINGTON AREA CHRISTIAN WRITERS. Contact: Kathi Adams, 9576 W. St. Rd. 48, Bloomington IN 47404. (812)876-8265. Membership (9) open.
*CENTRAL INDIANA ASSN. OF CHRISTIAN WRITERS. Indianapolis area. Contact: Brenda Dewar Purvis, 207 Mill Springs, Coatesville IN 46121. (317)386-7267. Membership (24) open.
*CREATIVE WRITERS. Marion. Contact: Mary M. Cain, 631 Candlewood Dr., Marion IN 46952. (317)662-6222. Membership (14) open.
+EVANSVILLE-AREA CHRISTIAN WRITERS' FELLOWSHIP. Contact: Cynthia Bezek, 5506 O'Hara Dr., Evansville IN 47711-2016. (812)471-9063. E-mail: jdbezek@evansville.edu. Membership (20) open.
FORT WAYNE CHRISTIAN WRITERS CLUB. Fort Wayne. Contact: Linda R. Wade, 739 W. Fourth St., Fort Wayne IN 46808-2613. (219)422-2772. Membership (30) open. Also publishes a bimonthly newsletter called Fort and Field (editor: Phyllis Posey, PO Box 127, Hicksville OH 43526).
+INDIANAPOLIS CHRISTIAN SCRIBES. Plainfield. Contact: Henry & Bernice Mercier, 1233 Raymond St., Plainfield IN 46168-2039. (317)838-8931. Fax (317)838-8951. Membership (8) open.
OPEN DOOR CHRISTIAN WRITERS. Westport. Contact: Janet Teitsort, PO Box 78, Westport IN 47283-0078. Phone/fax (812)591-2210. Membership (15-20) open. Sponsors a seminar about every two years in May.
*SEYMOUR CHRISTIAN WRITER'S CLUB. Contact: Anna Belle Stewart, 2379

N. US Hwy 31, Seymour IN 47274. (812)523-8178. Membership open.

IOWA
CEDAR RAPIDS CHRISTIAN WRITER'S CRITIQUE GROUP. Contact: Helen Hunter, 1132-21st St. SE, Cedar Rapids IA 52403. Phone/fax (319)362-4777. E-mail: Authorhh@aol.com. Membership (15) open. A day and a night group.
***RIVER CITY WRITERS.** Council Bluffs. Contact: Dee Barrett, 16 Susan Lane, Council Bluffs IA 51503. (712)322-7692. Membership (10+) open.
SIOUXLAND CHRISTIAN WRITERS. Sioux City. Contact: William B. Tucker, 4881 Bradford Ln., Sioux City IA 51106-9519. (712)943-1412. Membership (15) open.

KANSAS
***CHRISTIAN WRITERS GROUP OF TOPEKA.** Contact: Charles White, 4102 NW Dondee Ln., Topeka KS 66618. (913)286-0388. Membership (14) open.
***CREATIVE WRITERS FELLOWSHIP.** Newton, Halsted, Hesston. Contact: Chester Osborne, 429 N Weaver, Hesston, KS 67062. Membership (15) open.
+KANSAS CITY CHRISTIAN WRITERS' NETWORK. Olathe. Contact: Teresa Vining, 1438 N Lucy Montgomery Way, Olathe KS 66061-6706. Phone/fax: (913)764-4610. E-mail: KCCWN@aol.com. Membership (156) open. Sponsors a spring retreat (May 10, 1997) and a fall writers' conference (October 11, 1997). Contest for those who attend conference.
***LAMPLIGHTERS CHRISTIAN WRITERS CLUB.** Andover. Contact: Sharon Stanhope, Box 415, Benton KS 67017. (316)778-1043. Membership (20) open.
LEARNERS CHRISTIAN WRITING CLUB. Medicine Lodge. Contact: Ruth E. Montgomery, PO Box 308, Medicine Lodge KS 67104-0308. (316)886-9863. Membership (10) open.
PITTSBURG CHRISTIAN WRITERS FELLOWSHIP. Pittsburg. Contact: LeAnn Campbell, 267 SW 1st Ln., Lamar MO 64759. (417)682-2713. Membership (20) open. Sponsors an April seminar.
***PRAIRIE CHRISTIAN WRITERS.** Larned. Contact: Marilyn Phemister, 206 E 10th St., Larned KS 67550. (316)285-6217. Membership (3-4) open.

KENTUCKY
AMERICAN CHRISTIAN WRITERS LOUISVILLE CONFERENCE. February 1, 1997. Contact: Reg Forder, Box 110390, Nashville TN 37222. 1-800-21-WRITE. Attendance: 50-150.
JACKSON CHRISTIAN WRITERS' CLUB. Vancleve. Contact: Donna J. Woodring, PO Box 10, Vancleve KY 41385-0010. (606)666-5000. Fax 606-666-7744. E-mail: kmbc@harold.eastky.com. Membership (9) open.
OHIO VALLEY FELLOWSHIP OF CHRISTIAN WRITERS. Merged with Evansville-Area Christian Writers Fellowship. See that listing in Indiana.

LOUISIANA
SCRIBES OF NEW ORLEANS. Contact: Jack Cunningham, PO Box 55601, Metairie LA 70055-5601. (504)837-4397. Membership (10) open.

MAINE

*MAINE FELLOWSHIP OF CHRISTIAN WRITERS. China Lake. Contact: Ken Parker, China Lake Conference Center, PO Box 149, China ME 04926. (207)968-2101. Membership (10-20) open.

MARYLAND

ANNAPOLIS FELLOWSHIP OF CHRISTIAN WRITERS. Annapolis. Contact: Mark Littleton, 5350 Eliot's Oak Rd., Columbia MD 21044. Phone/Fax (410)995-0831. E-mail: MarkLitt@aol.com. Membership (20) open. Sponsors occasional seminars.

MASSACHUSETTS

WESTERN MASSACHUSETTS CHRISTIAN WRITERS FELLOWSHIP. Springfield. Contact: Barbara A. Robidoux, 127 Gelinas Dr., Chicopee MA 01020-4813. (413)594-4741. Fax 592-5395. Membership (50) open. Monthly newsletter.

MICHIGAN

*SOUTHEASTERN CHRISTIAN WRITERS GROUP. Royal Oak. Contact: Audrey Perry, 255 W 14 Mile Rd. #1518, Clawson MI 48017-1955. (810)288-0913. Membership (15) open.

MINNESOTA

MINNESOTA CHRISTIAN WRITERS GUILD. Edina. Contact: Jane Kise, 5504 Grove St., Edina MN 55436. (612)926-4343. Membership (100) open. Sponsors an annual spring seminar in April.

MISSOURI

CHRISTIAN WRITERS WORKSHOP. St. Louis. Contact: Ruth McDaniel, 15233 Country Ridge Dr., Chesterfield MO 63017-7432. (314)532-7584. Membership (25) open.

*INSPIRATIONAL WRITERS WORKSHOP OF GREATER ST. LOUIS. St. Charles. Contact: Lila Wold Shelburne, 707 Gran Lin Dr., St. Charles MO 63303-6025. (314)946-8533. Membership (2-3) open to writers.

*NORTHLAND CHRISTIAN WRITERS. Kansas City. Contact: Margaret Owen, 207 NW 67th St., Gladstone MO 64118. (816)436-5240.

*SPRINGFIELD CHRISTIAN WRITERS CLUB. Contact: Owen Wilkie, 4909 Old Wire Rd., Brookline MO 65619-9655. (417)882-5185. Membership (6) open.

MONTANA

*HELENA CHRISTIAN WRITERS. Contact: Lenore Puhek, 1215 Hudson, Helena MT 59601. (406)443-2552. Membership (12) open as space allows. Has one-day writers retreat for members.

*MONTANA CHRISTIAN WRITERS. Contact: Margaret Wilkison, 2007 Sweet Grass Rd., Helena MT 59061. (406)442-9939.

NEW HAMPSHIRE
THE WORDSMITHS. Nashua. Contact: Cynthia Vlatas, 5 Jeremy Ln., Hudson NH 03051. (603)882-2851. Fax (603)883-7518. E-mail: sasacindy@aol.com. Membership (26) open. Sponsors occasional workshop.

NEW JERSEY
*RAINBOW WRITERS. Bridgewater Contact: Dr. Megan D. Simpson, 9 Iroquois Trail, Branchburg NJ 08876-5451. (908)231-9437. Membership (8) open.
*SOUTH JERSEY CHRISTIAN WRITERS FELLOWSHIP. Atlantic City. Contact: Sandi Cleary, 308 Clark Pl., Northfield NJ 08225. (609)646-5694.

NEW MEXICO
+MESILLA VALLEY CHRISTIAN WRITERS. Las Cruces. Contact: Jewell Johnson, 2050 Thomas Dr., Las Cruces NM 88001. (505)521-0316. Membership (6) open.
*SOUTHWEST CHRISTIAN WRITERS ASSOCIATION. Farmington. Contact: Patti Cordell, #74 RD 3535, Flora Vista NM 87415. (505)334-2258. Membership (18) open. Sponsors annual one-day seminar the third Saturday in September.
SOUTHWEST WRITERS WORKSHOP. Albuquerque. Contact: SWW, 1338 Wyoming Blvd. NE, Ste. B, Albuquerque NM 87112-5067. (505)293-0303. Fax (505)237-2665. Membership (900-1,000) open. Sponsors a contest and a conference at Hilton Hotel in Albuquerque in August.

NEW YORK
*BROOKLYN WRITER'S CLUB. Contact: Ann Dellarocco, Box 184, Bath Beach Station, Brooklyn NY 11214. (718)837-3484. Membership (500) open.
INTERNATIONAL BLACK WRITERS. New York & Chicago. Contact: Mable Terrell, PO Box 1030, Chicago IL 60690-1030. (312)409-2292. Membership (2,000) open. Sponsors a contest open to nonmembers. Conference in Chicago, June 27-29, 1997.
NEW YORK CHRISTIAN WRITERS GROUP. Manhattan. Contact: Zoe Blake, 361 Clinton Ave., #7H, Brooklyn 11238. (718)430-5898. Membership (10-12) open.
SOUTHERN TIER CHRISTIAN WRITERS' FELLOWSHIP. Binghamton/ Johnson City area. Contact: Kenneth Cetton, 20 Pine St., Port Crane NY 13833-1512. (607)648-7249. E-mail: KC1933@juno.com. Membership (12) open.
*SYRACUSE CHRISTIAN WRITERS' GUILD. Liverpool. Contact: Pat Spencer, 108 Woodpath Rd., Liverpool NY 13090. (315)652-3178. Membership (25-60) open. Sponsors annual seminar.

NORTH CAROLINA
*CHRISTIAN WRITERS CLUB. Contact: David F. Browning, Box 4311, Rocky Mount NC 27801. (919)442-7119.
COVENANT WRITERS. Lincolnton. Contact: Janice Stroup, 403 S. Cedar St., Lincolnton NC 28092-3342. (704)735-8851. Membership (7) open.

OHIO
*AKRON MANUSCRIPT CLUB. Contact: Tom Raber, Box 966, Cuyahoga Falls OH 44223. (216)928-7268. Membership open. Sponsors annual writers' conference in May.

+CHRISTIAN WRITERS GUILD. Youngstown area. Contact: Susan K. Virgalitte, 240 Sawmill Run Dr., Canfield OH 44406. Phone/fax (330)533-5833. E-mail: TOVIR@aol.com. Membership (30) open.

COLUMBUS CHRISTIAN WRITERS ASSN. Contact: Brenda Custodio, 3069 Bocastle Ct., Reynoldsburg OH 43068. (614)861-1011. E-mail: custodiob1@ aol.com. Membership (40) open. Sponsors a spring workshop and a contest open to non-members.

DAYTON CHRISTIAN SCRIBES. Kettering. Contact: Lois Pecce (secretary), Box 613, Dayton OH 45441-0613. (937)433-6470. Fax (937)435-2175. Membership (35) open.

GREATER CINCINNATI CHRISTIAN WRITERS' FELLOWSHIP. Contact: Teresa Cleary, 895 Garnoa St., Cincinnati OH 45231-2618. Phone/fax (513)521-1913. E-mail: tmicleary@aol.com. Membership (20) open.

NORTHWEST OHIO CHRISTIAN WRITERS. Bowling Green. Contact: Linda R. Tippett, 4221 Woodmont Rd., Toledo OH 43613. (419)475-9169. Membership (30) open. Sponsors a Saturday seminar in September.

*OHIO FELLOWSHIP OF CHRISTIAN WRITERS. Contact: John G. Hoffman, 233 W. Church St., Marion OH 43302. (614)387-6683. Membership open. Sponsors annual writers' conference.

PATASKALA CHRISTIAN WRITERS. . Contact: Melissa Morgan, PO Box 667, Pataskala OH 43062. (614)927-7773. Membership (6-20) open.

*SET FORTH WRITERS GUILD. North Central OH/Mansfield area. Contact: Donna Caudill, 836 Delph Ave., Mansfield OH 44906. (419)747-1755. Membership (35) open. Planning seminar for July 1997.

STATELINE CHRISTIAN WRITER'S CLUB. Celina. Contact: Shirley Knox, 54106 Club Island Rd., Celina OH 45822. (419)268-2040. Membership (20) open. Sponsors a People in Print Seminar, October 18, 1997.

+WEST-DAYTON CHRISTIAN WRITERS GUILD. Contact: Tina V. Toles, PO Box 7403, Dayton OH 45407. (937)832-0541. Membership (50) open. Sponsoring an August 1997 seminar.

*WESTERN OHIO CHRISTIAN WRITERS. Sidney. Contact: Alice Linsley, 231 N. Miami Ave., Sidney OH 45365. (513)663-4131/492-8584. Membership (43) open.

OKLAHOMA
TULSA CHRISTIAN WRITERS. Contact: Eugene C. Scott, 930 E. 95th Pl., Tulsa OK 74133. (918)459-0004. E-mail: 104676.1742@compuserve.com. Membership (50) open.

+WEST-DAYTON CHRISTIAN WRITER'S GUILD. Contact: Tina, PO Box 45407, Dayton OH 45407. (513)263-3492. Fax (513)268-9002. E-mail: Tina1poet @aol.com. Membership open.

WORDWRIGHTS. Oklahoma City. Contact: Irene Martin. PO Box 890003, Oklahoma City OK 73189-0003. (405)793-9424. Membership (40-50) open. Sponsor a fall 1997 seminar; send SASE for information.

OREGON

*EMERALD CHRISTIAN WRITERS GROUP. Eugene. Debbie Hedstrom, 3191 Kentwood Dr., Eugene OR 97401. Membership (6) open.

EUGENE CHRISTIAN WRITERS GROUP. Contact: Dorothy A. Grant, PO Box 502, Eugene OR 97440. (541)343-2187. Membership (11) may be open.

HOCKETT CRITIQUE GROUP. Contact: Betty Hockett, 1100 N. Meridian #38, Newberg OR 97132. (503)538-9871. E-mail: milogh@aol.com. Membership (10) not currently open.

*LEBANON/ALBANY CHRISTIAN WRITERS GROUP. Contact: Rebecca Brown, 36135 Bohlken Dr., Lebanon OR 97355-9675. (503)258-6978. Membership (6) open.

*MONMOUTH CHRISTIAN WRITERS GROUP. Contact: Cathy Verley, 14100 Kings Valley Hwy., Monmouth OR 97361. (503)838-0394. Membership (5) open.

+OREGON CHRISTIAN SCRIBES. Portland. Contact: Blanche B. Butler, 11351 Corvallis Rd., Independence OR 97351-9748. (503)838-2470. Membership (15) open. Annual conference in Yakima WA, May 4, 1997, May 3, 1998.

OREGON CHRISTIAN WRITERS. Contact: Kris Ingram, pres., 955 S. 59th St., Springfield OR 97478-5452. (503)726-8320. Meets three times annually: February in Salem, May in Eugene, and October in Portland. All-day Saturday conferences. Membership (250) open. Sponsors annual conference in August (in Salem). Newsletter & critique groups.

ROCK CREEK CHRISTIAN WRITERS GROUP. Contact: Karen Taylor, 5530 NW Osprey Pl., Portland OR 97229-1089. (503)645-4906. Membership (5) open.

SMITH ROCK CHRISTIAN WRITERS. Redmond. Contact: Josephine Manes, 2135 NE O'Neil Way, Redmond OR 97756. (541)548-8872. Membership (5) open.

WORDSMITHS. Gresham/Portland/Vancouver/Battle Ground. Contact: Susan Thogerson Maas, 27526 SE Carl St., Gresham OR 97080-8215. (503)663-7834. E-mail: Smaas@wow.com. Membership (5) open. Christian and secular writers.

PENNSYLVANIA

+BETHEL WORDSPINNERS. Bethlehem. Contact: Wanda Dean, 4100 Birch Dr., Bethlehem PA 18017-4512. Membership (7) open. Monthly meetings and critique by mail.

THE FIRST WORD. Sewickley. Contact: Shirley Stevens, 326 B Glaser Ave., Pittsburgh PA 15202-2910. (412)761-2618. Membership (15) open.

GREATER JOHNSTOWN CHRISTIAN WRITERS' GUILD. Contact: Betty Rosian, 108 Deerfield Ln., Johnstown PA 15905-5703. (814)255-4351. E-mail: brosian@twd.com. Membership (15) open.

GREATER PHILADELPHIA CHRISTIAN WRITERS' FELLOWSHIP. Broomall. Contact: Marlene Bagnull, 316 Blanchard Rd., Drexel Hill PA 19026. Phone/fax (610)626-6833. E-mail: mbagnull@aol.com. Membership (40) open. Sponsors annual writers' conference.

HARRISBURG AREA CHRISTIAN WRITERS' FELLOWSHIP. Middletown. Contact: Georgia Burkett, 220 Dock St., Middletown PA 17057-1609. (717)944-4427. Membership (50) open.

LANCASTER CHRISTIAN WRITERS FELLOWSHIP. Contact: John Brenneman, 258 Brenneman Rd., Lancaster PA 17603-9623. (717)872-5183. Membership (10) open.

MONTROSE CHRISTIAN WRITERS FELLOWSHIP. Contact: Patti Souder, PO Box 159, Montrose PA 18801-1059. (800)598-5030. Membership (13) open. Holding a conference July 7-11,1997.

WEST BRANCH CHRISTIAN WRITERS. Williamsport. Contact: Eileen Berger, RR 2 Box 378, Hughesville PA 17737. (717)584-2280. Membership (15-20) open. Sponsors annual writers workshop, October 1997.

SOUTH CAROLINA

CHRISTIAN WRITERS GROUP. Greenville. Contact: Nancy Parker, 2530 E North St. Apt. 6A, Greenville SC 29615-1448. (864)322-5593. Fax (864)322-5596. Membership (8) open.

SOUTH DAKOTA

+BLACK HILLS CHRISTIAN WRITERS. Rapid City. Contact: Loma Davies Silcott, 1777 Zinnia St., Rapid City SD 57701-6240. Phone/fax (605)393-2246. E-mail: 73500,3633@compuserve.com. Membership (12) open. Instruction at each meeting.

TENNESSEE

CHATTANOOGA CHRISTIAN WRITERS WORKSHOP. Chattanooga Bible Institute. Contact: Peter Snyder, 181 Lovella Dr., Ringgold GA 30736. (706)891-0858. Fax (706)891-3931. E-mail: 103473.2322@compuserve.com. Membership (20) open.

TEXAS

AUSTIN CHRISTIAN WRITERS' GUILD. Contact: Bob Rose, 309 Summit Ridge North, Leander TX 78645-8645. (512)267-3630. Fax (512)219-5444 (voice activated). Membership (50) open. Seminar February 21-22, 1997.

*CHRISTIAN WRITERS ASSN. Contact: Dolores Beringer, 1400 FM 509 #B-115, San Benito TX 78586-9730. (210)399-8763. Membership (12) open.

INSPIRATIONAL WRITERS ALIVE! Pasadena. Contact: Maxine E. Holder, Rt 4 Box 81H, Rusk TX 75785-9410. (903)795-3986. Membership (90-100) open. Sponsors summer seminar, monthly newsletter, and annual contest (November 1-April 1).

INSPIRATIONAL WRITERS ALIVE!/AMARILLO CHAPTER. Contact: Helen Luecke, 2921 S. Dallas, Amarillo TX 79103-6713. (806)376-9671. Membership (30) open. Seminar April 5, 1997 in Amarillo.

INSPIRATIONAL WRITERS ALIVE!/HOUSTON CHAPTER. Houston. Contact: Wanda Shadle (713)862-1115 or Pam Binkley (713)467-2041. Membership (30) open.

INSPIRATIONAL WRITERS ALIVE!/NORTHWEST HOUSTON CHAPTER. Spring. Contact: Claire Ottensteen, (713)376-7613. Membership open.

INSPIRATIONAL WRITERS ALIVE!/JACKSONVILLE CHAPTER. Contact: Maxine Holder, Rt. 4 Box 81H, Rusk TX 75785. (903)795-3986. Membership open.

INSPIRATIONAL WRITERS ALIVE!/TRINITY CHAPTER. Barbers Hill. Contact: Mary Ann Evans, PO Box 1027, Anahuac TX 77514. (409)267-3284. Membership (13) open.

*LOWER RIO GRANDE VALLEY CHRISTIAN WRITERS LEAGUE. Harlingen. Contact: Herschel Whittington, 2910 Treasure Hills, Harlingen TX 78550. (210)423-8048. Membership (30) open.

*SOUTHWESTERN CHRISTIAN WRITERS GUILD. Dallas. Contact: Jan Winebrenner, 2709 Winding Hollow, Plano TX 75093. (214)867-1119. Membership (60) open. Sponsors fall seminar.

UTAH

*UTAH CHRISTIAN WRITERS FELLOWSHIP. Salt Lake City & suburbs. Contact: Kimberly Malkogannis, 117 W Park St., Bingham Canyon UT 84006-1134. (801)568-7761. Membership (20+) open. Monthly newsletter $12 (free sample copy).

VERMONT

+CENTRAL VERMONT CHRISTIAN WRITERS LEAGUE. Central Vermont and Eastern New York. Contact: Celeste Perrino Walker, RR #3 Box 4913, Rutland VT 05701. (802)773-0535. Membership open. Instruction given at monthly meetings.

VIRGINIA

NEW COVENANT WRITER'S GROUP. Hampton. Contact: Mary Tatem, 451 Summer Dr., Newport News VA 23606. (757)930-1700. Membership (20) open. Sponsors an annual writers seminar.

NORTHERN VIRGINIA CHRISTIAN WRITERS FELLOWSHIP. Tyson's Corners. Contact: Jennifer Ferranti, dir., PO Box 629, Dunn Loring VA 22027-0629. Phone/fax (703)698-7707. E-mail: 75327.3147@compuserve.com. Membership (135) open. Sponsors a spring seminar (March 15, 1997).

S.O.N. WRITERS. Alexandria. Contact: Susan Lyttek, 2434 Temple Ct., Alexandria VA 23307-1524. Phone/fax (703)768-5582. E-mail: SusanAJL@aol.com. Membership (10+) open. May hold poetry event in 1997.

*WINCHESTER CHRISTIAN SCRIBES. Stephens City. Contact: Traci Noe, 208 Hackberry Dr., Stephens City VA 22655-2131. (540)869-0446. Membership (8) open.

WASHINGTON

ADVENTIST WRITERS ASSOCIATION OF WESTERN WASHINGTON. Renton. Contact: Marian Forschler, 18115 - 116th Ave. SE, Renton WA 98058-6562. (206)235-1435. Membership (40) open. Newsletter $10/yr. Sponsors annual writers' conference.

+CAPITOL CHRISTIAN WRITERS ASSN. Olympia. Contact: Teresa Graham, 2009 Aqua Ct. NW, Olympia WA 98502. Membership (19) open.

CHILDREN'S WRITERS CRITIQUE GROUP. Spokane. Contact: Pat Pfeiffer, PO Box 104, Otis Orchards WA 99027-0104. (509)927-7671 or 226-3532 (evenings). Or call Christine at (509)448-0593. Membership open.

CHRISTIAN WRITERS. Walla Walla. Contact: Dolores Walker, 904 Ankeny, Walla Walla WA 99362-3705. (509)529-2974. Membership (10) open.

KITSAP COUNTY CHRISTIAN WRITERS SUPPORT GROUP. Bainbridge Island. Contact: Kay Stewart, 7584 Meadowmeer Ln., Bainbridge Island WA 98110. (206)842-4269.

NORTH SPOKANE CRITIQUE GROUP. Contact: Larry Clark, 2709 W. La-Crosse, Spokane WA 99205. (509)324-6465. Membership (7) open.

*NORTHWEST CHRISTIAN WRITERS ASSN. Bellevue. Contact: Beth Harris, 14313 - 130th Ave. NE, Kirkland WA 98034. (206)821-5672. Membership (90) open.

SPOKANE CHRISTIAN WRITERS. Contact: Niki Anderson, 1405 E 54th Ave., Spokane WA 99223-6374. (509)448-6622. Membership (12+) open.

SPOKANE NOVELISTS. Contact: Joan Mochel, 12229 N. Ruby Rd., Spokane WA 99218-1924.(509)466-2938. E-mail: MOCHEL@aol.com. Membership (10) open. Secular group with mostly Christian members.

SPOKANE WRITERS. Contact: Pat Pfeiffer, PO Box 104, Otis Orchards WA 99027-0104. (509)927-7671/226-3532. Membership (20) open by vote.

WASHINGTON CHRISTIAN WRITERS. Seattle. Contact: Elaine Wright Colvin, Box 11337, Bainbridge Island WA 98110. Phone/fax (206)842-9103. Membership (350+) open. Holds four annual meetings.

WENATCHEE CHRISTIAN WRITERS' FELLOWSHIP. East Wenatchee. Contact: Shirley R. Pease, 1818 Skyline Dr. #31, Wenatchee WA 98801. (509)662-8392. Membership (35-50) open. Holds one-day seminar in September.

WHATCOM CHRISTIAN WRITERS CLUB. Group does not meet regularly. Area contact: Judy Slotemaker, 840 E. Pole Rd., Lynden WA 98264. (206)354-2636.

WISCONSIN

WORD & PEN CHRISTIAN WRITERS CLUB. Menasha. Contact: Don Derozier, 4850 Island View Dr., Oshkosh WI 54901-1318. (414)235-7905. Membership (18) open. Seminar tentatively planned for fall 1998.

CANADA

ALBERTA CHRISTIAN WRITERS' FELLOWSHIP. Calgary & Edmonton. Contact: Elsie Montgomery, pres., 34 - 1130 Falconer Rd., Edmonton AB T6R 2J6, Canada. (403)988-5622. Fax (403)430-0139. E-mail: elsie_montgomery@enabel. ccinet.ab.ca. Membership (122) open. Sponsors seminars the last week-end of April & September. See conference listing.

ARTISTIC LICENSE. Langley, BC. Contact: Christy Bowler, Box 56040, Valley Center PO, Langley BC V3A 8B3 Canada. (604)532-0401. Membership (20) open.

CHRISTIAN WRITERS CLUB. Montreal, Quebec. Contact: Mary Ann Lipscombe , 7428 Stuart (Park Extension District), Montreal QB H3N 2R4 Canada. (514)273-5356. Annual membership fee, $15. Membership (18) open. Holds occasional writers' seminar.

FRASER VALLEY CHRISTIAN WRITERS GROUP. Abbotsford. Contact: Ingrid Shelton, 2082 Geneva Ct., Clearbrook BC V2T 3Z2 Canada (Box 783, Sumas WA 98295). (604)859-7530. Membership (30) open.

*MANITOBA CHRISTIAN WRITERS ASSN. Winnipeg. Contact: Eleanor Bilsland, 208 - 211 Watson St., Winnipeg MB R2P 2E1 Canada. 697-4559. Membership (15) open.

SOUTHERN MANITOBA FELLOWSHIP OF CHRISTIAN WRITERS. Winkler or Roland. Contact: Isabel Allison, Box 208, Roland MB R0G 1T0 Canada. (204)343-2119. Membership (5) open.

SPIRITWOOD SCRIBES. Meets 19X/yr. Contact: Elmer Bowes, Spiritwood SK, S0J 2M0. (306)883-2003. Annual dues $5. Membership open.

*SWAN VALLEY WRITERS GUILD. Swan River, Manitoba. Contact: Julie Bell, Box 2115, Swan River MB R0L 1Z0 Canada. (204)734-7890. Membership (7-8) open. Sponsors a seminar.

FOREIGN

THE FELLOWSHIP OF CHRISTIAN WRITERS. London, England. Contact: Juliet Hughes, 74 Longleaze, Wootton Bassett, Swindon Wilshire, England SN4 8AS. Telephone: 00-44-1793-852296. Membership (700) open. Sponsors a contest (open to non-members) and 3 writer's days a year: March 1 (London), July 5 (Swindon Wilshire), and October 4 (London) in 1997.

NATIONAL/INTERNATIONAL GROUPS (no state location)

AMERICAN CHRISTIAN WRITERS SEMINARS. Sponsors conferences in various locations around the country (see individual states for dates and places). Call for dates and locations. Sponsoring a Caribbean cruise, November 16-23, 1997. Contact: Reg Forder, Box 110390, Nashville TN 37222. 1-800-21-WRITE.

CHRISTIAN WRITERS FELLOWSHIP INTL. Contact: Sandy Brooks, Rt. 3 Box 1635, Jefferson Davis Rd, Clinton SC 29325-9542. (864)697-6035. E-mail: CWFI@aol.com. No meetings, but offers market consultations, critique service, writers books and conference workshop tapes. Connects writers living in the same area, and helps start writer's groups.

NAZARENE CHRISTIAN WRITERS CLUBS. Puts out a quarterly newsletter to encourage writers and would-be writers. Contact: Bonnie Perry, ed, %Communications division, 6401 The Paseo, Kansas City MO 64131.

THE PRESBYTERIAN WRITERS GUILD. No regular meetings. National writers organization with a quarterly newsletter. Dues $15 per year. Contact: Ann Barr Weems, 6900 Kingsbury Blvd., St. Louis MO 63130. (314)725-6290. E-mail: AWEEMS7@aol.com. Membership (212) open. Sponsors a couple of contests for members each year. Sponsors annual conference (April 7-12, 1997).

*THE WRITING ACADEMY. Contact: Nora Buys, 11534 Hillpark Ln., Los Altos CA 94024. Membership (56) open. Sponsors year-round correspondence writing program and annual seminar in August (held in various locations).

Note: If your group is not listed here, please send information to: Sally Stuart, 1647 SW Pheasant Dr., Aloha OR 97006. October 20 is deadline for the next year's edition.

EDITORIAL SERVICES

The following listing is included because so many writers contact me looking for experienced/qualified editors who can critique or evaluate their manuscripts. These people from all over the country offer this kind of service. I cannot personally guarantee the work of any of those listed, so you may want to ask for references or samples of work.

The following abbreviations indicate what kinds of work they are qualified to do: GE indicates general editing/manuscript evaluation; LC—line editing or copy editing; GH—ghostwriting; CA—co-authoring; B—brochures; NL—newsletters; SP—special projects; and BC—book contract evaluation. The following abbreviations indicate the types of material they evaluate: A—articles, SS—short stories, P—poetry, F—fillers, N—novels, NB—nonfiction books, BP—book proposals, JN—juvenile novels, PB—picture books, BS—Bible studies, TM—technical material, E—essays, D—devotionals, S—scripts.

Always send a copy they can write on and an SASE for return of your material.

(*) Indicates that editorial service did not return questionnaire.
(+) Indicates new listing.

ALABAMA
ELLA ROBINSON, 735 - 7th Pl., Pleasant Grove AL 35127. Phone/fax (205)744-4925. Send $18 deposit. LC/N/SP. Does NB/BS/D. Charges $18 (estimates for longer projects).

ARIZONA
CARLA'S MANUSCRIPT SERVICE/CARLA BRUCE, 4326 N. 50th Ave., Phoenix AZ 85031-2031. Phone/fax (602)247-0174. Call/write. GE/LC/GH. Does A/SS/NB/BS/TM. Charges by the page or gives project estimate after evaluation. Does ghostwriting for pastors & teachers; professional typesetting.

JOY P. GAGE, 2370 S. Rio Verde Dr., Cottonwood AZ 86326-5923. (520)646-6534. Send material with $25 deposit. GE. Does A/N/NB/BS. Charges $25/hr.

DONNA GOODRICH, 648 S. Pima St., Mesa AZ 85210. (602)962-6694. Call/write. GE/LC. Does A/SS/P/F/N/NB/BP/D. Also types ($1/pg) and proof-reads ($15/hr) manuscripts. Editing $1.50/pg.

*KAREN MARTELL, 5829 N. 81st St., Scottsdale AZ 85250. (602)991-1134. Fax (602)949-1041. Call/write. GE/LC. Does A/SS/F/N/NB/JN/BS/TM/D. Charges $15/hr-$1.50/pg.

'LEEN POLLINGER, 12610 Westgate Dr, Sun City West AZ 85375-5137. (602)546-4757. Write. GE/LC. Does SS/F/N/NB/BP/JN/BS/D. Charges $12-35/hr depending on work done. Fee schedule available for SASE.

CALIFORNIA
CHRISTIAN COMMUNICATOR MANUSCRIPT CRITIQUE SERVICE/SUSAN TITUS OSBORN, 3133 Puente St., Fullerton CA 92835-1952. (714)990-1532.

Fax (714)990-0310. E-mail: Susanosb@aol.com. Call/write. For book, send material with $80 deposit. Staff of 11 editors. GE/LC/SP/book contract evaluation. Edits all types of material. Articles/stories $60. Three-chapter book proposal $80. Additional editing $20/hr.

DINA DONOHUE, 1633 Diamond St. #9, San Diego CA 92109-3161. (619)272-2890. Write. GE. Does A/SS/F/D. Articles/1,500 wds/$20, short stories/3,000 wds/$25; $5 each additional 1,000 wds; fillers/to 750 wds/$10.

*DIANE FILLMORE PUBLISHING SERVICES, 13776 Starhill Ln., LaPuente CA 91746-2733. (818)336-5899. E-mail: 73554.461@compuserve.com. Call. GE/LC/GH/CA/B/NL/SP. Does A/SS/N/NB/BP/JN/BS/E/D/small group or SS curriculum. Charges $15/hr. Member of Assn. of Professional Writing Consultants.

VICKI HESTERMAN, PhD, PO Box 6788, San Diego CA 92166. (619)224-4549. Call/write. GE/LC/CA/SP. Does A/NB/BP/TM/E/D. Specializes in helping people tell their personal stories. Charges standard rates.

DARLENE HOFFA, 512 Juniper St., Brea CA 92621. (714)990-5980. Write. GE. Does A/F/NB/BP/BS/D. Charges $35/article or short piece; $65 for book ms up to 52 pgs, plus $1.25/pg; or $15/hr.

+MAIN ENTRY EDITIONS/REBECCA JONES, 1057 Chestnut Dr., Escondido CA 92025. (619)741-3750. Fax (619)480-0252. E-mail: Perejone@mailhost2. csusm.edu. Call/e-mail. GE/LC/GH/B/NL/basic formatting. Does A/SS/P/F/N/ NB/BP/JN/PB/BS/E/D. Send payment and SASE. Content $20-25/hr; copy-editing $15-20/hr; rewriting $25-30/hr, formatting/indexing $25/hr.

KIMURA CREATIONS/DENELLA KIMURA, 785 Barton Way, Benicia CA 94510-3807. (707)746-8421. Write/$10 deposit. GE/LC (for poetry). SS/P/D/poetry book proposals & chapbooks. Charges $10/poem for detailed critique; $30-50 for poetry book evaluation; $10/devotional & $25/story.

LIGHTHOUSE EDITING/DR. LON ACKELSON, 13326 Community Rd., #11, Poway CA 92064. Phone/fax: (619)748-9258. E-mail: JER333@aol.com. Write, or call first if faxing. GE/LC/BC. Does A/SS/NB/BP/BS/D. Charges $25 for article/short story critique; $35 for book proposal; $25-35 + $4/pg for critique and revision.

+LONNIE HULL DUPONT & ASSOCIATES, 21 Columbus Ave. Ste 210, San Francisco CA 94111. (415)296-8944. Fax (415)296-8854. GE/LC. Help with proposals and more. Call for details.

MARY CARPENTER REID, 925 Larchwood Dr., Brea CA 92821. (714)529-3755. E-mail: MARYCREID@aol.com. Call/write. GE. Does A/SS/N/BP/JN/PB/E. Charges $25/hr., $75 minimum.

JANE RUMPH, 1130 Leonard Ave., Pasadena CA 91107-1746. (818)351-8703. Fax (818)822-1022. E-mail: rumph@alumni.caltech.edu. Write. GE/LC. Does A/F/ NB/BS/TM/E/D/theses/dissertations. Charges $15-20/hr.

LAURAINE SNELLING, 952 Marie Ave., Martinez CA 94553-3519. (510)372-9047. Fax (510)372-3622. E-mail: TLSnelling@aol.com. Call. GE. Does N/BP/JN. Charges $50/hr ($50 minimum), or by the project after discussion with client.

COLORADO
ARIEL COMMUNICATIONS/DEBBIE BARKER, 67 Seminole Ct., Lyons CO

80540. Phone/Fax (303)823-5718. Fax (303)823-6408. E-mail: dkbarker@cris.com. Call or send with $150 deposit. GE/LC. Does A/SS/F/N/NB/BP/JN/PB/E/D. Negotiable rates on a project basis.

+**COLORADO WORDMASTER/DEAN MERRILL**, 915 Big Valley Dr., Colorado Springs CO 80919-1008. Phone/fax (719)535-0288. E-mail: DeanColo@aol.com. GE/LC/CA/SP/consulting. Does NB/BP. Evaluates each project individually on its level of complexity and also its appeal—then sets a package price.

+**ECLIPSE EDITORIAL SERVICES/TRACI MULLINS**, 901 N. El Paso St., Colorado Springs CO 80903. (719)587-1201. Fax (719)578-0230. E-mail: 73041. 3440@compuserve.com. Call or write (preferred). GE/LC/GH/CA/B/SP/BCE/ book proposal preparation and/or critique. Does A/NB/BP/D. Charges $35-45/hr., depending on service.

*****EDITH QUINLAN**, 9030 W. 3rd Pl., Lakewood CO 80226. (303)237-8358. Call/ write. GE/LC/NL. Does A/F/NB. Charges $10/hr.

CONNECTICUT

KAREN ORFITELLI, 105 Shepard Dr., Manchester CT 06040. (860)645-1100. E-mail: KarenOrf@aol.com. Send ms/$20 deposit. GE/LC. Does A/SS/P/F/JN/ BS/E/D. Charges $20/hr. Estimates given.

FLORIDA

JULIA LEE DULFER, 705 Hibiscus Trail, Melbourne Beach FL 32951. (407)727-8192. Call. GE/LC/B/NL/SP. Does A/SS/F/N/NB/BP/JN/PB/BS/TM/E/D/S. Charges $20/hr for all functions.

*****LESLIE SANTAMARIA**, PO Box 780066, Orlando FL 32878-0066. Write. GE/ LC/GH/CA/SP. Does A/SS/N/NB/BP/JN/BS/TM/E/D/S/query & cover letters/ resumes. Charges $1/page for GE; $2/page for LC; $30 minimum.

GEORGIA

+**SANDRA A. HUTCHESON**, 210 Montrose Dr., McDonough GA 30253. (770)474-8880. Fax (770)389-9662. Call. GE/LC/CA/B/NL/SP. Does A/SS/F/N/NB/BP/ JN/PB/BS/TM/E/D. Charges $25/hr ($25 min.), plus expenses (telephone, research, postage).

IDAHO

*****IN PRINT/KAY YOUNKIN**, 9125 Edwards Rd., Rathdrum ID 83858. (208)687-1079. Fax (208)687-1079. Write or send with deposit. GE/LC/GH/B/NL/SP/book contract evaluation. Does A/SS/P/F/N/NB/BP/JN/PB/BS/TM/E/D. Fee is by the page or hourly with minimum deposit of $25.

ILLINOIS

DEBORAH CHRISTENSEN, PO Box 354, Addison IL 60101. (630)665-3044. Send with $20 deposit. GE/LC. Does A/SS/F/N/NB/JN. Charges $20 for first hour; $15 for each additional hour.

*****EDITECH/DOUGLAS C. SCHMIDT**, 872 S. Milwaukee Ave., Ste. 272, Libertyville IL 60048. Write. GE/LC/SP. Does A/SS/F/BS/D; Sunday school curriculum. Charges $25/hr or negotiated flat fee.

VIRGINIA J. MUIR EDITORIAL SERVICES, 130 Windsor Park Dr. #C205, Carol Stream IL 60188. (708)665-2994. Write. GE/LC/CA. Does A/SS/N/NB/JN/BS/TM/E/D. Charges $30/hr; $30 minimum, plus telephone, research expenses and postage.

*****JIM RIORDAN**, 4207 W. Josephine Dr., Kankakee IL 60901. Write. GE. Does N/NB/BP/TM. Book proposal $250; books under 200 pgs. $400; books over 200 pgs. $400 + $50/100 pgs.

THE WRITER'S EDGE, PO Box 1266, Wheaton IL 60189. No phone calls. A manuscript screening service for 35 cooperating Christian publishers. Charges $45 to evaluate a book proposal and if publishable, they will send a synopsis of it to 35 publishers who might be interested. If not publishable they will tell how to improve it. If interested, send an SASE for guidelines and a Book Information Form.

INDIANA

DENEHEN, INC./DR. DENNIS E. HENSLEY, 6824 Kanata Ct., Fort Wayne IN 46815-6388. Phone/Fax (219)485-9891 (Fax 10 a.m-6 p.m., M-F). Call/write. GE/LC/GH/SP. Does A/SS/N/NB/BP/JN/E/D/academic articles. Rate sheet for SASE.

PMN PUBLISHING/GEORGE ALLEN, Box 47024, Indianapolis IN 46247. (317) 888-7156. Fax (317)791-8113. Write. Various editorial services and newsletters Call or write for services available and charges.

KANSAS

*****SHAUERS COMMUNICATIONS/MARGARET SHAUERS**, 1411 - 12th, Great Bend KS 67530. (316)792-1683. Christian author with 1,000+ published children's stories will critique children's fiction: $20 and up for 6 double-spaced pgs; $3 for each pg. over. Market appraisal included. Send SASE.

ESTHER L. VOGT, 113 S. Ash, Hillsboro KS 67063. (316)947-3796. Call or send $10 deposit/material. GE/LC/CO/GH. Does SS/N/JN. $15 for first chapter (to 20 pgs); $12 for each chapter thereafter.

LOUISIANA

*****BLUE-PENCIL SPECIALISTS/JOHN M. CUNNINGHAM, JR.**, Box 55601, Metairie LA 70055-5601. (504)837-4397. Send material with $10 deposit. GE/LC. Does A/SS/F/BS/T/E/D. Charges according to word count; rate sheet for SASE.

*****GLORY ARTS/BARBARA NAUER**, 1808 Brightside Dr., Apt.11-A, Baton Rogue LA 70820-4710. (504)673-6481. Fax (504)673-6330. Does editing, re-writing, ghosting, graphics, radio promo, and author advising. Charges by the hour. Send SASE for price list.

*****SHILOH REVISIONS/MELINDA JOY LEMMON**, 4635 Baccich St., New Orleans LA 70122-6115. (504)282-9464. Call, write or send with $20 deposit. GE/LC/CA. Does A/SS/F/N/NB/BP/JN/PB/BS/TM/E/D/S. Articles/stories $25-$75; books $175-450.

MARYLAND
NEE EDITORIAL SERVICES/KATHIE NEE, 7115 Varnum St., Landover Hills MD 20784. (301)577-9072. Call/write. GE/LC/B/SP. Does A/F/NB/BP/BS/E/D/ tracts/pamphlets/resumes/job application letters/biographical sketches. Charges $10-12/hr. Brochure available for SASE.

MASSACHUSETTS
MARION VUILLEUMIER, 579 Buck Island Rd. #147, West Yarmouth MA 02673. (508)775-4811. Call or write. GE (readies mss for presentation to publishers). Does A/NB. Contact for estimate on projects; consultations $75; ten-session writing classes $100.

WORD PRO/BARBARA ROBIDOUX, 127 Gelinas Dr., Chicopee MA 01020-4813. (413)594-4741. Fax (413)592-5395. Call. GE/LC/GH/B/NL. Does A/F/ NB/TM/E/D. Fee negotiable; estimate given.

MICHIGAN
+WORD FOR WORD/SHAUNNA HOWAT and LINDA WACYK, 9523 Riverside Dr., Grand Ledge MI 48837. (517)626-2419. E-mail: HOWATK@aol.com. Call/write. GE/LC/GH/CA/B/NL/SP/curriculum/educational materials. Does A/ SS/F/N/NB/BS/TM/E/D. Charge $25/hour or call for a quote.

MINNESOTA
+PTL SECRETARIAL SERVICES/CONNIE PETTERSEN, R 4 Box 289, Aitkin MN 56431. (218)927-6176. E-mail: pett289@emily.net. Call/write. Manuscript typing; IBM compatible computer, WordPerfect 6.1 software; Internet/e-mail access. Published freelance writer; 20 years secretarial and Dictaphone transcription experience. Fees charged by the page; rates negotiable.

MISSOURI
*TIM PATRICK MILLER, 4131 Manchester Blvd., St. Louis MO 63110. Line edit, $1/pg; copy edit, $2/pg; structural edit, $7/hr; proofing, .95/pg. literary consultations/new writers, $10/hr; literary consultations/published writers, $25-150/hr.

+PRO WORD WRITING & EDITORIAL SERVICES/MARY R. RUTH, PO Box 155, Labadie MO 63055-0155. (314)742-3663. Call/write. GE/LC/SP/manuscript or script typing, scan hard copy to disk, proofreading, indexing. Does A/SS/N/ NB/BP/JN/BS/TM/E/D/S/biographies/textbooks. Call to discuss your project. Reasonable rates/professional results. MC/Visa available.

DEBI STACK, Box 11805, Kansas City MO 64138-0305. Phone/fax: (816)763-5743. E-mail: Stackedits@aol.com. Send with $50 deposit. GE/LC/SP. Does A/SS/N/ NB/BP/JN/BS/E/D/customized marketing analyses & consulting. Speaks to groups. Send for rate sheet.

NEW HAMPSHIRE
*SALLY WILKINS, Box 393, Amherst NH 03031-0393. (603)673-9331. Write. GE/LC. Does A/F/JN/PB/ BS/TM. Rate sheet for SASE.

NEW JERSEY

BURNING LIGHT PRESS/CARL SIMMONS, 59 Treetop Ct., Bloomingdale NJ 07403-1016. (201)283-9516. Call/write. GE/LC/B/NL/SP. Does A/SS/P/N/NB/ JN/PB/BS/E/D. Charges $15-20/hr.

DAYSTAR COMMUNICATIONS/DR. MARY ANN L. DIORIO, Box 405, Millville NJ 08332-0405. (609)327-1231. Fax (609)327-0291. E-mail: 72602,1027@ compuserve.com; or madiorio@aol.com. Call/write. GE/LC. Does A/SS/P/F/E/ D/copy for ads and PR material/resumes/business letters; also translations in French, Italian and Spanish. Rate sheet for SASE.

NEW MEXICO

*K.C. MASON, 1882 Conejo Dr., Santa Fe NM 87501. Write for information, fees, and availability.

NEW YORK

*STERLING DIMMICK, 86 Route 34, Waverly NY 14892-9793. (607)565-4470. Write. GE/GH/CA. Does A/SS/P/F/N/NB/BP/JN/PB/BS/TM/E/D/S. Charges $15-20/hour or by the project.

SWANSON EDITYPE SERVICES/NANCY SWANSON, PO Box 946, Elizabethtown NY 12932-0946. (518)873-3405, days; (518)962-8702, eves. GE/LC/ GH/CA/NL/SP. Does A/SS/N/NB/JN/BS/TM/E/D/S. Charges negotiable, according to project; $10 minimum.

WILLIAM H. GENTZ, 300 E. 34th St. (9C), New York NY 10016-4976. (212)686-5737. Call/write. Works primarily as a book doctor—looking at proposals, ideas, projected projects, etc. to eventually shape the material into a book. If interested in this kind of help, write for an estimate of costs. Has 30 years experience as a book editor.

NORTH CAROLINA

*ANNA FISHEL, 3416 Hunting Creek Dr., Pfafftown NC 27040. (910)924-5880. Call. GE/CA/SP. Does A/SS/N/JN. Charges variable rates depending on job.

OHIO

BOB HOSTETLER, 2336 Gardner Rd., Hamilton OH 45013-9317. Phone/fax (513)737-1102. E-mail: 102163.3045@compuserve.com. Call/write. GE/LC/GH/ CA/B/N. Does A/SS/P/N/NB/BP/JN/PB. Rate sheet available for SASE.

+A WRITE IMPRESSION/KELLY BOYER SAGERT, PO Box 3181, Lorain OH 44052. (216)245-1569. Call for fax. E-mail: DarkPrint@aol.com. Call/write/e-mail. GE/LC/GH/CA/B/NL/SP. Does A/SS/F/N/NB/BP/JN/E. Charges contract price or $25/hr.

OKLAHOMA

*KATHRYN FANNING, Critique Service, PO Box 18472, Oklahoma City OK 73154-0472. N/NB; no poetry. Charges $3.50/page.

THE WRITE WORD/IRENE MARTIN, PO Box 300332, Midwest City OK 73140. (800)799-9424. Write. GE/LC/GH. Does A/SS/N/JN/PB. For fee schedule send SASE/query letter detailing project. Charges $3/pg or $15/hr.

OREGON

*NASIRA ALMA, 8851-A SE 11th Ave #2, Portlend OR 97202-7050. Call. GE/GH. Does A/SS/P/N/NB/BP/BS/E/D. For an initial overview, which includes a single-spaced report of not less than 10 pgs, charges $400 (for book of average size). Sometimes negotiates a flat fee for the project.

BOOKPARTNERS, INC./URSULA BACON, PO Box 922, Wilsonville OR 97070. (503)682-9821. Fax (503)682-8684. Write. GE/LC/GH/CA. Does A/SS/N/NB/ BP/PB/TM. Fees are quoted on a per project basis. Ms evaluation for 250-325 pgs starts at $550. Full report and chapter-by-chapter recommendations included. Secular, but handles Christian books.

*CHRISTIAN WRITING SERVICES/ED STEWART, 3540 SE Spring Dr., Hillsboro OR 97123. (503)640-2522. Call. LC/GH/CA. Does NB/BP. Charges by the project based on $35/hr.

GAIL DENHAM, Box 89, Newberg OR 97132. (503)538-4691. Call. GE. Does A/SS/P/F/JN/PB/E/D/brochures/newsletters. Has photos to go with articles or books. Charges $20/hour; $25 minimum.

MARION DUCKWORTH, 2495 Maple NE, Salem OR 97303. (503)364-9570. Call/write. GE. Does A/SS/F/NB/BP/PB/BS/D. Charges $20/hr. Consultations or private lessons, $25/hr.

LIT.DOC/KRISTEN INGRAM, 955 S. 59TH St., Springfield OR 97478. (503)726-8320. Fax (503)988-9126. E-mail: 72734.3354@Compuserve.com. GE/LC. Does GH/CA/B/NL/SP. Edits A/SS/P/F/N/NB/BP/JN/TM/E/D. General evaluation $40/hr; copy editing $45/hr. Send SASE for rate sheet (includes project prices).

*LYON'S LITERARY SERVICES/ELIZABETH LYON, 2123 Marlow Ln., Eugene OR 97401-6431. (541)344-9118. Fax (541)485-2216. Call/write. GE/LC/ SP. Does A/SS/N/NB/BP/JN/PB/TM/E/D. Charges $45/hr or $75, plus $3/pg. for longer projects.

*PRIMA FACIE PUBLISHERS/BEN RIGALL, 13002 SE Alder St., Portland OR 97233-1629. (503)255-2199. Write or call. GE/LC. Contact for information and fees.

CONNIE SOTH, 4890 SW Menlo Dr., Beaverton OR 97005-2612. (503)644-4972. Call/Write. GE/LC/book doctoring & guidance. Does N/NB/BP/JN. Realistic rates by the hour.

ANNA LLOYD STONE, PO Box 2251, Lake Oswego OR 97035. (503)638-3705. Fax (503)638-3811. Call. LC/special projects/word processing. Does A/SS/P/ F/N/NB/BP/JN/PB/BS/TM/E/D/S. Charges $20/hr for copyediting or word processing; $30/hr for both.

SALLY STUART, 1647 SW Pheasant Dr., Aloha OR 97006. (503)642-9844. Fax (503)848-3658. E-mail: stuartcwmg@aol.com. Call/write. GE. Does A/SS/N/NB/ BP/JN/PB/E. Charges $25/hr. for critique; $35/hr. for consultations. Comprehensive publishing contract evaluation $50-80.

PENNSYLVANIA

*VAL CINDRIC EDITING & PUBLISHING SERVICES, 536 Monticello Dr., Delmont PA 15626. Phone/Fax (412)468-6185. Call/write. GE/GH/CA. Does NB. Charges $20/hr.

IMPACT COMMUNICATIONS/DEBRA PETROSKY, 11331 Tioga Rd., N. Huntingdon PA 15642-2445. Phone/fax (412)863-5906. E-mail: Editing 4U@aol.com. Call. GE/LC/B/NL/typesetting. Does NB/BP. Charges $20/hr. 10% discount for nonprofits.

SPREAD THE WORD/MAURCIA DELEAN HOUCK, 1618 Rockwell Rd., Abington PA 19001. Phone/fax (215)659-2912. Write. GE/LC/B/N/SP/BC. Does A/SS/F/N/NB/BP/JN/BS/E/D. Charges $1.75/pg., or as quoted.

WRITE HIS ANSWER MINISTRIES/MARLENE BAGNULL, 316 Blanchard Rd., Drexel Hill PA 19026-3507. Phone/fax: (610)626-6833. E-mail: mbagnull@aol.com. Call/write. GE/LC/typesetting. Does A/SS/F/N/NB/BP/JN/BS/E/D. Charges $20/hr; estimates given.

SOUTH CAROLINA

CHRISTIAN WRITERS FELLOWSHIP INTL./SANDY BROOKS, Rt. 3 Box 1635, Jefferson Davis Rd., Clinton SC 29325. Phone/fax (803)697-6035. E-mail: CWFI@aol.com. Call. GE/LC. Does A/F/N/NB/BP/JN/PB/D. Charges $1/pg ($25 min.) for general editing; $2/pg ($25 min.) for line editing. Enclose payment.

TENNESSEE

+CHRISTIAN WRITERS INSTITUTE MANUSCRIPT CRITIQUE SERVICE, PO Box 110390, Nashville TN 37222. (800)21-WRITE. Send material with payment. GE/LC. Does A/SS/P/N/NB/BP. Send SASE for rate sheet and submission slip.

+JOHNSON LITERARY AND TALENT SERVICES/JOSEPH S. JOHNSON JR., 2915 Walnut Crest Dr., Antioch TN 37013-1337. Phone/fax (615)361-8627. Call. GE/LC/GH/CA/SP/BC. Does A/SS/P/F/N/NB/BP/JN/PB/BS/TM/E/D/S/advice on song writing. Reasonable rates; negotiable.

WILLIAM PENS/WILLIAM D. WATKINS, 342 Alden Cove Dr., Smyrna TN 37167. (615)355-4455. Fax (615)355-9977. E-mail: 76612.32@compuserve.com. Write. GE/CA/B/NL/SP/BC/consulting, contract negotiations, book proposal evaluations & creations, market analysis of book ideas. Does A/SS/N/NB/BP/BS/TM/E/D. Send SASE for rate sheet.

TEXAS

SYLVIA BRISKEY, PO Box 9053, Dallas TX 75209-9053. (214)521-7507. Call/send ms/full payment. GE/LC. Does SS/P/N/JN/PB/children's stories/secular articles. Poetry, charges $5.60 plus $1/line; fiction $30 to 2,000 wds, $2.50/page thereafter.

JAN E. KILBY, Ph.D. , PO Box 17494, San Antonio TX 78217-0494. (210)657-0171. Fax (210)657-0173. Call. GE/LC. Does A/SS/P/F/N/NB/BP/JN/PB/TM/E/D/speeches. Call for prices/information.

VIRGINIA

CREATIVE CHRISTIAN MINISTRIES/BETTY ROBERTSON, PO Box 12624, Roanoke VA 24027-2624. Phone/fax (540)342-7511. E-mail: ccmbbr@worldnet.att.com. Send with full payment. GE/LC. Does A/SS/F/NB/BP/BS/D/S. Charges $2/page for everything.

IRENE BOYER, 8836 Burbank Rd., Annandale VA 22003-3859. (703)425-1080. Fax (703)425-1090. E-mail: caboyer@mnsinc.com. Write. LC/GH/CA/B/NL/SP. Does A/F/NB/BS/E/D. Word processing, typesetting, hard copy, electronic. Charge depends on type/scope. Brochure for SASE.

***HCI EDITORIAL SERVICES/DAVID HAZARD**, Box 71, Lincoln VA 22078. (703)338-7032. Write or call. GE. Does N/NB/BP. Works with agents and self-publishers. Fees on request.

PUBLICATIONS MANAGEMENT, INC./JANETTE G. BLACKWELL, 4039 Hallman St., Fairfax VA 22030-5213. (703)691-1853. Call. GE/LC/GH/CA/B/NL/SP. Does A/SS/N/NB/TM/E/D/biographies; design and production of brochures, newsletters, books. Charges $25/hr. for writing/editing, or as negotiated.

WASHINGTON

***DUE NORTH PUBLISHING/SCOTT R. ANDERSON**, 7372 Guide Meridian, Lynden WA 98264. Phone/fax (360)354-0234 (call first for fax). Write. GE/LC/GH/CA/B/NL/SP. Does A/SS/P/N/NB/BP. Charges $35-60/hr or by the project (estimate given). Offers wide range of editorial & pre-press (design/layout) services.

+MARY ARMSTRONG LITERARY SERVICES, 8018 - 38TH Dr. NE, Marysville WA 98270. (360)653-6548. Call/write; send fee for line editing. GE/LC/GH/CA/B. Does A/SS/F/N/NB/BP/JN/BS/TM/E/D. Line-editing $1.50/pg.; evaluations $25/hr.

BIRDIE ETCHISON, Box 877, Ocean Park WA 98640. (206)665-6576. Write. GE/LC. Does A/SS/F/N/BP/PB. Charges according to length, $15 minimum.

JAN GREEN, 1616 SW Henderson St., Seattle WA 98106. (206)763-2760. Call/write. GE/LC/GH/CA/B/NL/SP. Does A/SS/P/F/N/NB/JN/BS/T/E/D. Negotiable rates.

KALEIDOSCOPE PRESS/PENNY LENT, 2507 - 94th Ave. E., Puyallup WA 98371-2203. Phone/Fax (206)848-1116. Call/write. GE/LC/GH/CA/B/NL/ SP/BC. Does A/SS/F/N/NB/BP/JN/PB/E/D. Also market analysis. Line item editing $3/pg; other projects negotiated individually.

AGNES C. LAWLESS, 17462 NE 11th St., Bellevue WA 98008-3814. (206)644-5012. Write. GE/LC/CA. Does A/SS/P/F/N/NB/BP/JN/BS/E/D. Send SASE for rate sheet; $15/hr.

VIRGINIA A. MOODY, 17402 - 114th Pl. NE, Granite Falls WA 98252-9667. (360)691-5402. Call/write. GE/LC/CA/B/NL/BC. Does SS/F/N/NB/BP/JN/PB/BS/D. Charges $@/pg or as agreed.

PATRICIA H. RUSHFORD, 3600 Edgewood Dr., Vancouver WA 98661. (360)695-2263. E-mail: PRushford@aol.com. Call. GE/personal consultation and conference; Weekend With a Writer. Does A/SS/N/NB/BP. Fee $15-35/hr (negotiable). Offers private week-end workshop for $300, plus expenses.

PAULINE SHEEHAN, Box 801, Lake Stevens WA 98258. (206)334-7049. Fax (206)397-0854. E-mail: DAT1johns@aol.com. Writet. GE/GH. Does SS/F/N/NB/BP/JN/S. Book proposals. Charges $2/pg, $20 minimum.

WRITE AWAKE! EDITORIAL SERVICES/GLORIA KEMPTON, 13115 NE 123rd Pl, #204, Kirkland WA 98034. Phone/fax: (206)823-6008. Call/write. GE. Does A/SS/F/N/NB/BP/JN/E. Free estimates; generally $25-50 for article/short story, $100-250 for book proposal.

WRITERS INFORMATION NETWORK/ELAINE WRIGHT COLVIN, Box 11337, Bainbridge Island WA 98110. Phone/fax (206)842-9103. Send material/ $100 deposit. GE/LC/GH/CA/B/NL/SP/BC. Does A/SS/P/N/NB/BP/JN/PB/BS/ E/D/S. Send SASE for rate sheet & list of all services.

WISCONSIN

BETHESDA LITERARY SERVICE/MARGARET L. BEEN, South 63 West 35530 Piper Rd., Eagle WI 53119-9726. (414)392-9761. Fax (414)547-8871. E-mail: MLJBeen@aol.com. Write. GE/LC. Does A/SS/P/F/NB/BS/E/D. Charges $15/hr. Also does devotional & inspirational readings. Teaches writers' classes/poetry seminars for all ages, with emphasis on classical literature.

MARGARET HOUK, 514 S Buchanan, Appleton WI 54915. (414)739-4997. Call/write. GE/LC. Does A/NB/BP/BS. Charges $20/hr.

CANADA

*A. BIENERT, Box 1358, Three Hills AB T0M 2A0 Canada. 443-2491. GE/LC. Does N/NB. Charges negotiable.

BERYL HENNE, 541 - 56 Street, Delta BC V4L 1Z5 Canada (U.S. address: Box 40, Pt. Roberts WA 98281-0040). (604)943-9676. Fax (604)943-9651. Write. GE/LC/ B/NL. Does A/SS/NB/BP/E/D. Charges $20/hr.

*WINDFLOWER COMMUNICATIONS/THE WRITER'S EDGE, 844-K McLeod Ave., Winnipeg MB R2G 2T7, Canada. (204)668-7475. Fax (204)661-8530. Write first. Charges $100.

WRITING SERVICES INSTITUTE (WSI)/MARSHA DRAKE, Box 27113, Collingwood PO, Vancouver BC V5R 6A8, Canada. Phone/fax (604)438-7507. E-mail: 103270.2051@compuserve.com. Call/write. GE/LC/GH/CA/B/SP; also biographies or resumes. Does A/SS/F/N/NB/BP/D. Offers correspondence course: Write for Fun and Profit. Charges $20/hr. for critique; $30/hr for consultation. Write for details and info on correspondence course.

CHRISTIAN LITERARY AGENTS

(*) Indicates that publisher did not return questionnaire.
(#) Indicates that listing was updated from guidelines or other sources.
(+) Indicates new listing.

ALIVE COMMUNICATIONS, 1465 Kelly Johnson Blvd. #320, Colorado Springs CO 80920-3955. (719)260-7080. Fax (719)260-8223. Agents: Rick Christian/ Greg Johnson/Kathy Yanni. Well known in the industry. Est. 1989. Represents over 50 clients. Open to unpublished authors occasionally. Occasionally open to clients at this time. Handles fiction and nonfiction for all ages, gift books. Deals in both Christian (80%) and general market (20%). Also runs a speaker's bureau.
> **Contact:** Query with letter, previous history and future ideas (no calls)/ SASE.
> **Commission:** 15%
> **Fees:** Only extraordinary costs with client's pre-approval; no review fee.

*ALLEGRA LITERARY AGENCY, 2806 Pine Hill Dr., Kennesaw GA 30144-2834. Phone/fax (770)795-8318. Agent: Cynthia Lambert. Est. 1994. Establishing reputation. Represents 4 clients. Open to unpublished authors. Handles adult & teen (rarely) novels, adult nonfiction, scripts (rarely). Interested in Christian science fiction, romance and mainstream novels. Books only.
> **Contact:** By mail, phone, or fax.
> **Commission:** 12%.
> **Fees:** Requires a $150 retainer for postage and copying: 100% refundable when manuscript sells.
> **Tips:** "We're interested in fictional manuscripts that are spiritually uplifting as well as educational."

*AUTHOR AID ASSOCIATES, 340 E. 52nd St., New York NY 10022. (212)758-4213. Agent: Arthur Orrmont. Not known in industry but expanding Christian/religious client list. Est. 1967. Represents 10 Christian clients. Open to unpublished authors. Handles novels for all ages, nonfiction for all ages, and scripts.
> **Contact:** By mail or phone.
> **Commission:** 15%.
> **Fees:** Evaluation fees for new/unpublished authors.

BK NELSON LITERARY AGENCY, 84 Woodland Rd., Pleasantville NY 10570. (914)741-1322. Fax (914)741-1324. E-mail: 105011.426@compuserve.com. Internet: http://www.CMONLINR.Com/bknelson. Agent: John W. Benson. Recognized in the industry. Est. 1979. Represents 4 clients. Open to unpublished authors & new clients. Handles adult fiction and nonfiction, motion picture and television scripts. Also CD-ROM, audio tapes and lecturers.
> **Contact:** Send inquiry and SASE.
> **Commission:** 20%, foreign 25%.
> **Fees:** $350 reading fee or $2/pg for proposals with sample chapter.
> **Comments:** "Allow us the opportunity to evaluate and if the material is salable,

we will give you the best representation in the publishing/literary field."

BRANDENBURGH & ASSOCIATES LITERARY AGENCY, 24555 Corte Jaramillo, Murrieta CA 92562. (909)698-5200. Agent: Don Brandenburgh. Recognized in industry. Est. 1986. Represents 5 clients. Open to unpublished authors (limited). Open to new clients only in special circumstances. Handles adult novels and nonfiction. Specializes in nonfiction for the religious market only. Books only.

  Contact: Query/SASE (or no response).

  Commission: 10%; 20% for foreign or dramatic rights.

  Fees: $35 for mailing/materials when contract is signed.

PEMA BROWNE LTD., Pine Rd., HCR Box 104B, Neversink NY 12765. (914)985-2936. Fax (914)985-7635. Agents: Perry & Pema Browne. Recognized in industry. Est. 1966. Represents 7 clients. Open to unpublished authors and to new clients. Handles novels and nonfiction (preferred) for all ages; picture books. Only wishes mss not sent previously to publishers.

  Contact: Letter query with credentials & SASE.

  Commission: 15%; 20% foreign

  Fees: None.

CISKE & DIETZ LITERARY AGENCY, 10605 W. Wabash, Milwaukee WI 53224. (414)355-8915. Agent: Andrea Boeshaar. Recognized in industry. Open to unpublished authors and new clients at this time. Handles romance novels only, contemporary and historical.

  Contact: One-two page query letter, with an SASE.

  Commission: 15%.

  Fees: None.

  Tips: We prefer query letters that sum up the book in one paragraph, giving word length and whether contemporary or historical. If historical, give date. Additional info on the author is important if it pertains to their writing or the manuscript.

+CREATIVE CONCEPTS LITERARY AGENCY, PO Box 128, Troy MI 48083. (810)524-0864. Agent: Michele Glance. Recognized in the industry. Est. 1987. Open to unpublished authors and new clients. Handles Adult/teen/children's novels, adult/children's nonfiction, poetry books, and gift books.

  Contact: Send brief description of book in letter, plus sample chapters.

  Commission: Negotiable.

  Fees: Charges $95 to critique a full manuscript.

  Tips: Write from the heart, that's how the best books always start. Persist in your efforts to be published. Having the right attitude is 95% of the key to success.

LOIS CURLEY ENTERPRISES, 18755 W. Bernardo Dr., Suite 1039, San Diego CA 92127-3010. (619)675-2031. Fax (619)675-2026. Agent: Lois L. Curley. Recognized in industry. Est. 1979. Represents 24 clients. May be open to unpublished authors. Handles adult fiction and nonfiction. Books only. Currently has a waiting list of new clients.

  Contact: Query, fax, or call. Send SASE for submission guidelines.

  Commission: 15% on first 35,000 copies, 10% thereafter.

  Fees: Charges normal office expenses.

Comments: "We have a waiting list of writers from which we select one or two new clients each quarter for representation."

+CVK INTERNATIONAL, 277 Smith St., New York NY 11231. (718)237-4570. Fax (718)237-4571. Agent: Cynthia Neeseman. Handles adult fiction and nonfiction; screenplays; and seeks foreign sales for translations of books published in the US.

    Contact: Query.

DEERING LITERARY AGENCY, 106 N. Main St. Ste. A, Nicholasville KY 40356-1234. (606)887-5862. Fax (606)885-0254. E-mail: DEERINGLIT@aol.com. Agent: Charles Deering. Recognized in the industry. Est. 1988. Represents 91 clients. Open to unpublished authors and new clients. Handles novels and nonfiction for all ages, picture books, screenplays, scripts, poetry books, gift books and short story collections. Book length material only; nothing over 125,000 wds.

    Contact: Query letter and synopsis, fax or e-mail.

    Commission: 15%

    Fees: Reading fee, plus expenses, i.e., postage, phone calls, faxing, etc.

    Tips: "I see so many mss that are not in the appropriate format. Please edit for spelling, tense, sentence structure, etc. Good religious material is so needed in our society today. Write uplifting material."

JOYCE FARRELL AND ASSOCIATES, 669 Grace St., Upper Montclair NJ 07043. (201)746-6248. Fax (201)746-6348. (January-April, Phone/fax 941-966-2922). Agent: Joyce Farrell. Recognized in the industry. Est. 1985. Represents 15-20 clients. Open to unpublished authors; selectively open to new clients. Handles fiction and nonfiction for children and adults. No fantasy novels. In nonfiction, prefers issue books, or books with historical, scientific, psychological or theological orientation.

    Contact: Prefers phone or fax. If by mail, send query letter, author bio, synopsis and SASE.

    Commission: 15%

    Fees: Reading fee: up to 50 pgs, $35; complete manuscript $65 additional. Author provides copies for multiple submissions.

    Tips: "Check the marketplace to see what is currently available, and whether your treatment of a subject presents a fresh, somewhat different angle than books already published. If not, choose another subject."

+SARA A. FORTENBERRY, PO Box 8177, Hermitage TN 37076-8177. (615)902-9471. Fax (615)902-9479. E-mail: safberry@aol.com. Contact before submitting material.

GOOD NEWS LITERARY SERVICE, Box 587, Visalia CA 93279. Phone/fax (209)627-6241 (call first for fax). Agent: Cynthia A. Wachner. Recognized in industry. Est. 1986. Not accepting mss at this time.

+STEPHEN GRIFFITH, PO Box 939, Leicester NC 28748. Unlisted phone. Fax (704)683-2851. Recognized in industry. Est. 1990. Not open to unpublished authors. Open only to referrals from existing clients. Handles novels for all ages and adult nonfiction.

    Contact: By mail or fax.

    Commission: 15% (10% on reprinted books).

    Fees: None.

HARTLINE LITERARY AGENCY, 123 Queenston Dr., Pittsburgh PA 15235.

(412)829-2483. Fax (412)829-2450. Agent: Joyce Hart. Recognized in industry. Est. 1992. Represents 14 clients. Published authors preferred. Open to new clients. Handles adult or teen novels (no science fiction) and adult or teen nonfiction. Handles books only.

Contact: Phone or query.
Commission: 15%.
Fees: Fee schedule available on request.
Tips: "Send your manuscript as professionally done as possible; on disk and the hard copy printed on a laser or inkjet printer is best."

*HOLUB & ASSOCIATES, 24 Old Colony Rd., North Stonington CT 06359. (203)535-0689. Agent: William Holub. Recognized by Catholic publishers. Est. 1966. Open to unpublished authors. Handles adult nonfiction; possibly picture books; Christian living in secular society.

Contact: Query with outline, 2 sample chapters, intended audience, and bio.
Commission: 15%.
Fees: Postage and photocopying.

*JEAN V. NAGGAR LITERARY AGENCY, 216 E. 75th St., New York NY 11201. (212)794-1082. Agent: Jean Naggar. Not recognized in industry. Est. 1978. Represents 5 clients. Open to unpublished authors. Handles adult/teen/children's novels and nonfiction, picture books. Handles articles/short stories only if handling book-length as well.

Contact: Query letter/1-2 pg. synopsis.
Commission: 15%; 20% foreign.
Fees: No reading fee, but Xerox, telephone & overseas mailing for clients.

*PEN & INK LITERARY AGENCY, 4319 Toll Gate Ln., Bellbrook OH 45305-1238. (513)434-0686. Agent: Theresa Freed. Recognized in industry. Est. 1993. Building client list. Open to unpublished authors. Handles fiction and nonfiction for all ages, picture books, scripts, poetry books; informational, motivational and how-to. Books only.

Contact: Send SASE for information.
Commission: 15%; 20% foreign.
Fees: Charges a $90 reading fee that is refunded on receipt of advance from publisher; also office expenses and marketing fee.
Tips: "Please submit ms in proper form. This will save everyone time and money."

A RISING SUN LITERARY GROUP, 5 Galleon Ct., Savannah GA 31406-8801. (912)356-5366. Fax (912)355-4053. E-mail: Wrdman95@aol.com. Agents: Chris & Vicki Scott. Limited recognition in the industry. Est. 1989. Represents 46 clients. Open to unpublished authors and to new clients. Handles fiction and nonfiction for all ages, picture books, scripts, poetry books, gift books, stage plays, cookbooks, audio books on tape, coffee-table books, photography and art work. Wants to see entire work, not just samples.

Contact: By phone, mail, fax or e-mail.
Commission: 12% domestic; 20% foreign; 18% dramatic.
Fees: A $50 reader's fee and a retainer charge only for first-time authors.
Comments: "We are looking for new work—interesting—family-oriented—fresh new ideas. We sell many works overseas as well."

*THE SHEPARD AGENCY, Pawling Savings Bank Bldg., Brewster (Rt. 22) NY 10509. (914)279-2900/3236. Fax (914)279-3239. Agents: Jean or Lance Shepard. Recognized in the industry. Est. 1986. Represents 8 clients. Open to unpublished authors. Handles fiction and nonfiction for all ages; no picture books; especially business, reference, professional, self-help, cooking and crafts. Books only.

    Contact: Query letter and sample material.

    Commission: 15%

    Fees: None except long-distance calls and copying.

WOLGEMUTH & HYATT, INC., 8012 Brooks Chapel Rd., Ste. 243, Brentwood TN 37027. (615)370-9937. Fax (615)370-9939. Agents: Michael S. Hyatt and Robert D. Wolgemuth. Well recognized in the industry. Est. 1992. Represents 30 clients. No unpublished authors. Handles only adult nonfiction.

    Contact: By letter, phone or CompuServe.

    Commission: 15%

    Fees: Charges fees.

    Other Services: Offers a manuscript evaluation service for unpublished authors to assist them in increasing their chances of getting published.

    Comments: "We work with authors who are either best-selling authors or potentially best-selling authors. Consequently, we want to represent clients with broad market appeal."

THE WRITER'S EDGE—See listing under Editorial Services—Illinois.

ADDITIONAL AGENTS

NOTE: The following agents did not return a questionnaire, but have been identified as agents who handle religious manuscripts. Be sure to send queries first if you wish to submit to them.

(*) Indicates they are known in the industry.

Julian Bach Literary Agency
E. 71st St.
New York NY 10021
(212)753-2605
nonfiction/fiction

Elizabeth H. Backman
PO Box 762
Pine Plains NY 12567
(518)398-6408
nonfiction/fiction

Bonnie Crown
B R Crown Intl. Literary & Arts Agency
50 E. 10th St.
New York NY 10003
(212)475-1999
nonfiction/fiction

Al Hart
Fox Chase Agency Inc.
Rm. 930/Public Ledger Bldg
Independence Square
Philadelphia PA 19106
(215)625-2450
nonfiction

Lawrence Jordan
Lawrence Jordan Literary Agency
250 W 57th St. Ste 1527
New York NY 10107
(212)690-2748
nonfiction/fiction

Ned Leavitt
The Ned Leavitt Agency
70 Wooster St. #4F
New York NY 10012
(212)334-0999
nonfiction/fiction

Pamela G. Ahearn
Southern Writers
635 Gravier St. #1020
New Orleans LA 70130
(504)525-6390
nonfiction/fiction

Mark Sullivan
Mark Sullivan Assoc.
521 Fifth Ave. #1700
New York NY 10175
(212)682-5844
nonfiction/fiction

DENOMINATIONAL LISTING OF BOOK PUBLISHERS AND PERIODICALS

An attempt has been made to divide publishers into appropriate denominational groups. However, due to the extensive number of denominations included, and sometimes incomplete denominational information, some publishers may have inadvertently been included in the wrong list. Additions and corrections are welcome.

ASSEMBLIES OF GOD
Periodicals:
American Horizon
At Ease
CE Counselor
Club Connection
Enrichment
High Adventure
Junior Trails
Live
Memos
On Course
Paraclete
Pentecostal Evangel
Pentecostal Testimony
   (Canada)
Resource (Canada)
Teen Life
Take Five
Woman's Touch
Youth Leader

BAPTIST, SOUTHERN
Book Publishers:
Baylor Univ. Press
Broadman & Holman
New Hope Publishers
Renewal Press
Southern Baptist Press
Woman's Missionary Union
Periodicals:
Baptist History & Heritage
Challenge
Christian Recreation
Christian Single
Church Administration
Church Media Library
Church Musician
Crusader
Discipleship Training
Experiencing God
Glory Songs
Home Life
Journey
Living With Teenagers

Mature Living
Music Leader
Music Makers
Music Time
National Drama Service
ParentLife
Proclaim
Senior Musician
Stand Firm
Young Musicians

BAPTIST, OTHER
Book Publishers:
Judson Press (American)
National Baptist (Missionary)
Sword of the Lord Publishers-
   (Independent)
Periodicals:
American Baptist
Atlantic Baptist
Baptist Beacon
Baptist Informer (General)
Baptist Leader (American)
The Canadian Baptist
Certainty (Regular)
Challenge (Regular)
Co-Laborer (Free Will)
Conquest
Contact (Free Will)
Courage (Regular)
The Five Stones (American)
Fundamentalist Journal
God's Special People (Inde-
   pendent)
Heartbeat (Free Will)
LIGHT...For/Christian Walk
   (Independent)
The Link (Fellowship/Canada)
Link & Visitor
Messenger, The (Pentecostal
   Free Will)
Moments with God (North
   American)
Primary Pal (Regular)
Secret Place (American)

Standard, The (General)
Writer's Forum

CATHOLIC
Book Publishers:
ACTA Publications
Alba House
American Catholic Press
Don Bosco Publications
Brown Publishing
Catholic Book Publishing
Catholic University of Amer-
   ica Press
Christendom Press
Christian Classics
Cistercian Publications
Dimension Books
Faith Publishing Co.
Franciscan University
   Press
Harper SF (Cath. bks)
Hi-Time Publishing
ICS Publications
Libros Liguori
Liguori Publications
Liturgical Press
Loyola University Press
Thomas More Press
Orbis Books
Our Sunday Visitor
Pastoral Press
Pauline Books
Paulist Press
Regina Press
Regnery Gateway
Resurrection Press
Riehle Foundation
Servant Publications
St. Anthony Messenger
St. Bede's Publications
Sheed & Ward
Tabor Publishing
Periodicals:
America
Annals of St. Anne

Light and Life
Light From the Word
Response (SPU)
World Mission People

FREE WILL BAPTIST
Periodicals:
CoLaborer
Heartbeat

LUTHERAN
Book Publishers:
Augsburg Press (ELCA)
Concordia
Langmarc Publishing
Periodicals:
Canada Lutheran (ELCC)
Christmas (ELCA)
Cresset
Diaconalogue
Esprit (ELCC)
Evangelism (MO Synod)
Lutheran, The (ELCA)
Lutheran Digest
Lutheran Educ. (MO Synod)
Lutheran Forum
Lutheran Journal
Lutheran Laymen (MO Synod)
LutheranPartners (ELCA)
Lutheran Witness (MO Synod)
Lutheran Woman's Quarterly (MO Synod)
Lutheran Woman Today (ELCA)
Northwestern Lutheran
Parenting Treasures (MO Synod)
Parish Teacher (ELCA)
Word & World (ELCA)
Teachers Inter. (MO Synod)

MENNONITE
Book Publishers:
Faith & Life Press
Herald Press
Kindred Press
Periodicals:
Christian Leader, The
Christian Living
Companions
Mennonite Brethren Herald
Mennonite Historian
Mennonite Reporter
Mennonite Weekly Review
The Messenger
On the Line

Partners
Purpose
Story Friends
Story Mates
With

MISSIONARY CHURCH
Book Publisher:
Bethel Publishing
Periodicals:
Emphasis/Faith & Living
Ministry Today

PENTECOSTAL HOLINESS CHURCH
Periodicals:
CE Connection
Helping Hand, The
Evangelism USA
Worldorama

PRESBYTERIAN
Book Publishers:
John Knox Press
Presbyterian & Reformed
Westminster Press
Periodicals:
Covenanter Witness
Horizons (USA)
PCA Messenger
Presbyterian Layman (USA)
Presbyterian Outlook (USA)
Presbyterian Record
Presbyterian Today

QUAKER/FRIENDS
Book Publishers:
Barclay Press
Friends United Press
Periodicals:
Evangelical Friend
Friends Journal

REFORMED CHURCHES
Periodicals:
Perspectives
Reformed Worship
Vision (MI)

SEVENTH-DAY ADVENTIST
Book Publishers:
Pacific Press
Review and Herald
Periodicals:
GUIDE Magazine
Insight (MD)
Journal/Adventist Ed
Kids' Stuff

Liberty
Listen
Message
Ministry
Our Little Friend
Primary Treasure
Signs of the Times
Vibrant Life
Young and Alive

UNITED METHODIST
Book Publishers:
United Methodist Publishing House
Imprints: Abingdon Press
Cokesbury
Discipleship Resources
Upper Room Books
Periodicals:
alive now!
Christian Social Action
Circuit Rider
Good News
Kaleidoscope
Leader/Church School Today
Magazine/Christian Youth!
Mature Years
Methodist History
New World Outlook
Pockets
Quarterly Review
Upper Room

UNITED PENTECOSTAL
Periodicals:
Conqueror, The
Pentecostal Homelife
Teen Life
Vision
Youth World

WESLEYAN CHURCH
Periodicals:
Changing Lives
Friend
In Touch
Wesleyan Advocate
Wesleyan World

MISCELLANEOUS DENOMINATIONS
Armenian Holy Apostolic
Pourastan
Brethren Church
Brethren Evangelist
Christian Reformed
The Banner
Brethren in Christ

LIST OF BOOK PUBLISHERS AND PERIODICALS BY CORPORATE GROUP

For the first time this year, we are including a listing of book publishers and periodicals that belong to the same group or family of publications.

CHRISTIAN BOOKSELLERS ASSN.
CBA Frontline
CBA Marketplace

CHRISTIANITY TODAY, INC.
Campus Life
Christian History
Christianity Today
Christian Reader
Leadership Journal
Marriage Partnership
Your Church

CHRISTIAN MEDIA
Christian Media (books)
The Apocalypse Chronicles
Christian Composer
Christian Media

COOK COMMUNICATIONS MINISTRIES
Accent Bible Curriculum
Accent Publications (books)
Bible Discovery (books)
Chariot Books
Chariot Family Publishing (books)
Lion Publishing (books)
Victor Books
Bible-in-Life Pix

Christian Parenting Today
Counselor
I.D.
Power for Living
Primary Days
Quiet Hour, The
The Rock
Single Adult Ministries Journal
Teen Power
Virtue
Zelos

FOCUS ON THE FAMILY
Focus on the Family (books)
Breakaway
Brio
Clubhouse
Clubhouse Jr.
Focus on the Family
Pastor's Family
Physician
Single-Parent Family
Teachers in Focus

GUIDEPOSTS
Guideposts Books
Angels on Earth
Guideposts
Guideposts for Kids

THOMAS NELSON PUBLISHERS
Thomas Nelson Publishers (books)
Release
Release Ink
7 Ball
Word

STANDARD PUBLISHING
Standard Publishing (books)
Christian Standard
The Lookout
R-A-D-A-R
Seek
Straight

STRANG COMMUNICATIONS
Creation House (books)
Charisma & Christian Life
Christian Retailing
Ministries Today
New Man

THE UPPER ROOM
Upper Room Books
Alive Now!
Devo'Zine
The Upper Room
Weavings

GLOSSARY OF TERMS

NOTE: This is not intended to be an exhaustive glossary of terms. It includes primarily those terms you will find within the context of this market guide.

Advance. Amount of money a publisher pays to an author up front, against future royalties.

All rights. An outright sale of your material. Author has no further control over it.

Anecdote. A short, poignant, real-life story, usually used to illustrate a single thought.

Assignment. When an editor asks a writer to write a specific piece for an agreed-upon price.

Avant-garde. Experimental; ahead of the times.

Bible Versions. KJV—King James Version; NAS—New American Standard; NIV—New International Version; NKJV—New King James Version; NRSV—New Revised Standard Version; RSV—Revised Standard Version.

Bimonthly. Every two months.

Biweekly. Every two weeks.

Book proposal. Submission of a book idea to an editor, usually includes a cover letter, thesis statement, chapter-by-chapter synopsis, market survey, and 1-3 sample chapters.

Byline. Author's name printed just below the title of a story, article, etc.

Circulation. The number of copies sold or distributed of each issue of a publication.

Clips. See "Published Clips."

Column. A regularly appearing feature, section, or department in a periodical using the same heading; written by the same person or a different freelancer each time.

Contributor's copy. Copy of an issue of a periodical sent to the author whose work appears in it.

Copyright. Legal protection of an author's work.

Cover letter. A letter that accompanies some manuscript submissions. Usually needed only if you have to tell the editor something specific, or to give your credentials for writing a piece of a technical nature.

Critique. An evaluation of a piece of writing.

Devotional. A short piece which shares a personal spiritual discovery, inspires to worship, challenges to commitment or action, or encourages.

Editorial guidelines. See "Writer's guidelines."

EPA/Evangelical Press Assn. A professional, trade organization for periodical publishers and associate members.

Essay. A short composition usually expressing the author's opinion on a specific subject.

Evangelical. A person who believes that one receives God's forgiveness for sins through Jesus Christ, and believes the Bible is an authoritative guide for daily living.

Feature article. In-depth coverage of a subject, usually focusing on a person, event, process, organization, movement, trend or issue; written to explain, encourage, help, analyze, challenge, motivate, warn, or entertain—as well as to inform.

Filler. A short item used to "fill" out the page of a periodical. It could be a timeless news item, joke, anecdote, light verse or short humor, puzzle, game, etc.

First rights. Editor buys the right to publish your piece for the first time.

Freelance. As in 50% freelance: means that 50% of the material printed in the publication is supplied by freelance writers.

Freelancer or freelance writer. A writer who is not on salary, but sells his material to a number of different publishers.

Free verse. Poetry that flows without any set pattern.

Genre. Refers to type or classification, as in fiction or poetry. In fiction, such types as westerns, romances, mysteries, etc., are referred to as genre fiction.

Glossy. A black and white photo with a shiny, rather than matte finish.

Go-ahead. When a publisher tells you to go ahead and write up or send your article idea.

Haiku. A Japanese lyric poem of a fixed 17-syllable form.

Holiday/seasonal. A story, article, filler, etc. that has to do with a specific holiday or season. This material must reach the publisher the stated number of months prior to the holiday/season.

Humor. The amusing or comical aspects of life that add warmth and color to an article or story.

Interdenominational. Distributed to a number of different denominations.

International Postal Reply Coupon. See "IRC."

Interview article. An article based on an interview with a person of interest to a specific readership.

IRC or IPRC. International Postal Reply Coupon: can be purchased at your local post office and should be enclosed with a manuscript sent to a foreign publisher.

Journal. A periodical presenting news in a particular area.

Kill fee. A fee paid for a completed article done on assignment that is subsequently not published.

Light verse. Simple, light-hearted poetry.

Mainstream fiction. Other than genre fiction, such as romance, mystery or science fiction. Stories of people and their conflicts handled on a deeper level.

Ms. Abbreviation for manuscript.

Mss. Abbreviation for more than one manuscript.

NASR. Abbreviation for North American serial rights.

Newsbreak. A newsworthy event or item sent to a publisher who might be interested in publishing it because it would be of interest to his particular readership.

Nondenominational. Not associated with a particular denomination.

Not copyrighted. Publication of your piece in such a publication will put it into public domain and it is not then protected. Ask that the publisher carry your copyright notice on your piece when it is printed.

On acceptance. Periodical pays a writer at the time an article is accepted for publication.

On assignment. Writing something at the specific request of an editor.

On publication. Periodical pays a writer when his/her article is published.

On speculation. Writing something for an editor with the agreement that he will buy it only if he likes it.

One-time rights. Selling the right to publish a story one-time to any number of publications (usually refers to publishing for a non-overlapping readership).

Payment on acceptance. See "On acceptance."

Payment on publication. See "On publication."

Pen Name. Using a name other than your legal name on an article in order to protect your identity or the identity of people included in the article. Put the pen name in the byline under the title, and your real name in the upper, left-hand corner.

Personal experience story. A story based on a real-life experience.

Personality profile. A feature article that highlights a specific person's life or accomplishments.

Photocopied submission. Sending an editor a photocopy of your manuscript, rather than an original. Some editors prefer an original.

Published clips. Copies of actual articles you have had published.

Quarterly. Every three months.

Query letter. A letter sent to an editor telling about an article you propose to write and asking if he or she is interested in seeing it.

Reporting time. The number of weeks or months it takes an editor to get back to you about a query or manuscript you have sent in.

Reprint rights. Selling the right to reprint an article that has already been published elsewhere. You must have sold only first or one-time rights originally, and wait until it has been published the first time.

Royalty. The percentage an author is paid by a publisher on the sale of each copy of a book.

SAE. Self-addressed envelope (without stamps).

SASE. Self-addressed, stamped envelope. Should always be sent with a manuscript or query letter.

Satire. Ridicule that aims at reform.

Second serial rights. See "Reprint rights."

Semiannual. Issued twice a year.

Serial. Refers to publication in a periodical (such as first serial rights).

Sidebar. A short feature that accompanies an article and either elaborates on the human interest side of the story or gives additional information on the topic. It is often set apart by appearing within a box or border.

Simultaneous rights. Selling the rights to the same piece to several publishers simultaneously. Be sure everyone is aware that you are doing so.

Simultaneous submissions. Sending the same manuscript to more than one publisher at the same time. Usually done with non-overlapping markets (such as denominational) or when you are writing on a timely subject. Be sure to state in a cover letter that it is a simultaneous submission and why.

Speculation. See "On speculation."

Staff-written material. Material written by the members of a magazine staff.

Subsidiary rights. All those rights, other than book rights, included in a book contract—such as paperback, book club, movie, etc.

Subsidy publisher. A book publisher who charges the author to publish his book, as opposed to a royalty publisher who pays the author.

Tabloid. A newspaper-format publication about half the size of a regular newspaper.

Take-home paper. A periodical sent home from Sunday School each week (usually) with Sunday School students, children through adults.

Think piece. A magazine article that has an intellectual, philosophical, or provocative approach to a subject.

Third World. Reference to underdeveloped countries of Asia and Africa.

Transparencies. Positive color slides, not color prints.

Trade magazine. A magazine whose audience is in a particular trade or business.

Traditional verse. One or more verses with an established pattern that is repeated throughout the poem.

Unsolicited manuscripts. A manuscript an editor did not specifically ask to see.

Vanity publisher. See "Subsidy publisher."

Vitae/Vita. An outline of one's personal history and experience.

Work-for-hire assignment. Signing a written contract with a publisher stating that a particular piece of writing you are doing for him is "work for hire." In the agreement you give the publisher full ownership and control of the material.

Writers' guidelines. An information sheet provided by a publisher which gives specific guidelines for writing for the publication. Always send an SASE with your request for guidelines.

GENERAL INDEX

This index includes only periodicals, books, and greeting cards. Conferences, groups, and editorial services are listed alphabetically by state; agents are listed alphabetically by the name of the agency. Check the Table of Contents for the location of these supplementary listings.